NARRATIVE AND DRAMATIC SOURCES OF SHAKESPEARE

Volume VII
MAJOR TRAGEDIES:
HAMLET
OTHELLO
KING LEAR
MACBETH

Volumes published

I. EARLY COMEDIES, POEMS, ROMEO AND JULIET

II. THE COMEDIES (1597–1603)

III. EARLIER ENGLISH HISTORY PLAYS:
HENRY VI, RICHARD III, RICHARD II

IV. LATER ENGLISH HISTORY PLAYS:
KING JOHN, HENRY IV, HENRY V,
HENRY VIII

V. THE ROMAN PLAYS:
JULIUS CÆSAR
ANTONY AND CLEOPATRA
CORIOLANUS

VI. OTHER 'CLASSICAL' PLAYS:
TITUS ANDRONICUS
TROILUS AND CRESSIDA
TIMON OF ATHENS
PERICLES, PRINCE OF TYRE

VII. MAJOR TRAGEDIES:
HAMLET
OTHELLO
KING LEAR
MACBETH

NARRATIVE
AND DRAMATIC
SOURCES OF
SHAKESPEARE

Edited by
GEOFFREY BULLOUGH

Emeritus Professor of English Language and Literature,
King's College, London

Volume VII
MAJOR TRAGEDIES:
HAMLET
OTHELLO
KING LEAR
MACBETH

LONDON: Routledge and Kegan Paul
NEW YORK: Columbia University Press
1973

First published 1973
by Routledge and Kegan Paul Ltd
Broadway House, 68–74 Carter Lane
London EC4V 5EL
and Columbia University Press
Columbia University, New York
Made and printed in Great Britain
by Richard Clay (The Chaucer Press) Ltd
Bungay, Suffolk

© *Geoffrey Bullough 1973*

RKP   ISBN 0 7100 7287 2
CUP   ISBN 0 231 08897 3

Library of Congress Catalog Card Number: 57–9969

To the Librarians who
(usually with great amiability)
have helped in this work

PREFACE

UNTIL a late stage in collecting material on the later plays of Shakespeare I hoped to get an adequate amount of it into one volume, but (as wiser friends forewarned me) this proved almost impossible, and it was decided, rather than 'scamp' the 'great' tragedies, to devote this volume to them and a final volume to the 'romances'. Consequently I am able to include here not only the obvious pieces but a number of minor analogues which may help to throw light on the plays and the conditions in which they were written. A particular feature of this volume, and of the next, is the suggestion that the plays were rather more topical than has sometimes been supposed, e.g. that the *Ur-Hamlet* may have been affected, if not prompted, by the negotiations for the marriage of James VI and Anne of Denmark, and that Shakespeare may have taken advantage of current political issues in his references to England and Poland as well as in Hamlet's adventure with the pirates. Moreover, I have ventured to supplement a suggestion made many years ago that the play-within-the-play contained elements originally derived from some account of the murder of Francesco Maria I, Duke of Urbino.

If it be thought that I have occasionally trespassed beyond my brief by giving material which is barely narrative or dramatic, I plead guilty but am not repentant. In the section on *King Lear* there is a chapter from S. Harsnett's *Declaration of Egregious Popish Impostures*, the importance of which has been shown by Professor Kenneth Muir. I wish that I could have given more, but I have restricted myself to one of the more 'narrative' parts of that clever piece of controversial writing.

So much has been written about these tragedies, especially in recent years, that the Bibliography (though only a small fraction of what it might have been) is longer than in previous volumes. I have separated the major from the minor sources and analogues of *Hamlet*, and listed the critical studies of minor sources, etc., along with the texts. I have also inserted a section on the political and historical background of this play. For *Hamlet* and *Lear* I have also given a list of writings which, although not specifically concerned with sources, contain diverse ideas about Shakespeare's creative use of his materials.

I am grateful to the Council of the Malone Society for permission to use its edition of *The True Chronicle History of King Leir* as the basis of my text, and to the Scottish Text Society for permission to use (in slightly modernized form) an excerpt from *The Original Chronicle of Andrew of Wyntoun*, edited by F. J. Amours. As in previous volumes references to Shakespeare's plays are to the three-volume edition by W. J. Craig. Like many previous editors, I have made use of the late Oliver Elton's translation of *The First Nine Books of Saxo Grammaticus* (1894), and of H. Howard Furness's translation of *Der bestrafte Brudermord* (which I have revised somewhat). My debt to other scholars is incalculable, but I wish especially to thank the colleagues and friends who have sent me offprints or answered queries. These include Professors Vittorio Gabrieli of Rome and Piero Pieri of Turin, A. P. Stabler of Washington State University and Harold Fisch of Bar-Ilan, Mr K. Brown, Dr R. Freudenstein, Miss Emily Lyle, Sir Peter Noble and Mr Yngve Olsson. The librarians to whom I gratefully dedicate this volume include those at University of London King's College, Edinburgh University Library, the British Museum, and the National Library of Scotland.

CONTENTS OF VOLUME VII

ILLUSTRATIONS

NOTE ON THE ILLUSTRATIONS

1. Francesco Maria I, Duke of Urbino, from P. Giovio, *Elogia Virorum bellica Virtute illustrium*, 1575, p. 321.

   Paolo Giovio (1483–1552), born at Como, was encouraged by Leo X to write a history of his own times. Falling out of favour with Paul III he retired to his birthplace, where he lavishly adorned his villa with antiquities and portraits of famous soldiers and men of learning. Among them was the portrait of Francesco Maria, painted by Titian not long before the Duke's death in 1538. Giovio wrote short biographies to accompany the portraits, which were engraved and first published in 1551.

2. The tree of Banquo's royal descendants, from John Leslie, *De Origine, Moribus, et Rebus Gestis Scotorum, Rome, 1578,* p. 260.

   Leslie (1527–96), made Bishop of Ross in 1566, followed Queen Mary to England and was imprisoned before going to France in 1574. A doughty defender of his Queen against detractors such as Buchanan and Knox, he maintained her right (and James VI's) to succeed Queen Elizabeth on the English throne.

3. R. Holinshed, *The Chronicles of Scotland*, 1577 edn.

   The small cuts reproduced on pp. 489, 491, 494 and 497 were not given in the 1587 edition. They were probably the work of Marcus Gheeraerts the Elder, who was living in London in 1576. Edward Hodnett regards the illustrations as 'the finest specifically designed for an English book before 1600, and among the most successful in an English book of any period'. (*Marcus Gheeraerts the Elder*, Utrecht, 1971, pp. 48–57.)

All these illustrations are taken from copies of the books in the National Library of Scotland, by kind permission of the Trustees.

LIST OF ABBREVIATIONS

1. **Shakespeare's Works and Apocrypha**

A&C	Antony and Cleopatra
Ado	Much Ado about Nothing
AFev	Arden of Feversham
AShrew	The Taming of A Shrew
AYL	As You Like It
CE	Comedy of Errors
Cor	Coriolanus
Cym	Cymbeline
Ham	Hamlet
1H4	Henry the Fourth, Part I
2H4	Henry the Fourth, Part II
H5	Henry the Fifth
1H6	Henry the Sixth, Part I
2H6	Henry the Sixth, Part II
3H6	Henry the Sixth, Part III
H8	Henry the Eighth
JC	Julius Caesar
KJ	King John
LComp	Lover's Complaint
Lear	King Lear
LLL	Love's Labour's Lost
Luc	The Rape of Lucrece
Mac	Macbeth
MM	Measure for Measure
MND	A Midsummer Night's Dream
More	Sir Thomas More
MV	The Merchant of Venice
MWW	The Merry Wives of Windsor
NobKin	Two Noble Kinsmen
Oth	Othello
Per	Pericles
PhT	The Phoenix and the Turtle
PPil	The Passionate Pilgrim
R2	King Richard the Second
R3	King Richard the Third
RJ	Romeo and Juliet
Son	Sonnets
TA	Titus Andronicus
Tem	The Tempest
TGV	Two Gentlemen of Verona
Tim	Timon of Athens
TN	Twelfth Night
TrC	Troilus and Cressida
TSh	The Taming of The Shrew
VA	Venus and Adonis
WT	The Winter's Tale

2. **Modern Editions and Other Works**

Arden	The Arden Shakespeare (original)
Camb	The New Cambridge edition, edited by J. Dover Wilson, A. Quiller-Couch, &c.
Coll	Shakespeare's Library, ed. J. P. Collier
Conf	John Gower, Confessio Amantis
ELH	English Literary History (Johns Hopkins University, Baltimore)
ElSt	E. K. Chambers, The Elizabethan Stage

EngHist Soc	English Historical Society	*ShJb*	Jahrbuch der deutschen Shakespeare—Gesellschaft
EngStud	*Englische Studien*	*ShLib*	*Shakespeare's Library*, 6 vols. 2nd Edn. 1875, edited by J. P. Collier and W. C. Hazlitt
E Studies	*English Studies*		
FP	*Fratricide Punished*		
Hol.	Holinshed's *Chronicles*		
JEGP	*The Journal of English and Germanic Philology*	*ShQ*	*Shakespeare Quarterly*
		Sh.Soc. Trans.	*Transactions of the New Shakespeare Society*
Jest Books	*Shakespeare Jest Books*, edited W. C. Hazlitt	*SPhil*	*Studies in Philology*
		SpT	*The Spanish Tragedy*
Lee	Sir Sidney Lee, *Life of Shakespeare*	*Sh Survey*	*Shakespeare Survey*
		Texas	*University of Texas Studies in English*
MalSoc	Malone Society Reprints		
MedSt	E. K. Chambers, *The Medieval Stage*	*TLS*	*The Times Literary Supplement* (London)
		TR	*The Troublesome Raigne of King John*
MLN	*Modern Language Notes*		
MLR	*The Modern Language Review*	*Var.*	*The New Variorum edition*, ed. H. H. Furness, &c.
MPhil	*Modern Philology*		
New Arden	The Arden Edition of Shakespeare (revised and reset)	*WSh*	E. K. Chambers, *William Shakespeare.*
N&Q	*Notes & Queries*		
Oxf.	The Oxford Edition of Shakespeare, text by W. J. Craig; Introductory Studies by E. Dowden	**3. *Other Abbreviations***	
		Arg	Argument
		Chor	Chorus
		Prol	Prologue
PhilQ	*Philological Quarterly*	*Rev.*	Review
PMLA	Publications of the Modern Language Association of America	F	Folio edition
		n.d.	No date
		Q	Quarto edition
RES	*The Review of English Studies*	S.R.	The Stationers' Register
SEL	*Studies in English Literature* (Rice Institute)	STC	*A Short-Title Catalogue of Books printed . . . 1475–1640* (1950)

HAMLET

INTRODUCTION

THERE were two major versions of *Hamlet* before the first Folio. On 26 July 1602 there was entered in the Stationers' Register to James Roberts 'A booke called the Revenge of Hamlett Prince Denmarke as yt was latelie Acted by the Lord Chamberlayne his servants'. Next year, after the accession of James I, appeared the first Quarto, 'The Tragicall Historie of Hamlet Prince of Denmarke. By William Shakespeare. As it hath beene diverse times acted by His Highnesse servants in the Cittie of London: as also in the two Universities of Cambridge and Oxford, and elsewhere. At London printed for N.L. [Nicholas Ling] and John Trundell.' The second Quarto of 1604 was claimed to be 'Newly imprinted and enlarged to almost as much againe as it was, according to the true and perfect Coppie. Printed by J.R. [James Roberts] for N.L.'

The relationship between the three texts has puzzled editors and bibliographers, but it is now generally agreed that whereas Q2 and F1 are authentic texts approved by the King's Men, Q1 was a pirated version based on memories of the play as performed either in full or in abridgment. The main reporter may have been the actor who played Marcellus and Lucianus. Greg believed that this busy man also played the ambassador Voltemar. The theory accounts for the difference between the perfect intelligibility of some parts of Q1 and various degrees of imperfect reproduction found in others.

Q2 is widely held to be a text based on Shakespeare's own 'foul papers' which were set up by two compositors having different habits. At times, when the manuscript was confusing owing to bad writing or interpolations, the compositors may have referred to a copy of Q1.[1] The Q2 manuscript was the 'author's final draft which had been handed to the company in

---

[1] A. Walker, 'The Textual Problem of *Hamlet*: A Reconsideration', *RES* n.s. II, pp. 328–38; J. M. Nosworthy, *Shakespeare's Occasional Plays*, 1965, Ch. 10.

all its untidiness'.[1] A fair copy of this would be made for the production, and this probably 'served as the Folio copy', with the omission of 225 lines and the insertion of others not in Q2. A copy of the printed Q2 itself was also used for F1, but to what extent is still debated.[2]

The Folio text is slightly shorter than Q2, and since *Hamlet* is an unusually long play (nearly 4,000 lines) F1 may represent the piece as it was performed by 1620. Most modern editions provided a 'maximum' text made up from Q2 and F1.

If Q1 was a pirated text, from what version of the play was it taken? The detailed analysis made by the late G. I. Duthie proves that 'practically everything in (Q1) depends upon the full Shakespearian text of Q2 or upon a stage version of that'.[3] 'Practically everything'; but not everything, for there are remarkable differences between the two not explicable by a simple failure of verbal memory. Thus Polonius is called Corambis and his servant Reynaldo is Montano; the nunnery-scene is introduced earlier than in Q2, immediately after Corambis suggests that Ophelia be used to test Hamlet's madness; there is an important difference in the treatment of Gertrude, for at the end of the closet-scene she not only protests her innocence but promises to help her son get his revenge: 'I sweare by heaven I never knew of this most horride murder', and 'I vow . . . I will conceale, consent, and doe my best / What stratagem soe're thou shalt devise.' There is also a scene between the Queen and Horatio in which she is told of Hamlet's return to Denmark and says that she will help Hamlet by deceiving her husband. Moreover, although in Q1 Horatio says in that scene that he has had a letter from Hamlet 'Where as he writes how he escap't the danger', the letter is never read aloud, and Hamlet does not personally tell him (and the audience) the story of his voyage. Nor are the pirates mentioned. Horatio merely says:

> Being crossed by the contention of the windes,
> He found the Packet sent to the King of England . . .

[1] Nosworthy, *op. cit.* p. 139.
[2] A. Walker, *Textual Problems of the First Folio*, 1953, pp. 121–37; H. Jenkins, *Studies in Bibliography*, vii, pp. 69–83, xiii, 47n.; Nosworthy, *op. cit.* pp. 142–63.
[3] G. I. Duthie, *The 'Bad' Quarto of Hamlet*, 1941, p. 273.

and that Hamlet will tell his mother all about it when they meet. We never see him doing so. Only the changing of the letter is briefly described, then 'He being set ashore, they went for England'. Some topical allusions are omitted from Q1, e.g. in the discussion about the Players' leaving the city (Q2, II.2).

These differences could be the result of abridgment and invention by actors or reporters—modern productions of Shakespeare have afforded ample evidence of changes equally sweeping. It is also possible that the version behind Q1 differed from that represented in Q2, and that the play underwent some revision by Shakespeare. I cannot enter here into this intricate problem, but I believe that the play was mainly written between 1598 and 1601, and that alterations were made, probably in 1601 or 1602.[1]

The name Amlotha appears out of the mists of Icelandic antiquity in a quotation from the poet Snaebjorn preserved by Snorri Storlason in his *Prose Edda* (*c.* 1230) referring to 'the Nine Maidens of the Island mill stirring the baleful quern of the Skerries, they who in ages past ground Amleth's meal'. This may allude to one of the riddling sayings of the hero Amleth who in Saxo Grammaticus fools the courtiers who when they are walking by the sea bid him 'look at the meal'—i.e. the seashore sand; whereupon the hero, pretending to be mad, replies solemnly 'that it has been ground small by the white waves of the sea'. It is possible therefore that there was a legend about an Amleth who assumed madness two or more centuries before his life story was told by the Dane Saxo Grammaticus at the end of the twelfth century, who was asked to write his *Danish History* by Archbishop Absalon of Lund, who died in 1201. First printed in 1514, *Historiae Danicae* had several editions at Basle and Frankfurt and was translated into Danish in 1575. An English version of the first nine books was made by Oliver Elton in 1894,[2] and this has been used for the present reprint [Text I].

As a collector of legends Saxo was to Denmark what Geoffrey

[1] Cf. J. D. Wilson, *Camb.*, pp. xix–xxii: 'Shakespeare may first have handled the play sometime after Lodge's reference of 1596 and then revised it in 1601.' E. K. Chambers, *WSh*, i, p. 423, thought that it was written between 1598 and 'the death of Essex in February, 1601'. Cf. also the discussion in Duthie, *op. cit.* pp. 78–84.

[2] *The First Nine Books of the Danish History of Saxo Grammaticus*, trans. by Oliver Elton, 1894; excerpts in I. Gollancz, *The Sources of Hamlet*, 1926.

of Monmouth was to Britain. He drew on Latin histories such as
Bede and Adam of Bremen, on Icelandic and Danish MSS., and
on oral traditions. He tells of gods and heroes, monsters and
warriors. Women figure frequently as inciters to love and battle.
Books I and II describe the origins of the Danes and the adventures of mythical personages such as Gram and Groa, Hadding
and Hardgrep, the god Odin, Frode (who invaded England),
Ragnar and Swanhwid. In Book III we read of Hother's rivalry
with Balder, and of Rorik, under whom Amleth's father Horwendil ruled Jutland with his brother Feng.

The Amleth saga belongs to a common type of revenge-story
in which the hero feigns insanity or stupidity to save his life and
gain an opportunity for a coup. In Saxo's Book VI Harald and
Halfden, the dispossessed sons of a murdered father and an unfaithful mother, pretend madness when attacked by their uncle
Frode, who then desists, 'thinking it shameful to attack with the
sword those who seemed to be turning the sword against themselves. But he was burned to death by them on the following
night and was punished as befitting a fratricide. For they
attacked the palace, and first crushed the queen with a mass of
stones; and then, having set fire to the house, they forced Frode
to crawl into a narrow cave. . . . There he perished, stifled by
the reek and smoke' (Elton, p. 263).

The wise-fool theme appears also in the life of Wiglaf's grandson, Uffe, who 'surpassed all his age in stature, but in his early
youth was supposed to have so dull and foolish a spirit as to be
useless for all affairs public or private.' He never laughed or
talked, until his father, now blind, was challenged by the King
of Saxony. Then the dumb fool spoke, became his father's
champion, and with the aid of a rusty sword overcame his
enemies, and became known as King Olaf the Gentle (*ibid.*,
Bk. IV, pp. 130–43).

As told by Saxo the Amleth story owes something to the
Roman legend of Lucius Junius Brutus, who expelled the Tarquins after the rape of Lucrece. When his father and his elder
brother were murdered by Tarquin the Proud, Lucius escaped
by pretending to be an imbecile; hence the nickname 'Brutus'
(stupid). Being sent with Tarquin's two sons to the oracle at
Delphi, he gave as offering a hollow wooden staff filled with
gold, an emblem of his own condition. He showed greater in-

telligence than his companions in interpreting the oracle, and after Lucrece's suicide revealed himself and became the liberator of Rome. Saxo would read this in Livy, I. Ch. 56. (Text II). Plutarch does not relate this part of Brutus's life; Shakespeare would know it from Livy. He is less likely to have known Saxo's version of the Amleth story, though some scholars have seen traces of it in the play. The story falls into two parts linked by similar themes and incidents; the first (Bk. III) tells of Amleth's survival in his uncle's court, and of his revenge; the second (in Bk. IV) describes his life as ruler of Jutland, his second marriage and how he died.

Two brothers, Horwendil and Feng, are joint governors of Jutland under the King of Denmark. The former, married to Gerutha, has a son, Amleth. The jealous Feng murders his brother, and, declaring that he did so to save Gerutha from Horwendil's cruelty, marries her. The boy grows up afraid of death and pretends to be soft-witted; yet he has suspicious flashes of intelligence, as when, making wooden hooks with steel barbs, he says that they are javelins to avenge his father.

Pranks are played on Amleth by his uncle's courtiers to test his folly. Always he baffles them with ambiguities containing some truth, gravely turning nonsensical suggestions into extravagant sense by witty metaphoric wordplay. A climax comes when they set on his foster-sister to tempt him sexually in the forest, arguing that no man in his sense would fail to take advantage of the girl. Amleth is warned by his foster-brother, and although he possesses her in secret, he boasts of it so ridiculously that the courtiers believe the girl's denials. Finally, when one of Feng's intimates urges that Amleth be watched while talking to his mother, the youth kills the eavesdropper, treats the body with great savagery, reproves his mother, and mocks at the King.

Resolving to have Amleth murdered by the King of England his tributary, Feng sends him off with two men bearing a letter ordering his death.[1] Before leaving, Amleth bids his mother

---

[1] This trick is used in the *Iliad*, Bk. VI, where Bellerophon is sent by King Proetus to King Rheuns, who obediently sends him against the Chimaera, the Solymi and the Amazons in turn. He defeats them and finally gains Rheuns's daughter (Chapman, VI, 151–200). According to Cornelius Nepos (trans. J. S. Watson, 1882, p. 327), Pausanias, tiring of his love-affair with a young man, tried to get rid of him thus. Sir Bevis of Hampton has a similar adventure with King

surround the hall with tapestry and mourn his death at the end of a year. On the way to England he changes the wording of the letter, instructing the English King to execute his companions and to give Amleth his daughter in marriage.

In England Amleth behaves outrageously at the welcome-feast, speaking in riddles which prove to be true, though un-favourable to the English royal family. Realizing the Prince's wisdom, the King gives him his daughter and hangs the two companions—at which Amleth (as if ignorant of the letter) demands blood-money. He melts down the gold and pours it into two hollow wands (an obvious echo of the Brutus-legend).

With nothing but these wands Amleth returns to Jutland, disguised in his former insanity and filth, and arrives as his death is being mourned. Asked about his two friends he says that they are in his sticks. He is mocked, but the courtiers regard him as dangerous, and when he has drawn his sword several times and drawn blood from his fingers, they nail the sword and scabbard together. When the drunken lords are asleep Amleth lets down the hangings from the walls and fastens them tight round his enemies with his hooks, then sets fire to the hall. Awakening Feng in his chamber, he challenges him, ex-changes swords, and kills his father's murderer after long years of waiting.

In Book IV Amleth justifies himself to the people in a long oration and is acclaimed King of Jutland. Then he sails for England, taking with him a splendid shield on which are painted the principal events of his life. The King of England has sworn an oath of blood-brotherhood with Feng and must avenge his death. He therefore sends Amleth to Scotland to woo on his behalf the fierce Queen Hermutrude, who has slain all her previous suitors. She however loves Amleth at first sight, changes the commission to require that she marry him, and

---

Ermyn and King Bredmond. These heroes do not change the letter, but Herodotus tells of a traveller who, asked to deliver a letter to a Vizier, and finding from it that he is to be slain, changes the message. Sir Coustans (see *Old French Romances*, trans. W. Morris, 1894) is sent by a Moslem emperor to the Burgrave of Byzan-tium with a letter ordering his immediate execution. Falling asleep in the palace-garden, he is found by the Emperor's daughter, who opens the letter and alters its message to command that she be married to the young man. The Emperor accepts the *fait accompli* and Coustans succeeds him. This parallels Amleth's later adventure with the King of Scotland's daughter.

persuades him to marry her. On his return to England Amleth's first wife accepts the situation and warns him that her father intends to kill him. After a campaign in which his father-in-law is slain, Amleth returns to Jutland with his two wives.

Amleth's career ends when the new King of Denmark, Wiglek, regarding him as an usurper, illtreats Amleth's mother and challenges the hero. Before Amleth goes out to certain death his Scottish wife Hermutrude swears not to survive him, but after he is killed she gives herself to the victor. Saxo comments bitterly on feminine frailty.

The second part of the story may originally have belonged to a different hero, but there are likenesses between the two, notably his cunning, the sending of him to another country to be killed, the changing of a sinister message, and the betrayal of her dead lord by the wife he has loved.

The mythological origins and analogues of the Amleth story in Scandinavian and Celtic lore do not concern us now.[1] It was referred to in various histories, notably in Albert Krantz's *Chronica Regnorum Aquilonarium*, published in German in 1545, in Latin in 1548.[2] Hans Sachs used this for a version in loose rhyme (1558). The discovery by J. F. Bladé in the nineteenth century of a remarkable analogue told by illiterate peasants in several Gascon villages made Marcel Schwob and other *littérateurs* think that it might go back so far as the English occupation of Guyenne during the Hundred Years War. There is no wicked uncle. In order to preserve her position of power a Queen poisons her husband when he arranges for their son to marry a neighbouring princess. The son succeeds to the throne, but his father's ghost comes and demands justice. The son tells his best friend, 'Misfortune has come on me' and sends him to inform the princess that they can never be married and that she should 'Retire to a convent. Take the black veil, and pray to God for your friend until you are carried to the cemetery.' To escape his task the King disguises himself as a beggar and goes far away to a high mountain where he builds a cabin to live in. The ghost appears to him and repeats its demand for justice.

---

[1] See I. Gollancz, *op. cit.*, for many references.

[2] Yngve Olsson, 'In Search of Yorick's Skull', *Sh. Studies*, iv, 1968, gives the relevant passage, with translation, and argues that the author of *Hamlet* knew the work.

The King returns to his homeland, where his friend tells him that his betrothed is dead and that his mother is misruling the country. Once more the ghost appears to demand justice. Next morning the King arms himself and rides to his mother's castle where she welcomes him and they dine together. He tells her that he has just married his betrothed and that she will arrive tomorrow. The Queen says nothing but leaves the room, returning with a poisoned draught. She proposes a toast to the bride. Then her son makes her choose between drinking from the goblet or being slain with his sword. She drinks and dies. The young King kneels and prays, then mounts his horse and rides away, never to be seen again.

The story contains much not in Saxo: a ghost, a reluctant avenger, a faithful friend, a girl whom the hero loves but to whom he says farewell and bids enter a nunnery, death by poison. The collocation of all these features makes it certain that A. H. Krappe was right in arguing that the tale developed from memories of a French translation of Shakespeare's play made in the eighteenth or early nineteenth century.[1] In its simplicity and verbal repetition however, the tale has the true flavour of folk-story.

Amleth entered Elizabethan drama through the agency of François de Belleforest's *Histoires Tragiques*. Belleforest(1530–83) was a minor follower of the Pléiade who compiled chronicles and published seven collections of tragic stories between 1564 and 1582. Much of his material came from Bandello and classical and medieval historians. He knew Saxo's *Danish History* well, as several other tales beside that of Amleth show.[2] An undistinguished writer, Belleforest modernized and moralized what he borrowed, marring the clarity of Bandello and Saxo with 'tedious expansion', adding harangues, reflections, religious digressions, letters and poems, and displaying conventional prejudices against women and the pleasures of the senses. His collection however went into many editions, and was used by English translators such as William Painter. Shakespeare seems

[1] J. F. Bladé, *Contes Populaires de la Gascogne*, 3 vols, Paris, 1886. Vol. I, pp. 57–66. 'La reine châtiée'; Marcel Schwob, *Mercure de France*, 1 Jan. 1900, pp. 225–6, review of Dowden's *Hamlet*; A. H. Krappe, 'Shakespeare in Romance Folk-Lore', *Neuphilologische Mitteilungen*, xxvii, Helsinki, 1926, pp. 65–70. I am grateful to Dr. Sylvia Morton for calling my attention to the story and its commentators.

[2] Cf. *The French Bandello*, ed. F. S. Hook, U. of Missouri Studies, xxii, no. 1, 1948.

to have known Belleforest's version of Bandello's story of Timbreo and Fenicia when he wrote *Much Ado*.

At least ten editions were issued of the fifth volume of *Histoires Tragiques* which contains the Amleth story (1570, 1572, 1576, 1582, 1583, 1601, etc.). That of Paris, 1582, containing many textual alterations from 1576, was used by the anonymous English translator in *The Hystorie of Hamblet* (London, 1608) which is a dull, fairly close version but bears evidence in the Closet scene (p. 94) that its author had seen *Hamlet* performed. Probably the success of the play and its Quartos explains why the *Hystorie* was published. There is no evidence of a previous edition. Sir I. Gollancz, in *The Sources of Hamlet* (1926), re- printed the 1582 text of Belleforest with that of the *Hystorie*. In giving the latter below (Text III) I have indicated in footnotes its most important deviations from the French text, which Professor A. P. Stabler has examined closely.[1] He points out that the 1576 edition is occasionally more like Shakespeare than the 1582 text.

There are important differences between Belleforest's and Saxo's versions of the saga. Belleforest has a lengthy argument asserting the misery of rulers and the frequency of hatred be- tween relatives in all ages. He refers to 'the memorie of our fore- fathers in Scotland and England' and to recent French history, but his main reason for giving the Danish story is not so much its topicality as the nature of its revenge-theme. It was the 'great and gallant occurrences', the cunning and decisive nature of Amleth's vengeance, that interested Belleforest and his readers. The delay was as important as the inevitability and originality of the method used.

Belleforest does not understand the age of saga and its ethical code. Saxo had generalized against women with reference to Hermutrude's disloyalty. Belleforest increases the misogyny. He also apologizes for the savagery of his story, which happened 'long time before Denmark received the faith of Jesus Christ', when 'the common people were barbarous and uncivill and their princes cruell, without faith or loyaltie'. The custom of

---

[1] A. P. Stabler, 'The Histoires Tragiques de François de Belleforest', U. of Virginia Ph.D. dissertation, 1959 (Lib. Cong. Mic. 59–4246); 'The Sources of Hamlet: Some Corrections of the Record', *Research Studies*, xxxiii, 1964; 'Melancholy, Ambition and Revenge in Belleforest's Hamlet', *PMLA*, lxxxi, 1966, pp. 207–16.

piratical sea-roving has to be explained. Yet the story is no more
savage than many told by Boccaccio and Bandello. Every point
is obscured by laborious moralizing. At the close Belleforest
apologizes again for writing 'these strange histories, and of
people that were uncivilised, that the vertue of these rude
people may give more splendour to our nation.'

Some other changes made by Belleforest should be noted.
The murder of Horwendil in Saxo seems to be done in private
and then excused to the court; nothing is said of accomplices,
though the sycophantic courtiers accept Feng's lies. In Belleforest Fengon obtains abettors and then slays his brother at a
banquet; his excuse must therefore be known to be false by all
who were there. Belleforest has bungled this alteration of Saxo.

Geruth is made into an incestuous adultress before the
murder, and (although this is not explicitly stated) she must
have remained silent after her husband's death although she
knew that Fengon's story was untrue. This blackens her character and makes her later excuses to Amleth incredible. Inevitably
some Danes believe that she caused the murder so as to enjoy
her adultery.

Amleth's assumed insanity is compared with that of Brutus
and other dissimulators in history; and Belleforest insists more
explicitly than Saxo on the truth showing through his extravagant answers, 'that a wise man would soone have judged from
what spirite so fine an invention might proceede'. Some courtiers
indeed soon came to suspect him, and informed the King.

Belleforest alters the temptation in the forest. He omits the
twofold warning of Amleth's foster-brother—not to show 'the
slightest glimpse of sound reason' or to do 'the act of love
openly'. He omits Amleth's sitting on the horse facing its tail;
his riddling answers mingling 'craft and candour'; the straw in
the gadfly's tail;[1] and Amleth's dragging the girl off to a secret
place. Belleforest does not say clearly that Amleth possessed the
girl, though he asserts that she would have wished it. The
English translator thought that Amleth 'both deceived the
courtiers and the ladyes expectation', but he was led to this by
a misplaced comma in the 1582 French text (see p. 92).

---

[1] This trick has puzzled some commentators, but surely it was a warning to
Amleth to beware of 'the sting in the woman's tail'. Perhaps Amleth sat facing the
tail of his horse to show that he realized the need for caution.

In Saxo, having had the willing girl, Amleth says so and is mocked when the girl denies it. In Belleforest the girl denies it but he affirms it 'in subtilty', and is disbelieved. It is not clear whether he told a lie or not; Saxo's Amleth never lies; that is an aspect of his shrewdness. By omitting the fantastic details Belleforest has diminished the power of the incident.

The closet-scene is changed only slightly. Like Saxo's, Belleforest's spy hides beneath a quilt (Fr. loudier) on which Amleth tramples, suspecting some treason, and discovers the intruder. He disposes of the body in the same barbarous way before returning to upbraid his mother. She is contrasted with Rinde, daughter of King Rother, a princess celebrated for her chastity.[1]

Amleth searches the room, 'as if distrusting his mother as well as the rest'. His harangue is greatly lengthened, and he accuses her of abandoning him to his enemies. With unconscious irony he mentions a journey abroad, 'even to the English', as a means of saving his life. Belleforest now introduces a long defence by Geruth of her (enforced) marriage to Fengon, making no mention of her adultery. She never consented to her husband's murder; she hopes to see her son avenge him, and promises secrecy, but warns Amleth not to be 'hastie nor overfurious'. He expatiates on the glory he will gain by his revenge.

Belleforest follows closely Saxo's account of the voyage to England and the adventures there. He explains Amleth's clairvoyance by the theory that northern countries 'living as then under Satan's laws, were full of enchanters', and Amleth knew the 'devilish art'. Saxo on the other hand accepted divination as a natural characteristic of heroes. Belleforest wonders in passing whether Amleth's power sprang from 'the vehemence of his melancholy' and he refers to the prophetic frenzies of philosophers, 'Saturnists by complection', but it may be that 'a reasonable soul becometh the habitation of a meaner sort of devils, by which men learn the secrets of things natural.'[2]

---

[1] This comes from Saxo, Bk. III, in which Rinde, daughter of the King of the Ruthenians, modestly repulsed the advances of Odin. He got possession of her by trickery, and she bore a son Boe, who slew Hother, Rorik's father, in revenge for the slaying of his half-brother Balder.

[2] This supernatural digression may have influenced the *Hamlet* plays into making Hamlet wonder about the power of devils when thinking about the Ghost. *Macbeth* also depends somewhat on the idea that the Devil can know 'thinges that shall happen unto men'.

The rest of Amleth's stay in England follows Saxo. The comedy of his arrival home during his funeral feast turns sinister when his answer about his two missing companions makes some courtiers leave in apprehension. Omitting to tell how Amleth's sword came to be nailed into its scabbard, Belleforest misses an important point. He inserts an address of Amleth to his uncle ere he slays him and another as he cuts off his head. Saxo's commendation of Amleth's courage and cunning is expanded; he 'deceived the wise, pollitike and craftie, thereby not onely preserving his life from the treasons and wicked practises of the tyrant, but (which is more) by a new and unexpected kinde of punishment, revenged his father's death, many yeres after the act committed.' This throws light on why the Amleth story appealed to the Elizabethans, and why the *Hamlet* playwrights, in modernizing it, sought for witty devices and strange methods of murder.

In drawing out the hero's harangue to the populace Belleforest increases the rhetoric as he appeals to their loyalty and justice, begs forgiveness for his mother, and demands his reward, meaning the throne. As in Saxo he insists that he alone removed the tyrant and avenged his father without confiding in anybody. Following Saxo's account of Amleth's later adventures, the French translator does not appreciate the solemnity of the oath sworn between Feng and the English King, and the latter's dilemma when he discovered that his son-in-law had killed his friend. Belleforest calls him a 'barbarous king' for resolving to remove Amleth. He omits Amleth's shield and the use made of it by the Scottish Queen, also her changing of the letter. Instead she woos him at some length, and his marriage to her is not the result of 'the very trick . . . which he had himself used in outwitting his companions', but of her persuasiveness and his ambition. This infidelity is the beginning of Amleth's downfall. His end is a punishment for bigamy.

Belleforest makes more of the English wife's resentment. She preaches at Amleth, yet love overcomes her anger against the foreign concubine, and she warns him against her father. The King's attempts on Amleth's life are briefly told, and the battles which ended in the sacking of England. The catastrophe follows Saxo's account, but Belleforest emphasizes Amleth's intense love for Hermutrude, and concludes that his fault was

that he could not restrain 'the unbridled desires of his concupiscence'. He ends by asking readers to regard Amleth's
virtues and see him as an example of natural goodness in a
pagan age.

Undoubtedly the original play of *Hamlet* was based on the
French *novella*, and I see no proof that either Shakespeare or his
predecessor used Saxo Grammaticus at all.[1]

That a Hamlet play was known on the English stage by 1589
is shown by Nashe's address 'To the Gentlemen Students of
Both Universities' printed before Greene's romance *Menaphon*
in that year. Nashe was warning students against bad writers
such as the Mar-Prelate pamphleteers, bad dramatists and bad
translators. He showed special animus against ink-horn tragedi-
ans and rhetorical poets with their 'bragging blank verse'. Later
he attacked 'triviall translators' and Senecan dramatists:

'It is a common practise now a dayes amongst a sort of shifting
companions, that runne through every Art and thrive by
none, to leave the trade of *Noverint*, whereto they were borne,
and busie themselves with the indevours of Art, that could
scarcely Latinize their neck verse if they should have neede;
yet English *Seneca* read by Candlelight yeelds many good
sentences, as *Blood is a begger*, and so forth; and if you intreate
him faire in a frostie morning, hee will affoord you whole
Hamlets, I should say handfuls of Tragicall speeches. But O
griefe! *Tempus edax rerum*, whats that will last alwayes? The
Sea exhaled by droppes will in continuance bee drie, and
Seneca, let blood line by line and page by page, at length must
needes die to our Stage; which makes his famished followers
to imitate the Kid in *Aesop*, who, enamoured with the Foxes
newfangles, forsooke all hopes of life to leape into a newe
occupation; and these men, renouncing all possibilities of
credite or estimation, to intermeddle with Italian Translations: Wherein how poorely they have plodded, (as those that
are neither provenzall men, nor are able to distinguish of

---

[1] J. D. Wilson thought that Saxo was behind the description of Polonius as a
'rash, intruding fool', and Gertrude's cry, 'O Hamlet, thou hast cleft my heart in
twain!', but A. P. Stabler has shown that the ideas could have been suggested by
Belleforest's French (Cf. 'The Sources of *Hamlet*: Some Corrections of the Record',
Research Studies, xxxiii, 1964, pp. 207–16; and Text III).

Articles) let all indifferent Gentlemen that have travelled in that tongue discerne by their two-pennie Pamphlets.'[1]

There has been much discussion about this passage, especially concerning the likelihood that it refers to Thomas Kyd, the author of *The Spanish Tragedy*. It certainly fits what we know of him, for he was a scrivener's son who apparently never went to the University but loved the classics (though his translations are rarely accurate). He soon left the law for the theatre, and most of his original work was done before 1588[2] after which he published translations from Italian and French. The '*Noverint*' suggests Kyd and there are other apparent references to him in parts of Nashe's address not printed above. The identification is made almost certain by the allusion to 'the Kidde in *Aesop*', forcibly dragged in, not from Aesop but from Spenser's May Eclogue, where it does not really fit the situation Nashe had in mind.[3]

Even if Nashe was mocking at Kyd he did not say definitely that he was the author of a Hamlet play, only that he could write in that tragic manner. The innuendo however points to Kyd as the author, and the resemblances between *The Spanish Tragedy* and Shakespeare's *Hamlet* are so many that it seems very probable that Shakespeare rewrote an earlier *Hamlet* (hereinafter called the *Ur-Hamlet*) written either by Kyd or an imitator of Kyd.

Over a score of parallels in incidents and situations exist between *Hamlet* and *The Spanish Tragedy*.[4] These include: 1 A Ghost which repeatedly demands revenge; 2 A secret crime revealed but needing verification; 3 An oath taken on the cross of a sword-hilt; 4 The avenger falls into doubts which are removed; 5 The avenger assumes madness, and a woman really goes mad; 6 The revenge is delayed and the avenger reproaches himself; 7 A contrast is drawn between the tardy avenger and someone else whose father (*Hamlet*) or son (*The Spanish Tragedy*)

---

[1] R. B. McKerrow, *Works of Nashe*, iii, 1958, pp. 315–16.

[2] *The Works of Thomas Kyd*, ed. F. S. Boas, 1955 edn., p. xxv.

[3] Cf. V. Osterborg, *MLR*, xv, 1920, p. 439; G. I. Duthie, *The 'Bad' Quarto of Hamlet*, Ch. I; P. Edwards, ed. *SpT*, 1959, disagrees.

[4] E. E. Stoll, *Hamlet, an Historical and Comparative Study*, U. of Minnesota, 1919; *M.Phil*, xxxv, Aug. 1937, pp. 31–46, and xxxvii, Nov. 1939, pp. 173–86; F. Carrère, *Le Théâtre de Thomas Kyd*, Toulouse, 1951, pp. 146–7; F. T. Bowers, *Elizabethan Revenge Tragedy*, 1966, pp. 65–83.

has been murdered; 8 The avenger meditates on suicide; 9 He uses dissimulation, as do his enemies; 10 The woman loved by the son is warned by her father and brother; 11 The avenger discusses the art of the theatre; 12 A play-within-the-play is a decisive moment; 13 The catastrophe occurs during an alleged entertainment; 14 Both plays have a character (Horatio) who is a faithful friend; 15 Hamlet knows in the closet-scene that his father's Ghost comes to chide him: Hieronimo takes Bazulto to be his son's ghost; 16 Hieronimo pretends a reconciliation with his enemy Lorenzo: Hamlet offers Laertes a sincere reconciliation; Laertes dissembles; 17 A spy is set to watch the lovers; 18 A brother hates his sister's lover and kills him treacherously; 19 A woman dies by suicide; 20 Conflicts between two kingdoms involve the coming and going of ambassadors; moreover each play is set in a moral climate of intrigue, crime and hypocrisy. The mind of each hero is almost unhinged by grief and frustration, and there are violent Senecan speeches in each play.

There are a few verbal parallels between the two plays which need not be listed here. They are mainly found in Q1. Professor Duthie suggested that they were inserted by the reporter of Q1, whose mind was apparently well-stocked with snatches of Kyd and of Shakespeare's earlier plays. But if Q1 came (however corruptly) from a Shakespearian version prior to Q2 which contained elements from the *Ur-Hamlet* later removed, then these verbal links with Kyd might come from his version of the drama.

The relationship between the *Ur-Hamlet* and *The Spanish Tragedy* is impossible to define and we do not know which of the two came first. E. E. Stoll[1] and F. Carrère[2] regard the *Ur-Hamlet* as written first and suggesting to its author a companion-piece in which a father would seek revenge for a son and use madness as a weapon against his enemies. Unfortunately no source is known for the cumbrous plot of *The Spanish Tragedy*. If we can argue back from Shakespeare's *Hamlet* (a dangerous process) and assume that the *Ur-Hamlet* was like that in its main outlines, we see that the Ghost of old Hamlet plays a more important and integral part in the play than the Ghost of Andrea, and that the diplomatic activity, the play-within-the-

---

[1] E. E. Stoll, '*Hamlet* and *The Spanish Tragedy*', M.Phil., xxxv, 1937–8, pp. 31–46.
[2] Carrère, *op. cit.* p. 149, dating *Hamlet* in 1587.

B

play and the course of the action are more unified, suggesting that *Hamlet* came second. For our purpose it matters little. Shakespeare may have gone direct to Belleforest or he may not; he may have used the *Ur-Hamlet* much or little; he may have drawn on *The Spanish Tragedy*. Surmise helps us little to ascertain the imaginative process shaping his play.

A *Hamlet* play would have considerable topicality between 1587 and 1589 after the execution of Mary Queen of Scots and during the negotiations for her son's marriage. In 1585 when James VI was nearly 20 and his mother was a prisoner in England, Queen Elizabeth was disturbed when an embassy arrived in Edinburgh from Denmark ostensibly to demand the return to Danish rule of the isles of Orkney and Shetland, and also to suggest that James should marry a Danish princess. The Queen opposed the proposal but friendly relations were set up between Scotland and Denmark and Scottish ambassadors went over in 1588. The death of Frederick II delayed the match but in June 1589 a retinue sailed to Copenhagen to bring the bride, who was married to James by proxy on 20 August 1589. Contrary winds however prevented her crossing the North Sea and her ship was in peril and took shelter in Norway. Thither the eager bridegroom sailed, leaving Leith on 22 October 1589. He met Anne at Oslo on 19 November and married her in person four days later. They did not arrive in Scotland until 1 May 1590.

Nashe's address mentioning 'Hamlet' speeches was written before 23 August 1589, when Greene's *Menaphon* was registered. Presumably the play was well known by then but it may have been a newish piece. Fortinbras's demand for the return of the 'lands . . . by his father lost' (I.1.103) would strike a chord from 1585 onward. There was a sick king of Denmark in 1588 (cf. Norway in II.2.66).[1] The London audience would not expect close analogies. But the idea of a son's revenge might have had some slight topicality, for in 1587 James VI was called on by many Scottish nobles to avenge his mother's murder by Queen Elizabeth. James however was a careful man; he had never known his mother; he feared Elizabeth and hoped to be made

[1] And when Frederick II died the Chancellor had difficulty in preventing his brother Duke John from seizing the throne, although the nobles had recognized Christian, a boy of 11, as heir. The English Ambassador reported this to Burghley (H. Ellis, *Original Letters*, Ser. II., Vol. 3, Letter 233; G. Sjögren, *Sh Studies*, iv, pp. 221–30).

her heir. So he merely protested formally against his mother's execution.

Although the parallel between Amleth's situation and James's appears distant to us, the latter appears as a potential avenger of his father Lord Darnley (not his mother) in a Latin poem written in France soon after Mary's death, probably by John Gordon, a relative of the Queen and now First Gentleman of the Chamber to Henri III. Gordon was working for a union between England and Scotland under James on Elizabeth's death.[1] In the poem, which urges caution on the young monarch, the shade of Darnley, assuming an innocence which he lacked in life, reminds his son of his mother's infidelity and connivance at his murder, and of Bothwell's villainy and evil fate. The enormity of the Queen's third marriage is referred to, and the Prince is said to have narrowly escaped his father's fate. The word *'Vindicta'* is used more than once, but the Ghost tells his son that revenge has been obtained by the mother's recent execution, and that he should not seek further vengeance for his father, nor let himself be carried away by pity for his mother's fate (Text IV).[2]

The poem seems not to have been printed until 1875[3] but it probably circulated in MS. in Paris and Scotland and may have been known in London. It has significance as showing that King James's situation, his mother's failings and his father's murder could be treated as material for a Complaint in the manner of *The Mirror for Magistrates*, with Senecan undertones but a refusal to exhort an Orestean vengeance. If a relative could see matters thus, so might other people.[4] It seems likely therefore

[1] For the Latin poem see G. Lambin, 'Une première ébauche d'Hamlet', *Les Langues Modernes*, XLIX, Paris, 1955, pp. 37–45.

[2] More details are given in my notes to this poem.

[3] By A. Lemerre in *Librairie des Bibliophiles*, Paris, 1875.

[4] They had certainly done so in 1567 when broadsides and bills were printed in Edinburgh demanding punishment for Bothwell and the Queen. Thus, in a verse Complaint, 'Heir follows the testament and tragedie of umquhile king Henrie Stewart of gude memorie', Darnley tells how the Queen loved him and 'maid me ʒour King', then abandoned him to be blown up and strangled. 'O wickid women, venomous of nature' he cries, and lists other women who caused their husbands' deaths. Finally he appeals to the nobles: 'To ʒow, my Lordes, of my deid innocent, / For to revenge and I leif my Testament / My sackles [innocent] bluid, my murther and injure.' Another broadside, 'Exhortacion to the Lordis', urges them to 'Revenge in haist the cruell act'. See *Satirical Poems of the Time of the Reformation*, ed. J. Cranstoun, 2 vols. 1891, Vol. I, Nos. IV, V, etc.

that between 1587 and 1589 the Danish negotiations, the Scottish royal tragedy, and even maybe the inadequacy of James VI as an avenger, suggested to Kyd a play somewhat in the manner of his *Spanish Tragedy*, based not on recent Scottish history, which would be politically impossible, but on the Danish story in Belleforest.

The Spanish Tragedy was one of the most popular and influential of Elizabethan plays, being performed many times in the 1590s. Jonson made additions 'in Heronymo' in 1602, which gave the piece another lease of life on the stage and in print, as witness the Quartos of 1602, 1610 and 1615. The *Ur-Hamlet* was not so successful and maybe it was hastily written to take advantage of the other play's popularity. It seems to have been performed in June 1594 for Henslowe, at a time when a Danish piece would have some topicality—for Queen Anne of Scotland's first son, Henry, was born on 19 February in that year. If T. Lodge's reference in *Wit's Miserie* recalls a recent revival in 1596, that may have been because Anne's daughter the Princess Elizabeth was born on 15 August. It is noteworthy also that Q1 was printed soon after James's accession in England (he and Anne were crowned on 24 July). Because of plague their entry to London was postponed until 15 March 1604. No doubt Shakespeare's play was performed then; Q2 was published late in the year (some copies are dated 1605). More will be said later on the topicality of Shakespeare's play.

In addition to the above versions of the Hamlet story we must consider the German prose play *Der Bestrafte Brudermord oder Prinz Hamlet aus Dännemark*, the degenerate version of an English play probably taken over to the Continent by English actors before 1626, when a *Tragoedia von Hamlet einen Prinz in Danemark* was performed in Dresden by Green's company of English players. The piece was probably put on later by Carl Andreas Paul's German group who toured Germany and Scandinavia between 1660 and 1690. The extant text comes from a manuscript dated 27 October 1710, not now available. This seems to have belonged at one time to the famous actor Conrad Ekhof (d. 1778), from whom it was obtained by H. A. O. Reichard, who first published it in full in 1781.[1]

---

[1] Extracts appeared in Theater-Kalendar, 1779, Gotha. Reichard's text was in *Olla Potrida*, Pt. II, Berlin, 1781. It was reprinted by A. Cohn in *Shakespeare in*

The title has been translated as *Fratricide Punished*, and this I preserve. Its language is not homogeneous: 'Some passages are in High, some in Low German; some expressions are relatively early, some certainly later than 1650' (Brennecke, p. 252). Generations of actors played havoc with the original text and doubtless changed incidents as well as dialogue. The plot follows Shakespeare fairly closely but the action is telescoped and the effect is so crude as to approach burlesque. The translation below is based on H. H. Furness's (Text V).

From what version of *Hamlet* did *Fratricide Punished* emerge? Is it a debased abridgment of the Q1 text, of Q2, or of the *Ur-Hamlet*? Each view has had its exponents. The late Professor Duthie, to whom all students of *Hamlet* are greatly indebted, points out many 'parallels with Q2 and F1 where Q1 disagrees, and parallels with Q1 where Q2 and F1 disagree'. He also notes passages which might come from an earlier work. He concludes that when the English players made their version for performance abroad, the Q2 text was already in existence but probably not yet published, and that they 'relied mainly upon their recollection of that, from which however they deviated at certain points, incorporating in their version material taken in some cases from the Q1 text and in others from the *Ur-Hamlet*.'[1] This must have been a complicated process.

Duthie quotes thirty-six verbal parallels between *Fratricide Punished* and Q2, most of them acceptable (pp. 240–8). Since he believes that Q1 represents not a slightly earlier version of *Hamlet* but a derivant from Q2, he sees the Q2 version behind the German play. But if Q1 were based on a slightly earlier version than Q2, one which Shakespeare revised somewhat, some of the passages common to *FP* and Q2 may also have been in the text which Q1 mutilated.

Duthie also cites twenty-one resemblances to Q1 rather than to Q2 and F1 (pp. 248–52). Although fewer in number, these are on the whole more significant with regard to action and characters. Thus, *FP* and Q1 agree in naming Polonius

---

Germany, 1865, with a translation by Georgina Archer. Other trans. were made by R. G. Latham, 1870, H. H. Furness, *Var.* 1877 and E. Brennecke in *Shakespeare in Germany, 1590–1700*, Chicago, 1964.

[1] Duthie, *op. cit.* p. 254; R. Freudenstein, *Der Bestrafte Brudermord*, Hamburg, 1958, argues that *FP* is exclusively from Q1 and Q2.

Corambus or Corambis. They put the nunnery-scene immediately after it has been planned. They agree in having Hamlet expect his uncle to change colour during the play-scene (Q1, ix.62; *FP*, II.7. 92–4) but note that elsewhere Q2 and F1 have 'if a' do blench' (II.2.601). Both make Claudius admit that his sins are 'unpardonable' (Q1, x.7; *FP*, III.1). Both agree against Q2 in having the King on the stage with the Queen to be told that Ophelia is mad before Ophelia enters (Q1, xiii.6–8; *FP*, IV.6). In both, Hamlet's journey to England is crossed by contrary winds.

Unlike Q2 and F1 they make the King, not Laertes, suggest that one rapier in the fencing-match be poisoned. Other likenesses also suggest that the compilers of *Fratricide Punished* had a version like Q1 in mind, But perhaps the actors in Germany supplemented their text somewhat from a copy of Q2 after that was published in 1604.

Fratricide Punished has certain features peculiar to itself. In a prologue Hecate, Queen of Night, sends out the Furies to sow discord on earth. Some critics have taken this for a vestige of the *Ur-Hamlet*. It is certainly Senecan, but such prologues were not unknown in seventeenth-century German drama. Its content does not entirely suit the play, for Night tells her minions to 'sow the seeds of discord' between the King and Queen, 'mingle poison with their marriage and put jealousy into their hearts'. The prologue was probably taken from another German tragedy.

Hamlet says that 'the King has given him the Crown of Norway and has appealed to the election of the states' (I.4); and the Queen says (III.6) that her marriage 'robbed my son of the Crown of Denmark'. In the seventeenth century Denmark and Norway were a dual monarchy; the Emperor was elected by the German princes. 'Election of the states' was probably introduced in Germany to explain 'popp'd in between the election and my hopes'.

Hamlet's desire for a memorable revenge 'that posterity shall speak of it for ever' (I.6) resembles Belleforest (see p. 97). It may come from the dying Hamlet's wish that Horatio tell his story, or it may have been invented for *FP*.

Hamlet's vengeance may be difficult; he must 'find an opportunity'; 'wait on him until I find an opportunity' (I.6). His uncle is 'always surrounded by many guards'. In Belleforest

Fengon is surrounded by sycophantic accomplices. No external obstacle to revenge is explicitly mentioned in *Hamlet*, but surely it is assumed; otherwise why should Hamlet put 'an antic disposition' on, and be delighted when he finds the King alone at prayer?[1] The German play needs to stress this hindrance because it diminishes Hamlet's doubts by omitting soliloquies.

Ophelia's nature and her relations with Hamlet are very different. In II.3 she complains that he pesters her with his attentions, but in the next scene he reviles her and tells a silly anecdote about a lady undressing, of a kind which survived in Victorian burlesque (e.g. the parody, 'After the ball is over'). Ophelia has nothing to say during the play-scene. After her father's death she becomes a nymphomaniac, pursuing a new character, Phantasmo, in crudely comic madness (III.9,11). The courtier Phantasmo, who later plays the part of Q1's 'braggart gentleman' and Q2's Osric, is given a foil in Jens, who is seeking pardon for not paying his taxes (Jens must have strayed in from some other play).

German topical references abound. Thus the advice to the players is made to suit the German theatre and fashions. The guilty woman at the play is transferred to Strasbourg and more details are given than by Shakespeare.

In V.1 Hamlet reproaches Nemesis, not himself, for delaying his revenge. This is like Belleforest. He has not yet been able to reach his uncle, but will finish the business today. Ophelia commits suicide, we learn (V.6), by throwing herself from a high hill. In *The Spanish Tragedy* Hieronimo, telling the story of Soliman and Perseda, says that after Perseda had killed herself the lustful bashaw, 'Mov'd with remorse of his misdeeds, / Ran to a mountain-top, and hung himself' (IV.1.127–8). Did Shakespeare introduce the drowning to make Ophelia's end more pathetic?[2] Or did the *FP* actors provide an undoubted suicide

[1] An 'Answer of the Lords of Scotland to Sir Nicholas Throgmorton' in July 1567 asserts that Bothwell, having 'seased her [Mary's] persoun in his handes, envyroned with continuall garde of two hundreth harquebusers as weil day as nycht, quhair ever she went (besides a nomber of his servaundes and others naughty persouns, murtheres and pyrattis' so that 'gif any had to do with the prince, it behovit him, before he could come to hir presence, to go through the ranks of harquebusers under the mercy of a notorious tyran.' (*Illustrations of the Reign of Q. Mary*, ed. J. Stevenson (Maitland Club), 1837, pp. 223–4).

[2] It has been suggested that he recalled that a Katherine Hamlett had been accidentally drowned in the Avon in 1580 while fetching water.

when cutting out his lyricism? *FP* has no Churchyard scene, no rivalry in affection with Laertes.

In V.3 Hamlet's nose bleeds, an omen of misfortune, whereas in Q1 and Q2 his heart is sore. After killing his uncle in V.6 Hamlet kills Phantasmo who has 'brought the poisoned sword'. This is not in *Hamlet*. The German play entirely cuts out the diplomatic business between Denmark and Norway, and Fortinbras's passage through the land. Instead Hamlet has been made King of Norway by his uncle. When dying, however, he asks Horatio to take the crown to Fortinbras his cousin, who has not been mentioned hitherto. Through this abridgment *FP* entirely lacks the sense of national crisis, the wars and rumours of war found in Shakespeare's play.

From the above it appears that *Fratricide Punished* derived mainly from Shakespeare, and almost all those features in it which are not represented in Q1 or Q2 could have been due to the players in Germany. One scene not so far discussed, that with the two murderers on the island (IV.1) which takes the place of Hamlet's adventure with the pirates, will be treated later. Duthie believes that it may come from the *Ur-Hamlet*.[1] I think this unlikely, but memories of the Kydian piece may have affected the English text behind *FP*.[2]

Most of the material common to Shakespeare's play and Belleforest has now been covered. Something must be said about important features of the plot which have no counterpart in the French story. These are the Ghost, the method of the murder, the play-within-the-play, the name Claudius and the Pyrrhus speech, the prayer-scene, the political topicalities, Hamlet's adventure with the pirates, the fencing-match and the end of the tragedy.

There was no Ghost in Saxo or Belleforest, but it was the feature of the *Ur-Hamlet* which most affected spectators and lingered on in public memory, so that in 1596 Thomas Lodge (in *Wits Miserie*) described a devil looking 'as pale as the Visard of the ghost which cried so miserably at the Theatre, like an oister-wife, Hamlet, revenge'.

When Kyd, or whoever else wrote it, adapted Belleforest's

---

[1] Duthie, *op. cit.* pp. 190–3.
[2] Professor A. P. Stabler argues that *FP* owes much to 'a non-Shakespearean source closely related to Belleforest'. *Sh. Studies*, v, 1969, pp. 97–105.

tale in terms of Senecan drama, he dealt only with the first part of Amleth's life until his triumph over Fengon, and changed the climax of that to make it tragic and (no doubt) easier to stage. The main factors shaping the altered plot were the secrecy of Amleth's father's murder and the introduction of his Ghost to incite the hero to revenge. Whereas in *The Spanish Tragedy* the Ghost of Andrea (killed before the play opens) accompanies Revenge to watch the action and 'serve for Chorus in this tragedie', taking no part in the action save to express impatience at the slowness with which punishment falls on the wicked, in the *Ur-Hamlet* the father's Ghost really had some reason for demanding vengeance, and presumably started off the action by revealing it. This was a new departure in ghostly behaviour,[1] and it makes me believe that *Hamlet* was written after *The Spanish Tragedy*.

Seneca's dramas lacked the religious attitude of Greek tragedy and the theme of personal revenge superseded divine retribution; horror became a dominant effect, and the Senecan Chorus contributed to this.[2] Thus at the beginning of *Agamemnon*, Thyestes' Ghost rises from Hell to describe his own adultery with his brother Atreus' wife, and how Atreus took revenge by feasting him on the flesh of his own son; tells too how he raped his own daughter Pelopea (who later married Atreus) and had by her a son, Aegysthus, who is now Clytemnestra's paramour and will shortly help her murder Thyestes' nephew, her husband Agamemnon. The Ghost does not interfere in the action; it expounds the past and prepares the atmosphere of horror (Text VI.A.i). The *Agamemnon* also has a scene in which Electra accuses her mother of adultery and murder—a striking antici- pation of the closet-scene in *Hamlet* (Text VI.A.ii). The Amleth saga was in this tradition of fraternal hate and incest; hence no doubt its appeal to Elizabethan Senecan playwrights.

In *Troades* Talthybius tells how the Ghost of Achilles de- manded the sacrifice of Polyxena (whom he had loved while living) before the Greek fleet could sail from Troy. In the Latin play this ghost did not appear in person, but Jasper Heywood introduced it in Act II of his translation, craving revenge on the

---

[1] Cf. F. T. Bowers, *Elizabethan Revenge Tragedy*, Gloucester, Mass., 1940; E. Prosser, *Hamlet and Revenge*, Stanford, 1967.

[2] H. B. Charlton, *The Senecan Tradition in Renaissance Tragedy*, 1946.

Trojans.[1] Ignoring this proof of survival after death, Seneca's Chorus later doubts (371–408) whether the soul lives on (Text VI.B.ii). There is a resemblance here to the apparent inconsistency in *Hamlet* where, soon after accepting the Ghost as his 'father's spirit', the hero speaks of 'the undiscover'd country from whose bourn / No traveller returns' (III.1.79–80).

Professor Eleanor Prosser's study of the ghosts in Elizabethan drama shows that many act as Chorus or Prologue, or as the retributory voices of conscience, and that these are almost all pagan ghosts risen from Hades.[2] Few ghosts show Christian characteristics. After *Hamlet* three or four mingle Christian and pagan qualities. Only Andrugio in *Antonio's Revenge* (probably derived from the *Ur-Hamlet*) and the Ghost in *Hamlet* 'appear to a protagonist to command blood revenge'. (This occasionally occurred in Italian Senecan tragedies.) Andrugio's Ghost comes from his coffin to demand that his son

> Invent some stratagem of vengeance
> Which, but to think on, may like lightning glide
> With horror through thy breast. (III.1.48–50)

He combines delight in the most awful tortures with assurances that he is in league with Heaven. But the play is so confused in tone that some critics have regarded it as a parody. Old Hamlet's Ghost is unique in the problems it posits, and 'Shakespeare may well have intended to jolt his audience into a fresh response to what had become a hackneyed convention'.[3] It is extremely unlikely that the inventor of Andrea in *The Spanish Tragedy* also created a spirit so complex as that in *Hamlet* Q2.

This is not a suitable place in which to enter the debate about the nature of this ghost.[4] W. W. Greg's suggestion that it is a figment of Hamlet's imagination was countered by E. Stoll who thought it an objectivation of Elizabethan popular lore. For J. D. Wilson it was an occasion for Shakespeare to present three different attitudes to ghosts: the Catholic view (of Marcellus and Bernardo) that a soul could come from Purgatory; the

---

[1] Cf. G. Ll. Evans, 'Shakespeare, Seneca and the Kingdom of Violence', in *Roman Drama*, ed. T. A. Dorey and D. R. Dudley, 1965.

[2] E. Prosser, *op. cit.* Appendix A.

[3] Prosser, *op. cit.* pp. 101–2.

[4] For the following references see Bibliography.

sceptical view of Horatio (like Reginald Scot's) but soon
changed to belief; and Hamlet's Protestant view (held by L.
Lavater and James VI) that ghosts were probably devils but
might be angels, never the souls of men. Another school of
thought, including Roy W. Battenhouse and Miss Prosser,
argues that the Ghost is a damned spirit come to mislead Hamlet
into offending against the divine injunction against revenge.

My own view is nearer to that of I. J. Semper who saw the
Ghost as a visitant from Purgatory and that of Sister Miriam
who sees Hamlet as justifiably doubting and testing it. But we
should not exaggerate the doctrinal strictness of Shakespeare's
approach or assume that he was a Catholic because he used the
idea of Purgatory. P. N. Siegel was right to insist: 'The Hamlet
Ghost is a compound of the Senecan revenge ghost, the Catholic
purgatorial spirit and the popular graveyard spook, created for
an audience prepared by theatrical tradition, by what Cardinal
Newman called "floating religious opinions" (as against official
dogma) and by current folklore to give it dramatic credence.'[1]
The pagan element appears in the Ghost's insistence on quasi-
physical horrors unspeakable and the reference to 'Lethe
wharf' (I.5.33); its purgatorial quality in I.5.12–13. It has an
almost Miltonic apprehension of virtue and vice (53–7); it loves
the Sacraments and deeply regrets having died 'Unhousel'd,
disappointed, unaneal'd' (76–80). Its folklore features include
the hour when it walks and when it disappears, and its knocking
underground.

Two analogues to the purgatorial spirit are given below, one
from the Middle Ages (the *St. Albans Chronicle*) [Text VII], the
other having somewhat more relationship to the play since it
pretends to show the ghost of Richard Tarlton the stage-clown,
who though never a court-jester had been much in demand as an
entertainer in great houses, and is thought by some scholars to
have suggested Yorick, the 'fellow of infinite jest'[2] (Text VIII).
Tarlton died in 1588, about the time when the *Ur-Hamlet* was
being played. Soon afterwards *News out of Purgatory*, an undistinguished collection of *facetiae* and *novelle* lifted from Boccaccio and Straparola, etc., was put out with an amusing introduction in which the editor imagines himself seeing in a vision the

[1] P. N. Siegel, 'Discerning the Ghost in *Hamlet*', *PMLA*, lxxviii, 1963, p. 148.
[2] The name Yorick may come from the Danish Jorg.

ghost of Tarlton, who proves to him that Purgatory exists despite what Calvinists say, and describes the place and its inhabitants in a burlesque manner, satirizing popes and other church-
men, the professions, cuckolds, hardhearted virgins, etc. The
tone is anti-Catholic and flippant, but the piece suggests that
questions about the nature and origin of ghosts were interesting
to the general reader.

Whatever precisians and members of the old faith may have
thought, there can be little doubt that the average Elizabethan
playgoer would regard Hamlet's father's Ghost as truly his
'spirit in arms', benevolent to his son, watching mournfully over
his erring wife, and demanding a just vengeance on the incestuous fratricidal murderer.[1] 'It is an honest ghost' and the revenge
it requires is sanctioned not only by classical and modern
dramatic conventions and by the social practice of many
nations, but also by the Old Testament law of *lex talionis*. Like
Belleforest's hero, Hamlet is to be 'Heavens scourge and
minister' carrying out a just and unescapable duty. But that the
soldiers fear lest the Ghost may be a demon and that Hamlet
himself doubts it for a short time reveals a degree of sophistica-
tion in Shakespeare's treatment entirely lacking in *The Spanish
Tragedy* and probably only dimly foreshadowed in the *Ur-
Hamlet*.

At some stage, probably in the *Ur-Hamlet*, the saga already
somewhat modernized by Belleforest was brought into line with
Renaissance manners and current tales of court-murders and
revenge. This involved changing the ending by having Hamlet
achieve his vengeance during a modern fencing-match. It also
meant altering the way in which old Hamlet was killed, and the
Ghost's part was made important by substituting the Italianate
secret way of poison for open murder at a banquet. The Ghost
accuses Claudius of seducing his wife and of killing him while
'sleeping in my orchard':

> Upon my secure hour thy uncle stole,
> With juice of cursed hebona in a vial,
> And in the porches of mine ears did pour
> The leperous distilment . . . (I.5.41–79)

---

[1] Cf. R. H. West, 'King Hamlet's Ambiguous Ghost', *PMLA*, lxx, 1955, pp.
1107–17.

Arranging the performance of *The Murder of Gonzago* Hamlet says,

> One scene of it comes near the circumstance
> Which I have told thee of my father's death
> (III.2.76–7)[1]

but the play is somewhat differently described in Q1 and Q2:

Q1.   this play is
The image of a murder done in *guyana*, Albertus
Was the Duke's name, his wife Baptista.

Q2.   This play is the Image of a murther done in *Vienna*,
Gonzaga is the Dukes name, his wife Baptista, you shall see anon, 'tis a knavish peece of worke. . . . This is one *Lucianus*, Nephew to the King. . . . A poysons him i' the Garden for his estate, his names *Gonzago*, the story is extant, and written in very choice Italian, you shall see anon how the murtherer gets the love of *Gonzagoes* wife.

In the dumbshow the characters, according to the Q1 reporter, are a 'King and Queene'; the murderer is Lucianus, 'nephew to the King', but the speech-headings, a stage-direction, and the above speech describe them as a 'Duke and Dutchesse'. In Q2 they are 'a King and Queene' both in the dumbshow and in the text; yet there is a reference to the 'Duke'. These variants suggest that the original story concerned a duke and a duchess, that the players dressed in royal robes to point the reference to Hamlet's father and mother, and that in Q2 and F1 the text was brought into agreement with this practice, but not completely.

In the Q2 *Murder of Gonzago* both the murderer and his victim shared the Gonzago name. This clue has set scholars searching for the 'story written in very choice Italian' about a Gonzaga crime. G. Sarrazin pointed out that a relative of the Duke

---

[1] Plays as fiercely topical as this were rare, but on 14 May 1567, some weeks after Bothwell had been acquitted of Darnley's murder for lack of evidence, William Drury wrote to Cecil: 'There has been an interlude of boys at Stirling of the manner of the King's death and the arraignment of the Earl. He who represented the Earl was in sport so long hanged that hardly in a long time could life be renewed. This was before the Lords, who the Earl thinks were devisers of the same.' (*CSP. Foreign*, 1566–8, p. 87). Bothwell was not present, but no doubt he was as furious as Claudius.

Vincenzio Gonzaga (himself possibly the original Duke in *Measure for Measure*), the Marchese Alfonso Gonzaga di Castel-goffredo, was murdered by eight bravos while resting at his country villa near Mantua on 7 May 1592. They were hired by his nephew, the Marchese Rodolfo di Castiglione. His wife was named Hippolyta. On 3 January 1593, Rodolfo in his turn was murdered.[1] Sarrazin's authority was not published until after Shakespeare's death, and the event itself was too late for the *Ur-Hamlet* of 1587–9.

A more likely historical source was suggested by C. Elliot Browne who in 1876 noted that Albertus (as in Q1) was 'a more appropriate name for a duke of Austria . . . than Gonzago, but the story of the Play is certainly taken from the murder of the Duke of Urbano (*sic*) by Luigi Gonzaga in 1538, who was poisoned by means of a lotion poured into his ears. The new way of poisoning caused great horror throughout Europe.'[2] I question this last sentence, but in 1560 the great surgeon Ambroise Paré was wrongfully suspected of having murdered François II of France (Mary of Scots' first husband) by blowing a poisonous powder into his ear;[3] and Lightborn in Marlowe's *Edward II* (*c.* 1591) describes methods he learned in Naples:

> Or, whilst one is asleep, to take a quill,
> And blow a little powder in his ears;
> Or ope his mouth and pour quicksilver down.
>
> (V.4.34–6)

Dowden in his Arden edition drew on Browne for his note on III.2.251, making the same error but not mentioning his source. Browne got his information from James Dennistoun's *Memoirs of the Dukes of Urbino*[4] which showed the importance of Urbino in Italian cultural life after Federico da Montefeltro (1422–84) was made duke and married Battista Sforza. The picture of its brilliant court under Guidobaldo I and his wife Elisabetta Gonzaga given by Baldassarre Castiglione in *Il Cortegiano* (drafted 1508, published 1528) was little exaggerated. The characters of that week of dialogues held under the auspices of

---

[1] G. Sarrazin, 'Neu italienische Skizzen zu Shakespeare', *ShJb*, 31, 1895, based on *Antonio Possevini Gonzaga Mantuae*, 1628, p. 804.

[2] C. E. Browne, 'Notes on Shakespeare's Names', *Athenaeum*, 29 July 1876.

[3] R. R. Simpson, *Shakespeare's Medicine*, 1959, p. 135.

[4] 3 vols, 1851 (reprinted by E. Hutton, 1909).

1 Francesco Maria della Rovere, Duke of Urbino (engraved from a portrait by Titian, in P. Iovii, *Elogia Virorum Bellica Virtute Illustrium*, 1575.)

the Duchess included Pietro Bembo, Bibbiena, Giuliano de'
Medici, Bernado Accolti, and her son Francesco Maria della
Rovere (called 'the Lord General' although he was only seventeen at the time). There can be little doubt that Shakespeare
knew Hoby's translation (1561) and that it influenced his depiction of courtly manners. 'Without Castiglione we should not
have had a Hamlet.'[1] We do not know how far Shakespeare
drew upon the *Ur-Hamlet* for the method of old Hamlet's
murder and the play-within-the-play, but Shakespeare's
Hamlet combines with the Amleth story material taken from
the circumstances surrounding the death of Guidobaldo I's
nephew and successor.

Duke Francesco Maria I della Rovere (1490–1538) had a
varied career. He married Leonora, daughter of Francesco
Gonzaga and Isabella d'Este in 1508, and their son Guidobaldo
II was the eldest boy of five children. Twice driven from
his duchy, first by the Borgias and later by the Medici, he
spent most of his life in warfare and his leisure at the Villa
dell'Imperiale at Pesaro, which came to him through his wife.

Opinions of his generalship differed. Guicciardini asserted
that his inactivity contributed to the fall of Rome in 1527, but
Rusticelli called him 'the founder of the art of war as practised
in the sixteenth century'. According to his secretary Urbani, 'his
ideas and discourse tended to lofty themes. Ready of hand, he
dexterously managed, on horseback or on foot, the arms then in
use. Of high courage, he invariably bent his mind to objects
conducive to his honour and renown, especially in war....
He loathed incontinence and youthful excesses.'[2] Quick in
temper, he slew a man who he thought had seduced his sister,
and when the sly and treacherous Cardinal Alidosi, whom he
held responsible for his defeat by the French and loss of papal
Bologna, smiled at him maliciously after he had been berated
by Julius II, he killed the priest with one blow of his fist.

In 1538, as Captain-General of the Venetian forces, he was
preparing an expedition against Solyman the Great. Having
been unwell for some time he was recuperating in September at

---

[1] W. B. D. Henderson, ed., *The Courtier*, trans. Sir Thomas Hoby, pp. xii–xvi.
See also pp. 83–4, 133–5, 152–3, 166–7, for allusions to Francesco Maria and his
wit; and p. 259 for praise of his wife Leonora.

[2] Dennistoun, *op. cit.* iii, p. 76.

the Villa dell'Imperiale, which he was decorating magnificently. He had invited Titian (who had recently painted portraits of him and his wife) to help him inspect the work being done there. But on 6 September the Duke fell seriously ill and after lingering for six weeks he died during the night of 20/21 October. His body was taken to Urbino and buried in full armour.

Rumour quickly blamed the Duke's enemies for this unexpected death. Paolo Giovio in his eulogy declared that Francesco Maria died 'not through natural destiny, but through the malice of certain men who, it is said, had him given poison; as can be seen by the sure evidence of a law-suit and by a confession that this great crime had been committed.'[1] G. Leoni, the Duke's biographer, supplies no further details,[2] and contemporary historians were studiously careful, since no crime was ever proved and powerful families were involved. Elisa Viani, however, has pieced together subsequent events.[3]

When a post-mortem revealed traces of poison in his father's body Guidobaldo arrested his father's barber (i.e. barber-surgeon) who had visited him during his illness. The man confessed under torture that he had poured poison into the Duke's ears at the instigation of Luigi Gonzaga, Marchese di Castel-goffredo, and of Cesare Fregoso. Both of these men were Francesco Maria's enemies, and in 1513 he had protested against their employment in the Venetian army, objecting especially to Gonzaga, 'knowing the nature of Sig. Luigi, who is not only very malicious, but also very cunning in his conceits'. According to one chronicler Guidobaldo had the barber torn with pincers and then quartered in the streets of Pesaro.

Gonzaga and Fregoso indignantly denied the charge and demanded 100,000 scudi damages for wrongful accusation. Guidobaldo sought for several years to bring them to justice, without success. Angry letters and pamphlets were exchanged. Pietro Aretino, the 'Scourge of Princes', who owed gratitude to Francesco Maria, at first took Guidobaldo's side in a violent attack on the accused men (which unfortunately I have been unable to find). But he soon climbed down, and apologized for

---

[1] *Gli Elogi, Vite brevemente scritte d'Huomini illustri di Guerra* . . . Fiorenza, 1554. Latin original, 1548 (often reprinted). See below.

[2] *Vita di F. M.*, Venice, 1605, p. 459.

[3] E. Viani, *L'Avvelenatura di Francesco Maria, Duca di Urbino*, Mantua, 1902.

having connected two such honourable gentlemen with the crime of a vile barber. I give his letter and also one in which Luigi Gonzaga sought to exculpate himself (Text IX). In 1543 Guidobaldo dropped his case, perhaps at his mother's suggestion. She mourned her husband long and deeply, as did their intimate friend Pietro Bembo in his letters to the Duchess in the next few years, as when on the death of her relative Cardinal Gonzaga he tried to console her in her double loss: 'comfort your self with the King of Heaven, who has allowed it to be thus; and accept His will and judgement, which cannot err.'[1]

There are parallels between the Urbino story and *The Murder of Gonzago* besides the manner of the murder and its pleasant setting. In both the alleged murderer is related to the victim. Lucianus (perhaps a Latinized form of Luigi) is 'nephew to the King' (Q2); Luigi Gonzaga was a kinsman of Leonora Gonzaga, Francesco Maria's wife, and Fregoso was a kinsman of the Duke. The Player Duke's wife's name, Baptista, was also that of Federico da Montefeltro's Duchess. The Player King has been married for forty years in Q1, thirty years in Q2; Francesco Maria had been married for thirty years in 1538. Gonzago is unwell; his 'operant powers their functions leave to do' (III.2.177) before he is poisoned. This was true of the Duke of Urbino.

In the main play we also learn that old Hamlet and Gertrude have been married for over thirty years (V.1.146–68). Like Francesco Maria he was a famous soldier. His single combat with King Fortinbras comes from Belleforest, but both this and his 'angry parle' with the Poles recall the Duke's victories. Such resemblances may be fortuitous; but the many details about Hamlet's father's appearance and dress suggest that Shakespeare (rather than Kyd) knew the portrait of Francesco Maria by Titian as engraved in several editions of Paolo Giovio's *Elogia Virorum Bellica Virtute Illustrium*[2] (Text X). The engraving

---

[1] P. Bembo, *Opere*, Venice, 1729, iii, p. 262; iv, p. 330, etc. For other details about the case see my article, 'The Murder of Gonzago', *MLR*, xxx, 1935, 433–44.

[2] I have not found the portrait in several editions of the Italian translation of Giovio's work by Domenichi which I have consulted. Dennistoun gives the portraits of the Duke and his wife. A portrait which I once thought to be of Guidobaldo was shown by P. Rebora to be of someone else (see 'Echi di Urbino nella Cultura Inglese', *Studi Urbinati*, Ser. B, 1–2, xvi, Urbino, 1938). Bronzino did Guidobaldo's portrait, now in the Pitti Palace at Florence.

does scant justice to Titian's fine portrait (now in the Uffizi Gallery), yet even here one sees the strong warrior of Shakespeare's play, in 'complete steel', with 'Hyperion's curls' and beard 'grizzled', a 'sable silver'd'; here are the armour which impressed Horatio, the field-marshal's truncheon (held at hip) and behind him the helmet with its 'beaver up'.

The contrasting portraits used by Hamlet in III.4.53ff. may have been suggested by those in Giovio's book. It would be building speculation on speculation to argue that the dramatist also looked at the unprepossessing portrait of Alidosi (whom Giovio treated as a 'remorseless, treacherous . . . villain') and the verses telling how he was slain by the Duke; '*Quem tamen impavidus | Sustulit Hercules confossum Feltrius ictu.*'[1] The Duke was compared to Mars and Hercules in the Latin poem appended to Giovio's eulogy. So Hamlet indirectly compares his father to Hercules when he says that his uncle is 'No more like my father than I to Hercules' (I.2.153) and later that he had 'An eye like Mars, to threaten and command' (III.4.57). In *Fratricide Punished* the portraits hang in a near-by gallery.[2] English stage tradition has long made them miniatures, Claudius's worn by the Queen, his father's by Hamlet.[3]

The parallel between Hamlet and Brutus is by no means the only classical analogy in the play. Why is the wicked uncle's name changed from Fengon or Feng to Claudius?

As Mr William Montgomerie has pointed out[4] the Roman Emperor Claudius was the second husband of Agrippina, mother of Nero, whom she loved and dominated until finally he had her murdered. This matricide is referred to by Hamlet when, going towards his mother's chamber, he says:

> O heart! lose not thy nature; let not ever
> The soul of Nero enter this firm bosom;

[1] 1575 edn. Lib. III, pp. 207–10.

[2] Tapestry portraits of a hundred Danish monarchs hung in the Great Chamber at Kronbourg Castle, Elsinore. Stowe mentioned them in his *Annals* (Sjögren, *op. cit.*).

[3] A later anecdote bears on this. T. Forde in *A Theatre of Wits* (1660) tells of King Borislaus IV of Poland (1632–48) who 'bearing the picture of his Father hanged about his neck in a plate of gold, when he was to speak, or doe anything of importance, he took his picture, and kissing it, said, *Dear Father*, I wish I may not doe anything remissly, unworthy of thy name' (pp. 7–8).

[4] 'More an Antique Roman than a Dane', *Hibbert Journal*, lix, 1960, pp. 67–74.

Let me be cruel, not unnatural;
I will speak daggers to her, but use none.

(III.2.399–402)

Nero's mother would not let him divorce Octavia to marry Poppaea, who therefore kindled his resentment against the aggressive Agrippina. This was not all. Agrippina was alleged to have sought to commit incest with her son, and to have tempted him publicly at a banquet (Tacitus XIV, 1–2). Nero was warned by his concubine Acte that the army would revolt 'against a man plunged in vice of so deep a dye', so he had his mother killed in the most brutal fashion.

Agrippina may not have committed incest with Nero, but she had done so in marrying Claudius; for she was the daughter of his brother Germanicus, and when after the execution of the monstrous Messalina the Emperor had to choose another wife, he was seduced by Agrippina (widow of Domitius Aenobarbus), although as Tacitus writes: 'the marriage of an uncle with his brother's daughter was, at that time, without a precedent . . . an incestuous marriage' (XII.5).[1]

So Nero's great-uncle became his stepfather, as Hamlet's uncle became his. Shakespeare certainly intended the parallel when he called the incestuous uncle Claudius. Furthermore, Agrippina got rid of her husband, and most ingeniously. First she gave Claudius a dish of mushrooms containing 'a compound of new and exquisite ingredients such as would make directly to the brain, yet not bring on an immediate dissolution' (XII.66). When Claudius survived, though sick, she got her husband's physician to poison the feather with which he tickled the Emperor's throat to make him vomit (XII.67). Thus Agrippina made her son Nero's succession sure, and thoroughly deserved the end he gave her later.

The unusual manner of the murder had something in common with old Hamlet's taking off, and the several themes, mother's sexuality and incest, uncle-father, matricide, certainly must have added Roman associations to the conception of the play when Fengon was named Claudius. Shakespeare, however, did not make much use of the analogy. Indeed Claudius is named only in the stage-direction at his first entry and the

[1] Tacitus, *Annals*, trans. Arthur Murphy, 1793.

heading of his first speech in Q2; elsewhere he is always the 'King'. Maybe the name Claudius and the Nero allusion occurred first in the earlier play. But one recalls how passages in Tacitus came into Shakespeare's mind when writing *Henry V* (cf. Vol. IV, pp. 361–2). Claudius was certainly a suitable name for marking a contrast with Hamlet's father, for the Emperor Claudius was ugly, sensual, uxorious and cruel, an unworthy ruler.[1]

There was probably a cry of players in the *Ur-Hamlet* if that play, as I suppose, included a *Murder of Gonzago*; but it seems certain that Shakespeare enlarged this section of the piece to introduce references topical in 1599–1603, to the War of the Theatres, the popularity of child actors, etc. He probably also introduced the 'passionate speech' of the First Player and the Hecuba references in the hero's soliloquy.

The Troy tale was of course involved in some of Seneca's tragedies, e.g. *Troades* and *Agamemnon*, where revenge and ghosts were important, so it is not surprising that allusions to the siege and its heroes should be made in dramatizing the Norse saga. Shakespeare had introduced the fall of Troy into *The Rape of Lucrece*, where Lucrece gazes upon a skilful painting of it,

> To find a face where all distress is stell'd . . .
>> Till she despairing Hecuba beheld,
>> Staring on Priam's wounds with her old eyes,
>> Which bleeding under Pyrrhus' proud foot lies. (1444–9)

Her ruinous old age and grief are described:

>> Who nothing wants to answer her but cries,
>> And bitter words to ban her cruel foes.

Lucrece undertakes to provide the lamentations which the painter could not,

>> And drop sweet balm in Priam's painted wound,
>> And rail on Pyrrhus that hath done him wrong. (1466–7)

---

[1] Mr. Montgomerie, *op. cit.*, sees other parallels between Claudius the Roman and Claudius the Dane in their addiction to drink, sloth, gaming and bad temper; he also likens Hamlet to Nero in several respects!

In *Hamlet* Shakespeare pretends to take his description of Priam's death and his wife's grief from an English play on Dido and Aeneas in which Aeneas tells his story, somewhat as in *Aeneid*, Bk. II. That is, a son tells how his father was killed before his mother's eyes and how she grieved. There are resemblances to *The Tragedie of Dido Queene of Carthage*, by Marlowe and Nashe (published 1594), but *Dido* emphasizes the pathos of the scene, making Priam beg for his life, having Pyrrhus cut off the old man's hands before ripping his body from navel to throat, etc. The Player's speech comes nearer to Virgil, whose Priam makes an effort to attack Pyrrhus, but that Shakespeare remembered Marlowe's play is proved by the fact that in both *Dido* and *Hamlet* Priam is knocked down by the wind of Pyrrhus' sword (Text XI).[1]

Shakespeare would also know the translation of the *Troades* by Jasper Heywood (1559) in which Hecuba tells of the burning city and her husband's death (Text VI, B.i). A novel element in Shakespeare's version is the collapse of Troy walls as the King falls, and the momentary pause of Pyrrhus like a 'painted tyrant' before completing the murder. Possibly this pictorial moment was due to a memory of *Lucrece*, but in *Troades* the Nuntius tells how when Polyxena, doomed to die to satisfy the vengeful Ghost of Achilles, stands before Pyrrhus awaiting death,

> Her corage moves eche one, and loe a strange thing monstrous like,
> That Pyrrhus even himselfe stoode still, for dread, and durst not strike.

The style of the Player's speech is high-pitched, in a deliberate, solemn, epic manner (not unlike the Prologue to *Troilus and Cressida*), with plentiful epithets, more Latinate than usual. It is obviously not an imitation of Marlowe and Nashe's manner, and Shakespeare's gently mocks its portentous extravagance ('eyes like carbuncles', 'threatening the flames With bisson rheum'), yet he admires the piece as good of its time, and the 'passionate speech' has a deep effect on Hamlet.

[1] There was another *Dido and Aeneas* play acted on 8 Jan. 1598 by the Admiral's Men. It is unlikely that Shakespeare would praise this, but he might parody it.

As Professor Johnston points out, the position of Pyrrhus was not unlike that of Hamlet; he was seeking vengeance for the murder of his father Achilles in a temple, by Paris.[1] But Shakespeare ignores this. As in *Lucrece* his sympathy is wholly with Priam and Hecuba. Pyrrhus, as the brutal murderer of a defenceless old man, is like Claudius, and Hecuba is the faithful wife that Gertrude should have been. The actor who represents her grief breaks down in tears and this starts Hamlet off on a train of self-reproach, that he does not say enough, feel enough, do enough. He draws no parallel or contrast between himself and Pyrrhus. Instead he sums up the purpose of the whole scene when he tells us that he has doubts of the Ghost and will test it, seeing whether 'guilty creatures, sitting at a play' will reveal their guilt.

Plutarch tells how the tyrant Alexander of Pherae once left the theatre when Euripides' *Troades* was being performed, saying that he 'was ashamed his people should see him weepe to see the miseries of Hecuba and Andromache played, and that they never saw him pity the death of any one man, of so many of his citizens as he had caused to be slaine.'[2] This is not quite what Hamlet meant. Much nearer is the definite instance mentioned in the anonymous play *A Warning for Faire Women*, played by Shakespeare's company and published in 1599 (Text XII). Here after a murderer has been miraculously exposed when his victim's wounds began to bleed and the 'dead' man accuses him, the Mayor of Rochester and others discuss other examples of murders strangely revealed, among them the case of a guilty widow sitting at a play. This was probably Shakespeare's source.

Neither in Saxo nor in Belleforest did the wicked uncle show any sign of remorse, and the introduction of the prayer-scene indicates that the play had religious implications not present in the old saga. Such a scene provided an opportunity for Hamlet to take speedy revenge immediately after *The Murder of Gonzago* had proved the honesty of the Ghost and the justice of his own

[1] A. Johnston, 'The Player's Speech in *Hamlet*', *ShQ*, xiii, 1962, pp. 21–30. C. Leech, 'The Hesitation of Pyrrhus' in *The Morality of Art*, ed. D. W. Jefferson, 1969, writes, 'Hamlet sees himself as Pyrrhus, the revenger who pauses'.

[2] *Life of Pelopidas*, cited by Johnston, *op. cit.* p. 27. Plutarch also tells that Alexander's wife Phebe, disgusted by his cruelties, forced three young men to help her kill him in his bed.

cause. If it appeared in the *Ur-Hamlet* it must have resembled in broad outline the scene as we have it: a Kydian hero would surely put off the killing of his enemy, not out of religious scruples, but to make sure of damning his soul.[1]

The killing of a warrior at prayer was the original cause in the medieval Troy story for the vengeance of Pyrrhus, for his father Achilles was so slain by Paris in the tenth year of the siege when he had gone to the Temple of Pallas to discuss with Hecuba his marriage to Polyxena. In *Excidium Troiae* Paris shoots him in the foot (his only weak spot) while Achilles is praying to Apollo. Shakespeare would read the incident in Caxton's *Recuyell* (used for *Troilus* a little later). In Seneca's *Troades*, although Hecuba regrets that Paris did not slay Pyrrhus with his father, the shame of such a cowardly killing disgraces the slayer, especially since his victim was a man 'Whom e'en a god would not fight face to face' (348). Claudius is no Achilles, but Hamlet must not kill him at prayer, since not only would it end the play prematurely, but it would show the hero in a bad light and be inadequate vengeance besides, for the villain should surely realize what is happening to him and why.

Hamlet's stated reasons for sparing his uncle must be accepted and we must regard them as a triumph of Senecan and Italianate vengefulness over Christian piety. Miss Prosser and other critics are horrified by Hamlet's desire to damn his uncle to all eternity, and she demonstrates that nearly all proponents of 'Immortal vengeance' in Elizabethan drama lose the audience's sympathy.[2] But it would be strange in the circumstances were Hamlet to behave like Othello, who does not wish to damn Desdemona's soul. Hamlet does *not* kill his defenceless uncle; moreover we already know the irony of Hamlet's dilemma; for although Claudius has gone three steps up the ladder of repentance (contrition, confession and faith), he has not mounted the convincing fourth (amendment).[3] Nor can he, for he will not surrender 'those effects for which I did the murder' and at the close we know that, even had Hamlet killed him, his soul would scarcely have been saved:

[1] According to Gentillet, vengeful Italians 'seeke in slaying the bodie to damne the soule, if they could'. (*Against Machiavel*, 1608, trs. Patericke, Pt. iii, Max. 6. Cited by Bowers, *op. cit.* p. 52.)

[2] Prosser, *op. cit.* Appendix B.

[3] Prosser, *op. cit.* pp. 183–4.

My words fly up, my thoughts remain below:
Words without thoughts never to heaven go.

(III.3.97–8)

It seems likely that the prayer-scene was suggested by the
Pyrrhus material of the Players. In adopting it Shakespeare
humanizes Claudius by giving us a glimpse of his inner life
which shows him as a soul in conflict, while his confession con-
firms the Ghost's assertion of his guilt and justifies Hamlet's
desire for revenge. Had Hamlet done it 'pat', he would not have
been Hamlet. Laertes might more easily have played Paris's
part, 'To cut his throat i' the church' (IV.7.125).

The mental state of Claudius, believing himself incapable of
true penitence, was of course well known to religious psycholo-
gists. A dramatic analogue may be found in Nathaniel Woods's
didactic play *The Conflict of Conscience* (1581), based on the life of
Francesco Spira, an Italian who fell into despair after turning
to Roman Catholicism from Calvinism.[1] In the play Philologus,
threatened by a Cardinal and tempted by Sensual Suggestion,
chooses worldly goods instead of truth and martyrdom and falls
into 'confusion and horror of the mind'. His friends Eusebius
and Theologus urge him to trust God and pray. He tries, but in
vain:

My lippes have spoke the wordes in deede, but yet I feele my
                                                            heart
With cursing is replenished, with rancor, spight, and gall . . .

(Text XIII).

In the first edition he commits suicide by hanging; in the
second he is converted to God before dying. The parallel with
Claudius is not close. Philologus believes that he is beyond
pardon, whereas Claudius cannot give up his ill-gotten gains
though he knows that God's mercy is waiting for the truly
penitent.

Some topical reasons for the composition of a *Hamlet* play
between 1587 and 1599 have already been given. In Shakespeare's piece there are many details which an audience in the

[1] Woods knew a pamphlet translated by E. Aglionby, *A Notable and marvailous
epistle of the famous Doctor, Mathewe Gribalde* (1550) which described Spira's life and
agonies.

last years of Elizabeth's reign might well take as references to current topics. The Kydian play would probably, as in *The Spanish Tragedy*, have an international setting, fictitious but suggested by historical circumstances. Shakespeare may well have developed this, while preserving a medieval setting in which Norway and Denmark were separate countries.[1] The dual monarchy was elective and primogeniture was not invariably honoured.[2]

Denmark was now a Protestant country and had special connections with Hamlet's university, Wittenberg. Christian II had invited Lutheran theologians from there, and many prominent Danish clerics studied there.

As Hamlet says, the Danes were known as great drinkers. Jerome Horsey, returning from a mission to Russia, told how he met Magnus, King Frederick II's brother: 'He used me but roughly, by reason I could not drink excessively with him.' Again on another visit: 'I dined with the King but could not drink so well.'[3]

During Elizabeth's reign Anglo-Danish relations were warily friendly, for Denmark was a bulwark of Protestantism against possible Catholic advances from the Baltic. But the Scottish alliance with Denmark troubled Elizabeth; moreover Denmark traded with the Spanish Netherlands, and the stopping of Danish vessels by English ships (authorized or unauthorized) was a continual cause of friction. In 1591 the Danes complained that fifteen of their ships had been seized or pillaged. She replied, asserting that 'fifteen pirates, involved in robberies upon the Danes, had been executed'[4] and pointed out that the Danes were supplying the Spaniards, her enemies. Pirates of many nationalities swarmed in the North Sea and in the Bay of Biscay, and in 1588 the ambassador Daniel Rogers, at the Danish court to welcome the accession of Christian IV, when sending a messenger with a report on his reception, 'Hopes that he may

---

[1] There were wars between Norway and Denmark in 1289 ('Norway being the aggressor'), and in 1362–3, but dynastic union followed in 1380, and in 1536 Norway lost its administrative identity while remaining on paper a separate kingdom. (K. Larsen, *A History of Norway*, New York, 1948.)

[2] See Gunnar Sjögren, *Sh. Studies*, iv, 1968, for a discussion of Anglo-Danish problems.

[3] J. Horsey, *Memorials*, Hakluyt Soc. 20, ed. E. A. Bond, 1856 pp. 192, 244.

[4] *CSP. Foreign*, July 1590–May 1591, p. 440.

pass safely, for the seas are very full of pirates, and few or none from hence adventure by the long seas to England' (Text XIVA). Ten years later the position was no better.

Another cause of friction was the tolls and licences demanded by the Danes from traders and fishermen using their ports or the Sound. Frederick II had exempted the English Muscovy Company from paying an annual sum for permission to pass the North Cape (Larsen, *op. cit.* p. 259). Elsewhere the charges were much resented by traders who were often ignorant of Danish laws. In 1598 Dr Christopher Perkins, Dean of Carlisle went on a mission to Denmark to protest against injuries done to English merchants, and 'one Carey [George Carew], Secretary to the Lord Keeper, is going to Poland on some like errand'.[1] Perkins returned with a disappointing reply, only a promise of

> '40,000 dollars to be restored on condition his subjects may be satisfied for such injuries as they have received; and to that purpose he sent an ambassador along with him, who had audience on Sunday last, but his message was nothing pleasing, as being for the most part a complaint of our piracies. And as Dr. Perkins returned with half an answer, so they say Master Cary is come out of Poland with none at all, nor could get no audience.'[2]

Christian IV behaved arrogantly and supported his subjects' grievances in 'very indecent terms'. He even resorted to physical violence in 1599 when seizing five ships from Hull because they had not paid toll or got a licence to fish (Text XIVC). 'He and his brother with their own hands beat and misused the men very unprincely, and spoke contumeliously of the nation.'[3]

In such times of hostility old issues were revived, and the question of harbour-tolls and fishing or trading licences merged into demands for tribute allegedly paid or due by English shipmen from time immemorial. So in 1589 in an interview with Jerome Horsey the Danish King demanded for permission to trade in 'the northern ocean seas', 'a yearly pay of 100 rose nobles; it is but acknowledgement of our right, an homage ever

[1] John Chamberlain to Dudley Carleton, *CSP. Dom.* 1598–1600, 31 May 1598, p. 57. Perkins often sat on commissions dealing with alleged piracies.

[2] *ibid.* 20 Dec. 1598, p. 134.

[3] *ibid.*, 1 Aug 1599, p. 274.

done and payable by her Majesty's ancestors unto our predecessors, lords and Kings of Norway, and of all the said ocean seas adjacent ... the which we purpose to enjoy and not forgo.'[1] Horsey rejected the claim, 'neither can any such due or right be acknowledged, never paid by her Majesty's subjects ... no record, historie, nor chronicle doth make mention of any such thing.'

Recently a claim had been made on the Scots asserting that when Magnus of Norway sold the Hebrides and Isle of Man to Scotland by the Treaty of Perth (1266), 'besides a substantial purchase sum the Scots agreed to make a small annual payment. . . . Soon all payments ceased' (Larsen, p. 171). The claim was dropped when James VI married Princess Anne. We hear again about the claim on England in 1598 when rumours spread on the Continent that the Danish and Polish kings were strongly supporting James's desire to be named as Queen Elizabeth's heir (Text XIVB).

Thus in 1588/9 there was already talk of pirates in the North Sea and of tribute owed by England to Denmark. By 1598 these topics had become more serious factors in Anglo-Danish relations. Tension continued[2] until 1603 when the accession of James VI to the English throne brought smoother running. Probably then, if these subjects were mentioned in the *Ur-Hamlet* they were developed by Shakespeare in rewriting the play.

Fortinbras' Polish campaign is fictitious, and I have not found any victory of the Danes over 'sledded Polacks on the ice'. But Christian II defeated the Swede Sten Sture in a battle on the ice of Lake Asunden in January 1520,[3] and Magnus, Frederick II's brother, took the island of Osel from the Poles in 1561. Poland was Denmark's ally in the 'Seven Years' Northern War' (1563–70) but after 1586, when Sigismund of Sweden became King of Poland, there were fears in England that these two countries might overwhelm Denmark and combine with Spain. The danger passed, but Poland supplied grain to the Spanish Netherlands. In 1597 a Polish ambassador, protesting too vigorously against English privateers in the Baltic, provoked Elizabeth to magnificent scorn when she spoke of his King as

[1] Horsey, *op. cit.* pp. 241–2.
[2] Cf. *Hist. Mss. Comm. Salisbury*, xii, 1910, pp. 373–4.
[3] A. de Torquemada in *The Spanish Mandevile*, 1600, described the lakes in Gothland (South Sweden) which then belonged to Denmark: 'In time of Warre, they skirmish often upon these frozen lakes, yea, and sometimes fight maine battailes upon them.'

monarch 'not so much by right of blood as by right of election, and only newly elected at that' (Text XIVD). The Queen's speech in the 'angry parle' was hailed by Essex as a 'princely triumph' over the 'braving Polack'.[1]

The Danes were more afraid of the Swedes than of the Poles. In his 1589 audience Horsey complained that the Danes had enticed away her Majesty's servants and shipwrights to fashion the Danish navy, and had 'carried away out of her Majesty's kingdom much ordnance, both brass and iron, pieces and other munition, in the time of [their] greatest wars with the Swethian' (*op. cit.* p. 244). Christian IV also imported many Scottish shipwrights, especially after the accession of Charles IX to the Swedish throne in 1599 made him expect a conflict with Sweden which did not occur until 1611.[2] This probably lay behind Marcellus' inquiry about

> such daily cast of brazen cannon,
> And foreign mart of implements of war;
> Why such impress of shipwrights . . . (I.1.73–5)

But some foreign gossips believed that Denmark might be going to war against England.

For Fortinbras to march through Denmark's territory would be the natural land-route to Poland, though Denmark and Poland were no longer contiguous as in the time of Cnut.[3] I suspect that Poland was brought into *Hamlet* because it shared topicality with Denmark both before and after 1588, and was viewed as unfriendly, especially after 1597.

Probably the name Polonius for the King's confidential adviser was given in or after 1598, for in that year there was published an anonymous translation, *The Counsellor*,[4] by the

[1] See W. Chwalewik, *Anglo-Polish Renaissance Texts*, Warsaw, 1968, pp. 8–12.
[2] Camb. Mod. Hist., IV, p. 566.
[3] On the geography of *Hamlet* see K. Brown, 'Hamlet's Place on the Map', *Sh. Studies*, iv, 1968, pp. 160–82.
[4] *The Counsellor. Exactly pourtraited in two Bookes. Wherein the offices of Magistrates, The happie life of Subjectes, and the felicitie of Common-weales is pleasantly and pithilie discoursed. A Golden Worke, replenished with the chiefe learning of the most excellent Philosophers and Lawgivers, and not onely profitable, but verie necessarie for all those that be admitted to the administration of a well-governed Common-weale. Written in Latin by Laurentius Grimaldus, and consecrated to the honour of the Polonian Empyre. Newlie translated into English.* Richard Bradocke, 1598. Modern edn. (facsimile) in W. Chwalewik, *Anglo-Polish Renaissance Texts*, Warsaw, 1968. See his Introduction; also I. Gollancz, 'Bits of Timber', in *A Book of Homage to Shakespeare*, 1916.

Polish statesman Grimaldus Goslicius (Grzymala Goslicki), of
a Latin work originally published in Venice in 1563. The ver-
bose style of the translation and the somewhat commonplace
worldly wisdom of the contents make it almost certain that
Shakespeare enlarged the part of the spying courtier in the light
of it, mocking where it praised the statesman's wariness, senten-
tiousness and gravity, and making Hamlet take the side of that
objector to the counsellor's 'philosophy' who declares, 'that arte
of thine is rather to be tearmed the science of prating, then a
knowledge whereby men attaine unto felicitie'.[1] Hence of the
dead Polonius Hamlet declares:

> Indeed this Counsellor
> Is now most still, most secret and most grave,
> Who was in life a foolish, prating knave.
> (III.4.213–15)

The name 'Polonius' attached to such a character would have
comic point only after the publication of Goslicius' book and
when the dispute with Poland was still fresh, i.e. 1598–1602.
Maybe to avoid offence 'Corambis' was substituted in the
theatre-version from which Q1 was taken, but Polonius survived
in the Q2 and F1 copy. 'Corambis' may have been in the *Ur-
Hamlet*.

Hamlet's adventure with the pirates should be seen against
this background of contemporary events. The circumstances of
his escape from his uncle's 'English' plot and of his return to
Denmark differ from version to version of the story. In Saxo
and Belleforest Amleth reads the King's letters while his two
companions are asleep, and changes the message so as to have
the two men executed and himself married to the English
princess. It seems likely that the *Ur-Hamlet*, concentrating on
the main issue, cut out the English part of the saga and brought
back the hero to Denmark by some simple device such as we
find in Q1 where Horatio tells the Queen

> Being crossed by the contention of the windes,
> He found the Packet sent to the King of *England*,
> Wherein he saw himselfe betray'd to death,

and

[1] *Op. cit.* p. 41.

He being set ashore, they went for *England*,
And in the Packet there writ down that doome
To be perform'd on them poynted for him:
And by great chance he had his fathers Seale,
So all was done without discoverie. (Sc. 14).

Horatio promises that Hamlet will tell the Queen what happened in full next time he sees her, but there is no opportunity for this in the Q1 text. In Q2 and F1 Hamlet feels uneasy in the night, goes to his companions' cabin, finds the King's letter and alters it to ask that Rosencrantz and Guildenstern be put to death. Next day their vessel is chased by pirates; they grapple and Hamlet, boarding the enemy ship, is carried away, well-treated ('I am to do a good turn for them') and set down on the coast of Denmark, while his two 'friends' go to their deaths in England.

Fratricide Punished raises problems, for there the King orders two attempts on Hamlet's life. The 'attendants' are to try to murder him with dagger or pistol as soon as they reach England. Should this fail they are to take him with the letter to a place where he will be 'well cared for'. On an island 'near Dover' they propose to murder him, telling him why. He trickily makes them shoot each other, searches them, and finds the letter ('to an arch-hangman in England'). The English King is not mentioned. How Hamlet gets home is not clear from his confused remarks about taking the 'post' at the nearest town, and ordering the sailors 'back to Denmark'.

It looks as if the shooting plan was inserted into *Fratricide Punished* to let us see Hamlet on his journey and to provide a serio-comic scene in which he outwits the murderers. The traditional letter-scheme is thereby rendered futile, and I cannot believe that the island-scene was in either the *Ur-Hamlet* or the version behind Q1. On the other hand several authorities have suggested that the incident came from the *Ur-Hamlet*, and Professor Fredson T. Bowers has shown that the play *Alphonsus, Emperor of Germany*, (which he dated 1594–9) seems to echo a Hamlet-play in having a Laertes-like avenger who is used as a tool by the wicked monarch, and also several snatches of dialogue reminiscent of Shakespeare.[1] It includes a scene in which

[1] F. T. Bowers, '*Alphonsus, Emperor of Germany* and the *Ur-Hamlet*', *MLN*, 48, 1933, pp. 101–8; Duthie, *op. cit.* pp. 191–3.

Prince Richard of England, who has been robbed of a throne by a faked election, is to be murdered by two German boors, Hans and Jerick. He overhears them reading a letter promising them his wealth after he has been dispatched. When attacked he falls down and shams death. They plunder his clothes, then quarrel about a gold chain. Jerick kills Hans, and Richard kills Jerick and jests as he drags off the dead body. There are resemblances to *Fratricide Punished* here which have made Bowers and others believe that *Alphonsus* was indebted to the *Ur-Hamlet*, and that this latter contained the shooting-incident or something of the kind. But the date of *Alphonsus* is not certain; it was not published until 1654, and the adventure with the boors, which is almost all in German, may have been a late addition, made perhaps by a writer who had seen *Fratricide Punished* acted in Germany. Or the actors who made up *Fratricide Punished* may have remembered a performance of *Alphonsus* when they decided to enliven the account of Hamlet's voyage overseas. The two incidents are both age-old comic *lazzi*; in one the hero shams death and waits for the two villains to quarrel over their spoils; in the other the 'innocent' victim sets up the stooges and makes them strike each other unwittingly.[1]

The great swelling of allusions to Denmark, tribute, Poland and pirates from 1597 onwards for several years leads me to suggest that Shakespeare wrote a version of *Hamlet*, improving greatly on the *Ur-Hamlet*, between 1597 and 1600, and that he expanded the topical references and introduced the pirate-adventure between 1600 and 1603. Like the authors of *Fratricide Punished* he was dissatisfied with Belleforest's adverse winds as a means to get Hamlet home again, though this would not seem so weak a device as it does to us, since gales often drove ships far from their destination.[2] Those topical pirates were an obvious means of proving Hamlet's gallantry, short-circuiting the journey to England, and linking his northern tale with Mediter-ranean romances like *Apollonius of Tyre*[3] and Sidney's *Arcadia*. In particular the adventures of Musidorus and Pyrocles gradually

[1] The cross-shooting jest certainly survived; I remember seeing it in a Christmas pantomime in my boyhood.

[2] The ship bearing Princess Anne to Scotland in August 1589 was forced to seek shelter in Norway after being in great peril.

[3] Already used for *CE*, and to be used again for *Per.* In Belleforest Amleth's father was 'the most renowned pirate'.

revealed by Sidney seem to have influenced Shakespeare. In Book 2, ch. 24 of the 1590 *Arcadia* an old knight, to avenge a kinsman murdered by the evil Plexirtus (partial prototype of Edmund in *Lear*), gets the latter into his power by forging a letter from Artaxia promising him marriage. Plexirtus is saved by Pyrocles but ungratefully tries to get rid of Pyrocles and Musidorus, ordering a sea-captain to murder them on their way to Arcadia. A grave counsellor warns them and tries in vain to dissuade the captain ('who had been a pyrate from his youth, and often blouded in it'). The young men defend themselves; the ship gets on fire and they leap into the sea. Musidorus gets to land in Book I, ch. 1; Pyrocles is taken up by pirates (Bk. I, ch. 8) and forced to fight with them against the King of Lacedaemon, whose nephew he kills before being captured. He is released when the people revolt and he assists them so successfully that they elect him their chief (Text XV).[1]

Kyd could not have known these incidents before writing the *Ur-Hamlet*, but Shakespeare knew the *Arcadia* well. The letter-trick, the killing of a king's nephew, the proposed murder on a sea-journey, by their associations with the Hamlet story, may have helped to suggest the adventure with the pirates in Q2 and his good relations with them (IV.6.8–28).

How much of the incident in the last scene of the play was in the *Ur-Hamlet*, it is impossible to say. The climax of the story in Saxo and Belleforest, Amleth's catching Fengon's courtiers in the nets or tapestry hung round the walls of the hall, could hardly have been presented on an open stage, but the attack on Fengon in his chamber, the changing of the weapons (Amleth's sword being nailed in its scabbard) and the death of the villain, with appropriate speeches, could well be shown. However, remembering Kyd's use of a court-entertainment in *The Spanish Tragedy* we may imagine that the *Ur-Hamlet* contained, in addition to the play-within-the-play, a fencing-match in which sport concealed deadly earnest, Hamlet was wounded by a foul blow, the King was killed and the Queen died by drinking poison intended for her son. This even if there was no Laertes in the old play.

---

[1] *The Countesse of Pembrokes Arcadia*, 1590, ed. A. Feuillerat, 1912, pp. 302–7; 51–3. In *TGV* the banished Valentine is captured by outlaws (on land), and made their leader because he is 'a linguist' and 'beautified / With a good shape' (IV.2).

I incline to believe that accidental poisoning occurred in the *Ur-Hamlet*. The Queen must perish (whereas in the sources she lived on to be persecuted by the new King of Denmark). When the play was first written two accidental poisonings had recently been reported. In Italy Bianca Capello, having removed her husband so that she could marry Francesco Duke of Florence, had seen him die when a cup of poison or a tart which she had prepared for his brother Ferdinand, the Cardinal, was mistakenly handed to him.[1] This was in 1587. And the Earl of Leicester was rumoured to have sought to kill his second wife, Lettice, mother of the great Essex, in September 1588, but the attempt misfired. One story went that she anticipated him by giving him a poisonous cordial. Years later Ben Jonson told Drummond of Hawthornden 'The Earl of Leicester gave a botle of liquor to his Lady which he willed her to use in any faintness which she after his returne from court not knowing it was Poison gave him & so he died.'[2] No trace of poison was found in Leicester's body. It is possible that Kyd used the situation in the *Ur-Hamlet* after hearing one of these stories.

The careful details of the wager and fencing were probably introduced by Shakespeare, substituting dagger and rapier for sword and buckler. As J. D. Wilson showed,[3] in the nineties there was great rivalry between exponents of the two different styles, but 'Alla stoccata carries it away', as Mercutio said, and Hamlet and Laertes fight according to the new style of Vincentio Saviolo in his *Practice* (1595) rather than the old style of George Silver's *Paradoxes of Defence* (1599).

An exchange of weapons was already in Saxo and Belleforest where Amleth seized his uncle's sword, leaving him to take the one nailed in its scabbard. Dover Wilson explains how the exchange may have been effected in terms of rapier and dagger play so that Hamlet, already wounded by Laertes' (probably unfair) thrust, might wound Laertes with the poisoned weapon (V.2.300–7).

The full implications of the changed climax of the Amleth

---

[1] See Fynes Moryson, *Itinerary*, 1903 edn., p. 94. Middleton based *Women beware women* on this story.

[2] B. Jonson, *Conversations* (1619), ed. G. B. Harrison, 1923, p. 15.

[3] Introduction to G. Silver, *Paradoxes of Defence*, 1599, Shakespeare Association Facsimiles, No. 6, 1933.

story can be seen only in relation to the design of the play as a whole.

Compared with *Julius Caesar Hamlet* is a play of one hero, yet of all Shakespeare's tragedies it is the richest in incidents, in the variety of extraneous matter not essentially connected with the one plot running through the whole piece. To account for all this material in dramatic terms, to explain how it seems to occur quite naturally (despite anachronisms) and to fall into a satisfying pattern with the major interest is a task which critical enquiry has not yet fully achieved. Here I can merely suggest an approach in the light of the foregoing account of the manifold ingredients of the plot.

The source-story involved a period of waiting between the perpetration of the old King's murder and the accomplishment of his son's revenge. This was punctuated rather than filled by the various tests on Amleth, the sexual encounter in the forest, the closet-scene with the Queen and the killing of the spying counsellor, the letter-scheme and the journey towards England, the execution of the two companions, and a great deal not in our play, before Amleth's return to Denmark and the funeral-feast turned into a revenger's triumph. These incidents are almost all initiated by Amleth's enemies; he is lurking, avoiding all appearance of rational behaviour or vengeful planning, yet mingling sly mockery and disturbing *double entendres* with apparent imbecility. No doubt the Kydian *Ur-Hamlet* included all these elements; but making the murder secret and introducing a Ghost to reveal it complicated the story, for, as we find in *Hamlet*, the assumed madness loses some of its *raison d'être*, since the usurper has now no reason to suspect Hamlet of any dangerous knowledge. So in Shakespeare it becomes a means of putting Claudius on his guard as Polonius's theory about its cause fails to explain the young man's insulting innuendoes. The sexual test is transformed from a real or pretended attempt at seduction to a rejection by the hero of an innocent girl whom he has wooed with letters and gifts. And since the girl is made the daughter of the spying counsellor killed by Hamlet, the way is paved for her madness and possible suicide, both treated however with a tenderness alien to Kyd or to Seneca, Kyd's master.

Moreover the suddenness of Hamlet's 'madness' must be

explicable; hence the melancholy ascribed to him by Belleforest, which he well might suffer on his father's death and mother's 'o'erhasty marriage', becomes a lasting disease which he admits (II.2.609) and which increases, if it does not cause, the rapid changes of mood, the world-weariness and sexual disgust, the manic-depressive behaviour which mark him through most of the play. The secrecy of the murder means that Hamlet must provoke his uncle out of security and apparent goodwill into alarm and murderous intentions. In doing so by wild conduct entirely unlike what we are told he was before the play opens, he separates himself from the court and those who really love him and ensures the spiritual solitude revealed in the soliloquies. He must insult Claudius, be barely civil to his mother, abandon his love for Ophelia in an extravagant manner, mock at Polonius, make enemies of Rosencrantz and Guildenstern, behave rudely to Ophelia in the nunnery-scene, with a sidelong threat to the King ('those that are married already, all but one, shall live') which Claudius hears and at once decides to counter by sending him away; and this before the play-scene reveals that Hamlet knows about his father's murder and might make a public accusation in his hysteria. Little of all this was in Saxo or Belleforest.

For an audience much of the excitement of the play arises from the varied situations, the intellectual vivacity, the swift transitions from friendship or affection to suspicion or hostility, from clear-sighted sanity to pretended folly or passionate outbursts. Suspense is accompanied by, often forgotten in, our sheer delight in Hamlet's many-sided activity. But his activity is not directed solely towards his task, and since he has promised to 'sweep to his revenge', reasons for his long delay are justifiably sought, especially when in his soliloquies he reproaches himself. Unlike Kyd in *The Spanish Tragedy*, Shakespeare is not content to surround scenes of violence and suffering with incoherent emotion. He takes us more deeply into Hamlet's mind than into that of any of his previous tragic heroes. Yet he seems not to have completely thought out, or at least explained, the motivation behind some scenes and relationships.

Hamlet's relations with Ophelia are left mysterious. What would almost certainly have been a scene of farewell in the *Ur-Hamlet* is narrated in *Hamlet*, so that we hear only Ophelia's side of it (II.1.75–100). We are left wondering whether (some weeks after the Ghost's revelation) this is a sign of his self-dedication to vengeance, or whether he sees her as inevitably bound to prove that 'Frailty, thy name is woman', as a potential ally of the other side, or just as a pawn in his game of pretended madness. His love-letter is that of a conventional wooer, yet real pity struggles with his revulsion and disgust in the nunnery-scene, and his protest at her graveside rings true, 'I loved Ophelia', though mingled with the rhodomontade of pretended madness (V.1.261–91). Since the plot did not allow the dramatist to show the two together in a happier time, we are left with an unsolved puzzle.

His delay is inadequately explained to us, nor can Hamlet explain it to himself. Yet it is not enough to regard the self-reproaches as periodic proofs that the avenger has not forgotten his purpose, sprinkled about the play to keep the tension strong.[1] This might work in a Kydian piece, but Hamlet's mind is so keen and his penetration into other minds so deep that we expect a power of self-analysis when he speaks of himself greater than in fact he shows. It is of course wrong to expect of Shakespeare the full display and commentary found in Proust or Henry James; but the gap is such that critics in all ages have been encouraged to find in Hamlet qualities, and in his creator intentions, suited to their own cultural climates and personalities. No interpretation as yet covers all the facts perfectly while agreeing with Jacobean ways of thought. It may well be that in taking over the old *Hamlet* and preserving its outlines Shakespeare was much less interested in explaining the delay inherent in the story than in the many interesting scenes to be presented during it. His problem was, given the variegated material which we have discussed (as well as much that does not fall within the province of this book), how to pull it together and make it happen credibly to the avenger so as to occupy his mind and time until the catastrophe—and our minds too. The Icelandic saga-hero, regarded as a pagan by Belleforest, is Christianized and put into a Renaissance setting, with allusions to Christmas, Wittenberg, Paris as a finishing-school for young courtiers, the latest in fencing-fashions, etc. He becomes a modern, sophisticated University man faced with a task almost as likely to

[1] Cf. E. E. Stoll, *Hamlet*, Minneapolis, 1919, Ch. II.

befall a prince in the sixteenth century as in the Dark Ages. It seems that Shakespeare was not greatly interested in filling the gaps in Kyd's motivation of the delay. He sketched a partial explanation and left his audiences to fill it out, and they have been doing so ever since.

A clue may perhaps be found in lines from a soliloquy by Brutus in *Julius Caesar*, probably written just before *Hamlet*:

> Between the acting of a dreadful thing
> And the first motion, all the interim is
> Like a phantasma or a hideous dream.
> The Genius and the mortal instruments
> Are then in council, and the state of man
> Like to a little kingdom, suffers then
> The nature of an insurrection. (II.1.62–9)

Brutus shows little sign of such a mental 'insurrection', but in *Hamlet* it occupies most of the play. As soon as he hears of his father's murder his mind rushes hither and thither, mixing rage and resolve to remember the Ghost, 'while memory holds a seat / In this distracted globe' and a generalization for his tables, with a hysterical alternation of 'wild and whirling words' and serious admonitions. Although he is appalled by his task he never objects to revenge as such. One must ignore or go beyond the text if one wishes to regard Hamlet as too highly civilized and too Christian to kill his uncle. His doubts of the Ghost spring from his knowledge that ghosts are often demons, and that its story might then not be true. Like Othello he seeks 'ocular proof' of what he is convinced is true. He would be damned only if he slew his uncle unjustly. But the doubt comes late and seems an afterthought to justify the arrangement he has already made to use the Players to get some sign of guilt from his uncle (II.2).

So Hamlet does not delay out of any scruples about killing; here he is true to his prototype. Nor does he try to excuse himself by any difficulty of getting access to Claudius. He blames something in his own make-up:

HAM. Do you not come your tardy son to chide
      That lapsed in time and passion, lets go by
      The important acting of your dread command?

GHOST Do not forget; this visitation
    Is but to whet thy almost blunted purpose.
            (III.4.106–10)

'Lapsed in time and passion.' Hamlet has wasted both, and the soliloquies which show us the inner man below the student, deprived heir, play-actor and satirist, are meant to show also his consciousness of his own weaknesses. Almost as soon as the Ghost has gone he realizes the immensity of his task: 'The time is out of joint. O cursed spite, That ever I was born to set it right!' (I.5.189–90). When next alone he accuses himself of cowardice, empty rhetoric and indifference, and he certainly displays a tendency to 'unpack his heart with words' (II.2.555–613). Soon he is brooding on death, by action or by suicide, but not in a very personal way, when he says that only 'the dread of something after death' makes men endure this present life (III.1.55–88). The mood however is sombre, and when he says that 'conscience doth make cowards of us all', this may be Shakespeare's comment on Hamlet's self-conscious brooding 'too precisely on the event' which endangers his enterprise 'of great pith and moment'. When, on his way towards England, his encounter with Fortinbras' army fills him with shame, he is bewildered by his own failure:

       Now, whe'r it be
  Bestial oblivion, or some craven scruple
  Of thinking too precisely on the event,
  A thought, which, quarter'd, hath but one part wisdom,
  And ever three parts coward, I do not know
  Why yet I live to say, 'This thing's to do';
  Sith I have cause and will and strength and means to do't.
            (IV.4.32–66)

The only instances we have had of 'thinking too precisely on the event' were when he doubted the Ghost, and when he refused the opportunity to kill his uncle at prayer. Does he regret that he missed that chance?

'Bestial oblivion'? Forgetfulness there has certainly been, and when we recall the Ghost's insistence: 'Remember me', 'Do not forget', we glimpse an explanation. For Hamlet has not concentrated all his energies on his great task. He has dissipated his energies in all sorts of ways only obliquely touching on his mission. 'His emotions circle endlessly, but find no direction'; he makes 'everything, even what he deeply feels, into a matter of play-acting.'[1] As Miss Anne Righter has demonstrated, *Hamlet* is 'riddled with theatrical language, with various uses of the "play the part" idiom.'[2] The inset-play, Hamlet's interest in the current theatre, his knowledge of actors and acting, his interpolation of a passage (unspecified) into *The Murder of Gonzago*, his intrusion as a malicious presenter in the play-scene, are all extensions of the major pretence taken over from the sources as Shakespeare puts Hamlet into a poisoned world where 'the characters are all watching one another, forming theories about one another, listening, contriving . . .'.[3] As the original Amleth fooled the courtiers, so Shakespeare's Hamlet fools his enemies at every encounter. His centrifugal imagination could justify reflections on any subject under the sun. This is how the dramatist brings into some sort of relevance all the topical allusions and other material which he takes over or introduces.

Hamlet's failure before he goes to England is indeed 'oblivion' in so far as he has 'lapsed in time and passion', but he is not simply 'passion's slave'; he is also the slave of an insatiable intelligence, a delighted curiosity about everything (whatever he may say to Rosencrantz and Guildenstern in II.2). The tragedy is one of 'distraction', in the several Elizabethan senses of the word. His mind is a 'distracted globe' (1.5.97), perplexed, confused, bewildered; he pretends to be 'distract', as Ophelia is by IV.5.2; he is divided against himself, and thinks and acts disjointedly: like Caesar's armies in a very different context, 'His power went out in such distractions as / Beguil'd all spies' (*AC.* III.7.76); but he also deceives himself that he is fulfilling his task. His manifold interests, love of mental activity (without always an eye to its purpose), his wordplay, passionate rhetoric, distract him (draw him aside) from planning his revenge. Is it true that he 'feels himself paralysed because an exclusive concentration on evil . . . is itself corrupting'[4]? Or is

---

[1] L. C. Knights, *An Approach to Hamlet*, 1960, pp. 65–6.
[2] A. Righter, *Shakespeare and the Idea of the Play*, 1967 edn., pp. 142–7.
[3] C. S. Lewis, *Hamlet, the Prince or the Poem*, Brit. Acad. Proc., xxviii, 1942, 139–54.
[4] L. C. Knights, *op. cit.* p. 43.

it because he cannot concentrate on evil for long enough? His equilibrium upset by grief, disgust and shock, he runs through most of the effects of melancholy in rapid succession, e.g. passionate fits, *taedium vitae*, suspicion; he is 'humorous' ('sometimes profusely laughing, extraordinarily merry, and then again weeping without a cause'), often 'of a deep reach, excellent apprehension, judicious, wise and witty', yet seeking solitude, inconstant but also obstinate.[1]

One must not exaggerate the systematic psychology of Shakespeare's portrayal of character, yet it is obvious that Hamlet suffers greatly from the variability noted by Burton and other writers on the subject:

'Inconstant they are in all their actions, vertiginous, restless, unapt to resolve of any business, they will and will not, persuaded to and fro upon every small occasion, or word spoken; and yet if once they be resolved, obstinate, hard to be reconciled. Yet in most things wavering, irresolute, unable to deliberate. . . . Now prodigal, and then covetous, they do, and by-and-by repent them of that which they have done, so that both ways they are troubled, whether they do or do not, want or have, hit or miss, disquieted of all hands, soon weary, and still seeking change, restless, I say, fickle, fugitive, they may not abide to tarry in one place long . . . no company long, or to persevere in any action or business.'[2]

Hamlet is 'so various that he seems to be / Not one but all mankind's epitome'; but he is no Buckingham, and ever and anon he remembers his mission and then will sacrifice anything and anybody to it.

Does Hamlet degenerate? I think not. Unlike his prototype he suffers the shock of his father's murder when he is no longer a child. He is thrown off his balance and from the end of Act I to the beginning of Act V he is struggling in the grip of the passions incidental to grief, melancholy, frustrated anger and disgust at the world and himself. He is not entirely ineffective: he reveals to himself and the audience the duplicity of Polonius, the hypocrisy of Rosencrantz and Guildenstern, and the weak

[1] Cf. the summary in R. Burton, *Anatomy of Melancholy* (1621), 1924 edn., I.3.i.2, pp. 252–60.

[2] Burton, *op. cit.* p. 256.

ignorance of Ophelia. He forces the King to betray his guilt by breaking up the entertainment, and he kills the spying Polonius who might well reveal that Hamlet is not mad. Although these actions are not directly focused on his revenge and his departure for England is the nadir of his fortunes, removing him from all possibility of carrying out his father's command, yet Hamlet is no worse a man for it. Indeed in his interview with his mother he performs an important subsidiary part of his task, as it was seen by Saxo and Belleforest, by making her realize her own sin and her ignorance of her second husband's true nature. He goes to her to make her confess and repent: 'I will speak daggers but use none'. He does not really believe that she was an accomplice in his father's murder and although his tirade shows him lapsing into passion, once she sees the 'black and grained spots' in her soul, he obeys the Ghost's injunction to 'step between her and her fighting soul' and speaks calmly and religiously: 'Confess yourself to heaven / Repent what's past; avoid what is to come.' He even asks forgiveness for his obtrusive preaching: 'And when you are desirous to be bless'd / I'll blessing beg of you.' What he has said is so effective that, if she does not promise actively to help him (as in Q1 and Belleforest), she keeps her knowledge of his sanity secret and pretends that he 'weeps' for killing Polonius (IV.1).

Hamlet has all our sympathy when he sets out for England. Whatever his motives, we are pleased that he has not slain Claudius while engaged in activity that might have some 'relish of salvation in it', and he has behaved well towards his mother. And although he himself reminds us of his failure so far to complete his mission, we know that he is plotting against the plotters (III.4.200–10), though his 'from this time forth / My thoughts be bloody, or be nothing worth!' has a familiar ring.

When he returns to Denmark Hamlet's mood has entirely changed. The dramatist knows that the period of marking time is over, and prepares us and the hero for a good end. His warlike spirit and gleeful energy appear in his story of the pirates. The meditations on death by the new grave mingle humour with seriousness. The passionate display over the body of Ophelia is mainly pretended madness, but it is mixed with sincere feeling for Ophelia and her brother. His account of how he circumvented Rosencrantz and Guildenstern (V.2) reveals not only his cunning and resource, but a lively sense of Providence:

> Our indiscretion sometimes serves us well
> When our deep plots do pall; and that should teach us
> There is a divinity that shapes our ends,
> Rough-hew them how we will. (V.2.8–11)

So Heaven was 'ordinant' in that he found his father's signet in his purse, which enabled him to seal the changed commission. He who was troubled to find himself 'Heaven's scourge and minister' still insists on the justice of personal revenge: 'is't not perfect conscience / To quit him with this arm?' (V.2.67–8), but he has lost his habit of wild and whirling words in a new sense of destiny ('a man's life's no more than to say "One"') and though he feels 'how ill all's here about my heart' before going to the fencing-match, he will 'defy augury; there's a special providence in the fall of a sparrow . . . the readiness is all' (V.2.219–24).[1]

I agree with Miss Prosser that Hamlet's state here is not 'classic despair or Stoic fatalism' but that 'in it Hamlet surrenders his will to Divine providence'.[2] He does so quietly and hopefully ('The interim is mine') for he has not given up his hope of punishing his uncle but believes that heaven will show him the way and means to do it. With the King listening he must still pretend, and to Laertes he explains his killing of Polonius as due to his madness. But in all sincerity he accepts Laertes' treacherous promise not to wrong his proffered friendship, and looks on the match as a 'brother's wager'. After all his cunning Hamlet's return to princely simplicity brings him to death, and he obtains his revenge not, like Hieronimo, through a planned holocaust, but through the mistakes of his enemies, who by overreaching themselves prove the inexorable justice which Belleforest saw Hamlet as meting out on God's behalf.

Hamlet is a Revenge play in a tradition of tragedy that depended on terrible happenings to be watched with mixed feelings. On the one hand revenge was justified in certain cir-

---

[1] 'Are not two sparrows sold for a farthing? and one of them shall not fall on the ground without your Father. But the very hairs of your head are numbered. Fear ye not therefore, ye are of more value than many sparrows.' *Matthew*, 10, 29–31.

[2] Prosser, *op. cit.* p. 229.

cumstances and in *Hamlet* it was a work of filial piety imposed on the hero by 'heaven and hell'. On the other hand Christian doctrine and the law were against it, and the revenge of such heroes as Hieronimo and Titus Andronicus must be viewed with mingled approval and horror as the agent of justice in pursuit of his right and duty violates the more refined ethics of modern civilization and involves himself in deeds of savage cruelty only credible if performed in a state of near-madness. At the climax the audience watches with fascinated horror a spectacle of inhuman ferocity and diabolical cunning.

In *Hamlet*, however, Shakespeare had long moved away from the ultra-Senecanism of *Titus*, and his aim was to lessen the horror both quantitatively and qualitatively by expanding the setting of his Orestean story so as to include a whole courtly society with international connections affording relief from the display of inordinate passions by means of wit, humour, satire, topical allusion, and moments of gracious courtesy. The story which the dramatist took over enabled him to avoid the almost continuous sanguinary ritual of *Titus* and to create a hero who preserves our sympathies throughout, the more so since he forestalls any critical comments we are likely to make on his failure speedily to avenge his father.

Indeed, just because the brilliant young prince plays a waiting game (although extraordinarily busy, physically alert and mentally a match for his enemies) and is more acted on than active in his chief purpose for most of the play, we are able to identify ourselves with him in his isolated and vulnerable position. Shakespeare very cleverly has it both ways; for since Hamlet (unlike his prototype) attains his end without pursuing a definite long-laid Machiavellian scheme of carnage, but because a cowardly attempt to murder him turns against its plotters, even the most pious opponent of blood-revenge should object little, while the unregenerate among us rejoice at the fulfilment of his task, though it comes late and at the expense of his noble life.

I. Source

From HISTORIAE DANICAE
by Saxo Grammaticus,
translated by Oliver Elton (1894)[1]

Book III

AT this time Horwendil and Feng, whose father Gerwendil had
been governor of the Jutes, were appointed in his place by Rorik
to defend Jutland. But Horwendil held the monarchy for three
years, and then, to win the height of glory, devoted himself to
roving. Then Koll, King of Norway, in rivalry of his great deeds and
renown, deemed it would be a handsome deed if by his greater
strength in arms he could bedim the far-famed glory of the rover;
and, cruising about the sea, he watched for Horwendil's fleet and
came up with it. There was an island lying in the middle of the
sea, which each of the rovers, bringing his ships up on either side,
was holding. The captains were tempted by the pleasant look of the
beach, and the comeliness of the shores led them to look through
the interior of the spring-tide woods, to go through the glades, and
roam over the sequestered forests. It was here that the advance of
Koll and Horwendil brought them face to face without any witness.
Then Horwendil endeavoured to address the king first, asking him
in what way it was his pleasure to fight, and declaring that one best
which needed the courage of as few as possible. For, said he, the
duel was the surest of all modes of combat for winning the meed of
bravery, because it relied only upon native courage, and excluded all
help from the hand of another. Koll marvelled at so brave a judgment in a youth, and said: 'Since thou hast granted me the choice
of battle, I think it is best to employ that kind which needs only the
endeavours of two, and is free from all the tumult. Certainly it is
more venturesome, and allows of a speedier award of the victory.
This thought we share, in this opinion we agree of our own accord.
But since the issue remains doubtful, we must pay some regard to

[1] *The First Nine Books of the Danish History of Saxo Grammaticus*, trans. by Oliver
Elton, 1894.

gentle dealing, and must not give way so far to our inclinations as to leave the last offices undone. Hatred is in our hearts; yet let piety be there also, which in its due time may take the place of rigour. For the rights of nature reconcile us, though we are parted by differences of purpose; they link us together, howsoever rancour estrange our spirits. Let us, therefore, have this pious stipulation, that the conqueror shall give funeral rites to the conquered. For all allow that these are the last duties of human kind, from which no righteous man shrinks. Let each army lay aside its sternness and perform this function in harmony. Let jealousy depart at death, let the feud be buried in the tomb. Let us not show such an example of cruelty as to persecute one another's dust, though hatred has come between us in our lives. It will be a boast for the victor if he has borne his beaten foe in a lordly funeral. For the man who pays the rightful dues over his dead enemy wins the goodwill of the survivor; and whoso devotes gentle dealing to him who is no more, conquers the living by his kindness. Also there is another disaster, not less lamentable, which sometimes befalls the living—the loss of some part of their body; and I think that succour is due to this just as much as to the worst hap that may befall. For often those who fight keep their lives safe, but suffer maiming; and this lot is commonly thought more dismal than any death; for death cuts off memory of all things, while the living cannot forget the devastation of his own body. Therefore this mischief also must be helped somehow; so let it be agreed, that the injury of either of us by the other shall be made good with ten tablets [marks] of gold. For if it be righteous to have compassion on the calamities of another, how much more is it to pity one's own? No man but obeys nature's prompting; and he who slights it is a self-murderer.'

After mutually pledging their faiths to these terms, they began the battle. Nor were their strangeness in meeting one another, nor the sweetness of that spring-green spot, so heeded as to prevent them from the fray. Horwendil, in his too great ardour, became keener to attack his enemy than to defend his own body; and, heedless of his shield, had grasped his sword with both hands; and his boldness did not fail. For by his rain of blows he destroyed Koll's shield and deprived him of it, and at last hewed off his foot and drove him lifeless to the ground. Then, not to fail of his compact, he buried him royally, gave him a howe of lordly make and pompous obsequies. Then he pursued and slew Koller's sister Sela, who was a skilled warrior and experienced in roving.

He had now passed three years in valiant deeds of war; and, in order to win higher rank in Rorik's favour, he assigned to him the best trophies and the pick of the plunder. His friendship with Rorik enabled him to woo and win in marriage his daughter Gerutha, who bore him a son Amleth.

Such great good fortune stung Feng with jealousy, so that he resolved treacherously to waylay his brother, thus showing that goodness is not safe even from those of a man's own house. And behold, when a chance came to murder him, his bloody hand sated the deadly passion of his soul. Then he took the wife of the brother he had butchered, capping unnatural murder[1] with incest. For whoso yields to one iniquity, speedily falls an easier victim to the next, the first being an incentive to the second. Also the man veiled the monstrosity of his deed with such hardihood of cunning, that he made up a mock pretence of goodwill to excuse his crime, and glossed over fratricide with a show of righteousness. Gerutha, said he, though so gentle that she would do no man the slightest hurt, had been visited with her husband's extremest hate; and it was all to save her that he had slain his brother; for he thought it shameful that a lady so meek and unrancorous should suffer the heavy disdain of her husband. Nor did his smooth words fail in their intent; for at courts, where fools are sometimes favoured and backbiters preferred, a lie lacks not credit. Nor did Feng keep from shameful embraces the hands that had slain a brother; pursuing with equal guilt both of his wicked and impious deeds.

Amleth beheld all this, but feared lest too shrewd a behaviour might make his uncle suspect him. So he chose to feign dulness, and pretend an utter lack of wits. This cunning course not only concealed his intelligence but ensured his safety. Every day he remained in his mother's house utterly listless and unclean, flinging himself on the ground and bespattering his person with foul and filthy dirt. His discoloured face and visage smutched with slime denoted foolish and grotesque madness. All he said was of a piece with these follies; all he did savoured of utter lethargy. In a word, you would not have thought him a man at all, but some absurd abortion due to a mad fit of destiny. He used at times to sit over the fire, and, raking up the embers with his hands, to fashion wooden crooks, and harden them in the fire, shaping at their tips certain barbs, to make them hold more tightly to their fastenings. When asked what he was about, he said that he was preparing sharp javelins to avenge his father. This answer was not a little scoffed at, all men deriding his idle and ridiculous pursuit; but the thing helped his purpose afterwards. Now it was his craft in this matter that first awakened in the deeper observers a suspicion of his cunning. For

---

[1] Unnatural murder] These words of the Ghost in *Hamlet*, I.5.25, exactly translate *parricidium*, which (with *parricida*) occurs constantly in this narrative, and has been variously rendered by 'slaying of kin', 'fratricide', etc. [E]

his skill in a trifling art betokened the hidden talent of the craftsman; nor could they believe the spirit dull where the hand had acquired so cunning a workmanship. Lastly, he always watched with the most punctual care over his pile of stakes that he had pointed in the fire. Some people, therefore, declared that his mind was quick enough, and fancied that he only played the simpleton in order to hide his understanding, and veiled some deep purpose under a cunning feint. His wiliness (said these) would be most readily detected, if a fair woman were put in his way in some secluded place, who should provoke his mind to the temptations of love; all men's natural temper being too blindly amorous to be artfully dissembled, and this passion being also too impetuous to be checked by cunning. Therefore, if his lethargy were feigned, he would seize the opportunity, and yield straightway to violent delights. So men were commissioned to draw the young man in his rides into a remote part of the forest, and there assail him with a temptation of this nature. Among these chanced to be a foster-brother of Amleth, who had not ceased to have regard to their common nurture; and who esteemed his present orders less than the memory of their past fellowship. He attended Amleth among his appointed train, being anxious not to entrap, but to warn him; and was persuaded that he would suffer the worst if he showed the slightest glimpse of sound reason, and above all if he did the act of love openly. This was also plain enough to Amleth himself. For when he was bidden mount his horse, he deliberately set himself in such a fashion that he turned his back to the neck and faced about, fronting the tail; which he proceeded to encompass with the reins, just as if on that side he would check the horse in its furious pace. By this cunning thought he eluded the trick, and overcame the treachery of his uncle. The reinless steed galloping on, with the rider directing its tail, was ludicrous enough to behold.

Amleth went on, and a wolf crossed his path amid the thicket. When his companions told him that a young colt had met him, he retorted, that in Feng's stud there were too few of that kind fighting. This was a gentle but witty fashion of invoking a curse upon his uncle's riches. When they averred that he had given a cunning answer, he answered that he had spoken deliberately: for he was loth to be thought prone to lying about any matter, and wished to be held a stranger to falsehood; and accordingly he mingled craft and candour in such wise that, though his words did lack truth, yet there was nothing to betoken the truth and betray how far his keenness went.

Again, as he passed along the beach, his companions found the rudder of a ship which had been wrecked, and said they had discovered a huge knife. 'This', said he, 'was the right thing to carve such a huge ham;' by which he really meant the sea, to whose infinitude, he thought, this enormous rudder matched. Also, as they passed the sandhills, and bade him look at the meal, meaning the sand, he replied that it had been ground small by the hoary tempests of the ocean. His companions praising his answer, he said that he had spoken it wittingly. Then they purposely left him, that he might pluck up more courage to practise wantonness. The woman whom his uncle had dispatched met him in a dark spot, as though she had crossed him by chance; and he took her and would have ravished her, had not his foster-brother, by a secret device, given him an inkling of the trap. For this man, while pondering the fittest way to play privily the prompter's part, and forestall the young man's hazardous lewdness, found a straw on the ground and fastened it underneath the tail of a gadfly that was flying past; which he then drove towards the particular quarter where he knew Amleth to be: an act which served the unwary prince exceedingly well. The token was interpreted as shrewdly as it had been sent. For Amleth saw the gadfly, espied with curiosity the straw which it wore embedded in its tail, and perceived that it was a secret warning to beware of treachery. Alarmed, scenting a trap, and fain to possess his desire in greater safety, he caught up the woman in his arms and dragged her off to a distant and impenetrable fen. Moreover, when they had lain together, he conjured her earnestly to disclose the matter to none, and the promise of silence was accorded as heartily as it was asked. For both of them had been under the same fostering in their childhood; and this early rearing in common had brought Amleth and the girl into great intimacy.

So, when he had returned home, they all jeeringly asked him whether he had given way to love, and he avowed that he had ravished the maid. When he was next asked where he did it, and what had been his pillow, he said that he had rested upon the hoof of a beast of burden, upon a cockscomb, and also upon a ceiling. For, when he was starting into temptation, he had gathered fragments of all these things, in order to avoid lying. And though his jest did not take aught of the truth out of the story, the answer was greeted with shouts of merriment from the bystanders. The maiden, too, when questioned on the matter, declared that he had done no such thing; and her denial was the more readily credited when it was found that the escort had not witnessed the deed. Then he who had marked the gadfly in order to give a hint, wishing to show Amleth that to his trick he owed his salvation, observed that latterly he had been singly devoted to Amleth. The young man's reply was apt. Not to seem forgetful of his informant's service, he said that he had seen a certain thing bearing a straw flit by suddenly, wearing a stalk of chaff fixed on its hinder parts. The cleverness of this speech, which made the rest split with laughter, rejoiced the heart of Amleth's friend.

Thus all were worsted, and none could open the secret lock of the young man's wisdom. But a friend of Feng, gifted more with assurance than judgment,[1] declared that the unfathomable cunning of such a mind could not be detected by any vulgar plot, for the man's obstinacy was so great that it ought not to be assailed with any mild measures; there were many sides to his wiliness, and it ought not to be entrapped by any one method. Accordingly, said he, his own profounder acuteness had hit on a more delicate way, which was well fitted to be put in practice, and would effectually discover what they desired to know. Feng was purposely to absent himself, pretending affairs of great import. Amleth should be closeted alone with his mother in her chamber; but a man should first be commissioned to place himself in a concealed part of the room and listen heedfully to what they talked about. For if the son had any wits at all he would not hesitate to speak out in the hearing of his mother, or fear to trust himself to the fidelity of her who bore him. The speaker, loth to seem readier to devise than to carry out the plot, zealously proffered himself as the agent of the eavesdropping. Feng rejoiced at the scheme, and departed on pretence of a long journey. Now he who had given this counsel repaired privily[2] to the room where Amleth was shut up with his mother, and lay down skulking in the straw.[3] But Amleth had his antidote for the treachery. Afraid of being overheard by some eavesdropper, he at first resorted to his usual imbecile ways, and crowed like a noisy cock, beating his arms together to mimic the flapping of wings. Then he mounted the straw and began to swing his body and jump again and again, wishing to try if aught lurked there in hiding. Feeling a lump beneath his feet, he drove his sword into the spot, and impaled him who lay hid. Then he dragged him from his concealment and slew him. Then, cutting his body into morsels, he seethed it in boiling water, and flung it through the mouth of an open sewer for the swine to eat, bestrewing the stinking mire with his hapless limbs. Having in this wise eluded the snare, he went back to the room. Then his mother set up a great wailing, and began to lament her son's folly to his face; but he said: 'Most infamous of women! dost thou seek with such lying lamentations to hide thy most heavy guilt? Wantoning like a harlot, thou hast entered a wicked and abominable state of wedlock, embracing with incestuous bosom thy husband's slayer,

[1] Cf. *Hamlet*, III.4: 'Thou wretched, rash, intruding fool . . .'
[2] 'ambobus inscius', unknown to both of them.
[3] 'Stramentum', possibly a straw mattress.

and wheedling with filthy lures of blandishment him who had slain the father of thy son. This, forsooth, is the way that the mares couple with the vanquishers of their mates; for brute beasts are naturally incited to pair indiscriminately; and it would seem that thou, like them, hast clean forgot thy first husband. As for me, not idly do I wear the mask of folly; for I doubt not that he who destroyed his brother will riot as ruthlessly in the blood of his kindred. Therefore it is better to choose the garb of dulness than that of sense, and to borrow some protection from a show of utter frenzy. Yet the passion to avenge my father still burns in my heart; but I am watching the chances, I await the fitting hour. There is a place for all things; against so merciless and dark a spirit must be used the deeper devices of the mind. And thou, who hadst been better employed in lamenting thine own disgrace, know it is superfluity to bewail my witlessness; thou shouldst weep for the blemish in thine own mind, not for that in another's. On the rest see thou keep silence.' With such reproaches he rent the heart of his mother and redeemed her to walk in the ways of virtue,[1] teaching her to set the fires of the past above the seductions of the present.

When Feng returned, nowhere could he find the man who had suggested the treacherous espial; he searched for him long and carefully, but none said they had seen him anywhere. Amleth, among others, was asked in jest if he had come on any trace of him, and replied that the man had gone to the sewer, but had fallen through its bottom and been stifled by the floods of filth, and that he had then been devoured by the swine that came up all about that place. This speech was flouted by those who heard; for it seemed senseless, though really it expressly avowed the truth.

Feng now suspected that his stepson was certainly full of guile, and desired to make away with him, but durst not do the deed for fear of the displeasure, not only of Amleth's grand-sire Rorik, but also of his own wife. So he thought that the King of Britain should be employed to slay him, so that another could do the deed, and he be able to feign innocence. Thus, desirous to hide his cruelty, he chose rather to besmirch his friend than to bring disgrace on his own head. Amleth, on departing, gave secret orders to his mother to hang the hall with knotted tapestry, and to perform pretended obsequies for him a year thence; promising that he would then return. Two retainers of Feng then accompanied him, bearing a letter graven on wood[2]—a kind of writing material frequent in old

---

[1] '*talis convicis laceratam matrem ad excolendum virtutis habitum revocavit*'; 'With such a reproach did he recall his wounded mother to cultivate the habit of virtue.' Cf. III. 4, 160–5.

[2] Carved with runic letters.

times; this letter enjoined the king of the Britons to put to death the youth who was sent over to him. While they were reposing, Amleth searched their coffers, found the letter, and read the instructions therein. Whereupon he erased all the writing on the surface, substituted fresh characters, and so, changing the purport of the instructions, shifted his own doom upon his companions. Nor was he satisfied with removing from himself the sentence of death and passing the peril on to others, but added an entreaty that the King of Britain would grant his daughter in marriage to a youth of great judgment whom he was sending to him. Under this was falsely marked the signature of Feng.

Now when they had reached Britain, the envoys went to the king, and proffered him the letter which they supposed was an implement of destruction to another,[1] but which really betokened death to themselves. The king dissembled the truth, and entreated them hospitably and kindly. Then Amleth scouted all the splendour of the royal banquet like vulgar viands, and abstaining very strangely, rejected that plenteous feast, refraining from the drink even as from the banquet. All marvelled that a youth and a foreigner should disdain the carefully-cooked dainties of the royal board and the luxurious banquet provided, as if it were some peasant's relish. So, when the revel broke up, and the king was dismissing his friends to rest, he had a man sent into the sleeping-room to listen secretly, in order that he might hear the midnight conversation of his guests. Now, when Amleth's companions asked him why he had refrained from the feast of yestereve, as if it were poison, he answered that the bread was flecked with blood and tainted; that there was a tang of iron in the liquor; while the meats of the feast reeked of the stench of a human carcase, and were infected by a kind of smack of the odour of the charnel. He further said that the king had the eyes of a slave, and that the queen had in three ways shown the behaviour of a bondmaid. Thus he reviled with insulting invective not so much the feast as its givers. And presently his companions, taunting him with his old defect of wits, began to flout him with many saucy jeers, because he blamed and cavilled at seemly and worthy things, and because he attacked thus ignobly an illustrious king and a lady of so refined a behaviour, bespattering with the shamefullest abuse those who merited all praise.

All this the king heard from his retainer; and declared that he who could say such things had either more than mortal wisdom or more than mortal folly; in these few words fathoming the full depth of Amleth's penetration. Then he summoned the steward and asked

---

[1] No doubts about their being accomplices!

him whence he had procured the bread. The steward declared that it had been made by the king's own baker. The king asked where the corn had grown of which it was made, and whether any sign was to be found there of human carnage? The other answered, that not far off was a field, covered with the ancient bones of slaughtered men, and still bearing plainly all the signs of ancient carnage; and that he had himself planted this field with grain in springtide, thinking it more fruitful than the rest, and hoping for plenteous abundance; and so, for aught he knew, the bread had caught some evil savour from this bloodshed. The king, on hearing this, surmised that Amleth had spoken truly, and took the pains to learn also what had been the source of the lard. The other declared that his hogs had, through negligence, strayed from keeping, and battened on the rotten carcase of a robber, and that perchance their pork had thus come to have something of a corrupt smack. The king, finding that Amleth's judgment was right in this thing also, asked of what liquor the steward had mixed the drink? Hearing that it had been brewed of water and meal, he had the spot of the spring pointed out to him, and set to digging deep down; and there he found, rusted away, several swords, the tang whereof it was thought had tainted the waters. Others relate that Amleth blamed the drink because, while quaffing it, he had detected some bees that had fed in the paunch of a dead man; and that the taint, which had formerly been imparted to the combs, had reappeared in the taste. The king, seeing that Amleth had rightly given the causes of the taste he had found so faulty, and learning that the ignoble eyes wherewith Amleth had reproached him concerned some stain upon his birth, had a secret interview with his mother, and asked her who his father had really been. She said she had submitted to no man but the king. But when he threatened that he would have the truth out of her by a trial, he was told that he was the offspring of a slave. By the evidence of the avowal thus extorted he understood the whole mystery of the reproach upon his origin. Abashed as he was with shame for his low estate, he was so ravished with the young man's cleverness, that he asked him why he had aspersed the queen with the reproach that she had demeaned herself like a slave? But while resenting that the courtliness of his wife had been accused in the midnight gossip of a guest, he found that her mother had been a bondmaid. For Amleth said he had noted in her three blemishes showing the demeanour of a slave; first, she had muffled her head in her mantle as bondmaids do; next, that she had gathered up her gown for walking; and thirdly, that she had first picked out with a splinter, and then chewed up, the remnant of food that stuck in the crevices between her teeth. Further, he mentioned that the king's mother had been brought into slavery from captivity, lest she should seem servile only in her habits, yet not in her birth.

Then the king adored the wisdom of Amleth as though it were inspired, and gave him his daughter to wife; accepting his bare word as though it were a witness from the skies. Moreover, in order to fulfil the bidding of his friend, he hanged Amleth's companions on the morrow. Amleth, feigning offence, treated this piece of kindness as a grievance, and received from the king, as compensation, some gold, which he afterwards melted in the fire, and secretly caused to be poured into some hollowed sticks.

When he had passed a whole year with the king he obtained leave to make a journey, and returned to his own land, carrying away of all his princely wealth and state only the sticks which held the gold. On reaching Jutland, he exchanged his present attire for his ancient demeanour, which he had adopted for righteous ends, purposely assuming an aspect of absurdity. Covered with filth, he entered the banquet-room where his own obsequies were being held, and struck all men utterly aghast, rumour having falsely noised abroad his death. At last terror melted into mirth, and the guests jeered and taunted one another, that he whose last rites they were celebrating as though he were dead, should appear in the flesh. When he was asked concerning his comrades, he pointed to the sticks he was carrying, and said, 'Here is both the one and the other.' This he observed with equal truth and pleasantry; for his speech, though most thought it idle, yet departed not from the truth; for it pointed at the weregild of the slain as though it were themselves. Thereon, wishing to bring the company into a gayer mood, he joined the cupbearers, and diligently did the office of plying the drink. Then, to prevent his loose dress hampering his walk, he girded his sword upon his side, and purposely drawing it several times, pricked his fingers with its point. The bystanders accordingly had both sword and scabbard riveted across with an iron nail. Then, to smooth the way more safely to his plot, he went to the lords and plied them heavily with draught upon draught, and drenched them all so deep in wine, that their feet were made feeble with drunkenness, and they turned to rest within the palace, making their bed where they had revelled. Then he saw they were in a fit state for his plots, and thought that here was a chance offered to do his purpose. So he took out of his bosom the stakes he had long ago prepared, and went into the building, where the ground lay covered with the bodies of the nobles wheezing off their sleep and their debauch. Then, cutting away its supports, he brought down the hanging his mother had knitted, which covered the inner as well as the outer walls of the hall. This he flung upon the snorers, and then applying the crooked stakes, he knotted and bound them up in such insoluble intricacy, that not one of the men beneath, however hard he might struggle, could contrive to rise. After this he set fire to the palace. The flames spread, scattering the conflagration far and wide. It enveloped the whole dwelling, destroyed the palace, and burnt them all while they were either buried in deep sleep or vainly striving to arise. Then he went to the chamber of Feng, who had before this been conducted by his train into his pavilion; plucked up a sword that chanced to be hanging to the bed, and planted his own in its place. Then, awakening his uncle, he told him that his nobles were perishing in the flames, and that Amleth was here, armed with his old crooks to help him, and thirsting to exact the vengeance, now long overdue, for his father's murder. Feng, on hearing this, leapt from his couch, but was cut down while, deprived of his own sword, he strove in vain to draw the strange one. O valiant Amleth, and worthy of immortal fame, who being shrewdly armed with a feint of folly, covered a wisdom too high for human wit under a marvellous disguise of silliness! and not only found in his subtlety means to protect his own safety, but also by its guidance found opportunity to avenge his father. By this skilful defence of himself, and strenuous revenge for his parent, he has left it doubtful whether we are to think more of his wit or his bravery.

Book IV

AMLETH, when he had accomplished the slaughter of his stepfather, feared to expose his deed to the fickle judgment of his countrymen, and thought it well to lie in hiding till he had learnt what way the mob of the uncouth populace was tending. So the whole neighbour-hood, who had watched the blaze during the night, and in the morning desired to know the cause of the fire they had seen, per-ceived the royal palace fallen in ashes; and, on searching through its ruins, which were yet warm, found only some shapeless remains of burnt corpses. For the devouring flame had consumed everything so utterly, that not a single token was left to inform them of the cause of such a disaster. Also they saw the body of Feng lying pierced by the sword, amid his blood-stained raiment. Some were seized with open anger, others with grief, and some with secret delight. One party bewailed the death of their leader, the other gave thanks that the tyranny of the fratricide was now laid at rest. Thus the occurrence of the king's slaughter was greeted by the beholders with diverse minds.

Amleth, finding the people so quiet, made bold to leave his hiding. Summoning those in whom he knew the memory of his father to be fast-rooted, he went to the assembly and there made a speech after this manner:

'Nobles! Let not any who are troubled by the piteous end of Horwendil be troubled by the sight of this disaster before you: be not ye, I say, troubled, who have remained loyal to your king and duteous to your father. Behold the corpse, not of a prince, but of a fratricide. Indeed, it was a sorrier sight when ye saw our prince lying lamentably butchered by a most infamous fratricide— brother, let me not call him. With your own compassionating eyes ye have beheld the mangled limbs of Horwendil; they have seen his body done to death with many wounds. Surely that most abominable butcher only deprived his king of life that he might despoil his country of freedom! The hand that slew him made you slaves. Who then so mad as to choose Feng the cruel before Horwendil the righteous? Remember how benignantly Horwendil fostered you, how justly he dealt with you, how kindly he loved you. Remember how you lost the mildest of princes and the justest of fathers, while in his place was put a tyrant and an assassin set up; how your rights were confiscated; how everything was plague-stricken; how the country was stained with infamies; how the yoke was planted on your necks, and how your free will was forfeited! And now all this is over; for ye see the criminal stifled in his own crimes, the slayer of his kin punished for his misdoings. What man of but ordinary wit, beholding it, would account this kindness a wrong? What sane man could be sorry that the crime has recoiled upon the culprit? Who could lament the killing of a most savage executioner? or bewail the righteous death of a most cruel despot? Ye behold the doer of the deed; he is before you. Yea, I own that I have taken vengeance for my country and my father. Your hands were equally bound to the task which mine fulfilled. What it would have beseemed you to accomplish with me, I achieved alone. Nor had I any partner in so glorious a deed, or the service of any man to help me. Not that I forget that you would have helped this work, had I asked you; for doubtless you have remained loyal to your king and loving to your prince. But I chose that the wicked should be punished without imperilling you; I thought that others need not set their shoulders to their burden when I deemed mine strong enough to bear it. Therefore I consumed all the others to ashes, and left only the trunk of Feng for your hands to burn, so that on this at least you may wreak all your longing for a righteous vengeance. Now haste up speedily, heap the pyre, burn up the body of the wicked, consume away his guilty limbs, scatter his sinful ashes, strew broadcast his ruthless dust: let no urn or barrow enclose the abominable remnants of his bones. Let no trace of his fratricide remain; let there be no spot in his own land for his tainted limbs; let no neighbourhood suck infection from him; let not sea nor soil be defiled by harbouring his accursed carcase. I have done the rest; this one loyal duty is left for you. These must be the tyrant's obsequies, this the funeral procession of the fratricide. It is not seemly that he who stripped his country of her freedom should have his ashes covered by his country's earth.

'Besides, why tell again my own sorrows? Why count over my troubles? Why weave the thread of my miseries anew? Ye know them more fully than I myself. I, pursued to the death by my stepfather, scorned by my mother, spat upon by friends, have passed my years in pitiable wise, and my days in adversity; and my insecure life has teemed with fear and perils. In fine, I passed every season of my age wretchedly and in extreme calamity. Often in your secret murmurings together you have sighed over my lack of wits: there was none (you said) to avenge the father, none to punish the fratricide. And in this I found a secret testimony of your love; for I saw that the memory of the King's murder had not yet faded from your minds.

'Whose breast is so hard that it can be softened by no fellow-feeling[1] for what I have felt? Who is so stiff and stony, that he is swayed by no compassion for my griefs? Ye whose hands are clean of the blood of Horwendil, pity your fosterling, be moved by my calamities. Pity also my stricken mother, and rejoice with me that the infamy of her who was once your queen is quenched. For this weak woman had to bear a two-fold weight of ignominy, embracing one who was her husband's brother and murderer. Therefore, to hide my purpose of revenge and to veil my wit, I counterfeited a listless bearing; I feigned dulness; I planned a stratagem; and now you can see with your own eyes whether it has succeeded, whether it has achieved its purpose to the full; I am content to have you to judge so great a matter. It is your turn: trample under foot the ashes of the murderer! Disdain the dust of him who slew his brother, and defiled his brother's queen with infamous desecration, who outraged his sovereign and treasonably assailed his majesty, who brought the sharpest tyranny upon you, stole your freedom, and crowned fratricide with incest. I have been the agent of this just vengeance; I have burned for this righteous retribution: uphold me with a high-born spirit; pay me the homage that you owe; warm me with your kindly looks. It is I who have wiped off my country's shame; I who have quenched my mother's dishonour; I who have beaten back oppression; I who have put to death the murderer;

---

[1] Fellow-feeling for what I have felt; *compassio passionum mearum*. The words are rare, and there is a play in them which it is hard to render closely. [E]

I who have baffled the artful hand of my uncle with retorted arts. Were he living, each new day would have multiplied his crimes. I resented the wrong done to father and to fatherland: I slew him who was governing you outrageously and more hardly than it beseemed men. Acknowledge my service, honour my wit, give me the throne if I have earned it[1]; for you have in me one who has done you a mighty service, and who is no degenerate heir to his father's power; no fratricide, but the lawful successor to the throne; and a dutiful avenger of the crime of murder. You have me to thank for the recovery of the blessings of freedom, for release from the power of him who vexed you, for relief from the oppressor's yoke, for shaking off the sway of the murderer, for trampling the despot's sceptre under foot. It is I who have stripped you of slavery, and clothed you with freedom; I have restored your height of fortune, and given you your glory back; I have deposed the despot and triumphed over the butcher. In your hands is the reward: you know what I have done for you: and from your righteousness I ask my wage.'

Every heart had been moved while the young man thus spoke; he affected some to compassion, and some even to tears. When the lamentation ceased, he was appointed king[2] by prompt and general acclaim. For one and all rested the greatest hopes on his wisdom, since he had devised the whole of such an achievement with the deepest cunning, and accomplished it with the most astonishing contrivance. Many could have been seen marvelling how he had concealed so subtle a plan over so long a space of time.

After these deeds in Denmark he equipped three vessels lavishly, and went back to Britain to see his wife and her father. He had also enrolled in his service the flower of the warriors, and arrayed them very choicely, wishing to have everything now magnificently appointed, even as of old he had always worn contemptible gear, and to change all his old devotion to poverty for outlay on luxury. He also had a shield made for him, whereon the whole series of his exploits, beginning with his earliest youth, was painted in exquisite designs. This he bore as a record of his deeds of prowess, and gained great increase of fame thereby. Here were to be seen depicted the slaying of Horwendil, the fratricide and incest of Feng; the infamous uncle, the whimsical nephew; the shapes of the hooked stakes; the stepfather suspecting, the stepson dissembling; the various temptations offered, and the woman brought to beguile him; the gaping wolf; the finding of the rudder; the passing of the sand; the

---

[1] '*regnum, si merui date*'.
[2] i.e. 'elected'. The people's agreement was necessary: '*rex alacri cunctorum acclamatione censetur*'. Cf. V.2.65, 355–6.

entering of the wood; the putting of the straw through the gadfly; the warning of the youth by the tokens; and the privy dealings with the maiden after the escort was eluded. And likewise could be seen the picture of the palace; the queen there with her son; the slaying of the eavesdropper; and how, after being killed, he was boiled down, and so dropped into the sewer, and so thrown out to the swine; how his limbs were strewn in the mud, and so left for the beasts to finish. Also it could be seen how Amleth surprised the secret of his sleeping attendants, how he erased the letters, and put new characters in their places; how he disdained the banquet and scorned the drink; how he condemned the face of the king and taxed the queen with faulty behaviour. There was also represented the hanging of the envoys, and the young man's wedding; then the voyage back to Denmark; the festive celebration of the funeral rites; Amleth, in answer to questions, pointing to the sticks in place of his attendants, acting as cup-bearer, and purposely drawing his sword and pricking his fingers; the sword riveted through, the swelling cheers of the banquet, the dance growing fast and furious; the hangings flung upon the sleepers, then fastened with the interlacing crooks, and wrapped tightly round them as they slumbered; the brand set to the mansion, the burning of the guests, the royal palace consumed with fire and tottering down; the visit to the sleeping-room of Feng, the theft of his sword, the useless one set in its place; and the king slain with his own sword's point by his stepson's hand. All this was there, painted upon Amleth's battle-shield by a careful craftsman in his choicest of handiwork; he copied truth in his figures, and embodied real deeds in his outlines. Moreover, Amleth's followers, to increase the splendour of their presence, wore shields which were gilt over.

The King of Britain received them very graciously, and treated them with costly and royal pomp. During the feast he asked anxiously whether Feng was alive and prosperous. His son-in-law told him that the man of whose welfare he was vainly inquiring had perished by the sword. With a flood of questions he tried to find out who had slain Feng, and learnt that the messenger of his death was likewise its author. And when the king heard this, he was secretly aghast, because he found that an old promise to avenge Feng now devolved upon himself. For Feng and he had determined of old, by a mutual compact, that one of them should act as avenger of the other. Thus the king was drawn one way by his love for his daughter and his affection for his son-in-law, another way by his regard for his friend, and moreover by his strict oath and the sanctity of their mutual declarations, which it was impious to violate. At last he slighted the ties of kinship, and sworn faith prevailed. His heart turned to vengeance, and he put the sanctity of his oath before family bonds. But since it was thought sin to wrong the holy ties of hospitality, he preferred to execute his revenge by the hand of another, wishing to mask his secret crime with a show of innocence. So he veiled his treachery with attentions, and hid his intent to harm under a show of zealous goodwill. His queen having lately died of illness, he requested Amleth to underake the mission of making him a fresh match, saying that he was highly delighted with his extra-ordinary shrewdness. He declared that there was a certain queen reigning in Scotland, whom he vehemently desired to marry. Now he knew that she was not only unwedded by reason of her chastity, but that in the cruelty of her arrogance she had always loathed her wooers, and had inflicted on her lovers the uttermost punishment, so that not one out of all the multitude was to be found who had not paid for his insolence with his life.

Perilous as this commission was, Amleth started, never shrinking to obey the duty imposed upon him, but trusting partly in his own servants, and partly in the attendants of the king. He entered Scotland, and, when quite close to the abode of the queen, he went into a meadow by the wayside to rest his horses. Pleased by the look of the spot, he thought of resting—the pleasant prattle of the stream exciting a desire to sleep—and posted men to keep watch some way off. The queen on hearing of this, sent out ten warriors to spy on the approach of the foreigners and their equipment. One of these, being quick-witted, slipped past the sentries, pertinaciously made his way up, and took away the shield, which Amleth had chanced to set at his head before he slept, so gently that he did not ruffle his slumbers, though he was lying upon it, nor awaken one man of all that troop; for he wished to assure his mistress not only by report but by some token. With equal address he filched the letter entrusted to Amleth from the coffer in which it was kept. When these things were brought to the queen, she scanned the shield narrowly, and from the notes appended made out the whole argument. Then she knew that here was the man who, trusting in his own nicely-calculated scheme, had avenged on his uncle the murder of his father. She also looked at the letter containing the suit for her hand, and rubbed out all the writing; for wedlock with the old she utterly abhorred, and desired the embraces of young men. But she wrote in its place a commission purporting to be sent from the King of Britain to herself, signed like the other with his name and title, wherein she pretended that she was asked to marry the bearer. Moreover, she included an account of the deeds of which she had learnt from Amleth's shield, so that one would have thought the shield con-firmed the letter, while the letter explained the shield. Then she told the same spies whom she had employed before to take the shield back, and put the letter in its place again; playing the very trick on Amleth which, as she had learnt, he had himself used in outwitting his companions.

Amleth, meanwhile, who found that his shield had been filched from under his head, deliberately shut his eyes and cunningly feigned sleep, hoping to regain by pretended what he had lost by real slumbers. For he thought that the success of his one attempt would incline the spy to deceive him a second time. And he was not mistaken. For as the spy came up stealthily, and wanted to put back the shield and the writing in their old place, Amleth leapt up, seized him, and detained him in bonds. Then he roused his retinue, and went to the abode of the queen. As representing his father-in-law, he greeted her, and handed her the writing, sealed with the king's seal. The queen, who was named Hermutrude, took and read it, and spoke most warmly of Amleth's diligence and shrewdness, saying that Feng had deserved his punishment, and that the unfathomable wit of Amleth had accomplished a deed past all human estimation; seeing that not only had his impenetrable depth devised a mode of revenging his father's death and his mother's adultery, but it had further, by his notable deeds of prowess, seized the kingdom of the man whom he had found constantly plotting against him. She marvelled therefore that a man of such instructed mind could have made the one slip of a mistaken marriage; for though his renown almost rose above mortality, he seemed to have stumbled into an obscure and ignoble match. For the parents of his wife had been slaves, though good luck had graced them with the honours of royalty. Now (said she), when looking for a wife, a wise man must reckon the lustre of her birth and not of her beauty. Therefore, if he were to seek a match in a proper spirit, he should weigh the ancestry, and not be smitten by the looks; for though looks were a lure to temptation, yet their empty bedizenment had tarnished the white simplicity[1] of many a man. Now there was a woman, as nobly born as herself, whom he could take. She herself, whose means were not poor nor her birth lowly, was worthy his embraces, since he did not surpass her in royal wealth nor outshine her in the honour of his ancestors. Indeed she was a queen, and but that her sex gainsaid it, might be deemed a king; nay (and this is yet truer), whomsoever she thought worthy of her bed was at once a king, and she yielded her kingdom with herself. Thus her sceptre and her hand went together. It was no mean favour for such a woman to offer her love, who in the case of other men had always followed her refusal with the sword. Therefore she pressed

---

[1] *'multorum candorem inaniter fucata detersit'*. [E]

him to transfer his wooing, to make over to her his marriage vows, and to learn to prefer birth to beauty. So saying, she fell upon him with a close embrace.

Amleth was overjoyed at the gracious speech of the maiden, fell to kissing back, and returned her close embrace, protesting that the maiden's wish was his own. Then a banquet was held, friends bidden, the chief nobles gathered, and the marriage rites performed. When they were accomplished, he went back to Britain with his bride, a strong band of Scots being told to follow close behind, that he might have its help against the diverse treacheries in his path. As he was returning, the daughter of the King of Britain, to whom he was still married, met him. Though she complained that she was slighted by the wrong of having a paramour put over her, yet, she said, it would be unworthy for her to hate him as an adulterer more than she loved him as a husband; nor would she so far shrink from her lord as to bring herself to hide in silence the guile which she knew was intended against him. For she had a son as a pledge of their marriage, and regard for him, if nothing else, must have inclined his mother to the affection of a wife. 'He', she said, 'may hate the supplanter of his mother, I will love her; no disaster shall put out my flame for thee; no ill-will shall quench it, or prevent me from exposing the malignant designs against thee, or from revealing the snares I have detected. Bethink thee, then, that thou must beware of thy father-in-law, for thou hast thyself reaped the harvest of thy mission, foiled the wishes of him who sent thee, and with wilful trespass seized over all the fruit for thyself.' By this speech she showed herself more inclined to love her husband than her father.

While she thus spoke, the King of Britain came up and embraced his son-in-law closely, but with little love, and welcomed him with a banquet, to hide his intended guile under a show of generosity. But Amleth, having learnt the deceit, dissembled his fear, took a retinue of two hundred horsemen, put on an under-shirt[1] [of mail], and complied with the invitation, preferring the peril of falling in with the king's deceit to the shame of hanging back. So much heed for honour did he think that he must take in all things. As he rode up close, the king attacked him just under the porch of the folding doors, and would have thrust him through with his javelin, but that the hard shirt of mail threw off the blade. Amleth received a slight wound, and went to the spot where he had bidden the Scottish warriors wait on duty. He then sent back to the king his new wife's spy, whom he had captured. This man was to bear witness that he

[1] Under-shirt of mail, '*subarmalem vestem*', lit. 'a robe under the shoulders' (*armi*). The context shows it must have been mail. [E]

had secretly taken from the coffer where it was kept the letter which
was meant for his mistress, and thus was to make the whole blame
recoil on Hermutrude, by this studied excuse absolving Amleth
from the charge of treachery. The king without tarrying pursued
Amleth hotly as he fled, and deprived him of most of his forces.
So Amleth, on the morrow, wishing to fight for dear life, and utterly
despairing of his powers of resistance, tried to increase his apparent
numbers. He put stakes under some of the dead bodies of his comrades to prop them up, set others on horseback like living men, and
tied others to neighbouring stones, not taking off any of their
armour, and dressing them in due order of line and wedge, just as if
they were about to engage. The wing composed of the dead was as
thick as the troop of the living. It was an amazing spectacle this, of
dead men dragged out to battle, and corpses mustered to fight. The
plan served him well, for the very figures of the dead men showed
like a vast array as the sunbeams struck them. For those dead and
senseless shapes restored the original number of the army so well, that
the mass might have been unthinned by the slaughter of yesterday.
The Britons, terrified at the spectacle, fled before fighting, conquered
by the dead men whom they had overcome in life. I cannot tell
whether to think more of the cunning or of the good fortune of this
victory. The Danes came down on the king as he was tardily making
off, and killed him. Amleth, triumphant, made a great plundering,
seized the spoils of Britain, and went back with his wives to his own
land.

Meanwhile Rorik had died, and Wiglek, who had come to the
throne, had harassed Amleth's mother with all manner of insolence
and stripped her of her royal wealth, complaining that her son had
usurped the kingdom[1] of Jutland and defrauded the King of Leire,
who had the sole privilege of giving and taking away the rights of
high offices. This treatment Amleth took with such forbearance as
apparently to return kindness for slander, for he presented Wiglek
with the richest of his spoils. But afterwards he seized a chance of
taking vengeance, attacked him, subdued him, and from a covert
became an open foe. Fialler, the governor of Skaane, he drove into
exile; and the tale is, that Fialler retired to a spot called Undensakre,
which is unknown to our peoples. After this, Wiglek, recruited with

---

[1] Usurped the kingdom (*regnum*) of Jutland . . . Amleth, like his father and uncle,
receives throughout the title of *Rex*, which has been translated literally; nor is there
any hint at his election that the Jutes are supposed to have had anyone but them-
selves to consult in choosing their 'king', though Rorik was reigning in Denmark . . .
That there was a certain allegiance of a practical kind implied is clear from
Horwendil giving the spoil to Rorik, and winning Amleth's mother to wife. On
Wiglek's accession, Amleth owns the tributary right by surrendering choice spoil.
[E]

the forces of Skaane and Zealand, sent envoys to challenge Amleth to a war. Amleth, with his marvellous shrewdness, saw that he was tossed between two difficulties, one of which involved disgrace and the other danger. For he knew that if he took up the challenge he was threatened with peril of his life, while to shrink from it would disgrace his reputation as a soldier. Yet in that spirit ever fixed on deeds of prowess the desire to save his honour won the day. Dread of disaster was blunted by more vehement thirst for glory; he would not tarnish the unblemished lustre of his fame by timidly skulking from his fate. Also he saw that there is almost as wide a gap between a mean life and a noble death as that which is acknowledged between honour and disgrace themselves. Yet he was enchained by such love for Hermutrude, that he was more deeply concerned in his mind about her future widowhood than about his own death, and cast about very zealously how he could decide on some second husband for her before the opening of the war. Hermutrude, therefore, declared that she had the courage of a man, and promised that she would not forsake him even on the field, saying that the woman who dreaded to be united with her lord in death was abominable. But she kept this rare promise ill; for when Amleth had been slain by Wiglek in battle in Jutland, she yielded herself up unasked to be the conqueror's spoil and bride. Thus all vows of women are loosed by change of fortune and melted by the shifting of time; the faith of their soul rests on a slippery foothold, and is weakened by casual chances; glib in promises, and as sluggish in performance, all manner of lustful promptings enslave it, and it bounds away with panting and precipitate desire, forgetful of old things, in the ever hot pursuit after something fresh. So ended Amleth. Had fortune been as kind to him as nature, he would have equalled the gods in glory, and surpassed the labours of Hercules by his deeds of prowess. A plain in Jutland is to be found, famous for his name and burial-place.

II. Possible Source

From THE ROMANE HISTORIE
by Titus Livius
translated by Philemon Holland (1600)

From The First Book

[Tarquinius Priscus alarmed by a portentous serpent, sent two of his sons to consult the Oracle at Delphi.]

Titus and *Aruns* were they that went this journie, having to beare them companie all the way, *L. Junius Brutus*. This *Brutus* was the sonne of *Tarquinia* the kings sister, a yoong gentleman of farre other nature and disposition, than he seemed in outward shew and semblance. He having heard say that certain principall citizens, and his own brother among them, had been by this his uncle put to death; to the intent that himselfe might have nothing left, eyther in the parts of his mind for the king to feare, or in his outward state for him to covet and desire: resolved under the cloake of base contempt to save himselfe, since that in right or justice he might repose small or no safegard at all. And therefore composing and framing himselfe of purpose to counterfeit a noddie and a verie innocent, as suffering himselfe, and all that he had to fall into the kings hands as an escheat, he refused not to be misnamed *Brutus*, a name appropriat to unreasonable creatures; that under the shadow and colour of that surname, that courage of his lying close hid, which should one day set free the cittie of Rome, might abide the full time and appeare in due season. This *Brutus* being by the *Tarquines* brought to Delphi, as their laughing stock to make them pastime by the way, rather than a meet mate to accompany them, carried with him (as men say) for to offer and present unto *Apollo*, a golden rod within a staffe of cornell wood, made hollow for the purpose: the very type and resemblance by secret circumstances, of his naturall disposition.[1]

Thither beeing arrived, the yong men having done their fathers commission accordingly, were very desirous and earnest to inquire and learne of the Oracle, which of them should be king of Rome. And from the bottome of the deepe vault, this answere as men say, was delivered in their hearing: WHICH OF YOU (O YONG

[1] Valerius Maximus wrote that Brutus 'carried Gold as a present to the Diety, hid in a hollow stick; fearing that it was not safe to worship the Celestial Deity with an open Liberality.' (*Romae Ant. Descript.*, trans. S. Speed., 1678, VII, p. 3.)

MEN) SHAL FIRST KISSE YOUR MOTHER, HE SHAL
BEARE CHIEFE AND SOVERAIGNE RULE IN ROME.
The *Tarquines* then intending that *Sextus* their brother who was left
behind at Rome, might neither know the answer, not yet obtaine the
kingdome, willed the matter should by all possible meanes be
caried so secret as might be, and concealed from him. They themselves agreed upon this together, to draw lots whether of them twaine,
when they were returned to Rome, should first kisse his mother. But
Brutus, supposing the speech of *Apollo* his priest tended to another
sence, made as though he stumbled forward and tooke a fall, and
so touched the ground with his mouth and kissed the earth, thinking
this with himselfe, that she was the common mother of all mortall
men. Then returned they to Rome. Where they found great pre-
paration for warre against the Rutilians.

[During this war the rape of Lucretia occurred, after which
Brutus incited the people against the king and his family, and the
Tarquins were banished.]

III. Analogue

THE HYSTORIE OF HAMBLET
Anon. (1608)

London: Imprinted by Richard Bradocke, for Thomas
Pavier, and are to be sold at his shop in Corne-hill, neere
to the Royall Exchange. 1608.

The Argument.

IT is not at this present, neither yet a small time since, that envy
raigning in the worlde hath in such sort blinded men,[1] that without
respect of consanguinitie, friendship, or favour whatsoever, they
forget themselves so much as that they spared not to defile their
hands with the blood of those men, who by all law and right they
ought chiefly to defend and cherish. For what other impression was
it that entered into Romulus heart, when, under pretence of I know
not what lawe, he defiled his hands with the blood of his owne

---

[1] *In margin*: 'The desire of rule causeth men to become traytors and murtherers.'
I print significant marginal notes from 1608 and some variants in Belleforest [B].

D

brother, but the abhominable vice of desire to raigne? which, if in all the accurrences, prosperities, and circumstances thereof, it were well wayed and considered, I know not any man that had not rather live at his ease, and privately without charge, then, being feared and honored of all men, to beare all the charge and burden upon his shoulders; to serve and please the fantasies of the common people; to live continually in feare, and to see himself exposed to a thousand occasions of danger, and most commonly assailed and spoiled when hee thinkes verily to hold Fortune as slave to his fantasies and will, and yet buyes such and so great misery for the vaine and fraile pleasures of this world, with the losse of his owne soule; making so large a measure of his conscience, that it is not once mooved at any murther, treason, deceit, nor wickednes whatsoever he committed, so the way may be opened and made plaine unto him, whereby hee may attaine to that miserable felicitie, to command and governe a multitude of men (as I said of Romulus), who, by a most abhominable action, prepared himselfe a way to heaven (but not by vertue).

The ambitious and seditious Orator of Rome supposed the degrees and steps to heaven, and the wayes to vertue,[1] to consist in the treasons, ravishments, and massacres committed by him that first layd the foundations of that citty. And not to leave the hystories of Rome, what, I pray you, incited Ancius Martinus to massacre Tarquin the Elder, but the desire of raigning as a king, who before had bin the onely man to move and solicite the saide Tarquinius to bereave the right heires and inheriters thereof? What caused Tarquinius the Proud traiterously to imbrue his hands in the blood of Servius Tullius, his father in law, but onely that fumish and unbridled desire to be commander over the cittie of Rome? which practise never ceased nor discontinued in the said principall cittie of the empire, as long as it was governed by the greatest and wisest personages chosen and elected by the people; for therein have been seen infinite numbers of seditions, troubles, pledges, ransommings, confiscations and massacres, onely proceeding from this ground and principle, which entereth into mens hearts, and maketh them covet and desirous to be heads and rulers of a whole common wealth. And after the people were deprived of that libertie of election, and that the empire became subject to the pleasure and fantasie of one man, commanding al the rest, I pray you peruse their bookes, and read diligently their hystories, and do but looke into the meanes used by the most part of their kings and emperours to attaine to such power and authoritie, and you shall see how poysons, massacres, and secret murthers, were the means to push them forwards that

[1] *In margin:* 'Cicero in his Paradoxes.'

durst not openly attempt it, or else could not compasse to make open warres.[1] And for that the Hystory (which I pretend to shew unto you) is chiefly grounded upon treason, committed by one brother against the other, I will not erre far out of the matter; thereby desiring to shew you, that it is and hath been a thing long since practised and put in use by men, to spill the blood of their neerest kinsmen and friends to attaine to the honour of being great and in authoritie; and that there hath bin some, that being impatient of staying till their just time of succession, have hastened the death of their owne parents: as Absolon would have done to the holy king David, his father; and as wee read of Domitian, that poysoned his brother Titus, the most curtious and liberall prince that ever swayed the empire of Rome. And God knowes we have many the like examples in this our time, where the sonne conspired against the father; for that Sultan Zelin, emperour of Turkes, was so honest a man, that fearing Baiazeth, his father, would die of his naturall death, and that thereby he should have stayd too long for the empire, bereaved him of his life; and Sultan Soliman, his successor, although he attempted not any thing against his father, yet being mooved with a certaine feare to bee deposed from his emperie, and bearing a hatred to Mustapha, his son (incited thereunto by Rustain Bassa, whom the Jewes, enemies to the yong prince, had by gifts procured thereunto), caused him to be strangled with a bowe string, without hearing him (that never had offended his father) once speake to justifie his innocencie.[2] But let us leave the Turkes, like barbarians as they are, whose throne is ordinarily established by the effusion of the blood of those that are neerest of kindred and consanguinitie to the empire, and consider what tragedies have bin plaid to the like effect in the memorie of our ancestors,[3] and with what charitie and love the neerest kindreds and friends among them have bin intertained. One of the other, if you had not the hystories extant before you, if the memorie were not in a manner fresh, and known almost to every man, I would make a long discourse thereof;[4] but things being so cleare and evident, the truth so much discovered, and the people almost, as it were, glutted with such treasons, I will omit them, and follow my matter, to shew you that, if the iniquitie of a brother caused his brother to loose his life, yet that vengeance was not long after delayed; to the end that traitors may know, although the punishment of their trespasses committed be stayed for awhile, yet that they may assure themselves that, without all doubt,

[1] *In margin:* 'Divers attained to the empire by murther.'
[2] The theme of F. Greville's tragedy *Mustapha*.
[3] B. adds 'in Scotland and England'.
[4] *In margin:* 'Great mischiefe in our age.'

they shal never escape[1] the puisant and revenging hand of God; who being slow to anger, yet in the ende doth not faile to shew some signes and evident tokens of his fearefull judgement upon such as, forgetting their duties, shed innocent blood, and betray their rulers, whom they ought chiefly to honour, serve, and reverence.

The Preface

ALTHOUGH in the beginning of this Hystorie I had determined not to have troubled you with any other matter than a hystorie of our owne time, having sufficient tragicall matter to satisfie the minds of men; but because I cannot wel discourse thereof without touching many personages whom I would not willingly displease, and partly because the argument that I have in hand, seemed unto me a thing worthy to bee offered to our French nobilitie, for the great and gallant accurrences therein set downe, I have somewhat strayed from my course, as touching the tragedies of this our age, and, starting out of France and over Neitherlanders countries, I have ventured to visit the hystories of Denmarke, that it may serve for an example of vertue and contentment to our nation (whom I specially seeke to please), and for whose satisfaction I have not left any flower what-soever untasted, from whence I have not drawne the most perfect and delicate hony, thereby to bind them to my diligence herein; not caring for the ingratitude of the time present, that leaveth (as it were rejecteth) without recompence such as serve the common wealth, and by their travell and diligence honour their countrey, and illustrate[2] the realme of France: so that oftentimes the fault proceedeth rather from them, then from the great personages that have other affaires which withdraw them from things that seeme of small consequence. Withall, esteeming my selfe more than satisfied in this contentment and freedome which I now injoy, being loved of the nobilitie, for whom I travell without grudging, favoured of men of learning and knowledge, for admiring and reverencing them according to their worthiness,[3] and honoured of the common people, of whom, although I crave not their judgement, as not esteeming them of abilitie to eternize the name of a worthy man, yet I account my selfe sufficiently happy to have attained to this felicitie, that few or no men refuse, or disdaine to reade my workes, many admiring and wondering thereat; as there are some that, provoked

---

[1] *In margin*: 'God stayeth his wrath, but yet revengeth wrong: read Plutarch Opuscules, of the slownesse of God's judgements.' B. introduced this religious motif.

[2] B. 'illustre', make famous.

[3] Cf. II. 2. 526–33.

by envie, blame and condemne it. To whom I confesse my selfe much bound and beholding, for that by their meanes I am the more vigelant, and so by my travell much more beloved and honored than ever I was; which to mee is the greatest pleasure that I can injoy, and the most abundant treasures in my coffers, wherewith I am more satisfied and contented then (if without comparison) I enjoyed the greatest treasures in all Asia. Now, returning to our matter, let us beginne to declare the Hystorie.

CHAP. I

How Horvendile and Fengon were made Governours of the Province of Ditmarse, and how Horvendile marryed Geruth, the daughter to Roderick, chief K. of Denmark, by whom he had Hamblet: and how after his marriage his brother Fengon slewe him trayterously, and marryed his brothers wife, and what followed.[1]

YOU must understand, that long time before the kingdome of Denmark received the faith of Jesus Christ, and imbraced the doctrin[2] of the Christians, that the common people in those dayes were barbarous and uncivill[3] and their princes cruell, without faith or loyaltie, seeking nothing but murther, and deposing (or at the least) offending each other, either in honours, goods, or lives; not caring to ransome such as they tooke prisoners, but rather sacrificing them to the cruell vengeance naturally imprinted in their hearts:[4] in such sort, that if ther were sometime a good prince or king among them, who beeing adorned with the most perfect gifts of nature, would adict himselfe to vertue, and use courtesie, although the people held him in admiration (as vertue is admirable to the most wicked) yet the envie of his neighbors was so great, that they never ceased untill that vertuous man were dispatched out of the world. King Rodericke,[5] as then raigning in Denmarke, after hee had appeased the troubles in the countrey, and driven the Sweathlanders and Slaveans from thence, he divided the kingdom into divers provinces, placing governours therein; who after (as the like happened in France) bare the names of Dukes, Marqueses, and Earls, giving the government of Jutie (at this present called

[1] No chapter headings in B.
[2] B. adds 'and holy baptism'.
[3] *In margin:* 'The Danes in times past barbarous and uncivill.'
[4] *In margin:* 'The crueltie of the Danes.'
[5] B. has Roric.

Ditmarsse) lying upon the countrey of the Cimbrians, in the straight or narrow part of land that sheweth like a point or cape of ground upon the sea, which neithward bordereth upon the countrey of Norway, two valiant and warlike lords Horvendile and Fengon, sonnes to Gervendile, who likewise had beene governour of that province.[1] Now the greatest honor that men of noble birth could at that time win and obtaine, was in exercising the art of piracie upon the seas, assayling their neighbours, and the countries bordering upon them; and how much the more they used to rob, pill, and spoyle other provinces, and ilands far adjacent, so much the more their honours and reputation increased and augmented: wherein Horvendile obtained the highest place in his time, beeing the most renouned pirate[2] that in those dayes scoured the seas and havens of the north parts: whose great fame so mooved the heart of Collere, king of Norway, that he was much grieved to heare that Horvendile surmounting him in feates of armes, thereby obscuring the glorie by him alreadie obtained upon the seas: (honor more than covetousnesse of riches (in those dayes) being the reason that provoked those barbarian princes to overthrow and vanquish one the other, not caring to be slaine by the handes of a victorious person). This valiant and hardy king[3] having challenged Horvendile to fight with him body to body, the combate was by him accepted, with conditions, that hee which should be vanquished should loose all the riches he had in his ships, and that the vanquisher should cause the body of the vanquished (that should bee slaine in the combate) to be honourably buried, death being the prise and reward of him that should loose the battaile: and to conclude, Collere, king of Norway (although a valiant, hardy, and couragious prince) was in the end vanquished and slaine by Horvendile, who presently caused a tombe to be erected, and therein (with all honorable obsequies fit for a prince) buried the body of king Collere, according to their aunxient manner and superstitions in these dayes, and the conditions of the combate, bereaving the kings shippes of all their riches; and having slaine the kings sister, a very brave and valiant warriour, and over runne all the coast of Norway, and the Northern Ilands, returned home againe layden with much treasure,[4] sending the most part thereof to his soveraigne, king Rodericke, thereby to procure his good liking, and so to be accounted one of the greatest favourites about his majestie.

The king, allured by those presents, and esteeming himselfe

---

[1] Old Hamlet was king of all Denmark.

[2] *In margin*: 'Horvendile a king and a pirate.'

[3] 'ambitious Norway.' I.1.61, 82–95.

[4] Hence I.1.82–95.

happy to have so valiant a subject, sought by a great favour and courtesie to make him become bounden unto him perpetually, giving him Geruth his daughter to his wife, of whom he knew Horvendile to bee already much inamored. And the more to honor him, determined himselfe in person to conduct her into Jutie, where the marriage was celebrated according to the ancient manner: and to be briefe, of this marriage proceeded Hamblet, of whom I intend to speake, and for his cause have chosen to renew this present hystorie.[1]

Fengon, brother to this prince Horvendile, who [not] onely fretting and despighting in his heart at the great honor and reputation wonne by his brother in warlike affaires,[2] but solicited and provoked by a foolish jealousie to see him honored with royall aliance, and fearing thereby to bee deposed from his part of the government, or rather desiring to be onely governour,[3] thereby to obscure the memorie of the victories and conquests of his brother Horvendile, determined (whatsoever happened) to kill him; which hee effected in such sort, that no man once so much as suspected him,[4] every man esteeming that from such and so firme a knot of aliance and consanguinitie there could proceed no other issue then the full effects of vertue and courtesie: but (as I sayd before) the desire of bearing soveraigne rule and authoritie respecteth neither blood nor amitie, nor caring for vertue, as being wholly without respect of lawes, or majestie devine; for it is not possible that hee which invadeth the countrey and taketh away the riches of an other man without cause or reason, should know or feare God. Was not this a craftie and subtile counsellor? but he might have thought that the mother, knowing her husbands case, would not cast her sonne into the danger of death. But Fengon, having secretly assembled certain men, and perceiving himself strong enough to execute his interprise, Horvendile his brother being at a banquet with his friends, sodainely set upon him,[5] where he slewe him as traiterously, as cunningly he purged himselfe of so detestable a murther to his subjects; for that before he had any violent or bloody handes, or once committed parricide upon his brother, hee had incestuously abused his wife, whose honour hee ought as well to have sought and procured as traiterously he pursued and effected his destruction.[6] And it is most certaine, that the man that abandoneth himselfe to

---

[1] *In margin:* 'Hamlet sonne to Horvendile.'
[2] *In margin:* 'Fengon, his conspiracie against his brother.'
[3] III.3.55.
[4] I.e. of plotting.
[5] *In margin:* 'Fengon killeth his brother.' Not secretly as in *Ham.* I.5.59–74.
[6] So in I.5.42–6.

any notorious and wicked action, whereby he becommeth a great sinner, he careth not to commit much more haynous and abhominable offences, and covered his boldnesse and wicked practise with so great subtiltie and policie, and under a vaile of meere simplicitie, that beeing favoured for the honest love that he bare to his sister in lawe, for whose sake, hee affirmed,[1] he had in that sort murthered his brother, that his sinne found excuse among the common people, and of the nobilitie was esteemed for justice: for that Geruth, being as courteous a princesse as any then living in the north parts, and one that had never once so much as offended any of her subjects, either commons or courtyers, this adulter and infamous murtherer, slaundered his dead brother, that hee would have slaine his wife, and that hee by chance finding him upon the point ready to do it, in defence of the lady had slaine him, bearing off the blows, which as then he strooke at the innocent princesse, without any other cause of malice whatsoever. Wherein hee wanted no false witnesses to approove his act,[2] which deposed in like sort, as the wicked calumniator himselfe protested, being the same persons that had born him company, and were participants of his treason;[3] so that instead of pursuing him as a parricide and an incestuous person, al the courtyers admired and flattered him in his good fortune, making more account of false witnesses and detestable wicked reporters, and more honouring the calumniators, then they esteemed of those that seeking to call the matter in question, and admiring the vertues of the murthered prince, would have punished the massacrers and bereavers of his life. Which was the cause that Fengon, boldned and incouraged by such impunitie, durst venture to couple himselfe in marriage with her whom hee used as his concubine during good Horvendiles life, in that sort spotting his name with a double vice,[4] and charging his conscience with abhominable guilt, and two-fold impietie, as incestuous adulterie and parricide murther: and that the unfortunate and wicked woman, that had receaved the honour to bee the wife of one of the valiantest and wiseth princes in the north, imbased her selfe[5] in such vile sort, as to falsifie her faith unto him, and which is worse, to marrie him, that had bin the tyranous murtherer of her lawfull husband; which made divers men thinke that she had beene the causer of the murther, thereby to live in her adultery without controle.[6] But where shall a man finde a more wicked and bold

[1] B. has 'for the love of whom'.
[2] Shakespeare's Denmark is not so corrupt.
[3] *In margin*: 'Slanderers more honoured in court then vertuous persons.'
[4] *In margin*: 'The incestuous marriage of Fengon with his brothers wife.'
[5] Cf. I.5.47: 'What a falling off was there.'
[6] Hence III.4.28–9.

woman, then a great parsonage once having loosed the bands of honor and honestie? This princesse, who at the first, for her rare vertues and courtesses was honored of al men and beloved of her husband, as soone as she once gave eare to the tyrant Fengon, forgot both the ranke she helde among the greatest names, and the dutie of an honest wife on her behalfe. But I will not stand to gaze and mervaile at women, for that there are many which seeke to blase and set them foorth, in which their writings they spare not to blame them all for the faults of some one, or few women. But I say, that either nature ought to have bereaved man of that opinion to accompany with women, or els to endow them with such spirits, as that they may easily support the crosses they endure, without complaining so often and so strangely, seeing it is their owne beastlinesse that overthrowes them.[1] For if it be so, that a woman is so imperfect a creature as they make her to be, and that they know this beast to bee so hard to bee tamed as they affirme, why then are they so foolish to preserve them, and so dull and brutish as to trust their deceitfull and wanton imbraceings? But let us leave her in this extreamitie of laciviousnesse, and proceed to shewe you in what sort the yong prince Hamblet behaved himselfe, to escape the tyranny of his uncle.[2]

CHAP. II

How Hamblet counterfeited the mad man, to escape the tyrannie of his uncle, and how he was tempted by a woman (through his uncles procurement) who thereby thought to undermine the Prince, and by that meanes to finde out whether he counterfeited madnesse or not: and how Hamblet would by no meanes bee brought to consent unto her, and what followed.

GERUTH having (as I sayd before) so much forgotten herself, the prince Hamblet perceiving himself to bee in danger of his life, as beeing abandoned of his owne mother, and forsaken of all men,[3] and assuring himselfe that Fengon would not detract the time to send him the same way his father Horvendile was gone, to beguile the tyrant in his subtilties (that esteemed him to bee of such a minde that if he once attained to mans estate he wold not long delay the

---

[1] *In margin:* 'If a man be deceived by a woman, it is his owne beastlinesse.' But Cf. III.1.140–1.

[2] This sentence is not in B.

[3] Hamlet makes his own solitude.

time to revenge the death of his father) counterfeiting the mad man
with such craft and subtill practises, that hee made shewe as if hee
had utterly lost his wittes: and under that vayle hee covered his
pretence, and defended his life from the treasons and practises of the
tyrant his uncle. And all though hee had beene at the schoole of the
Romane Prince, who, because hee counterfeited himselfe to bee a
foole, was called Brutus,[1] yet hee imitated his fashions, and his
wisedom. For every day beeing in the queenes palace, (who as then
was more carefull to please her whoremaster, then ready to revenge
the cruell death of her husband, or to restore her sonne to his
inheritance), hee rent and tore his clothes, wallowing and lying in
the durt and mire,[2] his face all filthy and blacke, running through
the streets[3] like a man distraught, not speaking one worde, but such
as seemed to proceede of madnesse and meere frenzie; all his actions
and jestures beeing no other than the right countenances of a man
wholly deprived of all reason and understanding, in such sort, that
as then hee seemed fitte for nothing but to make sport to the pages
and ruffling courtiers that attended in the court of his uncle and
father-in-law. But the yong prince noted them well enough, minding
one day to bee revenged in such manner, that the memorie thereof
should remaine perpetually to the world.

Beholde, I pray you, a great point of a wise and brave spirite in a
yong prince, by so great a shewe of imperfection in his person for
advancement, and his owne imbasing and despising, to worke the
meanes and to prepare the way for himselfe to bee one of the happiest
kings in his age. In like sort, never any man was reputed by any of
his actions more wise and prudent then Brutus[4] dissembling a great
alteration in his minde, for that the occasion of such his devise of
foolishnesse proceeded onely of a good and mature counsell and
deliberation, not onely to preserve his goods, and shunne the rage of
the proude tyrant, but also to open a large way to procure the
banishment and utter ruine of wicked Tarquinius, and to
infranchise the people (which were before oppressed) from the yoake
of a great and miserable servitude. And so, not onely Brutus, but
this man and worthy prince, to whom wee may also adde king
David that counterfeited the madde man among the petie kings of
Palestina to preserve his life from the subtill practises of those kings.
I shew this example unto such, as beeing offended with any great
personage, have not sufficient meanes to prevaile in their intents, or

[1] L. J. Brutus. See Text II.
[2] B. 'in the sweepings and dirt of the house.'
[3] B. 'rubbing his face with the mud of the streets through which he ran . . .'
[4] *In margin:* 'Brutus esteemed wise for counterfeiting the foole. Read Titus
Livius and Halicarnassus.'

revenge the injurie by them receaved. But when I speake of revenging
any injury received upon a great personage or superior, it must be
understood by such an one as is not our soveraigne, againste whome
wee maie by no means resiste, nor once practise anie treason nor
conspiracie against his life:[1] and hee that will followe this course
must speake and do all things whatsoever that are pleasing and
acceptable to him whom hee meaneth to deceive, practise his
actions, and esteeme him above all men, cleane contrarye to his
owne intent and meaning; for that is rightly to playe and counter-
feite the foole, when a man is constrained to dissemble and kisse his
hand, whome in hearte hee could wishe an hundred foote depth under
the earth, so hee mighte never see him more, if it were not a thing
wholly to bee disliked in a christian, who by no meanes ought to
have a bitter gall, or desires infected with revenge. Hamblet, in
this sorte counterfeiting the madde man, many times did divers
actions of great and deepe consideration, and often made such and so
fitte answeres, that a wise man would soone have judged from what
spirite so fine an invention mighte proceede,[2] for that standing by
the fire and sharpning sticks like poynards and prickes, one in smiling
manner asked him wherefore he made those little staves so sharpe at
the points? I prepare (saith he) piersing dartes and sharpe arrowes to
revenge my fathers death.[3] Fooles, as I said before, esteemed those
his words as nothing; but men of quicke spirits, and such as hadde
a deeper reache began to suspect somewhat, esteeming that under
that kinde of folly there lay hidden a greate and rare subtilty, such
as one day might bee prejudiciall to their prince, saying, that under
colour of such rudenes he shadowed a crafty pollicy, and by his
devised simplicitye, he concealed a sharp and pregnant spirit:[4] for
which cause they counselled the king to try and know, if it were
possible, how to discover the intent and meaning of the yong prince;
and they could find no better nor more fit invention to intrap him,
then to set some faire and beawtifull woman in a secret place, that
with flattering speeches and all the craftiest meanes she could use,
should purposely seek to allure his mind to have his pleasure of her:
for the nature of all young men, (especially such as are brought up
wantonlie)[5] is so transported with the desires of the flesh, and entreth
so greedily into the pleasures therof, that it is almost impossible to
cover the foul affection, neither yet to dissemble or hyde the same by
art or industry, much lesse to shunne it.[6] What cunning or subtilty

---

[1] *In margin:* 'Rom. viii.21.'
[2] As Claudius soon does.
[3] *In margin:* 'A subtill answere of Prince Hamlet.'
[4] Polonius sees no danger. II.2.210–13.
[5] B. 'à son aise', in luxury.
[6] *In margin:* 'Nature corrupted in man.'

so ever they use to cloak theire pretence, seeing occasion offered, and that in secret, especially in the most inticing sinne that rayneth in man, they cannot chuse (being constrayned by voluptuousnesse) but fall to naturall effect and working.[1] To this end certaine courtiers were appointed to leade Hamblet into a solitary place within the woods,[2] whether they brought the woman, inciting him to take their pleasures together, and to imbrace one another,[3] subtill practises used in these our daies, not to try if men of great account bee extract out of their wits, but rather to deprive them of strength, vertue and wisedome, by meanes of such devilish practitioners, and infernall spirits, their domestical servants, and ministers of corruption.[4] And surely the poore prince at this assault had bin in great danger, if a gentleman (that in Horvendiles time had been nourished with him) had not showne himselfe more affectioned to the bringing up he had received with Hamblet, then desirous to please the tirant, who by all meanes sought to intangle the sonne in the same nets wherein the father had ended his dayes. This gentleman bare the courtyers (appointed as aforesaide of this treason) company, more desiring to give the prince instruction what he should do, then to intrap him, making full account that the least showe of perfect sence and wisedome that Hamblet should make would be sufficient to cause him to loose his life: and therefore by certain signes, he gave Hamblet intelligence in what danger hee was like to fall, if by any meanes hee seemed to obaye, or once like the wanton toyes and vicious provocations of the gentlewoman sent thither by his uncle. Which much abashed the prince, as then wholy beeing in affection to the lady,[5] but by her he was likewise informed of the treason, as being one that from her infancy loved and favoured him, and would have been exceeding sorrowfull for his misfortune, and much more to leave his companie without injoying the pleasure of his body, whome shee loved more than herselfe. The prince in this sort having both deceived the courtiers, and the ladyes expectation,[6] that affirmed and swore that hee never once offered to have his pleasure of the woman, although in subtilty hee affirmed the contrary, every man there upon assured themselves that without all doubt

---

[1] Contrast *Hamlet*, II.2.314–16.

[2] *In margin:* 'Subtilties used to discover Hamblet's madnes.'

[3] *1608* inserts 'but the'.

[4] *In margin:* 'Corrupters of yong gentlemen in princes courts and great houses.'

[5] B. 'esmeu de la beauté de la fille'. Not in love with her, but 'moved by her beauty'.

[6] A mistranslation based on an awkward comma in B.*1582*. 'ayant le jeune seigneur trompé les courtisans, et la fille, soustenans qu'il ne s'estoit avancé en sorte aucune à la violer . . .' In *1572* etc. the girl affirmed that he had never tried to ravish her. It is left uncertain whether he had in fact enjoyed her. [Stabler]

he was distraught of his sences,[1] that his braynes were as then wholly void of force, and incapable of reasonable apprehension, [so that as then Fengons practise took no effect. but for al that he left not off, still seeking by al meanes to finde out Hamblets subtilty, as in the next chapter you shall perceive.][2]

CHAP. III.

How Fengon, uncle to Hamblet, a second time to intrap him in his politick madnes, caused one of his counsellors to be secretly hidden in the queenes chamber, behind the arras, to heare what speeches passed between Hamblet and the Queen; and how Hamblet killed him, and escaped that danger, and what followed.

AMONG the friends of Fengon, there was one that above al the rest doubted of Hamblets practises in counterfeiting the madman;[3] who for that cause said, that it was impossible that so craftie a gallant as Hamblet, that counterfeited the foole, should be discovered with so common and unskilfull practises, which might easily bee perceived, and that to finde out his politique pretence it were necessary to invent some subtill and crafty meanes, more attractive, whereby the gallant might not have the leysure to use his accustomed dissimulation; which to effect he said he knewe a fit waie, and a most convenient meane to effect the kings desire, and thereby to intrap Hamblet in his subtilties, and cause him of his owne accord to fall into the net prepared for him, and thereby evidently shewe his secret meaning.[4] His devise was thus, that King Fengon should make as though he were to goe some long voyage concerning affairs of great importance,[5] and that in the meane time Hamblet should be shut up alone in a chamber with his mother, wherein some other should secretly be hidden behind the hangings, unknowne either to him or his mother, there to stand and heere their speeches, and the complots by them to bee taken concerning the accomplishment of the dissembling fooles pretence; assuring the king that if there were any point of wisedome and perfect sence in the gallants spirit, that without all doubte he would easily discover it to his mother, as being

---

[1] Hamlet's rejection of Ophelia convinces Claudius otherwise, III.1.165.
[2] The passage within brackets is not in B.
[3] Polonius does not doubt.
[4] *In margin:* 'Another subtilty.'
[5] Not suggested in the play.

devoid of all feare that she would utter or make knowne his secret intent, beeing the woman that had borne him in her bodie, and nourished him so carefully; and withall offered himselfe to be the man that should stand to harken and beare witnesse of Hamblets speeches with his mother, that hee might not be esteemed a counsellor in such a case wherein he refused to be the executioner for the behoofe and service of his prince.[1] This invention pleased the king exceeding well, esteeming it as the onelie and soveraigne remedie to heale the prince of his lunacie; and to that ende making a long voyage, issued out of his pallace, and rode to hunt in the forrest. Meane time the counsellor entred secretly into the queenes chamber, and there hid himselfe behind the arras,[2] not long before the queene and Hamblet came thither, who beeing craftie and pollitique, as soone as hee was within the chamber, doubting some treason, and fearing if he should speake severely and wisely to his mother touching his secret practises[3] he should be understood, and by that meanes intercepted, used his ordinary manner of dissimulation, and began to crowe like a cocke beating with his armes, (in such manner as cockes use to strike with their wings) upon the hangings of the chamber:[4] whereby, feeling something stirring under them, he cried, A rat, a rat,[5] and presently drawing his sworde thrust it into the hangings, which done, pulled the counsellour (halfe dead) out by the heeles, made an end of killing him, and beeing slaine, cut his bodie in pieces, which he caused to be boyled and then cast it into an open vaulte or privie, that so it mighte serve for foode to the hogges.[6] By which meanes having discovered the ambushe, and given the inventor thereof his just rewarde, hee came againe to his mother, who in the meane time wepte and tormented her selfe to see all her hopes frustrate, for that what fault soever she had committed, yet was shee sore grieved to see her onely child made a meere mockery, every man reproaching her with his folly, one point whereof she had as then seene before her eyes, which was no small pricke to her conscience, esteeming that the gods sent her that punishment for joyning incestuously in marriage with the tyrrannous murtherer of her husband, who like wise ceased not to invent all the means he could to bring his nephew to his ende, accusing her[7] owne

[1] Polonius, III.1.187–8.

[2] B. has 'souz quelque loudier' (quilt); he hides 'unknown to both of them'.

[3] 'touching ... practises.' Not in B.

[4] In B. Amleth 'Jumped upon the quilt, and felt that something was hiding underneath, and at once struck right through it with his sword.'

[5] Not in B., but Cf. III.4.23, whence doubtless the *Hystorie* derived this incident.

[6] *In margin:* 'A cruell revenge taken by Hamblet upon him that would have betraid him.' Cf. IV.3.17–40.

[7] *1608:* his.

naturall indiscretion, as beeing the ordinary guide of those that so much desire the pleasures of the bodie, who shutting up the waie to all reason, respect not what maie ensue of of their lightnes and great inconstancy, and how a pleasure of small moment is sufficient to give them cause of repentance during their lives,[1] and make them curse the daye and time that ever any such apprehensions entred into theire mindes, or that they closed[2] their eies to reject the honestie requisite in ladies of her qualitie, and to despise the holy institution of those dames that had gone before her, both in nobilitie and vertue, calling to mind the great prayses and commendations given by the danes to Rinde, daughter to king Rothere,[3] the chastest lady in her time, and withall so shamefast that she would never consent to marriage with any prince or knight whatsoever; surpassing in vertue all the ladyes of her time, as shee herselfe surmounted them in beawtie, good behaviour, and comelines. And while in this sort she sate tormenting herselfe, Hamlet entred into the chamber,[4] who having once againe searched every corner of the same, distrusting his mother as well as the rest, and perceiving himselfe to bee alone, began in sober and discreet manner to speak unto her, saying,[5]

What treason is this, O most infamous woman! of all that ever prostrated themselves to the will of an abhominable whore monger, who, under the vail of a dissembling creature, covereth the most wicked and detestable crime that man could ever imagine, or was committed. Now may I be assured to trust you, that like a vile wanton adultresse, altogether impudent and given over to her pleasure, runnes spreading forth her armes joyfully to imbrace the trayterous villanous tyrant that murthered my father, and most incestuously[6] receivest the villain into the lawfull bed of your loyall spouse,[7] imprudently entertaining him in steede of the deare father of your miserable and discomforted sonne, if the gods grant him not the grace speedilie to escape from a captivity so unworthie the degree he holdeth, and the race and noble familie of his ancestors. Is this the part of a queene, and daughter to a king? to live like a brute beast[8] (and like a mare that yieldeth her bodie to the horse that hath beaten hir companion awaye), to followe the pleasure of an abhominable king that hath murthered a farre more honester

---

[1] 'Queene Geruth's repentance.'
[2] 'closed their eyes.' B. 'bandé,' blindfolded. Cf. III.4.77 'hoodman-blind'. One of the Hamlet playwrights knew French.
[3] 'Rinde a princes of an admirable chastitie.'
[4] Hamlet does not leave after killing Polonius.
[5] B. has a heading: 'Amleth's Harangue to his mother Queen Geruth.'
[6] B., like Shakespeare, emphasizes the incest.
[7] Hence I.2.156-7: 'to post with such dexterity to incestuous sheets.'
[8] I.2.150-1: 'a beast, that wants discourse of reason'

and better man then himself in massacring Horvendile, the honor
and glory of the Danes, who are now esteemed of no force nor valour
at all, since the shining splendure[1] of knighthood was brought to
an end by the most wickedest and cruellest villaine living upon
earth. I, for my part, will never account him for my kinsman, nor
once knowe him for mine uncle, nor you [for] my deer mother, for
not having respect to the blud that ought to have united us so
straightly together, and who neither with your honor nor without
suspicion of consent to the death of your husband could ever have
agreed to have marryed with his cruell enemie. O, queene Geruthe,
it is the part of a bitch to couple with many, and desire acquaintance
of divers mastiffes: it is licentiousnes only that hath made you deface
out of your minde the memory of the valor and vertues of the good
king your husband and my father: it was an unbrideled desire that
guided the daughter of Roderick to imbrace the tyrant Fengon, and
not to remember Horvendile (unworthy of so strange intertainment),
neither that he killed his brother traiterously, and that shee being
his fathers wife betrayed him, although he so well favoured and loved
her, that for her sake he utterly bereaved Norway of her riches and
valiant souldiers to augment the treasures of Roderick, and make
Geruthe wife to the hardyest prince in Europe: it is not the parte of
a woman, much lesse of a princesse, in whome all modesty, curtesse,
compassion, and love ought to abound, thus to leave her deare child
to fortune in the bloody and murtherous hands of a villain and traytor.
Bruite beasts do not so, for lyons, tygers, ounces and leopards fight
for the safety and defence of their whelpes; and birds that have
beakes, claws, and wings, resist such as would ravish them of their
yong ones; but you, to the contrary, expose and deliver mee to
death, whereas ye should defend me. Is not this as much as if you
should betray me, when you knowing the perversenes of the tyrant
and his intents, ful of deadly counsell as touching the race and image
of his brother, have not once sought, nor desired to finde the meanes
to save your child (and only son) by sending him into Swethland,
Norway, or England,[2] rather than to leave him as a prey to youre
infamous adulter? bee not offended, I praye you, Madame, if
transported with dolour and griefe, I speake so boldely unto you,
and that I respect you lesse then duetie requireth:[3] for you, having
forgotten mee, and wholy rejected the memorye of the deceased K.
my father, must not bee abashed if I also surpasse the bounds and
limits of due consideration. Beholde into what distresse I am now
fallen, and to what mischiefe my fortune, and your over great light-

---

[1] Hence perhaps the Hyperion image, III.4.56.

[2] B. 'ou plutost l'exposer aux Anglois.' Cf. III.4.200.

[3] III.4.178. B. 'si . . . je vous parle si rigoureusement'.

nesse, and want of wisdome have induced mee, that I am constrained to playe the madde man to save my life, in steed of using
and practising armes,[1] following adventures, and seeking all meanes
to make my selfe knowne to bee the true and undoubted heire of the
valiant and vertuous king Horvendile. It was not without cause, and
juste occasion, that my gestures, countenances, and words, seeme all
to proceed from a madman,[2] and that I desire to have all men esteeme
mee wholly deprived of sence and reasonable understanding, by-
cause I am well assured, that he that hath made no conscience to
kill his owne brother, (accustomed to murthers, and allured with
desire of governement without controll in his treasons), will not
spare, to save himselfe with the like crueltie, in the blood and flesh
of the loyns of his brother by him massacred: and, therefore, it is
better for me to fayne madnesse, then to use my right sences as
nature hath bestowed them upon me; the bright shining clearnes
therof I am forced to hide under this shadow of dissimulation, as
the sun doth hir beams under some great cloud, when the wether in
sommer time overcasteth. The face of a mad man serveth to cover my
gallant countenance, and the gestures of a fool are fit for me, to the
end that guiding my self wisely therein,[3] I may preserve my life
for the Danes, and the memory of my late deceased father; for the
desire of revenging his death is so engraven in my heart, that if I
dye not shortly, I hope to take such and so great vengeance, that
these countryes shall for ever speake thereof.[4] Neverthelesse, I must
stay the time, meanes, and occasion,[5] lest by making over great
hast, I be now the cause of mine owne sodaine ruine and overthrow,
and by that meanes end before I beginne to effect my hearts desire.
Hee that hath to doe with a wicked, disloyall, cruell, and discourteous
man must use craft and politike inventions, such as a fine witte
can best imagine, not to discover his interprise;[6] for seeing that by
force I cannot effect my desire, reason alloweth me by dissimulation,
subtiltie, and secret practises to proceed therein.[7] To conclude,
weepe not (madame) to see my folly, but rather sigh and lament your
owne offence, tormenting your conscience in regard of the infamie
that hath so defiled the ancient renowne and glorie that (in times
past) honoured queene Geruth; for wee are not to sorrowe and
grieve at other mens vices, but for our owne misdeedes, and great

[1] Hence 'forgone all custom of exercises.' II.2.302–3 (Stabler).
[2] Cf. III.4.141–2.
[3] B. *In margin:* 'In great enterprises one must not be hasty.'
[4] Cf. V.2.339–40; 348–9.
[5] Contrast Hamlet, IV.4.39–46.
[6] *In margin:* 'We must use subtiltie to a disloyal person.'
[7] III.4.188; 209–10.

follyes. Desiring you, for the surplus of my proceedings, above all things (as you love your owne life and welfare) that neither the king nor any other may by any meanes know mine intent;[1] and let me alone with the rest, for I hope in the ende to bring my purpose to effect.

Although the queene perceived herselfe neerly touched, and that Hamlet mooved her to the quicke, where [most] she felt herselfe interested,[2] neverthelesse shee forgot all disdaine and wrath, which thereby she might as then have had, hearing her selfe so sharply chiden and reprooved, for the joy she then conceaved, to behold the gallant spirit of her sonne, and to thinke what she might hope, and the easier expect of his so great policie and wisdome. But on the one side she durst not lift up her eyes to beholde him, remembering her offence, and on the other side she would gladly have imbraced her son, in regard of the wise admonitions by him given unto her, which as then quenched the flames of unbridled desire that before had moved her to affect K. Fengon, to ingraff in her heart the vertuous actions of her lawfull spouse, whom inwardly she much lamented, when she beheld the lively image and portraiture[3] of his vertue and great wisedome in her childe, representing his fathers haughtie and valiant heart: and so, overcome and vanquished with his honest passion, and weeping most bitterly, having long time fixed her eyes upon Hamlet, as beeing ravished into some great and deepe contemplation, and as it were wholy amazed, at the last imbracing him in her armes (with the like love that a vertuous mother may or can use to kisse and entertaine her owne childe), shee spake unto him in this manner.[4]

I know well (my sonne) that I have done thee great wrong in marrying with Fengon, the cruell tyrant and murtherer of thy father, and my loyal spouse: but when thou shalt consider the small meanes of resistance, and the treason of the palace, with the little cause of confidence we are to expect or hope for of the courtiers, all wrought to his will, as also the power hee made ready, if I should have refused to like of him,[5] thou wouldest rather excuse then accuse me of lasciviousnes or inconstancy much lesse offer me that wrong to suspect that ever thy mother Geruthe once consented to the death and murther of her husband: swearing unto thee (by the majestie of the Gods)[6] that if it had layne in my power to have resisted the

[1] Cf. III.4.181–99.

[2] B. 'Quoy que la Royne se sentist piquer de bien pres, et que Amleth la touchast vive-vivement ou plus elle se sentoit interessee . . .'

[3] Did this suggest the pictures at III.4.53–67?

[4] Gertrude does not defend herself.

[5] B. 'if I had refused to marry him' (son alliance).

[6] Cf. Q1, Sc.11.104.

tyrant, although it had beene with the losse of my blood, yea and my
life, I would surely have saved the life of my lord and husband with
as good a will and desire as, since that time, I have often beene a
meanes to hinder and impeach the shortning of thy life, which
being taken away, I will no longer live here upon earth. For seeing
that thy sences are whole and sound, I am in hope to see an easie
meanes invented for the revenging of thy fathers death.[1] Neverthelesse, mine owne sweet sonne, if thou hast pittie of thy selfe, or care
of the memorie of thy father (although thou wilt do nothing for her
that deserveth not the name of a mother in this respect), I pray thee,
carie thine affayres wisely: bee not hastie, nor over furious in thy
interprises,[2] neither yet advance thy selfe more then reason shall
moove thee to effect thy purpose. Thou seest there is not almost any
man wherein thou mayest put thy trust, nor any woman to whom
I dare utter the least part of my secrets, that would not presently
report it to thine adversarie, who, although in outward shew he
dissembleth to love mee,[3] the better to injoy his pleasures of me, yet
hee distrusteth and feareth mee for thy sake, and is not so simple to
be easily perswaded that thou art a foole or mad;[4] so that if thou
chance to doe any thing that seemeth to proceed of wisedome or
policie (how secretly soever it be done) he will presently be informed
thereof, and I am greatly afraid that the devils have shewed him
what hath past at this present between us, (fortune so much pursueth
and contrarieth our ease and welfare) or that this murther that now
thou hast committed be not the cause of both our destructions, which
I by no meanes will seeme to know,[5] but will keepe secret both thy
wisedome and hardy interprise; beseeching the Gods (my good
soone) that they, guiding thy heart, directing thy counsels, and
prospering thy interprise, I may see thee possesse and injoy that
which is thy right, and weare the crowne of Denmarke, by the tyrant
taken from thee; that I may rejoyce in thy prosperitie, and therewith content my self, seeing with what courage and boldnesse thou
shalt take vengeance upon the murtherer of thy father, as also upon
all those that have assisted and favoured him in his murtherous
and bloody enterprise. Madame (sayd Hamlet) I will put my trust
in you, and from henceforth meane not to meddle further with your
affayres, beseeching you (as you love your owne flesh and blood)
that you will from hence foorth no more esteeme of the adulterer,[6]

[1] Not in Q2, but in Q1: 'I will conceale, consent, and doe my best, What
stratagem soe're thou shalt devise.'

[2] Cf. her advice in Q1, Sc.14, 1764-7.

[3] mee. B. 'de m'aimer'. *1608* thee.

[4] As in the play.

[5] Gertrude tells Claudius but blames it on H's madness.

[6] Contrast Hamlet's vehemence at III.4.157-70.

mine enemie whom I wil surely kill, or cause to be put to death, in despite of all the devils in hel: and have he never so manie flattering courtezans to defend him, yet will I bring him to his death, and they themselves also shall beare him company therein, as they have bin his perverse counsellors in the action of killing my father, and his companions in his treason, massacre and cruell enterprise. And reason requireth that, even as trayterously they then caused their prince to bee put to death, that with the like (nay well, much more) justice they should pay the interest of their fellonious actions.

You know (Madame) how Hother your grandfather, and father to the good king Roderick, having vanquished Guimon, caused him to be burnt, for that the cruell vilain had done the like to his lord Gevare, whom he betrayed in the night time.[1] And who knoweth not that traytors and perjured persons deserve no faith nor loyaltie to be observed towardes them, and that conditions made with murtherers ought to bee esteemed as cobwebs, and accounted as if they were things never promised nor agreed upon:[2] but if I lay handes upon Fengon, it will neither be fellonie nor treason, hee being neither my king nor my lord, but I shall justly punish him as my subject, that hath disloyaly behaved himselfe against his lord and soveraigne prince. And seeing that glory is the rewarde of the vertuous, and the honour and praise of those that do service to their naturall prince, why should not blame and dishonour accompany traytors, and ignominious death al those that dare be so bold as to lay violent hands upon sacred kings, that are friends and companions of the gods, as representing their majestie and persons. To conclude, glorie is the crown of vertue, and the price of constancie, and seeing that it never accompanieth with infelicitie, but shunneth cowardize and spirits of base and trayterous conditions, it must necessarily followe, that either a glorious death will be mine ende,[3] or with my sword in hand, (laden with tryumph and victorie) I shall bereave them of their lives that made mine unfortunate, and darkened the beames of that vertue which I possessed from the blood and famous memory of my predecessors.[4] For why should men desire to live,[5] when shame and infamie are the executioners that torment their consciences, and villany is the cause that withholdeth the heart from valiant interprises, and diverteth the minde from honest desire of glorie and commendation, which indureth for ever? I

---

[1] Cf. Saxo, Bk. III, ed. Elton, p. 100.

[2] *In margin:* 'We must observe neither faithfulnesse or fidelitie to Traytors or parricides' (V.2.63–70).

[3] Stabler sees here the germ of III.1.57–60; but Hamblet has no doubts.

[4] This suggested the 'To be or not to be' speech, III.1.56–88.

[5] B. *In margin:* 'Life miserable when accompanied by infamy.'

know it is foolishly done to gather fruit before it is ripe,[1] and to seeke to enjoy a benefit, not knowing whither it belong to us of right; but I hope to effect it so well, and have so great confidence in my fortune (that hitherto hath guided the action of my life) that I shall not dye without revenging my selfe upon mine enemie, and that himselfe shall be the instrument of his owne decay, and to execute that which of my selfe I durst not have enterprised.

After this, Fengon (as if hee had beene out some long journey) came to the court againe, and asked for him that had received the charge to play the intilligencer, to entrap Hamlet in his dissembled wisedome, was abashed to heare neither newes nor tydings of him, and for that cause asked Hamlet what was become of him, naming the man.[2] The prince that never used lying, and who in all the answers that ever he made (during his counterfeit madnesse) never strayed from the trueth (as a generous minde is a mortal enemie to untruth) answered and sayd, that the counsellor he sought for was gone downe through the privie, where being choaked by the filthynesse of the place, the hogs meeting him had filled their bellyes.

CHAP. IIII.

How Fengon the third time devised to send Hamblet to the king of England, with secret letters to have him put to death: and how Hamblet, when his companions slept, read the letters, and instead of them counterfeited others, willing the king of England to put the two messengers to death, and to marry his daughter to Hamblet, which was effected; and how Hamblet escaped out of England.

A MAN would have judged any thing, rather then that Hamblet had committed that murther, nevertheless Fengon could not content himselfe, but still his minde gave him that the foole would play him some tricke of liegerdemaine,[3] and willingly would have killed him, but he feared king Rodericke, his grandfather, and further durst not offend the queene, mother to the foole, whom she loved and much cherished,[4] shewing great griefe and heavinesse to see him so

---

[1] Cf. V.2.219–22.
[2] Cf. IV.2.
[3] So Claudius, IV.3.1–3.
[4] Cf. IV.7.5–18.

transported out of his wits. And in that conceit, seeking to bee rid of him, determined to finde the meanes to doe it by the ayde of a stranger, making the king of England minister of his massacreing resolution,[1] choosing rather that his friende should defile his renowne with so great a wickednesse, then himselfe to fall into perpetuall infamie by an exploit of so great crueltie, to whom hee purposed to send him, and by letters desire him to put him to death.

Hamblet, understanding that he should be sent into England, presently doubted the occasion of his voyage, and for that cause speaking to the queene, desired her not to make any shew of sorrow or griefe for his departure, but rather counterfeit a gladnesse, as being rid of his presence; whom, although she loved, yet she dayly grieved to see him in so pittifull estate, deprived of all sence and reason: desiring her further, that she should hang the hall with tapestrie, and make it fast with nayles upon the walles, and keepe the brands for him which hee had sharpened at the points, then, when as he said he made arrowes to revenge the death of his father: lastly, he counselled her, that the yeere after his departure being accomplished, she should celebrate his funerals; assuring her that at the same instant she should see him returne with great contentment and pleasure unto her for that his voyage. Now, to beare him company were assigned two of Fengons faithfull ministers,[2] bearing letters ingraved in wood, that contained Hamlets death, in such sort as he had advertised the king of England. But the subtile Danish prince (beeing at sea) whilst his companions slept, having read the letters, and knowne his uncles great treason, with the wicked and villainous mindes of the two courtyers that led him to the slaughter,[3] rased out the letters that concerned his death, and in stead thereof graved others, with commission to the king of England to hang his two companions;[4] and not content to turne the death they had devised against him upon their owne neckes, wrote further, that king Fengon willed him to give his daughter to Hamlet in marriage. And so arriving in England[5] the messengers presented themselves to the king, giving him Fengons letters; who having read the contents, sayd nothing as then, but stayed convenient time to effect Fengons desire, meane time using the Danes familiarly, doing them that honour to sit at his table (for that kings as then were not so curiously, nor solemnely served as in these our dayes), for in these dayes meane kings, and lords of small revenewe

---

[1] Cf. IV.3.60–70.
[2] Originals of Rosencrantz and Guildenstern.
[3] *In margin:* 'Hamblets craft to save his life.'
[4] V.2.12–53.
[5] Hamlet never gets to England.

are as difficult and hard to bee seene, as in times past the monarches
of Persia used to bee: or as it is reported of the great king of Aethy-
opia, who will not permit any man to see his face, which ordinarily
hee covereth with a vaile. And as the messengers sate at the table
with the king, subtile Hamlet was so far from being merry with them,
that he would not taste one bit of meate, bread, nor cup of beare
whatsoever, as then set upon the table, not without great wondering
of the company, abashed to see a yong man and a stranger not to
esteeme of the delicate meates and pleasant drinkes served at the
banquet, rejecting them as things filthy, evill of tast, and worse prepared. The king, who for that time dissembled what he thought,
caused his ghests to be conveyed into their chamber, willing one of
his secret servantes to hide himselfe therein, and so to certifie him
what speeches past among the Danes at their going to bed.

Now they were no sooner entred into the chamber, and those
that were appointed to attend upon them gone out, but Hamlets
companions asked him, why he refused to eate and drinke of that
which hee found upon the table, not honouring the banquet of so
great a king, that entertained them in friendly sort, with such
honour and courtesie as it deserved? saying further, that hee did not
well, but dishonoured him that sent him, as if he sent men into
England that feared to bee poysoned by so great a king. The prince,
that had done nothing without reason and prudent consideration,
answered them, and sayd:[1] What, think you, that I wil eat bread
dipt in humane blood, and defile my throate with the rust of yron,
and use that meat that stinketh and savoureth of mans flesh, already
putrified and corrupted, and that senteth like the savour of a dead
carryon, long since cast into a valt? and how woulde you have mee
to respect the king, that hath the countenance of a slave; and the
queene, who in stead of great majestie, hath done three things more
like a woman of base parentage, and fitter for a waiting gentle-
woman than beseeming a lady of her qualitie and estate. And having
sayd so, used many injurious and sharpe speeches as well against the
king and queene, as others that had assisted at that banquet for the
intertainment of the Danish ambassadors; and therein Hamblet
said trueth, as hereafter you shall heare, for that in those dayes, the
north parts of the worlde, living as then under Sathans lawes, were
full of inchanters, so that there was not any yong gentleman whatsoever that knew not something therein sufficient to serve his turne,
if need required: as yet in those dayes in Gothland and Biarmy,
there are many that knew not what the Christian religion permitteth,
as by reading the histories of Norway and Gothland, you maie
easilie perceive: and so Hamlet, while his father lived, had bin

[1] B. *In margin:* 'Amleth's subtle reply'.

instructed in that devilish art, whereby the wicked spirite abuseth mankind, and advertiseth him (as he can) of things past.

It toucheth not the matter herein to discover the parts of devination in man, and whether this prince, by reason of his over great melancholy,[1] had received those impressions, devining that, which never any but himselfe had before declared, like the philosophers, who discoursing of divers deep points of philosophie, attribute the force of those divinations to such as are Saturnists by complection, who oftentimes speake of things which, their fury ceasing, they then alreadye can hardly understand who are the pronouncers; and for that cause Plato saith, many deviners and many poets, after the force and vigour of their fier beginneth to lessen, do hardly understand what they have written, although intreating of such things, while the spirite of devination continueth upon them, they doe in such sorte discourse thereof that the authors and inventers of the arts themselves by them alledged, commend their discourses and subtill disputations. Likewise I mean not to relate that which divers men beleeve, that a reasonable soul[2] becometh the habitation of a meaner sort of devels, by whom men learn the secrets of things natural; and much lesse do I account of the supposed governors of the world fained by magitians, by whose means they brag to effect mervailous things. It would seeme miraculous that Hamlet shold divine in that sort, which after prooved so true (if as I said before) the devel had not knowledg of things past, but to grant it he knoweth things to come I hope you shall never finde me in so grose an error.[3] You will compare and make equall derivation, and conjecture with those that are made by the spirit of God, and pronounced by the holy prophets, that tasted of that marvelous science, to whome onely was declared the secrets and wondrous workes of the Almighty. Yet there are some imposturious companions that impute so much devinitie to the devell, the father of lyes, that they attribute unto him the truth of the knowledge of thinges that shall happen unto men,[4] alledging the conference of Saul with the witch,[5] although one example out of the Holy Scriptures, specially set downe for the condemnation of wicked man, is not of force to give a sufficient law to all the world; for they themselves confesse that they can devine, not according to the universal cause of things, but by signes borrowed from such like causes, which are all waies alike, and by those con-

---

[1] B. 'pour la véhémence de la mélancholie.' Cf. II.2.607–11.

[2] B. 'une âme toute convertie en raison.'

[3] B. *In margin:* 'The Demons know the past well, but they do not know the future.'

[4] Cf. the Witches in *Macbeth*.

[5] B. *In margin:* 'Saul has the soul of Samuel called up' (*1 Kings*, 28).

jectures they can give judgement of thinges to come,[1] but all this beeing grounded upon a weake support, (which is a simple conjecture) and having so slender a foundation, as some foolish or late-experience, the fictions being voluntarie, it should be a great folly in a man of good judgment, specially one that imbraceth the preaching of the gospell, and seeketh after no other but the trueth thereof, to repose upon any of these likelihoods or writings full of deceipt.

As touching magical operations, I will grant them somewhat therein, finding divers histories that write thereof, and that the Bible maketh mention, and forbiddeth the use thereof:[2] yea, the lawes of the gentiles and ordinances of emperors have bin made against it in such sort, that Mahomet, the great hereticke and friend of the devell, by whose subtiltyes hee abused most part of the east countries, hath ordained great punishments for such as use and practise those unlawfull and damnable arts, which, for this time leaving of, let us returne to Hamblet, brought up in these abuses, according to the manner of his country, whose companions hearing his answere reproached him of folly, saying that hee could by no meanes show a greater point of indiscretion, then in despising that which is lawfull, and rejecting that which all men receaved as a necessary thing, and that hee had not grossely so forgotten himselfe as in that sort to accuse such and so excellent a man as the king of England, and to slander the queene, being then as famous and wise a princes as any at that day raigning in the ilands thereabouts, to cause him to be punished according to his deserts; but he, continuing in his dissimulation, mocked him, saying that hee had not done any thing that was not good and most true. On the other side, the king being advertised thereof by him that stood to heare the discourse, judged presently that Hamlet, speaking so ambiguously, was either a perfect foole, or else one of the wisest princes in his time, answering so sodainly, and so much to the purpose upon the demaund by his companions made touching his behaviour; and the better to find the trueth, caused the baker to be sent for,[3] of whome inquiring in what place the corne grew whereof he made bread for the table, and whether in that ground there were not some signes or newes of a battaile fought, whereby humaine blood had therein been shed? the baker answered that not far from thence there lay a field ful of dead mens bones, in times past slaine in a battaile, as by the greate heapes of wounded sculles mighte well appeare, and for that the ground in that parte was become fertiler than other grounds, by reason of the fatte and humours of the dead bodies,

---

[1] B. *In margin:* 'How magicians can divine.'
[2] B. *In margin:* 'Magicians do marvellous things.'
[3] B. 'boulanger'; *1608* 'babler'. Also below.

that every yeer the farmers used there to have in the best wheat
they could finde to serve his majesties house. The king perceiving it
to be true, according to the yong princes wordes, asked where the
hogs had bin fed that were killed to be served at his table? and
answere was made him, that those hogs getting out of the said
field wherein they were kepte, had found the bodie of a thiefe that
had beene hanged for his demerits, and had eaten thereof: whereat
the king of England beeing abashed, would needs know with what
water the beer he used to drinke of had beene brued? which having
knowne, he caused the river to bee digged somewhat deeper, and
therein found great store of swords and rustie armours, that gave an
ill savour to the drinke. It were good I should heere dilate somewhat
of Merlins prophesies,[1] which are said to be spoken of him before
he was fully one yeere old; but if you consider wel what hath al
reddy been spoken, it is no hard matter to divine of things past,
although the minister of Sathan therein played his part, giving
sodaine and prompt answeres to this yong prince, for that herein are
nothing but natural things, such as were wel known to be true, and
therefore not needfull to dreame of thinges to come. This knowne,
the king, greatly moved with a certaine curiositie to knowe why the
Danish prince saide that he had the countenance of a slave, suspecting thereby that he reproached the basenes of his blood, and that he
wold affirme that never any prince had bin his sire, wherein to
satisfie himselfe he went to his mother, and leading her into a
secret chamber, which he shut as soone as they were entered,
desired her of her honour to shewe him of whome he was ingendred
in this world. The good lady, wel assured that never any man had
bin acquainted with her love touching any other man then her
husband, sware that the king her husband onely was the man that
had enjoyed the pleasures of her body; but the king her sonne,
alreadie with the truth of the Danish princes answers, threatned
his mother to make her tell by force, if otherwise she would not
confesse it, who for feare of death acknowledged that she had
prostrated her body to a slave, and made him father to the king of
England; whereat the king was abashed, and wholy ashamed.[2] I
give them leave to judge who esteeming themselves honester than
theire neighbours, and supposing that there can be nothing amisse in
their houses, make more enquirie then is requisite to know the
which they would rather not have known. Neverthelesse dissembling
what he thought, and biting upon the bridle, rather then he would
deprive himselfe by publishing the lasciviousnes of his mother,
thought better to leave a great sin unpunished, then thereby to

[1] B. *In margin:* 'Merlin, prophet of the English.'
[2] B. *In margin:* 'The Englishman's mother confesses that her son is a Bastard.'

make himselfe contemptible to his subjects, who peradventure would have rejected him, as not desiring to have a bastard to raigne over so great a kingdome.

But as he was sorry to hear his mothers confession, on the otherside he tooke great pleasure in the subtilty and quick spirit of the yong prince, and that for cause went unto him to aske him, why he had reproved three things in his queene convenient for a slave, and savouring more of basenes then of royaltie, and far unfit for the majesty of a great prince?[1] The king, not content to have receaved a great displeasure by knowing him selfe to be a bastard, and to have heard with what injuries he charged her whom hee loved best in all the world,[2] would not content himself untill he also understood that which displeased him, as much as his owne proper disgrace, which was that his queen was the daughter of a chambermaid, and withall noted certaine foolish countenances she made, which not onely shewed of what parentage she came, but also that hir humors savored of the basenes and low degree of hir parents, whose mother, he assured the king, was as then yet holden in servitude. The king admiring the young prince, and behoulding in him some matter of greater respect then in the common sort of men, gave him his daughter in marriage, according to the counterfet letters by him devised, and the next day caused the two servants of Fengon to be executed, to satisfie, as he thought, the king's desire. But Hamlet, although the sport plesed him wel,[3] and that the king of England could not have done him a greater favour, made as though he had been much offended, threatning the king to be revenged, but the king, to appease him, gave him a great sum of gold, which Hamlet caused to be molten, and put into two staves, made hollow for the same purpose, to serve his tourne there with as neede should require;[4] for of all other the kings treasures he took nothing with him into Denmark but onely those two staves, and as soone as the yeere began to bee at an end, having somewhat before obtained licence of the king his father in law to depart, went for Denmarke; then, with all the speed hee could to returne againe into England to marry his daughter, and so set sayle for Denmarke.

[1] B. 'Princesse'; *1608* prince.
[2] B. *In margin:* 'Too great curiosity harmful to a man.'
[3] B. *In margin:* 'Treachery falls on the head of him who wishes to perform it.' Cf. III.4.206–9.
[4] Like L. J. Brutus in Text II. Brutus is mentioned in Chapter II above.

CHAP. V.

How Hamblet, having escaped out of England, arrived in Denmarke the same day that the Danes were celebrating his funerals, supposing him to be dead in England; and how he revenged his fathers death upon his uncle and the rest of the courtiers; and what followed.

HAMBLET in that sort sayling into Denmark, being arrived in the contry, entered into the pallace of his uncle the same day that they were celebrating his funeralls,[1] and going into the hall, procured no small astonishment and wonder to them all, no man thinking other but that hee had beene deade: among the which many of them rejoyced not a little for the pleasure which they knew Fengon would conceave for so pleasant a losse, and some were sadde, as remembering the honourable king Horvendile, whose victories they could by no meanes forget, much lesse deface out of theire memories that which apperteined unto him, who as then greatly rejoyced to see a false report spread of Hamlets death, and that the tyrant had not as yet obtained his will of the heire of Jutie, but rather hoped God[2] would restore him to his sences againe for the good and welfare of that province.

Their amazement at the last beeing tourned into laughter, all that as then were assistant at the funerall banquet of him whome they esteemed dead, mocked each at other, for having beene so simply deceived, and wondering at the prince, that in his so long a voyage he had not recovered any of his sences, asked what was become of them that had borne him company into Greate Brittain? to whome he made answere (shewing them the two hollow staves, wherein he had put his molten golde, that the King of England had given him to appease his fury, concerning the murther of his two companions), and said, Here they are both. Whereat many that already knewe his humours, presently conjectured that hee had plaide some tricke of legerdemane, and to deliver himselfe out of danger, had throwne them into the pitte prepared for him; so that fearing to follow after them and light upon some evil adventure, they went presently out of the court.

And it was well for them that they didde so, considering the tragedy acted by him the same daie, beeing accounted his funerall, but in trueth theire last daies, that as then rejoyced for their over-

---

[1] Ophelia's in the play; V.i.
[2] B. 'les Dieux'.

throw; for when every man busied himselfe to make good cheare,
and Hamlets arivall provoked them more to drinke and carouse, the
prince himselfe at that time played the butler and a gentleman
attending on the tables, not suffering the pots nor goblets to bee
empty, whereby hee gave the noble men such store of liquor, that
all of them being ful laden with wine and gorged with meate, were
constrained to lay themselves downe in the same place where they
had supt, so much their sences were dulled, and overcome with the
fire of over great drinking (a vice common and familiar among the
Almaines, and other nations inhabiting the north parts of the world)[1]
which when Hamlet perceiving, and finding so good opportunitie
to effect his purpose and bee revenged of his enemies, and by the
means to abandon the actions, gestures, and apparel of a mad man,
occasion so fitly finding his turn, and as it were effecting it selfe,
failed not to take hold therof, and seeing those drunken bodies,
filled with wine, lying like hogs upon the ground, some sleeping,
others vomiting the over great abundance of wine which without
measure they had swallowed up, made the hangings about the
hall to fall downe and cover them all over; which he nailed to the
ground, being boorded, and at the ends thereof he stuck the brands,
whereof I spake before, by him sharpned, which served for prickes,
binding and tying the hangings in such sort, that what force soever
they used to loose themselves, it was unpossible to get from under
them: and presently he set fire in the foure corners of the hal, in such
sort, that all that were as then therein not one escaped away, but
were forced to purge their sins by fire, and dry up the great aboun-
dance of liquor by them received into their bodies, all of them dying
in the inevitable and mercilesse flames of the whot and burning
fire: which the prince perceiving, became wise, and knowing that
his uncle, before the end of the banquet, had withdrawn himselfe
into his chamber, which stood apart from the place where the fire
burnt, went thither, and entring into the chamber[2] layd hand upon
the sword of his fathers murtherer, leaving his own in the place,
which while he was at the banket some of the courtiers had nailed
fast into the scaberd, and going to Fengon said: I wonder, disloyal
king, how thou canst sleep heer at thine ease, and al thy pallace is
burnt, the fire thereof having burnt the greatest part of thy
courtiers and ministers of thy cruelty, and detestable tirannies; and
which is more, I cannot imagin how thou sholdst wel assure thy
self and thy estate, as now to take thy ease, seeing Hamlet so neer
thee armed with the shafts by him prepared long since, and at this

---

[1] 'Drunkenes a vice over common in the north partes of the world.' This marginal
note is not in B. Cf. I.4.8–22.

[2] *In margin:* 'A strange revenge taken by Hamlet.'

present is redy to revenge the traiterous injury by thee done to his lord and father.[1]

Fengon, as then knowing the truth of his nephews subtile practise, and hering him speak with stayed mind, and which is more, perceived a sword naked in his hand, which he already lifted up to deprive him of his life, leaped quickly out of the bed, taking holde of Hamlets sworde, that was nayled into the scaberd, which as hee sought to pull out, Hamlet gave him such a blowe upon the chine of the necke, that hee cut his head cleane from his shoulders, and as he fell to the ground sayd, This just and violent death is a just reward for such as thou art: now go thy wayes, and when thou commest in hell, see thou forget not to tell thy brother (whom thou trayterously slewest), that it was his sonne that sent thee thither with the message, to the ende that beeing comforted thereby, his soule may rest among the blessed spirits, and quit mee of the obligation that bound me to pursue his vengeance upon mine owne blood, seeing that it was by thee that I lost the chiefe thing that tyed me to this aliance and consanguinitie. A man (to say the trueth) hardie, couragious, and worthy of eternall comendation, who arming himself with a crafty, dissembling, and strange shew of beeing distract out of his wits, under that pretence deceived the wise, pollitike, and craftie, thereby not onely preserving his life from the treasons and wicked practises of the tyrant, but (which is more) by an new and unexpected kinde of punishment, revenged his fathers death, many yeeres after the act committed[2]: in such sort[3] that directing his courses with such prudence, and effecting his purposes with so great boldnes and constancie, he left a judgement to be decyded among men of wisdom, which was more commendable in him, his constancy or magnanimitie, or his wisdom in ordring his affaires, according to the premeditable determination he had conceaved.

If vengeance ever seemed to have any shew of justice, it is then, when pietie and affection constraineth us to remember our fathers unjustly murdered,[4] as the things wherby we are dispensed withal, and which seeke the means not to leave treason and murther unpunished: seeing David a holy and just king, and of nature simple, courteous, and debonaire, yet when he dyed he charged his soone Salomon (that succeeded him in his throane) not to suffer certaine men that had done him injurie to escape unpunished. Not that this holy king (as then ready to dye, and to give account before God of all his actions) was carefull or desirous of revenge, but to leave this

---

[1] *In margin:* 'A mocke but yet sharp and stinging, given by Hamlet to his uncle.'
[2] 'Commendation of Hamlet for killing the tyrant.'   [3] *1608:* 'in no such sort'.
[4] B. *In margin:* 'When vengeance should be considered just.' *1608:* 'How just vengeance ought to be considered.'

example unto us, that where the prince or countrey is interessed, the desire of revenge cannot by any meanes (how small soever) beare the title of condemnation, but is rather commendable and worthy of praise: for otherwise the good kings of Juda, nor others had not pursued them to death, that had offended their predecessors, if God himself had not inspired and ingraven that desire within their hearts. Hereof the Athenian lawes beare witnesse, whose custome was to erect images in remembrance of those men that, revenging the injuries of the commonwealth, boldly massacred tyrants and such as troubled the peace and welfare of the citizens.

Hamblet, having in this manner revenged himselfe, durst not presently declare his action to the people, but to the contrary determined to worke by policie, so to give them intelligence, what he had done, and the reason that drew him thereunto: so that beeing accompanied with such of his fathers friends that then were rising, he stayed to see what the people would doe when they shoulde heare of that sodaine and fearefull action. The next morning the townes bordering there aboutes, desiring to know from whence the flames of fire proceeded the night before they had seene, came thither, and perceiving the kings pallace burnt to ashes, and many bodyes (most part consumed) lying among the ruines of the house, all of them were much abashed, nothing being left of the palace but the foundation. But they were much more amased to beholde the body of the king all bloody, and his head cut off lying hard by him; whereat some began to threaten revenge, yet not knowing against whom; others beholding so lamentable a spectacle, armed themselves, the rest rejoycing, yet not daring to make any shewe thereof; some detesting the crueltie, others lamenting the death of their Prince, but the greatest part calling Horvendiles murther to remembrance, acknowledging a just judgement from above, that had throwne downe the pride of the tyrant. And in this sort, the diversities of opinions among that multitude of people being many, yet every man ignorant what would be the issue of that tragedie, none stirred from thence, neither yet attempted to move any tumult, every man fearing his owne skinne, and distrusting his neighbour, esteeming each other to bee consenting to the massacre.

CHAP. VI.

How Hamlet, having slaine his Uncle, and burnt his Palace, made an Oration to the Danes to shew them what he done; and how they made him King of Denmark; and what followed.

HAMLET then seeing the people to be so quiet, and most part of them not using any words, all searching onely and simply the cause of this ruine and destruction, not minding to loose at any time, but ayding himself with the commodotie thereof, entred among the multitude of people, and standing in the middle spake unto them as followeth.[1]

If there be any among you (good people of Denmark) that as yet have fresh within your memories the wrong done to the valiant king Horvendile, let him not be mooved, nor thinke it strange to behold the confused, hydeous, and fearfull spectacle of this present calamitie: if there be any man that affecteth fidelitie, and alloweth of the love and dutie that man is bound to shewe his parents, and find it a just cause to call to remembrance the injuryes and wrongs that have been done to our progenitors, let him not be ashamed beholding this massacre, much lesse offended to see so fearfull a ruine both of men and of the bravest house in all this countrey: for the hand that hath done this justice could not effect it by any other meanes, neither yet was it lawfull for him to doe it otherwise, then by ruinating both sensible and unsensible things, thereby to preserve the memorie of so just a vengeance.

I see well (my good friends) and am very glad to know so good attention and devotion in you, that you are sorrie (before your eyes) to see Fengon so murthered, and without a head, which heeretofore you acknowledged for your commander; but I pray you remember this body is not the body of a king, but of an execrable tyrant, and a parricide most detestable. Oh Danes! the spectacle was much more hydeous when Horvendile your king was murthered by his brother. What, should I say a brother! nay, rather by the most abhominable executioner that ever beheld the same. It was you that saw Horvendiles members massacred, and that with teares and lamentations accompanied him to the grave; his body disfigured, hurt in a thousand places, and misused in ten times as many fashions. And who doubteth (seeing experience hath taught you) that the tyrant (in massacring your lawfull king) sought onely to infringe the ancient liberties of the common people? and it was one hand onely, that murthering Horvendile, cruelly dispoyled him of life, and by the same meanes unjustly bereaved you of your ancient liberties, and delighted more in oppression then to embrace the plesant countenance of prosperous libertie without adventuring for the same. And what mad man is he that delighteth more in the tyrany of Fengon then in the clemencie and renewed courtesie of Horvendile? If it bee so, that by clemencie and affabilitie the hardest and stoutest hearts are molified and made tractable,

[1] B. inserts a heading: 'Amleth's Harangue to the Danes.'

and that evill and hard usage causeth subjects to be outragious and unruly, why behold you not the debonair cariage of the first, to compare it with the cruelties and insolencies of the second, in every respect as cruell and barbarous as his brother was gentle, meeke, and courteous? Remember, O you Danes, remember what love and amitie Horvendile shewed unto you; with what equitie and justice he swayed the great affaires of this kingdome, and with what humanitie and courtisie he defended and cherished you, and then I am assured that the simplest man among you will both remember and acknowledge that he had a most peaceable, just, and righteous king taken from him, to place in his throane a tyrant and murtherer of his brother: one that hath perverted all right, abolished the auncient lawes of our fathers,[1] contaminated the memories of our ancestors, and by his wickednesse polluted the integritie of this kingdome, upon the necke thereof having placed the troublesome yoak of heavie servitude, abolishing that libertie wherein Horvendile used to maintaine you, and suffered you to live at your ease. And should you now bee sorrie to see the ende of your mischiefes, and that this miserable wretch, pressed downe with the burthen of his offences, at this present payeth the usury of the parricide committed upon the body of his brother, and would not himselfe be the revenger of the outrage done to me, whom he sought to deprive of mine inheritance, taking from Denmark a lawfull successor, to plant a wicked stranger, and bring into captivitie those that my father had infranchised and delivered out of misery and bondage? And what man is he, that having any sparke of wisdom, would esteem a good deed to be an injury, and account pleasures equal with wrongs and evident outrages? It were then great folly and temerity in princes and valiant commanders in the wars to expose themselves to perils and hazards of their lives for the welfare of the common people, if that for a recompence they should reape hatred and indignation of the multitude. To what end should Hother have punished Balder, if, in steed of recompence, the Danes and Swethlanders had banished him to receive and accept the successors of him that desired nought but his ruine and overthrowe? What is hee that hath so small feeling of reason and equitie, that would be grieved to see treason rewarded with the like, and that an evill act is punished with just demerit in the partie himselfe that was the occasion? who was ever sorrowfull to behold the murtherer of innocents brought to his end, or what man weepeth to see a just massacre done upon a tyrant, usurper, villaine, and bloody personage?

I perceive you are attentive, and abashed for not knowing the author of your deliverance, and sorry that you cannot tell to whom

---

[1] No sign of this in the play.

E

you should bee thankefull for such and so great a benefit as the
destruction of a tyrant, and the overthrow of the place that was the
storehouse of his villanies, and the true receptacle of all the theeves
and traytors in this kingdome: but beholde (here in your presence)
him that brought so good an enterprise to effect. It is I (my good
friends), it is I, that confesse I have taken vengeance for the violence
done unto my lord and father, and for the subjection and servitude
that I perceived in this countrey, whereof I am the just and lawfull
successor. It is I alone,[1] that have done this piece of worke, whereunto you ought to have lent me your handes, and therein have
ayded and assisted me. I have only accomplished that which all of
you might justly have effected, by good reason, without falling into
any point of treason or fellonie. It is true that I hope so much of
your good willes towards the deceased king Horvendile, and that the
remembrances of his vertues is yet so fresh within your memories,
that if I had required your aide herein, you would not have denied
it, specially to your naturall prince. But it liked mee best to doe it my
selfe alone, thinking it a good thing to punish the wicked without
hazarding the lives of my friends and loyall subjects, not desiring
to burthen other mens shoulders with this weight;[2] for that I made
account to effect it well inough without exposing any man into danger,
and by publishing the same should cleane have overthrowne the
device, which at this present I have so happily brought to passe.
I have burnt the bodyes of the courtiers to ashes, being companions
in the mischiefs and treasons of the tyrant; but I have left Fengon
whole, that you might punish his dead carkasse (seeing that when
hee lived you durst not lay hands upon him), to accomplish the full
punishment and vengeance due unto him, and so satisfie your
choller upon the bones of him that filled his greedy hands and coffers
with your riches, and shed the blood of your brethren and friends.
Bee joyful, then (my good friends); make ready the pyre[3] for this
usurping king: burne his abhominable body, boyle his lascivious
members, and cast the ashes of him that hath beene hurtful to all
the world into the ayre: drive from you the sparkes of pitie, to the
end that neither silver, nor christall cup, nor sacred tombe may be
the restfull habitation of the reliques and bones of so detestable a
man: let not one trace of a parricide be seene, nor your countrey
defiled with the presence of the least member of this tyrant without
pity, that your neighbours may not smell the contagion, nor our
land the polluted infection of a body condemned for his wickednes.
I have done my part to present him to you in this sort; now it belongs

---

[1] Shakespeare's Hamlet too becomes a solitary avenger.
[2] No such explanation is given in the play. Cf. I.5.189–90.
[3] 'pyre'. B. 'bûcher', pyre; *1608:* 'nosegay' by confusion with 'bouquet'! [Stabler]

to you to make an end of the worke, and put to the last hand of dutie whereunto your severall functions call you; for in this sort you must honor abhominable princes, and such ought to be the funerall of a tyrant, parricide, and usurper, both of the bed and patrimony that no way belonged unto him, who having bereaved his countrey of liberty, it is fit that the land refuse to give him a place for the eternal rest of his bones.

O my good friends, seeing you know the wrong that hath bin done unto mee, what my griefs are, and in what misery I have lived since the death of the king, my lord and father, and seeing that you have both known and tasted these things then, when as I could not conceive the outrage that I felt, what neede I recite it unto you? what benefit would it be to discover it before them that knowing it would burst (as it were with despight) to heare of my hard chance, and curse Fortune for so much imbasing a royall prince, as to deprive him of his majesty, although not any of you durst so much as shew one sight of sorrow or sadnes? You know how my father in law[1] conspired my death, and sought by divers meanes to take away my life; how I was forsaken of the queen my mother, mocked of my friends, and dispised of mine own subjects: hetherto I have lived laden with griefe, and wholy confounded in teares,[2] my life still accompanied with fear and suspition, expecting the houre when the sharp sword would make an ende of my life and miserable anguishes. How many times, counterfeiting the mad man, have I heard you pitty my distresse, and secretly lament to see me disinherited?[3] and yet no man sought to revenge the death of my father, nor to punish the treason of my incestuous uncle, full of murthers and massacres. This charitie ministred comfort, and your affectionate complaints made me evidently see your good wills, that you had in memorie the calamity of your prince, and within your harts ingraven the desire of vengeance for the death of him that deserved a long life. And what heart can bee so hard and untractable, or spirit so severe, cruel, and rigorous, that would not relent at the remembrance of my extremities, and take pitty of an orphan child, so abandoned of the world? What eyes were so voyd of moysture but would distill a field of tears, to see a poore prince assaulted by his owne subjects, betrayed by his mother, pursued by his uncle, and so much oppressed that his friends durst not shew the effects of their charitie and good affection?[4] O (my good friends) shew pity to him whom you have nourished, and let your harts take some compassion upon the memory of my misfortunes! I speak to you that

---

[1] stepfather.   [2] Hence perhaps I.2.78–80.
[3] Note the insistence on H. as the dispossessed heir.
[4] Hamlet is 'most dreadfully attended'; II.2.271.

are innocent of al treason, and never defiled your hands, spirits, nor desires with the blud of the greate and vertuous king Horvendile. Take pity upon the queen, sometime your soveraign lady, and my right honorable mother, forced by the tyrant, and rejoyce to see the end and extinguishing of the object of her dishonor, which constrained her to be lesse pitiful to her own blood, so far as to imbrace the murtherer of her own dear spouse, charging her selfe with a double burthen of infamy and incest, together with injuring and disannulling of her house, and the ruine of her race. This hath bin the occasion that made me counterfet folly, and cover my intents under a vaile of meer madnes, which hath wisdom and pollicy therby to inclose the fruit of this vengeance, which, that it hath attained to the ful point of efficacy and perfect accomplishment, you yourselves shall bee judges; for touching this and other things concerning my profit, and the managing of great affaires, I refer my self to your counsels, and therunto am fully determined to yeeld, as being those that trample under your feet the murtherers of my father, and despise the ashes of him that hath polluted and violated the spouse of his brother, by him massacred; that hath committed felony against his lord, traiterously assailed the majesty of his king, and odiously thralled his contry under servitude and bondage, and you his loyall subjects, from whom he, bereaving your liberty, feared not to ad incest to parricide, detestable to al the world. To you also it belongeth by dewty and reason commonly to defend and protect Hamlet, the minister and executor of just vengeance,[1] who being jealous of your honour and your reputation, hath hazarded himself, hoping you will serve him for fathers, defenders, and tutors, and regarding him in pity, restore him to his goods and inheritances. It is I that have taken away the infamy of my contry, and extinguished the fire that imbraced your fortunes. I have washed the spots that defiled the reputation of the queen, overthrowing both the tirant and the tiranny, and beguiling the subtilties of the craftiest deceiver in the world, and by that meanes brought his wickednes and impostures to an end. I was grieved at the injurie committed both to my father and my native country, and have slaine him that used more rigorous commandements over you, then was either just or convenient to be used unto men that have commaunded the valiantest nations in the world. Seeing, then, he was such a one to you, it is reason that you acknowledge the benefit, and thinke wel of for the good I had done your posterity, and admiring my spirit and wisdome, chuse me your king, if you think me worthy of the place. You see I am the author of your preservation, heire of my fathers kingdome, not straying in any point from his vertuous action, no murtherer,

[1] III.4.175.

violent parricide, nor man that ever offended any of you, but only the vitious. I am lawfull successor in the kingdom,[1] and just revenger of a crime above al others most grievous and punishable: it is to me that you owe the benefit of your liberty receaved, and of the subversion of that tyranny that so much afflicted you, that hath troden under feete the yoke of the tirant, and overwhelmed his throne, and taken the scepter out of the hands of him that abused a holy and just authoritie; but it is you that are to recompence those that have well deserved, you know what is the reward of so greate desert, and being in your hands to distribute the same, it is of you that I demand the price of my vertue, and the recompence of my victory.

This oration of the yong prince so mooved the harts of the Danes, and wan the affections of the nobility, that some wept for pity, other for joy, to see the wisedome and gallant spirit of Hamlet; and having made an end of their sorrow, al with one consent proclaimed him king of Jutie and Chersonnese, at this present the proper country of Denmarke.[2] And having celebrated his coronation, and received the homages and fidelities of his subjects, he went into England to fetch his wife, and rejoyced with his father in law touching his good fortune; but it wanted little that the king of England had not accomplished that which Fengon with all his subtilties could never attaine.

CHAP. VII.

How Hamlet, after his coronation, went into England; and how the king of England secretly would have put him to death; and how he slew the king of England, and returned againe into Denmarke with two wives; and what followed.

HAMLET, being in England, shewed the king what meanes hee had wrought to recover his kingdom; but when the king of England understood of Fengons death, he was both abashed and confused in his minde, at that instant feeling himselfe assailed with two great passions, for that in times past he and Fengon having bin companions together in armes, had given each other their faith and promises, by oath, that if either of them chanced to bee slaine by any man whatsoever, hee that survived (taking the quarrel upon him as his

[1] Cf. V.2.65.
[2] *In margin:* 'Hamlet king of one part of Denmark.' Note the suggestion that the people must consent to the accession of a new king, even if he were the legitimate heir.

owne) should never cease till he were revenged, or at the leaste
do his endeavour. This promise incited the barbarous king to
massacre Hamlet, but the alliance presenting it selfe before his eies,
and beholding the one deade, although his friend, and the other
alive, and husband to his daughter, made him deface his desire of
revenge. But in the end, the conscience of his oath and promise
obtained the upper hand, and secretly made him conclude the death
of his sonne in law, which enterprise after that was cause of his own
death, and overrunning of the whole country of England by the
cruelty and despight conceived by the king of Denmarke. I have
purposely omitted the discourse of that battaile, as not much pertinent to our matter, as also, not to trouble you with too tedious a
discourse, being content to shew you the end of this wise and valiant
king Hamlet, who revenging himselfe upon so many enemies, and
discovering all the treasons practised against his life, in the end
served for a sport to fortune, and an example to all great personages
that trust overmuch to the felicities of this world, that are of small
moment, and lesse continuance.

The king of England perceiving that hee could not easilie effect
his desire upon the king, his son in lawe, as also not being willing
to break the laws and rights of hospitality, determined to make a
stranger the revenger of his injury, and so accomplish his oath made
to Fengon without defiling his handes with the blood of the husband
of his daughter, and polluting his house by the traiterous massacring
of his friend. In reading of this history, it seemeth, Hamlet should
resemble another Hercules, sent into divers places of the world by
Euristheus (solicited by Juno) where he knew any dangerous adventure, thereby to overthrow and destroy him; or else Bellerophon sent
to Ariobatus to put him to death; or (leaving prophane histories)
an other Urias, by king David appointed to bee placed in the fore
front of the battaile, and the man that should bee first slain by the
barbarians. For the king of Englands wife being dead not long before
(although he cared not for marrying an other woman) desired his
sonne in lawe to make a voyage for him into Scotland, flattering him
in such sort, that he made him beleeve that his singular wisdome
caused him to preferre him to that ambassage, assuring himselfe that
it were impossible that Hamlet, the subtillest and wisest prince in the
worlde, should take any thing in the world in hand without effecting
the same.

Now the queen of Scots beeing a maid, and of a haughty courage,
despised marriage with al men, as not esteeming any worthy to be her
companion, in such manner that by reason of this arrogant opinion
there never came any man to desire her love but she caused him to
loose his life: but the Danish kings fortune was so good, that

Hermetrude (for so was the queens name) hearing that Hamlet was come thither to intreat a marriage between her and the king of England, forgot all her pride, and dispoiling herselfe of her sterne nature, being as then determined to make him (being the greatest prince as then living) her husband, and deprive the English princesse of her spouse, whome shee thought fit for no men but herself; and so this Amazon without love, disdaining Cupid, by her free wil submitted her haughtie mind to her concupiscence. The Dane arriving in her court, desired she to see the old king of Englands letters, and mocking at his fond appetites, whose blood as then was half congealed, cast her eies upon the yong and plesant Adonis of the North, esteeming her selfe happy to have such a prey fallen into her hands, wherof she made her ful account to have the possession: and to conclude, she that never had been overcome by the grace, courtesie, valor, or riches of anie prince nor lord whatsoever, was as then vanquished with the onelie report of the subtilties of the Dane; who knowing that he was already fianced to the daughter of the king of England, spake unto him and said: I never looked for so great a blisse, neither from the gods nor yet from fortune, as to behold in my countries the most compleate prince in the North, and he that hath made himselfe famous and renowned through all the nations of the world, as well neighbours as strangers, for the only respect of his vertue, wisdom, and good fortune, serving him much in the pursuite and effect of divers thinges by him undertaken, and thinke myselfe much beholding to the king of England (although his malice seeketh neither my advancement nor the good of you, my lord) to do me so much honor as to send me so excellent a man to intreate of a marriage (he being olde, and a mortal enemy to me and mine) with mee that am such a one as every man seeth, is not desirous to couple with a man of so base quality as he, whom you have said to be the son of a slave. . . . Think then, my Lord, how much I account of your alliance, who being accustomed with the sword to pursue such as durst imbolden themselves to win my love, it is to you only to whom I make a present both of my kisses, imbracings, scepter, and crown: what man is he, if he be not made of stone, that would refuse so precious a pawn as Hermetrude, with the kingdome of Scotland? accept, sweete king, accepte this queene, who with so great love and amitie, desireth your so great profit, and can give you more contentment in one day then the princesse of England wold yeeld you pleasure during her life: although shee surpass me in beauty, her bloud beeing base it is fitter for such a king as you are to chuse Hermetrude, lesse beautiful but noble and famous, rather then the English lady with great beawtie, but issuing from an unknown race, without any title of honor.

Now think if the Dane, hearing such forcible resons and under-standing that by her which he half doubted, as also moved with choller for the treason of his father in law, that purposely sent him thether to loose his life, and being welcomed, kist, and playd withal by this queen, yong and reasonable fair, if he were not easie enough to be converted, and like to forget the affection of his first wife, with this to enjoy the realme of Scotland, and so open the waie to become king of all Greate Britain: that, to conclude, he married her, and led her with him to the king of Englands court, which moved the king from that time forward much more to seek the meanes to bereave him of his life; and had surely done it, if his daughter, Hamlets other wife, more careful of him that had rejected her then of her fathers welfare, had not discovered the enterprise to Hamlet, saying: I know well, my Lord, that the allurements and perswasions of a bold and altogether shameles woman, being more lascivious then the chast imbracements of a lawful and modest wife, are of more force to intice and charm the sences of yong men; but for my part, I cannot take this abuse for satisfaction, to leave mee in this sorte without all cause, reason, or precedent faulte once known in mee, your loyall spouse, and take more pleasure in the aliance of her who one day will be the cause of your ruine and overthrow. . . . Manie reasons induce me to love and cherish you, and those of great consequence, but especially and above all the rest, I am and must bee carefull of you, when I feele your child stirring in my wombe; for which respecte, without so much forgetting yourselfe, you ought to make more account of me then of your concubine, whome I will love because you love her, contenting my selfe that your sonne hateth her, in regard of the wrong she doth to his mother; for it is impossible that any passion or trouble of the mind whatsoever can quench those fierce passions of love that made me yours, neither that I shold forget your favours past, when loyallie you sought the love of the daughter of the king of England. Neither is it in the power of that thiefe that hath stoln your heart, nor my fathers choller, to hinder me from seeking to preserve you from the cruelty of your dissembling friend (as heeretofore by counterfetting the madman, you prevented the practises and treasons of your uncle Fengon), the complot being determined to be executed upon you and yours. Without this advertisement, the Dane had surely been slain, and the Scots that came with him; for the king of England, inviting his son in law to a banquet, with greatest curtesies that a friend can use to him whom he loved as himself, had the means to intrap him, and cause him dance a pittiful galliard, in that sort to celebrate the marriage betweene him and his new lady. But Hamlet went thither with armour under his clothes, and his men in like sort; by which means he and his escaped with little hurt, and so after that hapned the battaile before spoken of, wherein the king of England losing his life, his countrie was the third time sacked by the barbarians of the ilands and countrie of Denmark.

CHAP. VIII.

How Hamblet, being in Denmarke, was assailed by Wiglerus his Uncle, and after betrayed by his last wife, called Hermetrude, and was slaine: after whose death she marryed his enemie, Wiglerus.

HAMLET having obtained the victory against the king of England, and slaine him, laden with great treasures and accompanied with his two wives, set forward to saile into Denmarke, but by the way hee had intelligence that Wiglere, his uncle, and sonne to Rodericke, having taken the royall treasure from his sister Geruth (mother to Hamblet) had also seazed upon the kingdome, saying, that neither Horvendile nor any of his helde it but by permission, and that it was in him (to whom the property belonged) to give the charge therof to whom he would. But Hamblet, not desirous to have any quarrell with the sonne of him from whom his predecessors had received their greatnes and advancement, gave such and so rich presents to Wiglere, that he, being contented, withdrew himselfe out of the countrey and territories of Geruths sonne. But within certaine time after, Wiglere, desirous to keepe all the countrey in subjection, intyced by the conquest of Scanie and Sialandie, and also that Hermetrude (the wife of Hamlet, whom he loved more then himselfe) had secret intelligence with him, and had promised him marriage, so that he would take her out of the handes of him that held her,[1] sent to defie Hamlet, and proclaimed open warre against him. Hamlet, like a good and wise prince, loving especially the welfare of his subjects, sought by all meanes to avoyde that warre; but againe refusing it, he perceived a great spot and blemish in his honor, and, accepting the same, he knewe it would bee the ende of his dayes. By the desire of preserving his life on the one side, and his honor on the other side pricking him forward, but, at the last, remembering that never any danger whatsoever had once shaken his vertues and constancy, chose rather the necessitie of his ruine, then to loose the immortall fame that valiant and honourable men obtained in the warres. And there is as much difference betweene a life

---

[1] *In margin:* 'Hermetrude betrayeth Hamlet her husband.'

without honour and an honourable death, as glory and renowne is more excellent then dishonour and evil report.

But the thing that spoyled this vertuous prince was the over great trust and confidence hee had in his wife Hermetrude, and the vehement love hee bare unto her, not once repenting the wrong in that case done to his lawfull spouse, and for the which (paradventure that misfortune had never hapned unto him, and it would never have bin thought that she, whom he loved above all things, would have so villainously betrayed him), hee not once remembring his first wives speeches, who prophesied unto him, that the pleasures hee seemed to take in his other wife would in the end be the cause of his overthrowe, as they had ravished him of the best part of his sences, and quenched in him the great prudence that made him admirable in all the countries in the ocean seas, and through all Germany. Now, the greatest grief that this king (besotted on his wife) had, was the separation of her whom he adored, and, assuring himselfe of his overthrowe, was desirous either that she might beare him company at his death, or els to find her a husband that should love her (he beeing dead) as well as ever hee did. But the disloyall queene had already provided herself of a marriage to put her husband out of trouble and care for that, who perceiving him to be sad for her sake, when shee should have absented her selfe from him, she, to blind him the more and to incourage him to set forward to his owne destruction, promised to follow him whether soever he went, and to take the like fortune that befell to him, were it good or evil, and that so she would give him cause to know how much shee surpassed the English woman in her affection towardes him, saying, that woman is accursed that feareth to follow and accompany her husband to the death: so that, to heare her speake, men would have sayd that shee had been the wife of Mithridates, or Zenobia queene of Palmira, shee made so greate a show of love and constancy. But by the effect it was after easily perceived howe vaine the promise of this unconstant and wavering princesse was; and howe uncomparable the life of this Scottish queene was to the vigor of her chastitie, being a mayd before she was marryed. For that Hamlet had no sooner entred into the field, but she found meanes to see Wiglere, and the battel begun, wherein the miserable Danish prince was slaine;[1] but Hermetrude presently yeelded her self, with all her dead husbands treasure, into the hand of the tyrant, who, more then content with that metamorphosis so much desired, gave order that presently the marriage (bought with the blood and treason of the sonne of Horvendile) should bee celebrated.

Thus you see that there is no promise or determination of a woman,

---

[1] *In margin:* 'Hamlet slaine.'

but that a very small discommoditie of fortune mollifieth and altereth the same, and which time doeth not pervert; so that the misfortunes subject to a constant man shake and overthrowe the naturall slipperie loyaltie of the variable steppes of women, wholy without and any faithfull assurance of love, or true unfained constancy: for as a woman is ready to promise, so is shee heavy and slowe to per-forme and effect that which she hath promised, as she that is without end or limit in her desires, flattring her selfe in the diversitie of her wanton delights, and taking pleasure in diversitie and change of newe things, which as soone shee doth forget and growe weary off: and, to conclude, such shee is in all her actions, she is rash, covetous, and unthankefull, whatsoever good or service can bee done unto her. But nowe I perceive I erre in my discourse, vomitting such things unworthy of this sects; but the vices of Hermetrude have made mee say more then I meant to speake, as also the authour, from whence I take this Hystorie, hath almost made mee hold this course, I find so great a sweetnesse and livelinesse in this kinde of argument; and the rather because it seemeth so much the truer, considering the miser-able successe of poore king Hamlet.

Such was the ende of Hamlet, sonne to Horvendile, prince of Jutie; to whom, if his fortune had been equall with his inward and naturall giftes, I know not which of the auncient Grecians and Romans had been able to have compared with him for vertue and excellencie[1] but hard fortune following him in all his actions, and yet hee vanquishing the malice of his time with the vigour of constancy, hath left us a notable example of haughtie courage, worthy of a great prince, arming himselfe with hope in things that were wholy without any colour or shewe thereof, and in all his honorable actions made himselfe worthy of perpetuall memorie, if one onely spotte had not blemished and darkened a good part of his prayses. For that the greatest victorie that a man can obtaine is to make himselfe victorious and lord over his owne affections, and that restraineth the unbridled desires of his concupiscence; for if a man be never so princely, valiant, and wise, if the desires and intice-ments of his flesh prevaile, and have the upper hand, hee will imbase his credite, and, gasing after strange beauties, become a foole, and (as it were) incensed, dote on the presence of women. This fault was in the great Hercules, Sampson; and the wisest man that ever lived upon the earth, following this traine, therein impaired his wit; and the most noble, wise, valiant, and discreet personages of our time, following the same course, have left us many notable examples of their worthy and notable vertues.

But I beseech you that shall reade this Hystorie not to resemble

[1] Cf. Fortinbras, V.2.397-8.

the spider, that feedeth of the corruption that shee findeth in the flowers and fruites that are in the gardens, whereas the bee gathereth her hony out of the best and fayrest flower shee can finde: for a man that is well brought up should reade the lives of whoremongers, drunkards, incestuous, violent, and bloody persons, not to follow their steps, and so to defile himselfe with such uncleannesse, but to shunne paliardize,[1] abstain the superfluities and drunkennesse in banquets, and follow the modestie, courtesie, and continencie that recommendeth Hamlet in this discourse, who, while other made good cheare, continued sober; and where all men sought as much as they could to gather together riches and treasure, hee, simply accounting riches nothing comparable to honor, sought to gather a multitude of vertues, that might make him equall to those that by them were esteemed as gods; having not as then received the lighte of the gospell, that men might see among the barbarians, and them that were farre from the knowledge of one onelye God, that nature was provoked to follow that which is good, and those forward to imbrace vertue, for that there was never any nation, how rude or barbarous soever, that tooke not some pleasure to do that which seemed good, therby to win praise and commendations, which wee have said to be the reward of vertue and good life. I delight to speak of these strange histories, and of people that were unchristned, that the vertue of the rude people maie give more splendor to our nation, who seeing them so compleat, wise, prudent, and well advised in their actions, might strive not only to follow (imitation being a small matter), but to surmount them, as our religion surpasseth their superstition, and our age more purged, subtill, and gallant, then the season wherein they lived and made their vertues knowne.

[1] debauchery.

IV. Analogue

HENRICI SCOTORUM REGIS MANES AD JACOBUM VI^{UM} FILIUM

by I.G. (John Gordon). Composed March 1587[1]

The Shade of Henry, King of Scotland to his Son James VI.[2]

Learn, Governors of Peoples, learn O Kings
To obey the Laws as the decrees of God.
Observe the rules of Nature and of Nations,
And by no action break a treaty made.
Should you so do, Vengeance attends the crime.
Great is the pow'r that Kings wield over men;
More great the sway of God o'er Kings themselves.
   If thou should'st seek examples, there's an Isle
Which rises hugely from the level Sea—
—An island often stained with blood of Kings—
Among whom Fortune's will may count me one.
The penalty does not the crime prove; I
Came blameless down to you, Ancestral Shades.[3]
Believe no crime of me, unless 'tis wrong
When any husband loves his wife too much.
And thou my wife, dearer to me than breath,
Whose heart so changed against me on behalf
Of a vile rascal pardoned in despite
Of Lords' just anger and the People's wrongs!

---

[1] In the *Registre-Journal* of P. de l'Estoile. Latin text printed in Lemerre, *Libr. des Bibliophiles*, 1875, and G. Lambin, 'Une Première Ebauche d'Hamlet (mars 1587)', *Les Langues Modernes*, 49, 1955, pp. 229–45. English translation by the editor.

[2] The speaker is Henry Stuart, Lord Darnley (1545–67), a beautiful but vain and unintelligent youth of nineteen when the widowed Queen Mary (aged twenty-two) married him in July 1565. He proved vicious and useless in state matters, but wished to be King, and out of jealousy had Mary's adviser Riccio murdered. Realizing his guilt the Queen turned against him and showed favour to Bothwell. Darnley would not attend the baptism of his son James at Stirling but sulked in his room. Fearing for his life he would have left Scotland, but fell ill, probably with smallpox or V.D., though Knox and Buchanan claimed that he was poisoned. Mary and he seemed to be reconciled but she was probably aware of the plot to murder him by blowing up his lodging at Kirk-o'-Field on 10 February 1567. His body was found in a garden near by.

[3] This was quite untrue. Darnley was a weaker, meaner man than the reckless, brave Bothwell.

To thee the evil life of such a boor
Was aphrodisiac until, forgot
Both royal fame and queen's decorum, thou,
First trying me with poison, drov'st out fear
Soon from thy mind, then murdered'st me with flames!
　　Nor rested here the wickedness. That Bothwell,
Chief foe to the gods, author of thy great crime,
Who after he the secrets of our couch
Had violated, taught the erring wife
Her hands to sprinkle with her husband's blood,
That vile adulterer trod our marriage-bed.[1]
　　But Fate denied enjoyment of the sin
Nor let the lovers sport there long secure;
For soon the nobles' anger broke the peace
And troubled their new marriage-songs with war.
The people murmured too, and wandered wide,
Girded with arms. A soldier, wild with wrath,
Paraded through the streets a picture showing
The deed of slaughter, while my tender babe
In cradle raised to heaven his arms in vain;
And as he strode the man reviled the crime.
　　Confounded and disgraced, the murderer fled
To th' Orkneys, thence to Cimbria, where in shame
His shameful life he ends in obscure gaol.
　　Straightway the Turtle, widowed of her Dove,
Her royal home deserting took a ship;
So she who erst to Hepburn gave her honour
Her Fortune now committed to the waves,
And glided to the hateful English shore
Where once again she mixed in tumult blind
(Daring, foul crime, to raise her steel against
Her cousin-german) till, when she had lived
Near twenty years 'neath watchful guard, at last

---

[1] James Hepburn (1536?–1578), fourth Earl of Bothwell, unruly and violent from his youth, was sent to England in 1564 for riotous conduct, but was pardoned by Queen Mary and became her confidant after Riccio's murder. The 'Casket Letters' were said to have proved her guilty love for Hepburn, who 'abducted' her on 24 April 1567 and married her on 15 May after he had obtained a divorce from his wife Jean Gordon. The storm caused by this rash act brought about the Queen's abdication. Bothwell fled to his dukedom in the Orkneys but was refused admission to Kirkwall and went on to the Shetlands in July 1567. He set up as a pirate, but had to seek shelter in Norway, whence he was taken to Denmark. There he was well treated at first on promising to cede the northern islands to the Danes, who claimed them. In 1573 he was moved from Malmö (Sweden) to rigorous confinement at Drangholm in Zeeland, where he gradually went insane, and died in April 1578.

The hapless woman felt the headsman's axe.[1]
   'Tis grievous that the English so should bear
It o'er the Scots; and I myself have grieved.
But Heaven's Moderator has not let
Me wander long a Shade still unavenged;
He sent this cleansing feast of sacrifice
Unto my ashes. Seek no other cause
For this late punishment. But thou, who scaped
That bitter shipwreck in a little trough,[2]
Thou whom thy angry mother hardly spared,[3]
My son, sole hope of Scotland's royal house,
If thou art mine, and if thou hear'st me right,
Learn thou from me thy Master, aye to seek
Justice o'er all, and ne'er despise the gods.
Fly the approach of flatterers, prudent fly
As well as canst the sting of envious tongues.
What aids the realm, or profit shall demand,
Or gives the people health, be strong to urge.
Ignore the rest, secure from rumours base;
Vain, Son, thy work if aught thou seek beside.
Nor should thy mother's death move thee so deep
As thou rejoic'st thy sire's death is avenged.[4]

I.G. st.
Me. Martio
1587.

[1] After her abdication Queen Mary was confined by her lords at Lochleven. She escaped in May 1568, but failing to regain power, soon fled to England, crossing the Solway Firth in a fishing-boat to Workington. From then until 1586 she was captive in England, but spent much time corresponding with the Catholic powers hostile to Elizabeth. In 1585 she was implicated in the Babington Plot; she was tried at Fotheringay Castle, and (after much vacillation on the part of Elizabeth) executed on 8 February 1586/7.

[2] Latin, *tabella*; used of the tray or trough which saved Romulus and Remus.

[3] On Mary's marriage to Bothwell the opposing lords met at Stirling and 'made a Bond to defend the young Prince from the Murderers of his Father; as already they had had ane Plot to cut him off, which God in his mercy did prevent.' On 12 June the lords at Edinburgh proclaimed that Bothwell had seduced the Queen 'into a dishonest and unlawful Marriage with himself' and was now 'stirring himself to get the young Prince in his Hands that he might murder the Child, as he had murdered the Father' (J. Knox, *History of the Reformation in Scotland*, 1732 edn., pp. 484, 487).

[4] King James never knew his mother and did not honour her in life or death. He also feared Elizabeth and hoped to be made her heir. So he would not be displeased by the poet's advice. He had protested against Mary's long imprisonment, but did not include her in the league made with England in 1585 and was angry when she disinherited him and willed her crown to Philip II.

V. Analogue

FRATRICIDE PUNISHED
(DER BESTRAFTE BRUDERMORD)
Anon.

Tragœdia. Der bestrafte Brudermord oder Prinz Hamlet aus Dannemark.[1]

PERSONS REPRESENTED

1 In the Prologue

NIGHT, in a car, covered with stars
ALECTO
THISIPHONE
MÆGERA

2 In the Tragedy

GHOST of the old King of Denmark
ERICO, brother to the King
HAMLET, Prince, son of the murdered King
SIGRIE, the Queen, Hamlet's mother
HORATIO, the Prince's friend, of high rank
CORAMBUS,[2] Lord Chamberlain
LEONHARDUS, his son
OPHELIA, his daughter
PHANTASMO, the clown
FRANCISCO, Officer of the guard
JENS, a peasant
CHARLES, the principal of the comedians
A CORPORAL of the guard
TWO RUFFIANS
TWO SOLDIERS
LIFE-GUARDS ⎫
SERVANTS ⎬ Mute persons
TWO COMEDIANS ⎭

---

[1] Printed in *Olla Potrida*, ed. H. A. O. Reichard, Pt. II, 1781, pp. 18–68, and in A. Cohn, *Shakespeare in Germany*, 1865, pp. 236ff., with translation by G. Archer. I have adapted H. H. Furness's version, bringing it nearer to the German text and making no attempt to smoothe the awkwardness of the latter.

[2] As in Q1, where, however, it is spelt 'Corambis'.

PROLOGUE

NIGHT, *from above* I am the sable Night; and all sleeps through
           my might.
Of Orpheus I'm the wife, playtime of vice and strife.
I'm guardian of the thief; of lovers friend in chief.
I am the sable Night, and have it in my might
To magnify excess, and mankind to depress.
My mantle hides the face of every whore's disgrace.
Ere Phoebus' light shall flame, I shall begin a game.
You offspring of my heart, daughters of lust, come start,
You Furies; up arise, and let yourselves appear;
Come diligently learn what soon must happen here.
ALECTO What says dark Night, the Queen of midnight still?
What is there new? What's your desire and will?
MÆGERA Hotfoot from Acheron's pit Mægera stands
To hear, Witch of Ill Fate, thy sweet commands.
THISIPHONE Thisiphone I; what hast in mind? now say
Black Hecate, how to serve thee best I may.
NIGHT Hearken, all ye three Furies, hear! offspring of darkness,
bearers of all misfortune, listen to your poppy-crowned Queen of
Night, protectress of thieves and robbers, friend and light to the
incendiary, lover of stolen goods, and most-beloved goddess of all
dishonourable loves, how often will my evil altar be honoured for
this deed! This night and during the coming day you must assist me,
for the king of this realm burns in lust for his brother's wife, for
whose sake he has murdered him that he may possess her and the
kingdom. Now is the hour at hand in which he will celebrate his
nuptials with her. I shall throw my mantle over them so that they
see not their sin. Wherefore be ready to sow the seeds of discord,
mix poison into their marriage and jealousy into their hearts.
Kindle a fire of revenge, and make its sparks fly throughout the
kingdom, entangle blood-brothers in the snare of incest, rejoice the
infernal regions with deeds of ruthless and rancorous malice; be
gone, hasten and fulfil my behests.
THISIPHONE Enough. I've heard; I'll finish, quickly too,
More than Night by herself could plan to do.
MÆGERA Pluto himself can not inspire in me
More ill than men shall very shortly see.
ALECTO I fan the sparks, and make the fire to burn.
Within two days, all joy I'll overturn.
NIGHT Then haste; I now ascend; your tasks attend!
                           [Ascends. Music.

Act I: Scene I

Two Soldiers

1 SENT. Who goes there?

2 SENT. A friend!

1 SENT. What friend?

2 SENT. The sentry.

1 SENT. Ho! comrade, thou com'st to relieve me. I hope that the time may not seem so long for thee as it has to me.

2 SENT. Nay, comrade, it's not so very cold now.[1]

1 SENT. Cold or no, I have had an infernal fright.

2 SENT. Why so timid? that is not right for a soldier; he must fear neither friend nor foe, nay, not the devil himself.

1 SENT. Ay, if he once grip thee by the short hairs thou'lt soon learn to say the *Miserere Domine*.

2 SENT. Tell me then, what has frightened thee?

1 SENT. Know then that a ghost has appeared on the platform of the castle; and it tried twice to cast me down from the battlements.

2 SENT. Run along, Fool; a dead dog bites not; I shall soon see whether a ghost that has neither flesh nor bones can do me any harm.

1 SENT. Just see if the trouble he gives you makes you see otherwise. I am going to the guard-house. Farewell.   [*Exit.*

2 SENT. Off you go, then;[2]—perhaps you were born on a Sunday; such people can all see ghosts. I must attend to my duty.

                    [*Healths within drunk, with a flourish of trumpets.*

2 SENT. Our new King makes merry; they are drinking healths.

Scene II

[*Ghost of the King approaches the Sentinel and startles him.   Exit.*

2 SENT. Oh! St. Anthony of Padua, defend me! Now I see for the first time what my comrade spoke of. Oh! St. Velten, if the main patrol were over I'd quit my post like any rogue.

                    [*Another flourish of drums and kettle-drums.*

2 SENT. Oh! for a draught of wine from the King's table to damp down my fearful, burning heart!

[*Ghost gives the Sentry a box on the ear from behind, and makes him drop his musket.   Exit.*

---

[1] Cf. I.1.8: 'tis bitter cold'. Cold not mentioned in Q1.

[2] 'Gehe du nur hin.' Cf. I.1.7: 'Get thee to bed'. No such dismissal in Q1.

2 SENT.   The devil in person is in this game. Oh! I'm too afraid to move from the spot.

Scene III

Horatio and Soldiers

2 SENT.   Who's there?

HORAT.   The patrol.

2 SENT.   Which?

HORAT.   The main patrol.

2 SENT.   Stand, patrol—corporal out! Present arms!

[*Francisco and patrol come out, give the word from the other side.*

HORAT.   Sentry, look well to your post; maybe the Prince himself will go the rounds; look to it you do not sleep at any time; otherwise it might cost you the best head on your shoulders.

2 SENT.   Oh! even if the whole company were here, not a man amongst them could sleep, and I must be relieved, or I'll run for it at the risk of hanging tomorrow on the highest gallows.

HORAT.   And why is that?

2 SENT.   Oh, sir, a ghost appears here in this place every quarter of an hour, and pesters me so much that I might fancy I was set down while still alive in purgatory.

FRANCISCO.   The first sentry who was relieved in the last hour, has just told me the same story.

2 SENT.   Ay, wait but a little while; it will not stay long away.

[*Ghost stalks across the stage.*

HORAT.   Upon my life, it is a ghost, and it looks extremely like the late King of Denmark!

FRANCISCO.   He bears himself sadly, and seems to want to say something.

HORAT.   There is some mystery behind this.

Scene IV

Hamlet.

2 SENT.   Who's there?

HAMLET.   Quiet!

2 SENT.   Who's there?

HAMLET.   Quiet!

2 SENT.   Answer, or I'll teach thee better manners.

HAMLET.   A friend!

2 SENT.   What friend?

HAMLET.   Friend to the kingdom.

FRANCISCO.   By my life, it is the Prince!

HORAT.   Your Highness, is it you or not?

HAMLET.   Ha! Horatio, is it you? What are you doing here?

HORAT.   Your Highness, I have gone the rounds, to see that all sentries are at their posts.

HAMLET.   You act like an honest soldier, for on you rests the safety of the king and kingdom.

HORAT.   My lord, a strange thing has happened, for a ghost appears here every quarter of an hour. To my mind, he is very like your father the late king. He does much harm to the sentries on their patrol.

HAMLET.   I hope not, for the souls of the faithful rest quietly till the day of their resurrection.

HORAT.   But it is so, your Highness; I have seen him myself.

FRANCISCO.   He frightened me most horribly, your Highness.

2 SENT.   And me he dealt a good box on the ears.

HAMLET.   What time is it now?

FRANCISCO.   It is just midnight.

HAMLET.   'Tis well, for it is at this time that the spirits usually show themselves when they walk.[1]

> [*Again healths drunk to sound of trumpets.*

HAMLET.   Hello! What does this mean?

HORAT.   I think that they are still very merry at court with their toasts.

HAMLET.   True, Horatio! my father and uncle makes merry indeed still with his friends and followers. Horatio, I know not why since my father's death I have all the time such sadness of heart;[2] whereas my royal mother has so soon forgotten him; but this king still sooner; for whilst I was in Germany, he had himself crowned in all haste King of Denmark, and with show of right made over to me the crown of Norway,[3] and appealed to the election of the states.[4]

Scene V

Ghost

2 SENT.   Beware, the spirit comes again!

HORAT.   Does your lordship see it now?

---

[1] Cf. I.4.5–6. Not in Q1.

[2] Cf. II.2.301–3. Not in Q1.

[3] Not so in *Hamlet*.

[4] Note the insistence on election. In *Hamlet* too Claudius is now legally King. Cf. V.2.65.

FRANCISCO. My lord, be not afraid.

[*The ghost stalks over the stage and beckons to Hamlet.*

HAMLET. The spirit beckons me. Gentlemen stand a little aside. Horatio, do not go too far. I will follow the ghost and learn his will.

[*Exit.*

HORAT. Gentlemen, let's follow to see that no misfortune befalls him.

[*Exeunt.*

[*The ghost beckons Hamlet to the middle of the stage, and opens his jaws several times.*

HAMLET. Speak![1] Who art thou? Say what thou desirest?

GHOST. Hamlet!

HAMLET. Sir!

GHOST. Hamlet!

HAMLET. What wishest thou?

GHOST. Hear me, Hamlet, for the time draws near when I must return to the place whence I came:[2] listen and mark well what I shall tell thee.

HAMLET. Speak, thou sacred shade of my royal father.

GHOST. Then listen, Hamlet, my son, to what I shall tell thee of thy father's unnatural death.

HAMLET. What? Unnatural death?

GHOST. Ay, unnatural death. Know that it was my custom, which nature had made habitual to me, to retire every day after the noon-time meal to walk in my royal garden, there to enjoy an hour's repose. One day, when doing this as usual, behold my brother comes to me, thirsting for the crown, bearing with him the subtle juice of what they call Hebenon. This oil or juice has this effect, that as soon as a few drops of it mix with the blood of man, they immediately stop up the veins, and take away life. While I slept, he poured this juice into my ear, and as it entered my head, I could not but die immediately; whereupon it was given out that I had suffered a severe apoplexy. Thus was I robbed of kingdom, wife, and life by this tyrant.

HAMLET. Just heaven, if this be true, I swear to avenge thee.

GHOST. I cannot rest until my unnatural murder be avenged.

[*Exit.*

HAMLET. I swear not to rest until I have taken my revenge on this fratricide.

---

[1] So at I.5.1. No imperative in Q1. Sc. 4.
[2] Cf. I.5.2–4. Q1, Q2 describe Purgatory.

Scene VI

Horatio, Hamlet, Francisco

HORAT.   How is it, my noble lord? Why so terror-stricken? Have you perhaps been disturbed?

HAMLET.   Why yes, Horatio, beyond all measure.

HORAT.   Have you seen the ghost, my lord?

HAMLET.   Indeed yes, I have seen it, and spoken with it too.

HORAT.   O Heaven! this bodes something strange!

HAMLET.   He has revealed to me a horrible thing; therefore, I pray you, gentlemen, stand by me in a matter that calls for vengeance.

HORAT.   Certainly you are assured of my loyalty; only explain it to me, my lord.

FRANCISCO.   Your lordship cannot doubt of my aid also.

HAMLET.   Gentlemen, before I make this matter known to you, you must swear an oath by your loyalty and honour.

FRANCISCO.   Your lordship knows how much I love you, and how gladly I will lend my life if you wish to be revenged.

HORAT.   Offer us the oath; we will stand by you faithfully.

HAMLET.   Then lay your finger on my sword. We swear!

HORAT. and FRANCISCO.   We swear.

GHOST.   We swear.

HAMLET.   What is this? Can there be an echo here, to give us back our words? Come, gentlemen, we will go to another spot. We swear.

GHOST.   We swear.

HAMLET.   This means something strange! Come, once more; we will go to the other side. We swear.

HORAT. and FRANCISCO.   We swear.

GHOST.   We swear.

HAMLET.   Ha, what is this? Again: We swear.

HORAT. and FRANCISCO.   We swear.

GHOST.   We swear.

HAMLET.   O! now I understand what it is. It appears that the spirit of my father is not pleased that I should make this matter known. Good friends, I pray you, leave me—tomorrow I shall reveal it all to you.

HORAT. and FRANCISCO.   Farewell, your Highness! [*Exit Francisco.*

HAMLET.   Come here, Horatio.

HORAT.   What is your Highness' will?

HAMLET.   Has the other fellow gone?

HORAT.   Yes, he has gone.

HAMLET. I know, Horatio, thou hast at all times been true to me; therefore I shall reveal to thee what the ghost told me, namely, that my father died an unnatural death. My father, he who is now my father, has murdered him.

HORAT. O heavens! what do I hear!

HAMLET. Thou know'st, Horatio, that my late father was accustomed to sleep an hour every day after dinner in his garden. Knowing this, the villain comes to my father and pours the juice of hebenon into his ear while he is asleep; so that through this strong poison, he immediately yields up the ghost. And this the accursed dog did to obtain the crown: but from this hour I will put on a feigned madness, and in this deceit I'll play my part so skilfully that surely I shall find an opportunity to avenge my father's death.

HORAT. My lord, if the matter stands thus, I shall offer you my loyal help.

HAMLET. Horatio, I will so revenge myself on this usurper, this adulterer, this murderer, that posterity shall speak of it to all eternity;[1] now I shall go, and with dissembling wait upon him until I find an opportunity to execute my vengeance. [*Exeunt.*

Scene VII

King, Queen, Hamlet, Corambus, and Attendants

KING. Though yet our brother's death is fresh in memory of all[2] and it befits us to suspend all state-celebrations, yet from this time it is needful for us to change our black mourning garb to crimson, purple, and scarlet, since my late departed brother's widow has now become our dearest spouse. Wherefore I pray you, let everyone show himself joyful and make himself a partner in our mirth. But you, Prince Hamlet, pray you, be happy. See here your mother, how sad and troubled she is by your melancholy. Also we have learned that you have resolved to go back to Wittenberg. For the sake of your mother, do not do so. Stay here, for we love you and like to see you, and should not wish any harm to overtake you. Stay with us at court,[3] or, if not, betake yourself to Norway, to your kingdom.

QUEEN. My much-loved son, Prince Hamlet, it greatly astonishes us to learn that you have planned to leave us and to go to Wittenberg. You know well that your royal father died a short time ago, which causes us great sadness and heaviness of heart, and should you go away from us, it would greatly increase our grief. Then, dearest son, stay here, and every pleasure and delight shall be yours without denial, if it so please you.

---

[1] Cf. Belleforest, *supra*, pp. 90, 97.   [2] Cf. I.2.1–2.

[3] Closer to Q1, Sc. 2.31, than to I.2.115–17.

HAMLET. I shall obey your command with all my heart, and for the present shall remain here and not go away.

KING. Do so, dearest Prince! Say, Corambus, how is it with your son Leonhard? Has he already set out for France?

CORAMB. Ay, my gracious lord and king, he has already gone.

KING. But was it with your consent, Corambus?

CORAMB. Ay, your majesty, with top consent, bottom consent, and middle consent.[1] Indeed he got a most glorious, wonderful, and superb consent from me.

KING. As he has your consent to go, I hope that he may prosper, and that the gods may speed him back here again in safety. Now it is our will to hold a carousal, so that our dear spouse's grief may end. And you, Prince Hamlet, and other noble persons of our court must show yourselves mirthful; but for the present we shall make an end of our festivities, for the day is approaching to put black night to flight. You, my dearest consort, I shall accompany to your bed-chamber.

> Come, arm in arm and hand in hand; tonight
> In pledge of Love and Rest we'll take delight.

Act II Scene I

King, Queen

KING. Dearest consort, whence comes it that you are so sad? Pray tell me the cause of your melancholy! You are indeed our Queen; we love you, and all that the entire Kingdom affords is your own. What is it then that troubles you?

QUEEN. My King, I am greatly troubled by the melancholy of my son Hamlet, who is my only prince; it is this that grieves me.

KING. What! is he melancholy? We will gather together all the learned doctors and physicians throughout our whole Kingdom, that they may help him.

Scene II

Corambus, *to the above.*

CORAMB. News, news! my gracious lord and king!

KING. What news, Corambus?

CORAMB. Prince Hamlet is mad, aye, as mad as ever the Greek madman was.[2]

---

[1] Cf. Q2: 'my hard consent'; Q1: 'a forced graunt'.

[2] Probably Hercules, driven mad by the shirt of Nessus, or Ajax who in a mad rage slaughtered a flock of sheep.

KING. And why is he mad?

CORAMB. Because he has lost his wits.

KING. Where has he lost his wits?

CORAMB. That I know not. Perhaps he may know, who has found them.

Scene III

Ophelia

OPHELIA. Alas! father, protect me.

CORAMB. What is it, my child?

OPHELIA. Alas! my father, Prince Hamlet plagues me; I can have no peace from him.[1]

CORAMB. Calm yourself, dear daughter. But he has not done anything else to you? O! now I know why Prince Hamlet is mad: he is certainly in love with my daughter.

KING. Has love then such power as to make a man mad?

CORAMB. My gracious master and king, most assuredly is love powerful enough to make a man mad. I remember when I myself was young, how love plagued me—indeed, but it made me as mad as a March hare. But now, I care for it no longer. I prefer to sit by the fire, to count my red pennies, and drink your Majesty's health.

KING. May we not ourselves see his raving and madness with our own eyes?

CORAMB. Yes, your Majesty. We will stand a little on one side, and my daughter shall show him the jewel which he gave her. Then will your Majesty be able to see his madness.

KING. Dearest wife, we beseech you, go to your chamber. Meanwhile we will be a witness of his madness.

[*Hide themselves.*

Scene IV

Hamlet, Ophelia

OPHELIA. I pray your Highness take back the jewel which you gave me.[2]

HAMLET. What, young lady! dost want a husband? Get thee away from me—nay, come back. Listen girl, you young women do make nothing but fools of us bachelors; you buy your beauty from apothecaries and pedlars. Listen while I tell you a tale. There was

---

[1] This replaces Polonius's warning to Ophelia (Q1. Sc.3; Q2.I.2) and her account of Hamlet's farewell visit (Q1. Sc. 5; Q2.II.1).

[2] As in Q1 the nunnery-scene precedes the arrival of the Players. Contrast III.1 in Q2, F1.

once a cavalier in Anion, who fell in love with a lady, who, to look at, was like the goddess Venus. Now when they were to go to bed together, the bride went first and began to undress. First she took out one eye, which had been set very cleverly—then the front teeth made of ivory, so finely that no one had ever seen the like. Then she washed herself, and the paint with which she had smeared herself disappeared also. At length came the bridegroom expecting to embrace his bride. But as soon as he caught sight of her, he started back, and thought it was a ghost. Thus it is ye deceive us young fellows; therefore listen to me. But wait young lady—nay go, go to a nunnery, but not to a nunnery where two pairs of slippers lie by the bedside.

[Exit.

CORAMB. Is he not truly and completely mad, my gracious King?

KING. Corambus, leave us. When we have need of you, we'll send for you. [*Exit Corambus*] We have heard the Prince's madness and raving with great astonishment. But it seems to us no real madness, but rather a pretence.[1] We must contrive to get rid of him from here, or perhaps indeed put an end to him altogether; otherwise some harm may come of it.[2]

[Exit.

Scene V

Hamlet, Horatio

HAMLET. Horatio, my good friend, I trust by my assumed madness to find an opportunity to avenge my father's death. You know that my father is at all times surrounded by many guards, so my attempt may fail. Should you perchance find my body, have it honourably buried, for on the first occasion that I find I shall make an attempt on him.

HORAT. I entreat your lordship to do nothing of the kind. Perchance the ghost has deceived you.

HAMLET. Oh no! his words were all too plain. I can believe him fully. Ha! what news is that old fool bringing now?

Scene VI

Corambus

CORAMB. News, news! my lord! The actors have come.

HAMLET. When Marus Russig[3] was an actor in Rome, what fine times those were!

---

[1] Cf. III.1.165–7. Not in Q1. [2] Cf. III.1.167–70. Not in Q1.
[3] Cf. II.2.395–6, 'Roscius'.

CORAMB.   Ha, ha, ha, how your Highness always teases me!

HAMLET.   O! Jephthah, Jephthah! what a fair daughter hast thou!

CORAMB.   Why, my lord, you are always harping on my daughter.

HAMLET.   Well, well, old man, let the master of the actors come in.

CORAMB.   I will, my lord.   [*Exit.*

HAMLET.   These actors come in the nick of time, for through them I shall prove whether the ghost told me the truth or not. Once I saw a tragedy wherein one brother murders the other in the garden; this shall they act. And if the king turns pale, then he has done what the ghost told me.

Scene VII

Actors, Charles, the principal

CHARLES.   May the gods bestow on your Highness many blessings, happiness, and health!

HAMLET.   I thank you, my friend. What do you desire?

CHARLES.   Pardon, your Highness, but we are strangers, High-German actors, and we wanted the honour of acting at his Majesty's wedding. But Fortune turned her back on us, and contrary winds their face towards us. We therefore beseech your Highness to allow us to act a story, that our long journey be not all in vain.

HAMLET.   Were you not some few years ago at the University at Wittenberg? It seems to me I have seen you act before.

CHARLES.   Yes, your Highness, we are the same actors.

HAMLET.   Have you the whole of the same company still?

CHARLES.   We are not quite so numerous, because some students took engagements in Hamburg. Nevertheless we are numerous enough for many merry comedies and tragedies.

HAMLET.   Could you give us a play tonight?

CHARLES.   Yes, your Highness, we are numerous enough, and well rehearsed.

HAMLET.   Have you still the three actresses with you? They used to play well.

CHARLES.   No, only two; one stayed behind with her husband at the court of Saxony.

HAMLET.   You acted good comedies that time when you were at Wittenberg. But you had some fellows in your company, who had good clothes, but dirty shirts; others who had boots but no spurs.

CHARLES.   Your Highness, it is often hard to procure everything; maybe they thought they would not need to ride.

HAMLET. Still it is better to have everything correct. But listen a little longer, and excuse me, for you do not often hear directly what judgments the spectators pass on you. There were also a few who wore silk stockings and white shoes, but had on their heads black hats full of feathers, nearly as many below as on the top; I think they must have gone to bed in them instead of nightcaps. Now that is bad, yet it may easily be reformed.[1] Moreover you may tell some of them, that when they have to act a royal or a princely personage, they should not make such eyes whenever they pay a compliment to a lady. Neither should they walk so many Spanish pavans or put on such airs. A man of rank laughs at such things. Natural ease is best. He who plays a king must in the play fancy himself a king; and he who plays a peasant, must fancy himself a peasant.

CHARLES. Your Highness, I accept your Highness's reproof with the deepest respect and will endeavour to do better in future.

HAMLET. I am a great lover of your art, and hold it not wrong, since by it one can, as in a mirror,[2] see one's failings. Hear me now; you once acted a piece in Wittenberg about a King Pyr, Pyr—Pyr something.

CHARLES. Ah, it was perhaps about the great King Pyrrhus?

HAMLET. Methinks it was, but I am not quite sure.

CHARLES. Perhaps your Highness would name some persons in it, or give me some idea of the matter.

HAMLET. It was about one brother murdering the other in the garden.

CHARLES. It will be the same piece. Did not the king's brother pour poison into the king's ear?

HAMLET. True, true, the same story; could you play that piece tonight?

CHARLES. Oh yes, we can do that easily enough, for there are few characters in the play.

HAMLET. Then go, prepare the stage in the great hall: whatever wood you may require, you can get from the master-builder; if you want anything from the armoury or if you have not dresses enough, make known your wants to the master of the robes or the steward; we wish you to be provided with everything.

CHARLES. I thank your Highness most humbly for your favour. We shall hasten to get ready. Farewell.

[*Exit.*

HAMLET. These actors come most opportunely for me. Horatio,

---

[1] Contrast II.2.439–54 and III.2.1–36, where Hamlet is more interested in speech than dress.

[2] Cf. III.2.23. No mirror in Q1.

pay good heed to the king; if he grow pale or alter favour,[1] then most surely has he done the deed, for play actors with their feigned fables often hit the target of truth. Listen, I'll tell you a fine tale. In Germany, at Strasburg, there was once a remarkable case in which a wife murdered her husband with an awl through the heart. Afterwards she and her paramour buried the man under the threshold. This deed remained hid nine whole years, till at last it chanced that some actors came that way, and played a tragedy of like import. The woman who was present at the play with her husband began to cry aloud (her conscience being touched) 'Alas! this hits at me, for thus did I murder my innocent husband.' She tore her hair, ran straight out of the theatre to the judge, freely confessed the murder, and when it was proved true, in deep repentance for her sins she received the holy unction from the priest, gave her body in true contrition to the executioner, and recommended her soul to God. Oh that my uncle-father[2] would thus take it to heart if he has committed this crime! Come Horatio, let us go and wait upon the King; but pray note all things exactly, for I must dissemble.[3]

HORAT. Your Highness, I shall make my eyes keep a sharp look-out. *[Exeunt.*

Scene VIII

King, Queen, Hamlet, Horatio, Corambus, Ophelia, Retinue

KING. Our dearest wife, I hope that you will now banish your sadness, and make it give place to joy; before supper there is to be a comedy, played by the German actors, and after the meal a ballet given by our own people.

QUEEN. Most gladly shall I see such sport; still, I hardly believe that my heart will be at ease, for gloomy forebodings of misfortune, I know not what, disturb my soul.

KING. Pray, be content. Prince Hamlet, we are informed that some players have arrived here who will perform a comedy tonight. Tell me, is it so?

HAMLET. Ay, father,[4] it is so. They asked my permission, and I have given it. I hope that your Majesty will also approve.

KING. What is the subject? There's nothing offensive or uncivil in it?

---

[1] Nearer to Q1. Sc. 9.66 than to III.2.80–1; but note II.2.605: 'if he but blench'.
[2] Cf. II.2.381: 'my uncle-father'. Not in Q1.
[3] III.2.90: 'I must be idle.' Not in Q1.
[4] So in Q1. Sc. 9.72.

HAMLET.   It is a good subject. We that have a good conscience, it touches us not.

KING.   Where are they? Let them begin at once; we should like to see what the Germans can do.

HAMLET.   Marshal, go and see whether the actors are ready; tell them to begin.

CORAMB.   Actors, where are you? Quick, you are to begin at once. Ah! here they come.

[*Here the play enters: The King with his consort. He wishes to lie down and sleep; the Queen entreats him not to do so; he lies down all the same. The Queen kisses him, and takes her leave. The King's brother comes with a phial and pours something into his ear, and exit.*

HAMLET.   That is King Pyrrhus who goes to sleep in the garden. The Queen entreats him not to do so, but he lies down. The poor wife goes away: see, there comes the King's brother bearing the poisonous juice of hebenon; and he pours into his ear that which, as soon as it mixes with the blood of a man, immediately destroys his life.

KING.   Bring torches, lanterns here! the play does not please us!

CORAMB.   Pages, lackeys, light the torches! The King wishes to depart: quick with the lights! The actors have made a mess of it.

[*Exeunt King, Queen, Corambus and retinue.*

HAMLET.   Bring torches here, the play does not please us! Now thou seest that the Ghost has not deceived me! Players, you can go from here with this verdict, that although you have not played the piece to its end, and it has not pleased the King, yet it pleased us all the same. Horatio shall reward you on my behalf.

CHARLES.   We thank you and ask for a passport.

HAMLET.   You shall have one. [*Exeunt Players.*] Now may I go boldly on to vengeance. Did you perceive how the king went pale when he saw the play?

HORAT.   Yes, your Highness; the thing is certain.

HAMLET.   My poor father was murdered, just as we have seen in this play! But I will punish him for this wicked deed.

Scene IX

Corambus

CORAMB.   The Players, I fear, will get a poor recompense, for their play has deeply displeased the King.

HAMLET.   What say'st thou, old man; they will get a recompense? And if they are ill-rewarded by the King, they will be all the better rewarded by Heaven.

CORAMB. Your Highness, do actors then get into heaven?

HAMLET. Think'st thou, old fool, that they will not find their place there? Wherefore go and treat these people well for me.

CORAMB. Yes, I shall treat them as they deserve.

HAMLET. Treat them well, I say; for there is no greater praise to be gained than through actors, for they travel far and wide in the world. If they are treated well at one place, they do not know how to praise it enough at the next; for their theatre is a little world, in which they represent all that takes place in the great world. They revive the old forgotten histories, and display to us good and bad examples; they publish abroad the justice and laudable government of princes; they punish vices, and exalt virtues, they praise the good, and show how tyranny is punished—wherefore you must reward them well.

CORAMB. Well, they shall certainly have their reward, since they are such great folk. Farewell, your Highness.   [*Exit.*

HAMLET. Come Horatio, I am going, and from this hour[1] I shall accordingly seek means to find the King alone, that I may take his life, as he has taken my father's.

HORAT. My lord, consider well, that you come to no harm.

Verse

HAMLET. I ought, I must, I will this crime repay
If not by craft, with force I'll make a way!

Act III, Scene I

King

A church and altar.

KING [*alone*]. Now my conscience begins to awaken: the sting of my treachery begins to prick me hard. It is time I turn to repentance, and confess to Heaven the evil I have done. I fear that my guilt is so great, that it could never be forgiven.[2] Yet I will pray fervently to the gods, that they will pardon my great sins.

[*Kneels before the altar.*

Scene II

Hamlet, *with a drawn sword.*

HAMLET. For so long have I followed the accursed dog, till at last I have found him. Now it is time, since he is alone. I will take

---

[1] Cf. IV.4.65–6: 'from this time forth', etc., but there Hamlet has already found Claudius alone.

[2] Cf. Q1. Sc. 10.7: 'sinnes that are unpardonable'.

his life at the height of his devotions [*he is about to stab him*]. But no, I will first let him finish his prayer. Ha! when I think of it, he did not leave my father so much time as to say a prayer first, but sent him to hell (perhaps) in his sleep, in his sins;[1] wherefore, I'll send him also to the same place [*again about to stab him from behind.*] Nay, hold Hamlet! Why dost thou want to take his sins upon thee? I shall let him end his prayer, and let him go this time, and will give him his life. But I shall wreak my vengeance at another time.

[*Exit.*

KING. My conscience is somewhat lightened, but still the dog lies gnawing at my heart. Now will I go and make my peace with heaven by fasting, alms, and also with fervent prayer. Ah cursed ambition! To what hast thou brought me?

[*Exit.*

Scene III

Queen, Corambus

QUEEN. Tell me, Corambus, how is my son, Prince Hamlet? Does his madness decrease at all, or will his ravings never come to an end?

CORAMB. Ah no, your Majesty, he is just as mad as he was before.

Scene IV

Horatio

HORAT. Most gracious Queen, Prince Hamlet is in the ante-chamber, and desires a private audience.

QUEEN. He is most dear to us; admit him immediately.

HORAT. It shall be done, your Majesty.   [*Exit.*

QUEEN. Hide yourself behind the arras, Corambus, till we call you.

CORAMB. Ay, ay, I will hide myself a little. [*He hides himself.*

Scene V

Hamlet

HAMLET. Mother, did you know your first husband well?

QUEEN. O! do not remind me of my former sadness. I cannot restrain my tears when I think of him.

---

[1] Q1. Sc. 10.16: 'he tooke my father sleeping, his sins brim full.' Contrast III.3.80-1.

HAMLET. You weep? Leave off doing that; they are only crocodile tears.[1] But look, there in that gallery hangs the counterfeit
resemblance of your first husband, and there hangs the counterfeit
of your present one. What think you now? Which of them is the
finer looking? Is not the first the nobler Lord?

QUEEN. Indeed that is so.

HAMLET. How then could you forget him so soon? Fie! Shame
on you! You celebrated his funeral and your wedding almost
on the same day! But hush! are all the doors shut fast?[2]

QUEEN. Why do you ask that?

[Corambus coughs behind the arras.

HAMLET. Ha! ha! who is that, listening to us?   *[Stabs him.*

CORAMB. O! Prince, what are you doing? I am slain![3]

QUEEN. O Heavens! My son, what have you done? It is
Corambus, the Lord Chamberlain!

Scene VI

Ghost stalks over the stage. [Lightning.]

HAMLET. Ah, gracious spirit of my father, stay. What dost thou
want? Dost thou demand revenge?[4] I shall execute it at the right
time.

QUEEN. What are you doing? With whom are you speaking?

HAMLET. See you not the spirit of your late husband? Look,
he beckons as if he would speak to you.

QUEEN. How? I see nothing.

HAMLET. Indeed I believe you see nothing, for you are no longer
worthy to look upon his form. Fie, shame on you! I shall say not
another word to you.

[Exit.

QUEEN [alone]. O Heavens! what great madness melancholy
has brought upon the Prince! Alas, my only son has entirely lost his
reason! And I am much to blame for it! Had I not taken in marriage
my brother-in-law, I should not have robbed my son of the crown of
Denmark. But what can be done about things that are done?
Nothing, they must stay as they are. Had not the Pope allowed such

[1] Not in *Hamlet*. Cf. Belleforest: 'souz le fard d'un pleur dissimulé' (''neath the
disguise of a pretended tear'); and I.2.154, 'the salt of most unrighteous tears'.

[2] Cf. Q1. Sc. 11.7: 'first weele make all safe.' Not in Q2, F1.

[3] 'Ich sterbe.' Cf. III.4.24: 'I am slain.' Not in Q1.

[4] Q1. Sc. 11. 62–70 has 'revenge' twice. Not in Q2, F1.

F

a marriage, it would never have happened. I shall go and try my utmost to restore my son to his former understanding and health.

[*Exit.*

Scene VII

Jens, *alone*

It's a long time since I was last at court and paid my taxes. I am afraid, go where I may, I shall be clapped in prison. If I could find only one good friend to put in a good word for me so that I might not be punished!

Scene VIII

Phantasmo

PHANT. There are queer goings on at court now. Prince Hamlet is mad, Ophelia is mad too. In sum, it's very queer here altogether, so that I have a good mind to take myself off.

JENS. My goodness! there I see my good friend Phantasmo. I couldn't find a better. I'll beg him to put in a good word for me. Good luck to you, Master Phantasmo!

PHANT. Thank you kindly! What do you want, Master Clown?

JENS. Eh, Master Phantasmo, 'tis a long time since I have been at court, and I am greatly in arrears. So prithee put in a good word for me, and I'll treat you to a good cheese.

PHANT. What, lout, dost think that I get nothing to eat at court?

Scene IX

Ophelia, *mad*

OPHELIA. I run and race and yet cannot find my sweetheart. He sent a messenger to tell me to come to him. We are to be married, and I have dressed myself for it already. But ah! there is my love. Art thou there, my lamb? Oh! I have sought thee so much; yes, I have sought thee. Ah, only think; the tailor has quite spoiled my calico gown! See! there's a pretty flower for thee, my heart!

PHANT. O the devil! I wish I were far away!—she thinks I am her lover.

OPHELIA. What say'st thou my love? We will go to bed together; I'll wash thee quite clean.

PHANT. Ay, ay, I'll soap you in return, and wash you out too.

OPHELIA. Listen my love, hast already put on thy beautiful new suit? Ay! how finely it is made, quite in the new fashion.

PHANT. I know that well without . . .

OPHELIA. Gracious me! what I had nearly forgotten! The King has asked me to supper, I must run quickly. Look, there's my little coach, my little coach![1]   [*Exit.*

PHANT. O Hecate, thou queen of witches, how glad I am that that mad thing's gone away! If she had stayed any longer, I should have gone mad with her. I must be off before the crazy thing comes back again.

JENS. Oh kind-hearted Master Phantasmo! Prithee, do not forget me.

PHANT. Come along, Brother Windy; I'll see if I can put you right with the tax-collector.

[*Exeunt.*

Scene X

King, Hamlet, Horatio, Two Attendants

KING. Where is the body of Corambus bestowed? Has it not yet been removed?

HORAT. He is still lying in the place where he was stabbed.

KING. It grieves us that Corambus has lost his life so unexpectedly. Go, have him carried away; we wish him to have honourable burial. Ah, Prince Hamlet, what have you done, stabbing that innocent old man? It grieves us deeply; still, because it was done unwittingly this murderous deed is perhaps somewhat to be pardoned. Nevertheless I fear that when this gets known amongst the nobles, it may easily excite a rising among my subjects, and they may avenge his death on you.[2] But out of our paternal care we have devised a way of avoiding this misfortune.

HAMLET. I am sorry for it, my uncle and father?[3] I wished to discuss something privately with the Queen, and this spy lay in wait for us. But I did not realise that it could be this silly old fool. What now does your Majesty propose it were best to do with me?

KING. We have determined to send you to England, because that crown is friendly to our own, so that you may cool down there somewhat, since the air is wholesomer, and may aid your recovery better than here.[4] We shall give you some of our attendants, who must accompany you, and serve you faithfully.

---

[1] Cf. IV.5.71: 'Come, my coach!'. Not in Q1.

[2] Cf. IV.3.42: 'for thine especial safety'. No danger mentioned in Q1.

[3] Cf. III.4.173 (to his mother). No regret in Q1. Sc.10.

[4] Closer to Q1. Sc.11.129–30: 'the aire and climate of the country . . .' than to III.1.172ff., etc.

HAMLET. Ay ay, King, just send me off to Portugal, that I may never come back again, that is the best plan.[1]

KING. No, not to Portugal, but to England, and these two shall accompany you on the journey. But when you arrive in England, you shall have more attendants.

HAMLET. Are those the lackeys? A pair of fine fellows!

KING. Listen, both of you! [*secretly to the two attendants.*] As soon as ye reach England, do as I have commanded you. Take a dagger or pistol each, and kill him. But should your attempt miscarry, take this letter and bring it along with the prince to the place written down on it; there he will be so well cared for that he will never come back from England again. But this I warn you, that ye make known this to no man. Your reward shall be given you immediately on your return.

HAMLET. Well, your Majesty, who are these fine fellows that are to travel with me?

KING. These two. The gods be with you, and give you a fair wind to reach your destination.

HAMLET. Now farewell, Mother!

KING. What, Prince! Why do you call us Mother?

HAMLET. Man and wife is one flesh—Father or Mother, it is all the same to me.

KING. Well, fare ye well. May Heaven be with you.

[*Exit.*

HAMLET. Now! you sprigs of nobility, are you to be my companions?

ATTEND. Yes, your Highness.

HAMLET. Come then, my noble sirs, [*taking each by the hand*], let's go, let's go to England! Take your little messages in your hand; you are indeed an honest fellow. Let's go, let's go to England!

[*Exeunt.*

Scene XI

Phantasmo, Ophelia

PHANT. Wherever I go or stay, that cracked girl runs after me from every corner. I can get not a moment's peace for her; she says continually that I'm her lover; and that's not true. If I could only hide where she couldn't find me! Oh, the devil's loose again; there she is once more!

OPHELIA. Where can my sweetheart be? The rogue will not stay with me, he'd rather flee from me—but see! there he is. Listen

---

[1] An allusion apt in 1589, but also in the 1660s.

darling, I've been to the priest, and he will unite us this very day; I have made all ready for the wedding; and bought pullets, hares, meat, butter, cheese. Now there is nothing more wanting than for the musicians to play us to bed.

PHANT. I can only say yes. Come then, we'll go to bed together.

OPHELIA. No, no, my puppet, we must first go to church together, afterwards eat and drink, and then dance—ah! how merry we shall be!

PHANT. Ay, it will be very merry; three will eat off one plate.

OPHELIA. What do you say? If you will not have me, I will not have you [*strikes him*]. There, there, is my dearest, he beckons me. Look there, what a beautiful suit he has on!—look, he wants to entice me to him, he throws me a lily and a rose; he wants to take me in his arms; he beckons me; I come, I come.

[*Exit.*

PHANT. At close quarters she's lost her wits, but further off she's clean mad. I wish she were hanged, and then the carrion could not pester me so.

[*Exit.*

Act IV, Scene I

Hamlet, Two Ruffians

HAMLET. It is a pleasant place here on this island! Let us stay here for a while and dine. There is a delightful wood, and here a cool spring of water. So fetch the best from our ship, and we'll make right merry here.

RUFF. 1. There's no dinner time here for you, my lord, since you will never leave this island, for here's the place destined for your grave.

HAMLET. What say'st thou, scoundrel, slave? Dost thou know who I am? Wouldst thou jest thus with a royal prince? However, on this occasion I pardon thee.

RUFF. 2. No, it is no jest, but grim earnest. Prepare yourself for death.

HAMLET. Wherefore this? What harm have I ever done you? I cannot recollect any; therefore speak out, why do ye have such wicked thoughts?

RUFF. 1. We have been ordered to do it by the King: as soon as we have brought your Highness to this island, we are to take your life.

HAMLET. Dear friends, spare my life! Say that you have done it properly, and I will never return to the King as long as I live.

Consider well, what do you gain by covering your hand with the innocent blood of a prince? Will you stain your consciences with my sins? What bad luck that I came here unarmed! If only I had something in my hand!   [*Grabs at a sword.*

RUFF. 2.   Take care of thy weapon, comrade!

RUFF. 1.   I'll take good care. Now Prince, prepare yourself; we haven't much time.

HAMLET.   Since it cannot be otherwise, and I must die at your hands, by the orders of the tyrannical king, I must submit, although I am innocent. And since you have been bribed through poverty, I freely pardon you. Yet this murderer of his brother and my father must answer for my blood at the Last Great Day.

RUFF. 1.   Eh! what is that great day to us? we must carry out our orders for today.

RUFF. 2.   That's true, brother! Quickly to work; it must be so! You fire from this side, I from the other.

HAMLET.   Listen to one word more from me. Since even the wickedest evildoer is not executed without being given time to repent, I, an innocent prince, beg you to let me first address a fervent prayer to my Creator; after which I shall willingly die. But I shall give you a sign: I shall raise my hands to heaven, and as soon as I spread out my arms, fire! Level both pistols at my sides, and when I say shoot, give me as much as I need, and be sure and hit me, that I may not suffer long.

RUFF. 2.   Well, we may do that much to please him; so go right ahead.

HAMLET.   [*Spreads out his hands.*] Shoot! [*Meanwhile he falls down forward between the two servants, who shoot each other.*] Just Heaven! Thanks be to thee for thy angelic inspiration; henceforth I will ever worship the guardian angel who working through my thoughts has saved my life. But these scoundrels, as they worked, so were they paid out. The dogs move still; they have shot each other, but for revenge I'll give them the coup de grace; otherwise one of the rogues might escape. [*He stabs them with their own swords.*] Now I'll search them, to see whether they have some warrant on them. This one has nothing. But here I find a letter on this murderer. I'll read it. This letter is written to an arch-murderer in England, so that should this attempt miscarry, they would hand me over to him, and he would soon blow out the light of my life! But the gods ever stand by the just. Now I will go back again to my 'father', to terrify him; but I will not trust to water again, for who knows whether the captain may not likewise prove a rogue. I shall go to the first town and take the post. The sailors I shall order back to Denmark, but these scoundrels I'll throw into the water.   [*Exit.*

Scene II

King, and retinue

KING. We long to hear how things have gone with our son, Prince Hamlet, and whether the companions we gave him for his journey have faithfully performed what we ordered.

Scene III

Phantasmo

PHANT. News, Monsieur the King! The very latest news!
KING. What is it, Phantasmo?
PHANT. Leonhardus has come back home from France.
KING. We are glad of it. Let him come into our presence.

Scene IV

Leonhardus

LEON. My gracious Lord and King, I demand my father or just vengeance for his grievous murder. If this is not granted, I shall forget that you are king, and avenge myself on the criminal.
KING. Be satisfied, Leonhardus, that we are guiltless of your father's death.[1] Prince Hamlet unwittingly ran him through behind the arras: but we shall see that he is punished for it.
LEON. Since your Majesty is innocent of my father's death, I humbly crave your pardon on my knees. My anger, together with my filial affection, so overcame me that I hardly knew what I was doing.
KING. It is forgiven thee, for we can easily believe that it must have gone deep into thy heart to lose thy noble father so piteously. But rest content; thou shalt find another father in ourselves.
LEON. I thank you for this most kingly favour.

Scene V

Phantasmo

PHANT. Uncle King, more news still!
KING. What fresh news do you bring?

[1] So at IV.5.148. Not in Q1.

PHANT.   Prince Hamlet has come back!

KING.   The devil has come back, not Prince Hamlet!

PHANT.   Prince Hamlet has come back and not the devil!

KING.   Leonhardus, hear. Now thou canst avenge thy father's death, for the Prince has come home again. But you must swear to us an oath to disclose it to no man.

LEON.   Doubt me not, your Majesty; what you reveal shall be as secret as if you had spoken to a stone.

KING.   We shall arrange a match between thyself and him on these terms: you shall fence with rapiers, and the one of you who makes the first three hits, shall have won a white Neapolitan horse. But in the middle of this bout you must let your foil drop, and instead of it, you must have a rapier with a sharp point ready to hand, which must be made exactly like the foil, but you must rub the point of it with a strong poison;[1] as soon as you shall wound his body with it, he will certainly die, but you shall win the prize, and your king's favour as well.

LEON.   Your Majesty must excuse me! I dare not undertake this, for the Prince is a skilled fencer[2] and might well turn the tables on me.

KING.   Leonhardus, do not refuse, but do it to please thy King; do it to revenge thy father's death. For know, the Prince as assassin of your father deserves such a death. But we cannot do justice on him, because his mother backs him, and my subjects love him dearly. If therefore we avenged ourselves on him openly, a rebellion might easily follow.[3] But that we now reject him as our step-son and nephew is the will of sacred Justice, since he is bloodthirsty and insane, and for the future we must ourselves be afraid of so wicked a man. If you do what we desire, you will relieve your King of his fear, and secretly avenge yourself on the murderer of your father.

LEON.   It is a difficult thing which I scarcely dare venture. For should it come out, it would cost me my life.

KING.   Do not doubt; if this should fail we have already devised another trick. We shall have an oriental diamond powdered fine, and this, when he is hot, we shall offer to him in a goblet[4] filled with wine mixed with sugar: thus shall he drink death to our health.

LEON.   Well then, your Majesty, under this protection I will carry it out.

---

[1] In Q1 (not in Q2, F1) Claudius suggests the poisoned rapier.

[2] Cf. V.2.211. Hamlet has been 'in continual practice'. Not in Q1.

[3] Cf. IV. 7.5–24.

[4] 'Becher'. Cf. IV. 7.159: 'chalice'. Not in Q1. Sc. 15, but 'poysned cup' in Sc. 17.

Scene VI

Queen

QUEEN. My gracious lord and King, my dearest consort, I bring you bad news.[1]

KING. What is it, dear soul?

QUEEN. My dearest maid-in-waiting, Ophelia, runs up and down, and cries, and screams, and neither eats nor drinks; they think that she has entirely lost her wits.

KING. Alas! One hears nothing but the most sad and unhappy news!

Scene VII

Ophelia, *with flowers*

OPHELIA. Look, there's a flower for thee; for thee too, and for thee too [gives a flower to each]. But gracious me, what had I clean forgotten! I must run quickly, I have forgotten my jewels. Ah! my diadem. I must go quick to the court goldsmith and ask what new fashions he has got. So, so, set the table quick; I shall soon be back again. [*Runs off.*

LEON. Am I then born to every misfortune! My father dead, and my sister robbed of her reason![2] My heart will almost burst for very grief!

KING. Take comfort, Leonhardus, thou shalt live supreme in our favour. But you, sweet Queen, be pleased to walk inside with us, for we have something to reveal to you in private. Leonhardus, do not forget what we have told you.

LEON. I shall be diligent to perform it.

QUEEN. My King, we must find some means by which this unhappy maiden may be restored to her senses.

KING. Let the case be handed over to our own physician. Follow us, Leonhardus. [*Exit.*

Act V, Scene I

Hamlet

Unhappy Prince, how long must thou live without rest! How long a time, O just Nemesis, dost thou appoint for whetting thy just

---

[1] In Q1 also (Sc. 13) the Queen tells him of Ophelia's madness before the girl enters. Contrast IV.5.

[2] Cf. Laertes in Q1. Sc. 13.114–15. 'Griefe upon griefe, my father murdered, My sister thus distracted.'

sword of vengeance[1] against my uncle, the fratricide! Now am I back here once more, and cannot yet attain to my revenge, because this fratricide is at all times surrounded by many people.[2] But I swear, that ere the sun has finished his journey from east to west, I will avenge myself on him.

Scene II

Horatio

HORAT. Your Highness, I am heartily glad to see you here again in good health. But I pray you, tell me why you have come back again so soon.

HAMLET. Alas! Horatio, thou hast very nearly not seen me alive again, for my life was already at stake, had not the Divine Power specially protected me.[3]

HORAT. How? What does your Highness say? How did it happen?

HAMLET. You know that my father gave me two fellow-travellers as servants to accompany me. Now it chanced that one day we had contrary winds,[4] and we cast anchor by an island not far from Dover. With my two attendants I left the ship to breathe the fresh air. There the cursed villains came and wished to take my life, saying that the King had hired them to do so. I begged for my life, saying that I would give them as much reward, and that if they would report my death to the King, I would never show myself at court again. But there was no mercy in them. At length the gods put an idea in my mind: I begged them that I might say a prayer before my end, and when I called 'Shoot!' they were to fire at me. But as I called, I fell flat on the ground, so that they shot each other. Thus I escaped this time with my life. But my arrival will not be very agreeable to the King.

HORAT. O unheard of treachery!

Scene III

Phantasmo

HAMLET. Look Horatio, this fool is much dearer to the king than my person. Let's hear what he has to say.

---

[1] Belleforest too regards the delay as outside human control.

[2] This obstacle is not stated in *Hamlet*.

[3] In Q2, F1 also the story is told by Hamlet to Horatio; in Q1. Sc. 14 by Horatio to the Queen, who thanks Heaven.

[4] Cf. Q1. Sc. 14.5: 'crossed by the contention of the windes.' Not in Q2, F1.

PHANT. Welcome home, Prince Hamlet! Have you heard the news? The King has laid a wager on you and young Leonhardus. You are to fight together with foils, and he who gives his opponent the first two hits is to win a white Neapolitan horse.

HAMLET. Is this certain that you say?

PHANT. Yes, nothing else!

HAMLET. Horatio, what can this mean? Leonhardus and I to fight each other! I believe they have been mocking this fool, for one can make him believe what one likes. Observe. Signor Phantasmo, it is terribly cold.

PHANT. Ay, it is terribly cold—

[*His teeth chattering with cold.*

HAMLET. Now it is not so cold any more.

PHANT. You're right my lord, just the happy medium.

HAMLET. But now it is very hot indeed.

[*Wiping his face.*

PHANT. O what a dreadful heat!

[*Also wiping away the perspiration.*

HAMLET. Now it is neither very cold nor very warm.

PHANT. Yes, now it is just temperate.

HAMLET. Do you see, Horatio, one can make him believe what one will. Phantasmo, go back to the King, and tell him that I'll wait upon him instantly.[1] [*Phant. exit.*] Come, Horatio, I go this very minute, and present myself to the King. Ha! What does this mean? Drops of blood fall from my nose; my whole body trembles! Alas! what is happening to me?

[*Faints.*

HORAT. Most noble Prince! O Heavens! what does this mean? Come to your senses my lord! My noble Prince, what is it? what is the matter with you?

HAMLET. I do not know Horatio. When I thought of going to court, a sudden faintness came over me. The gods alone know what it signifies.

HORAT. Heaven grant that this omen foretells nothing bad!

HAMLET. Be it what it may, I shall nevertheless go to court, even should it cost me my life.

[*Exeunt.*

Scene IV

King, Leonhardus, Phantasmo

KING. Leonhardus prepare, for Prince Hamlet will also be here directly.

[1] Nearer to Q1. Sc. 18.33 than to V.2.173–81.

LEON. I am prepared, your Majesty, and will do my utmost.

KING. Look well to it; here comes the Prince already.

Scene V

Hamlet, Horatio

HAMLET. All health and happiness wait on your Majesty!

KING. We thank you, Prince! We are extremely glad that your melancholy has somewhat left you; wherefore today we have arranged a friendly match between you and young Leonhardus. You are to fight him with foils and the one of you who makes the first three hits will have won the prize, a white Neapolitan horse with saddle and all the trappings.

HAMLET. Your Majesty will pardon me, for I am little practised with the foils, while Leonhardus comes direct from France, where he had undoubtedly had plenty of practice; wherefore will you please excuse me.

KING. Prince Hamlet will do it to please us, for we are curious to learn what feints the Germans and French use.

Scene VI

Queen

QUEEN. Gracious Lord and King, I am the bearer of sad tidings.

KING. Heaven forbid; what is it?

QUEEN. Ophelia has climbed a high hill, and cast herself down and taken her own life.[1]

LEON. Ill-fated Leonhardus! In a short time thou hast lost a father and a sister! Whither will misfortune lead thee? I could for grief wish myself to die.

KING. Be comforted, Leonhardus! You enjoy our favour; only begin the contest. Phantasmo, fetch the foils. You, Horatio, shall be umpire.

PHANT. Here is the warm beer.

HAMLET. Well then, Leonhardus, come on; let's see who is to put the fool's cap and bells on the other. Should I make a mistake, pray excuse me, for I have not fought for a long time.

LEON. I am your Lordship's servant; you are only jesting.[2]

[*During the first bout they fence fairly. Leonhardus receives a thrust.*

---

[1] Contrast the method of her death in *Hamlet*, where also she dies before Hamlet's return home.

[2] Cf. V.2.255–7. Not in Q1.

HAMLET.   One!¹ That was a hit, Leonhardus!

LEON.   True, your Highness. Now for my revenge! [*He lets his foil fall, and seizes the poisoned sword which is lying ready, and gives the Prince a thrust in carte in the left arm. Hamlet parries on Leonhardus, so that both drop their weapons. They run to pick them up. Hamlet takes the poisoned sword and mortally wounds Leonhardus.*

LEON. Alas! I am mortally wounded! I receive the reward which I thought to pay another. Heaven, have mercy on me!

HAMLET.   What the devil is this, Leonhardus? have I pierced you with the foil? How is this possible?

KING.   Go quick, and fetch my goblet, with wine to refresh our swordsmen a little. Go, Phantasmo, and fetch it. [*Descends from the throne. Aside.*] I hope that they may both drink of the wine and die, and this trick may not be exposed.

HAMLET.   Tell me, Leonhardus, how did this come about?

LEON.   Alas! Prince, I have been misled into this mishap by the King!² Look at what you have in your hand! It is a poisoned sword.

HAMLET.   O! Heavens, what is this! Preserve me from it!

LEON.   I was to wound you with it, for it is so strongly poisoned that whoever receives the slightest wound from it must die.

KING.   Ho! gentlemen, take this cup and drink. [*Whilst the King is rising from his chair and speaking these words, the Queen takes the cup out of Phantasmo's hand and drinks; the King exclaims:*] Ah! where is the cup? Dear wife, what are you doing? This drink is mixed with the strongest poison. Alas! what have you done!

QUEEN.   Alas! I die!

[*The King stands before the Queen.*

HAMLET.   And thou, tyrant, shalt bear her company in death.³

[*Stabs him from behind.*

KING.   Alas! I receive the reward of my wickedness!

LEON.   Farewell, Prince Hamlet! Farewell, world! I die too. Ah, forgive me, Prince!

HAMLET.   May heaven receive thy soul for thou art guiltless.⁴ But for this tyrant, I wish that he may purge his black sins in Hell. Ah, Horatio! now my soul is at peace, now I am avenged on my enemies. 'Tis true I have received a hit on the arm, but I hope that it means nothing. It grieves me that I have slain Leonhardus. I do not know how the fatal rapier came into my hand; but as the work is, so is the pay,⁵ and he has received his reward. Nothing afflicts me

¹ V.2.280: 'One.'
² Cf. V.2.320: 'The king's to blame.' No such direct statement in Q1.
³ Cf. V.2.327: 'Follow my mother.' Not in Q1.
⁴ Not in Q1.
⁵ Cf. III.3.79; 'this is hire and salary, not revenge.'

so much as my mother; yet by her sins she has somewhat deserved this death. But tell me, who gave her the cup that poisoned her?

PHANT. I, your Highness. I also brought the poisoned sword, but the poisoned wine was meant for you alone.

HAMLET. Hast thou been an instrument of this woe? There, then; thou too hast thy reward!

[Stabs him.

PHANT. Stab away, till your blade grows weak!

HAMLET. O Horatio, I fear that taking my revenge will cost me my life, for I am sorely wounded in the arm. I grow faint; my limbs grow weak and my legs refuse to support me. My voice fails.[1] I feel the poison in all my members. Gentle Horatio, take the crown to my cousin, Duke Fortenbras of Norway,[2] so that the kingdom may not fall into other hands. Alas! I am dying!

HORATIO. Noble Prince, help may still come! Heavens! he is dying in my arms. Ah, how this Kingdom of Denmark has been scourged. First long wars; then scarcely has peace been established when it is filled with new internal disturbances, ambitions, strifes and murders. It may well be that in no age of the world has such a grievous Tragedy happened as this which we have just lived through in this court. And now, with the help of all true Counsellors, I shall make arrangements to have these high personages buried according to their rank. After which I shall go at once to Norway with the crown, and deliver it as this unhappy Prince has commanded me.

Verse.

Thus, if a Prince obtains the Crown by craft,
        And treacherously takes it as his prey,
He nothing gains but purest hate and scorn,
        For 'as the labour is, so is the pay'.

---

[1] Cf. Q1. Sc. 18.106–7. Not in Q2, F1.
[2] Cf. V.2.356. In Q1 he does not mention the succession.

VI. Possible Sources

From
SENECA HIS TENNE TRAGEDIES
edited by Thomas Newton (1581)[1]

A. AGAMEMNON
translated by John Studley

(i) [The Ghost of Thyestes is sent from Hell to torment the house of Atreus.]
[Act I]

DEPARTINGE from the darkned dens which Ditis low doth
keepe,
Loe heere I am sent out agayne from Tartar Dungeon deepe,
Thyestes I, that wheather coast to shun doe stande in doubt,
Th'infernall fiendes I fly, the foalke of earth I chase about.
My conscience lo abhors, that I should heather passage
make,
Appauled sore with feare and dread my trembling sinewes
shake:
My fathers house, or rather yet my brothers I espy,
This is the olde and antique porche of Pelops progeny.
Here first the Greekes on prynces heads doe place the royall
crowne,
And heere in throne aloft they lye, that jetteth up and
downe,   10
With stately Scepter in theyr hand, eake heere theyr courts
do ly,
This is theyr place of banquetting, returne therefore will I.
Nay: better were it not to haunt the lothsome Limbo lakes,
Where as the Stygion porter doth advaunce with lusty crakes
His tryple gorge be hong with Mane shag hairy, rusty, blacke:
Where Ixions Carkasse linked fast, the whirling wheele doth
racke,
And rowleth still upon him selfe: where as full oft in vayne
Much toyle is lost (the tottring stone down tumbling backe
agayne)

---

[1] *Seneca His Tenne Tragedies*, ed. T. Newton, 1581; modern edn., Tudor Translations, 2 vols, 1927. *Agamemnon*, translated by J. Studley, orig. edn., 1566; *Troas*, translated by Jasper Heywood, orig. edn., 1559.

Where growing guts the greedy gripe do gnaw with ravening
bits.

Where parched up with burning thirst amid the waves he
sits,   20

And gapes to catch the fleeting flood with hungry chaps
beguilde,

That payes his paynefull punishment, whose feast the Gods
defilde:

Yet that olde man so stept in yeares at length by tract of
time,

How great a part belonges to mee and portion of his crime?

Account wee all the grisly ghostes, whom guilty sounde of
ill,

The Gnosian Judge in Plutoes pyts doth tosse in torments
still:

Thyestes I in driery deedes will farre surmount the rest. . . .   27

But valyant *Agamemnon* he graund captayne of the oste

Who bare the sway among the kinges, and ruled all the
roste, . . .   50

Retournd he is to yeld his throte unto his traytresse wyfe,

That shall with force of blooddie blade beryve him of hys
lyfe.

The glytering swerd, the hewing axe, and woundyng weapons
mo,

With blood for blood new set a broche shall make the floore to
flow.[1]   60

With sturdy stroke, & boysteous blow, of pythye Pollax geven

His beaten braynes are pasht abroad, his cracked skull is
reven.

Now myschiefe marcheth on a pace, Now falshod doth
appeare,

Now butchers slaughter doth approach, and murther
draweth neare.

(ii) [Act V. Sc. 4] [Electra upbraids her mother and will not say
where Orestes is.]

Clytemnestra. Electra. Ægisthus. Cassandra

CLY. O THOU thy Mothers Enemy, ungracious saucy face,

After what sorte dost thou a mayde appeare in publyque
place?   1150

EL. I have wyth my virginity the bowres of Baudes forsooke.

CLY. What man is hee, that ever thee to bee a vyrgin tooke?

[1] Such alliteration is mocked at in *MND*.

EL. What your own daughter? CLY. With thy mother more modest should thou be.[1]

EL. Doe you at length begin to preach, such godlines to me?

CLY. A manly stomacke stout thou hast with swelling hawty hart,
Subdued with sorrow learne thou shall to play a womans part.

EL. A swerd and buckler very well a woman doth beseeme,
(Except I dote.) CLY. Thy selfe dost haylefellowe with us esteeme?

EL. What Agamemnon new is this, whom thou hast got of late?

CLY. Hereafter shall I tame, and teach thy gyrlish tongue to　　1160
prate.
And make thee know, how to a Queene thy taunting to forbeare.

EL. The whilst (thou Wyddow) aunswere me directly to this geare.
Thy husband is bereved quight of breath, his lyfe is donne.

CLY. Enquier where thy brother is, go seeke about my sonne.

EL. Hee is departed out of Greece. CLY. Goe fetch him out of hande.

EL. Fetch thou my father unto mee. CLY. Give me to understande,
Where doth he lurking hyde his head? where is he shrunke away?

EL. All plunge of perills past hee is, and at a quiet stay
And in another Kyngdome where no harme hee doth mistrust,
The aunswere were sufficient, to please a Parent just.　　　　1170
But one whose breast doth boyle in wrath, it cannot satisefy.

CLY. To day by death thou shalt receyve thy fatall destiny.

EL. On this condition am I pleasde, the Aulter to forsake,
If that this hand shall doe the deede, my death when I shall take.
Or els if in my throate to bath thy blade, thou doe delight,
Most willingly I yeelde my throate, and give thee leave to smite.
Or if thou will chop of my heade in brutishe beastly guise,

---

[2] Cf. *Hamlet*, III.4.9–12.

My necke a wayting for the wounde out stretched ready
lies.
Thou hast committed sinfully a great and grievous guilt.
Goe purge thy hardned hands, the which thy husbande
bloud have spilt.   1180
CLY. O thou that of my perills all dost suffer part with mee,
And in my realme dost also rule with egall dignity,
Ægisthus, art thou glad at this? (as doth her not behove,)
With checks and taunts the daughter doth her mothers
mallice move.
Shee keepes her brothers counsell close conveyde out of the
way.
ÆGI. Thou malipert and witlesse wenche, thyne elvishe
prating stay,
Refrayne those wordes unfit thy Mothers glowing eares to
vex.
EL. What shall the breeder of this broyle controll me with his
checks,
Whose fathers guilt hath caused him to have a doubtfull
name,
Who both is to his sister, sonne, and Nephew to the same?   1190
CLY. To snap her head of with thy swerd Ægist dost thou
refrayne?
Let her give up the ghost: or bryng her brother straight
agayne:
Let her be lockt in dungeon darck, and let her spend her
dayes
In Caves and Rocks, with painefull pangues, torment her
every wayes . . .
EL. Graunt me my doome by meanes of death to passe unto
my grave.
CLY. I would have graunted it to thee, if thou should it
deny.
Unskilfull is the tyraunt, who by suffring wretches dy
Doth ende theyr paynes.   EL. What, after death doth any
thing remayne?
CLY. And if thou doe desyre to dye, the same see you
refrayne.
Lay hands sirs on this wondrous wretch, whom being caryed
on,
Even to the furthest corner of my jurisdiction,
Farre out beyond Mycœnas land in bonds let her be bound,
With darknesse dim in hiddeous holde let her be closed
round.   1200

B. TROAS

translated by Jasper Heywood

(i) [At the beginning of Act I Hecuba describes burning Troy:]

With fire and sworde thus battered lie her Turrets downe to nought.
The walles but late of high renowne lo here their ruinous fall:
The buildings burne, and flashing flame sweepes through the pallas
  al.
Thus every house ful hie it smoakes, of old Assarackes lande:
Ne yet the flames with holdes from spoyle the greedy Victors hand.
The surging smoake, the asure skye, and light hath hid away:
And (as with cloude beset) Troyes Ashes staynes the dusky day . . .

[She foretold it all]

My fyre it is wherwith ye burne, and Parys is the brand
That smoaketh in thy towres (O Troy) the flowre of Phrygian land.
But ay (alas) unhappy age, why did thou yet so sore
Bewayle thy Countries fatall fall, thou knewest it long before?
Behold thy last calamityes, and them bewayle with teeres:
Account as old Troys overturne, and past by many yeares.
I saw the slaughter of the King, and how he lost his life:
By th'aulter side (more mischiefe was) with stroake of Pyrrhus
  knife
When in his hand he wound his lockes, and drew the King to
  grounde,
And hid to hiltes his wicked sword, in deepe and deadly wound.
Which when the gored King had tooke, as willing to bee slayne,
Out of the old mans throate he drew his bloudy blade agayne.
Not pitty of his yeares (alas) in mans extreamest age,
From slaughter might his hand withhold, ne yet his yre asswage:[1]
The Gods are witnes of the same, and eake the sacrifyes
That in his Kingdome holden was, that flat on ground now lies.

[In Act 4 when Hecuba knows that she is to be Ulysses' captive, her
ravings include Pyrrhus:]

But Pyrrhus comes with swiftned pace and thretning browes doth
  wrest.
What staye thou Pyrrhus? strike thy sword now through this
  woful brest,

[1] Cf. II.2.472–96; not a close parallel.

And both at ones the parents of thy fathers wife now slay.
Murderer of age, likes thee her bloud? . . .

(ii)
[Act II]

Chorus

May this be true, or doth the Fable fayne,
When corps is deade the Sprite to live as yet? 1095
When Death our eies with heavy hand doth strain,
And fatall day our leames of light hath shet,
And in the Tombe our ashes once be set,
Hath not the soule likewyse his funerall,
But still (alas) do wretches live in thrall? 1100

Or els doth all at once together die?
And may no part his fatal howre delay.
But with the breath the soule from hence doth flie?
And eke the Cloudes to vanish quite awaye,
As danky shade fleeth from the poale by day?
And may no jote escape from desteny,
When once the brand hath burned the body?

What ever then the ryse of Sunne may see,
And what the West that sets the Sunne doth know,
In all Neptunus raygne what ever bee, 1110
That restless Seas do wash and overflow,
With purple waves stil tombling to and fro,
Age shal consume: each thing that livth shal die,
With swifter race then Pegasus doth flie.

And with what whirle, the twyse sixe signes do flie,
With course as swift as rector of the Spheares,
Doth guide those glistering Globes eternally,
And Hecate her chaunged hornes repeares,
So drauth on death, and life of each thing weares,
And never may the man returne to sight 1120
That once hath felt the stroke of Parcas might.[1]

For as the fume that from the fyre doth passe,
With tourne of hand doth vanish out of sight
And swifter then the Northren Boreas
With whirling blaste and storme of raging might,

---

[1] Cf. III.i.79–80.

Drivth farre away and puttes the cloudes to flight,
So fleeth the sprighte that rules our life away,
And nothing taryeth after dying day.

Swift is the race we ronne, at hand the marke
Lay downe your hope, that wayte here ought to win,   1130
And who dreads ought, cast of thy carefull carke:
Wilt thou it wot what state thou shalt be in,
When dead thou art as thou hadst never bin.
For greedy tyme it doth devoure us all,
The world it swayes to Chaos heape to fall.

Death hurtes the Corpes and spareth not the spright,
And as for all the dennes of Tænare deepe,
With Cerberus kingdome darke that knowes no light,
And streightest gates, that he there sittes to keepe,
They Fancies are that follow folke by sleepe.   1140
Such rumors vayne, but fayned lies they are,
And fables like the dreames in heavy care.

VII. Analogue

From THE ST. ALBAN'S CHRONICLE
in Bodley MS. 462[1]

[A Son meets his Father's Ghost.]

The following things happened round about the present year [1343]
in England. While a certain priest was walking to a church about
three miles distant from the house in which he was staying, he
observed, afar off, at about the third hour of the day, two riders
coming towards him. As soon as he saw them a continual shuddering
and horror invaded him, so that he approached a cross which stood
by the wayside, and embraced it, trembling. When the riders drew
near the said priest recognised his father, who had died fourteen
years previously, leading with him a woman, and carrying before
him on the neck of his horse a boy lying in a cradle.

When he saw this the priest was terrified. The other, noticing

---

[1] The Latin text is given in the Appendix to *The St. Albans Chronicle, 1406–1420*,
ed. V. H. Galbraith, Oxford, 1937, pp. 128–31. The translation is by the present
editor.

it, said as he approached: 'The Lord be with thee, my son; fear not but speak confidently to me.' The priest said, wondering; 'Who art thou, and what dost thou desire?' The other: 'Dost thou not know me?' And the priest: 'Yes indeed; it seems to me that thou art my father.' 'That is true, my son,' he said, 'I am thy father who died fourteen years ago and am now come to speak with thee.' 'And how dost thou fare?', he asked. 'Until now, badly; for I have been in great and hard torments. But now I am freed from them all, and have no other punishment but to serve this woman and to carry this boy, who is very heavy. But both from these and all other pains I shall be released by God's mercy on All Souls' Day after the feast of All Saints.'

The priest said to him: 'Who now are this woman and that infant?' he replied: 'She was once our lady-mistress, who as thou knowest died six years past.' Then the priest: 'I pray thee let me see her face.' He answered: 'It is not expedient, my son, for thee to see it, for she has been placed in great and hard torments and her face is horrible.' Said the priest: 'Who then is that boy?' 'Her son,' he said, 'And I must tell thee about it. My lord loved me much and placed great trust in me. He was a faithful soldier and wealthy, and set out on pilgrimage to Jerusalem, first committing to my care all his possessions, his house and his wife. But after he had set forth a certain soldier fell in love with his wife, and was loved by her. When they dared not fulfil their desires because of me, they spoke to me flatteringly, and, broken in will by that and their gifts, I consented and let them come together. She conceived by the soldier and bore this son, who soon after birth died unbaptised. After I had confessed all these things I did penance and obtained forgiveness from my lord, and, as I said, I shall be freed from all these pains after Mass on All Souls' Day. If however the woman had not been confessed before she died, she would certainly have been condemned to Hell without end. But now she is tormented with great and hard pains until she be completely purged of her sins, and then she will be saved. And God does this because His mercy is great.'

Then said the priest: 'Where, or in what pains are repentant souls after they go out from the body?' His father said to him: 'If only it were permissible for me to tell thee!'. Said the priest: 'Who will ever give thee leave?' But he answered; 'I shall not conceal from thee, my son, that for all men from their birth are deputed personal angels, one for each man, who are with them everywhere until their deaths, and report to God their good deeds or their bad. And he is a happy man whose holy conversation delights the angel who is with him; for when his soul shall go out from his body his angel will present it to God with rejoicing. He who sins and makes confession before he dies, if, prevented by death, he cannot do his penance, his angel will be with him in Purgatory to console him, nor will he be troubled by an immeasurable fierceness of anguish. And God acts thus out of His great kindness. For in Hell there is no consolation, but eternal confusion. And whosoever is plunged therein does not come forth again. Those again who are perfectly righteous, as soon as they depart from the body, go to their rest. The utterly evil on the other hand must proceed straightway into Hell. The less perfect who, prevented by death, cannot do their penance, will be purged in Purgatory until they are completely cleansed, some more heavily, some more lightly, according to their works; and being thus cleansed they will go to their rest.'

After this he said to the priest: 'Lift up thine eyes.' And he lifted them up and saw all that region and the neighbouring vale filled with fire and sulphur, and on the other side with hail and darkness, snow and ice and terrible cold. And the place was filled with men who alternated their anguish, going now from fire to frost, now from cold to fire; and some were clad in secular garb and some with white cowls, and some with black, looking like wild animals. Some also were naked and black, some half-black and half-white. From the mouths of some sulphurous flame came out and went in again, and they cried out with a great howling: 'Woe, woe, woe, hard are our torments. Why ever were we born?' And again, consoling themselves they cried: 'Thou art just, O Lord, good, pious and numberless are thy mercies; and thy judgements are true and holy and full of mercy, who dost not wish us to perish eternally. So thou purgest us with such torments because when we could we did not wish to cleanse ourselves with lighter penances.' And once more they called out, saying: 'We give thanks to thee, Lord Jesus Christ, who hast redeemed us with thy blood and will give us cooling when thou shalt so wish.'

When the said priest saw and heard these things he groaned and said to his father: 'Hard is this place. Woe to its inhabitants!' And his father: 'It is so,' he said, 'but Hell is harder. For this will have an end; but in Hell are perpetual grief and eternal horror.'

The priest said: 'What are those people clothed and those others unclothed? I should like to know the differences between them.' His father replied: 'Those who are clad in secular dress are men who were righteous in their time, who gave of their riches to the poor and lived soberly and correctly with their wives and also with their fellowmen; but who were negligent in small matters and died not fully purified, so they must be cleansed; and then they will enter into the joy of their Lord. Those who are clad in black and white were vowed to religion, but lived more neglectfully than was fitting, so they do penance here so that when completely purged they may go to their rest. Those who are naked, or half black or half white, are men of all professions who lived shamefully and did not repent until their last moments (*in extremis*); so they are tormented here until they become wholly white. But those from whose nostrils and mouth proceeds sulphurous fire were men of the worst possible behaviour who sinned against nature and committed flagrant sins with the beasts; but nevertheless in the end, coming to themselves they groaned in remorse, confessed their sins, and undertook penance. For God, who is benign and merciful in compassion for their sufferings, did not despise the tears of penitents, but ordered them to be punished here until all the rust of sinners is consumed with flame of pains. And nevertheless their angels are with them and console them. Also they themselves are comforted by hope since they know that they will be saved.' Then the priest: 'Why then has man been made?' And again he asked: 'Of what value to the dead are the alms and oblations made for them?' he answered: 'For some they are of much value; for some a little; for others none at all. They are of great value to those who while they lived gave alms to others freely and devotedly. But for those who did nothing for others they are of little or no value.'

The priest then asked: 'Are there souls in Purgatory elsewhere in England as well as here?' He replied: 'Also in Derbyshire and round London, but not so many as here, except on the mountain of Monseya. There are innumerable souls there, and shall be until they are cleansed from every stain.'

And the priest asked: 'Where is my mother?'. He replied: 'She is in May.' Hearing this the priest fortified himself with the sign of the Cross, thinking that all he saw must be a phantasm. His father asked: 'Why dost thou cross thyself, my son? What dost thou think May is?' The priest: 'A month of the year.' And the other: 'I speak not of that, but of an island in the sea near Scotland, where there are very frequent storms. And just as when she was here she lived in the heat of lust, so there she is in great torments because, unknown to me, she led a most depraved life. But because when dying she confessed her sins, she is placed there until she be purified, which is done by the blessed mercy of Jesus; otherwise she would burn in Hell with the Devil.'

The priest asked: 'Do you know what we living men do on earth?' He said: 'We do not know what you do on earth unless the angels who are around us will tell us, or the souls that come day by day inform us of it. Therefore, my son, beware that thou comest not to a more grievous state, and do penance while thou art alive; and pray for me.' Thus saying, all the aforementioned vision vanished. But these things happened near the country-seat of Braham in the county of ——.[1]

VIII. Analogue

From
TARLTONS NEWES OUT OF
PURGATORIE
Anon. (*c.* 1590)

Tarltons Newes out of Purgatorie. Onelye such a jest as his Jigge, fit for Gentlemen to laugh at an houre, &c. Published by an old companion of his, Robin Goodfellow. Printed for Edward White.

[The Introduction]

Sorrowing, as most men doo, for the death of Richard Tarlton, in that his particular losse was a generall lament to all that coveted either to satisfie their eies with his clownish gesture, or their ears with his witty jestes. The woonted desire to see plaies left me in that although I saw as rare showes, and heard as lofty verse, yet I injoyed not those wonted sports that flowed from him, as from a fountaine of pleasing and merry conceits. For although he was only superficially seene in learning, having no more but a bare insight into the Latin tung, yet he had such a prompt wit, that he seemed to have that *salem ingenij*, which Tullie so highly commends in his *Oratorie*.[2] Well, howsoever, either naturall or artificiall, or both, he was a mad merry companion, desired and loved of all[3] amongst the rest of whose wel wishers myselfe, being not the least, after his death I mourned in conceite, and absented myselfe from all plaies, as wanting that merrye Roscius of plaiers, that famosed all comedies so with his pleasant and extemporall invention; yet at last, as the longest sommers day hath his night, so this dumpe had an end: and

---

[1] The name of the county is left blank in the MS. The place may have been Bramham, ten miles north-east of Leeds, where there is still a fine park and a partly seventeenth-century mansion. Local feeling might explain the allusion to Derbyshire! But that county was always regarded as a wild region, with its Peak and its caverns.

[2] Lib. i., c. 25.

[3] Cf. V.1.189–97.

forsooth upon Whitson Monday last I would needs to the Theatre[1]
to a play, where when I came, I founde such concourse of unrulye
people, that I thought it better solitary to walk in the fields, then to
intermeddle myselfe amongst such a great presse. Feeding mine
humour with this fancie I stept by dame Anne of Cleeves well, and
went by the backside of Hogsdon, where, finding the sun to be hotte,
and seeing a faire tree that had a coole shade, I sat me downe to
take the aire, where after I had rested me a while, I fell asleepe.
As thus I lay in a slumber, me thought I sawe one attired in russet,
with a buttond cap on his head, a great bag by his side, and a strong
bat in his hand, so artificially attired for a clowne as I began to call
Tarltons woonted shape to remembrance, as he drew more neere
and he came within the compasse of mine eie, to judge it was no
other but the verye ghoast of Richard Tarlton, which pale and wan,
sat him down by me on the grasse. I that knew him to be dead, at
this sodaine sight fell into a great feare, in somuch that I sweat in my
sleep; which he perceiving, with his woonted countenance full of
smiles, began to comfort me thus: What, olde acquaintance, a man
or a mouse? Hast thou not heard me verifie, that a souldier is a
souldier if he have but a blew hose on his head? feare not me, man,
I am but Dick Tarlton, that could quaint it in the court, and clowne
it on the stage; that had a quarte of wine for my friend, and a swoord
for my foe, who hurt none being alive, and will not prejudice any
being dead: for although thou see me heere in likenes of a spirite, yet
thinke me to bee one of those *Familiares Lares* that were rather pleasantly disposed then endued with any hurtfull influence, as Hob
Thrust, Robin Goodfellow and such like spirites, as they tearme
them of the buttery, famozed in every olde wives chronicle for their
mad merrye prankes. Therefore sith my appearance to thee is in
a resemblance of a spirite, think that I am as pleasant a goblin as
the rest, and will make thee as merry before I part, as ever Robin
Goodfellow made the cuntry wenches at their Cream-bowles. With
this he drewe more neere me, and I, starting backe, cried out:—
In nomine Jesu, avoid Sathan, for ghost thou art none, but a very
divell[2] for the soules of them which are departed, if the sacred
principles of theologie be true, never returne into the world againe
till the generall resurrection,[3] for either are they plast in heaven,
from whence they came not to intangle themselues with other cares,
but sit continuallye before the seat of the Lambe, singing Alleluia[4]

---

[1] A playhouse so called, situated in Shoreditch. In Nash's *Pierce Penilesse*, Tarlton
is mentioned as playing there. [Note by Halliwell]

[2] Cf. Horatio's fear, I.1.127, I.4.69, and Hamlet's doubt, I.4.39–44.

[3] So Hamlet, III.1.79–80.

[4] *Revelation*, Ch. 19.

to the highest; or else they are in hell. And this is a profound and
certain aphorisme, *Ab inferis nulla est redemptio*. Upon these conclusive
premises, depart from me, Sathan, the resemblance of whomsoever
thou doost carrye. At this, pitching his staffe downe on the end,
and crossing one leg over another, he answered thus:—why you
horson dunce, think you to set Dick Tarlton *non plus* with your
aphorismes? no, I have yet left one chapter of choplogick[1] to
tewslite[2] you withall, that were you as good as George à Greene[3]
I would not take the foile at your hands, and that is this, I perceive
by your arguments your inward opinion, and by your wise discretion
what pottage you love: I see no sooner a rispe[4] at the house end or a
maipole[5] before the doore, but I cry there is a paltry alehouse: and
as soon as I heare the principles of your religion, I can saye, Oh,
there is a Calvinist; what, doo you make heaven and hell *contraria
immediata*—so contrarie, that there is no meane betwixt them, but
that either a mans soule must in post haste goe presently to God, or
else with a whirlewind and a vengeance goe to the divell! yes, yes,
my good brother, there is *quoddam tertium*, a third place that all our
great grandmothers have talkt of, that Dant hath so learnedlye
writ of, and that is purgatorie. What, sir, are we wiser then all our
forefathers? and they not onlye feared that place in life, but found it
after their death: or els was there much land and annuall pensions
given in vaine to morrowe-masse priests for dirges, trentals and such
like decretals of devotion, whereby the soules in purgatorie were
the sooner advanced into the quiet estate of heaven? Nay, more,
how many popes and holy bishops of Rome whose cannons cannot
erre, have taught us what this purgatory is: and yet if thou wert so
incredulous that thou wouldest neither beleeve our olde beldames,
nor the good Bishops: yet take Dick Tarlton once for thine authour,
who is now come from purgatory, and if any upstart Protestant
deny, if thou hast no place of Scripture ready to confirme it, say as
Pithagoras' schollers did *Ipse dixit* and to all bon[6] companions it
shall stand for a principle. I could not but smile at the madde merrye
doctrine of my freend Richard, and therefore taking hart at grasse,[7]
drawing more neere him, I praied him to tell me what Purgatory is,

[1] 'Will you chop with me? *voulez vous troquer avec moi?* or thus, in a burlesk sense,
as to chop logick with one, *disputer avec quêcun*.'—*Miege*. [H.]

[2] To perplex. [H.]

[3] An allusion to the old play of 'George a Greene, the Pinner of Wakefield,' 1599,
ascribed by some to Robert Greene; or the old prose history upon which that play
is founded. [H.]

[4] A branch. [H.] Perhaps 'wisp', a bunch of hay or greenery as an ale sign.

[5] The ale-stake, frequently explained as may-pole in the old glossaries. [H.]

[6] boon—convivial.

[7] taking heart of grace—plucking up my courage.

and what they be that are resident there; as one willing to doo me
such a favour, he sat him downe, and began thus:—

[The burlesque account need not trouble us.]

IX. Possible Historical Source

THE MURDER OF
FRANCESCO MARIA I,
DUKE OF URBINO

A. [Luigi Gonzaga protests his innocence of the Duke of
Urbino's murder.][1]

. . . It does not seem likely to me (if it be true, as I have heard, that
his late Excellency was already sick of an infirmity which was
regarded as serious before the barber arrived) that the Secretary[2]
would not have wished to see the illness diminished before placing
himself in such danger.[3] And I cannot imagine how in a serious
illness occasion can have occurred to bathe the Duke's ears many
times (that is, if the rumour be true which is spread abroad, that the
barber had the opportunity to give him the poison many times
through the ears), because in a grave and dangerous sickness it does
not seem probable that the ears would be bathed much and often.
And before going to Venice this last time he had never done such a
thing.

Nor could it be supposed that I might have known about, or
instigated it, since I had not seen him [the Duke] for two years.
Although he was here twice during these past two years, that was
during the time when I was with the Emperor's army.

B. [Pietro Aretino apologizes to Luigi Gonzaga.]

To Luigi Gonzaga,

Do not believe, Marquis, that my mind has
ever inclined in the least to the belief that the villainy which has
murdered not only the Duke of Urbino but the reputation of mankind, the oracle of the soldier and the grace of speech, could have

---

[1] From *L'Avvelenatura di Francesco Maria, Duca di Urbino*, by Elisa Viani, Mantua,
1902.

[2] Probably Lionardi, the Duke's confidant, who accused Gonzaga.

[3] By letting the barber work on his master; but he would be a barber-surgeon,
used to nursing sick people.

sprung from you. Of course I am not a judge in such a case. It could however, well be, that on hearing of the sad fate of the great Francesco Maria, there fell from my mouth some words against so cruel an excess; for the effect of terrible things presents itself with so horrible an aspect that in that moment the heart does not know how to preserve its customary caution. On the contrary, overwhelmed by the iniquity of the deed, the mind grows dark in the same way as when thunder shakes the soul. It is very true, also, that just as we laugh at a rumour which makes us fear, so we repent of the falsity that makes us talk scandal. As to prejudicing you, however, my tongue is innocent; nor would I injure the sincerity of your nature with so malign a presumption.

But what cannot a wicked man do when he resolves to exercise his criminal will on another's head? Certainly at that point he puts aside all respect for God and fear of Justice, and, set out of tune in his entire body and soul, he behaves just as if neither God nor Justice could injure him either in soul or body. If it happens that the severity of the one and the scourge of the other confine him in prison, then, putting on audacity in his baseness, when the rope is nearer than death, he not only confesses to the crime at the approach of torture, hoping that in the interval between admission of guilt and the penalty he may escape it, but also, believing that a sin carried out at the instigation of another may be excusable, he frequently tries to shift the burden of the crime on to the shoulders of his betters. . . .

So do not be disturbed. And if it happens that the teeth of any jesting word bite the finger-tips of your honour, do not take it for mine, seeing that I am ever unwilling to think that the magnanimous blood of the Gonzagas, so abundant always in virtue and glory, could lack my devotion.

From Venice, 21 August 1538[1]

[1] From P. Aretino, *Il Secondo Libro delle Lettere*, ed. F. Nicolini, Bari, 1916, Part i, CDX, pp. 99–100. The date must be wrong; probably written in 1539. On 1 April 1540 Aretino sent the Duke of Mantua (another Gonzaga) a copy of a letter he had written to Luigi Gonzaga declaring that he did not believe him to blame for the death of the Duke of Urbino (Letter DXV, p. 242).

X. Possible Source

From
EULOGIES OF MEN FAMOUS FOR WARLIKE VIRTUE
by Paolo Giovio,[1] translated by the editor

None of the great generals is portrayed more elegantly and more faithfully in a picture according to his true likeness than this Duke of Urbino, who with his arms and embellishments, and the triple insignia of military command is seen as depicted by the hand of the great painter Titian. The son of Sr Giovanni della Rovere, lord of Sinigallia and Prefect of Rome (who was blood-brother of Pope Julius II) and of the lady Joanna, daughter of Federigo, Duke of Urbino, he earned his adoption into the family of Montefeltro by Duke Guido Ubaldo, his mother's brother (whom destiny had given no children), and to be made by the latter heir to his estate. It can therefore easily be believed that in his honourable temper he mingled the force and ready energy of his father's race with the valiant wisdom and discipline in war characteristic of the house of Montefeltro, so that he might carry off the highest military honours.

While yet a youth he bore himself in arms in such a way that, almost before he became a soldier, he was made Captain General of his uncle's forces in the war whereby Cervia, Ravenna, Ariminio and Faenza, occupied by the Venetians, were restored to the Church. Not long afterwards, the French war broke out owing to the summoning of the Council by means of which the King of France, ever vigorous in arms, freed himself to destroy completely the authority of the Pope.

In that war the Duke of Urbino, with inferior forces, was defeated and deprived of his quarters by the great general Trivulzio, and Bologna, which was badly defended by Cardinal Alidosi fell once more into the hands of its ancient rulers, the Bentivogli. The Duke's great soul could not endure such a disgrace, and filled with grief for his broken army and the lost city, he slew the Cardinal, author of so much evil, when he came into his presence at Ravenna.

This homicide, committed on a prelate—even though he had deserved it for his misconduct—so altered the Pope's attitude that Duke Francesco Maria thought of offering his services to the French

---

[1] Pauli Iovii ... *Elogia Virorum bellica virtute illustrium, Septem libris jam olim ab Authore comprehensa, Et nunc ex eiusdem Musae ad vivum expressis Imaginibus exornata,* Basil, 1575 edn.

King. But not long afterwards the terrible anger of Julius cooled when after the Battle of Ravenna which drove the French out of Italy he was crowned with victory.

[Leo X proved a dangerous enemy to the Duke, who was deprived of his possessions in Umbria, which he did not regain until after the death of that Pope.]

These great troubles in the wars made him so practical a soldier that the fame of his valour grew and was confirmed until both by the Florentines (formerly his enemies) and by the Venetians, he was appointed supreme commander. When he was made Captain General of the Venetian army, he began, as was required by the times and the customs of a most prudent Signoria, to temper the ancient ardour of his warlike spirit with a valuable admixture of just and sagacious gravity when it now seemed to him that the most courageous and hitherto undefeated infantry of foreign nations might be withstood much more surely by holding back rather than by provoking them to battle. For the Venetian nobles, having learned that lesson twice already through the rashness and rout of the Liviano, appreciated a captain like Q. Fabius much more than one like M. Marcellus. The Duke Francesco Maria therefore earned the reputation of serving the Signoria most usefully if he lost nothing and if he did not risk the uncertainties of a battle in which he might be defeated; if he mocked the fury of the enemy by means of skirmishes and taking up the best possible fortified positions; if he continually harassed them when they were in need of money and victuals; though he was ready to fight a pitched battle when he believed it necessary.

By such artifices, therefore, against the opinion of a few who rashly thought that the brute strength of foreign troops was enough to ensure victory, he saved all Italy by his distinguished conduct. Francesco Sforza was restored to his hereditary princedom, and the tranquil peace was established by which we still breathe. In this peace Duke Francesco Maria in his every thought desired nothing else but that the Christian Princes might agree together to turn their just and invincible arms against the Turks.

In this most honourable purpose, however, he was snatched away, not by natural destiny, but through the malice of a few men who, it is said, had him given poison; as can be seen from the certain evidence of a law-suit and by the confession that this great crime had been committed.[1] He left by inheritance not only the state of

---

[1] Francesco Sansovino, *Dell'Origine delle Case Illustri d'Italia*,1582, ended his account: 'Towards the end of the year 1538 he died at Pesaro on 21 October, poisoned through the hatred and malice of his enemies. Guido Baldo II . . . ruled after his father. Universally praised by everyone for the magnificence and splendour

Urbino but also the Generalship of the Venetian Signoria to the Duke Guido Ubaldo, who is esteemed by everyone for his meritorious virtues.

by Antonio Francesco Rainieri

The mace from Hercules, from Mars the sword,
 Thy buckler by Bellona's self was given;
 And Jove bestowed the splendour bright of heaven
Which by the wondering world is so adored.
The truth transparent of thy eloquence
 Makes all minds swift and ready to thy will.
 Thy valour is a testimony still
To the great name, thy prime inheritance.
Thou quellest monsters, and the hostile press
 Cleavest with steel; and with unconquered pace
Returnest thy old kingdom to possess:
 Blest son of Jove, who godlike dost outrace
The ancient heroes, and transcend'st no less
 The moderns with thy power and wisdom's grace.

XI. Possible Source

From
THE TRAGEDIE OF DIDO
QUEENE OF CARTHAGE
by Christopher Marlowe and Thomas Nash (1594)

The Tragedie of Dido Queene of Carthage. Played by the Children of her Maiesties Chappell. Written by Christopher Marlowe, and Thomas Nash. Gent. Printed by the Widdowe Orwin, for Thomas Woodcocke . . . 1594.

[Aeneas describes to Dido and her household how Troy fell and how he escaped.]

---

of his building as of his every other action. A lover of letters and music. And although he was not found in person at the wars, he was nevertheless of excellent judgement in the requirements of arms, and many men thronged to his Court for his decisions in disputes about duelling and arms; for he loved and favoured greatly men who were excellent in them.'

By this the Campe was come unto the walles,
And through the breach did march into the streetes,
Where meeting with the rest, kill, kill they cryed.
Frighted with this confused noyse, I rose,
And looking from a turret, might behold
Yong infants swimming in their parents bloud,
Headles carkasses piled up in heapes,
Virgins halfe dead dragged by their golden haire,   490
And with maine force flung on a ring of pikes,
Old men with swords thrust through their aged sides,
Kneeling for mercie to a Greekish lad,
Who with steele Pol-axes dasht out their braines.
Then buckled I mine armour, drew my sword,
And thinking to goe downe, came *Hectors* ghost
With ashie visage, blewish sulphure eyes,
His armes torne from his shoulders, and his breast
Furrowd with wounds, and that which made me weepe,
Thongs at his heeles, by which *Achilles* horse   500
Drew him in triumph through the Greekish Campe,
Burst from the earth, crying, *Æneas* flye,
Troy is afire, the Grecians have the towne.
   DIDO.   O *Hector* who weepes not to heare thy name?
   ÆN.   Yet flung I forth, and desperate of my life,
Ran in the thickest throngs, and with this sword
Sent many of their savadge ghosts to hell.
At last came *Pirrhus* fell and full of ire,
His harnesse dropping bloud, and on his speare
The mangled head of *Priams* yongest sonne,[1]   510
And after him his band of Mirmidons,
With balles of wilde fire in their murdering pawes,
Which made the funerall flame that burnt faire *Troy*:
All which hemd me about, crying, this is he.
   DIDO.   Ah, how could poore *Æneas* scape their hands?
   ÆN.   My mother *Venus* jealous of my health,
Convaid me from their crooked nets and bands:
So I escapt the furious *Pirrhus* wrath:
Who then ran to the pallace of the King,
And at *Joves* Altar finding *Priamus*,   520
About whose withered necke hung *Hecuba*,
Foulding his hand in hers, and joyntly both
Beating their breasts and falling on the ground,
He with his faulchions poynt raisde up at once,
And with *Megeras* eyes stared in their face,

---

[1] Cf. II.2.457–63.

   G

Threatning a thousand deaths at every glaunce.
To whom the aged King thus trembling spoke:
Achilles sonne, remember what I was,
Father of fiftie sonnes, but they are slaine,
Lord of my fortune, but my fortunes turnd,   530
King of this Citie, but my *Troy* is fired,
And now am neither father, Lord, nor King:
Yet who so wretched but desires to live?
O let me live, great *Neoptolemus.*
Not mov'd at all, but smiling at his teares,
This butcher whil'st his hands were yet held up,
Treading upon his breast, strooke off his hands.
  DIDO. O end *Æneas,* I can heare no more.
  ÆN. At which the franticke Queene leapt on his face,
And in his eyelids hanging by the nayles,   540
A little while prolong'd her husbands life:
At last the souldiers puld her by the heeles,
And swong her howling in the emptie ayre,
Which sent an eccho to the wounded King:
Whereat he lifted up his bedred lims,
And would have grappeld with *Achilles* sonne,
Forgetting both his want of strength and hands,
Which he disdaining whiskt his sword about,
And with the wind thereof the King fell downe:[1]
Then from the navell to the throat at once,   550
He ript old *Priam*: at whose latter gaspe
Joves marble statue gan to bend the brow,
As lothing *Pirrhus* for this wicked act:
Yet he undaunted tooke his fathers flagge,
And dipt it in the old Kings chill cold bloud,
And then in triumph ran into the streetes,
Through which he could not passe for slaughtred men:
So leaning on his sword he stood stone still,
Viewing the fire wherewith rich *Ilion* burnt.[2]

---

[1] Cf. II.2.476-8.

[2] Compare Virgil's account (*Aeneid*, II.469 ff.) in which he describes Pyrrhus 'in his glory, gleaming with spear and sword, and with all the brilliance of steel. . . . But the palace within is a confused scene of shrieking and piteous disorder. . . . The terror-stricken matrons are running to and fro through the spacious courts. . . . On presses Pyrrhus with his father's might. . . . I saw Hecuba and her hundred daughters-in-law and Priam at the altar, polluting with his blood the flames he had himself made holy. . . . Here about the altar Hecuba and her daughters, all helpless, huddled together and clinging to the statues of the gods, were sitting . . .' [Priam had donned his armour but she forced him to take sanctuary with her by the altar. Pyrrhus came and slew their son Polites before his parents' eyes. Priam]

XII. Probable Source

From
A WARNING FOR FAIRE WOMEN
Anon.[1] (1599)

Enter the Mayor of Rochester, with Browne, and Officers.

BARNES. As I take it, maister Mayor of Rochester.

MAYOR. The same good master *Barnes*.

BARNES. What happie fortune sent you here to Woolwich: That
yet your company may give us comfort, in this sad time?

MAYOR. Beleeve me sad in deed, and verie sad,
Sir the Councels warrant lately came to me
About the search, for one Captaine *George Browne*,
As it should seeme suspected for this murther,
Whom in my search I hapt to apprehend.
And hearing that the bodies of the murdred
Remained here, I thought it requisite,
To make this in my way unto the Court,
Now going thither with the prisoner.

BARNES. Beleeve me sir ye have done right good service,
And shewne your selfe a painfull Gentleman,
And shall no doubt deserve well of the state.

M. JAMES. No doubt you shall, and I durst assure you so,
The Councel wil accept well of the same.

BARNES. Good maister Mayor this wretched man of mine,
Is not yet dead: looke you where he sits,
But past all sense, and labouring to his end.

'hurled at him a dart unwarlike, unwounding, which the ringing brass at once
shook off, and left hanging helplessly from the end of the shield's boss . . . [Pyrrhus
then slew the old man] . . . he dragged him to the very altar, palsied and sliding in
a pool of his son's blood, wreathed his left hand in his hair, and with his right
flashed forth and sheathed in his side the sword to the hilt. Such was the end of
Priam's fortunes, such the fatal lot that fell on him, with Troy blazing and Perga-
mus in ruins before his eyes—upon him, once the haughty ruler of those many
nations and kingdoms, the sovereign lord of Asia.' (Conington's translation.)

[1] Title page: '*A Warning for Faire Women. Containing, The most tragicall and lamentable murther of Master George Sanders of London Marchant, nigh Shooters hill. Consented
unto By his owne wife, acted by M. Browne, Mistris Drewry and Trusty Roger agents therin:
with their severall ends. As it hath beene lately diverse times acted by the right Honorable, the
Lord Chamberlaine his Servantes. Printed at London by Valentine Sims for William Aspley
1599.*'

MAYOR.   Alas poore wretch.

BARNES.   Is this the *Browne* that is suspected to have done
The murther? a goodly man beleeve me:
Too faire a creature for so fowle an act.

BROWNE.   My name is *Browne* sir.

M. JAMES.   I know you well, your fortunes have beene
Faire, as any Gentlemans of your repute.
But *Browne*, should you be guiltie of this fact,
As this your flight hath given shrewde suspition,
Oh *Browne*, your hands have done the bloodiest deed
That ever was committed.

BROWNE.   He doth not live dare charge me with it.

M. JAMES.   Pray God there be not.

MAYOR.   Sergeants bring him neere: see if this poore soule know
him.

BARNES.   It cannot be: these two dayes space
He knew no creature.

BROWNE.   Swounds, lives the villaine yet?   [*aside.*
O how his very sight affrights my soule!
His very eies will speake had he no tongue,
And will accuse me.

BARNES.   See how his wounds break out afresh in bleeding.[1]

M. JAMES.   He stirs himselfe.

MAYOR.   He openeth his eyes.

BARNES.   See how he lookes upon him.

BROWNE.   I gave him fifteene wounds,   [*aside.*
Which now be fifteene mouthes that doe accuse me,
In ev'ry wound there is a bloudy tongue,
Which will all speake, although he hold his peace,
By a whole Jury I shalbe accusde.

BARNES.   *John*, dost thou heare? knowest thou this man?

BEANE.   Yea, this is he that murdred me and M. Sanders.[2]
                                        [*He sinckes downe.*

M. JAMES.   O hold him up.

MAYOR.   *John* comfort thy selfe.

M. JAMES.   Bow him, give him ayre.

BARNES.   No he is dead.

BROWNE.   Me thinks he is so fearefull in my sight,
That were he now but where I saw him last,
For all this world I would not looke on him.

BARNES.   The wondrous worke of God, that the poore creature,

---

[1] As they were supposed to do in the presence of the murderer.

[2] So Desdemona comes back to life, but not to accuse Othello. She tries to save
her murderer. (*Oth.* V.2.120–3.)

not speaking for two dayes, yet now should speake to accuse this
man, and presently yeeld up his soule.

    M. JAMES.   Tis very strange, and the report thereof
Can seeme no lesse unto the Lords.

    MAYOR.   Sergeants, away, prepare you for the court,
And I will follow you immediatly.

    BARNES.   Sure the revealing of this murther's strange.

    M. JAMES.   It is so sir: but in the case of blood,
Gods justice hath bin stil myraculous.[1]

    MAYOR.   I have heard it told, that digging up a grave.
Wherein a man had twenty yeeres bin buryed,
By finding of a naile knockt in the scalpe,
By due enquirie who was buried there,
The murther yet at length did come to light.

    BARNES.   I have heard it told, that once a traveller,
Being in the hands of him that murdred him,
Told him, the fearne that then grew in the place,
If nothing else, yet that would sure reveale him:
And seven yeares after, being safe in London,
There came a sprigge of fearne borne by the wind,
Into the roome where as the murtherer was,
At sight whereof he sodainely start up,
And then reveald the murder.

    M. JAMES.   Ile tell you (sir) one more to quite your tale,
A woman that had made away her husband,
And sitting to behold a tragedy
At Linne a towne in Norffolke,
Acted by Players travelling that way,
Wherein a woman that had murtherd hers
Was ever haunted with her husbands ghost:
The passion written by a feeling pen,
And acted by a good Tragedian,
She was so mooved with the sight thereof,
As she cryed out, the Play was made by her,
And openly confesst her husbands murder.[2]

    BARNES.   How ever theirs, Gods name be praisde for this:
You M. *Mayor* I see must to the Court:
I pray you do my duety to the Lords.

    MAYOR.   That will I sir.

    M. JAMES.   Come, Ile go along with you.   [*Exeunt.*

---

[1] Cf. II.2.601–2.
[2] Cf. II.2.596–600.

XIII. Analogue

From
THE CONFLICT OF CONSCIENCE
by Nathaniel Woods (1581)[1]

An excellent new Commedie. Intituled: The Conflict of Conscience. Contayninge, The most lamentable Hystorie, of the desperation of Frauncis Spera, who forsooke the trueth of Gods Gospell, for feare of the losse of life and worldly goodes. Compiled by Nathaniell Woodes. Minister in Norwich. . . . At London. Printed by Richard Bradocke . . . 1581.

PHILOLOGUS.   Oh would my soule were sunke in hell, so body were in grounde! 2053
That angrie God now hath his will, who sought mee to confounde.
THEOLOGUS.   Oh say not so Philologus, for God is gracious,
And to forgive the penitent, his mercy is plentious.
Do you not know that all the earth with mercy doth abound,
And though the sinnes of all the world uppon one man were layde,
If he one only sparke of grace or mercy once had found, 2060
His wickednes could not him harme? wherefore be not dismayde,
Christes death alone for all your sinnes, a perfect raunsome payde . . .

PHIL.   But I alas, am reprobate, God doth my soule reprove. 2116
Moreover, I will say with tongue what so you wyll require,
My harte I feele with blasphemy and cursing is repleate.
THEOL.   Then pray with us, as Christ us taught, we doo you all desire.
PHIL.   To pray with lips unto your God, you shall mee soone intreate.
My spirit to Sathan is in thrall, I can it not thence get . . .

---

[1] Text from *MalSoc* edn. 1952, but with punctuation somewhat modernized. The original title page showed how the eighteen characters could be played by six actors.

EUSEBIUS.   God shall renue your spirit againe, pray onely as you can,
And to assist you in the same, we pray ech Christian man.

PHIL.   O God which dwellest in the Heavens, and art our father deare,
Thy holy name throughout the world be ever sainctified,   2129
The kingdome of thy word and spirit uppon us rule might beare,
Thy will in earth, as by thy saincts in heaven be ratified,
Our dayly bread, we thee beseech, O Lord for us provide,
Our sinnes remit (Lord unto us) as we ech man forgive,
Let not tentation us assayle, in all evill us releeve. Amen.

THEOL.   The Lord be praysed, who hath at length thy spirit mollified.
These are not tokens unto us of your reprobation.
You morne with teares, and sue for grace, wherefore be certified,
That God in mercy giveth eare unto your supplication,   2139
Wherfore dispayre not thou at all of thy soules preservation,
And say not with a desperat heart, that God against thee is,
He will no doubt, these paynes once past, receive you into blisse.

PHIL.   No, no, my friends, you only heare and see the outward part,
Which though you thinke they have don wel, it booteth not at all.
My lippes have spoke the wordes in deede, but yet I feele my heart
With cursing is replenished, with rancor, spight, and gall,
Neither do I your Lord and God in hart my father call,
But rather seeke his holy name for to blaspheame and cursse.
My state therfore doth not amend, but waxe still worse and worse.   2150
I am secluded cleane from grace, my heart is hardened quight,
Wherefore you do your labour loose, and spend your breth in vayne.

EUS.   Oh say not so Philologus, but let your heart be pight
Uppon the mercyes of the Lord, and I you assertayne,
Remission of your former sinnes you shall at last obtayne:
God hath it sayde (who cannot lye) at whatsoever time
A sinner shall from heart repent, I will remitt his cryme...

PHIL.   The healthfull neede not Phisicks art, and ye which
    are all haile,   2174
Can give good counsell to the sick, their sicknesse to eschew:
But here alas, confusion, and hell, doth mee assaile,
And that all grace from me is reft, I finde it to be true.
My hart is steele, so that no faith can from the same insue.
I can conceive no hope at all, of pardon or of grace,
But out, alas, Confusion is alway before my face . . .

EUS.   We have good hope Philologus, of your salvation
    doubtlesse.   2194
PHIL.   What your hope is concerning mee, I utterly
    contempne.
My Conscience, which for thousands stand, as guiltie mee
    condemne. . . .

XIV. Probable Historical Allusions

A. From C.S.P. FOREIGN, ELIZABETH, 1588, JULY–DECEMBER

[On the accession of Christian IV (aged 19) Daniel Rogers
was sent to pay Queen Elizabeth's respects. He was lodged in the
Castle at Elsinore, 'unequalled in Europe, for situation, magnificence,
force, and revenues'.]

'Had audience on the 7th (July, Sunday) . . . The King, with his
second brother, Ulric, attended by many guards and gentlemen,
after the salutations desired him to accompany him to the chapel,
it being then 9 o'clock. The King gave him always the right hand,
saying that his father had always done so. The sermon and prayers
lasted an hour and a half. Afterwards had public audience with the
Queen his mother in the presence chamber, the King, the four
Governors and Rammell attending her. . . .' 'The Queen . . . is a
right virtuous and godly princess, which very severely and with
great wisdom ruleth her children.'

[Rogers sends his report by a messenger] 'Hopes he may pass
safely, for the seas are very full of pirates, and few or none from hence
adventure by the long seas to England.' (July 24. pp. 75–6)

[He mentions George Rosenkrantz of Rosenholm, Master of the
Palace, Axel Guildenstern of Lyngbye, Viceroy of Norway, and
Peter Guildenstern, Marshal of Denmark.]

B. From C.S.P. DOMESTIC, ELIZABETH, 1598–1600

[Rumours in 1598]

June 4/14. John Petit to Peter Halms, from Antwerp. '. . . If I were not acquainted with Scottish brags, I might believe England was already more than half theirs. They say that the King of Denmark's brother, a lusty young fellow, is to bring men from Denmark to do wonders in England; that the Queen, having promised the King of Scots, at his marriage with the Dane, to declare him her successor, she must perform it; and that the Dane will demand a certain old payment which England was accustomed to give Denmark.' (p. 59)

C. From C.S.P. DOMESTIC, ELIZABETH, 1598–1600

[Christian IV and the English mariners.]

1599. July 2/12. From the Mayor and seven Aldermen of Kingston-upon-Hull to Robert Cecil. Divers merchants and mariners of this town have sustained great loss, to the undoing of most of them, through the King of Denmark. Five of our ships being at the Ward-house in his dominions to provide fish, as they have done for years past, the King himself, with his brother, came there with a small fleet, and took the whole of them prize, with all their goods and victuals, spoiled the men of their very apparel, beat and put some of them to torture, and then caused them to be put in irons. He took four of the ships home with him, and all the goods, together with the most serviceable men; the rest he put in the worst ships, giving them a small quantity of his own refuse victuals, and so sent them home. . . . We crave some relief from Council, and your furtherance in the cause.

D. A POLISH AMBASSADOR (1597)

A Letter from Robert Cecil to the Earl of Essex.[1]

. . . There arrived three daies since in the cittie an ambassador out of Poland, a gentleman of excellent fashion, witte, discourse, language, and person; the Quene was possessed by some of our new counsellours, that are as cunning in intelligence as in decyphering, that his negotiation tendeth to a proposition of peace. Her Majestie,

[1] From *Queen Elizabeth and her Times: A series of Original Letters*, ed. Thomas Wright, 2 vols., 1838, I. pp. 478–81.

in respect that his father the Duke of Finland had so much honored her, besydes the lyking she had of this gentleman's comeliness and qualities, brought to her by reporte, did resolve to receive him publiquely, in the chamber of presence, where most of the erles and noblemen about the Court attended, and made it a great day. He was brought in attired in a longe robe of black velvett, well jewelled and buttoned, and came to kisse her Majestie's hands where she stood under the state, from whence he straight returned ten yards of, and then begun his oration aloude in Latin, with such a gallant countenance, as in my lyfe I never behelde. The effect of it was this, that 'the King hath sent him to putt her Majestie in mynde of the auncient confederacies between the Kings of Poland and England; that never a monarche in Europe did willingly neglect their friendship, that he had ever frendly received her merchants and subjects of all quality, that she had suffered his to be spoyled without restitution, not for lacke of knowledge of the violences, but out of meere injustice, not caring to minister remedy, notwithstanding many particular petitions and letters received, and to confirme her disposition to avowe these courses (violating both the law of nature and nations) because there were quarrells betweene her and the King of Spaine, she therefore tooke upon her, by mandate, to prohibite him and his countries, assuming thereby to herself a superioritie (not tollerable) over other Princes, nor he determined to endure, but rather wished her to knowe, that if there were no more than the auncient amitie between Spain and him, it were no reason to look that his subjects should be impedited, much less now, when a stricte obligation of bloud had so conjoined him with the illustrious howse of Austria;' concluding that if her Majestie would not reforme it, he would.

To this I swear by the living God, her Majestie made one of the best aunswers *extempore*, in Latin, that ever I heard, being much moved to be challenged in publick, especially against her expectation. The wordes of her beginning were these, '*Expectavi legationem, mihi vero querelam adduxisti.* Is this the business your King has sent you about? surelie I can hardly believe, that if the King himself were present, he would have used such language, for if he should, I must have thought that his being a King of not many years, and that *non de jure sanguinis, sed jure electionis, imo noviter electus*, may leave him uninformed of that course which his father and auncestors have taken with us, and which, peradventure, shall be observed by those that shall come to live after him. And as for you' saith she to the ambassador, 'although I perceave you have read many books, to fortifie your arguments in this case, yet I am apt to believe that you have not lighted upon the chapter that prescribeth the forme to be used between kings and princes; but were it not for the place you hold, to have so publickly an imputation throwne upon our justice, which as yet never failed, we would aunswer this audacitie of yours in another style; and for the particulars of your negotiations, we will appoint some of our counsell to conferre with you, to see upon what ground this clamor of yours hath his foundation, who shewed yourself rather an heralde than an ambassador.'

I assure your Lordship, though I am not apt to wonder, I must confesse before the living Lord that I never heard her (when I knew her spirits were in a passion) speake with better moderation in my lyfe.[1]

You will think it strange that I am thus idle, as to use another bodie's hand. I assure you I have hurte my thumb at this hour, and because the Quene tould me, she was sorry you heard not his Latin and hers, I promised her to make you partaker of as much as I could remember, being, as I knew, the worst you would expect from her, and yet the best could come from any other. If, therefore, this letter finde you, and that you write backe before your going, I pray you to take notice that you were pleased to heare of her wise and eloquent aunswer.

I am half ashamed to take this much tyme from you, but when I hope it shall be the last which shall come to you before you go out of England, I am contented in this to be censured idle, though in all things els upon the face of the earth I will be founde,

Your faithful and affectionate poore frende, to do you service.[2]

I feare nothing, but your Lordship will speed the worse for having some of those in your companie that have robbed the Dantsickers and many other merchantes, *exempli gratia*, the Capten of the Warspight, for whom I have laied out 50*l.* for the Rowbuck, for which I will stay some of his billetts and canarie wine, that he hath sent for out of my sellar at Chelsey.

From the Court at Greenwich, the 26th of July, 1597.

[1] It was on this occasion that the Queen, after her speech, turning to her court, exclaimed, 'God's death! my Lords, (for that was her oath even in anger,) I have been enforced this day to scour up my old Latin, that hath lain long in rusting!'

[2] The signature is cut off.

XV. Analogue

From
THE COUNTESSE OF PEMBROKES ARCADIA
by Sir Philip Sidney (1590)

From Lib. I. Ch. 8.

But first at *Musidorus* request, though in brief manner, his mind much running upon the strange storie of *Arcadia*, he did declare by what course of adventures he was come to make up their mutuall happinesse in meeting. When (cosin, said he) we had stript our selves, and were both leapt into the Sea, and swom a little toward the shoare, I found by reason of some wounds I had, that I should not be able to get the lande, and therefore turned backe againe to the mast of the shippe, where you found me, assuring my selfe, that if you came alive to the shore, you would seeke me; if you were lost, as I thought it as good to perishe as to live, so that place as good to perish in as an other. There I found my sworde among some of the shrowds, wishing (I must confesse) if I died, to be found with that in my hand, and withall waving it about my head, that saylers by it might have the better glimpse of me. There you missing me, I was taken up by Pyrates, who putting me under boorde prisoner, presentlie sett uppon another shippe, and mainteining a long fight, in the ende, put them all to the sworde. Amongst whom I might heare them greatlie prayse one younge man, who fought most valiantlie, whom (as love is carefull, and misfortune subject to doubtfulnes) I thought certainely to be you. And so holding you as dead, from that time till the time I sawe you, in trueth I sought nothing more then a noble ende, which perchance made me more hardie then otherwise I would have bene. Triall whereof came within two days after: for the Kinges of *Lacedæmon* having sett out some Galleys, under the charge of one of their Nephews to skowre the Sea of the Pyrates, they met with us, where our Captaine wanting men, was driven to arme some of his prisoners, with promise of libertie for well fighting: among whom I was one, and being boorded by the Admirall, it was my fortune to kil *Eurileon* the Kings nephew: but in the end they prevailed, & we were all taken prisoners: I not caring much what became of me (only keeping the name of *Daiphantus*, according to the resolution you know is betweene us,) but beyng laid in the jayle of *Tenaria*, with speciall hate to me for the death of *Eurileon*, the popular sort of that towne conspired with the *Helots*, and so by night opened them the gates; where entring and killing all of the gentle and riche faction, for honestie sake brake open all prisons, and so delivered me; and I mooved with gratefulnesse, and encouraged with carelesnesse of life, so behaved my selfe in some conflictes they had in fewe dayes, that they barbarouslie thinking unsensible wonders of mee, and withall so much they better trusting mee, as they heard I was hated of the Kinge of *Lacedæmon*, (their chiefe Captayne beyng slayne as you knowe by the noble *Argalus*, who helped thereunto by his perswasion) having borne a great affection unto me, and to avoyde the daungerous emulation whiche grewe among the chiefe, who should have the place, and all so affected, as rather to have a straunger then a competitour, they elected mee, (God wotte little prowde of that dignitie,) restoring unto mee such thinges of mine as being taken first by the pyrates, and then by the *Lacedæmonians*, they had gotten in the sacke of the towne. Now being in it, so good was my successe with manie victories, that I made a peace for them to their owne liking, the verie daie that you delivered *Clitophon*, whom I with much adoo had preserved. And in my peace the King *Amiclas* of *Lacedæmon* would needes have mee bannished, and deprived of the dignitie whereunto I was exalted: which (and you may see howe much you are bounde to mee) for your sake I was content to suffer, a newe hope rising in mee, that you were not dead: and so meaning to travaile over the worlde to seeke you; and now here (my deere *Musidorus*) you have mee.

OTHELLO
THE MOOR OF VENICE

INTRODUCTION

THIS PLAY, though popular on the stage, was published late, being entered in the Stationers' Register on 6 October 1621, to Thomas Walkley as 'The Tragedie of Othello, the moore of Venice'. A Quarto appeared in 1622, with authorship attributed to William Shakespeare; the first Folio in 1623. A second Quarto (1630) was apparently based on F1 with emendations from Q1.

The relationship of Q1 and F1 has been disputed. The Quarto has more stage directions, but is shorter than F1 by about 160 lines, some of them obvious theatrical cuts. Miss Alice Walker concluded (*Camb.* p. 125) that Q1 represented 'a licentious transcript of a late acting version of *Othello* further mangled in its printing', and that F1 derived 'from the collation of an example of Q1 with a reputable manuscript (which) stood at no more than one remove from Shakespeare's foul papers'. Greg thought that the Quarto was printed from a transcript made about 1620 'from the foul papers by a scribe of rather careless habits', and the Folio text from a copy of Q1 'first collated with the prompt-book'.[1] M. R. Ridley (*New Arden*, pp. xvi–xlv) argued that 'in Q1, amplified by the reinstatement of the cuts, we have as near an approximation as we are likely to get to the play as Shakespeare first wrote it with nothing between us and him but the blunders of an honest but not always skilful transcriber and compositor. On the other hand I think that in F we have probably a good deal of Shakespeare's second thoughts.'

'The Moor of Venis' by 'Shaxberd' was performed on 1 November 1604 (Hallowmas) 'in the Banketinge house att Whit Hall'. This record in the Revels Accounts, at one time suspected to be a forgery, is now held to be authentic, and the play was the first of several performed before the new King and his Danish wife by his recently accredited players. Its position as

---

[1] W. W. Greg, *The Shakespeare First Folio*, 1955, pp. 357–74.

first may indicate that the piece was newer than the rest, which included *The Merry Wives* and *Measure for Measure*.

The 'bad' Quarto of *Hamlet* (published in summer, 1603) may have echoes from *Othello*; on the other hand Iago's 'I'll pour this pestilence into his ear' recalls the murder of old Hamlet. In *The Honest Whore* (1604) the reference to Hippolyto (accused of murdering Infelice) as 'more savage than a barbarous Moor', is too general to be taken as necessarily an allusion to Othello. Details probably taken by Shakespeare from R. Knollys's *History of the Turks* (1603), which was dedicated to James I, place the play between March 1603 and October 1604.

The main narrative source was Giraldi Cinthio's *Gli Hecatommithi* (Decade 3, Story 7), first published in 1565. A ballad in BM. Add. MS. 32380 was forged by J. P. Collier, who printed it in his *New Facts* (1835).[1] No English translation of Cinthio's novella is known before 1753, but a close French version was made by Gabriel Chappuys in 1584, and Shakespeare may have read this,[2] as he probably read the story behind *All's Well* in Le Macon's version of Boccaccio.[3] Emilia's 'I'll have the work ta'en out' (III.3.296) comes very near to 'en tirer le patron', which has no equivalent in the Italian. On the other hand Othello's demand, 'give me the ocular proof. . . . Make me to see't' (III.3.361–5) is nearer to Cinthio's 'se no mi fai . . . veder cogl' occhi' than to Chappuys's 'se tu ne me fais voir'.[4] Since there is no certainty I supply a translation from the Italian (Text I).

Cinthio's stories, like Boccaccio's, had a frame. Fleeing after the Sack of Rome in 1527 five ladies and five gentlemen sailed for Marseilles and beguiled the time with stories, each day on one particular topic. In the Introduction the gentlemen under the wise old Fabio discuss how a peaceful life in love may be achieved. Fabio insists that it is only in marriage, where reason and high ideals conquer appetite, and after great care in choosing a partner (Text IA). The Introduction itself contains ten short exemplary tales; the main body of the work falls into

---

[1] Cf. *Var*, pp. 398–402.

[2] In *Premier Volume des Cent Excellentes Nouvelles*, 1584. E. A. J. Honigmann, *N & Q*, n.s. 13, 1966, pp. 136–7, supports this claim with several parallels.

[3] Cf. H. G. Wright, 'How did Shakespeare come to know the *Decameron*?', *MLR*, xlix, 1955, pp. 45–8.

[4] Cf. W. Wokatsch, *Archiv.*, clxii, 1932, pp. 118–19.

two parts with five Decades in each. Here also the main theme is marriage, and includes instances of love affairs conducted against the wishes of parents, of infidelity, treachery and intrigue, of fidelity and generosity, of changes of fortune. Many of the stories are horrific, like that on which Cinthio wrote his sensational tragedy *Orbecche* (Dec. 2, Story 2). In the third edition (1574) Cinthio asserted that his tales were founded on fact. We must take this with more than a grain of salt, for many were lifted from the classics and given a modern setting. But realism is a characteristic of his melodrama, and the tale of Disdemona, succinctly and flatly related, and anticlimactic in its close, is marked by a verisimilitude of detail which has made some scholars suspect that it was based on some police-court case of the sixteenth century (Text IB).

Eduard Engel suggested that Cinthio's Moor was one of the Italian Moro family, citing Marino Sanuto's *Diaries*[1] Vol. vii, p. 656, under 27 October 1508: 'This morning Christopher Moro, lately arrived as Lieutenant from Cyprus, and now elected Captain in Crete, was before the committee, with acrimony, his wife having died on the way from Cyprus, as has already been indicated. . . .' On 5 November 'Another captain was chosen for Crete, since Moro had refused the post.'[2] That is all.

Ross O'Connell[3] found in the *Vecchie Storie* of Molmenti (Venice, 1882, p. 77) part of a letter written to Vincenzo Dandolo by the theologian Domenico Bollani, ending thus: 'The other night a certain Sanudo who lives in the Rio della Croce by the Giudecca forced his wife (who was a Cappello) to make her confession, and the following night he stabbed her in the throat with a stiletto and killed her; they say, because she was unfaithful; but the neighbours consider her a saint.' The letter was dated 1 June 1602. Since the man and his wife were of illustrious families Molmenti thought that the Venetian ambassador in England would soon hear of the case, and that Shakespeare might have heard of it too and been impelled to write his Venetian tragedy. Making the wife confess before murdering her parallels V.2. There is no evidence, however,

---

[1] M. Sanuto, *I Diarii*, 58 vols., Venice, 1879–1903, vii, p. 656.
[2] *ShJb* xxxv, 1899, pp. 271–3: 'Zur Urgeschichte des Othello.'
[3] *N & Q*, s.6, xi, 1885, p. 147: 'Desdemona in the Flesh'.

that the murder caused any stir in England; and Hamlet's father's ghost shows that Shakespeare realized the enormity of sending a soul out 'unhousell'd, disappointed, unanneal'd'.

Another possible analogue was discovered by Andrea da Mosto in the records of the Council of Ten.[1] In 1544 Captain Francesco da Sessa, called 'the Moor', was brought in chains from Cyprus, where he was serving in the army, along with two alleged accomplices, Paolo da Padua and his sergeant Alessandro della Mirandola. The case lasted some months, at the end of which da Sessa was banished for ten years; Paolo da Padua was released, having become ill in prison, but he was not declared innocent; Alessandro della Mirandola, who had gone mad in gaol, was declared innocent. Unfortunately the extant minutes of the Council of Ten give no hint of the charge or evidence, and the Cyprus records vanished after the Turks took the island. So there is a hollow at the core of this 'analogue', no evidence of wife-murder, nor that da Padua was the Ensign and Alessandro the 'capo di squadra' of Cinthio's tale. This 'Moro' was not a Moor but, like Ludovico Sforza (d. 1510), also nicknamed 'Il Moro', a dark-skinned European.

A literary parallel was found by A. H. Krappe in the tenth-century Byzantine epic from Asia Minor, *Digenis Akritas*. There the son of a Moorish emir and a Byzantine lady falls in love with a general's daughter (Eudocia), and woos her with his lyre. They elope and are pursued, but after a battle reconciliation is effected. Eudocia follows her husband to the wars. When he is dying he kisses her good-bye, then suddenly, in a paroxysm of jealousy lest she marry again, he chokes her to death.[2]

This tale contains elements not in Cinthio: an elopement, a happy married life, death by suffocation. Krappe sees resemblances to *Othello*; but Othello's is not properly an elopement but a secret marriage at once revealed, and the jealousy is different. Krappe suggested that the dramatist may have followed, not Cinthio, but another version, fuller and containing more of the Greek story. This is pure speculation.

In Cinthio's story only the wife is named (Disdemona). The

---

[1] A. da Mosto, 'Il Moro di Venezia', in *Bollettino degli Studi Inglese in Italia*, April 1933, Florence, pp. 3–10.

[2] A. H. Krappe, 'A Byzantine Source of Shakespeare's *Othello*', *MLN*, xxxix, 1924, pp. 156–61; answered by W. L. Bullock in *MLN* xl, 1925, pp. 226–8. The jealousy is like that of Bandello's Albanian captain [Text II].

others are a Moorish Captain (Capitano Moro), an Ensign or Standard-bearer (Alfieri) and a 'Capo di squadra'. In view of Shakespeare's modifications of these ranks it is well to have their values clear. As Professor Paul A. Jorgenson has argued,[1] a 'Capo di squadra' was an officer of low degree in charge of training one part of a company of infantry. This is confirmed by Lelio Brancaccio in *I Carichi Militari* (Anversa, 1610), who wrote (Ch. II)

'It is the practice in the militia to give to every twenty-five soldiers a "Capo di squadra" or Corporal (as they call him in Italy); the choice of whom is at the will of the Captain. He has not authority over the soldiers as much as the other officers, nor can he command them at any time. His office is properly to take note of all the soldiers in his group and to know them by sight and by name ... his place on the march must be at the head of the company, in the first file of arque-busiers, therefore the arquebus has to be his weapon, so that he may be more ready to obey and to command' (pp. 17–21).[2]

The Ensign was of much higher rank.

'The office of Ensign (Alfiero) of a company is one of great confidence and honour, because on him falls the duty, in the absence of his Captain, of commanding the company; also because he raises and upholds with his hand the honoured standard which is the emblem and guide of valiant soldiers; wherefore with good reason this office may be awarded to some very noble and much-honoured person. The choice of this officer lies with the Captain, with the approval of the 'maestro di campo'. .... It is proper then for an Ensign, so that he may carry out his duty to look after his standard, and now and then to command his company, that he should be gifted with great valour and the best of judgement; and his valour needs to be accompanied by great bodily size, liveli-ness and agility of limbs, in order that he may in battle more

[1] P. A. Jorgenson, *Shakespeare's Military World*, Berkeley, 1956, Ch. III.

[2] More details of his duties are in Mario Savorgnano, *Arte Militare Terrestre e Maritima*, Venetia, 1614 edn. Captains 'must take all care that their Corporals do their duty, to control the soldiers well, teaching them to be ready for action, obedient, skilful in arms, enduring in fatigue, bold in danger, frugal in food and clothing, and pleasant in converse one with another' (pp. 8, 9).

easily display, hold up and manage his standard' (pp. 34–40).[1]

A Captain was in charge of a company. Cinthio's Moor however was (at least temporarily) of higher rank than this, since he was made commandant of the troops sent to Cyprus; his actual position is not made clear, since it is of no significance in the story. Undoubtedly, however, the Ensign is of higher rank than the 'Capo di squadra' and his resentment would be all the greater when he thought that Disdemona was in love with the Corporal. Apparently there was nothing surprising in the sixteenth century in the fact that the Corporal should be invited frequently to dine at his Captain's house.[2]

The tale, like many others by Giraldi, is ingeniously worked out, with plenty of circumstantial detail to give it plausibility. It is dryly told, with no analysis of character and a complete lack of that 'sensibility' frequent in English euphuistic stories; and it falls naturally into a series of scenes, with little dialogue. It is long drawn out in time, occupying many months. First comes the wooing, the marriage, and a period of happiness in Venice before the move to Cyprus and time to settle down there. Then the Ensign falls in love with Disdemona, and some time must elapse before he despairs and resolves to upset the marriage: 'he set himself to wait'. 'Not long afterwards' the Corporal is demoted; Disdemona intercedes 'many times'. The Ensign starts his campaign and the Moor 'became quite melancholy'; he has to 'wait for the day' when the Ensign will provide evidence.

The handkerchief business occupies several days. Disdemona realizes its loss 'a few days later'. The Ensign must wait for an opportunity to leave it in the Corporal's room. Next day the latter tries to return it; the Ensign promises more evidence. More waiting is involved before the Moor sees the Corporal laughing with the Ensign. 'One day after dinner' the Moor asks for the handkerchief. Thereafter he is obsessed 'day and night' with the idea of killing his wife, who asks him 'many

---

[1] I owe these references to my friend Prof. Vittorio Gabrieli of the University of Rome, who obtained them from Prof. Piero Pieri, the eminent authority on Renaissance military history.

[2] Most previous translations of Cinthio call the 'Capo di squadra' a Lieutenant or Captain. I call him a Corporal. Cf. Jorgenson, *op. cit.*

times' what is wrong, and 'sometimes' confides her troubles to the Ensign's wife. After the sempstress is seen copying the handkerchief 'much entreaty' is needed to make the Ensign agree to kill the Corporal. 'One dark night' the Corporal is attacked. 'Next day' they plot Disdemona's murder but must await 'a suitable occasion'. 'One night' the deed is done.

After the funeral a considerable time passes during which the Moor goes half-demented and then, filled with hatred towards the Ensign, dismisses him. A feud grows between them. The Ensign travels to Venice with the Corporal; there they accuse the Moor; he is brought to Venice, imprisoned, tortured, tried, and exiled. A vague stretch of time ensues during which the Moor is killed by Disdemona's relatives, and the Ensign tries his tricks, is caught and fitly punished.

Cinthio deliberately lingers over the action, maybe because this was what occurred in fact, but also to show the Ensign as a determined man content to bide his time. There are frequent pauses between the stages of the plot, but the delays are followed by sudden activity as the Ensign achieves the steps in his general plan by cleverly adapting his tactics to the circumstances of the moment. The main action in Cyprus is sandwiched between an exposition covering some months and an epilogue which describes how in the end condign punishment came to the criminals.

Some features of Cinthio's characterization should be noted. Following Fabio's advice in the Introduction to the collection, Disdemona loves the Moor not merely through sexual appetite (though they make love frequently after marriage), but for his noble nature. She is aware of the difference in race and background, but continues to love him even when that difference becomes ominous. They are not newly married when they move to Cyprus. To emphasize the Moor's considerate nature and his wife's resolute affection Cinthio elaborates the discussion about her accompanying him overseas. Their voyage is peaceful.

Only in Cyprus are we introduced to the other main characters. When the Ensign, hoping to possess her, hints at his passion, Disdemona does not even notice it. Her nature is sweet and gentle, and she remains obedient to the last, yet she expostulates with her husband when his moods change and she dares to comment on his Moorish temperament. Her appeals for the

Corporal are made out of sheer kindness, and are not prompted by anyone else. She dies protesting her innocence.

We are told of the Moor's noble nature, but we see no evidence of it in Cyprus, and there is little reference to military duties or state business there. The island is at peace. The tragedy is purely *à quatre*, with no political implications. The Moor is kindly and sociable but is quickly led to suspect his wife with the Corporal once the latter has been guilty of breaking discipline. There have been frequent opportunities for them to meet in his absence. Little mention is made of his colour, but the Ensign uses it at a critical moment to explain why his wife might be unfaithful. He is clearly intended to be an instance of the man of different race and manner of life whom a Venetian girl should hesitate to marry, according to Cinthio's Introduction. This emerges when Disdemona tells him 'you Moors are so hot by nature that any little thing moves you to anger and revenge'. And more explicitly when she fears that she will 'be a warning to young girls not to marry against their parents' wishes; and Italian ladies will learn by my example not to tie themselves to a man whom Nature, Heaven and manner of life separate from us' (see p. 248). The Ensign's insinuations make him bewildered, then suspicious; he demands evidence but is easily led to interpret what he sees in the way the Ensign suggests and, instead of openly accusing his wife, he becomes melancholy, surly and withdrawn.

When Disdemona cannot produce the handkerchief he pretends to dismiss the matter. He becomes completely dependent on the Ensign, bribes him to kill the Corporal, takes his advice on how to murder his wife, then sends her from bed to her death, and taunts her while the Ensign is killing her most brutally. This is Revenge for Honour of a most sordid kind, and (true to the Mediterranean custom that sexual dishonour and its punishment should be kept secret) the criminals cunningly make it appear an accident and escape scot-free, until after the Moor has realized his loss and dismissed his accomplice. He is accused and tortured, but remaining steadfastly silent is banished, only to die at the hands of Disdemona's relatives. The noble Moor has lapsed into bestial savagery, but those who hear the tale blame him for foolish credulity, not for any racial characteristics.

The Ensign is a consummate double-dealer, devious and ever-careful of his own safety. He is married, with a little daughter. He dominates his wife by fear, but cannot make her take part in his schemes. When he desires Disdemona and she fails to respond, he assumes, not that she loves her husband, but that she must be in love with the Corporal. His enmity is rather to her and the Corporal than to the Moor, and though he is jealous of the latter his purpose is to use him as a means to destroy the other two. He is assisted several times by chance, of which he takes skilful advantage. So the Corporal's demotion, for which the Ensign is not responsible, excites Disdemona's pity, thus giving the villain an opportunity to arouse the Moor's sexual doubts. Having to provide evidence, he seizes the opportunity of stealing Disdemona's handkerchief while she is nursing his child. Then the fact that the Corporal's sempstress is sitting by the window allows him to show her in possession of the handkerchief. Moreover, fate plays into the Ensign's hands when the Moor's unexpected return home prevents the Corporal from returning the handkerchief (which would have ended that plot), and the Moor catches a glimpse of him stealing away from the house. Another characteristic, rapacity, is shown when the Ensign extorts money from the Moor to persuade him to kill the Corporal. In this crime he is not fully successful—but he makes use of the Corporal later. The plan for Disdemona's murder reveals both the Ensign's fiendish cruelty and his fear of discovery. He instigates and carries out the crime, and together they hoodwink the authorities. Once the deed is done the Moor's dependence on the Ensign ceases and, suspecting the truth, he dismisses him from his post. Even now the latter's self-possession does not fail. Fearing to work openly against his enemy in Cyprus, he gets himself and the Corporal to Venice, where he accuses the Moor. There his connection with his victim ceases, and he is finally punished, not for the plot against Disdemona, but for another false accusation. So ends a malicious rogue who loved duplicity and plotting for the sheer joy of manipulating events and other people.

The Ensign's wife is a shadowy, ambiguous figure; 'honest and fair' we are told, but her honesty is limited. She is intimate with Disdemona and sees much of her, but her affection for her is less than her fear of her own husband. She knows that the

Ensign is plotting against her friend and refuses to be his
accomplice, but she does no more to help Disdemona than warn
her to try to keep the Moor's trust. Only after the Ensign's death
does she reveal the whole story.

Lastly there is the Corporal, a simple, honourable man whose
(unexplained) breach of discipline when on guard causes his
demotion but would not make him forfeit the Moor's goodwill
for long. Even the Ensign calls it a trivial offence. He never asks
Disdemona to intercede for him, and there is no indication that
he ever meets her after his dismissal, for in his discomfiture he
avoids meeting his Captain, and is unable to return the handkerchief which he finds in his room. The woman (*donna*) in his
quarters is not his wife, as some critics have assumed, but a
housekeeper or sempstress. He is certainly not in love with
Disdemona, and he makes a habit of visiting a whore in the
town. When attacked on leaving the latter's house he defends
himself gallantly, though wounded so sorely that he loses a leg.
His 'wooden leg' seems a grotesque touch, but it may be true to
fact; it indicates that his military career is ruined and explains
his desire to be avenged on his alleged attacker.

Another possible source[1] is the fourth of Geoffrey Fenton's
Certaine Tragicall Discourses (1567), translated from Belleforest's
Histoires Tragiques (1561, etc.), themselves adapted from Bandello. Belleforest had moralized on the Italian tale; Fenton
went much farther, expanding Bandello's 2,200 words to
10,500. As C. S. Lewis comments: he 'loads, or stuffs, every rift
with rhetorical, proverbial, and moral lore',[2] and repeatedly
expresses horror at what he has chosen to tell. Yet Fenton has
some originality. Bandello's story of a jealous husband who
killed his patient wife lest some other man might enjoy her after
his death, was mainly concerned with the external facts. Fenton
tried to enter the minds of the characters, and described in
detail the symptoms of melancholy and the needless turmoil of
jealousy. I give the significant portions of the wordy narrative
(Text II).

To suggest that Shakespeare needed to read the psychological
embroideries of a second-rate adapter before he could create

---

[1] Cf. L. J. Ross, *Diss. Abstracts*, xx, 1959, p. 2302; P. N. Siegel, 'A New Source for
Othello?' PMLA, lxxv, 1960, p. 480; W. E. McCarron, *N & Q*, n.s. 13 April 1966, pp.
137–8.   [2] *English Literature in the Sixteenth Century*, 1954, p. 311.

the tragedy of Othello would be absurd, and the situation of the Albanian captain and his wife is very different. Regina has already been widowed after having a daughter by her first husband before meeting Don Spado (Spada in Bandello). The latter never focuses his jealousy on any one person; it is self-generated and general. He confines and ill-treats his faithful wife for an indefinite period before falling into a decline. When she rashly declares that she would not live on if he died, he stabs her and himself to death.

It is possible that here as elsewhere Shakespeare took hints from material with some slight resemblance to his main source and theme. Bandello's *novella* begins with a reference to the Turkish invasions, and the first husband has been a wanderer 'in woodes and deserte places unknowne'. He has risen by military skill to be 'generall of the whole armie of footemen' in Mantua. When he dies Regina is under twenty and inexperienced in worldly affairs. The second husband, Spado, is an Albanian soldier who has had nothing to do with women previously. Within a month he becomes jealous, for excess of love turns into 'a jealous loathing of the thing we chiefly love and hold most deare'. The Albanian's ambivalence applies to Othello too. A suggestion of erotic satiety is made by Iago. The wife's youth, inexperience, modesty and obedience resemble Desdemona's, but the latter, unlike Regina, does not understand Othello's changed attitude.

Fenton has a long digression asserting that 'the restraint of lybertye of women, together with a distrust proceding of none occasion, is the chiefest meane to seduce her that ells hath vowed an honeste and integrety of lyfe.' This is one of Emilia's arguments when she is explaining why some women 'do abuse their husbands' (IV.3.85–95).

Don Spado's sickness reaches its climax after he has lost his master by death; Othello's after he is recalled from Cyprus. As in Cinthio, the jealous husband murders his wife in their bedroom. Before he does so he has a paroxysm of frenzy, 'with owlinge, cryeng, and foaminge at the mouth . . .' Similarly in IV.1, Othello becomes incoherent and falls into a fit which Iago calls an epilepsy, saying: 'The lethargy must have his quiet course, / If not, he foams at the mouth, and by and by / Breaks out to savage madness.'

Before stabbing her the husband in Bandello, 'lay down with her, and pleasured her more than usual, so that there was no part of her white, innocent body that he did not kiss, taking that loving pleasure with her that men seek from their ladies.' Fenton more restrainedly writes that he 'embraced and kissed her, in such sorte as Judas kissed our Lorde the same night he betraied him'; and the dagger was already in his hand. So Othello kisses Desdemona, three times, before she wakes. Fenton describes rather well Don Spado's grief, love and jealous fear leading to an ecstasy of suicidal madness. He shows, as Desdemona says, 'That death's unnatural that kills for loving.' There is no pretence that the murder is an act of justice.

One resemblance in language should be noted. Fenton writes of Spado's 'hagarde mynde' (an early adjectival use meaning 'wild', 'uncontrollable', from 'haggard', a wild, untrained hawk): cf. III.3.260, 'If I do prove her haggard', with the hawk-association to the fore. The savagery of Don Spado is given an animal reference to Africa: 'far excedinge the brutishe maner of the tiger, lyon, or libarde, bredd in the dessertes of Affrike, the common norsse of monsters and creatures cruell without reason.' Dying, he commends his carcase to 'ravenous wolves', 'venemous serpentes', and 'his soule to the reprobate societie of Judas and Cayne, with other of the infernall crew.' In *Othello* the animal-imagery is mostly of insects, cats, toads, goats and monkeys; but Othello commends himself to devils when he realizes his folly (V.2.276–9).

Fenton (but not Bandello) twice writes of his narrative in theatrical terms which might appeal to Shakespeare. In the Argument his story is 'a bloody skaffolde, or theaterye, wherin are presented such as play no partes but in mortal and furious tragedeis'; later Spado's jealousy 'wolde not dismisse him from the stage till he had playd th' uttermost acte of his malicious tragedie.'

These points of resemblance do not prove that Shakespeare used Fenton, but they suggest that he *may* have done so in filling out Cinthio's bare tale and making the tragedy one of great mental suffering. Possibly the Turkish allusion encouraged him to introduce the Turkish menace to Cyprus; or perhaps, having decided to glorify Cinthio's Moor by making him a bulwark of Venice against the Muslim, Shakespeare recalled Bandello's story of another foreign captain with its detailed symptoms of jealousy and its patient heroine murdered in her bedroom in a manner somewhat less sordid than that described by Cinthio.

Did Shakespeare know Bandello in the original Italian? There are interesting coincidences. At the end of Fenton's tale[1] the husband is dead and the wife has just enough breath to ask to be buried with her first husband. In Bandello, however, the maid (like Emilia) calls for help; neighbours break in and find the dead husband lying stretched out face downward on the almost lifeless body of his wife. (Compare Othello's end, stabbed by himself and dying upon a kiss.) The wife revives sufficiently to make her confession to a priest and to insist that her husband was not to blame for her death, which was caused by her own misfortune (*disgrazia*). Similarly Desdemona revives enough to assert her guiltlessness and to answer, when asked, 'O, who hath done this deed?':

> Nobody; I myself; farewell!
> Commend me to my kind lord! (V.2.117–22)

Are these resemblances the results of chance? If not a source, Bandello's story, whether in Italian or in English, is an interesting analogue.

Further evidence of Shakespeare's addiction to modern short stories and his use of details from them when recalled to his mind by associative memory may be afforded by George Pettie's story of Cephalus and Procris.[2] Procris, a young woman of Venice just passing out of girlhood, meets Cephalus at the Duke's court, where he is celebrated for his story-telling. The company discusses various practitioners of the art, but Procris 'seemed to prefer the histories of Cephalus, both for that, saith she, his discourses differ from the rest, and besides that, me-thinks the man amendeth the matter much.' He offers to be her servant, and she encourages him modestly, until 'love remained mutual between them; which her father perceiving, and not liking very well of the match, for that he thought his daughter not old enough for a husband, nor Cephalus rich enough for such a wife, to break the bond of this amity went this way to

[1] And Belleforest's.
[2] G. Pettie, *A Petite Pallace of Pettie his Pleasure*, ed. I. Gollancz, 2 vols., 1908, Vol. II, p. 61. (Modernized text.)

work.' He gets Cephalus sent as ambassador to the Turk. Procris weeps as the ship sails away and pines so much that a marriage is made of 'hasty, foolish and fond affection'. Cephalus goes away, but returns in disguise and to test her says that her husband has forsaken her. She mourns, but when the newcomer tempts her with gold, she is willing to accept him. Cephalus reveals himself and forgives her, but she becomes needlessly jealous of him and in the end he shoots her accidentally when she is spying on him, out hunting. This of course is a modern, shortened version of Ovid's tale in *Metamorphoses*, VII, 26. It seems likely that, remembering its jealousy-theme, the Venetian setting, the reluctant father and the Turkish connection, Shakespeare was led to adapt the idea of an inexperienced girl falling in love primarily because of a man's skill in story-telling. Othello's tales, however, reveal the fineness of his mind as well as his romantic career, and Desdemona's love is anything but 'hasty, foolish and fond affection'.

It is rarely possible with any confidence to assert why Shakespeare wrote a particular play and at a particular time. But one can make suggestions. In the first years of the new century he was much occupied with themes of hypocrisy, treachery and intrigue against innocent people. This is true of *Hamlet*, *Measure for Measure* and *Lear*. In *Hamlet* the villain's main plot has already been successful when the play opens; his campaign against Hamlet is a consequence of the other, forced on him to avert discovery and punishment. Perhaps Shakespeare was attracted to Cinthio's tale because it would let him show (more fully, credibly and tragically than in *Much Ado*) an intriguer of even greater malevolence initiating and carrying out his plot to the end.

In the theatre at the end of the sixteenth century, as in verse-satire, the cynical denigrator, the malicious commentator on other characters, and the malcontent were all the rage. Thersites in *Troilus* (written about the same time as *Othello*) spat bile and attributed base motives to all around. The trickery of Jonson's villains had not yet reached its peak in *Volpone* and *The Alchemist*, but there was cynical commentary in *Every Man Out of his Humour*, *Cynthia's Revels*, and *The Poetaster*. As Quadratus exclaims in Marston's *What You Will* (1601), 'What's out of railing's out of fashion' (II.1.).

The plotter who delighted in wickedness for its own sake and for the sense of power and vitality it afforded him, had been popular since Marlowe's *Jew of Malta* and *Massacre at Paris*. Also there was a tradition of Moorish villains which had entered drama from ballads and stories.[1] Aaron the Moor in *Titus Andronicus* was a Machiavellian lover of 'policy and stratagem', of any plot

> Which cunningly effected, will beget
> A very excellent piece of villainy (II.3.5–7)

and he rejoiced in his negritude:

> Let fools do good, and fair men call for grace,
> Aaron will have his soul black like his face (III.1.204–5)

Peele's *Battle of Alcazar* had as villain Muly Hamed, son of a Negro mother and a King of Morocco, Abdelmelec. Nearer to the date of *Othello*, *Lust's Dominion* (*c.* 1600), a tragedy which Greg and others have thought related to the lost *Spanish Moor's Tragedy* by Dekker, Haughton and Day, commissioned for the Admiral's Men in 1598/9, has a Moor as wicked as Aaron, an ambitious climber, Aleazar, who knows that Fernando is in love with his wife, and uses it as a means to rise:

> The Spaniard loves my wife: she swears to me
> She's chaste as the white moon. Well, if she be,
> Well too if she be not; I care not, I,
> I'll climb up by that love to dignity.

Does Iago's notion that Othello and Cassio have enjoyed Emilia come from this? Was Shakespeare consciously writing a play in rivalry with the other theatre's *Lust's Dominion*, with a white man as the evil manipulator and the Moor as a good man betrayed?

Another possibility is that both the author of *Lust's Dominion* and Shakespeare were affected by the visit to London in August 1600 of an embassage from Muley Hamet, King of Barbary. The Ambassador, Abd-el-Oahed ben Massaood (a grave, sly, hawk-faced man)[2] was accompanied by an inter-

---

[1] Cf. Vol. VI, Introduction, *Titus Andronicus*.
[2] B. Harris, 'A Portrait of a Moor', *Sh. Survey* II, 1958, pp. 89–97, provides a full account and a portrait. Cf. also E. Jones, *Othello's Countrymen*, 1965.

preter who spoke Spanish and Italian and two other notabilities.
Their official aim was to suggest an alliance to invade and
conquer Spain by means of an English navy and African troops;
but they also sought to find out 'the prices, weights, measures,
and kinds of differences in such commodities as either their
country sent hither or England transported thither' (Stow,
Annales). They made a bad impression in London, for they
pleaded poverty, gave no gifts either at court or to the poor, and
during their six months' stay they cost the City over £230 for
their keep. 'They are very strangely attired and behavioured',
wrote Roland White. The oldest Barbarian, probably their
Imam ('a kind of priest or prophet') died in London, and popular rumour said he was poisoned by his colleagues 'lest he
should manifest England's honour to their disgrace' (Stow).
They left in February 1601, and nothing came of the proposed
alliance, for the Queen was already putting out peace-feelers
towards Spain. The same year she ordered 'negars and Black-
moores' to be expelled. Thus the embassage confirmed Londoners in their dislike of the Barbary pirates who had maltreated
many English sailors and merchants and who manifested 'their
inveterate hate unto our Christian religion and estate' (Stow).
Shakespeare must have known this, and it must have added
piquancy to his presentation of a new kind of Moor, a Christian
of generous instincts and lofty ideals, employed against the
Muslim invaders.

A direct result of the embassage was the publication in
November 1600 of John Pory's *A Geographical Historie of Africa*,
translated from the Latin of Leo Africanus,[1] which Shakespeare almost certainly consulted.[2]

Leo Africanus distinguished two kinds of Moor: the 'white
and tawnie Moores, and Negroes, or blacke Moores'. The
'tawny Moors' inhabited North Africa as far as the deserts
beyond the Atlas Mountains.[3] Further south in Senegal and the

---

[1] Born in Granada about 1495 but reared in North Africa, this man led an
adventurous life as merchant, diplomat and troubadour till he was captured in
1520 by pirates who took him to Pope Leo X, whose name he was given after his
conversion. He lived long in Rome but seems to have died in Tunis in 1552. His
book gave a first-hand account of the places and peoples he had known.

[2] Cf. Lois Whitney, 'Did Shakespeare know Leo Africanus', *PMLA*, xxxvii, 1922,
pp. 470–88.

[3] Leo Africanus, *The History and Description of Africa*, trans. John Pory, 1600; ed.
R. Brown, 3 vols., Hakluyt Soc. 1896, I, p. 130.

regions watered by the Niger, 'the inhabitants are extremely black, having great noses and blubber lips'.

Shakespeare's Aaron in *Titus Andronicus* was a Negro, 'coal-black' with 'woolly hair' and 'thick lipp'd'. The Prince of Morocco in *The Merchant of Venice* was a tawny Moor, but the maid whom Launcelot Gobbo got with child was a 'Negro'. Othello is a Negro, not a 'tawny Moor'. He says, 'I am black' (III.3.263); Iago calls him 'an old black ram'; Roderigo calls him 'the thick-lips', and Emilia at the end, 'black devil'. On the other hand Iago calls him a 'Barbary horse' and 'an erring barbarian', thus identifying him with the 'tawny Moors' of Barbary. Maybe Shakespeare's ethnology was not consistent, but probably Iago was reminding the audience of the recent unpopular visitors from North Africa. The imagery of blackness so frequent in the play loses its point if Othello is not played as a Negro.

There is no reason to suppose that the dramatist tried to delve deeply into African psychology, but Othello's honest simplicity agrees with what Leo Africanus wrote of the Moors of Barbary (among whom he had been brought up) and the Libyans; the Berbers were

'most honest people . . . and destitute of all fraud and guile; not onely imbracing all simplicitie and truth, but also prac-tising the same throughout the whole course of their lives. . . . They keepe their covenant most faithfully; insomuch that they had rather die than breake promise. No nation in the world is so subject unto jealousie; for they will rather leese their lives, then put up any disgrace in the behalfe of their women.'[1]

The Libyans were also 'somewhat civill of behaviour, being plaine dealers, voide of dissimulation, favourable to strangers, and lovers of simplicitie' (I. p. 184).

Jealousy was a characteristic of many Africans. Thus the Numidian women

'sometimes . . . will accept of a kisse; but whoso tempteth them farther, putteth his own life in hazard. For by reason of jealousie you may see them daily one to be the death and

[1] *Ibid.*, I, p. 183.

H

destruction of another, and that in such savage and brutish manner, that in this case they will shew no compassion at all. And they seeme to be more wise in this behalfe then divers of our people, for they will by no meanes match themselves unto an harlot.' (I. p. 154)

Shakespeare did not need to read Leo Africanus to know that men born under the hot sun could be gentle and savage, simple and vengeful by turns; the popular ethical books asserted that, and it was in Cinthio. But he may well have read in Pory's translation the juxtaposition of 'antres vast and desarts idle' (I.3.140),[1] and maybe the 'cisterns' and 'fountains' which haunt Othello's imagery were a reminiscence of the cisterns in Fez, 'alwaies kept sweete and cleane, neither are they covered but onely in summer time, when men women and children bathe themselves therein' (II. p. 420), and the 'more then six hundred cleere fountaines walled round about, and most closely kept' in the eastern part of that city.

It has even been suggested that the idea of making Othello a great traveller came from Pory's eulogy of Leo Africanus in his Introduction:

'Moreover as touching his exceeding great Travels, had he not at the first beene a Moore and a Mahumetan in religion, and most skilfull in the languages and customes of the Arabians and Africans, and for the most part travelled in Caravans, or under the authoritie, safe conduct, and commendation of great Princes: I marvell much how ever he should have escaped so manie thousands of imminent dangers. And (all the former notwithstanding) I marvel much more, how ever he escaped them. For how many desolate cold mountaines, and huge drie, and barren deserts passed he? How often was he in hazard to have beene captured, or have had his throte cut by the prouling Arabians, and wilde Moores? And how hardly manie times escaped he the Lyons greedie mouth, and the devouring jawes of the Crocodile. . . .' (I. p. 6)

---

[1] 'That sandie, barren and desert part of Africa which lieth betweene Nilus and the Red sea, especially the south of the Tripilie, was in olde times inhabited by the Troglodytae, a people so called, bicause of their dwelling in caves under the ground.' (I. pp. 25–7).

We must not make too much of Leo Africanus; but there can be no doubt that, although Shakespeare wrote fast, he prepared his ground well and, while hatching a plot or considering how to add details to a major source, he read round his subject, maybe in a desultory way but with an eye for the useful trifle, often dipping into books published in the last few years and recalling what he had long since read, conflating material from many places. So if he dipped into Pory he also turned up Philemon Holland's translation (1601) of Pliny's *Natural History*, where he would find the 'hollow caves' of the Troglodites, the Blemmyi with 'no heads, but with mouth and eyes both in their breast', the 'many kinds of them that feed ordinarily of man's flesh', including 'Scythians called Anthropophagi', Mount Atlas, mounting 'up to the sky, all rough, ill-favoured and overgrown on that side that lieth to the shore of the ocean', and many other references to things found in Africa and the Near East, all of which give solidity to the setting of the tragedy.[1]

Also, as E. H. W. Meyerstein showed,[2] Othello's denial that he had used magic drew several phrases from Pliny's story of a former bondslave, C. Furius Cresinus, who was accused of amassing wealth 'by indirect means, as if he had used sorcerie, and by charmes and witchcraft drawne into his owne ground that encrease of fruits.' Cresinus thereupon brought into the common place his plough and other implements, 'likewise . . . his own daughter, a lusty strong lass and big of bone . . . well fed and as well clad.' 'My Maisters' [he said] 'Behold, these are the sorceries, charmes, and all the inchauntments that I use.'

Shakespeare's determination to give credibility to his theme is to be seen nowhere more than in the suggestion of a historical setting at a time of national crisis. Cinthio's Moor was sent as Commandant of the garrison in Cyprus, but nothing was said about war or any urgent need. Shakespeare elevates Othello in dignity and importance by having him sent to defend the island against imminent Turkish invasion, and the perils of the sea-voyage are magnified thereby. Othello's secret espousals are at once followed by 'business of some heat' (I.2.) caused by 'a

[1] Cf. K. Muir, *Shakespeare's Sources*, pp. 127-8.
[2] Letter in *TLS*, 1942, p. 72. Cf. *Oth.* 'bondslaves and pagans' (I.2.99); 'indirect and forced courses' (I.3.111); 'My . . . good Masters' (1.3.77); 'what charms, / What conjuration, and what mighty magic . . . This only is the witchcraft I have used' (1.3.91-94, 169).

dozen sequent messengers' from the Venetian fleet. In I.3 we learn of several discrepant accounts of the strength of the enemy fleet, and doubts whether this 'makes for Rhodes' or intends to attack Cyprus. Another messenger makes it clear that the Turks have been reinforced off Rhodes and are now sailing for Cyprus. An attack is certain; hence the all-importance of strengthening the garrison there, and the local commander Signor Montano 'prays you to relieve him'.[1] Othello is sent off at once 'with full commission', leaving his wife to follow. Act II.1 opens in Cyprus, probably Famagusta, at the ebb of a great storm which has temporarily scattered the Turks, and one of Othello's first acts is to order six hours of rejoicing.

These alarms Shakespeare found in the story of the Venetian–Turkish wars which he had probably read in Richard Knolles's *History of the Turks* (1603). He also drew from William Thomas's *History of Italy* (1549) and from Sir Lewis Lewkenor's *The Commonwealth and Government of Venice* (translated in 1599 from the Italian version of G. Contarini's *De Magistratibus et Republica Venetorum*, Paris, 1543).

Throughout the sixteenth century the Turks had menaced southern and eastern Europe. Bosnia and Croatia fell to them in the twenties, and Vienna was besieged in 1529 but did not fall. In 1522 they took Rhodes, and held it until 1912; in 1551 they took Tripoli. After Selim II came to the Ottoman throne in 1566 he demanded the cession of Cyprus. Though greatly afraid, the Venetians chose to fight, ordered local governors to strengthen their walls, and 'at the same time made choyse of their most valiant and expert captaines both by sea and land' to defend 'their dispersed Seignorie'. 'Other meaner captaines were sent also with lesse charge [authority]' to various places, including Cyprus (see p. 263). The fact that the 'noble gentleman' Eugenius Singliticus was to go there first and be followed by 'Countie Martinengus', may have suggested to Shakespeare the convenience of separating Othello from Iago and Desdemona on the sea-journey.

The doubts about the Turkish strength expressed in I.3 could have been suggested by more than one episode in Knolles's *History*, but the question whether their fleet was making for

[1] W. J. Craig's Oxford edn. (I.3.42) has 'believe', following Q1 and F; but 'relieve', as in *Camb* and others, seems preferable.

Rhodes or Cyprus (I.3.14–39) must come from the passage in Knolles which explains how in April 1571 the Turkish admiral Piall Basha, sent out 'to keep the Venetians from sending aid to Cyprus', attacked Tenedos, then desisted, for his superior, Mustapha, 'had before appointed *Piall Bassa* at a time prefixed, to meet him at the Rhodes'.

Shakespeare, apparently ignorant that Rhodes was already in Turkish hands, makes the First Senator consider (and reject) the possibility that they were going to attack that island (I.3.17–30). The Messenger then announces that the Turks

> Steering with due course toward the isle of Rhodes
> Have there injoined them with an after fleet . . .
> Of thirty sail; and now they do re-stem
> Their backward course, bearing with frank appearance
> Their purposes toward Cyprus. (1.3.33–9)

Knolles (Text III, p. 262) also solves a minor mystery which has puzzled editors, e.g. M. R. Ridley, *New Arden*, I.3.16n. 'Signior Angelo: And who is he? And why, whoever he is, is his name mentioned? . . . Angelo is therefore presumably the commander of the galleys. But his introduction by name seems almost as irrelevant as that of Luccicos later (1.3.44), and rather suggests some hitherto undiscovered source for this part of the scene.' Angelo was 'Angelus Sorianus' who with his galley was sent to meet the Venetian ambassador bearing the Turkish ultimatum. Shakespeare probably picked up his name casually and used it to give concreteness to the sailor's information. If he also read G. P. Contarini's *De bello Turcico contra Venetos* (Basle, 1573), or its Italian version, he would find that after the fall of Nicosia Angelo Soriano brought news to Crete of an attack by Turkish vessels in which a ship that was with him in reserve was destroyed. I have not come upon 'Luccicos' in Knolles or Contarini. He may have been a Cypriot or Greek.[1]

The Turks invaded Cyprus and captured Nicosia, whose governor, Nicolo Dandolo, was inadequate. They had a harder task at Famagusta, but took it in November 1571. The island remained Turkish until 1878, when the British took possession of it. To avoid this defeat Shakespeare imagined the Turkish

---

[1] But a 'Marco Lucchese' owned an Italian ordinary in London in Shakespeare's day (J. S. Smart, *MLR*, 1916, p. 339).

fleet shattered by a storm. English audiences would appreciate this divine intervention, for England had been thus saved from invasion several times in the past fifteen years. The Spanish Armada was scattered in 1588, as were later Armadas in 1596 and 1597. In 1598 a fourth reached Calais, where half its ships were wrecked. A last fleet never sailed for England, but rumour spread that the Isle of Wight was invaded and the City of London gates were shut, the train-bands were called out, and all round the coast preparations were made to repel the Spaniards. So the watch on the promontory in II.1, based no doubt on the description of Famagusta in Knolles Text (III, p. 264),[1] the glad news of the 'segregation of the Turkish fleet' (II.1.10), and the festivities proclaimed by the Herald in II.2, would strike home to Londoners.

When he introduced the Turkish war and went to some trouble to get his facts right Shakespeare must have known that he was meeting one of the King's interests; for at the age of nineteen James VI had written a poem, *Lepanto*, on the naval victory of 1571. The piece contains nothing to our purpose, but it was well known and a new edition was printed in 1603.[2] Dedicating his *Generall Historie of the Turkes* to the King in that year, Knolles referred to his 'Heroicall Song'. This would encourage Shakespeare to set his tragedy in the period shortly before the great and glorious victory.

To give the story of the noble Moor an international setting and modern associations was in line with what Shakespeare had done in *Hamlet* and was soon to do in *Macbeth*. In this way additional interest and importance were added to the theme; and one of his chief preoccupations in using Cinthio's material was to dignify it, to transform it from a seedy drama of sordid crime into a poetic tragedy of human nature at its highest and lowest. So the social setting and the ranks of many characters were changed. Desdemona becomes the daughter of one of the

[1] The small vessel, the Veronesa, in which Cassio reached Cyprus first, may indeed have come from Verona (where the Po was navigable), for Veronese ships are in the long list given by G. P. Contarini, *op. cit.*

[2] It was first published in *His Majesties Poeticall Exercises at Vacant Houres* (1591); separately (1603); and translated into Latin by T. Moray (1604). Cf. Emrys Jones, '*Othello Lepanto*, and the Cyprus Wars', *Sh. Survey* 21, 1968, pp. 47–52, which notes passages in Knolles; as does G. R. Hibbard, '*Othello* and the Pattern in Shakespearian Tragedy', in the same volume, pp. 39–46.

Council, a 'magnifico' whose absence from an important meeting is noted with regret (I.3.50–1). Brabantio's kinsmen Gratiano and Lodovico are also high in state affairs. The Corporal becomes a Lieutenant of sufficient stature to replace Othello as ruler of Cyprus (V.2.331); and Othello himself is made Governor and Commander there. Only Iago remains an Ancient or Ensign, a disgruntled Warrant Officer.

There are changes consequent on the alterations in setting, rank, and above all, tone. Some are also the result of dramatizing the story in a way suited to the Elizabethan popular theatre. If Cinthio had written a play on the theme he would, no doubt, as in *Epitia*, have tried to keep the unities by placing the entire tragedy in Cyprus, as Verdi and his librettist Arrigo Boito did so successfully in their opera.[1] This, however, was not Shakespeare's way. He liked to trace the progression of a story from nearer its beginning, to show the diverse interplay of character and circumstance, to present contrasts in mood, varying the tempo and emotional stress. Hence he is at pains to explain why and how a Venetian maiden came to marry a Moorish mercenary, how opposition to the marriage arose and was overcome, and why the Moor was transferred to Cyprus. All this was to be enriched with details of Venetian life and military and seafaring activity so that the domestic tragedy in Cyprus would emerge from a firmly realized Mediterranean environment.

Like Cinthio's story the play falls into two distinct phases, the first in Venice, the second in Cyprus. In Cinthio the first phase is a preamble describing the Moor, his marriage, and how Disdemona persuaded him to take her with him to Cyprus. The wicked Ensign and the Corporal are not mentioned until the happy pair have settled down there, and the Ensign begins his plot only after he has tried to woo Disdemona and failed to make any impression on her. Shakespeare, however, not only expands the preliminary phase by introducing much new material, e.g. the Turkish menace, the Senate scenes, Brabantio's attempt to undo the marriage, but he shows Iago at work from the first moment, expressing his envy of Cassio and hatred of Othello, and revealing his cynicism and skill as a confidence-

---

[1] Cf. 'Verdi's *Othello*: A Shakespearian Masterpiece', by Winton Dean, *Sh. Survey* 21, 1968, pp. 87–96. I agree that '*Otello* is the only opera to challenge a Shakespeare tragedy and emerge undimmed by the comparison.'

trickster in his gulling of Roderigo—a newly invented character and a natural dupe of a very different sort from Othello but equally at the mercy of Iago.

In a stimulating essay Miss de Mendonça[1] has argued that *Othello* owed much to the Italian *commedia dell'arte*, as performed in London by Flaminio Curteise and his company in 1602. This is possible. Brabantio might be a Pantalone and Roderigo a gull, Othello the cuckold, and Iago the perverse, self-seeking Zanni. But how untypical they are in their individuality! The Roderigo scenes were more affected by the current English fashion for a realistic comedy of gulls and schemers, as much classical as Italianate in origin, and represented in early comedies by Jonson, Chapman and Middleton.

The first two acts build whole scenes on a few sentences in Cinthio. Only in Acts III and IV is the Italian story followed closely, and this no doubt because what attracted Shakespeare to the subject originally was the clever way in which Cinthio's Ensign played on the Moor's simplicity and perverted him from a noble officer and loving husband into a brutal murderer. As Segre wrote, Cinthio was 'a pioneer in psychological motivation', and Shakespeare learned something from him about the presentation of a gradual debasement. Shakespeare, however, makes numerous changes. The Ensign's resentment against Disdemona is transformed into hatred for her husband. The demotion of the Corporal is for a more serious offence when performed by Cassio. The business with the handkerchief is altered. Whereas Cinthio's Ensign has a little daughter whom he uses to distract Disdemona's attention while he filches the handkerchief from her girdle, Iago has no child—doubtless to avoid difficulties of casting and staging—and the accidental dropping of the handkerchief is used to show his ability to turn every occurrence to his purpose, and ultimately (V.2.211–30) to prove his guilt.

Of course the end of the story must be changed: the method of the murder and the mood in which it is done. The actual crime is Othello's alone; and he does not, unlike his prototype, try to escape the consequences of his misdeed. So the end comes quickly, both for the Moor and his tempter. About Shakespeare's use of time in the play more must be said, but this and

---

[1] 'Othello: A Tragedy built on a comic structure', *Sh. Survey* 21, 1968, pp. 31–8.

the characters which he created can best be discussed after a brief analysis of the tragedy and its varied moods.

The first scene takes us at once to the heart of the theme when Iago expounds to Roderigo (whom he has already gulled of much money on the pretence of helping his suit for Desdemona's hand) his reasons for hating Othello. They are prompted at present by the 'unjust' promotion of the 'bookish theoric' Cassio to be the General's Lieutenant over the more experienced, less educated, Ensign (I.1.8–33). That Iago is a Florentine makes it worse, because of the ancient enmity between the two cities. Iago's grudge is also directed more generally against the modern tendency to replace promotion by seniority with promotion by capacity, or as he thinks it, favouritism. Such malcontents were common at a time when new methods of warfare, artillery, fortification, were revolutionizing military science.[1] By line 65 we realize Iago's essential dishonesty ('I am not what I am'), and that we must not trust a word that he says to anyone else without further testing. That he hates Othello on racial grounds is also evident ('And I—God bless the mark!— his Moorship's ancient'; 'Were I the Moor I would not be Iago') and these remarks gain force if we remember that Sant'Iago (St. James of Compostella) was 'Matamoros' ('Killer of Moors'), as well as patron saint of Spain.[2]

Not surprisingly therefore Iago and Roderigo make Othello's race and colour the chief ground of their clamour before Brabantio's house:

> Even now, now, very now, an old black ram
> Is tupping your white ewe. (I.1.88)

All the stock sexual racial prejudices are called up, and the shocked father (who has been pleased to have the distinguished soldier as his guest) thinks at once that his daughter must have been put under some African 'charm'. Having started trouble

---

[1] Cf. P. A. Jorgenson, *Shakespeare's Military World*, Berkeley, 1956. Sixteenth-century Italy saw great changes in the arts of war. England lagged behind and some authorites were still advocating bows and arrows in the 'nineties (*supra*, IV, p. 374).

[2] Single-handed, at the Battle of Clavijo, he slew sixty thousand Moors, and the military Order of St. James had as its motto 'Red is the sword with the blood of Moors'. Cf. 'A Note on Iago's Name', by G. N. Murphy, *Literature and Society*, ed. B. Slote, Lincoln, Neb., 1964, pp. 38–43.

Iago is too cautious to appear as an accuser. His double game is made obvious to Roderigo and the audience.

In I.2 outside the inn (the *Sagittary*, or *Centaur*) where Othello has taken Desdemona after their marriage, Iago warns Othello against Roderigo and Brabantio, but fails to frighten him, for the Moor knows his own honourable career and princely birth, and has married only for love. He greets Brabantio and his officers of the law with debonair courage ('Keep up your bright swords, for the dew will rust them') and refuses to be enraged by Brabantio's insults ('sooty bosom', etc.) and accusations of magic. He cannot be arrested since he has been summoned to the Duke's council, so they will go together, Brabantio insulting him as they go ('Bondslaves and pagans shall our statesmen be').

In the Council chamber (I.3) the urgency of the military situation is exercising the Senators. There are conflicting reports of the Turkish naval strength and of their intentions. The young Governor of Cyprus, Montano, has sent an appeal for relief. Othello's entry is welcomed by the Duke before Brabantio can pour out his accusations, which the Moor meets with a dignified admission of his love and an account of his wooing which incidentally provides proofs of his arduous life and travels as a soldier, and tells how Desdemona's girlish interest grew into a responsive love (I.3.76–94; 128–69). At Desdemona's brief assertion of her love and loyalty to Othello her father's fury dwindles into grudging acceptance of the *fait accompli*, as the Duke urges; but in effect he has cast her off (1.3.239–40). Later we learn that he has died of grief (V.2.202–4).

Instead of the unduly long passage in Cinthio where Disdemona pleads with her husband to be allowed to accompany him to Cyprus, Shakespeare makes them both ask the Duke to allow it, in speeches which assert that their love is not merely sensual. 'I saw Othello's visage in his mind', says Desdemona, and Othello insists that he is not ruled by 'the palate of my appetite' or likely to become uxorious (I.3.249–75). He will leave his wife to follow; before that they can have 'but an hour / Of love, of worldly matters and direction' together. To Brabantio's parting shot, 'She has deceiv'd her father, and may thee', Othello's rejoinder, 'My life upon her faith!' is ironic in the light of future events, as is his leaving her in the charge of 'Honest Iago' (I.3.292–301).

Left alone with the despairing Roderigo, Iago tries to put heart into him by expounding his own philosophy of life which is based, not on virtue, but on the power of the individual will: 'tis in ourselves that we are thus, or thus.' Love is merely 'a lust of the blood and a permission of the will', to be controlled by reason, which is itself an instrument of self-interest. Cynicism mingles with greed in his reiterated demand to the dupe he promises to help, 'Put money in thy purse'. For him Desdemona is merely a 'guinea-hen', to be straddled or bought; her marriage will not last. 'These Moors are changeable in their wills'; she herself 'must change for youth; when she is sated with his body, she must find the error of her choice.' He boasts that he can break the marriage between 'an erring barbarian and a super-subtle Venetian', if he be given money enough. Something of this he may believe, but not all.

When the credulous Roderigo has left him Iago lets his active mind range enjoyably, seeking an excuse for tormenting the Moor and a method of doing so. He does not really believe the story he has heard that Othello may have slept with Emilia, but it suggests the idea of making the Moor jealous of Desdemona by raising his suspicions of Cassio. The plan at present is only vaguely engendered, but he rejoices at the thought of using Cassio ('a proper man') and Othello's 'free and open nature' to ensnare them both, and also to get Cassio's place (I.3.385ff.).

In this marvellous exposition Shakespeare has by the end of Act I introduced all his chief characters (except Emilia), sketched their personalities and relations, and prepared the audience for some devilish intrigue against Cassio and the newly married pair. Act II brings Iago's general plan to the end of its first phase by his adroit use of circumstance, Roderigo's help, and Cassio's own weakness. In Cyprus (probably Famagusta) we learn of a great storm which has scattered the Turkish fleet and separated the vessels sailing from Venice. Cassio arrives first with news of Othello's coming and his marriage to a wondrous maid; then Iago with Desdemona, his wife and Roderigo. Cassio welcomes Emilia with a kiss (an English habit rather than an Italian one) and this starts a discussion about women in which Iago is disrespectful to his wife and cynical about women in general. Desdemona sees rightly that most of his witticisms are 'old fond paradoxes to make fools laugh in the alehouse'. She regards him as a sardonic humorist and, asked to rhyme upon 'a deserving woman', he produces six satiric couplets worthy of Pope. With a trace of condescension Cassio calls him 'more . . . the soldier than . . . the scholar'. Whereupon in a long aside Iago shows his secret hatred, and his suspicion that Cassio may have designs on Desdemona (II.1.167–77).

The arrival of Othello brings a reunion whose hyperboles of bliss and expectation of further growth in love are given a sinister background by the presence of Iago, who, left alone with Roderigo, sets to work at once, asserting that Desdemona is in love with Cassio, for she cannot possibly love the Moor, who lacks 'loveliness of favour, sympathy in years, manner and beauties' (II.1.218–61). With lecherous suggestions worthy of Thersites he excites his dupe against Cassio and persuades him to try to tempt the quick-tempered Lieutenant to anger while on guard-duty that evening. In the soliloquy which ends the scene Iago whips up his own envy and malice by inventing excuses for them which for the moment he makes himself believe—that the Moor has had Emilia, and (an afterthought) so has Cassio too; that he himself might like to possess Desdemona, and failing that would even the score by making Othello madly jealous of her and of Cassio. He will do this while pretending to be the Moor's friend; but how he is not yet sure. So the audience is left wondering, uneasy with ominous expectation.

Act II.2 proclaims a brief respite in the watch against invasion from five to eleven p.m. during which the people may feast to celebrate the destruction of the Turkish fleet and the marriage of the new Governor. In II.3. Cassio is instructed to keep good guard that night, and Othello takes in his bride to make love—perhaps for the first time. Iago tries to elicit from Cassio some sign of sensual desire for Desdemona, but Cassio shows a proper respect and reserve. He does not wish to drink on guard-duty, but he is persuaded against his better judgement and is soon made drunk before he is reminded by Montano to set the watch. Suggesting to Montano that Cassio is often drunk and may sleep on guard, Iago sends Roderigo in to annoy Cassio. In the affray Montano is injured, and to exaggerate the affair Iago has mutiny called and the alarm bell rung. When Othello enters, 'honest' Iago, all reluctant frankness, puts the blame on Cassio whose grievous crime is the worse because done 'in a town of war, / Yet wild, the people's hearts brimful of fear' (II. 3.210–14). Seeing, as he thinks, through Iago's pretended 'honesty and love' for Cassio, Othello is made firmer in his resolve to punish the offence, dismisses Cassio ('Never more be officer of mine'), and orders Iago to calm the town.[1]

Before going to do so, Iago works on Cassio's grief and shame, urging him not to despair but to beg Desdemona to intercede for him, since (like Cinthio's Corporal) he is afraid to face his commandant himself. When he is alone Iago rejoices that his perfectly sound advice may be used against both Cassio in his repentance and Desdemona in her innocent generosity (II.3. 333–59). His plan to excite Othello's jealousy is now clear in his mind and after telling Roderigo, still smarting from Cassio's blows, that things are going well ('Thou know'st we work by wit and not by witchcraft, / And wit depends on dilatory time'), he says that he will get Emilia to persuade Desdemona to meet Cassio when Othello is absent, then bring back the Moor to find Cassio 'Soliciting his wife'. Thus by the end of Act II the foundation is laid on which Iago intends to build suspicion and unfounded jealousy.

If Shakespeare knew Cinthio in Italian he may have read Dec. X, Nov. 8 in which Louis IX of France is disturbed in his chamber by two knights in his army who come to blows. Furious with them both he is inclined to have them executed,

'knowing with what religious care the military must be ruled, since on their virtue depend the quiet and security of kingdoms and empires; and he who does not bridle the overweening audacity of soldiers, especially in times of war, so that

[1] B. della Valle wrote 'I declare that if the Captain is disobeyed on guard-duty or on the watch, and if any soldiers disobey his orders on parade, it is proper not only to deprive them of their arms, horses, pay and belongings, but also to decide on some penalty and punishment, and even to condemn them to death and (as is the custom) to make them run the gauntlet of pikes ...' (*Vallo: libro continente apertenientie ad capitano*, Venice, 1524, Ch. iii, 'De la Punitione del Disobediente et traditore al suo capitano'.) S. Goulart, *Trésors d'histoires admirables*, cites examples of towns captured while their guards were drunk. Belleforest in his fifth collection (1583) tells how a Captain, lusting after the innocent wife of a quarrelsome young soldier, gets him into a brawl for which he is condemned to death [Cf. Vol. II, p. 405].

they fear their king more than their enemy, endangers the state; for by indulging in untimely brawls they put armies into discord and the life of their prince in peril, reducing others also to disobedience, whereby the enemy may be given the victory.'

In the end Louis sentences them both to the galleys until further notice, and does not release them for a year. Cassio's punishment is comparatively light, but it means the end of his military career. In making Iago engineer his disgrace Shakespeare departs from Cinthio, where the Ensign has no responsibility for it and does not start putting his evil desires into effect until Disdemona has already 'tried many times to reconcile the Moor' with the Corporal.

Act III is perhaps the most closely-packed, the fastest moving act in Elizabethan drama, as Iago fulfils his maxim 'Dull not device with coldness and delay'. At the beginning Othello is still completely happy in the consummation of his marriage. By the end he is tormented with jealousy and alienated from his wife. The brilliance of Shakespeare's psychological insight and inventiveness is nowhere better shown than here.

In III.1 Cassio shows his dutiful affection by paying musicians to serenade the General and his wife in the morning. Apparently the Moor has no music in his soul at the moment, for he pays them to go away, thus unconsciously rebuffing Cassio who, however, thanks the ubiquitous Iago for getting him access to Desdemona: 'never knew a Florentine more kind and honest.' Emilia brings good news: Othello is well-disposed. III.2 shows him going off to inspect the fortifications. When III.3 opens Cassio has easily persuaded Desdemona to do her best for him, but unfortunately (and in a sense the tragedy springs from this) when Othello unexpectedly returns, Cassio (like the Corporal at the Moor's house) is afraid to meet him and slinks away, thus giving Iago his first opportunity faintly to insinuate that there is something wrong between Cassio and Desdemona. She is importunate until Othello, delighted with her, gives way, and as she goes off happily, he utters the fateful words:

> Excellent wretch! Perdition catch my soul,
> But I do love thee! and when I love thee not,
> Chaos is come again. (III.3.90–2)

At once the serpent strikes. Iago tries to insinuate vague suspicions of Cassio's sincerity when he 'came a-wooing' with Othello. When the Moor speedily tires of his beating about the bush he excuses himself by asserting (rightly) that he is 'vicious in my guess', apt 'To spy into abuses' instead of keeping silent about thoughts which might disturb his friend's peace. He talks of reputation (very differently from Cassio at II.3.259–69) and advises Othello to beware of jealousy in such a way as to excite the very passion that he warns against (III.3.148–74).

As yet Othello is not greatly perturbed. The trustful man of action has not the normal jealous husband's fear when his wife 'loves company, / Is free of speech, signs, plays, and dances well,' and he will not jump to conclusions: 'I'll see before I doubt', not knowing his own nature, or 'honest Iago's'. Admitting 'I speak not yet of proof', the latter bids him 'observe her well with Cassio' (197), and suggests that Venetian ladies are known to be successful deceivers of their husbands.[1] Desdemona has already deceived her father. Othello begins to be moved from his assumption that his wife is 'honest', and when Iago suggests that her refusal of 'many proposed matches / Of her own clime, complexion and degree' might argue 'a will most rank, / Foul disproportion, thoughts unnatural', the simple Moor, instead of striking Iago down for his insult, is stunned and hastily dismisses him, asking him to set Emilia on to watch and agreeing to postpone restoring Cassio to his post until they have seen whether Desdemona is unduly importunate on his behalf. Othello is completely taken in by the Ancient's apparent honesty and knowledge of the world. He thinks to himself that his colour, age and lack of social graces may well have turned Desdemona against him. If so, his pride will not let him endure it (225–77). As soon as she enters his sick fancies are almost dissipated, yet he has a pain in his forehead, where traditionally

---

[1] According to W. Thomas, *The History of Italy*, 1549, Venetian women were gay in apparel, and 'none, young or old, unpainted'. It was a city of courtesans since, to keep the population down, only one brother of a family would marry: 'wherefore the rest of the brethren do keep courtesans to the intent they may have no lawful children.' It was a very free and easy city, 'For no man marketh another's doings, or meddleth with another man's living' (ed. G. P. Parks, 1963, p. 83). Because of all this the 'gorgeous dames' of Venice were said to be very licentious, and this reputation lasted till the days of Byron.

a cuckold's horns would grow, and her handkerchief is not big enough to bind it up.

Desdemona drops the handkerchief in agitation that her husband is unwell. Emilia picks it up and steals it to give to Iago, although she knows that both her mistress and the Moor set great store by it. Iago snatches it from her and at once plans to put it in Cassio's lodging. Something may come of it, the bold opportunist thinks, for he knows that he has destroyed Othello's peace for ever (320–31).

While Othello has been offstage Iago's poison has taken effect, and he is now assuming his wife's guilt (presumably before their marriage). At one moment he wishes that he had never known of it; at the next he is demanding 'ocular proof' (III.3.361). He sees not only his marriage but his military glory destroyed. He mistrusts Iago for a moment and Iago is in a difficulty because he *has* no proof. Othello begins to press him hard, but by inventing an incident in which Cassio betrayed himself in gross dreams about Desdemona (410–29), and by asserting that Cassio has wiped his beard on Desdemona's precious handkerchief, Iago raises the Moor to fury while himself counselling caution. In a Senecan rage Othello kneels and swears revenge, and the hypocritical Iago mimics him, promising every assistance, at which the Moor orders Cassio to be killed. When Iago mentions Desdemona Othello includes her too, and makes Iago his lieutenant. So Iago's ambition is satisfied; his devilish love of mischief is not.

In III.4 Desdemona shows that she does not even know where Cassio's lodging is, when she bids a Clown ask him to come and see Othello, since she hopes 'all may be well'. She has missed her handkerchief, and Emilia lies, pretending to know nothing of it. Othello comes and pretends to be cheerful, but his words hint sexual accusations (III.4.27–47), and when his unlucky wife tells him that she has sent for Cassio he demands the handkerchief and terrifies her by speaking of its magical properties and that 'To lose't or give't away, were such perdition / As nothing else could match.' She denies that she has lost it and tries to distract his attention by speaking of Cassio again, till he storms out (III.4.50–96). In his behaviour Emilia sees signs of jealousy, yet does not tell Desdemona about the handkerchief. Desdemona has to inform Cassio that the time

is not propitious since Othello is angry about something, perhaps some official or military matter; but Emilia still scents
jealousy.

Cassio meets his 'sweet love' Bianca, who seems to mingle the
functions in Cinthio of the courtesan and the 'woman' in the
Corporal's house whom he let copy the handkerchief 'before it
went back', and who was seen doing so by the Moor. Bianca
reproaches Cassio for not having visited her for a week (a
discrepancy if Cassio landed in Cyprus only a day or two ago,
but the time-problem will be discussed later). Apparently Iago
has put the handkerchief in Cassio's room and he has found it.
Doubtless it will be enquired after, but he would like Bianca to
'take out' the pattern before it is returned to whoever owns it.
Thus unwittingly Iago's victims bring doom upon themselves.

At the start of Act IV the resourceful villain is insisting on
the handkerchief while exciting the Moor with suggestions of
'harmless' play between Desdemona and Cassio—'an un-
authoriz'd kiss', 'Or to be naked with her friend a-bed, / An
hour or more, not meaning any harm', until, when he asserts
that Cassio has boasted of lying with Desdemona, Othello falls
into frenzy and a swoon. On his recovery Iago cheerfully tells
him that hosts of married men are cuckolds and that he at least
now knows his position. He offers to let Othello hide and watch
him while he gets Cassio to speak mockingly of his conquest.
Actually they talk about Bianca, but Othello assumes that it is
about Desdemona. They are interrupted by Bianca, who
returns the handkerchief to Cassio, having become suspicious
that he got it from some other woman. This plays into Iago's
hands, for Othello sees the handkerchief, and it is easy for the
Ancient to taunt him: 'to see how he prizes the foolish woman
your wife! she gave it him, and he hath given it his whore'
(IV.1.178–80). This is 'ocular proof' enough for the half-
demented Othello. Even in his murderous fury and despair he
cannot forget his wife's sweetness: 'O Iago, the pity of it, Iago!',
yet the next moment on a reminder from his 'friend' he cries, 'I
will chop her into messes. Cuckold me!', and as in Cinthio they
discuss how to get rid of her. Othello suggests poison, but at
once sees the poetic justice of Iago's scheme: 'strangle her in her
bed, even the bed she hath contaminated' (IV.1.198–211).
Nothing is said here, as in Cinthio, about concealing the crime.

Othello does not think of his own safety, and Iago's part will be
to be Cassio's 'undertaker'.

At this moment Lodovico enters with a message from the
Venetian Senate, and his niece Desdemona is with him. Othello
who is reading the despatch while she is telling Lodovico about
the breach between her husband and Cassio, overhears her
mention 'the love I bear to Cassio'; and when Lodovico says
that Othello is recalled and Cassio must succeed him as Governor, and she says 'Trust me, I'm glad on't' (IV.1.241), Othello,
imagining that his wife is publicly rejoicing that the man who
supplanted him in bed is now to have his post, strikes her in
front of the Venetian emissaries and upbraids her abominably
(IV.1.242–65). Lodovico is amazed at the change apparent in the
great General, and Iago hints that he could disclose more if
asked. So Othello's private chaos is ruining his public life.

The Moor's mind is now completely lacking in judgement
and obsessed with prurient thoughts. In IV.2 he questions
Emilia about her mistress, and when Emilia protests her
innocence he treats her as a bawd. He refuses to believe Desdemona's protestations of fidelity, but grieves over her alleged
betrayal of him (IV.2.30–63) till, his fury rising, he calls her a
'cunning whore of Venice', and goes out as if from a brothel
(66–93). Ignorant of his meaning but afraid that she must somehow have deserved blame, Desdemona is in the utmost distress.
Iago comes to gloat, but for once has little to say, and his wife
almost stumbles on the truth, that he is the instigator of the
misunderstanding: 'The Moor's abus'd by some most villanous knave, / Some base notorious knave, some scurvy fellow'
(IV.2.110–47), but he shuts her up, and there ensues a terrible
moment when the innocent Desdemona kneels before her tor-
mentor, vowing her love for her husband and asking Iago to
help her win him back (IV.2.148–64).

After Desdemona has gone with his promise 'All things shall
be well', Iago must encourage the wretched Roderigo who is
demanding results for the gifts which Iago says he has passed on
to Desdemona. He does so by promising him that he shall possess her the next night if he will kill Cassio tonight as he returns
from supping 'with a harlotry' (Bianca). But this is urgent, for
Othello is being transferred to Mauretania where Roderigo
cannot accompany him; a lie of course.

In IV.3 Desdemona, obedient to her husband's every wish, is preparing for bed, still sad, and with premonitions of grief or death. She sings the Willow Song and asks Emilia whether there are indeed women unfaithful to their husbands. The coarse-grained Emilia admits frankly that she herself might be tempted, and blames the men who ill-treat their wives. Desdemona prays that she will never give ill for ill, but may rather learn by her own errors.

The first attempt at murder occurs in V.1. where Roderigo, set on by Iago, attacks Cassio harmlessly and is himself wounded. Iago then wounds Cassio and Othello, watching, rejoices and goes to perform his own crime (1–36). When Lodovico and Gratiano approach, hearing groans, Iago returns, and pretending to aid Cassio, stabs Roderigo, thus removing a nuisance who might have betrayed him. He accuses Bianca of being in league with the assailants and sends his wife to tell Othello that Cassio is wounded.

In the bedchamber Othello (V.2) broods sadly over his sleeping wife: 'It is the cause, it is the cause, my soul', he says, meaning her beauty and the sensuality it incarnates and evokes; 'Yet she must die, else she'll betray more men.' He loves her still, but must execute justice upon her; he kisses her thrice, and weeps 'cruel tears'. But when she wakes the solemn calm with which he tells her he must kill her soon breaks down when she denies any infidelity with Cassio and begs him, 'Send for the man and ask him.' This obvious step has never occurred to the perverted mind of Othello, who believes that Cassio has confessed, and that he is now dead, killed by 'honest Iago'. The Moor has offered her time to prepare for death by confession, but when she weeps for Cassio his rage mounts and he suffocates her. The coming of Emilia interrupts him and causes the discovery of Desdemona dying, but able to assert her innocence and to try to exculpate her husband. Othello, however, makes no real effort to deny his guilt but glories in his act of justice. When he tells Emilia that his information came from Iago, 'My friend, thy husband, honest, honest Iago', she cannot take it in, but her loyalty to Desdemona's goodness rises above her shock and fear. She raises the alarm, and when Iago and the others run in she is the means by which her husband's lying and misuse of the handkerchief are made clear. He kills her, but too late, escapes but is recaptured, is wounded by Othello but preserved to suffer lingering tortures later. As for Othello himself, we see him return to sanity and to the realization of his deluded folly and his eternal loss. He must remain a prisoner to await the decision of the Venetian Senate. He asks for impartial justice, a fair report:

> then must you speak
> Of one that lov'd not wisely but too well;
> Of one not easily jealous, but being wrought,
> Perplex'd in the extreme; of one whose hand
> Like the base Indian, threw a pearl away,
> Richer than all his tribe . . .
> And say besides, that in Aleppo once,
> Where a malignant and a turban'd Turk
> Beat a Venetian and traduc'd the state,
> I took by the throat the circumcised dog,
> And smote him, thus. (V.2.337–55)

Stabbing himself, he falls on Desdemona's body, and dies 'upon a kiss'.

I have given so much space to this sketch of the action in the hope of suggesting the careful construction, the interaction of private and public affairs, and the variety of incident and mood introduced by Shakespeare into Cinthio's story. Calling now for some particular comment are the treatment of time, the nature of Iago's plotting, and the variety of interpretation given by scholars to the two main characters.[1]

Much has been written about the handling of time in *Othello*, and not surprisingly. Cinthio's story, as I have already indicated, is a long-drawn-out affair, for the Moor lived happily in Venice with Disdemona for some months before leaving for Cyprus, and the Ensign began to plot against her only after making advances which she ignored. Indications are given that several weeks, or months, elapsed before she was murdered, and the deaths of the two killers were long delayed and separate.

In remaking the story Shakespeare, while inventing a fuller version of the preamble in Venice, set out to speed up the whole

---

[1] Cf. the discussions in A. C. Bradley, *Shakespearean Tragedy*, 1920 edn., note I; K. Muir, *Shakespeare's Sources*, I, pp. 136–7; H. B. Charlton, *Shakespearian Tragedy*, 1948, pp. 130–2.

action, beginning with the night of the marriage and having the Moor sent off at once to Cyprus. There is a time-gap between Acts I and II for the sea-journey; then, having lost his first battle, Iago starts his campaign in earnest as soon as they all land, and during that night the marriage has been consummated and Cassio has been cashiered. Next morning Cassio asks Desdemona to intercede for him, and she does so; but by the end of the same scene (III.3) Iago has her handkerchief, Othello is madly jealous, and Cassio and Desdemona are to be killed—one day after arriving in Cyprus. III.4 seems to fall on the same day, although Iago has had the opportunity to leave the handkerchief in Cassio's room, for the latter gives it to Bianca to copy. IV.1 follows at once, for she comes back angrily to return the handkerchief 'which you gave me even now'. She asks Cassio to supper that night, and Othello invites Lodovico. In IV.2 Roderigo is told to kill Cassio as he leaves Bianca's house and in IV.3 Lodovico leaves after supper with Othello, and Desdemona is sent to bed. The murder and the 'discovery' (Act V) take place that night. So the whole action in Cyprus occurs within two days.

Cutting across this is another set of time-indications which conform somewhat to Cinthio's time-scale. Before leaving Venice Iago promises 'After some time to abuse Othello's ear / That [Cassio] is too familiar with his wife' (I.3.394–5). In II.3.310–14 he tells Cassio, 'Our general's wife is now the general . . . he hath devoted and given himself up to her'. This implies that they have been together for some time. In III.3.292–3 Emilia says that Iago 'hath a hundred times woo'd me to steal' Desdemona's handkerchief. But when, unless since they came together to Cyprus? On the voyage? Iago suggests that she has tired of her husband, and Othello believes it possible. This does not suggest a bridal couple. In III.3.339–41 he speaks of Cassio's and Desdemona's 'stolen hours of lust', in IV.1 of their being in bed together 'an hour or more'. When could that have been? At V.2.210 Othello says that she has sinned 'a thousand time'. Bianca accuses Cassio of neglecting her for a whole week.

Affairs of state too involve considerable passage of time. From Cyprus Othello sends letters to Venice (III.2). In IV.1 Lodovico arrives with Othello's recall, not in disgrace, but probably because the destruction of the Turkish fleet has made his presence in Cyprus unnecessary. There has been time for news of the storm to reach Venice (if not by Othello's own letters), and for a ship to sail from there and reach Cyprus. That would involve a week or two. The complaints of Roderigo about Iago's delays and the money he has had to spend also suggest the passage of many days.

As Christopher North first showed,[1] Shakespeare here, whether consciously or unconsciously, made use of two time-scales, 'the Short Time for the mounting tension of the passion . . . the Long for a thousand general needs.' The Long Time on the whole agrees with Cinthio's story, and is found in the Cyprus part of the play. Another interpretation of these and other discrepancies has been put forward by Ned B. Allen,[2] namely that Shakespeare wrote Acts III–V first, before making up his mind about the details of Acts I and II, and that he 'remembered Cinthio better when he started to write than when he came to fill in with Acts I and II'. He probably meant to revise the second half to agree with what he wrote in the first half, but decided not to 'dull device by coldness and delay', so left it. But 'Shakespeare *always* in the last three acts of the drama thought of Othello and Desdemona as long married and long resident in Cyprus.' Nevertheless the speed of the action in Acts III–V seems to conflict with this idea, and the discrepancies may equally have arisen if Shakespeare began with Acts I and II, taking little from Cinthio, then went to him for many external facts, but was forced by his desire for rapidity of movement to speed up Iago's plotting and the progress of the Moor's jealousy. There was a weakness in Cinthio's tale in that over the weeks and months the Moor would surely have tested the Ensign's story, if only by questioning the Corporal and his wife. And the longer they had been married the less likely would he have been to suspect his loving wife. To avoid this Shakespeare makes them only just married—and separated after their first night. Cassio's fall from grace, on which Iago works so speedily, is placed on the very night of their arrival in Cyprus, the night when Othello's marriage is consummated, the night when

---

[1] Excerpts from North's and other discussions were given in *Var.* pp. 358–72.

[2] N. B. Allen, 'The Two Parts of *Othello*', *Sh. Survey* 21, pp. 13–30. An excellent essay which deserves more of an answer than I can give here.

public rejoicings make it possible to make Cassio tipsy and quarrelsome. In the theatre the ingenious concatenation of events from then on, and our participation in the minds of the characters, woo us into accepting both Long and Short Times as they emerge, for our attention is not on the clock. Shakespeare must have realized that there were discrepancies, as he now accepted, now hastened, Cinthio's timing; but he covered the temporal improbabilities with the rising tide of excitement and suspense, and with changes of pace within and between scenes.[1]

One may regard it as the result of an inadequate assimilation or transmutation of Cinthio's tale; as a piece of theatrical trickery; or as a triumph of dramatic organization over the laborious verisimilitude which Cinthio sought. This last is my view. I suggest that there are not two but three Times in *Othello*. The third is Psychological Time, the shifting sense of duration within the mind of a character (e.g. Hamlet's in his first soliloquy in which we hear him telescoping the period between his father's death and his mother's re-marriage: 'two months dead . . . within a month. . . . A little month', etc. I.2.138–57) and of the sympathetic audience. By this the discrepancies between the implied historical time (Cinthio's) necessary to make the sequence of events possible, and the shorter dramatic times indicated in the play, are counterpointed and overruled. Thus Shakespeare transcends external probabilities in a poetic vision of Iago's evil mind working with lightning rapidity to destroy the innocent, and of an agonized victim whose sense of past and present is increasingly confused under the stress of his jealousy.

Certainly one major effect of Shakespeare's use of time is to make clear not only the inexorable advance of Iago's plotting but also his serpentine flexibility and unusual ability to extemporize at need. Interest in Machiavellian villains in drama came partly from watching the twists and turns of their ingenuity in response to obstacles and opportunities as they arose. Their plans often grew from small beginnings. Thus Eleazar in *Lust's Dominion*, who has something of Iago's ready invention, a similarly cold-blooded attitude to his own wife, and an ability

[1] Cf. J. W. Draper, *The Tempo-Patterns of Shakespeare's Plays*, Heidelberg, 1957, Ch. XI.

to assume jealousy when it suited his purpose, expounded the idea:

> for this chaos,
> This lump of projects, ere it be lick'd over,
> 'Tis like a bear's conception; stratagems
> Being but begot and not got out, are like
> Charg'd cannons not discharg'd—they do no harm
> Nor good. True policy, breeding in the brain,
> Is like a bar of iron, whose ribs, being broken
> And soften'd in the fire, you then may forge it
> Into a sword to kill, or to a helmet to defend,
> Life. 'Tis therefore wit to try all fashions
> Ere you append villany. (IV.4.2620–30)[1]

Originally Iago does not intend to drive the Moor to murder, but he is the embodiment of a cold malignity which needs no external motive to prompt it but will make use of any occasion and excuse to justify and exacerbate it.[2] This is accompanied by great cunning, a flashing intelligence limited in imaginative range and ignorant of the good in human nature, but eminently practical and casuistical.

Iago understands selfish motives but not unselfish ones, and in the end this brings his downfall, for he does not understand his own wife, that a woman who will steal and lie for him may, when she realizes the depth of his depravity, expose him fearlessly out of loyalty and affection for Desdemona.

Iago is neither Vice nor Devil, though he combines both traditions;[3] he is a Machiavellian plotter of a highly individual kind, mingling the comic abilities of the cony-catching sharper and the mischief-making slave-confidant with the more fundamental evil of the marriage-wrecker and the soul-destroyer. He is given several 'proximate' motives for his actions: he is an 'outsider', a Florentine among Venetians. A good, experienced soldier, he lacks advancement, envying Cassio his promotion and the main reason for it, Cassio's theoretic knowledge of war.

---

[1] *Lust's Dominion: or The Lascivious Queene*, ed. J. le G. Brereton, *Materialien*, n.s. V. Louvain, 1931.

[2] Cf. Helen Gardner, 'The Noble Moor', Brit. Acad. Lecture, 1955: 'Ultimately, whatever its proximate motives, malice is motiveless.'

[3] Cf. S. Spivack, *Shakespeare and the Allegory of Evil*, N.Y., 1958, p. 83 etc.; L. Scragg, 'Iago—Vice or Devil', *Sh. Survey* 21, 1968, pp. 53–65.

He hates Moors with a profound repugnance which easily attaches itself to any sexual excuse; and he envies Othello his military rank. But in addition, he hates both of his superior officers for being virtuous and high-principled men of honour. His own philosophy, as we have seen, is little more than barrack-room cynicism and self-interest. Like Milton's Satan he recognizes the virtue he despises, that Cassio 'hath a daily beauty in his life / That makes me ugly' (V.1.19–20) and that Othello is indispensable to Venice and also has 'A constant, loving and noble nature' (II.1.290).[1] He at once despises Othello for his lack of worldly caution, which he will turn to his own purpose, and envies the trustful generosity which he wishes to destroy.

As Professor N. Coghill has demonstrated,[2] Iago is given to strong sexual fantasies of crude copulation, and he passes them on to Othello in order to work him up into jealous rage. Essentially, however, Iago has a cold nature in which sensuality is less potent than delight in power and in the exercise of his ability to manipulate other men. His jealousy of his wife comes and goes at will; he has no 'absolute lust' for Desdemona but toys with sexual suggestions about her to Cassio. His greed for money (hinted at by Cinthio whose Ensign extorts money from the Moor for killing the Corporal) is subsidiary to his pleasure in gulling the Venetian gallant and using him as an instrument against Cassio. Moreover, Roderigo is so stupid that with him Iago can let himself go, revealing to him (and the audience) the brutality and coarseness he elsewhere hides under his mask as 'honest Iago'. There is nothing Iago loves more than to make someone else 'egregiously an ass', to sit secure in his hypocrisy while others trust and praise him, to contemplate his own cleverness while others do his dirty work for him.

There has been more controversy about Othello's character than about Iago's, because Othello is so fully drawn that as many interpretations are possible of him as of a person in real life. Cinthio's virtuous Moor soon becomes as ignoble as his tempter. Shakespeare's is many-sided and even in his downfall a splendid figure. Yet there must have been many in the Jacobean audience who took Emilia's view of the black murderer: 'O gull! O dolt! / As ignorant as dirt!', 'O thou dull Moor', 'O

[1] Cf. Scragg, *ibid.* p. 64.
[2] N. Coghill, *Shakespeare's Professional Skills*, 1964.

murderous coxcomb!' and to whom 'Othello proves himself the
black savage after all'.[1] Thomas Rymer's objection to the
marriage of Othello and Desdemona as improbable and monstrous is well known.[2] For some critics Othello is a 'tawny
Moor', not a Negro, and his race is not an important feature of
the tragedy. R. B. Heilman considers that 'Othello's Moorish-
ness, if it is anything more than a neutral heritage from Cinthio,
is less a psychological or moral factor than a symbol of . . .
"insecurity" and "rejection".'[3] For G. K. Hunter,[4] Othello,
black in countenance, is white in soul, whereas Iago, white in
appearance, is black in soul and in effect, he 'reduces the
"white" reality of Othello to the "black" appearance of his
face' until the last scene.

On the other hand, holding Othello to be essentially a military man, M. N. Proser argues that 'Shakespeare takes a
soldier and places him in a situation with which his military
training cannot cope',[5] and compares him with Coriolanus,
another general who is unaware of his own nature and cannot
adapt to changing circumstances. He is said to be 'rigid with
self-approbation', to be a noble *poseur*, given to self-dramatiza-
tion.[6] There is also the suggestion that Iago may be right in
accusing Othello of sinking his reason and his generalship in his
uxorious passion for Desdemona.[7]

To discuss these opinions here is impossible.[8] Instead I wish
to suggest a manysided approach to a play which is as complex
as any that Shakespeare ever wrote. Othello is a negroid Moor,
probably from Mauretania, and his blackness is intended (as
G. K. Hunter asserts) to bring out the paradox of his and Iago's
minds. He has an African prince's dignity, amiability, tenderness and sense of splendour. His strong passions are disciplined
by war and a natural love of moderation. He can meet the

---

[1] L. Lerner, *Essays in Crit.* ix, 1959, pp. 339–65. Contrast Eldred Jones in *E.I.C.* x,
1960, and his *Othello's Countrymen.*

[2] Cf. N. Alexander, 'Thomas Rymer and *Othello*', *Sh. Survey 21*, 1968, pp. 67–77.

[3] R. B. Heilman, *Magic in the Web*, Lexington, 1956.

[4] *Othello and Colour Prejudice*, Brit. Acad. Lecture, 1968.

[5] *The Heroic Image in Shakespeare's Tragedies*, Princeton, 1965, p. 92.

[6] F. R. Leavis, 'Diabolic Intellect and the Noble Hero' in *The Common Pursuit*,
1952, pp. 136–59.

[7] R. N. Hallstead, 'Idolatrous Love: A new Approach to Othello', *ShQ.*, 1968.

[8] I recommend the admirable essay '*Othello:* A Retrospect' by Helen Gardner,
Sh. Survey 21, pp. 1–11.

Senators on equal terms, revealing a gift of eloquence and a mind stored with manly experience and images of travel in exotic places. He is an 'outsider' in Venice, but this does not mean that he is always conscious of his race. By long custom, the Venetians 'held it a better course to defend their dominions upon the Continent with foreign mercenary souldiers, than with their homeborn citizens'; once there was a law 'that no Gentleman of *Venice* should have the charge and commaundement of above five and twentie souldiers'; and the commanders of the army were always foreigners (Lewkenor, *op. cit.* pp. 131–2). Othello's race is brought to our notice by the vituperation of his enemies; but the Duke, Lodovico and Gratiano seem unaffected by it. The Moor himself knows that his military standing places him above racial barriers in his public life; but once the racial question enters his marriage he realizes that it may be a sexual barrier which might contribute to his wife's disloyalty. Yet the play cannot be summarized as simply a tragedy of colour. The untypical Moor is betrayed by an untypical soldier.[1]

Othello is equally a tragedy of misplaced trust, of credulity, as the relatively simple soldier, unused to the manners and intrigues of urban society, comes to trust his proven male friend rather than his new bride, and does not think of testing Iago's stories by confronting him with Cassio or Desdemona, or even of questioning them. Fenton's Albanian Captain is melancholic sick and moody from the first and his jealousy is self-generated. Cinthio's Moor gives himself entirely up to the persuasions of a more sophisticated mind, and Shakespeare takes this over, making Othello aware of his ignorance about Venetian women and Venetian morals. But his credulity is not like that of the gull, Roderigo. He brings out a more subtle aspect of Iago's knavery, which operates so skilfully that we do not have a constant sense of Othello's folly. Without completely identifying ourselves with him we quickly appreciate Othello's quality and our adverse criticism is swept away by the speed of the action and the spectacle of his anguish. In the study, reading analytically, we may think that despite his claim that he was 'not easily jealous', he was too easily 'wrought', but this makes too little of Elizabethan theatrical technique and Elizabethan psychology.

[1] Cf. Eldred Jones, *Othello's Countrymen*, 1965, pp. 64ff.

It is commonplace to call the play 'a Tragedy of Jealousy', and indeed 'we observe the operations of jealousy in several different characters—in the comic dupe Roderigo, in Bianca, in Iago, and in Othello himself',[1] and it operates differently in each person. Miss L. B. Campbell demonstrated that for the Renaissance jealousy was a compound passion: 'It is a species of envy, which is in turn a species of hatred.'[2] The close ties between envy and jealousy give a special force to the story of the Ensign and the Moor, for Iago is an embodiment of Envy, with sexual jealousy as only one of its symptoms. But he is not the typical envious man of *The French Academie* (1589).[3] Cinthio's Ensign has a 'handsome presence', 'the likeness of a Hector or an Achilles', and we may assume from Iago's general popularity that his appearance belies his mind. He creates in Othello a passion of envy and jealousy 'so strong / That judgement cannot cure'.

According to Benedetto Varchi as translated by Robert Tofte: 'Jealousie commeth in respect of a mans Reputation and Honor, according as his nature is, or as his Breeding hath beene, of after the fashion and manner of the Country in which hee is borne and liveth.'[4]

Hence *Othello* is also a tragedy of Honour. The tale is of a type common in the Renaissance, based on the notion of marital honour widespread in Mediterranean countries until our own time. In Spain or Italy an injured husband had the right—and the duty—to avenge himself on his wife and her lover in case of adultery. Vengeance should be secret if there had been no public scandal; otherwise it might be public. A man must preserve his reputation, his good name, above all else. A cuckold was a comic figure, so one must not publish one's shame in removing its cause.[5]

[1] *Othello*, ed. K. Muir, New Penguin Shakespeare, 1968, p. 21.

[2] L. B. Campbell, *Shakespeare's Tragic Heroes, Slaves of Passion*, 1961 edn., p. 148.

[3] 'Constrained to bite on his bridle, to locke up his owne miserie in the bottome of his heart . . . (he) becommeth pale, wanne, swart and leane; the eyes sinke into the head, the lockes are askew, and the whole countenance is disfigured.' (1594 edn., p. 317.) Cited by Campbell, who does not contrast it with Iago.

[4] *The Blazon of Jealousie*, 1615, pp. 21–3. Cited by Campbell.

[5] Cf. E. M. Wilson, 'Family Honour in the Plays of Shakespeare's Predecessors and Contemporaries', *Essays and Studies*, 1953, pp. 19–40: 'In Spain the general assumption was that honour represented a greater good than life; so that loss of honour could only be made good by killing those responsible for it.' This was true

In the eyes of the world Honour was largely a matter of reputation; hence Cinthio's Moor and Ensign plan two secret murders. Reputation is twice discussed in *Othello* by Iago, who of course is careful to keep up his own reputation as an 'honest' fellow, all things to all men. When Cassio is mourning his drunkenness and the loss of his reputation, 'the immortal part of myself', Iago says, 'Reputation is a most idle and most false imposition. . . . You have lost no reputation at all, unless you repute yourself such a loser' (II.3.259–68). But pushing Othello into suspicion and jealousy he is soon preaching that 'he that filches from me my good name / Robs me of that which not enriches him, / And makes me poor indeed' (III.3.155–61). Othello takes this seriously, for he is rightly proud of his good fame. But to him Honour concerns not just what other people think of him but what he thinks of himself. The 'fleers, the gibes, and notable scorns' which Iago pretends to show him in Cassio's banter about Bianca (IV.1.81–9) are infuriating, but much worse is the fear that he might have to 'keep a corner in the thing I love / For others' uses' (III.3.270–3). Having lost his wife, he has lost not only her but his ambition, military glory, and self-esteem.

Pride indeed, as M. N. Proser asserts,[1] is one of Othello's marked qualities, but I cannot find this a fault, or agree with George Meredith, who likened Othello to Sir Willoughby Patterne because 'He is a man whose pride, when hurt, would run his wife to perdition to solace it.'[2] This is too simple a view; not only is his pride 'hurt'; his love for Desdemona is, he imagines, violated by her infidelity and his mind fills with horrible sexual and animal images—toads, asps, dogs, goats and monkeys, as he reels in disgust. His moral sense is revolted by her apparent deception and hypocrisy; hence her death is to be a sacrifice to justice and purity. And at the end, when the justice he has meted out, not solemnly but in a sudden frenzy, proves to have been the foul murder of his innocent wife, he

---

in Italy also; hence Cinthio's Moor. In '*Othello*, a Tragedy of Honour', *Listener*, 5 June 1952, pp. 926–7, Wilson argues that Iago attacks Brabantio's honour, and ruins Cassio's for a time, besides destroying Othello's for ever.

[1] *Op cit.* pp. 92–5.

[2] *The Egoist*, Ch. 35. Cf. F. N. Lees, 'George Meredith and Othello', *N&Q*, n.s. 12, 3, 1965, p. 96.

accepts his position as an outsider, a barbarian (as the images of the 'base Indian' and the 'malignant . . . Turk' imply), and executes justice on himself. He now knows the depths of his own nature, but in the simple grandeur of his farewells he regains his nobility and much of the romantic glamour with which Shakespeare invested him before his fall.

I. Source

From GLI HECATOMMITHI
by Giovanni Battista Giraldi Cinthio, (1566 edn.),
translated by the editor

From the Introduction

[The Introduction gives a vivid account of the Sack of Rome, 1527, with all the horrors of war, famine and plague. A group of noble men and ladies sail for Marseilles to escape the devastation. On the way the men discuss how peace in love may be obtained. The various kinds of love are described: religious love towards the Divine, human love governed by reason and judgement, base appetite. The debate turns mainly on married love. Fabio, the wise old leader says:]

I hold firmly that peace can be found only in the love that comes of counsel and chooses well. For in such a love appetite is ruled by reason, which reins it in and prevents it from trespassing beyond what accords with ends both honest and suitable. And because I do not see any love among us (I refer to that which pertains to generation) which is not wholly appetite except that which is between husband and wife, I hold without any doubt that in the love of which we speak there cannot be a quiet and reposeful life except where husbands and wives . . . join together, seeking wisdom and prudence, and desiring honest repose so as to live peacefully in this mortal state. In conclusion I say that the only rational love is that which has marriage as its goal, and that this is the quiet of true and wise lovers, coupled together, cooling their amorous flames with sage discourse and in legitimate union.

[Ponzio disagrees with Fabio, for there is ample proof that there is not in marriage the peace and quiet of which you endeavour to persuade us. Women are dangerous beings; hence fathers pay large dowries to get rid of them. He quotes Menander ('Better bury a woman than marry her') and other authorities, including King Alfonso of Naples who said, 'For there to be peace between husband and wife the husband must be deaf and the wife blind.' To take a wife is to enter into intolerable trouble. Fabio answers that there must be understanding in marriage:]

Excellent it is, Ponzio, to take a wife, but one needs to use judgement, and a man must not let himself be prey to appetite; nor should any man take any woman indifferently to wife, nor any woman any man as husband. They should not let their eyes be dimmed by greed for possessions or greatness of blood, nor beauty of body, nor any other condition; but first they should consider only the nature and quality of the persons with whom they might join themselves in perpetual bonds. In this more than in any other affair it is needful to take reason and counsel for guide, and with discerning eye to consider the quality, manners, life and habits of the men or women, their mothers, fathers, families, antiquity, rank, and other such factors which are manifest signs of the natures and lives of other people.[1] Those who are joined together, not by chance or vanity or greed, but with sound reasoning, will live in that quiet and tranquil life of which I spoke, and none of the murmurings and discords of which you spoke will occur.

[They discuss whether love can exist outside marriage, and whether the world would not be equally well peopled by the fruits of illicit relationships. Fabio attacks courtesans:]

There is no beauty, Flamminio, where there is no virtue, and where there is no virtue, there cannot be love, for love is born only among good things. Hence he who wishes to form a true judgement of beauty must admire not only the body, but rather the minds and habits of those who present themselves to his view;[2] and if you find there a mind in harmony with the body's beauty, that soul will be loveable and gentle, and will excite those who desire it to something other than a dishonourable lasciviousness.

He warns them against women who 'with beauty of body and under a semblance of virtue, for instance in singing, playing, dancing lightly and speaking sweetly, hide an ugly and abominable soul.[3] One can say, "How foul must that room be which is given up to so evil a tenant!"'

[The Introduction contains ten stories; then there are ten Decades of ten stories each. After the Introduction the men rejoin the ladies, and some of the tales are told by the latter.
Novella 9 of the Introduction has a plot not unlike that of *Othello*, but with a female Iago. A woman falls in love with a married man

---

[1] Brabantio would agree.   [2] Cf. Desdemona, I.3.252–4.
[3] Contrast Othello, III.3.183–6.

and gets into his house as a serving-maid. Hoping so to win him she arouses his suspicion of his wife, and promises to give him proof. She gets her own paramour into the house, enjoys him, then makes it appear that is he coming away from the wife's bed when the husband comes seeking his proof. The husband tries to kill the intruder, who gets away. Then he attacks his wife with a knife, but she escapes and finds refuge until her innocence is proved by a kind benefactress.

At the beginning of the third Decade the troop of friends have been ashore and had a feast of talk and song. Next day Fabio gets them aboard again and they start their stories anew. The theme of this Decade is 'The infidelity of husbands and wives'. In Story 1 a King of Scotland falls in love and tries to have his wife poisoned. (This was the basis of Greene's *Scottish History of James IV*.) In No. 2 a Mayor is untrue to his wife, but although she knows it she refuses to be untrue to him. In No. 4 a husband discovers that his wife is in love with another man, substitutes himself in her bed for her lover, and after giving her great pleasure, reveals himself. She is penitent and he forgives her. Both Nos. 6 and 7 concern revenge for honour. In No. 6 a husband who finds his wife in adultery with a servant lets the man go and pretends that nothing has happened. Some time later the servant is accidentally drowned in the Arno. Then the husband ingeniously arranges for his wife also to be drowned 'accidentally' in the river.]

The Third Decade, Story 7

A Moorish Captain takes to wife a Venetian lady, and his Ensign accuses her to her husband of adultery; he desires the Ensign to kill the man whom he believes to be the adulterer; the Captain kills his wife and is accused by the Ensign. The Moor does not confess, but on clear indications of his guilt he is banished; and the scoundrelly Ensign, thinking to injure others, brings a miserable end on himself.

The ladies would have had great pity for the fate of the Florentine woman had her adultery not made her appear worthy of the severest punishment; and it seemed to them that the gentleman's patience had been unusually great. Indeed they declared that it would be hard to find any other man who, discovering his wife in such a compromising situation, would not have slain both of the sinners outright. The more they thought about it the more prudently they considered him to have behaved.

After this discussion, Curzio, on whom all eyes were turned as they waited for him to begin his story, said: I do not believe that either men or women are free to avoid amorous passion, for human nature is so disposed to it that even against our will it makes itself powerfully

I

felt in our souls.[1] Nevertheless, I believe that a virtuous lady has the power, when she feels herself burning with such a desire, to resolve rather to die than through dishonourable lust to stain that modesty which ladies should preserve as untainted as white ermine. And I believe that they err less who, free from the holy bonds of matrimony, offer their bodies to the delight of every man, than does a married woman who commits adultery with one person only. But as this woman suffered well-deserved punishment for her fault, so it sometimes happens that without any fault at all, a faithful and loving lady, through the insidious plots (*tesele*) of a villainous mind, and the frailty of one who believes more than he need, is murdered by her faithful husband; as you will clearly perceive by what I am about to relate to you.

There was once in Venice a Moor, a very gallant man, who, because he was personally valiant and had given proof in warfare of great prudence and skilful energy, was very dear to the Signoria, who in rewarding virtuous actions ever advance the interests of the Republic. It happened that a virtuous Lady of wondrous beauty called Disdemona, impelled not by female appetite but by the Moor's good qualities, fell in love with him, and he, vanquished by the Lady's beauty and noble mind, likewise was enamoured of her. So propitious was their mutual love that, although the Lady's relatives did all they could to make her take another husband,[2] they were united in marriage and lived together in such concord and tranquillity while they remained in Venice, that never a word passed between them that was not loving.

It happened that the Venetian lords made a change in the forces that they used to maintain in Cyprus; and they chose the Moor as Commandant of the soldiers whom they sent there.[3] Although he was pleased by the honour offered him (for such high rank and dignity is given only to noble and loyal men who have proved themselves most valiant), yet his happiness was lessened when he considered the length and dangers of the voyage, thinking that Disdemona would be much troubled by it. The Lady, who had no other happiness on earth but the Moor, and was very pleased with the recognition of his merits that her husband had received from so noble and powerful a Republic, could hardly wait for the hour when he would set off with his men, and she would accompany him to that honourable post. It grieved her greatly to see the Moor troubled; and, not knowing the reason for it, one day while they were dining together she said to him: 'Why is it, my Moor, that after being given such an honourable rank by the Signoria, you are so melancholy?'

---

[1] Iago takes a different view, I.3.329–37.   [2] Not Roderigo, certainly. (I.1.94–8.)
[3] No reason is given, no mention of the Turkish menace.

The Moor said to Disdemona: 'The love I bear you spoils my pleasure at the honour I have received, because I see that one of two things must happen: either I must take you with me in peril by sea, or, so as not to cause you this hardship, I must leave you in Venice. The first alternative must inevitably weigh heavily on me, since every fatigue you endured and every danger we met would give me extreme anxiety. The second, having to leave you behind, would be hateful to me, since, parting from you I should be leaving my very life behind.[1]

'Alas, husband,' said Disdemona, hearing this, 'What thoughts are these passing through your mind? Why do you let such ideas perturb you? I want to come with you wherever you go, even if it meant walking through fire in my shift instead of, as it will be, crossing the water with you in a safe, well-furnished galley. If there really are to be dangers and fatigues, I wish to share them with you; and I should consider myself very little beloved if, rather than have my company on the sea, you were to leave me in Venice, or persuaded yourself that I would rather stay here in safety than be in the same danger as yourself.[2] Get ready then for the voyage in the cheerfulness that befits the high rank you hold.'

Then the Moor joyously threw his arms round his wife's neck and said, with a loving kiss: 'God keep us long in this love, my dear wife!' Shortly afterwards,[3] having donned his armour and made all ready for the journey, he embarked in the galley with his lady and all his train; then, hoisting sail, they set off, and with a sea of the utmost tranquillity[4] arrived safely in Cyprus.

The Moor had in his company an Ensign of handsome presence but the most scoundrelly nature in the world. He was in high favour with the Moor, who had no suspicion of his wickedness; for although he had the basest of minds, he so cloaked the vileness hidden in his heart with high sounding and noble words, and by his manner, that he showed himself in the likeness of a Hector or an Achilles. This false man had likewise taken to Cyprus his wife, a fair and honest young woman. Being an Italian she was much loved by the Moor's wife, and spent the greater part of the day with her.

In the same company there was also a Corporal who was very dear to the Moor. This man went frequently to the Moor's house and often dined with him and his wife. The Lady, knowing him so well liked by her husband, gave him proofs of the greatest kindness, and this was much appreciated by the Moor.

The wicked Ensign, taking no account of the faith he had pledged

---

[1] Othello proposes to leave her in Venice. (I.3.236–9.)

[2] Desdemona asks the Duke for permission to accompany him. (I.3.249–60.)

[3] Cf. I.3.279: 'You must away tonight.'   [4] Cf. II.1.1–19: storm.

to his wife, and of the friendship, loyalty and obligations he owed the Moor, fell ardently in love with Disdemona,[1] and bent all his thoughts to see if he could manage to enjoy her; but he did not dare openly show his passion, fearing that if the Moor perceived it he might straightway kill him. He sought therefore in various ways, as deviously as he could, to make the Lady aware that he desired her. But she, whose every thought was for the Moor, never gave a thought to the Ensign or anybody else. And all the things he did to arouse her feelings for him had no more effect than if he had not tried them. Whereupon he imagined that this was because she was in love with the Corporal;[2] and he wondered how he might remove the latter from her sight. Not only did he turn his mind to this, but the love which he had felt for the Lady now changed to the bitterest hate, and he gave himself up to studying how to bring it about that, once the Corporal were killed, if he himself could not enjoy the Lady, then the Moor should not have her either. Turning over in his mind divers schemes, all wicked and treacherous, in the end he determined to accuse her of adultery, and to make her husband believe that the Corporal was the adulterer.[3] But knowing the singular love of the Moor for Disdemona,[4] and his friendship for the Corporal, he recognized that, unless he could deceive the Moor with some clever trick, it would be impossible to make him believe either charge. Wherefore he set himself to wait until time and place opened a way for him to start his wicked enterprise.

Not long afterwards the Moor deprived the Corporal of his rank for having drawn his sword and wounded a soldier while on guard-duty. Disdemona was grieved by this and tried many times to reconcile the Moor with him. Whereupon the Moor told the rascally Ensign that his wife importuned him so much for the Corporal that he feared he would be obliged to reinstate him. The evil man saw in this a hint for setting in train the deceits he had planned, and said: 'Perhaps Disdemona has good cause to look on him so favourably!' 'Why is that?' asked the Moor. 'I do not wish', said the Ensign, 'to come between man and wife, but if you keep your eyes open you will see for yourself.' Nor for all the Moor's inquiries would the Ensign go beyond this: nonetheless his words left such a sharp thorn in the Moor's mind, that he gave himself up to pondering intensely what they could mean. He became quite melancholy, and one day, when his wife was trying to soften his anger towards the Corporal,

[1] Contrast Iago's cold statement, II.1.294-9, and his mockery of Desdemona, II.1.144-60.
[2] Iago does not believe this.
[3] Cf. Iago on Cassio, I.3.396-7.
[4] Cf. II.1.291-4.

begging him not to condemn to oblivion the loyal service and friendship of many years just for one small fault, especially since the
Corporal had been reconciled to the man he had struck, the Moor
burst out in anger and said to her, 'There must be a very powerful
reason why you take such trouble for this fellow, for he is not your
brother, nor even a kinsman, yet you have him so much at heart!'

The lady, all courtesy and modesty, replied: 'I should not like you
to be angry with me. Nothing else makes me do it but sorrow to see
you deprived of so dear a friend as you have shown that the Corporal
was to you. He has not committed so serious an offence as to deserve
such hostility.[1] But you Moors are so hot by nature that any little
thing moves you to anger and revenge.'

Still more enraged by these words the Moor answered: 'Anyone
who does not believe that may easily have proof of it! I shall take
such revenge for any wrongs done to me as will more than satisfy
me!' The lady was terrified by these words, and seeing her husband
angry with her, quite against his habit, she said humbly: 'Only a
very good purpose made me speak to you about this, but rather than
have you angry with me I shall never say another word on the
subject.'

The Moor, however, seeing the earnestness with which his wife
had again pleaded for the Corporal, guessed that the Ensign's words
had been intended to suggest that Disdemona was in love with the
Corporal, and he went in deep depression to the scoundrel and urged
him to speak more openly. The Ensign, intent on injuring this unfortunate lady, after pretending not to wish to say anything that
might displease the Moor, appeared to be overcome by his entreaties
and said: 'I must confess that it grieves me greatly to have to tell you
something that must be in the highest degree painful to you; but
since you wish me to tell you, and the regard that I must have of
your honour as my master spurs me on, I shall not fail in my duty to
answer your request. You must know therefore that it is hard for your
Lady to see the Corporal in disgrace for the simple reason that she
takes her pleasure with him whenever he comes to your house. The
woman has come to dislike your blackness.'

These words struck the Moor's heart to its core; but in order to
learn more (although he believed what the Ensign had said to be
true, through the suspicion already sown in his mind) he said, with
a fierce look: 'I do not know what holds me back from cutting out
that outrageous tongue of yours which has dared to speak such insults
against my Lady!'[2] Then the Ensign: 'Captain,' he said, 'I did not
expect any other reward for my loving service; but since my duty

[1] Cf. III.3.63–7.
[2] Cf. III.3.360–74.

and my care for your honour have carried me so far, I repeat that the matter stands exactly as you have just heard it, and if your Lady, with a false show of love for you, has so blinded your eyes that you have not seen what you ought to have seen, that does not mean that I am not speaking the truth. For this Corporal has told me all, like one whose happiness does not seem complete until he has made someone else acquainted with it.'[1] And he added: 'If I had not feared your wrath, I should, when he told me, have given him the punishment he deserved by killing him. But since letting you know what concerns you more than anyone else brings me so undeserved a reward, I wish that I had kept silent, for by doing so I should not have fallen into your displeasure.'

Then the Moor, in the utmost anguish, said, 'If you do not make me see with my own eyes[2] what you have told me, be assured, I shall make you realize that it would have been better for you had you been born dumb.' 'To prove it would have been easy', replied the villain, 'when he used to come to your house; but now when, not as it should have been, but for the most trivial cause, you have driven him away, it cannot but be difficult for me, for although I fancy that he still enjoys Disdemona whenever you give him the opportunity, he must do it much more cautiously than he did before, now that he knows you have turned against him. Yet I do not lose hope of being able to show you what you do not wish to believe.'[3] And with these words they parted.

The wretched Moor, as if struck by the sharpest of darts, went home to wait for the day when the Ensign would make him see that which must make him miserable for ever. But no less trouble did the Ensign suffer by his knowledge of the Lady's chastity, for it did not seem possible to find a way of making the Moor believe what he had falsely told him, till, his thoughts twisting and turning in all directions, the scoundrel thought of a new piece of mischief.

The Moor's wife often went, as I have said, to the house of the Ensign's wife, and stayed with her a good part of the day; wherefore seeing that she sometimes carried with her a handkerchief embroidered most delicately in the Moorish fashion, which the Moor had given her and which was treasured by the Lady and her husband too, the Ensign planned to take it from her secretly, and thereby prepare her final ruin. He had a little girl of three years old, much loved by Disdemona. One day, when the unfortunate Lady had gone to pass some time at the villain's house, he took the child in his arms and carried her to the Lady, who took her and pressed her to her breast.

[1] Iago invents an erotic dream.
[2] III.3.360–74: 'Give me the ocular proof.'
[3] III.3.395–409.

The deceiver, who had great sleight of hand, lifted the handkerchief from her girdle so warily that she did not notice it; and he took his leave of her in great joy.[1]

Disdemona, knowing nothing of it, went back home and, being occupied with other thoughts, did not miss the handkerchief. But a few days later, she looked for it, and not finding it she became afraid that the Moor might ask for it, as he often did. The wicked Ensign, seizing a suitable opportunity, went to the Corporal's room, and with cunning malice left the handkerchief at the head of his bed.[2] The Corporal did not notice it till the next morning when, getting out of bed, he put his foot upon the handkerchief, which had fallen to the floor. Not being able to imagine how it had come into his house, and knowing that it was Disdemona's, he determined to give it back to her. So he waited till the Moor had gone out, then went to the back door and knocked. Fortune, it seems, had conspired with the Ensign to bring about the death of the unhappy lady; for just then the Moor came home, and hearing a knock on the door went to the window and shouted angrily: 'Who is knocking?'. The Corporal, hearing the Moor's voice and fearing that he might come down and attack him, fled without answering.[3] The Moor ran down the stairs, and opening the outside door went out into the street and looked around, but could see nobody. Then returning full of evil passion, he asked his wife who had knocked on the door below.

The Lady replied truthfully that she did not know. The Moor then said, 'It looked to me like the Corporal.' 'I do not know', she said, 'whether it was he or somebody else.' The Moor restrained his fury, though he was consumed with rage. He did not want to do anything before consulting the Ensign, to whom he went at once and told him what had occurred, praying him to find out from the Corporal all that he could about it. Delighted with what had happened, the Ensign promised to do so. Accordingly he spoke to the Corporal one day while the Moor was standing where he could see them as they talked; and chatting of quite other matters than the Lady,[4] he laughed heartily and, displaying great surprise, he moved his head about and gestured with his hands, acting as if he were listening to marvels. As soon as the Moor saw them separate he went to the Ensign to learn what the other had told him; and the Ensign, after making him entreat him for a long time, finally declared: 'He has hidden nothing from me. He tells me that he has enjoyed your wife

---

[1] Shakespeare omits the child and makes Desdemona drop the handkerchief. (III.3.279-331.)
[2] Cf. III.3.322-3; III.4.177-86.
[3] Cf. III.3.1-45, at an earlier stage.
[4] Of Bianca at IV.1.93-144.

every time you have given them the chance by your absence. And on the last occasion she gave him the handkerchief which you gave her as a present when you married her.'[1] The Moor thanked the Ensign and it seemed obvious to him that if he found that the Lady no longer had the handkerchief, then all must be as the Ensign claimed.

Wherefore one day after dinner, while chatting with the Lady on various matters, he asked her for the handkerchief.[2] The unhappy woman, who had greatly feared this, grew red in the face at the request, and to hide her blushes (which the Moor well noted), she ran to the chest, pretending to look for it. After much search, 'I do not know', she said, 'why I cannot find it; perhaps you have had it?' 'If I had had it,' said he, 'why should I ask for it? But you will look more successfully another time.'[3]

Leaving her the Moor began to think how he might kill his wife, and the Corporal too, in such a way that he would not be blamed for it.[4] And since he was obsessed with this, day and night, the Lady inevitably noticed that he was not the same towards her as he was formerly. Many times she said to him, 'What is the matter with you? What is troubling you? Whereas you used to be the gayest of men, you are now the most melancholy man alive!'

The Moor invented various excuses, but she was not at all satisfied, and although she knew no act of hers which could have so perturbed the Moor, she nevertheless feared that through the abundance of lovemaking which he had with her he might have become tired of her. Sometimes she would say to the Ensign's wife, 'I do not know what to make of the Moor. He used to be all love towards me, but in the last few days he has become quite another man;[5] and I fear greatly that I shall be a warning to young girls not to marry against their parents' wishes; and Italian ladies will learn by my example not to tie themselves to a man whom Nature, Heaven, and manner of life separate from us. But because I know that he is very friendly with your husband, and confides in him, I beg you, if you have learned anything from him which you can tell me, that you will not fail to help me.' She wept bitterly as she spoke.[6]

The Ensign's wife, who knew everything (for her husband had wished to use her as an instrument in causing the Lady's death, but she had never been willing to consent), did not dare, for fear of her husband, to tell her anything. She said only: 'Take care not to give

[1] IV.1.174–80.   [2] III.4.52–84.
[3] Othello is more demanding. (III.4.84–96.)
[4] Cf. III.3.461–79. Iago plays a bigger part here.
[5] The Brothel scene proves this. (IV.2.)
[6] Desdemona begs Iago to help her. (IV.2.148–51.)

your husband any reason for suspicion, and try your hardest to make him realize your love and loyalty'.[1] 'That indeed I do', said Disdemona, 'but it does not help.'

In the meantime the Moor sought in every way to get more proof of that which he did not wish to discover, and prayed the Ensign to contrive to let him see the handkerchief in the Corporal's possession; and although that was difficult for the villain, he promised nonetheless to make every effort to give him this testimony.

The Corporal had a woman at home who worked the most wonderful embroidery on lawn,[2] and seeing the handkerchief and learning that it belonged to the Moor's wife, and that it was to be returned to her, she began to make a similar one before it went back. While she was doing so, the Ensign noticed that she was working near a window where she could be seen by whoever passed by on the street. So he brought the Moor and made him see her,[3] and the latter now regarded it as certain that the most virtuous Lady was indeed an adulteress. He arranged with the Ensign to kill her and the Corporal, and they discussed how it might be done. The Moor begged the Ensign to kill the Corporal, promising to remain eternally grateful to him. The Ensign refused to undertake such a thing, as being too difficult and dangerous, for the Corporal was as skilful as he was courageous; but after much entreaty, and being given a large sum of money, he was persuaded to say that he would tempt Fortune.[4]

Soon after they had resolved on this, the Corporal, issuing one dark night from the house of a courtesan with whom he used to amuse himself, was accosted by the Ensign, sword in hand, who directed a blow at his legs to make him fall down; and he cut the right leg entirely through,[5] so that the wretched man fell. The Ensign was immediately on him to finish him off, but the Corporal, who was valiant and used to blood and death, had drawn his sword, and wounded as he was he set about defending himself, while shouting in a loud voice: 'I am being murdered!'

At that the Ensign, hearing people come running, including some of the soldiers who were quartered thereabouts, began to flee, so as not to be caught there; then, turning back he pretended to have run up on hearing the noise. Mingling with the others, and seeing the leg cut off, he judged that if the Corporal were not already dead, he

---

[1] Emilia hints that he is jealous, III.4.26–30; and tries to convince Othello that his wife is honest, IV.2.11–18.

[2] Bianca combines the functions of this woman and the courtesan.

[3] Othello sees her give it back to Cassio. (IV.1.146–77.)

[4] Cf. IV.1.203–15. Iago needs no bribe.

[5] V.1.1–72. Iago uses Roderigo. Cassio: 'My leg is cut in two.' An exaggeration, one hopes, like Montano's at II.3.161.

soon would die of the wound, and although he rejoiced inwardly, he outwardly grieved for the Corporal as if he had been his own brother.[1]

In the morning, news of the affray was spread throughout the city and reached the ears of Disdemona;[2] whereupon, being tender-hearted and not thinking that evil would come to her by it, she showed the utmost sorrow at the occurrence. On this the Moor put the worst possible construction. Seeking out the Ensign, he said to him: 'Do you know, my imbecile of a wife is in such grief about the Corporal's accident that she is nearly out of her mind!' 'How could you expect anything else?' said the other, 'since he is her very life and soul?'

'Soul indeed!' replied the Moor, 'I'll drag the soul from her body, for I couldn't think myself a man if I didn't rid the world of such a wicked creature.'

They were discussing whether the Lady should perish by poison or the dagger, and not deciding on either of them, when the Ensign said: 'A method has come into my head that will satisfy you and that nobody will suspect.[3] It is this: the house where you are staying is very old, and the ceiling of your room has many cracks in it. I suggest that we beat Disdemona with a stocking filled with sand until she dies. Thus there will not appear on her any sign of the blows. When she is dead, we shall make part of the ceiling fall; and we'll break the Lady's head, making it seem that a rafter has injured it in falling, and killed her. In this way nobody will feel any suspicion of you, for everyone will think that she died accidentally.'[4]

The cruel plan pleased the Moor, and they waited for a suitable opportunity. One night the Moor concealed the Ensign in a closet which opened off the bedchamber, and when the husband and wife were in bed, the Ensign, in accordance with their plan, made some sort of noise. Hearing it the Moor said to his wife:

'Did you hear that noise?'

'Yes, I heard it', she replied.

'Get up', said the Moor, 'and see what it is.'

The unfortunate Disdemona got out of bed, and as soon as she was near the closet, the Ensign came out and, being strong and muscular, he gave her a frightful blow in the small of her back, which made the Lady fall down at once, scarcely able to draw her breath. With the little voice she had she called on the Moor to help her. But he, jump-

---

[1] V.1.69–102.
[2] Desdemona is dead before morning.
[3] Othello suggests poison, Iago strangulation. (IV.1.207–13.)
[4] Othello makes no preparations to avoid discovery.

ing out of bed, said to her, 'You wicked woman, you are having the reward of your infidelity. This is how women are treated who, pretending to love their husbands, put horns on their heads.'[1]

The wretched Lady, hearing this and feeling herself near to death (for the Ensign had given her another blow), called on Divine Justice to witness to her fidelity, since earthly justice failed; and as she called on God to help her, a third blow struck her, and she lay still, slain by the impious Ensign. Then, placing her in the bed, and breaking her skull, he and the Moor made the ceiling fall as they had previously planned, and the Moor began to call for help, that the house was falling. Hearing his cries the neighbours ran in and found the bed, and the Lady dead under the rafters—which made everyone grieve, for they knew what a good life she had led.

Next day Disdemona was buried, amid the universal mourning of the people. But God, the just observer of men's hearts, did not intend such vile wickedness to go without proper punishment. He ordained that the Moor, who had loved the Lady more than his life, on finding himself deprived of her should feel such longing that he went about like one beside himself, searching for her in every part of the house. Realizing now that the Ensign was the cause of his losing his Lady and all joy in life, he held the villain in such abhorrence that he could not bear even to see him; and if he had not been afraid of the inviolable justice of the Venetian lords, he would have slain him openly. Not being able to do this with safety, he took away his rank and would not have him in his company, whereupon such a bitter hatred sprang up between them that no greater or more deadly feud could be imagined.

The Ensign, that worst of all scoundrels, therefore set all his mind to injuring the Moor, and seeking out the Corporal, who had now recovered and went about with a wooden leg instead of the one that had been cut off, he said to him, 'It is time you got your revenge for the leg you lost. If you will come to Venice with me, I shall tell you who the miscreant was, for here I dare not tell you, for many reasons; and I am willing to bear witness for you in court.'

The Corporal who felt himself deeply wronged but did not know the real truth, thanked the Ensign and came with him to Venice. When they arrived there the Ensign told him that it was the Moor who had cut off his leg because of a suspicion he had formed that he was Disdemona's lover, and that for the same reason he had murdered her, and afterwards made it known that the fallen ceiling had killed her. Hearing this, the Corporal accused the Moor to the Signoria, both of cutting off his leg and of causing the Lady's death, and called as witness the Ensign, who said that both accusations were

[1] Contrast Othello's attempt at a ritual murder.

true, for the Moor had approached him and tried to induce him to commit both crimes; and that, having then killed his wife through the bestial jealousy that he had conceived in his mind, he had told him how he had killed her.

When the Signoria learned of the cruelty inflicted by the Barbarian upon a citizen of Venice, they ordered the Moor to be apprehended in Cyprus and to be brought to Venice, where with many tortures they tried to discover the truth. But enduring with great steadfastness of mind every torment, he denied everything so firmly that nothing could be extorted from him. Although by his constancy he escaped death, he was, however, after many days in prison, condemned to perpetual exile, in which he was finally slain by Disdemona's relatives, as he richly deserved.

The Ensign returned to his own country; and not giving up his accustomed behaviour, he accused one of his companions, saying that the latter had sought to have him murder one of his enemies, who was a nobleman. The accused man was arrested and put to the torture, and when he denied that what his accuser said was true, the Ensign too was tortured, to compare their stories; and he was tortured so fiercely that his inner organs were ruptured. Afterwards he was let out of prison and taken home, where he died miserably.[1] Thus did God avenge the innocence of Disdemona. And all these events were told after his death by the Ensign's wife, who knew the facts, as I have told them to you.

[Story 8 is (as usual) prefaced by a linking passage commenting on the tale just heard:]

It appeared marvellous to everybody that such malignity could have been discovered in a human heart; and the fate of the unhappy Lady was lamented, with some blame for her father, who had given her a name of unlucky augury.[2] And the party decided that since a name is the first gift of a father to his child, he ought to bestow one that is grand and fortunate, as if he wished to foretell success and greatness. No less was the Moor blamed, who had believed too foolishly. But all praised God because the criminals had had suitable punishment.

[1] Cf. the tortures promised for Iago. (V.2.302–4; 366–8.)
[2] In Greek, 'unfortunate'.

II. Possible Source

CERTAINE TRAGICALL DISCOURSES
of Bandello, translated by Geoffrey Fenton (1567)

Discourse IV

An Albanoyse Capteine, beinge at the poynte to dye, kylled his wyfe, because no man should enjoye her beawtie after his deathe.

The Argument

It may seame to some that delighte in the reporte of other men's faltes, with respect rather to take occasion of synister exclamacion then be warned by their evils to eschewe the like harmes in themselves, that I have bene to prodigall in notinge the doinges and lives of diverse ladies and gentle women declininge by misfortune from the path of vertue and honour, only to sturre up cause of reproche and leave to confirme their fonde opinion. Albeit, as their errour appereth sufficiently in the integretye of my meaninge, so I hope th' indifferent sort will geve an other judgement of my entente; the rather for that I have preferred these discourses, both for the proffit of the present glorye of them that bee paste, and instruction of suche as bee to come; seing withal they discover more cause of rebuke and vices more heynous in men, then any we finde committed by women. Albeit the historye last recyted hath set fourth in lyvely collours, the furye and madd dispocition of a woman forced by disloyaltie, yet if a man maye any waie excuse synne, it maye in some sorte be dispensed withall, or at leaste with more reason then the tyranous execution followinge; where[1] a certaine jelousye spronge of an unjuste myslyke (as she thought) is readie to cover the falte of Pandora.[2] For what is he so ignorante in the passions of love that will not confesse that jelosye is an evill excedinge all the tormentes of the world, supplantynge oftentymes bothe wytt and reason in the moste wise that be, specially when appeareth the lyke treason that Pandora perswaded herselfe to receive by him that forsoke her. But for the other, how can he be acquited from an humor of a frantike man,

---

[1] whereas.

[2] Raging in jealousy against her lover Parthonope who had married another woman, the pregnant Pandora brought on an abortion by cruelly maltreating herself, then dashed out the baby's brains and tore it to pieces. This was the story in Discourse III.

who, without any cause of offence in the world, committes cruel execution upon his innocente wife, no lesse fayre and fournished in al perfections, then chast and verteous without comparison. . . . I have here to expose to you a myserable accident, happening in our tyme, whiche shall serve as a bloddy skaffolde, or theaterye, wherin are presented such as play no partes but in mortal and furious tragidies.

Duringe the sege and miserable sacke of Modona (a cytye of the Morea, confyning upon the sea Peloponese, not farr from the straite of Ysthmyon, by the whiche the Venetians conveighe their great traffique and trade of marchandise)[1] Bajazeth, th' emperour of the Turkes, and great grandfather to Sultan Solyman who this daye governeth the state of th' oriente, used so many sortes of inordinat cruelties in the persecution of those wretches whom fate, with extreme force of his warr, had not onlye habandoned from the soyle of their ancient and naturall abode, but also . . . forced them to crave harbour of the lymytrophall[2] townes adjoyning their country . . .

And . . . amongest the unhappie crewe of these fugitives and creatures full of care, there was one gentleman no lesse noble by discente then worthelye renowmed by the glorye of his own actes . . . This gentleman (whom mine author termeth by the name of Pietro Barzo) wearie even nowe with drawinge the heavie yoke of harde exile, left the rest of his contrymen and companions of care complaininge their mutuall myseries together, and retired to the ryche and populous cytie of Mantua; where his cyvell governmente, and prudent behavior (accompanied with a singular dexteritie in exploytes of armes, and other exercises of chevalrye, arguinge th' unfayned noblenes of his mynde) gave suche a shewe of his vertue, that he was not onlye in shorte tyyme intertained of the Marques and governour there, but also made generall of the whole armie of footemen.[3] Where, enjoyinge thus the benefyt of his vertue—who commonly yeldes no lesse successe to suche as imbrace her with true ymytacion, and treade the pathe of her loare with semblable sinceritie of mynde —he had there with him at the same instant his wyfe, beinge also of Modona, derived of no lesse nobilytie then he, and nothing inferiour in all gyftes of nature and ornamentes of vertue.

For touchinge her bewtie, seaming of suche wonderfull perfection that it was thoughte nature was dryven to the ende of her wittes in framinge a pece of so great excellancie, they dowted not to geve her therby the tytle of the faire Helene of Greece. Nether was she lesse meritorious for her vertues; being blessed therwith so plentifully at

---

[1] Modon, a city in the S.W. Morea, captured from the Venetians in 1460.
[2] I.e. on the frontier. Belleforest, 'pays limitrophes'.
[3] Belleforest, 'colonnel de la fanterie'.

the handes of th' Almighty, that it was doubted to the writers of that tyme whether God or nature deserved the greatest prayse in forminge so perfecte a creature.

If this were a consolation and singuler contentment of the pore Modonyse—waighinge earste in the ballance of his unhappye fortune, denied anye more to enjoye the fredome of his contreye, dryven by force from the auncient succours and solace of his frendes, wandringe in wooddes and deserte places unknowne, and (that whiche worse is) lefte onely to the mercie of hunger and coulde, with expectation to fall eftesones into the handes of hys enemyes; and nowe to bee taken from the malice of all theis miseries and restored to a place of abode, richesse and entertainement sufficient for sustentation, to beare office and authoritie amongeste the best, and rampired besydes within th' assured good will and opinion of the chiefe governor of a contreye—I appeale to th' opinions of those who earst have changed their miserable condicion, or state of adversytie, with the benefyt and goodnes of the lyke fortune.[1] Or if, againe, he had cause to rejoyce and make sacrifice to his fortune, that had gyven hym a wyfe, noted to be the odd image of the world for beautye, behaviour, courtesey, and uprighte dealyng, constant without cause or argument of dishonesty, and (that whiche is the chiefest ornement and decoracion of the beautie of a woman) to bee of disposition readye to obeye her husbande, yeldinge hym suffraintye with a deutifull obedience,[2] with other vertues that made her an admiration to the whole multitude, and her lyfe a spectacle to the ladyes of our age to beholde and imitate the lyke vertues—I leave it to the judgement of that smal number of happy men who (by a speciall grace from above) are ordeined to enjoye the benfyt of so rare and precious a gyfte. This couple, thus rejoycinge the retourne of happy lyfe, resigned withall their teares of auncient dule, and embraced the gyfte of present time, with intent to spend the remainder of their yeres in mutual consolacion and contentement of mynde.

[They had a little daughter (who does not appear in the story). But before long the husband died, 'in the flower of his yeres, and she not yet confermed in age and discretion able to beare and withstande the ordinary assaultes of the worlde.' She went to live with her brother. At church she was seen by an Albanian (Albanoys) captain, 'a noble gentelman thereabout, havinge for the credit of his vertue and valiantnes in armes the charge of certayne troopes of horsemen.' The captain wooed her in vain, then begged her brother to help him.]

---

[1] This digression is not in Bandello.
[2] *In margin:* 'The chiefest vertue in a wife is to be obedient to her husband.'

'And, albeit I have hetherto reserved the maydenhed of my affection, and lyved no lesse free from th' amarous delites or desyres of women, yet being nowe overtaken and tyed in the chaines of true affection, I had rather become captive, and yelde myselfe prisoner in the pursute of so fayre a ladye, then to have the honor of the greatest victorye that ever happened to captayne, by prowesse, or pollicie, or dynt of cruell sworde of his valiaunt soldiours.'

[The brother tries to persuade her. She is unwilling to marry again, not only because her husband has not been dead a year, but also because she believes that widows should not re-marry, and 'my hart, devininge diverslye of the successe of this mariage, threatneth a further mischiefe to fall upon me.' She gives way, however, and is married to the captain, Don Spado, with all ceremony.]

But nowe this Albanoys, enjoyeing thus the frutes of his desier, coulde not so wel brydel his present pleasure, nor conceile the singuler contentment he conceived by the encounter of his new mystres, but, in public show, began to prate of his present felicitye . . . But as in every thing excesse is hurtful, bringinge with it a doble discomoditie—I meane both a sourfet to the stomake by the pleasure we delite in, and a jelouse loathing of the thing we chiefly love and hold most dere—so the extreme and superfluitye of hoate love of this fonde husbande towards his wife, began, within the very month of the mariage, to converte itselfe into a contrary disposition, not much unlike the loving rage of the she ape towardes her yonge ones; who, as the poetes do affirme, doth use to chuse among her whelpes one whom she loves best, and keping it alwaies in her armes, doth cherish and loll it in such rude sorte that, or she is ware, she breketh the boanes and smothereth it to death, killing by this meanes with over-much love the thing which yet wold live if it were not for th' excesse of her affection.

In like sort this Albanoyse, doating without discrecion uppon the desyer of his newe lady, and rather drowned beastely in the super-fluitie of her love then waighing rightly the meryte and vertue of true affection, entred into such tearmes of fervant jelowsie, that every fle that wafteth afore her made hym sweate at the browes with the suspicion he had of her bewty. Wherin he suffered himselfe to be so much subject and overcome with the rage of this follie, that, according to the jelowse humor of th' Ytalyan,[1] he thoughte every man that loked in her face, wente about to grafte hornes in his forehed.

[Fenton expatiates on the folly of the man who keeps his wife close.]

[1] Not in Bandello.

And in vaine goeth hee aboute to make his wife honest, that eyther lockes her in his chamber, or fylles his house full of spyes to note her doinges, considering the just cause he gyves her hereby to be revenged of the distrust he hath of her without occasion . . . Neyther hath this folyshe humor of jelowsy so much power to enter into the hart of the vertuous and wise man; who neyther wyll gyve his wife such cause to abuse herselfe towardes hym, nor suspect her wythout great occasyon nor yet gyve judgement of any evill in her, withoute a sewer grounde and manifest proofe. And yet is he of suche governemente for the correction of such a falte, that he had rather cloke and disgest it with wisedome then make publication with open punishement in the eye of the slaunderous worlde. By whiche rare patience and secret dissimulation, he dothe not only choke the mouth of the slaunderor, buryinge the faulte with the forgetfulnes of the facte, but also reclaymes her to an assured honestie and faith hereafter, that earst had abused him by negligence and yl fortune. . . .

. . . what greater sign or argument can a man geve of his owne follie, then to believe that to be true, which is but doutfull, and yeldinge rashelye to the resolution and sentence of his owne conceites, thinks his wife as light of the seare and apt to deceive him, as he is readie to admit synister suspicion; which procedes but of an ymperfection in himselfe, judginge the disposition of an other, by his owne complexion. Which was one of the greatest faltes in this valyante Albanoyse; who, fearing even nowe that which he nede not to dowte, began to stande in awe of his owne shadow, perswadinge himselfe that his wife was no lesse liberall of her love towards others then to him, and that the benefit of her bewtie was as common to strangers as to himselfe.

Albeit, the good ladye, espyeng well enough the greefe of her husband, was not ydle, for her parte, to studie the meanes to please him, and also to frame her life in such wise every waye, that her chaste and discrete governement towardes hym might not only remove the vaile of his late suspicion, but also take awaye the thicke miste of frantike jelowsie that put him in suche disquiet, and made him so farre excede the lymites and bondes of discrecion. Albeit, her honeste endevor herein received a contrarye effecte; and as one borne under a crabbed constellation, or ordeined rather to beare the malice of a froward desteinye, she colde not devise a remedie for his disease, nor any hearbe to purge his suspicious humor; but the more she sought to prefer a show of sinceritie and honestie of life, the more grew the furye and rage of his perverse fancie, thinking the companye and fellowship of his wife to be as indifferente to others as peculiar to himselfe.

[He proceeded 'to dogge the doinges of hys wife with secret spies in every corner, to abridge her libertie in goinge abrode, and barr the accesse of any to come to her;' yet she, realizing his sickness, strove ever to moderate his passion.]

Wherin, for her part, she forgat not to make pacience her chiefest defence, agaynst the folish assaultes of his wilful follies; not only requitinge his extraordinary rage and fits of furie wyth a dutifull humylitye and obedience of a wife, but also ceassed not to love him no lesse then her honour and dutie bounde her therunto; hopinge, with th' assistance of some conveniente tyme, and her discrete behavior towardes hym, both to take awaye the disease, and mortifye the cause of his evill.

She seamed neyther to reprehend his falte openly, nor with other tearmes thenne argued her great humilitie; and for herselfe, howe evill so ever he intreated her, she gave an outwarde showe of thankefull contentmente. And when it was his pleasure to shutt her close in a chamber, as a birde in the cage, shee refused not his sentence, but, embrasinge the gifte of her present fortune, toke suche consolation as the harde condition of her case wolde admitt; givinge God thankes for his visitation, and cravinge with like intercession to have her husbande restored to the use of his former wittes.

Albeit, all these dutifull showes of obedience, and pacient digesting of his unnatural discourtesies, together with a rare and redie disposition in her to frame herselfe whollie to th' appitit of his will, prevailed no more to enlarge her libertie, or redeme her from the servile yoke of close ymprisonmente, then to reclayme his hagarde[1] mynde to th' understandinge of reason, or restore the traunce of his frantique humor; raging the more (as it seamed) by the incredible constancye he noted in this mirror of modestie, obedience, wisedome, and chastetie . . .

[When he took her off suddenly to the court of his master 'the Lord James Trivoulse' [Triulzo] she made no complaint. But Triulzo fell into disfavour with his overlord Louis XII[2] and came to Lombardy, where he died. Don Spado was inconsolable, fell sick, and began to talk of suicide. The wife sought to reconcile him to life, and declared that, having lost one husband, she could not bear to lose another, and would not live on if he died. This moved Don Spado greatly, and he told her why he was ill.]

And because I wil cleare in few wordes the misterie which seames to amaze you, you shall note that there be iii onely ministers and occasyons of my disease; wherof the firste (and of leaste importance)

---

[1] Cf. Othello, 'If I do prove her haggard', III.3.260.
[2] Fenton, III; Belleforest, XII, correctly.

is for the death of my late lorde and maister, Don Jhon Tryvoulso, whereof you are not ignorant; the second (excedinge the firste in greatnes of grefe and force against me) is to thinke that the rigour of my destinies, and violence of sicknes, yeldynge me into the handes of death, will dissolve and breake by that meanes, the league of longe and loyall love whiche from the beginnynge my harte hath vowed unto you; but the thirde and laste (of a more strange qualitie then eyther of the reste) is to thinke that when I am dead, and by time worne out of your minde, another shal enjoye the sweete and pleas-aunt benefit of that devine beautie of yours, whiche ought to serve but for the dyet of the gods, the simple viewe whereof seames hable (yf it were possible) to make me suffer the martiredome of ii deaths. Whereunto she replied with persuacions to drive hym from his fonde devise, profering herselfe eftesones to dye for companye wherin (callyng the majestie of the Highest to witnes) she protested againe that, if he wolde not be reclaimed from his desyer to dye within a veray shorte moment of tyme, she woulde bee as redye to yelde death his tribute as he.

[She said this to help cure her husband, not expecting to have to die.]

But alas! the infortunat ladye brewed heare the brothe of her owne bane, and spon the thredd of her owne destruction, for fallynge nowe unhappilye into the malice of her destenie, thinkyng nothinge lesse then of the secret ambushe of mortall treason her husband had layed for her, went unhappelye to bed wyth hym the same nighte; where, for his parte (preferinge in his face a shew of fayned contente-ment and consolation to the eye) he forced a further quiet of mynde by the joye he ymagined in the acte he ment to do, but chieflye for that he had devised howe th' innocent ladye (throughe the rage of his villainy) sholde bee forced to an effecte of her promisse.

For the spedie execution wherof, they had not bene longe in bedd together, but he rise from her, faynynge a desier to performe the necessitie of nature in the closset or chamber of secretes; his erraund in dede being to fetche his dagger, which (without makyng her privye) he conveyed under the bolster of his bed, beginnynge even then to preferre a preamble afore the parte he ment to playe. For, fallinge from his former complaintes of sicknes, he retired into tearmes of extreme frenezy and madnes, brainge out such groanes and sighes of hideus disposicion, with owlynge, cryeng, and foaminge at the mouth,[1] like one possessed with an evill sprit, that who had seene his often change of collor and complexion in his face, his ghastly regardes arguinge ententes of desperacion, and his eyes

---

[1] Cf. Othello in IV.1.

(flaming with furye) sonke into his head, with the order of his passion every waye, mighte easely have judged the desyer of his harte to be of no smal importance, and the thyng he went about neither common nor commendable. Wherein he was assisted with iii enemies of diverse disposicions, love, jealousie, and death: the least of the whiche is sufficient of himselfe to make a man chafe in his harneys, and take away the courage of his hart in the middest of the combat. For the one presented a certain feare by reason of the horrour of the acte; the other sewed (as it were) for an abstinence, or at least a moderation, of the crueltie he had commenced against his innocent wife; but the third, being the beginner of al, and excedinge the rest in power, wolde not dismiss him from the stage till he had playd th' uttermost acte of his malicious tragedie.

Marke here (good ladyes) the desolation of this unfortunat gentle-woman, and dispose yourselves to teares on the behalfe of hir distresse. Wherin, certainlye, you have no lesse reason to helpe to bewaile her wretched chaunce, then juste occasion to joyne in generall exclamation againste the detestable acte of her tyrannous husband; who, disclayminge even nowe his former state and condition of a man, retires into th' abite of a monster, and cruell enemye to nature; and in convertinge the vertue of his former love, and remembrance of the sondrie pleasures he had heretofore receyved of his deare and lovynge wyfe, into present rage and unnaturall furye (far excedinge the savage and brutishe maner of the tiger, lyon, or libarde, bredd in the desertes of Affrike, the common norsse of monsters and creatures cruell without reason) whettyng his teeth for the terrible suggestion of the devill, who at th' instante put into his hande the dagger; wherewith, after he had embraced and kissed her, in such sorte as Judas kissed our Lorde the same night he betraied him, he saluted her with ten or xii estockados,[1] one in the necke of another in diverse partes of her bodye, renewynge the conflict with no lesse nomber of blowes in her head and armes; and because no parte shoulde escape free from the stroke of his malice, he visyted her white and tender legges, with no lesse rage and furye then the rest.

Wherewith, beholdinge in her diverse undoubted argumentes of death, [he] began the lyke warre with himselfe, usinge the same meane and ministers with his owne handes, enbrewed yet with the blood of his innocent wyfe; shewyng (notwithstandyng this horrible part and acte of dispaire) diverse and sondrye signes of speciall gladnes and pleasure in his face, wherin he contynued till the laste and extreame gaspe of lyfe—chieflie for that he sawe him accompanied to death with her whome he was not hable to leave behinde hym on lyve, and who, being overcharged (as you have harde) with

[1] stabs.

the nomber of woundes, the violence whereof ... did presse her so muche with the hastie approche of death, that the want of breath abridged her secret shryft and confession to God, with lesse leasure to yeld her innocent soule (wyth humble praier) into the handes of her Redemer, and commende the forgevenes of her synnes to the benefit of his mercie. Only she had respyte (with great ado to speake) to give order that her bodie mighte be layde in the tombe of her firste husbande, Signeur Barzo.

But the cursed and execrable Albanoys (so whollie possessed with the devill that the gyfte of grace was denied him) abhorred to the laste mynute of his lyfe the remembrance of repentance; for, laughinge (as it were) at the fowlenes of the facte even untill life left him senceles and voyde of breathe, he commended his carkes to the gredie jawes of ravenous wolves, serving also as a fyt praie for the venemous serpentes and other crepinge wormes of the earthe, and his soule to the reprobate socyetie of Judas and Cayne, with other of th' infernall crewe.

[Fenton moralizes lengthily on the tale, and urges 'the lighte and harebrained husbandes not too easelie, or for smal occasions, to enter into suspicion with their wyves'.]

Compare Bandello's account of the climax:
the cruel and inhuman Albanian, taking up a dagger which he had hidden in the bed when he went out of the room, gave the lady a stab on the head and at the same instant stabbed himself in the chest; and kept wounding now himself and now his wife, till the poor unfortunate woman in a low and broken voice said, 'Alas, I am slain!'—no more. Then the ferocious wife-murderer gave himself a thrust right through his heart and drove out his vile criminal soul to the house of a hundred thousand devils; while his unhappy wife remained more dead than alive.

The maid who had heard an unaccountable noise had gone to her master's room, and heard the sounds of the villain's blows. Being unable to enter, she had gone to a window and called to the neighbours for help. Some of them came and broke down the door of the room, and having lights with them they perceived the treacherous husband lying face downward on the almost lifeless body of his unhappy wife.[1] They realized at once that she was not quite dead; so, lifting her up bodily and placing her on another bed, they sent for a doctor, who, seeing the lady's deep wounds, treated them but said that she could not live more than a day or two.

The wife, returning somewhat to consciousness, sent for one of the priests of Saint George, and made confession, pardoning her husband

[1] Cf. Othello's end, V.2.357-8.

with all her heart, not being willing to let anyone speak ill of him, but accusing nobody but her own misfortune.[1] She made her will and left everything to her daughter by her first husband and, dying, asked to be buried in the Barza tomb. [This was done.] The body of the cursed Albanian was dragged (amid the execrations of all the women of Mantua) out of the city and was left as he deserved to be food for dogs and wolves.

III. Probable Source

From THE GENERALL HISTORIE
OF THE TURKES
by Richard Knolles (1603)

[After Selim II came to the Turkish throne in 1566 he and his counsellor Mustapha decided to take Cyprus. But first he decided] that one *Cubates* should be sent embassadour to Venice, to prove the minds of the Senatours, whether they would willingly deliver the island, or adventure to have it taken from them by force. These things and such like as were then done at Constantinople, being by letters sent in post from the embassadour, made knowne at Venice, brought a generall heavinesse upon the Citie: for why, that understanding and provident State, warned by their former harmes, of all others most dread the Turks forces. *Cubates* the embassadour accompanied with *Aloysius Barbarus* the embassadours sonne, and *Bonricius* his secretarie, departing from Constantinople, came by long journeies to Ragusium, where Angelus Sorianus[2] sent from Venice to meet him, was readie to receive him, who, being taken into his gallie, brought him to Venice . . . (p. 839)

The greater the danger was now feared from the angrie Turke, the more carefull were the Venetians of their state; wherefore they forthwith sent messengers with letters unto the Governours of Cyprus, charging them with all carefulnesse and diligence to make themselves readie to withstand the Turke, and to raise what power they were able in the island, not omitting any thing that might concerne the good of the state, and at the same time made choice of their most valiant and expert captaines both by sea and land, unto whom they

[1] Cf. Desdemona, V.2.120–3.

[2] Cf. I.3.16 'Signior Angelo'. Angelo Soriano commanded a galley before the invasion of Cyprus, and after the fall of Nicosia brought news to Crete of an attack by Turkish vessels. (G. P. Contarini, *Historia della Guerra*, Venice, 1645 edn., f. 20ᵛ.)

committed the defence of their dispersed Seignorie, with the leading of their forces. *Hieronimus Zanius* was appointed Admirall, *Lucas Michaell* was sent into Crete, *Franciscus Barbarus* into Dalmatia, *Sebastianus Venerius* into Corcyra, all men of great honour, experience and valour. Other meaner captaines were sent also with lesse charge into the aforesaid places, as *Eugenius Singliticus*, a noble gentleman, with a thousand footmen into Cyprus, who had also the leading of all the horsemen in the island: after whom Countie *Martinengus* promised to follow with two thousand footmen moe. The strong Cities were now by the Venetians in all places new fortified, armour, ordnance, and victuall provided, and whatsoever else they thought needfull for defence of their state. (pp. 841–2.)

[Knolles gave a long account of Cyprus and its wealth.]

. . . It was in antient times called *Macaria*, that is to say, Blessed. The people therein generally lived so at ease and pleasure, that thereof the island was dedicated to *Venus*, who was there especially worshipped, and thereof called *Cypria* . . .

In the heart of the island standeth Nicosia, sometime the regall and late metropoliticall citie thereof: and in the East end thereof Famagusta, sometime called Tamarta, a famous rich citie, the chiefe and onely port of that most pleasant island. (p. 843.)

[Naval movements in 1570 were described.]

About the middle of April following, [Selim] sent *Piall Bassa* with fourescore gallies and thirtie galliots to keep the Venetians from sending aid into Cyprus . . .

[*Piall*] understanding by his espials, that the Venetians, greevously visited with the plague, and slowly relieved by their friends, were not like in hast to come out, hee tooke his course to Tenos, an island of the Venetians, to have taken it from them . . . [For two days he attacked it] but at length the Turks shamefully gave over the assault, and abandoning the island, directed their course toward Cyprus. For *Mustapha*, author of that expedition (for his antient hatred against the Christians, made Generall by *Selymus*) had before appointed *Piall Bassa* at a time prefixed, to meet him at the Rhodes, and that he that came first should tarrie for the other, that so they might together saile unto Cyprus. (pp. 845–6.)

[Mustapha] at the Rhodes met with Piall, as he had before appointed. The whole fleet at that time consisted of two hundred gallies, amongst whom were divers galliots and small men of war, with divers other vessels prepared for the transportation of horses: with this fleet *Mustapha* kept on his course for Cyprus. They of the island in the meane time carefully attending the enemies coming, from their watch towers first discovered the fleet at the West end of the island not farre from Paphos: from whence the Turks turning upon the right hand, and passing the promontorie *Curio*, now called *De le Gate*, landed divers of their men, who burned and spoiled certaine villages . . .

[Nicosia was besieged.]

There was not in the citie any valiant or renowned Captaine, who as the danger of that time required, should have taken upon him the charge: neither any strong armie in the island to oppose against the enemie. The Governour of the citie was one *Nicholaus Dandulus*, a man too weak for so great a burthen; who alwayes brought up in civile affaires, was to seeke how to defend a siege. (p. 847.) [The city had recently been fortified.] Neverthelesse, they found by experience in this warre, That fortifications are strengthened by the defendants, rather than the defendants by the fortifications.

[A Christian fleet failed to relieve Cyprus because of divisions between the Venetian and Spanish admirals, who finally parted company.]

Thus this mightie fleet, which had all this Sommer filled the Mediterranean with all the countries thereabout with the expectation of some great matter, was by the discord of the Generals dissolved, having done nothing at all worth the remembrance . . . The Venetian fleet was no sooner arrived at Corcyra but *Augustinus Barbadicus* was sent from the Senat to discharge *Zanius* the Admirall of his office, and to send him prisoner to Venice: in whose roome was placed *Sebastianus Venerius*, Governour of that island.[1] (pp. 853–4.)

[Nicosia was captured and its defenders maltreated. An ambassador, 'Ragazonius,[2] a coole and advised man' was sent to Constantinople to treat for peace. Famagusta was besieged and bravely defended. Knolles describes the city.]

. . . almost in two parts beaten upon with the sea . . . Upon the gate that leadeth to Amathus standeth a six cornered tower; other towers stand out also in the wall, everie of them scarce able to containe six peeces of artillerie. It hath a haven opening toward the Southeast, defended from the injurie of the weather by two great rockes, betwixt which the sea commeth in by a narrow passage about

---

[1] Othello did better than the 'mightie fleet', and, but for Iago, he would have been the right man in the right place.

[2] Did Shakespeare recall the name in *Measure for Measure* and bestow it on 'One Ragozine, a most notorious pirate' (IV.3.70–4)? Cf. G. Hibbard in *Sh. Survey* 21, 1968, p. 46, who also points out that the Bishop of Famagusta was Hieronimus Ragazonius.

40 paces over; but after opening wider, giveth a convenient harbour to ships, whereof it cannot containe any great number, and was now shut up with a strong chaine. Neere unto the haven standeth an old castle with foure towers, after the auntient manner of building. There was in the citie one strong bulwarke, built after the manner of the fortifications of our time, with palisadoes, curtaines, casaments, and such like, in such manner, as that it seemed almost impregnable.

[On the whole the city was not strong.] . . . but what it wanted by reason of the situation and weake fortification, that the Governour and other noble Captaines supplied in best sort they might, with a strong garrison of most valiant soldiours, the surest defence of strong places. (p. 863.)

[After a gallant defence the military leaders began to fear destruction, and the citizens, perceiving it, 'came flocking to the Governour, craving of him aid and comfort' which he could not give. Finally, in 1571, the city was taken and there was great slaughter. Knolles describes the terror in the other islands as the Turks attacked them one by one, until the Battle of Lepanto destroyed the Ottoman fleet.]

KING LEAR

INTRODUCTION

AN ENTRY in the Stationers' Register on 26 November 1607, for Nathaniel Butter and John Busby, refers to 'A booke called Master William Shakespeare his historye of Kinge Lear as yt was played before the Kinges Majestie at Whitehall uppon Sainct Stephens night at Christmas Last, by his majesties servantes playing usually at the Globe on the Bancksyde.' This definite entry was probably to avoid confusion with the earlier play *Leir*, printed in 1605. The new piece was printed in 1608.[1] Q2, dated 1608, was in fact taken from a copy of Q1 and printed in 1619. The F1 text was printed from a copy of Q1 heavily corrected, perhaps to agree with a prompt-book, for 300 lines were omitted and 100 not in Q1 were inserted. Q1 is generally agreed to have been a memorial reconstruction.[2] The F1 text is nearer to what Shakespeare probably wrote.

When performed before the King during Christmas 1606, the play may have been fairly new, for the 'late eclipses in the sun and moon' (I.2.108) may have been those of 27 September (sun) and 2 October (moon), 1605. It was certainly written after the publication of Samuel Harsnett's *Declaration of Popish Impostures* (1603), to which Shakespeare was much indebted (Text XI, p. 414). If we agree with E. K. Chambers that Edward Sharpham imitated *King Lear* in *The Fleir*, which was in existence before February 1606, we must put the tragedy earlier than that.

The old *King Leir* was registered in May 1605, and published later in that year. The S.R. entry called it a 'Tragedie' (altered to 'Tragecall historie'). Because the old play is really a tragi-comedy it has been suggested that Shakespeare's play had been

---

[1] '*M. William Shak-speare: His True Chronicle Historie of the life and death of King Lear and his three daughters. With the unfortunate life of Edgar, sonne and heire to the Earle of Gloster, and his sullen and assumed humor of Tom of Bedlam . . .*'
[2] See G. I. Duthie, *Shakespeare's King Lear*, 1949, Ch. III.

performed and that the publishers of *Leir* were hoping to palm off their piece as his. Maybe, but do S.R. entries usually describe accurately the genre of plays? And is not *Leir* a 'tragedy with a happy ending'? W. W. Greg and others have found it 'very difficult to believe that this respectable but old-fashioned play, dating back in all probability to about 1590' had been acted in 1605, 'especially if the playhouse manuscript had been for years in the hands of stationers'.[1] But the players may have got it back, or kept another copy, and revivals of old-fashioned pieces were not unknown. *Mucedorus*, a much looser piece of romantic writing, was revived in 1611, with some additions, by Shakespeare's company, before the King. That Shakespeare knew the old *Leir* is certain. He may have seen it on the Jacobean stage, and it is easier to believe that he read it in print than that he used a manuscript which had somehow 'come into the possession of the Chamberlain's men', as Greg and the *New Cambridge* editors have suggested.

A topical reason for the revival of *Leir*, if not for Shakespeare's rewriting of it, has been found in a remarkable historical parallel.[2] In October 1603 an old servant of Queen Elizabeth, Brian Annesley, was somewhat in Lear's situation. A wealthy Kentish courtier and 'Gentleman Pensioner', Annesley had three daughters, Grace, married to Sir John Wildgose, Christian, married to William, 3rd Baron Sandys, and Cordell, still unmarried. Christian played no public part in the affair, but Grace tried to get her father judged lunatic because he was senile and 'altogether unfit to govern himself or his estate'.

Cordell protested to Robert Cecil that her father's long service 'deserved a better agnomination, than at his last gasp to be recorded and registered a Lunatic'. She refused to let Sir John Wildgose make an inventory of her father's domestic property and seems to have succeeded in keeping him and his wife at bay. When Annesley died in July 1604, they disputed his will, which left them little and most of his property to Cordell.[3] The Prerogative Court upheld the will on 3 December. One of the execu-

---

[1] W. W. Greg, *The Library*, xx, pp. 381–4.

[2] By C. C. Stopes, *The Third Earl of Southampton*, 1922, p. 274; G. M. Young, 'Shakespeare and the Termers', Brit. Acad. Lecture, 1947; G. Bullough, '*King Lear* and the Annesley Case', in *Festschrift Rudolf Stamm*, Berne, 1969, pp. 43–50.

[3] See my article for some details of the will.

tors was Sir William Harvey,[1] third husband of the Dowager Countess of Southampton, mother of Shakespeare's early patron. And after that lady's death in 1607, he married Cordell Annesley.

Some biographers have fancied that Harvey was the Mr W. H. who procured Shakespeare's Sonnets for the press in 1609. For this there is no evidence, nor that Shakespeare knew either Harvey or Cordell Annesley. Yet it is possible. As an occasional attender at court the dramatist probably knew of the Annesley case, and that Cordell's behaviour suited her name, although (unlike Cordelia) she was always the old man's favourite daughter.[2] [Text I gives letters, etc. about the case.]

Perhaps the affair was responsible (in part at least) for the revival of the old *Leir* and its publication in 1605. How far Shakespeare was affected by the domestic dispute we cannot say. Did Leir's faithful companion become the Earl of Kent because Kent was Annesley's county, or merely because some of the action occurs round Dover? I believe that *King Lear* was written late in 1605 or early in 1606.

King Lear may have been a creature of Celtic legend, but his story belongs to a class well known in European and Oriental folk-lore. There were many ancient stories in India (in the *Mahabharata*, etc.) about filial ingratitude, the contrast between good and bad children's treatment of aged parents. In Europe the love-test appeared in the story of the Goosegirl-Princess who told her father that she 'loved him like salt'.[3] Cordelia has affinities with Cinderella, who suffered from her two ugly sisters. Perrett refers to twenty-six variants of the Lear story, in twenty-five of which the father, ignoring the significant reference to salt, is angry with his daughter, until he realizes what she meant.[4] The father makes the test for varying reasons: to find an easy way of dividing his kingdom; to get ready for death; to make sure that the daughter who loves him best will get most,

---

[1] Harvey had won glory in fighting the Armada, and he too was a 'Gentleman Pensioner' of Q. Elizabeth. Another 'overseer' of the will was Thomas Fanshawe, Queen's Remembrancer.

[2] C. J. Sisson, in *Shakespeare's Tragic Justice*, 1963, pp. 80–3, mentions two earlier Elizabethan instances of daughters' unkindness.

[3] Grimm's *Hausmärchen*, 179, trans. M. Hunt, *Grimm's Household Tales*, 1884, ii, pp. 286–7.

[4] W. Perrett, 'The Story of King Lear from Geoffrey of Monmouth to Shakespeare', *Palaestra*, xxxv, Berlin, 1904. § 1.

or all, of the land; because the wicked daughters make him suspect that the good one does not love him.

The Lear story does not appear in Welsh national literature, but it came into England with Geoffrey of Monmouth's *Historia regium Britanniae* (*c.* 1135), in which Lear is the tenth British king after Brut. The name Leir, however, was that of a Celtic seagod, and the name Leicester may have had nothing to do with the king until Geoffrey made him founder of the city.

Geoffrey adapted the tale but altered it, omitting the 'salt' and making more of the natural relationship between children and parent. When Cordeilla says, 'I have ever loved thee as a father, nor ever from that love will I be turned aside. . . . So much as thou hast, so much art thou worth, and so much do I love thee', she is being jestingly ironical about her sisters' exaggerations. She speaks plainly enough at first, but then riddles in a way which suggests to Lear that she loves him only for his possessions. What she means of course is that he has all that a father should have—affection for his children and the rights to love of a good parent; so her love for him is great. The narrative which follows is more full of feeling and more detailed than most of Geoffrey's other stories. Cordeilla's sad fate is not a punishment for her cryptic answer; it is a different story, arising from the 'divided land' motif which recurs often in the chronicle; for almost invariably the partition of the kingdom leads to war—as when Brut divides Britain between his sons Albanact, Camber and Locrine; when Mempricius and Malin quarrel about who should rule the island; when Belinus and Brennius fall out. The death of Cordeilla in prison after being dispossessed by the two sons of her sisters is an instance of evil reviving in a family. After this Margan and Cunedag quarrel and Margan is slain. Discord after Gorboduc's division of Britain recurs between Ferrex and Porrex and results in the destruction of the line of Brut.

The widespread diffusion of Geoffrey of Monmouth's History in England and on the Continent made the Lear story known (about 170 MSS. still survive), and when Henry VII appointed a commission to trace the British ancestry of the Tudors the work returned to favour and many accounts based on it were used by English chroniclers. There was no Elizabethan translation of the *Historia* into English; the version given below is from the late seventeenth century [Text II]. Shakespeare may well have read the original Latin or taken details from citations of Geoffrey by more recent writers. Perrett traced to Laʒamon's *Brut* and to Geoffrey the conception of Lear as a rash, intemperate man who learned wisdom the hardest way. His anger is well portrayed in the *Historia* and he does not break down until he finds himself slighted on the sea-crossing to Gallia. When received by Cordeilla he is able to accept rule over the whole country. This is no senile man.

Geoffrey anticipates Shakespeare in the pretexts made for reducing the King's train, in suggesting that he had only two companions in misery, in having him nursed and rested before meeting his lost daughter. A distinction between the characters of the two Dukes was first made by Geoffrey. The French King's 'My love should kindle to inflam'd respect' (I.1.256) may come from Geoffrey's Latin, '*Amore virginis inflammatus*'.

Perrett discussed a great number of Lear-allusions. I confine myself to those Tudor chroniclers and versifiers most likely to have been known to Shakespeare. Caxton printed a fourteenth-century English version of the French prose *Brut* in which Lear appeared. This work was well known in the sixteenth century for there were already eleven editions by 1528. Polydore Vergil's *Anglicae Historiae* (1534) introduced a new detail in having Cordilla allude to the love she would bear to her husband when she married. The *New Chronicles* of Robert Fabyan (1516), based on Geoffrey and Caxton, omitted much of the former's detail. Leyr's test was merely 'to knowe the mynde of his iii doughters'. Their marriages are not mentioned. Cordeilla, 'entendynge to prove her father', accuses her sisters of dissimulation and will not vie with them, but says that she has loved him 'ever as my naturall fader', and 'as moche as thou arte worthy to be beloved'.

Fabyan doubts whether Aganippus could be a King of France. He does not specify in what ways the two bad daughters were unkind. Leyr's journey to Gallia and reception there are passed over in a few words, for Fabyan is impatient with Geoffrey's romantic details ('Longe it were to shewe you the Circumstance . . .') but he accepts the rest of the story and Cordeilla's end. His account and a brief one in Hardyng were

K

used by John Stow in his *Summarie of Englyshe Chronicles* (1563) and his *Annales* (1592).

Holinshed too followed Fabyan in the main, but he knew Caxton and other sources [Text III]. His Leyr devised the love-test 'to understand the affections of his daughters towards him, and preferre hir whome he best loved to the succession over the kingdome.' Cordeilla answers as in Fabyan. Contrary to Fabyan, Aganippus was 'one of the twelve kings that ruled Gallia'. The Dukes rebelled when Leyr's survival hindered their unfettered rule. They grudged him everything, and 'scarcelie they would allow him one servant to wait upon him'. Cordeilla sends him money, 'to apparell himselfe withall' before meeting him. The invasion of Britain is described and Leyr promises to leave Cordeilla all his kingdom. Her suicide was no weakness, for she was 'a woman of manlie courage'.

Shakespeare seems to have taken nothing from Fabyan and little specifically from Holinshed. He did not follow the latter in making Goneril marry Cornwall and Regan Albany. Like Warner and *The Mirror*, he changed the husbands round. Goneril's boast: 'She loved him more than toong could ex-presse' may have suggested 'Sir, I love you more than word can wield the matter'; and Shakespeare seems to have wished to refute Holinshed's implication (after Caxton) that Cordelia in invading Britain wanted 'to take possession of the land', for in *King Lear* she declares: 'It is thy business that I go about; . . . No blown ambition doth our arms incite' (IV.4.23ff.).

In William Harrison's *Description of England*, which preceded the chronicle in Holinshed's first volume, the dramatist would read about the customs of the ancient Britons and the changes in their religion from nature-worship to polytheism before the birth of Christ in the time of Cymbeline [Text IV]. Of this more later. In Camden's *Remaines* (1605) he may have found the Lear-story transferred to Ina, King of the West-Saxons, and using Polydore Vergil's assertion that the good daughter would love her husband more than her father [Text V].

In addition to these prose chronicles, the Elizabethan age produced verse-accounts which Shakespeare may well have read and remembered. These occurred in John Higgins's addi-tions to *The Mirrour for Magistrates* (1574), in Spenser's *The Faerie Queene*, and in William Warner's *Albions England*.

In the first edition of *The Mirror* (1559), Ferrers had hoped that the series of 'complaints' might be augmented, 'to searche and discourse our whole storye from the beginning of the inhabiting of this Isle.'[1] This led John Higgins some fifteen years later to add sixteen legends extending 'from the coming of Brute to the incarnation'. He did not include King Lear but Cordila, who is there not so much for her early sufferings as because she committed suicide in prison, tells his story. In the next piece her nephew, Morgan of Albany, attributes his destruction by his brother Cunedag to his ill-treatment of her. In the 1574 edition Higgins's poem had fifty-one stanzas in a variation of rhyme royal; he made alterations in the 1575 and 1587 editions [Text VI].

In his Preface Higgins asserted that he had seen a manuscript of Geoffrey of Monmouth ('which I lost by misfortune') and one of Hardyng, besides the printed works of Caxton, Grafton, Stow, etc. Because these told the stories so briefly (he declared), 'I was often fayne to use mine owne simple invention, yet not swarving from the matter.'[2]

According to his Cordila, the love-test was made because Leire 'thought to give, where favoure most he fande'. He 'did not me mislike', but she was not his favourite. Cordila admits that 'In age my father had a childishe minde'. Leire's division of the kingdom was meant to take place after his death, but the sisters (not the sons-in-law) rebelled and seized 'his crown and right'. Higgins gave more details than usual of the gradual diminution of the old man's retinue, his leaving Gonerell for Ragan after six months, Ragan's welcome turning after a year to 'dayly spite'; so back to Gonerell, who 'Bereavde him of his servantes all save one'. Leire's journey to France takes only one line. Cordila left her husband behind in France, perhaps because Higgins did not want a foreigner to conquer Britain.

In the second part of the poem, describing Cordila's sufferings in prison, she is visited by Despair, who tempts her to suicide and offers her the knife used by Dido. By killing herself Cordila falls into deadly sin.

From *The Mirror* Shakespeare probably took the 'squires' of Lear's train (I.4.240), its reduction by a half (*ibid.* 293),

[1] *The Mirror for Magistrates*, ed. L. B. Campbell, 1938.
[2] *Parts added to the Mirror for Magistrates*, ed. L. B. Campbell, 1946, pp. 35–6.

the suggestion that he should content himself with one 'or none', and Cordelia's begging her husband to help her father (IV.4.25–6). Maybe Higgins's emphasis on Cordila's wretched end affected the dramatist. The captain at V.3.254 has been instructed 'To lay the blame upon her own despair / That she fordid herself.' But there is no allegory here. Edmund's excuse for imprisoning Lear and Cordelia, lest they gain popular support, may have been suggested by Margan's motive: 'Fearing lest she should recover ayde.'

Spenser's *Faerie Queene*, Bk. II, Canto 10, tells of Lear in the 'chronicle of Briton kings' read by Sir Guyon in the House of Alma. This gives the main points of Geoffrey's narrative with a few deviations. Leyr proposes to divide his realm equally until Cordelia disappoints him by her 'simple answere'. The manner of her death is new, for, maybe to give Spenser a rhyme, having been kept 'in prison long', 'her selfe she hong' [Text VII]. Spenser gave Shakespeare both Cordelia's name and the manner in which she was murdered. The images of light going out and wick thrown away (St. 30) may lie behind the Fool's 'So out went the candle and we were left darkling' (I.4.217) and Gloucester's reference to his wick burning out when he tries to kill himself (IV.6.40–1).

In William Warner's *Albions England*, a popular verse-chronicle which grew from four books in 1584 to sixteen by the sixth edition in 1606, Leir's life follows that of Locrine, and occupies 48 lines (Bk. III, Ch. xiv), bewailing his miseries and asserting that Gonoril 'did attempt / Her fathers death'. His restoration is described; Cordella's fate is not mentioned [Text VIII]. Nothing suggests that Shakespeare was influenced by this piece.

Doubtless Shakespeare had read all these poetic versions, but his major source was the anonymous play *The True Chronicle Historie of King Leir and his Three Daughters; Gonorill, Ragan, and Cordella*, published in 1605, 'As it hath bene divers and sundry times lately acted.' A Lear play was performed at the Rose by 'the Quenes men and my lord of Sussexe to geather' twice in April 1594 when Henslowe's share was 38s and 26s respectively.[1] It was probably not a new play then. Soon afterwards the Queen's company 'broke and went into the countrey to playe'

[1] *Henslowe's Diary*, ed. R. A. Foakes and R. T. Rickert, 1961, p. 21.

(*Diary*, 8 May 1594) and nine of their plays were registered for publication within a year, including *Friar Bacon*, *The Famous Victories of Henry V*, *The True Tragedy of Richard III*, Peele's *Old Wives' Tale*, and (on 14 May 1594) 'A booke entituled The most famous Chronicle historye of Leire kinge of England and his Three Daughters.' No publication followed, and the play was registered again on 8 May 1605, as 'The Tragecall historie . . .'. That there was no intention of misleading the public is proved by the title-page as published, 'The True Chronicle Historie'; and there is no reason to doubt that the phrase 'As it was latelie Acted' in the S.R. entry was true; but 'lately' might mean within two or three years.

The old play of *King Leir* printed below [Text IX], belongs to that numerous group of pieces concerned with early British history which extends from *Gorboduc* to Middleton's *Hengist, King of Kent*, and beyond. Such plays may be placed in four classes according to their handling of historical material.

1 Plays such as *Gorboduc*, written with a definitely didactic purpose; 2 Plays using chronicle-material fairly closely but bringing out the characters and passions involved, e.g. *Macbeth*, *Edmund Ironside*; 3 Plays using chronicle material together with romantic or comic ingredients, e.g. *A Knack to Know a Knave*, *Cymbeline*; 4 Plays with no historical pretensions but using a few historical names, e.g. *Old Fortunatus*, *Grim the Collier of Croydon*.[1] *Leir* belongs to the third rather than the second class. In Henslowe's 1594 list it comes with other pieces on early history: *William the Conqueror* (4 Jan.), *King Lud* (18 Jan.), *Leire* (6 and 8 April), *Cutlack* (16 May).[2] Of these *King Lud* and *Cutlack* are lost. If *William the Conqueror* was, or resembled, the 'Pleasant Comedie of Faire Em, the Millers Daughter of Manchester. With the love of William the Conqueror', not published until 1631, its only connection with history lay in his name.

Leir has been called 'a sentimental fairy-story with no historical pretensions'.[3] The author, however, kept the main outline of the Lear-story, embroidering it freely with pathos and romantic invention. Its sources, according to Perrett, were *The*

[1] See my essay 'Pre-Conquest Historical Themes in Elizabethan Drama', in *Medieval Literature and Civilization: Studies in Memory of G. N. Garmonsway*, ed. D. A. Pearsall and R. A. Waldron, 1969, pp. 289–321.
[2] *Henslowe's Diary*, pp. 20–1.
[3] I. Ribner, *The English History Play in the Age of Shakespeare*, Princeton, 1957, p. 247.

Mirror for Magistrates, Spenser's *Faerie Queene* and *Albions England* and 'there remains nothing which can suggest that he ever saw Holinshed's *Chronicle* or Geoffrey.'[1] The following analysis will show the relationship of this by no means contemptible play to the traditional story.

The reason for Leir's abdication is novel. The burial of Leir's wife has just taken place, and she is mourned in Christian terms as having lived 'a perfit patterne of a vertuous life'. Without her the old King feels lost and wishes to divide his kingdom and then abdicate. Like Gorboduc, Locrine, and other heroes of plays written under Morality influence, Leir has two counsellors, one (Skalliger) bad, the other (Perillus) good. Skalliger is a flatterer and an evil influence on Gonorill. Perillus, after warning his master against misunderstanding Cordella, tries to help her, and accompanies Leir on his wanderings.

The love-test becomes a device to make Cordella do her father's will. Skalliger suggests that the girls be given 'a Joynter more or lesse, / As is their worth, to them that love professe'. This idea comes from *The Mirror for Magistrates*. Leir (as in Spenser) disapproves of an unequal division of the land, but is willing to match Gonorill and Ragan with their suitors, the Kings of Cambria and Cornwall. Cordella has refused to marry 'unlesse love alowes', and shows no sign of wanting any of her many suitors. If she can be made to promise to do anything her father wishes he will 'match her with a King of Brittany' (actually, of Hibernia). The good counsellor protests, 'Do not force love'. Skalliger tells the other sisters about their marriages and the test, suggesting (despite what Leir has said) that those who answer most pleasingly 'shall have most unto their marriages' (155). They decide to spite Cordella by anticipating the answer their father expects from her. He 'dotes as if he were a child agayne', says Ragan. Thus before Scene 3 we have a good idea of the chief characters. When required to vie with her sisters Cordella rebukes them, saying:

> I cannot paynt my duty forth in wordes,
> I hope my deeds shall make report for me:
> But look, what love a child doth owe the father,
> The same to you, I beare, my gracious Lord. (277–80)

[1] W. Perrett, *op. cit.* pp. 99–120.

The irate monarch misunderstands her meaning, the sisters attack her, and she is driven out. She confides herself 'Unto him which doth protect the just' (331).

The coming of the sisters' suitors is presented in parallel scenes. Whereas in Geoffrey the King of the Franks sends envoys to ask for Cordelia's hand, the play shows (Sc. 4) the Gallian King setting out with his comic courtier Mumford, spurred by 'the wondrous prayse / Of these three Nymphes' to view 'the gallant Brittish Dames' in disguise as palmers. In Sc. 5 the Kings of Cornwall and Cambria having been sent for, meet *en route* for Leir's court.

As in Spenser all three sisters are beautiful, but, as in *The Mirror*, the other two envy Cordella's surpassing loveliness (481-4). Ragan says mockingly that she is fit to be a parson's wife, since she is both fair and dowerless. When the British princes arrive the kingdom is divided equally between them, but by lot (550), maybe, as Perrett suggests, because Spenser used 'lots' to make a rhyme with 'Scots' (258ff).

Cordella makes a romantic love-match. In Sc. 7, 'turn'd into the world, to seeke my fortune', she encounters the Gallian pair, who overhear her resolve to earn her living by her needle. The King of Gallia pretends that he is his own envoy sent to woo her (a memory of Geoffrey here). With characteristic directness she says that she would sooner marry the Palmer himself; so the King reveals his identity. They will marry on the same day as her sisters and then go to France. Mumford would like to marry another such 'honest and playne dealing wench' (727).

The play greatly elaborates the other daughters' ill-treatment of their father. Gonorill halves his allowance, angry at the 'quips and peremptory taunts' (775), the 'old, doltish, withered wit' with which he has rebuked her extravagance. Skalliger urges her to cut off all Leir's allowance. Cornwall is kind (Sc.10) but Gonorill tells Leir to leave, at which he weeps and bewails to the compassionate Perillus the wicked ways of the world. He feels that he is being punished for his unkindness to Cordella (911-16). He will go to Ragan.

A soliloquy by Ragan however (Sc. 11) shows her to be no kinder than her sister ('Ide send him packing somewhere else to go'). Gonorill intercepts a letter from the kindly Cornwall to

Ragan asking her if Leir is with her (Sc. 12). She substitutes another letter accusing her father of vile conduct.

In contrast we see Cordella (Sc. 13) blaming herself for neglecting her religious duties and mourning her loss of her father's love. When Leir reaches Cambria's castle, the latter is kind (Sc. 14) and Ragan pretends joy (as in Geoffrey, *The Mirror*, and Spenser) but she is a hypocrite, and when she has read Gonorill's lying letter she tempts the Messenger to kill Leir and Perillus (Sc. 17). Cordella meanwhile gets her husband to send an ambassador to invite Leir to Gallia.

The nadir of Leir's fortunes comes about the middle of the play when the Messenger tries to murder the two old men, who have been lured out into the countryside, where they fall asleep and Leir has an ill-boding dream. Awakened by the murderer, Leir, conscious of his guilt, thinks him sent by Cordella, but he soon learns the truth. When the villain proposes to swear by Hell, he is warned by thunder and lightning and shaken by their pleading and Perillus's stern admonitions. When the heavens speak again he spares their lives and leaves them (1755). The repentant Leir is easily persuaded to go to Cordella.

Having been coldly received by Gonorill (Sc. 18) the Gallian ambassador goes on to Ragan's court in search of Leir. Ragan accuses Cordella of murdering their father and strikes the envoy, against 'the law of Armes' (Sc. 22). Cambria regrets this, and is sincerely anxious for Leir's safety, but will support his wife against the Gallian King.

As in the sources the reconciliation of Leir and Cordella takes place in France. To give the meeting romance and pathos the dramatist makes Cordella and her husband resolve to sail to Britain to find her father, but first to go 'in progresse' to the sea-coast, disguised as plain country people (Sc. 21), with jesting Mumford as Roger their man. Leir and Perillus too arrive in France incognito, having changed their fine clothes for the sea-men's gowns and caps in order to pay their fares (Sc. 23). All this is peculiar to the play, but no doubt influenced by romances and other plays (e.g. the play *Damon and Pythias* by R. Edwards (1566) in which the two friends, travelling to see the world, arrive in Syracuse disguised as mariners).[1] Leir is now despair-

---

[1] Cf. *Old English Plays*, ed. R. Dodsley, 1744; modern edn. by W. C. Hazlitt, 1874, Vol. IV, p. 22.

ing of Cordella's forgiveness. The two parties meet, but neither recognizes the other till Cordella hears Perillus offering his blood to the famished Leir, and the latter's rehearsal of his sins and sufferings.

Here the play may have been influenced by T. Lodge's *Rosalynde* (1590) in which old Adam and Rosader wander starving in France and Adam offers his blood to save his master's life.[1] Given food and drink, the old men try to pay for it, and there follows a long and affecting recognition-scene, only marred by an excessive amount of kneeling. First Cordella kneels to ask Leir's blessing; then he kneels to beg her forgiveness; and later the Gallian King and Mumford kneel to swear revenge.

The restoration of King Leir follows soon. When Ragan's Messenger fails to return she rages at the thought that the old men have escaped, wishing that she had been a man (Sc. 25). The invasion of Britain is made easy by the neglect of the beacon-watchers who (in a Hardy-like scene) prefer the alehouse (Sc. 27). When the Gallian army lands, these defenders are quickly put to flight (Sc. 29), as are Cambria and Cornwall (Sc. 31), and the play ends with Leir's realizing the true inwardness of Cordella's expression of her love ('Thou lovedst me dearely, and as ought a child').

The tragi-comedy ekes out the slender chronicle-story (less detailed in Tudor accounts than in Geoffrey of Monmouth) with romantic material, but it is more than 'a sentimental fairy-story'. It is a tale in which parental unkindness and filial ingratitude, sins against natural and divine law, are contrasted with loyalty, truth, and piety. Leir's folly is set alongside Perillus's wisdom, the selfish cruelty of the bad sisters, those 'fell vipers', and Cordella's simple devotion.

That the play has strong religious implications has already been suggested. At the beginning they appear in Leir's pious wishes for his dead wife and his desire to 'resigne these earthly cares, / And thinke upon the welfare of my soule' (27–8). Cordella is submissive to God's will when rejected (610–11) and eager to help her Palmer-lover in his 'holy Prayers' (702). She feels guilt when she has not been to 'the Temple of my God / To

[1] See Vol. II, pp. 195–6. In Geoffrey of Monmouth, Bk. 12, Ch. 4, Brian feeds King Cadwallo with a roasted slice from his own thigh.

render thanks for all his benefits' (1061–2). The whole of Sc. 13 displays both her and her husband's goodness. Towards her father she feels love and Christian forgiveness. So it is not surprising that Perillus says of her, 'the perfit good indeed, / Can never be corrupted by the bad' (2065–6).

The union of divine and natural law is repeatedly stressed. 'No worldly gifts but grace from God on hye, / Doth nourish vertue and true charity', says Perillus (1772–3); and Leir's cruelty 'makes not her love to be any lesse. / If she do love you as a child should do.' So the nature and exercise of 'kindness', of human nature at its best, working in grace within Cordella and Perillus, make a major theme of the old play; and 'unkindness' is exemplified in the bad sisters, who are differentiated, Gonorill being more forthright in villainy, Ragan more hypocritical and slyly cruel.

As in the original story, Leir must learn the error of his ways. This he quickly does, for in Sc. 8 Perillus says that 'he, the myrrour of mild patience, / Puts up all wrongs, and never gives reply' (755–6). There are some good touches of characterization, as when Leir makes excuses for Gonorill's harshness, saying that she must be with child (844–5). He is, however, given to self-pity. There are occasional reflections on the 'iron age' (761) and the decay of human conduct. Neither he nor Perillus realizes how completely Gonorill and Ragan have reversed 'natures sacred law' until the Messenger swears thrice that they have sent him and shows Gonorill's letter (Sc. 19). Then Perillus bursts out in protest against God, but Leir urges pious submission.

The thunder and lightning which occur twice in this scene, first apparently as a warning against the Messenger's triple oath (1634) and then at the mention of Hell's punishment (1739), are a sign of divine Providence, but are not the only reason why the assassin spares the old men. He is moved by their pleas, thus proving that he has 'some sparke of grace'. So Perillus's question is answered, and the rest of the play, with its kindly mariners, reconciliation and victory, justifies the ways of God to men. Leir recognizes ever more clearly that his fault has 'sowrd the sweet milk of dame Natures paps', and 'chokt the flowr of grace' (2060–2). The union of nature and grace recurs when Cordella says that for her father to kneel to his daughter is against the law of 'God, world and nature' (2315). Leir then blesses her in biblical terms. So the anonymous dramatist of this very successful play has convincingly interpreted the story as more than a political and domestic affair, seeing it as concerned with the inmost laws of human nature and of the Divine Will.

We cannot be sure why Shakespeare altered the *Leir* play in the way he did. The change of ending may have been first thought of merely because his company wanted a tragedy from him. But his own creative mood led him to take a stage further the presentation of confused aims and sinister passions which he had explored in *Hamlet*, *Troilus* and *Othello*. His reading of the chronicles with their culmination in Cordelia's death as a direct result of the discord in the family, would support any inclination to rewrite the old play so as to make it much more of a 'Tragical Historie'—more tragic and more historical. Hence, and to concentrate the action, he struck out several scenes: Skalliger's conversation with the bad daughters before the love-test, the coming of the suitors, the ballad-like wooing of the French King, the abortive attempt on Lear's life, etc. But, having recently composed a highly intense and closely-knit tragedy in *Othello*, he was led by the epic nature of the Lear-material to revert to the manner of *Hamlet*, to follow his dramatic source in tracing events from beginning to end, and to enrich the social background and make it not so neutral as in *Othello* but pervaded with a moral and poetic atmosphere suited to the tragic perplexities of the chief characters.

With accurate details of place and time Shakespeare was not greatly concerned[1] as his imagination immersed itself in the emotional and ethical implications of the story and initially with obvious themes embodied there, e.g. ingratitude, discord in the family, parent against child, child against parent, greed, the pathos of old age maltreated, the war of good against evil. With his mind thus filled, and especially with the moral blindness of the self-centred Lear as noted by Perillus (577), and wanting

[1] A. C. Bradley, *op. cit.* pp. 256–60 and note U, discusses many improbabilities and obscurities which show that Shakespeare, in seeking broad effects and passionate scenes, ignored geography and likelihood. Where does the action take place? Does Cornwall live at Gloucester (I.5.1) or is that a slip of the pen? Does Gloster live in the middle of the heath (II.4.304)? Why must he go to Dover to kill himself? Why should Edgar have written a letter to Edmund, living in the same house? Similarly, how casually the Fool and Cordelia's husband are dismissed when no longer wanted!

some ancillary material to act as counterpoise, he recalled the story of the blind Paphlagonian king in Sidney's *Arcadia* (1590), who believed his wicked son and rejected his good one and was physically blinded by the former and cherished by the latter—a remarkable parallel to the Lear-story, though with different circumstances.

So the Edmund–Edgar–Gloucester plot emerges from the episode in which the heroes of Sidney's romance meet the blind King, led by his devoted son Leonatus, and hear how he was deceived by his bastard, Plexirtus, blinded, cast out, and brought to the brink of suicide. The good son returns, like Cordelia, from exile, and with foreign help thwarts the efforts of Plexirtus to murder him and his father. There is a fight between Leonatus and the villain with his men and later on Plexirtus manoeuvres two brothers. Tydeus and Telenor, into killing each other. The defeated Plexirtus returns with a rope round his neck to beg his brother's pardon, and goes free to plot further evil. As Dr F. Pyle has demonstrated, the Arcadian story influenced Shakespeare's treatment of the Lear-story[1] as well as that of Gloucester. Gloucester, like the Paphlagonian king, is let out to wander by enemies 'delighting to make me feele my miserie'; but so is Lear. The sufferings of the father who could barely subsist as a beggar at men's doors are transferred to Edgar, but also to Lear. The chivalric fights in *Arcadia* suggested the trial by combat between Edgar and Edmund (V.1, V.3). The storm in *Arcadia* from which the two princes shelter in a 'hollow rocke' and the 'poorely arayed, extreamley weather-beaten' appearance of the aged man and his son, joined with the thunder in *Leir* to evoke the central storm in *King Lear*. The tone of the episode certainly affected Shakespeare's treatment. Moreover not only Gloucester, like the Paphlagonian king, dies between joy and grief, but so does Lear, fondly hoping that Cordelia may be alive. And the rope round Plexirtus' neck, who so deserved to die, may have associated itself with Spenser's account of Cordelia's hanging, to reinforce Shakespeare's resolve for an ironic ending [Text XA].

Shakespeare augmented this strong story with other material from Sidney which also concerned a credulous king tricked into

[1] Fitzroy Pyle, '*Twelfth Night, King Lear,* and *Arcadia*', *MLR* XLIII, 1948, pp. 449–55.

mistrusting his virtuous son. The King of Iberia is made jealous of Plangus by his second wife, who makes him fear that Plangus is plotting to murder him. The device by which Edmund tricks Edgar into what seems to Gloucester an attempt at parricide (II.1) is developed from this [Text XB]. Plangus escapes overseas and (like Cordella in *Leir*) lives yearning for reconciliation with his father.

Another feature of Plangus' life is relevant, for he is in love with Queen Erona who has been captured and condemned to death. In Bk. II, Ch. 12, a *terza rima* poem of his is read in which he expresses deep despair (for which he is rebuked by Basilius), calling men

> Balles to the starres, and thralles to Fortunes raigne,
> Turnd from themselves, infected with their cage,
> Where death is feard, and life is held with paine.
> Like players plas't to fill a filthy stage. . . .
> Griefe onely makes his wretched state to see
> (Even like a toppe which nought but whipping moves)
> This man, this talking beast, this walking tree.
> Griefe is the stone which finest judgement proves . . .

Plangus goes further and maligns the gods:

> O heaven (if heaven there be)
> Hath all thy whirling course so small effect?
> Serve all thy starrie eyes this shame to see?
> Let doltes in haste some altars faire erect
> To those high powers, which idly sit above,
> And virtue do in greatest need neglect.

In reply Basilius defends the gods in conventional fashion:

> Alas, while we are wrapt in foggie mist
> Of our selfe-love (so passions do deceave)
> We thinke they hurt, when most they do assist . . .

The many references to providence and questions about heaven's guidance of men's lives in *King Lear* may also owe something to the celebrated dialogue between Cecropia and Pamela in the 1590 *Arcadia*, Bk. 3 [Text XC] in which Cecropia tries to convert Pamela to atheistic hedonism and

Pamela proves the dependence of nature on a benevolent order.[1]

As R. G. Moulton pointed out long ago,[2] the two plots work side by side, each producing three tragic actions, emerging inevitably from the initial error committed by the protagonist. Lear's tragedy is one of excessive retribution for his pride and for the injustice he showed Cordelia and Kent. Cordelia and Kent suffer greatly in consequence, but because they are unselfish they 'make a heaven in hell's despite' until the parthian shot by which evil destroys Cordelia. The tragedy of Goneril and Regan is one of increasing villainy and intrigue culminating in the destruction of both, as the malice at first used against their father is mingled with lust and turned against each other.

In the Gloucester-plot the old Earl is not the dramatic protagonist, but his is the ultimate responsibility for making Edmund what he is, for making Edmund at all. 'The gods are just, and of our pleasant vices, / Make instruments to plague us', as Edgar says. His lust of long ago results now in his downfall as Edmund's callous plotting against Edgar and his father leads to Gloucester's cruel blinding. The sufferings of Edgar parallel those of the good characters in the other plot; like them he fights back and with selfless devotion cherishes the father who has been unjust to him, before acting as his brother's executioner. As for Edmund, his tragedy, like that of the two sisters, is one of mounting ambition as his scope widens from dispossessing his brother to dispossessing and destroying his father, and exciting the desire of the two evil Queens through which he hopes to rule the whole land. His is the tragedy of Machiavellian atheism, and his last minute attempt to do some little good is futile.

In this play Shakespeare wished to insist on the resemblances rather than the contrasts between the two plots, and their emotional relationships and final interweaving are so close that it is misleading to speak of 'main-plot' and 'under-plot'. But there *are* differences between the two stories, and of these the dramatist takes every advantage, so that, as Moulton wrote, they are constantly 'by their antithesis throwing up one another's effect; the contrast is like the reversing of the original

---

[1] Cf. W. A. Armstrong, *TLS*, 14 Oct. 1949.
[2] R. G. Moulton, *Shakespeare as a Dramatic Artist*, 1885, pp. 205–8.

subject in a musical fugue' (p. 207). The musical analogy can be applied also in the sense in which Aldous Huxley uses it in *Point Counter Point* with regard to the 'musicalization of fiction'.[1] Changes of mood, 'abrupt transitions', 'modulations and variations' are certainly found in *King Lear*, and the following survey of the action may indicate how Shakespeare used them in combining his plots and adapting his sources to his own purposes.

Right at the beginning of the play there is a faint adumbration of the Edmund–Gloucester relationship when the imperceptive father introduces his bastard casually and insultingly to Kent before we are shown the more comprehensive folly of Lear himself in a court-scene which corresponds to the old play's third scene. So Shakespeare omits all reference to Leir's dead wife, Skalliger's betrayal of his intentions to Gonorill and Ragan, and their agreement to outsmart Cordella; nor are we shown the summoning of the suitors and their arrival. The division of the land has already been decided: equal amounts to all three daughters. The two older daughters' suitors are already present, and Cordelia's two, France and Burgundy, are 'long in our court' but offstage.

The love-test is less thoroughly explained than in *Leir*. Apparently it is a mere whim of the old King, who at the moment of abdication wants to be assured that he is much beloved. The reward will be 'our largest bounty': probably the richest of the three parts of Britain. As her sisters speak hyperbolically of their love Cordelia (oppressed by their extravagance) knows that she cannot rival their rhetoric and prepares us by her asides for her refusal to compete with them. Her answer is abrupt and, on the face of it, ungracious; but a more sensitive father would have looked below 'I cannot heave / My heart into my mouth' (I.1.91–2). By omitting the preparatory matter of the old play, Shakespeare makes her bald understatement a hammer-blow to the audience as well as to Lear himself. Her union of love and duty will be understood at once by those who already know the story; others may be puzzled for a time. In rebuking her sisters she draws on *The Mirror for Magistrates*

---

[1] 'A novelist modulates by reduplicating situations and character. He shows several people falling in love, or dying, or praying in different ways—dissimilars solving the same problem. Or vice versa, similar people confronted with dissimilar problems.' A. Huxley, *Point Counter Point*, 1947 edn., pp. 408–9.

(1587) or Camden's *Remaines*, and also anticipates the Christian marriage-service and the New Testament saying that a wife must leave her parents and cleave to her husband. She does not speak so riddlingly as in Holinshed and many other versions of the story, but sets cold truth above flattery in revulsion against her sisters' insincerity; yet we have as yet no reason to suspect that they are bad women. Blinded by self-love and the thwarting of his generosity, Lear falls into a rage, curses her and deprives her of her dowry: 'Let pride, which she calls plainness, marry her' (129). Proud she may be, but with the self-respect of a noble soul, not vain like her father. (In *Leir* Gonorill calls her 'stately' (494).)

Lear's pride is revealed when in abdicating he keeps 'a hundred knights . . . / The name and all the addition of a king.' Not perhaps an excessive retinue, but Kent is not only thinking of Cordelia's wrongs when he says, 'To plainness honour's bound / When majesty falls to folly' (148-9). The abdication itself is crass folly, as most Elizabethan historians and statesmen would agree. The King, being divinely appointed, cannot surrender his sacred mission; this was one lesson of *Gorboduc* and the *Arcadia*. Like Perillus, Kent calls Lear blind, as the latter will come to admit; and doubtless Shakespeare is thinking of what will happen to another rash old man. Kent also mentions madness (I.1.146).

Cordelia is given two suitors, to contrast the true love and perceptiveness of the French King with the financial caution of Burgundy. France's surprise at finding her cast off enables her to make clear that her fault is to have displeased her father by want of 'A still-soliciting eye, and such a tongue / As I am glad I have not'. 'A tardiness in nature' France calls it, and takes her gladly.

That she knows her sisters' natures appears when Goneril and Regan, left alone, discuss Lear's 'poor judgement' and capriciousness in banishing her and Kent. Regan sums him up contemptuously, 'Tis the infirmity of his age; yet he hath ever but slenderly known himself'; and Goneril calls him 'rash' at best and now subject to the 'unruly waywardness' of 'infirm and choleric years' (289-300). There is much truth in this, and the audience knows by the end of the first scene that Lear is a violent and 'difficult' person. The moral problem of the play is made more pointed than if he had been a wise and equable parent. These two daughters see only his faults; Cordelia remembers only, 'You have begot me, bred me, lov'd me' (96). It is a child's duty to show the utmost forbearance towards an erring parent because the natural bond between them implies perpetual 'kindness'.

In *Leir* the Gallian King does not arrive in Britain until Cordella has been driven out, and he meets and woos her in his disguise as a pilgrim. Shakespeare avoids the mild humour and naive sentiment of this scene by having the French King take her publicly in full court. Moreover, having ended I.1 with the unruly daughters, he begins I.2 with the unruly son Edmund who, after letting the audience know his deep 'atheism' and resentment at his bastard birth, begins his campaign against Edgar and his father by showing the latter a forged letter in which Edgar wished him to plot against Gloucester on the ground that, 'sons at perfect age, and fathers declined, the father should be as ward to the son, and the son manage his revenues' (I.2.74–7).

The parallel to the main plot is close, and Gloucester sees the resemblance: 'there's son against father: the king falls from the bias of nature; there's father against child', not realizing that he will follow Lear's pattern of behaviour in trusting the false child against the true. For him the situation is a proof that the age is in decline, as astrological portents suggest. Edmund mocks at astrology; like Cassius and Iago he believes in the individual will. Having persuaded Edgar that their father is estranged from him and seeks to injure him, he rejoices, like Iago, in tricking 'a credulous father and a brother noble'.

Shakespeare's dramatic judgement is shown in approaching Goneril's ill-treatment of Lear, for he omits the soliloquy in *Leir* (Sc. 8) in which Perillus bewails the King's plight now that she wishes to get rid of him and says that Leir, 'the myrrour of mild patience, / Puts up all wrongs, and never gives reply.' This robs the scene with Gonorill of much of its force. Instead, Shakespeare goes directly into a conversation between Goneril and Oswald in which she explains what she proposes to do and why: 'His knights grow riotous, and himself upbraids us / On every trifle' (I.3.7–8). 'Idle old man' (she calls him), 'That still would manage those authorities / That he hath given away.' She will goad him into leaving her house for Regan's. How far Lear is to blame we cannot tell; but that a daughter should speak so harshly about him to a servant casts an ill light on her character. Now Kent, another retainer but loyal to the monarch who banished him, appears in disguise (I.4) and gets employment with Lear, just in time to hear Oswald twice treating the old man with studied discourtesy. Kent trips the fellow up. The Fool makes his first bitter jests reproaching Lear for giving his golden crown away and giving his daughters the rod. His reference to 'That lord that counsell'd thee / To give away thy land' (I.4.139–40) is to Skalliger in *Leir*. Shakespeare's Lear needed no counsellor to make himself a 'bitter fool', and his Goneril does not ask advice about cutting down her father's allowance (Cf. *Leir*, Sc. 9). Her complaint is centred on his large retinue and its conduct. Lear meets her accusations with sarcasm, bewilderment and then violent rage (251–62). He now realizes what a small fault Cordelia committed and how mistaken he was:

> O Lear, Lear, Lear!
> Beat at this gate that let thy folly in,
> And thy dear judgement out. (270–2)

In both plays Goneril's husband is amiable and mild. In *Leir* (where he is Cornwall) he listens to his wife's tirade until he can bear it no longer and goes out. In *King Lear* Albany misses Goneril's accusations and does no more than urge Lear to be patient: he is easily borne down by his wife's pretended fears of her father's riotous knights. Lear stamps out after calling on the goddess Nature to make Goneril infertile or mother of an ungrateful monster. He re-enters almost at once, having discovered that orders have been given dismissing fifty of his followers. Weeping with rage and humiliation he will go to Regan who 'is kind and comfortable'. But Goneril sends Oswald on ahead with a letter explaining her fears and wishes. (Compare *Leir*, Sc. 12, where Cornwall sends to Leir, and Gonorill substitutes letters to her sister.)

This is not the broken man who mourns with Perillus at the end of *Leir*, Sc. 10, though both kings regret their unkindness to Cordelia and hope that Regan will be kinder than her sister.

Lear too is sending letters ahead, by Kent, to Gloucester,

where apparently Regan will be (I.5). The Fool keeps up his flow of gibes ('Thou shouldst not have been old before thou hadst been wise' (44–5)) and hints doubts of Regan's fidelity. Lear now begins to fear for his sanity: 'I will forget my nature'; 'O let me not be mad, sweet heaven, Keep me in temper; let me not be mad!' (46–7).

Instead of moving to France where Cordella in *Leir*, Sc. 13, is rejoicing in her marriage and only regretting her alienation from her father, Shakespeare uses II.1 to bring both plots together. Already there are hints of quarrels between the Dukes of Cornwall and Albany (II.1.10–11). At Gloucester's castle Edmund persuades Edgar to flee and pretends to their father that Edgar has attacked him (II.1.21–80). When Cornwall and Regan arrive she says that Edgar has been egged on by Lear's 'riotous knights', and Cornwall takes Edmund into his service.

In *Leir* the Messenger reaches Ragan after she has (however insincerely) welcomed her father. In *King Lear* Goneril's messenger Oswald reaches Gloucester's home and quarrels with Kent, who is put in the stocks, before Lear arrives. Putting Kent in the stocks is a parallel to Ragan's striking the ambassador in *Leir*, Sc. 22. Kent in his misery is given some hope by word from Cordelia (II.2.125–70).

Another wretched man, Edgar, on the run in II.3, decides to disguise himself as a mad beggar, 'the basest and most poorest shape / That every penury, in contempt of man / Brought near to beast' (II.3.7–9). Thus Shakespeare is preparing for the great scenes to come by bringing all the main characters close together. The insulting meanness of Regan and Cornwall in leaving home rather than receive Lear there is made clear by Kent when the old King, finding them absent, comes to Gloucester's place and sees Kent in the stocks (II.4). The Fool in his droll way explains why the King's entourage is so reduced: 'Let go thy hold when a great wheel runs down a hill' and why he is faithful: 'But I will tarry: the fool will stay, / And let the wise man fly' (II.4.63–84). Lear now fears that his mind is going, with 'hysterica passio' rising from his belly to his heart and head (56–7, 120), but he cannot restrain his indignation as (through the alarmed Gloucester) he commands the appearance of the Duke and his wife. When they come, unwillingly, Regan takes Goneril's part, advises him to ask forgiveness and to return to Albany's castle, and is disgusted by his histrionic fury (137–69). Kent is freed, but the coming of Goneril terrifies Lear (189–92) and fortifies Regan in her cruelty. When he refuses to return to Goneril with half his knights, she will have him only with less. The sisters take a perverse pleasure in cutting him down:

> *Gon.* What need you five-and-twenty, ten, or five,
>   To follow in a house, where twice as many
>   Have a command to tend you?
> *Reg.*   What need one?

Shakespeare jettisons the device by which Gonorill rouses Ragan against Leir (Sc. 12, 15). Regan needs no false libels to make her hostile; her parsimony, her dislike of Lear's entourage, and her lack of generous warmth are enough. She meets his pleadings with weak excuses which he finally sees through, and crying to the gods for patience—which he entirely lacks—he curses both daughters with futile threats of revenge and goes out into the night crying 'O fool! I shall go mad', leaving them somewhat abashed and making excuses to each other before they bid Gloucester shut his doors against the imminent storm.

Instead of using Ragan's plot against Lear's life (Sc. 15, 17) and the Messenger's attempt on the two old men (Sc. 19) from which he is deterred by thunder and their appeals to religion, Shakespeare evokes from the thunder (sign in *Leir* of divine displeasure) the great storm in which Lear vies with the elements in rage and rhetoric until he goes truly mad (III.2). Most of Act III is devoted to the King's breakdown in body and mind and his tardy realization of what poverty and desolation imply. The interest is shifted from external events to 'the agonies and strife of human hearts', though the hapless wandering of Lear and his Fool were suggested by *Leir* (Sc. 14), where the two old men are creeping towards Ragan's home, and by their later extremity in France (Sc. 24). Kent's note from Cordelia tells him that her husband is about to invade Britain, where the two Dukes are already at odds, and he sends her his ring as proof of his identity and faithfulness (III.1). In the next scene he finds Lear half-deranged, now calling on the storm to destroy the world, now full of self-pity, blaming it for siding with his daughters, now promising to be (as Leir was after the first scene) 'the pattern of all patience' (III.2.37), now calling on the gods to judge all 'close pent-up guilts'. Here for the first time the once-arrogant monarch feels sympathy for another, when he is sorry for the plight of his Fool (68–73).

In III.3 Gloucester (like Kent) has had a letter telling him that the King's injuries will be avenged. He warns Edmund to walk warily (III.3.20): 'We must incline to the King.' But Edmund will betray his father to Cornwall, for 'this must draw me/That which my father loses'.

Meanwhile Lear has ceased to feel the outer storm; 'the tempest in my mind / Doth from my senses take all feeling else / Save what beats there' (III.4.12–14). Though his mind is tottering he is able to think of the others, whom he orders into shelter. Now he pities all 'poor naked wretches: O! I have ta'en / Too little care of this' (III.4.32–6). His lifelong egoism broken down at last, experience and fellow-feeling bring an impulse of practical charity. This is not madness, but when Edgar, almost naked, darts out from the hovel and, playing his part of 'Bedlam beggar' indulges in demented nonsense, the King wishes to emulate this natural man and begins to tear off his clothes. The arrival of Gloucester to offer the King shelter, fire and food, initiates another round of mad conversation of a most poignant kind, during which Edgar keeps his identity secret and does not hear his father say that his own wits are crazed with grief because his beloved son has sought his life.

The other son is even now seeking Gloucester's life, having told Cornwall that his father is privy to the King of France's intentions (III.5); his reward is to have his father's title. Gloucester meanwhile has taken Lear and the others to some proper shelter, but Lear's wits have entirely gone, and in III.6 the man driven mad by grief, the clever simpleton and the pretended demoniac rival each other in oddity as they arraign the evil daughters before their insane court. The timid Gloucester comes, defying Cornwall, to see his old master off towards Dover in a litter. On his return home he is seized, haled before Regan and Cornwall and blinded (III.7), but it is Goneril who first suggests, 'Pluck out his eyes' (5). Edmund knows that his father is to be cruelly punished, and Gloucester is informed of his treachery. A servant who intervenes is killed by Regan, but not before he has wounded Cornwall (fatally, it turns out). The two plots are now intertwined, and the wicked sisters are responsible for the double horror of 'madding' Lear and blinding Gloucester.

In Act IV the powers of good gain ground. Gloucester, given into the mad beggar's care, recognizes his past errors—'I stumbled when I saw' (IV.1.19)—and longs for the maligned Edgar. He has lost all hope: 'As flies to wanton boys, are we to the gods; / They kill us for their sport.' But he feels gratitude for every assistance, and (like Lear before him) preaches charity: 'So distribution should undo excess, / And each man have enough' (71–2); and he knows the social irony of his plight: 'Tis the time's plague, when madmen lead the blind.' (46)

To intensify the action Shakespeare now makes his most considerable omissions from the old play: Cordella's envoy sent to invite her father to France (Sc. 16); her journey with her husband in disguise, Leir's crossing and exchange of clothes with the seamen (Sc. 23); and, later, the embarcation of the Gallian forces, the beacon-watchers (Sc. 27, 29), the landing and the capture of Dover. Shakespeare wished to have Lear meet his daughter on British soil, to avoid emphasizing the French invasion and to bring all his characters together for the catastrophe. So Dover is often mentioned. Lear is to be taken there at III.1.36; Oswald says that over thirty of his knights have gone after him (III.7.16) and Gloucester bravely boasts of sending him there (III.7.51–67) before being blinded and set free to 'smell his way to Dover'. In IV.1 he bids Edgar take him to Dover cliff—obviously to commit suicide there.

A surprising turn comes in IV.2 when Albany proves to be no longer the 'milk-liver'd man' Goneril calls him, but condemns her for her monstrous behaviour and promises revenge on Edmund for his treatment of Gloucester, ignorant that Goneril has already promised herself to the bastard.

Since the play is to end tragically there is no place for Cordelia's husband (who in the chronicles died soon after her father). His sudden removal in IV.3.1–10 is weakly motivated but obviates the embarrassment of a French king warring on British soil, helps to explain the defeat of his army, and allows Cordelia to devote herself entirely to her father henceforth, after the Gentleman's account of how she received news of Lear's coming to Dover with such joy, love and pity (IV.3.11–

34). As in *Leir* (Sc. 23), the old King feels 'a sovereign shame' which keeps him from going to her. Still insane, he has wandered off into the fields, and she sends to find him; meanwhile her forces are ready to meet the British attack: 'O dear father! / It is thy business that I go about.'

No such loyalty dwells in Regan's bosom as she shows Oswald her jealousy of Goneril with regard to Edmund and claims that since Cornwall is dead, 'more convenient is he for my hand / Than for your lady's'. Edmund knows it, she asserts, threatening her sister (IV.5). Gloucester is to be murdered, if found.

But Gloucester has been led by the mad beggar to what the latter claims is the top of Dover cliff (IV.6), and when the despairing old man has renounced the world, leapt forward and fallen half-senseless, Edgar plays one last trick on him, pretending to be a countryman who saw him fall and be preserved by some miracle of 'the clearest gods'. There follows a poignant meeting between the blind Earl and the mad King when Lear wanders in decked with flowers, uttering snatches of old memories and playing the king, satirizing the monstrous work of ingratitude and lust, the topsy-turvydom of society where 'a dog's obey'd in office' and the justice is no better than the thief. There's insight in this madness, and he has flashes of sanity too, but he runs away from Cordelia's messengers. In the same scene Edgar slays the 'serviceable villain' Oswald and by reading Goneril's letter to Edmund finds the means to turn her husband finally against her.

That other guardian angel, Kent, makes himself known to Cordelia (but will keep his disguise) before the great scene in which she and her father (restored by sleep) are brought together and he gradually comes to himself (IV. 7), first thinks she is 'a soul in bliss' looking down on him in Purgatory: 'You are a spirit, I know; when did you die?' (48), and wishes to kneel to her when she asks for his blessing (57–9), then recognizes her and expects her to poison him for the wrong he has done her (68–75). Pathos too deep to analyse, yet springing, however distantly, from the Recognition scene in *Leir*, Sc. 24.

Reconciliation between the good characters: jealousy and complete egoism among the bad. In V.1. the hostility of Goneril and Regan is made clear, Albany's reluctance in the war and desire for peace with Lear and Cordelia, Edmund's determination to use them all for his own supremacy and to ensure that Lear and Cordelia perish.

Shakespeare omits the conventional altercation between army-leaders in *Leir*, Sc. 30; but as in *Leir*, Sc. 31, the battle is merely sketched in V.2. In the old play it was the means by which Leir was restored to his throne—by foreign aid, however. Here it is the means by which he is captured by Edmund; the military aspect is entirely subordinate to the spiritual, but is no defeat of British by French forces. Edgar and his father must try to escape (V.2); Lear looks forward happily to imprisonment with Cordelia in his newfound innocence (V.3.3–26): but Edmund gives sinister orders before Albany as victorious Duke demands the prisoners, and tells him flatly, 'I hold you but a subject of this war, / Not as a brother' (61–2). Regan's defence of Edmund and proposal to marry him brings the jealousy between the two sisters to a head. Albany, no longer the mild man of earlier scenes, arrests both Edmund and Goneril, and proposes to prove Edmund's treason through trial by combat in chivalric fashion, as suggested by Edgar at V.1.41–4. Edgar is of course the antagonist, and he defeats and wounds Edmund before revealing his identity. Goneril, self-condemned by her letter to Edmund, goes out and kills herself, having already poisoned her sister. All this has distracted attention from the situation of Lear and Cordelia, but the faithful Kent reminds us of them and Edmund, who has accepted his defeat (V.3.174–5) and will die grateful for the evil love of his two women, repents of his murderous intent and tells them to save Lear and Cordelia.

Suspense is not long kept up. When Lear staggers in carrying the body of Cordelia the tragic end is certain. Though with a flash of his old vigour he 'kill'd the slave that was a-hanging thee' too late to save her, his mind now wanders and he cannot recognize Kent. Albany begins, as he must, to settle state affairs, promising to give Lear 'absolute power', but Lear faints and dies, still hoping that Cordelia may be alive. Albany gives the care of the realm to Edgar and Kent, but the latter, old and worn-out, knows that he must soon follow his master.

This outline, inadequate though it must be to show either the depth of characterization or the poetic movement of thought in *King Lear*, at least may suggest some of the universal themes evoked and embodied by Shakespeare in combining his two plots by parallel and contrast. Such themes were: anger and despair, madness, the relations between parents and children, 'nature' and questionings of divine justice. These ethical themes are stated more explicitly in this play than in any previous one (perhaps because those in *Leir* were made obvious and didactic), yet not so obtrusively as to turn the story into an allegory. They are worked out through character and incident, with a technique of concrete representation and inner motivation, not by parable.

To regard *King Lear* as a study of 'Wrath in Old Age' (L. B. Campbell)[1] is to oversimplify, yet various kinds of anger play a large part. The explosive, impetuous rage of Lear himself is set beside the impatience of Goneril, the hypocritical venom of Regan, the physical cruelty of Cornwall, the intriguing malice of Edmund, and the virtuous wrath of Kent and Edgar.

In *Leir* the King is a weak old man, sketched without depth or complexity, who after his outburst against Cordella endures without anger except for an occasional flash of bitter irony. Shakespeare's monarch is violent, intemperate, resistant to the wrongs he has to suffer, an irascible tyrant who probably, as Regan declares, 'hath ever but slenderly known himself'. Habitual arrogance has become an 'unruly waywardness'. His abdication, division of the kingdom, and rejection of Cordelia are one 'hideous rashness' after another, and his banishment of Kent proves once more how unsound his judgement is. His lack of self-control, his tendency to curse and rave are shown on several occasions. Before long he may be 'more sinned against than sinning', but he has far to go before he becomes 'the pattern of all patience', and his pilgrimage through madness to self-knowledge, altruism, humility and repentance is traced with the skill of genius.

Associated with anger in the sources was flattery, which avoids anger by appealing to self-love. The extravagant affection expressed by the two elder sisters is contrasted with the inability or refusal of the youngest to unpack her heart with words. The sycophantic ill-counsel or subservience of Skalliger or Oswald is contrasted with the blunt wisdom of Perillus or Kent and their readiness to endure all in their master's service.

[1] *Shakespeare's Tragic Heroes, Slaves of Passion*, 1930, Ch. 14.

Another important motif is despair. Present in the chronicle versions where Cordelia committed suicide in prison, despair became the other principal character in Higgins's poem in *The Mirror of Magistrates*, putting the knife into Cordila's hand and guiding it to take her life. In *Leir* the theme appears only briefly. When threatened with assassination the old King says 'Let us submit us to the will of God: / Things past all sence, let us not seeke to know' (1656-7). When in France and afraid to meet Cordella lest she now hate him he loses hope: 'Cease to beguile me with thy hopeful speaches: / O joyne with me, and thinke of nought but crosses', but is at once overcome by Perillus' 'strong argument' that 'death is better then for to despaire' (2073-82).

Shakespeare shifts the condition to Gloucester, whose original in the *Arcadia* sought suicide as the Earl does at Dover. The latter touches the bottom of his misery when he fails: 'Is wretchedness depriv'd that benefit / To end itself by death?' (IV.6.62-3). But he is soon persuaded by Edgar that he has been preserved from a demon, and accepts the situation: 'henceforth I'll bear / Affliction till it do cry out itself / "Enough, enough", and die' (76-8). He relapses when he hears that Lear and Cordelia are captured: 'No further, sir: a man may rot even here.' But again he is restored to patience by Edgar's profound words: 'What! in ill thoughts again! Men must endure / Their going hence, even as their coming hither: / Ripeness is all' (V.2.6-11).

The close connection between anger and madness was well known. Anger was '*brevis furor*', 'a short madnesse, for she is as little Mistresse of her selfe as the other' (Lodge's *Seneca*). It was 'a passion so like to furye and madnes, as nothing in the world more' (T. Newton).[1] There was no madness in *Leir*, but Shakespeare traces with great care the gradual deterioration of the King's mind as his explosive temper breaks up his personality and the conflict between memories of grandeur and actual impotence results in fits of violent rhetoric punctuated by fears of madness which are fulfilled when his attempts to rival the thunder end in mental collapse and hallucinations.

The gradual madness of Lear is set off by other kinds of mental aberration, in the Fool and Edgar, and the despair of Gloucester. The Fool is a professional jester of the 'inspired

---

[1] L. B. Campbell, *op. cit.*, Ch. 14, gives many authorities.

simpleton' kind, a youth whose pawky humour, sly malice and perceptiveness let him act as an embodied conscience to the King and turn the knife in the wound as he 'labours to out-jest / His heart-struck injuries'. Here, as in *As You Like It*, 'The wise man's folly is anatomis'd / Even by the squandering glances of the fool' (II.7.56–7), and Lear's fool was probably Robert Armin, who also played Feste in *Twelfth Night*. Indeed the Fool adapts Feste's song (*TN*, V.1.398) as he goes to the hovel in the storm (III.2.74–7), no doubt recalling the lines 'Gainst knaves and thieves men shut their gates, / For the rain it raineth every day' as he reminds Lear that they both of them have only 'a little tiny wit' and must manage as best they can.

Edgar's original in Sidney did not assume madness. No doubt Shakespeare recalled Hamlet when he needed to keep Edgar in Britain—and on the stage—though with a price on his head. His assumed madness would supply contrast and additional poignancy as Lear slipped into insanity and came to realize the extremes of poverty and suffering. Moreover the dramatist had recently read a book which supplied an entirely different style and set of images for Edgar's 'madness'. This was Samuel Harsnett's *A Declaration of Egregious Popish Impostures . . . Practised by Edmunds alias Weston, a Jesuit* (1603) in which the Chaplain to the Bishop of London attacked belief in witches and 'possession' and exposed the 'wickedness' of lurking Jesuits who had pretended to exorcize demons by the use of relics, fumigation, holy water and the Sacraments.[1] Inquiries made since 1598 had disclosed that in 1585–6 there had been an epidemic of 'possession' centred in the household of Edward Peckham where three chambermaids (Anne Smith and two sisters, Sarah and Friswood Williams) were strongly affected. Male sufferers were named Mainy, Marwood and Tyrrell. Harsnett's book, wittily written in a strain of bantering irony and mockery of superstition and deceit, had something of Nashe's boisterous eloquence in its mixture of learned and colloquial language. It would please James I, who liked himself to investigate cases of abnormal behaviour (cf. *Macbeth*, Introduction, p. 466), by its

[1] Samuel Harsnett (1561–1631) had sat on a commission in 1597–8 which condemned a Puritan exorcist. He acted as licenser of books for printing. He became Archdeacon of Essex in 1603 when by order of the Privy Council he published his exposure of Roman Catholic exorcists. Later (1628) he was elected Archbishop of York.

lavish details of symptoms and methods of cure, as well as by its anti-Catholic vehemence.

The full extent of Harsnett's considerable influence on Shakespeare has been shown by Professor K. Muir.[1] I give below [Text XI] the whole of one chapter (10) and some other excerpts of a narrative kind to illustrate its effect in the scenes where Edgar is involved. Harsnett argued that the so-called 'possession' by devils was partly due to weak-mindedness, sickness and delusion, and partly to deceit, when the Jesuits, eager to make converts and to gain power over their patients, encouraged the latter to exaggerate their symptoms and invent fantastic explanations. Edgar is a pretended demoniac and as such his speeches from III.4 to IV.6 are full of material from Harsnett whose derisive account of the multifarious devils named in the case-histories affects his wild rhetoric and grotesque humour. Lear too shows the influence, e.g. at II.4.56–8, which recalls Harsnett's Mainy, who had 'a spice of the *Hysterica passio*, as seems, from his youth, hee himselfe termes it the Moother'. And the word 'meiny' ('Household') is used in the same scene. As 'Poor Tom' Edgar is, he tells Lear (III.4.82) 'a servingman' like some of the 'possessed' witnesses, and in his ravings he declares that he has been occupied by five devils, naming some of those named by Sara Williams. One of them, Flibberdigibbett, he says, 'possesses chambermaids and waiting-women' (IV.1.62–4). From Harsnett come Frateretto, Flibberdigibbett, Hoberdidance, Modo, Mahu, Smulkin and Purr, and some of their activities—though Edgar varies these. He borrows the suggestion that they embody the deadly sins and have animal 'similitudes' (III.4.83–92). When the Fool sees Gloucester as 'a walking fire' (III.4.111) he is probably recalling that some of the demons, when exorcized, went out 'like a flame of fire' (Text XI, p. 420).

Some details not illustrated in my excerpts below may be of interest: the 'pittiful creature' Marwood, like Edgar, lay 'abroade in the fieldes' and 'was scared with lightning and thunder, that happened in the night' (Harsnett, p. 24). This may have encouraged Shakespeare to bring madmen together in a storm. Edgar's speech, III.4.49ff. suggested the spells of

[1] Cf. *RES*, 1951, pp. 11–21; *Shakespeare's Sources I*, 1957, pp. 147–61; *Arden Lear*, 1952, pp. 253–6.

Puck in misleading the lovers, but also the suicidal remark of Mainy, who thought 'a new haulter and two blades of knives' left on the gallery floor were placed there for them to use. Edgar's 'Purr! the cat is grey' (III.6.46) combines the devil Purre and the fact that Sara Williams was much haunted by cats (Harsnett, p. 138). Lastly, the devil described to Gloucester at IV.6.70–3 is based on the folk-devil in Harsnett (p. 134) 'with ougly hornes on his head, fire in his mouth . . . eyes like a bason, fangs like a dogge, clawes like a Beare, skinne like a Neger, and a voyce roaring like a Lyon . . .'

Muir gives many examples of the manner in which Shakespeare picked up words or phrases from Harsnett and used them in a different context. A striking instance occurs in Lear's attack on women: 'But to the girdle do the gods inherit, / Beneath is all the fiend's' (IV.6.127–8). This combines a reference to Edmund Campion's girdle, used as a saintly relic, and to Sara Williams's assertion that 'the Priests did pretend that the devill did rest in the most secret part of my body' (p. 122) and that he passed out that way when driven from her.

The name of Shakespeare's major villain too came from Harsnett, where two important characters were Edmunds and Edmund Campion;[1] but Edgar's brother has no other connection with the tract. Harsnett's tract is a most important source, for it contributed greatly to the play's atmosphere of trickery, deceit, and the sense of a wickedness inexplicable by reason. It helped Shakespeare to introduce a recognition that poverty, misery and sickness of mind and body were widespread in the world. Harsnett's pity for Marwood, Mainy and Sara in their delusions and fantasies was extended by Shakespeare to 'Bedlam beggars' and the homeless in their windswept crannies. The book gave him touches of extravagant comedy and satire; it increased his knowledge of psychological eccentricity, of human nature in distress. Above all, it added a new dimension to the Lear story by making him show the arrogant old king reduced to the lowest level of human existence, mad among madmen, yet recognizing his own lifelong indifference to other people's sufferings ('O! I have ta'en / Too little care of this' (III.4.32))

[1] Campion had been hanged in 1581; William Weston, *alias* Edmunds, after a long imprisonment, was allowed to go into exile in 1603, and in 1605 was made Spiritual Father of the English College at Seville.

and wishing to become 'a poor, bare, forked animal' like the mad beggar. Harsnett's 'possessed' folk were dupes or deceivers. Lear rises through madness to self-knowledge and innocence.

The story of Lear and his daughters was regarded as that of a father who treated his most loving daughter unnaturally by driving her out for a selfish whim, and of her deep love which triumphed when the unnatural behaviour of the other two proved their monstrous ingratitude. So Holinshed's Cordeilla says that she will continually love Lear as 'my naturall father'—putting into the epithet a world of generous meaning which he fails to perceive; and the historian writes of 'the unkindnesse, or (I may saie) the unnaturalnesse which he found in his two daughters'.

In the old play too there is talk about nature. Leir insists (896–905) on the duties owed him by his daughters 'by natures sacred law', and Cordelia asks her husband, 'What can stop the course of natures power?', thus explaining her love for the un-kind father (1264–74). On these and similar references to the natural bond of love and duty between parent and child Shake-speare builds a much more elaborate complex of associations, using the word 'nature' in a variety of senses and contexts in accordance with Elizabethan usage.[1] Nature was the whole universal order created by God, and was seen in external phenomena, in the influence of the stars on physical and mental life, and in the workings of human nature too. But since the Fall had caused a breach which has never been filled, there was a division in nature. Hence human nature might tend upwards towards its Divine origin, or it might obey the pull of Satan downwards to the passions and senses. And in the later Renais-sance the idea of nature not as links in the Great Chain of Being but as a collection of physical phenomena to be applied to utili-tarian purposes without necessarily any recourse to religion began to make headway. The division between the higher and the lower views of nature appears in *King Lear*.

Edmund is all for the 'lower' nature, doubtless, as he says, because he is a 'natural' son, illegitimate:

> Thou Nature art my Goddess, to thy Law
> My services are bound . . . etc. (I.2)

---

[1] Cf. J. F. Danby, *Shakespeare's Doctrine of Nature; A Study of King Lear*, 1949.

He worships Nature as opposed to any divinity above Nature; he regards the 'kindness' (obedience to nature) which others think based on the innate moral feelings of mankind as merely a matter of custom and convenient law. As well as being a Machiavellian and a supreme egoist (like Iago) he is also the seventeenth century 'atheist' delineated later by Samuel Butler.[1]

So whereas Lear calls on Nature only when cursing an unnatural daughter (I.4.275ff.) Edmund vows himself to her and denies that there is any spiritual influence in the universe. When Gloucester regards the alleged treachery of Edgar as foretold by 'these late eclipses in the sun and moon' (I.2.108) Edmund mocks at the idea of blaming the heavens for human frailties. He will not blame the stars because he is 'rough and lecherous', but accepts responsibility for his evil acts and glories in his freedom from moral ties (cf. Richard III's 'I am myself alone'). Bradley calls Edmund 'an adventurer pure and simple'; but he is neither an adventurer only, nor pure and simple! He is a philosophic villain who plans his future ruthlessly because other people exist only to make his way.

The diversity of human nature is a matter of wonder throughout the play, as when Kent wonders how 'one self mate and make could ... beget / Such different issues' as Cordelia and her sisters (IV.3.35–6). Lear wonders at the reasons for Regan's evil conduct: 'Let them anatomize Regan, see what breeds about her heart. Is there any cause in nature that makes these hard hearts?' (III.6.77–9). Goneril is a natural 'disease that's in my flesh' (II.4.222). And the nearness of human life to the animal level, the precariousness of civilization, are enforced by the frequent imagery of beasts and birds of prey.

Another meaning of 'nature', as the minimal life of man unassisted by civilization, appears when Lear expostulates with Regan for suggesting that he needs no retainers. 'O reason not the need', he exclaims, 'Allow not nature more than nature

[1] 'He draws a Map of Nature by his own Fancy, and bounds her how he pleases, without Regard to the Position of the Heavens, by which only her Latitude is to be understood, and without which all his Speculations are vain, idle, and confused ... He commits as great an Error in making Nature (which is nothing but the Order and Method by which all Causes and Effects in the World are governed) to be the first Cause, as if he should suppose the Laws, by which a Prince governs, to be the Prince himself.' *Characters*, ed. A. R. Waller, 1908, pp. 112–13.

needs, / Man's life is cheap as beast's' (II.4.266–8). What make
life bearable are the 'superfluities', and (ironically) so that Lear
may learn the need to distribute wealth generously he has to
descend to the bottom of the social scale, to become almost 'the
thing itself', bare forked unaccommodated man.

Nature is embodied in yet another way in the elemental
storm which increases Lear's sufferings and helps to destroy his
reason. Out of the thunder in *Leir*, the rainstorm in *Arcadia*,
Shakespeare created scenes which raise questions about the
benevolence of the universe, questions left unanswered at the
end of the tragedy.

I have already indicated that the old play contains several
references to the Christian religion, without any suggestion that
Leir lived before the coming of Christ. So Cordella's soliloquy
in Sc. 13 ends with a prayer for forgiveness: 'I will to Church,
and pray unto my Saviour'; and there is an echo of the Litany
when Perillus echoes the Messenger's demand, 'Deliver!' with
'Deliver us, good Lord, from such as he' (1506). Later in that
scene are lines which seem to have influenced Shakespeare
greatly—when Perillus cries,

> Oh just *Jehova*, whose almighty power
> Doth governe all things in this spacious world,
> How canst thou suffer such outragious acts
> To be committed without just revenge? (1649–52);

to which Leir replies:

> Let us submit us to the will of God:
> Things past all sence, let us not seeke to know:
> It is God's will, and therefore must be so.

This piece of dialogue seems to have set Shakespeare thinking
about Providence and Divine justice to such effect that in re-
shaping the old play as a tragedy he included an unusual
number of assertions and questions about the supernatural
order and its presence in the world.

Shakespeare paid more attention to British legends than did
his predecessor.[1] In W. Harrison's account of 'the Ancient
Religion Used in Albion' [Text IV] he would read that the first

---

[1] A trivial instance: Lear's 'Come not between the dragon and his wrath' may
have been suggested by Uther's title, handed on to his descendants, 'Pendragon'.

Druid preached a benevolent theism, 'that God is omnipotent, mercifull as a father in shewing favour unto the godlie, and just as an upright judge in punishing the wicked; that the secrets of mans hart are not unknowne, and onelie knowne to him.' This doctrine was soon contaminated by the idea of reincarnation, and after Albion religion decayed into 'idolatrie, honoring of the starres, and brood of inferiour gods'. After Brut came the worship of the Greek and Roman deities.

Realizing the composite nature of pre-Christian religion in Britain, Shakespeare introduced into *King Lear* many allusions to the stars, the classical gods, and the worship of nature. His decision to make the play a tragedy was connected with a revulsion against the sentimentality and piety of the good characters in *Leir*, and while retaining their Christian feelings he wished also to lend the domestic and national events a cosmic significance, and to project questions about ultimate causes. This decision may have been fostered by the discussions about nature and chance in *Arcadia* [Text X] and by his reading in Florio's Montaigne.

King Lear contains four overlapping but separable levels of religious reference: the Græco-Roman gods; Nature in relation to the Divine; the idea of a moral divinity which should protect the weak and condemn the guilty; Christian ideas. Most frequent are references to the gods. Lear disowns Cordelia 'by the sacred radiance of the sun, / The mysteries of Hecate and the night, / By all the operation of the orbs / From whom we do exist and cease to be' (I.1)—uniting the mythology and astrological beliefs regarded by Harrison as typical of early Britain. He refuses to revoke his banishment of Kent, 'by Jupiter'. Kent commends Cordelia to the gods' 'dear shelter' (183) and France calls on the gods when he joyfully takes Cordelia to be his wife (255).

Many other references to the classical gods are ejaculations or expletives: e.g. 'Now, gods that we adore!' cries Albany, amazed at Lear's cursing Goneril and Regan (I.4.290). Often, however, they are concerned with questions of justice or injustice. Suffering from Goneril's ill-conduct, Lear says that he will not shoot arrows with messages to the heavens (Cf. *TA*, IV.3.49–60), yet appeals to them for the patience he needs, and complains that the gods 'stir these daughters' hearts / Against

L

their father' (II.4.272-8). In the storm it is the gods 'that keep this dreadful pother o'er our heads', and he assumes that these 'dreadful summoners' are coming to judge the wicked (III.2.49-59).

Similarly Gloucester hopes to see 'the winged vengeance' overtake Lear's daughters, and although he calls on the gods in vain a minute or two later when his eye is put out (III.7.65-70), he exclaims, 'Kind gods, forgive me,' when he realizes Edgar's innocence (92). That the gods are more than a rhetorical flourish appears in IV.1 when Gloucester's realization of his own guilt accompanies a revulsion against the higher powers as he says bitterly, 'As flies to wanton boys, are we to the gods; / They kill us for their sport' (IV.1.36-7).

The alternation of attitudes continues when Gloucester pities Edgar and offers him his purse; but seeing that his own misery is a means to make the beggar happier by his charity he hopes that the 'heavens' will treat other 'superfluous and lust-dieted' men as he has been treated. 'So distribution should undo excess / And each man have enough' (IV.1.65-72). The gods therefore are not simply tormentors but humblers of pride, and they sometimes (though not often enough) bring good out of evil. This humble attitude of Gloucester's does not prevent his seeking suicide at Dover, where he calls on the 'mighty gods' to witness that he dies because he can bear his affliction no longer without quarrelling 'with your great opposeless wills' (IV.6.35-41). When he is greeted by Edgar (IV.6.74-8) the latter tells him that he has been saved by 'the dearest gods', and Gloucester resolves to bear his affliction manfully.

This pendulum swing from one to the other view of the divine order appears also when Albany, realizing the unnatural behaviour of Goneril and Regan, cries out—echoing Perillus in *Leir*—

> If that the heavens do not their visible spirits
> Send quickly down to tame these vile offences,
> It will come,
> Humanity must perforce prey on itself,
> Like monsters of the deep (IV.2.46-50)

The last two lines recall Ulysses' vision of disorder in *Troilus and Cressida* after the shaking of degree, by which

> Strength should be lord of imbecility
> And the rude son should strike his father dead

With the loss of a sense of right and wrong would come a descent from Power to Will to Appetite,

> And appetite, a universal wolf
> So doubly seconded with will and power,
> Must make perforce a universal prey,
> And last eat up himself. (I.3.103–24)

This is fully borne out in *King Lear*, which may be considered as a tragedy conceived in accordance with these lines.

But Albany quickly sheds his cosmic fear when, hearing that Cornwall's servant has been slain, he cries out:

> This shows you are above,
> You justicers, that these our nether crimes
> So speedily can venge!

The play seems to work a see-saw of belief and doubt about the participation of the gods in human affairs. When Lear and Cordelia are sent to prison to be murdered, Lear says that they will be happy in prison 'And take upon's the mysteries of things, / As if we were Gods spies' and then 'Upon such sacrifices, my Cordelia / The gods themselves throw incense' (V.3.16–21). This notion of a beneficent providence judging and reproving recurs when Edgar reveals himself to the fallen Edmund and says of Gloucester:

> The gods are just, and of our pleasant vices
> Make instruments to plague us:
> The dark and vicious place where thee he got
> Cost him his eyes. (V.3.171–4)

And Albany speaks of Goneril's death as 'This judgment of the heavens, that makes us tremble' (V.3.231). A moment later, hearing that Edmund has ordered Cordelia's death, he cries 'The gods defend her!' But they do not, nor are they mentioned at the end, for it seems they would be an irrelevance when we are immersed in so much human suffering. In earthly terms Shakespeare follows out the moral logic of the situation to its ultimate conclusion. Evil plays its last card and the 'deathbed repentance' of Edmund comes too late. Cordelia is hanged and her father dies pitifully. As Kent says, 'All's cheerless, dark and deadly' and there is no alleviation save death itself:

> Vex not his ghost. O let him pass! He hates him
> That would upon the rack of this tough world
> Stretch him out longer. (V.3.316)

And Albany reflects that this is an occasion which calls for no conventional condolences:

> The weight of this sad time we must obey;
> Speak what we feel, not what we ought to say.
> (V.3.324–5)

Like the Old Testament prophets Shakespeare has the courage to admit that in this world the results of evil are sometimes uncontrollable. The end of *Lear* does not give Shakespeare's own considered judgement on all human life: but this is one facet of our existence, and a natural corollary to *Troilus*, *Othello* and *Macbeth*.

I. Possible Historical Source

CORDELL ANNESLEY DEFENDS HER FATHER'S SANITY AND PROPERTY
From *Salisbury MSS.*
Historical Manuscripts Commission, Vol. XV, 1930.

A. Sir John Wildegos and others to Lord Cecil (p. 262)

1603, Oct. 18.—According to your letter of the 12th of this present, we repaired unto the house of Bryan Annesley, of Lee, in the county of Kent, and finding him fallen into such imperfection and distemperature of mind and memory, as we thought him thereby become altogether unfit to govern himself or his estate, we endeavoured to take a perfect inventory of such goods and chattels as he possessed in and about his house. But Mrs. Cordall, his daughter, who during the time of all his infirmity hath taken upon her the government of him and his affairs, refuseth to suffer any inventory to be taken, until such time as she hath had conference with her friends, by reason whereof we could proceed no farther in the execution of your letter.— From Lee, 18 Oct, 1603.

Signed: John Wildegos, Tymothe Lawe, Samuel Lennard.

B. Sir Thomas Walsingham and others to the Same (p. 265)

1603, Oct. 23.—According to the authority given us by your letters, we repaired to the house of Mr. Bryan Annesley, and there in the presence of his two daughters, Lady Wildgosse and Mrs. Cordell Annesley, have sealed up all such chests and trunks of evidence, and other things of value, as they showed us to be his. We are informed that he holdeth divers things by lease, which for not payment of the rent might be in danger to be forfeited. We have therefore requested Sir James Croftes, whom your lordship hath associated to us in this business, to take care of the payment of such rents as are reserved upon any lease made to the said Mr. Annesley and also for the receipts of rents due to him. As touching the government of his person and family, though by nature his two daughters may seem fittest to perform this duty, yet respecting the absence of Sir John Wildgosse at this time, and the present emulation between the two gentlewomen we have referred the determination thereof to your lordship.—From Scadbury, 23 Oct., 1603.

Signed: Tho. Walsingham: James Croftes: Samuel Lennard.

C. Cordell Annesley to Lord Cecil[1]

1603, Oct. 23.—I most humbly thank you for the sundry letters that it hath pleased you to direct unto gentlemen of worship in these parts, requesting them to take into their custodies the person and estate of my poor aged and daily dying father: But that course so honorable and good for all parties, intended by your Lo., will by no means satisfy Sr. John Willgosse, nor can any course else, unless he may have him begged for a Lunatic, whose many years service to our late dread Sovereign Mistress and native country deserved a better agnomination, than at his last gasp to be recorded and registered a Lunatic, yet find no means to avoid so great an infamy and endless blemish to and our posterity, unless it shall please your Lo. of your honourable disposition, if he must needs be accompted a Lunatic, to bestow him upon Sir James Croft, who out of the love he bare unto him in his more happier days, and for the good he wisheth unto us his children, is contented upon entreaty to undergo the burden and care of him and his estate, without intendment to make one penny benefit to himself by any goods of his, or ought that may descend to us his children, as also to prevent any record of Lunacy that may be procured hereafter. Lewsham, 23 October, 1603. Cordell Annesley.

D. Epitaph from a slab let in the wall of what was formerly the tower of the church at Lee, Kent[2]

Here lyeth buried the bodyes of Bryan Anslye Esquier, late of Lee in the county of Kent, and Audry his wife, the only daughter of Robert Turell, of Burbrocke in the county of Essex Esquier. He had issue by her one sonne and three daughters, Bryan who died without issue; Grace married to Sr John Wilgoose, Knight; Christian married to the Lord Sands; and Cordell married to Sir William Hervey, Knight.[3] The said Bryan the father died on the Xth of July 1604; he served Queene Elizabeth as one of the band of Gentlemen Penciours to her Matie the space of XXX^tye yeares. The said Awdry died on the XXVth of Novebeber (*sic*) 1591. Cordell, the youngest daughter, at her owne proper cost and chardges, in further testimonie of her

---

[1] From C. C. Stopes, *The Third Earl of Southampton*, Cambridge, 1922, p. 274. The version in *Salisbury MSS.*, XV, p. 266, is abridged.

[2] In J. W. Hales, *Notes and Essays on Shakespeare*, 1884, pp. 271–2.

[3] In 1628 he became Baron Harvey of Kidbroke, Kent, taking his title from one of the manors inherited by Cordell.

dutifull love unto her father and mother, caused this monument to be erected for the p'petuall memorie of their names against the ingratefull nature of oblivious time.

> 'Nec primus, nec ultimus; multi ante,
> Cesserunt, et omnes sequetitur' (*sic*).

II. Probable Source

From HISTORIA ANGLICANA
by Geoffrey of Monmouth,
translated by Aaron Thompson (1718)[1]

Book IV. Chap. XI

Leir, the Son of Bladud, having no Son, divides his Kingdom among his Daughters.

After this unhappy Fate of *Bladud*, *Leir* his Son was advanced to the Throne, and nobly governed his Country sixty Years. He built upon the River *Sore* a City called in the *British* Tongue *Kaerleir*, in the *Saxon Leircestre*. He was without Male Issue, but had three Daughters whose Names were *Gonorilla*, *Regan*, and *Cordeilla*, of whom he was doatingly fond, but especially of his youngest *Cordeilla*. When he began to grow old, he had Thoughts of dividing his Kingdom among them, and of bestowing them on such Husbands, as were fit to be advanced to the Government with them. But to make Tryal who was the worthiest of the best Part of his Kingdom, he went to each of them to ask, which of them loved him most. The Question being proposed, *Gonorilla* the Eldest made Answer, 'That she called Heaven to Witness, she loved him more than her own Soul.' The Father reply'd, 'Since you have preferred my declining Age before your own Life, I will marry you, my dearest Daughter, to whomsoever you shall make Choice of, and give with you the third Part of my Kingdom.' Then *Regan*, the second Daughter, willing after the Example of her Sister, to prevail upon her Fathers good Nature, answered with an Oath, 'That she could not otherwise express her

[1] Title page: 'The British History, Translated into English From the Latin of *Jeffrey* of *Monmouth*. With a large Preface concerning the Authority of the History. By Aaron Thompson, late of Queen's College, Oxon. ... London: Printed for *J. Bowyer* at the *Rose* in *Ludgate-Street*, *H. Clements* at the *Half-Moon*, and *W.* and *J. Innys* at the *Princes-Arms* in *St. Paul's Church-Yard*. MDCCXVIII.'

Thoughts, but that she loved him above all Creatures.' The credulous Father upon this made her the same Promise that he did to her elder Sister, that is, the Choice of a Husband, with the third Part of his Kingdom. But *Cordeilla* the youngest, understanding how easily he was satisfied with the flattering Expressions of her Sisters, was desirous to make Tryal of his Affection after a different Manner. 'My Father,' said she, 'Is there any Daughter that can love her Father more than Duty requires? In my Opinion, whoever pretends to it, must disguise her real Sentiments under the Veil of Flattery. I have always loved you as a Father, nor do I yet depart from my purposed Duty; and if you insist to have something more extorted from me, hear now the Greatness of my Affection, which I always bear you, and take this for a short Answer to all your Questions; Look how much you have, so much is your Value, and so much I love you.' The Father supposing that she spoke this out of the Abundance of her Heart, was highly provoked, and immediately reply'd; 'Since you have so far despised my Old-age, as not to think me worthy the Love that your Sisters express for me, you shall have from me the like Regard, and shall be excluded from any Share with your Sisters in my Kingdom. Notwithstanding I do not say but that since you are my Daughter, I will marry you to some Foreigner, if Fortune offers you any such Husband; but will never, I do assure you, make it my Business to procure so honourable a Match for you as for your Sisters; because though I have hitherto loved you more than them, you have in Requital thought me less worthy your Affection than they.' And without farther Delay, after Consultation with his Nobility, he bestowed his two other Daughters upon the Dukes of *Cornwal* and *Albania*,[1] with half the Island at present, but after his Death, the Inheritance of the whole Monarchy of *Britain*.

It happened after this, that *Aganippus* King of the *Franks*, having heard of the Fame of *Cordeilla*'s Beauty, forthwith sent his Ambassadors to the King to desire *Cordeilla* in Marriage. The Father retaining yet his Anger to her, made Answer; 'That he was very willing to bestow his Daughter, but without either Money or Territories; because he had already given away his Kingdom with all his Treasure, to his elder Daughters, *Gonorilla* and *Regan*.' When this was told *Aganippus*, he being very much in Love with the Lady, sent again to King *Leir*, to tell him, 'That he had Money and Territories enough, as he possessed the third Part of *Gaul*, and desired no more than his Daughter only, that he might have Heirs by her.' At last the Match was concluded, and *Cordeilla* was sent to *Gaul*, and married to *Aganippus*.

[1] Albany, Scotland, roughly east of Strathspey and north of a line between Edinburgh and Fort William.

CHAP. XII

Leir finding the Ingratitude of his two eldest Daughters, betakes himself to his youngest Cordeilla in Gaul.

A long time after this, when *Leir* came to be infirm through Old-age, the two Dukes, upon whom he had bestowed *Britain* with his two Daughters, made an Insurrection against him, and deprived him of his Kingdom, and of all Regal Authority which he had hitherto exercised with great Power and Glory. But at last they came to an Agreement, and *Maglaunus* Duke of *Albania*, one of his Sons-in-law, was to allow him and sixty Soldiers, who were to be kept for State, a Subsistence at his own House. After two Years Stay with his Son-in-Law, his Daughter *Gonorilla* grudged at the Number of his Men, who began to upbraid the Ministers of the Court with their scanty Allowance; and having spoke to her Husband about it, gave Orders that the Number of her Fathers Attendants be reduced to thirty, and the rest discharged. The Father resenting this Treatment, left *Maglaunus*, and went to *Henuinus*, Duke of *Cornwal*, to whom he had married his Daughter *Regan*. Here he met with an honourable Reception, but before the Year was at an End, a Quarrel happened between the two Families, which raised *Regan*'s Indignation; so that she commanded her Father to discharge all his Attendants but five, and to be contented with their Service. This second Affliction was unsupportable to him, and made him return again to his former Daughter, with Hopes that the Misery of his Condition might move in her some Sentiments of Filial Piety, and that he with his Family might find a Subsistence from her. But she not forgetting her Resentments, swore by the Gods, He should not stay with her, unless he would dismiss his Retinue, and be contented with the Attendance of one Man; and with bitter Reproaches, told him how ill his Desire of vain-glorious Pomp suited with his Old-age and Poverty. When he found that she was by no Means to be prevailed upon, he was at last forced to comply, and dismissing the Rest, to take up with one Man. But by this Time he began to reflect more sensibly with himself upon the Grandeur from which he had fallen, and the miserable State he was now reduced to, and to enter upon Thoughts of going beyond Sea to his youngest Daughter. Yet he doubted whether he should be able to move her Commiseration, whom (as was related above) he had treated so unworthily. However disdaining to bear any longer such base Usage, he took Shipping to *Gaul*. In his Passage, he observed he had only the third Place given him among the Princes that were with him in the Ship, at which with deep Sighs and Tears, he burst forth into the following Complaint.

'O irreversible Decrees of the Fates, that never swerve from your stated Course! Why did you ever advance me to an unstable Felicity, since the Punishment of lost Happiness is greater than the Sense of present Misery? The Remembrance of the Time when vast Numbers of Men obsequiously attended me at the taking of Cities and wasting the Enemies Countries, more deeply pierces my Heart, than the View of my present Calamity, which has exposed me to the Derision of those who formerly laid at my Feet. O Rage of Fortune! Shall I ever again see the Day, when I may be able to reward those according to their Deserts who have forsaken me in my Distress? How true was thy Answer, *Cordeilla*, when I asked thee concerning thy Love to me, *As much as you have, so much is your Value, and so much I love you?* While I had any Thing to give they valued me, being Friends not to me, but to my Gifts: They loved me then indeed, but my Gifts much more: When my Gifts ceased, my Friends vanished. But with what Face shall I presume to see you my dearest Daughter, since in my Anger I married you upon worse Terms than your Sisters, who, after all the mighty Favours they have received from me, suffer me to be in Banishment and Poverty?'

As he was lamenting his Condition in these and the like Expressions, he arrived at *Karitia*, where his Daughter was, and waited before the City while he sent a Messenger to inform her of the Misery he was fallen into, and to desire her Relief to a Father that suffered both Hunger and Nakedness. *Cordeilla* was startled at the News, and wept bitterly, and with Tears asked him how many Men her Father had with him. The Messenger answered, he had none but one Man, who had been his Armour-bearer, and was staying with him without the Town. Then she took what Money she thought might be sufficient, and gave it the Messenger, with Orders to him to carry her Father to another City, and there give out that he was Sick, and to provide for him Bathing, Clothes, and all other Nourishment. She likewise gave Orders that he should take into his Service forty Men well cloathed and accoutred, and when all Things were thus prepared that he should then notify his Arrival to King *Aganippus* and his Daughter. The Messenger quickly returning carried *Leir* to another City, and there kept him concealed, till he had performed every Thing that *Cordeilla* had commanded.

CHAP. XIII

He is very honourably received by Cordeilla, and the King of Gaul.

As soon as he was provided with his Royal Apparel, Ornaments and Retinue, he sent Word to *Aganippus* and his Daughter, that he was driven out of his Kingdom of *Britain* by his Sons-in-Law, and was come to them to procure their Assistance for the Recovering of his Dominions. Upon which they being attended with their chief Ministers of State and the Nobility of the Kingdom, went out to meet him, and received him honourably, and submitted to his Management the whole Power of *Gaul*, till such Time as he should be restored to his former Dignity.

CHAP. XIV

Leir by the Help of his Son-in-law and Cordeilla, being restored to the Kingdom dies.

In the mean Time *Aganippus* sent Officers over all *Gaul* to raise an Army, in Order to restore his Father-in-Law to his Kingdom of *Britain*. Which done, *Leir* returned to *Britain* with his Son and Daughter and their Forces they had raised, where he fought with his Sons-in-Law, and routed them. Thus having reduced the whole Kingdom under his Power, he died in the third Year after. *Aganippus* also died; so that *Cordeilla* now obtaining the Government of the Kingdom, buried her Father in a certain Vault, which she ordered to be made for him under the River *Sore* in *Leicester*. The Subterraneous Place where he was buried, had been built to the Honour of the God *Janus*. And here all the Workmen of the City, upon the anniversary Solemnity of that Festival, used to begin their yearly Labours.

CHAP. XV

Cordeilla being imprisoned kills herself. Margan aspiring to the whole Kingdom is killed by Cunedagius.

After a peaceable Possession of the Government for five Years, *Cordeilla* began to meet with Disturbances from the two Sons of her Sisters, being both young Men of great Spirit, whereof one, named

Margan, was born to *Maglaunus,* and the other, named *Cunedagius,* to *Henuinus.* These after the Death of their Fathers succeeding them in their Dukedoms, were incensed to see *Britain* subject to the Power of a Woman, and raised Forces in Order to make an Insurrection against the Queen; nor desisted from their Hostilities, till after a general Waste of her Countries, and several Battles fought, they at last took her and put her in Prison; where for Grief at the Loss of her Kingdom she killed herself. After this they divided the Island between them, of which the Part that reaches from the North Side of *Humber* to *Cathness,* fell to *Margan*; the other Part from the same River Westward was *Cunedagius*'s Share. At the End of two Years, some restless Spirits that took Pleasure in the Troubles of the Nation had Access to *Margan,* and inspired him with vain Conceits by representing to him, how mean and disgraceful it was for him not to govern the whole Island, which was his due by Right of Birth. Stirred up with these and the like Suggestions, he marched with an Army through *Cunedagius*'s Country, and began to burn all before him. A War thus breaking out, he was met by *Cunedagius* and all his Forces, and upon an Attack made he killed no small Number of his Men, put *Margan* to Flight, and pursued him from one Province to another, till at last he killed him in a Town of *Kambria,* which since his Death has been by the Country People called *Margan* to this Day. After the Victory, *Cunedagius* gained the Monarchy of the whole Island, which he governed gloriously for three and thirty Years. At this Time flourished the Prophets *Isaiah* and *Hoshea,* and *Rome* was built upon the eleventh of the Calends of *May* by the two Brothers, *Romulus* and *Remus.*

III. Source

From THE SECOND BOOKE OF THE HISTORIE OF ENGLAND, by R. Holinshed (1587 edn.)

[XII.2.59] LEIR the sonne of Baldud was admitted ruler over the Britaines,[1] in the yeare of the world 3105, at what time Joas reigned in Juda. This Leir was a prince of right noble demeanor, governing his land and subjects in great wealth. He made the towne of Caerleir now called Leicester, which standeth upon the river of Sore.[2] It is

[1] *In margin:* 'Leir *The* 10. *Ruler.*' Baldud, usually called Bladud.
[2] *In margin:* 'Leicester is builded (Mat. West.)'

written that he had by his wife three daughters without other issue, whose names were Gonorilla, Regan, and Cordeilla, which daughters he greatly loved, but specially Cordeilla the yoongest farre above the two elder. When this Leir therefore was come to great yeres, & began to waxe unweldie through age, he thought to understand the affections of his daughters towards him, and preferre hir whome he best loved, to the succession over the kingdome.[1] Wherupon he first asked Gonorilla the eldest, how well she loved him: who calling hir gods to record, protested that she 'loved him more than hir owne life, which by right and reason should be most deere unto hir'. With which answer the father being well pleased, turned to the second, and demanded of hir how well she loved him: who answered (confirming hir saiengs with great othes) that she loved him 'more than toong could expresse, and farre above all other creatures of the world.'

Then called he his yoongest daughter Cordeilla before him, and asked of hir what account she made of him, unto whome she made this answer as followeth:[2] 'Knowing the great love and fatherlie zeale that you have alwaies borne towards me (for the which I maie not answere you otherwise than I thinke and as my conscience leadeth me) I protest unto you, that I have loved you ever, and will continuallie (while I live) love you as my naturall father. And if you would more understand of the love that I beare you, assertaine your selfe, that so much as you have, so much you are woorth, and so much I love you, and no more'. The father being nothing content with this answer, married his two eldest daughters,[3] the one unto Henninus the duke of Cornewall, and the other unto Maglanus the duke of Albania, betwixt whome he willed and ordeined that his land should be divided after his death,[4] and the one halfe thereof immediatlie should be assigned to them in hand: but for the third daughter Cordeilla he reserved nothing.'

Nevertheles it fortuned that one of the princes of Gallia (which now is called France) whose name was Aganippus, hearing of the beautie, womanhood, and good conditions of the said Cordeilla, desired to have hir in mariage, and sent over to hir father, requiring that he might have hir to wife: to whome answer was made, that he might have his daughter, but as for anie dower he could have none, for all was promised and assured to hir other sisters alreadie. Aganippus notwithstanding this answer of deniall to receive anie thing by

---

[1] *In margin:* 'A triall of love.'

[2] *In margin:* 'The answer of the yoongest daughter.'

[3] *In margin:* 'The two eldest daughters are maried.'

[4] *In margin:* 'The realme is promised to his two daughters.' No immediate abdication.

way of dower with Cordeilla, tooke hir to wife, onlie moved thereto (I saie) for respect of hir person and amiable vertues. This Aganippus was one of the twelve kings that ruled Gallia in those daies, as in the British historie it is recorded.[1] But to proceed.

After that Leir was fallen into age, the two dukes that had married his two eldest daughters, thinking it long yer the government of the land did come to their hands, arose against him in armour, and reft from him the governance of the land, upon conditions to be continued for terme of life:[2] by the which he was put to his portion, that is, to live after a rate assigned to him for the maintenance of his estate, which in processe of time was diminished as well by Maglanus as by Henninus. But the greatest griefe that Leir tooke, was to see the unkindnesse of his daughters, which seemed to thinke that all was too much which their father had, the same being never so little: in so much that going from the one to the other, he was brought to that miserie, that scarslie they would allow him one servant[3] to wait upon him.

In the end, such was the unkindnesse, or (as I maie saie) the unnaturalnesse which he found in his two daughters, notwithstanding their faire and pleasant words uttered in time past, that being constreined of necessitie, he fled the land, & sailed into Gallia, there to seeke some comfort of his yongest daughter Cordeilla, whom before time he hated. The ladie Cordeilla hearing that he was arrived in poore estate, she first sent to him privilie a certeine summe of monie to apparell himselfe withall,[4] and to reteine a certeine number of servants that might attend upon him in honorable wise, as apperteined to the estate which he had borne: and then so accompanied, she appointed him to come to the court, which he did, and was so joifullie, honorablie, and lovinglie received, both by his sonne in law Aganippus, and also by his daughter Cordeilla, that his hart was greatlie comforted: for he was no lesse honored, than if he had beene king of the whole countrie himselfe.

Now when he had informed his sonne in law and his daughter in what sort he had been used by his other daughters, Aganippus caused a mightie armie to be put in a readinesse, and likewise a great navie of ships to be rigged, to passe over into Britaine with Leir his father in law, to see him againe restored to his kingdome. It was accorded, that Cordeilla should also go with him to take possession

---

[1] *In margin:* 'He governed the third part of Gallia as *Gal. Mon.* saith.'

[2] Cf. I.1.130-8. Lear makes his own conditions.

[3] Cf. Regan at II.4.263. In *Leir* he has Perillus, in *King Lear* the Fool, but also numerous knights. (III.7.16-20.)

[4] In *Leir*, 216-80, she gives him food; Cf. IV.7.21-2, where he is clothed while asleep.

of the land, the which he promised to leave unto hir, as the rightfull inheritour after his decesse, notwithstanding any former grant made to hir sisters or to their husbands in anie maner of wise.

Hereupon, when this armie and navie of ships were readie, Leir and his daughter Cordeilla with hir husband[1] tooke the sea, and arriving in Britaine, fought with their enimies, and discomfited them in battell, in the which Maglanus and Henninus were slaine: and then was Leir restored to his kingdome, which he ruled after this by the space of two yeeres, and then died, fortie yeeres after he first began to reigne. His bodie was buried at Leicester in a vaut under the chanell of the river of Sore beneath the towne.

The Sixt Chapter.

The gunarchie[2] of queene Cordeilla, how she was vanquished, of hir imprisonment and selfe-murther: the contention betweene Cunedag and Margan nephewes for governement, and the evill end thereof.

CORDEILLA the yoongest daughter of Leir was admitted Q. and supreme governesse of Britaine, in the yeere of the world 3155, before the bylding of Rome 54, Uzia then reigning in Juda, and Jeroboam over Israell. This Cordeilla after hir fathers decease ruled the land of Britaine right worthilie during the space of five yeeres, in which meane time hir husband died, and then about the end of those five yeeres, hir two nephewes Margan and Cunedag, sonnes to hir aforesaid sisters, disdaining to be under the government of a woman, levied warre against hir, and destroied a great part of the land, and finallie tooke hir prisoner, and laid hir fast in ward, wherewith she tooke such griefe, being a woman of a manlie courage, and despairing to recover libertie, there she slue hirselfe, when she had reigned (as before is mentioned) the tearme of five yeeres.

[The two cousins divided the land between them but soon quarrelled. Margan was slain in battle in Wales (hence the place-name 'Glamorgan'), and Cunedag ruled over all Britain.]

Moreover our writers doo report, that he builded three temples, one to Mars at Perth in Scotland, another to Mercurie at Bangor, and the third to Apollo in Cornewall.

---

[1] In *Leir* he defeats the enemy. Cf. IV.2.1–2, where after landing he has returned to France on urgent business.

[2] gynarchy, government by a woman.

IV. Possible Source

From AN HISTORICAL DESCRIPTION OF THE ILAND OF BRITAINE
by William Harrison[1]

CHAP. IX
Of the Ancient Religion Used in Albion

... In the beginning this Druiyus did preach unto his hearers, that the soule of man is immortall, that God is omnipotent, mercifull as a father in shewing favor unto the godlie, and just as an upright judge in punishing the wicked; that the secrets of mans hart are not un-knowne, and onelie knowne to him; and that as the world and all that is therein had their beginning by him, at his owne will, so shall all things likewise have an end, when he shall see his time. He taught them also with more facilitie, how to observe the courses of the heavens and motions of the planets by arithmeticall industrie, to find out the true quantities of the celestiall bodies by geometricall demonstration, and thereto the compasse of the earth, and hidden natures of things contained in the same by philosophicall contempla-tion. But alas, this integritie continued not long among his successors, for unto the immortalitie of the soule, they added, that after death it went into another bodie ... The second or succedent, being alwaies either more noble, or more vile than the former, as the partie deserved by his merits, whilest he lived here upon earth ... For said they (of whom Pythagoras also had, and taught this errour) if the soule apperteined at the first to a king, and he in this estate did not leade his life worthie this calling, it should after his decease be shut up in the bodie of a slave, begger, cocke, owle, dog, ape, horsse, asse, worme, or monster, there to remaine as in a place of purgation and punishment for a certeine period of time. ....

After the death of Druiyus, Bardus his sonne, and fift king of the Celts, succeeded not onelie over the said kingdome, but also in his fathers vertues, whereby it is verie likelie, that the winding and wrapping up of the said religion, after the afore remembred sort into verse, was first devised by him, for he was an excellent poet, and no lesse indued with a singular skill in the practise and speculation of musicke. ....

[1] Printed in R. Holinshed, *Chronicles*, Vol. I.

Thus we see as in a glasse the state of religion, for a time, after the first inhabitation of this Iland: but how long it continued in such soundnesse, as the originall authors left it, in good sooth I cannot say, yet this is most certeine, that after a time, when Albion arrived here, the religion earst imbraced fell into great decaie. For whereas Japhet & Samothes with their children taught nothing else than such doctrine as they had learned of Noah: Cham the great grandfather of this our Albion, and his disciples utterlie renouncing to follow their steps, gave their minds wholie to seduce and lead their hearers headlong unto all error. Whereby his posteritie not onelie corrupted this our Iland, with most filthie trades and practises; but also all mankind, generallie where they became, with vicious life, and most ungodlie conversation . . .

Thus we see in generall maner, how idolatrie, honoring of the starres, and brood of inferiour gods were hatched at the first, which follies in processe of time came also into Britaine, as did the names of Saturne & Jupiter, etc: as shall appeare hereafter. . . .

After Brute, idolatrie and superstition still increased more and more among us, insomuch that beside the Druiysh and Bardike ceremonies, and those also that came in with Albion and Brute him-selfe: our countriemen either brought hither from abroad, or dailie invented at home new religion and rites, whereby it came to passe that in the stead of the onelie and immortall God (of whom Samothes and his posteritie did preach in times past) now they honored the said Samothes himselfe under the name of Dis and Saturne: also Jupiter, Mars, Minerva, Mercurie, Apollo, Diana; and finallie Hercules, unto whome they dedicated the gates and porches of their temples, entrances into their regions, cities, townes and houses, with their limits and bounds (as the papists did the gates of their cities and ports unto Botulph & Giles) bicause fortitude and wisedome are the cheefe upholders and bearers up of common-wealths and kingdoms, both which they ascribed to Hercules (forgetting God) and divers other idols whose names I now remember not. In lieu moreover of sheepe and oxen, they offred mankind also unto some of them, killing their offendors, prisoners, and oft such strangers as came from farre unto them, by shutting up great numbers of them togither in huge images made of wicker, reed, haie, or other light matter: and then setting all on fire togither, they not onelie consumed the miserable creatures to ashes (sometimes adding other beasts unto them) but also reputed it to be the most acceptable sacrifice that could be made unto their idols . . . But to proceed with our owne gods and idols, more pertinent to my purpose than the rehersall of forreine de-meanours: I find that huge temples in like sort were builded unto them, so that in the time of Lucius, when the light of salvation began stronglie to shine in Britaine,[1] thorough the preaching of the gospell, the Christians discovered 25 Flamines or idol-churches, beside three Archflamines, whose preests were then as our Archbishops are now, in that they had superior charge of all the rest, the other being reputed as inferiours, and subject to their jurisdiction in cases of religion, and superstitious ceremonies.

V. Possible Source

From
REMAINES CONCERNING BRITAINE
by William Camden (1606)[2]

From *Grave Speeches and wittie Apothegmes of worthy Personages of this Realme in former times*

Ina King of West-Saxons, had three daughters, of whom upon a time he demanded whether they did love him, and so would do during their lives, above all others; the two elder sware deeply they would; the yongest, but the wisest, told her father without flattery: That albeit she did love, honour, and reverence him, and so would whilst shee lived, as much as nature and daughterly duty at the uttermost could expect: Yet she did thinke that one day it would come to passe, that she should affect another more fervently, meaning her husband, when she were married:[3] Who being made one flesh with her, as God by commandement had told, and nature had taught her, she was to cleave fast to, forsaking father and mother, kiffe and kinne. (Anonymous.[4]) One referreth this to the daughters of King *Leir*.

---

[1] Lucius, a descendant of Cymbeline, was said to have organized Christianity in Britain, and to have died in A.D. 156.

[2] Text from 1636 edition.

[3] Cordelia (I.1.95–102) will keep half her love for Lear.

[4] Camden apparently had no chronicle source for this anecdote.

VI. Source

From
THE MIRROR FOR MAGISTRATES
by John Higgins (1574)

The First parte of the Mirour for Magistrates, containing
the falles of the first infortunate Princes of this lande:
From the comming of Brute to the incarnation of our
saviour and redemer Jesu Christe. Ad. Romanos. 13.2.
Quisquis se opponit potestati, Dei ordina resistit.
Imprinted at London by Thomas Marshe. Anno. 1574.
Cum Privilegio.

Cordila shewes how by despaire when she was in prison she slue herselfe. the
yeare before Christe. 800.

> Yf any wofull wight have cause, to waile her woe:
> Or griefes are past do pricke us Princes tel our fal:
> My selfe likewise must needes constrained eke do so,
> And shew my like misfortunes and mishaps withal.
> Should I keepe close my heavy haps and thral?
> Then did I wronge: I wrongde my selfe and thee,
> Which of my facts, a witnes true maist bee.

>   A woman yet must blushe when bashfull is the case,
> Though truth bid tell the tale and story as it fell:
> But sith that I mislike not audience time nor place   10
> Therefore, I cannot still keep in my counsaile well:
> No greater ease of hart then griefes to tell,
> It daunteth all the dolours of our minde,
> Our carefull harts thereby great comfort finde.

       . . . . . .

>   Therefore if I more willing be to tell my fall,   22
> And shew mishaps to ease my burdened brest and minde:
> That others haply may avoide and shunne like thrall,
> And thereby in distresse more ayde and comfort finde.
> They maye keepe measure where as I declinde,
> And willing be to flye like bruite and blame:
> As I to tell, or thou to write the same.

For sith I see the[e] prest to heare that wilt recorde,
What I *Cordilla* tell to ease my inward smart: 30
I will resite my storye tragicall ech worde,
To the that givst an eare to heare and ready art,
And lest I set the horse behinde the cart,
I minde to tell ech thinge in order so,
As thou maiste see and shewe whence sprang my wo.

My grandsyre *Bladud* hight that found the Bathes by skill,
A fethered king that practisde for to flye and soare:
Whereby he felt the fall God wot against his will,
And never went, roode, raignde nor spake, nor flew no more.
Who dead his sonne my father *Leire* therefore, 40
Was chosen kinge, by right apparent heyre,
Which after built the towne of *Leircestere*.

He had three daughters, first and eldest hight *Gonerell*:
Next after hir, my sister *Ragan* was begote:
The thirde and last was, I the yongest namde *Cordell*,
And of us all, our father *Leire* in age did dote.
So minding hir that lovde him best to note,
Because he had no sonne t'enjoye his lande:
He thought to give, where favoure most he fande.[1]

What though I yongest were, yet men me judgde more wise 50
Then either *Gonorell*, or *Ragan* had more age,
And fayrer farre: wherefore my sisters did despise
My grace, and giftes, and sought my praise t'swage:[2]
But yet though vice gainst vertue die with rage,
It cannot keepe her underneth to drowne,[3]
But still she flittes above, and reapes renowne.

Yet nathelesse, my father did me not mislike:
But age so simple is, and easye to subdue:
As childhode weake, thats voide of wit and reason quite:
They thincke thers nought you flater fainde, but all is true: 60
Once olde and twice a childe, tis said with you,
Which I affirme by proofe, that was definde:
In age my father had a childishe minde.[4]

---

[1] Skalliger in *Leir* (37–8) suggests an unequal division; *Lear* is ambiguous at
I.1.52–3.
[2] 'and sought my wrecke to wage', *1587;* hence their plot in *Leir*, Sc. 2.
[3] Shakespeare goes into this more deeply in his tragedy.
[4] Ll.57–63 omitted from *1587*. He is nearer dotage in *Leir* than in Shakespeare's
play.

He thought to wed us unto nobles three, or Peres:
And unto them and theirs, devide and part the lande:
For both my sisters first he sent as first their yeares
Requirde their mindes, and love, and favour t'understand.
(Quod he) all doubtes of duty to abande,
I must assaye and eke your frendships prove:
Now tell me eche how much you do me love.   70

Which when they aunswered, they lovde him wel and more
Then they themselves did love, or any worldly wight:
He praised them and said he would againe therefore,
The loving kindnes they deservde in fine requite:
So found my sisters favour in his sight,
By flatery fayre they won their fathers hart:
Which after turned him and mee to smart.

But not content with this he minded me to prove,
For why he wonted was to love me wonders[1] well:
How much dost thou (quoth he) *Cordile* thy father love?   80
I will (said I) at once my love declare and tell:
I lovde you ever as my father well,
No otherwise, if more to know you crave:
We love you chiefly for the goodes[2] you have.

Thus much I said, the more their flattery to detect,
But he me answered therunto again with Ire,
Because thou dost thy fathers aged yeares neglect,
That lovde the more of late then thy desertes require,
Thou never shalt, to any part aspire
Of this my realme, among thy sisters twayne,   90
But ever shalt undoted ay remayne.

Then to the king of *Albany* for wife he gave
My sister *Gonerell*, the eldest of us all:

---

[1] wondrous.

[2] Word-play. He is all goodness to them so they should love him accordingly;
but the sisters may love him for his wealth. Ll.79–84, *1587* substitutes:

> If I did not him love and honour well.
> No cause (quod I) there is I should your grace despise:
> For nature so doth binde and duty mee compell,
> To love you, as I ought my father, well.
> Yet shortely I may chaunce, if Fortune will,
> To finde in heart to beare another more good will.

Lear, (I.1.95–104) uses this allusion to a husband.

And eke my sister *Ragan* for *Hinnine* to have,
Which then was Prince of *Camber* and *Cornwall*:
These after him should have his kingdome all
Betwene them both, he gave it franke and free:
But nought at all, he gave of dowry mee.

At last it chaunst the king of *Fraunce* to here my fame,
My beutie brave, was blazed all abrode eche where: 100
And eke my vertues praisde me to my fathers blame
Did for my sisters flattery me lesse favoure beare.
Which when this worthy king my wrongs did heare,
He sent ambassage likte me more then life,
T'intreate he might me have to be his wife.[1]

My father was content with all his harte, and sayde,
He gladly should obtaine his whole request at will
Concerning me, if nothing I herin denayde:
But yet he kept by their intisment hatred still
(quoth he) your prince his pleasure to fulfill,   110
I graunt and give my daughter as you crave:
But nought of me for dowry can she have.[2]

King *Aganippus* well agreed to take me so,
He deemde that vertue was of dowries all the best:
And I contentid was to *Fraunce* my father fro
For to depart, & hoapte t'enjoye some greater rest.
I maried was, and then my joyes encreaste,
I gate more favoure in this prince his sight,
Then ever princesse of a princely wight.

But while that I these joyes enjoyd, at home in *Fraunce*   120
My father *Leire* in *Britayne* waxed aged olde,
My sisters yet them selves the more aloft t'advaunce,
Thought well they might, be by his leave, or sans so bolde,
To take the realme & rule it as they wold.
They rose as rebels voyde of reason quite,
And they deprivde him of his crowne and right.[3]

Then they agreed, it should be into partes equall
Devided: and my father threscore knightes & squires[4]
Should always have, attending on him still at cal.

---

[1] In both plays he comes himself.   [2] I.1.203–6, 251–62.
[3] In both plays Lear has abdicated, on his own conditions.
[4] *1587* has 'sixtie Knights', no squires. *Leir* has neither; Cf. I.4.240.

But in six monthes so much encreasid hateful Ires, 130
That *Gonerell* denyde all his desires,
So halfe his garde she and her husband refte:[1]
And scarce alowde the other halfe they lefte.

Eke as in *Scotlande*[2] thus he lay lamenting fates,
When as his daughter so, sought all his utter spoyle:
The meaner upstarte gentiles, thought themselves his mates
And better eke, see here an aged prince his foyle.
Then was he faine for succoure his, to toyle,
With all his knightes, to *Cornewall* there to lye:
In greatest nede, his *Raganes* love to trye. 140

And when he came to *Cornwall*, *Ragan* then with joye,
Received him and eke hir husbande did the lyke:[3]
There he abode a yeare and livde without a noy,
But then they tooke, all his retinue from him quite
Save only ten, and shewde him dayly spite,
Which he bewailde complayning durst not strive,
Though in disdayne they laste alowde but five.

On this he deemde him selfe was far that tyme unwyse,
When from his doughter *Gonerell* to *Ragan* hee
Departed erste yet eache did him poore king despise, 150
Wherfore to *Scotlande* once againe with hir to bee
And bide he went:[4] but beastly cruell shee,
Bereavde him of his servauntes all save one,[5]
Bad him content him self with that or none.

Eke at what time he askte of eache to have his garde,
To garde his grace where so he walkte or wente:
They calde him doting foole and all his hestes debarde,
Demaunded if with life he could not be contente.

---

[1] 'What, fifty of my followers at a clap?' (I.4.294–5.)
[2] *Albany*, *1587*.
[3] So Ragan, dissembling, in *Leir*, 1226–40. Regan leaves home to avoid him, (II.1.104–5).
[4] He offers to go back with Goneril at II.4.258 but she does not want his followers.
[5] Cf. Regan, II.4.263: 'What need one?' Ll. 148–52, *1587* substitutes:
> What more despite could develish beasts devise,
> Then joy their fathers woefull dayes to see?
> What vipers vile could so their King despise,
> Or so unkinde, so curst, so cruell bee?
> Fro thence agayn hee went to *Albany*.

Lear has serpent imagery at I.4.288 and V.3.85.

Then he to late his rigour did repente,
Gainst me and sayde, *Cordila* now adieu: 160
I finde the wordes thou toldste me to to true.

And to be short, to *Fraunce* he came alone[1] to mee,
And tolde me how my sisters him our father usde:
Then I besought my king with teares upon my knee,
That he would aide my father thus by them misusde
Who nought at all my humble heste refusde:
But sent to every coste of *Fraunce* for ayde,
Wherwith my father home might be conveide.

The soldiers gathered from eche quarter of the land,
Came at the length to know the king his mind & will   170
Who did commit them to my fathers aged hand,
And I likewise of love and reverent mere goodwill
Desirde my king, he would not take it ill,
If I departed for a space withall:
To take a parte, or ease my fathers thrall.

This had: I partid with my father from my fere,[2]
We came to *Britayne* with our royall campe to fight:
And manly fought so long our enemies vanquisht were
By martiall feates, and force by subjectes sword and might.[3]
The Britishe kinges were fayne to yelde our right,   180
And so my father well this realme did guide,[4]
Three yeares in peace and after that he dide.

Then I at *Leircester* in *Janus* temple made,
His tombe and buried there his kingly regall corse,
As sondry tymes in life before he often bade:
For of our fathers will we then did greatly force,
We had of conscience eke so much remorce,
That we supposde those childrens lives to ill,
Which brake their fathers testament, and will.[5]

And I was queene the kingdome after still to holde,   190
Till five yeares paste I did this Iland guyde:

[1] With Perillus in *Leir*.
[2] In both plays her husband comes to Britain, but in *Lear* he returns home and takes no part in the battle.
[3] Ll. 177–8, *1587* has: 'And of our *Britaynes* came to aide likewise his right / Full many subjects, good and stout that were.'
[4] *1587*: 'Which wonne, my father well?'
[5] *1587* omits 183–9, and 197–203.

I had the *Britaynes* at what becke & bay I wolde,
Till that my loving king myne *Aganippus* dyde.
But then my seate it faltered on eache side,
Two churlishe Impes began with me to Jarre,
And for my crowne wadgde with me mortal warre.

The one hight *Morgan* th' elder sonne of *Gonerell*
My sister, and that other *Conidagus* hight
My sister *Ragans* sonne, that lovde me never well:
Both nephewes mine, yet wolde against me *Cordel* fight,   200
Because I lovde always that semed right:
Therfore they hated me, and did pursue,
Their aunte and queene as she had bene a Jewe.

This *Morgane* was that time the prince of *Albany*,
And *Conidagus* king of *Cornewale* and of *Wales*:
Both which, at once provided their artillery,
To worke me wofull wo, & mine adherentes bales:
What nede I fill thyne eares with longer tales?
They did prevaile by might and powre so faste
That I was taken prisoner at laste.   210

In spitefull sorte, they used then my captive corse,
No favoure shewde to me, extincte was mine estate.
Of kinred, princesse bloud, or pere was no remorce,
But as an abjecte vile and worse they did me hate,
To lie in darksome dongeon was my fate:
As twere a thiefe mine aunswers to abyde,
Gainst right and justice, under Jaylours guyde.

For libertie at lengthe I suid, to subjectes were:
But they kepte me in pryson close devoyde of truste,
If I might once escape, they were in dreade and feare,   220
Their fawning frendes with me would prove untrue and just.
They tolde me take it paciently I muste,[1]
And be contented that I had my life:
Sithe with their mothers I began the strife.

Whereby I saw might nothing me prevayle to pray,
Or pleade, or prove, defende, excuse or pardon crave.
They herde me not, despisde my plaintes, sought my decay,
I might no lawe, nor love, nor right, nor justice have:
No frendes, no faith, nor pitie could me save:

---

[1] Compare Lear's attitude to prison (V.2.8–19).

But I was from all hope of licence barde,   230
Condemde my cause like never to be herde.

Was ever lady in such wofull wreckfull wo:
Deprivde of princely powre, berefte of libertie,
Deprivd in all these worldly pompes, hir pleasures fro,
And brought from welthe, to nede, distresse, and misery?
From palace proude, in prison poore to lye:
From kingdomes twayne, to dungion one no more:
From Ladies wayting, unto vermine store.

From light to darke, from holsom ayre to lothsom smell:
From odewr swete, to sweate: from ease, to grievous payne: 240
From sight of princely wights, to place where theves do dwel:
From deinty beddes of downe, to be of strawe full fayne:[1]
From bowres of heavenly hewe, to dennes of dayne:
From greatest haps, that worldly wightes atchieve:
To more distresse then any wretche alive.

· · · · · ·

Thus as I pyning lay my carkas on couch of strawe,[2]
And felte that payne erste never creature earthly knewe:
Me thought by night a gryzely ghost in darkes I sawe,
Eke nerer still to me with stealing steps she drewe.   270
She was of coloure pale, a deadly hewe:
Hir clothes resembled thousand kindes of thrall,
And pictures playne, of hastened deathes withall.

I musing lay in paynes and wondred what she was,
Mine eyne stode still, mine haire rose up for feare an ende.
My fleshe it shoke and trembled: yet I cryde alasse,
What wight art thou, a foe or else what fawning frende?
If death thou arte, I praye thee make an ende.
But th' arte not death: arte thou some fury sente?
My wofull corps with paynes to more tormente?   280

With that she spake: I am (quoth she) thy frend *Despaire*
Which in distresse eache worldly wight with spede do ayde:
I rid them from their foes, if I to them repayre,
To[o] long from thee by other caytives was I stayde.

[1] This contrast may have led Shakespeare to invent the hovel and Lear's realization of what poverty means. III.2.69: 'Where is this straw, my fellow?'
[2] I omit ll.246–66 which continue her moan.

Now if thou arte to die no whit affrayde,
Here shalt thou choose of instrumentes (beholde)
Shall ridde thy restlesse life, of this be bolde.[1]

And therwithall she spred her garmentes lap asyde,
Under the which a thousand thinges I sawe with eyes:
Both knyves, sharpe swordes, poynadoes all bedyde   290
With bloud, and poysons prest which she could well devise.
There is no hope (quoth she) for thee to ryse,
And get thy crowne or libertie agayne:
But for to live, long lasting pining payne.

Loe here (quoth she) the blade that *Did'* of *Carthage* highte,
Whereby she was from thousande panges of payne let passe:
With this she slewe hir selfe, after *Aeneas* flighte:
When he to sea from *Tyrian* shores departed was,
Do chouse of these thou seest from woes to passe,
Or bid the ende prolonge thy paynefull dayes,   300
And I am pleasde from thee to get my wayes.

With that was I (poore wretche) content to take the knife,
But doubtfull yet to dye, and fearefull faine would bide:
So still I lay in study with my selfe at bate and strife,
What thing were best of both these deepe extreames untride.
My hope all reasons of dispayre denide,
And she againe replide to prove it best
To dye, for still in life my woes increast.

[Despair went on describing the irrevocable change in Cordila's
fortunes (309–22).]

Whereby I wretch devoide of comfort quite and hope,
And pleasures past comparde with present paines I had:
For fatall knife slipt forth my fearfull hand did grope,   325
Dispaire in this to ayde my sencelesse limmes was glad,
And gave the blade to ende my woes she bad.
I will (quoth I) but first with all my hart:
Ile pray the Gods, revenge my wofull smart.

If any wronge deserve the wrecke I pray you skyes,   330
And starres of light, if you my wofull plight do rue:
O *Phoebus* cleare I thee beseech and pray likewise,
Beare witnes of my plaints well knowne to Gods are true.

[1] In *Lear* suicidal despair is transferred to Gloucester.

You see from whence these injuries they grue,
Then let like vengeaunce hap and light on those
Which undeserved were my deadly foes.

[Cordila cursed her nephews and said farewell to France, partly
in French (337–50).]

And therewithall the sight did faile my dazeling eyne,
I nothing sawe save sole *Dispayre* bad mee dispatch,
Whom I behelde, she caught the knife from mee I weene,
And by hir elbowe carian death for mee did watch.   354
Come on (quoth I) thou hast a good catch,
And therewithal *Dispayre* the stroke did strike:
Whereby I dyde, a damned creature like.

Which I alasse lament, bid those alive beware,
Let not the losse of goodes or honour them constraine:
To play the fooles, and take such carefull carke and care,   360
Or to dispaire for any prison pine or paine.
If they be giltlesse let them so remaine,
Farre greater follye is it for to kill,
Themselves dispayring, then is any ill.

Sith first thereby their enmyes have, that they desyre:
By which they prove to deadly foes unwares a frende:
And next they cannot live, to former blisse t'aspyre
If God do bring their foes in time to sodaine ende:
They lastly as the damned wretches sende,
Their soules to hell, when as they undertake   370
To kill a corps: which God did lively make.

VII. Source

From THE FAERIE QUEENE
by Edmund Spenser (1596 edn.)

Book II, Canto X.

[Lear reigned after Bladud]

27

Next him king *Leyr* in happie peace long raind,
    But had no issue male him to succeed,
    But three faire daughters, which were well uptraind,

In all that seemed fit for kingly seed:
Mongst whom his realme he equally decreed
To have divided.[1] Tho when feeble age
Night to his utmoste date he saw proceed,
He cald his daughters; and with speeches sage
Inquyrd, which of them most did love her parentage.

28

The eldest *Gonorill* gan to protest,
That she much more then her owne life him lov'd:
And *Regan* greater love to him profest,
Then all the world, when ever it were proov'd;
But *Cordeill* said she lov'd him, as behoov'd:
Whose simple answere, wanting colours faire
To paint it forth, him to displeasance moov'd,
That in his crowne he counted her no heire,
But twixt the other twaine his kingdome whole did shaire.

29

So wedded th' one to *Maglan* king of Scots,
And th' other to the king of *Cambria*,[2]
And twixt them shayrd his realme by equall lots:
But without dowre the wise *Cordelia*[3]
Was sent to *Aganip* of *Celtica*.
Their aged Syre, thus eased of his crowne,
A private life led in *Albania*,
With *Gonorill*, long had in great renowne,
That nought him griev'd to bene from rule deposed downe.

30

But true it is, that when the oyle is spent,
The light goes out, and weeke is throwne away;
So when he had resigned his regiment,
His daughter gan despise his drouping day,
And wearie waxe of his continuall stay.
Tho to his daughter *Regan* he repayrd,
Who him at first well used every way;
But when of his departure she despayrd,
Her bountie she abated, and his cheare empayrd.

[1] Hence *Leir*, 27–31; apparently also intended in *Lear* I.i.79–82. 'Opulent',
I.i.86, means 'richer' not 'larger'.
[2] Cambria and Cornwall in *Leir*.
[3] Hence her name in *Lear*.

31

The wretched man gan then avise too late,
    That love is not, where most it is profest,
    Too truely tryde in his extreamest state;
    At last resolv'd likewise to prove the rest,
    He to *Cordelia* him selfe addrest,
    Who with entire affection him receav'd,
    As for her Syre and king her seemed best;
    And after all an army strong she leav'd,[1]
To war on those, which him had of his realme bereav'd.

32

So to his crowne she him restor'd againe,
    In which he dyde, made ripe for death by eld,
    And after wild, it should to her remaine:
    Who peaceably the same long time did weld:
    And all mens harts in dew obedience held:
    Till that her sisters children, woxen strong
    Through proud ambition, against her rebeld,
    And overcommen kept in prison long,
Till wearie of that wretched life, her selfe she hong.[2]

33

Then gan the bloudie brethren both to raine:
    But fierce *Cundah* gan shortly to envie
    His brother *Morgan*, prickt with proud disdaine,
    To have a pere in part of soveraintie,
    And kindling coles of cruell enmitie,
    Raisd warre, and him in battell overthrew:
    Whence as he to those woodie hils did flie,
    Which hight of him *Glamorgan*, there him slew:
Then did he raigne alone, when he none equall knew.

---

[1] Her husband takes no part in it. 'leav'd', levied.

[2] This probably suggested the manner of her death in *Lear*, and Edmund's intention to suggest suicide by hanging. (V.3.253–6.)

VIII. Possible Source

From ALBION'S ENGLAND
by William Warner (1589 edn.)[1]

Book 3, Chap. XIV

About a thirtie yeares and five did Leir rule this Land,
When, doting on his Daughters three, with them he fell in hand
To tell how much they loved him. The Eldest did esteeme
Her life inferior to her love, so did the Second deeme:
The Yongest sayd her love was such as did a childe behove,
And that how much himselfe was worth, so much she him did love.
The formost two did please him well, the yongest did not so:
Upon the Prince of *Albanie* the First he did bestoe:
The Middle on the *Cornish* Prince: their Dowrie was his Throne,
At his decease: *Cordellas* parte was very small or none.   10
Yet for her forme, and vertuous life, a noble Gallian King[2]
Did her, un-dowed, for his Queene into his Countrie bring.
    Her Sisters sicke of Fathers health, their Husbands by consent
Did joyne in Armes: from Leir so by force the Scepter went:
Yet, for they promise pentions large, he rather was content.
In *Albanie* the qondam King at eldest Daughters Court
Was setled scarce, when she repynes, and lessens still his Port.
His second Daughter then, he thought, would shewe her selfe
    more kinde,
To whom, he going, for a while did franke allowance finde.
Ere long, abridging almost all, she keepeth him so loe,   20
That of two badds, for betters choyse he backe agayne did goe.
But *Gonorill* at his returne, not only did attempt
Her fathers death,[3] but openly did hold him in contempt.
    His aged eyes powre out their teares, when holding up his hands,
He sayd: O God, who so thou art, that my good hap withstands,
Prolong not life, deferre not death, my selfe I over-live,
When those that owe to me their lives, to me my death would give.[4]

---

[1] Title page: *The First and Second parts of Albions England. The former revised and corrected, and the latter newly continued and added ... With Historical Intermixtures, Invention, and Varietie: profitably, briefly, and pleasantly performed in Verse and Prose by William Warner.* Imprinted at London by Thomas Orwin, for Thomas Cadman, dwelling at the great North-doore of Sainct Paules Church at the signe of the Bible. 1589. The 1606 edn. contained no important variants.

[2] Called this in *Leir*, 582 (s.d.), etc.

[3] This probably suggested the attempt in *Leir*, Sc. 12, 15, 17, 19.

[4] Cf. *Leir*, 860–5.

Thou Towne, whose walles rose of my wealth, stand evermore to tell
Thy Founders Fall, and warne that none do fall as *Leir* fell.　　29
Bid none affie in Frends, for say, his Children wrought his wracke:
Yea those, that were to him most deare, did lothe and let him lacke.
Cordella,[1] well *Cordella* sayd, she loved as a Childe:
But sweeter words we seeke than sooth, and so are men begilde.
She only rests untryed yet: but what may I expect
From her: to whom I nothing gave, when these do me reject.
Then dye, nay trye, the rule may fayle, and Nature may ascend:
Nor are they ever surest frends, on whom we most do spend.
　　He ships himselfe to *Gallia* then: but maketh knowne before[2]
Unto *Cordella* his estate, who rueth him so poore,
And kept his there arivall close, till she provided had
To furnish him in every want. Of him her King was glad,　　40
And nobly intertayned him: the Queene, with teares among,
(Her duetie done) conferreth with her father of his wrong.
Such duetie, bountie, kindnes, and increasing love, he found
In that his Daughter and her Lord, that sorrowes more abound
For his unkindly using her, then for the others crime:
And King-like thus in *Agamps* Court did Leir dwell, till time
The noble King his Sonne-in-law transports an Armie greate,
Of forcie *Gawles*, possessing him of dispossessed Seate,
To whom *Cordella* did succeede, not raigning long in queate.
　　Not how her Nephewes warre on her, and one of them slew th'
　　　　other
Shall followe: but I will disclose a most tyrannous mother.[3]　　51

[1] Hence her name in *Leir*.
[2] Not so in either play.
[3] Queen Iden, wife of Gorboduc, and mother of Ferrex and Porrex.

IX. Source

THE TRUE CHRONICLE HISTORIE OF KING LEIR
and his three daughters.
Anon. (1605)

ACTUS I

[Sc. 1]   *Enter King Leir and Nobles.*

Thus to our griefe the obsequies performd
Of our (too late) deceast and dearest Queen,
Whose soule I hope, possest of heavenly joyes,
Doth ride in triumph 'mongst the Cherubins;[1]
Let us request your grave advice, my Lords,
For the disposing of our princely daughters,
For whom our care is specially imployd,
As nature bindeth to advaunce their states,   10
In royall marriage with some princely mates:
For wanting now their mothers good advice,
Under whose government they have receyved
A perfit patterne of a vertuous life:
Lest as it were a ship without a sterne,
Or silly sheepe without a Pastors care;
Although our selves doe dearely tender them,
Yet are we ignorant of their affayres:
For fathers best do know to governe sonnes;
But daughters steps the mothers counsell turnes.   20
A sonne we want for to succeed our Crowne,
And course of time hath cancelled the date
Of further issue from our withered loynes:
One foote already hangeth in the grave,
And age hath made deepe furrowes in my face:
The world of me, I of the world am weary,
And I would fayne resigne these earthly cares,[2]
And thinke upon the welfare of my soule:
Which by no better meanes may be effected,
Then by resigning up the Crowne from me,   30

---

[1] Cf. *Tamburlaine*, II.4.26.
[2] Cf. *Lear*, I.1.38–41. But he is not so obviously weary.
    M

In equall dowry to my daughters three.[1]

SKALLIGER.   A worthy care, my Liege, which well declares,
The zeale you bare unto our *quondam* Queene:
And since your Grace hath licens'd me to speake,
I censure thus; Your Majesty knowing well,
What severall Suters your princely daughters have,
To make them eche a Joynter more or lesse,
As is their worth, to them that love professe.[2]

LEIR.   No more, nor lesse, but even all alike,
My zeale is fixt, all fashiond in one mould: 40
Wherefore unpartiall shall my censure be,
Both old and young shall have alike for me.

NOBLE.   My gracious Lord, I hartily do wish,
That God had lent you an heyre indubitate,
Which might have set upon your royall throne,
When fates should loose the prison of your life,
By whose succession all this doubt might cease;
And as by you, by him we might have peace.
But after-wishes ever come too late,
And nothing can revoke the course of fate: 50
Wherefore, my Liege, my censure deemes it best,
To match them with some of your neighbour Kings,
Bordring within the bounds of Albion,
By whose united friendship, this our state
May be protected 'gainst all forrayne hate.[3]

LEIR.   Herein, my Lords, your wishes sort with mine,
And mine (I hope) do sort with heavenly powers:
For at this instant two neere neyghbouring Kings
Of Cornwall and of Cambria, motion love
To my two daughters, *Gonorill* and *Ragan*.   60
My youngest daughter, fayre *Cordella*, vowes
No liking to a Monarch, unlesse love allowes.
She is sollicited by divers Peeres;[4]
But none of them her partiall fancy heares.
Yet, if my policy may her beguyle,
Ile match her to some King within this Ile,[5]
And so establish such a perfit peace,
As fortunes force shall ne're prevayle to cease.

PERILLUS.   Of us & ours, your gracious care, my Lord,   70
Deserves an everlasting memory,

---

[1] Less clear in I.1.52–3; 79–82.
[2] Reflected in I.1.52–4?
[3] Lear dreads 'future strife', I.1.44.
[4] Cf. I.1.45: by France and Burgundy.   [5] 'the Irish King', 190.

To be inrol'd in Chronicles of fame,
By never-dying perpetuity:
Yet to become so provident a Prince,
Lose not the title of a loving father:
Do not force love, where fancy cannot dwell,
Lest streames being stopt, above the banks do swell.

   LEIR.   I am resolv'd, and even now my mind
Doth meditate a sudden stratagem,
To try which of my daughters loves me best:
Which till I know, I cannot be in rest.   80
This graunted, when they joyntly shall contend,
Eche to exceed the other in their love:
Then at the vantage will I take *Cordella*,
Even as she doth protest she loves me best,
Ile say, Then, daughter, graunt me one request,
To shew thou lovest me as thy sisters doe,
Accept a husband, whom my selfe will woo.
This sayd, she cannot well deny my sute,
Although (poore soule) her sences will be mute:
Then will I tryumph in my policy,   90
And match her with a King of Brittany.

   SKAL.   Ile to them before, and bewray your secrecy.

   PER.   Thus fathers think their children to beguile,
And oftentimes themselves do first repent,
When heavenly powers do frustrate their intent.

                                  [Exeunt.

        [Sc. 2]   *Enter Gonorill and Ragan.*[1]

   GON.   I marvell, *Ragan*, how you can indure
To see that proud pert Peat, our youngest sister,
So slightly to account of us, her elders,
As if we were no better then her selfe!   100
We cannot have a quaynt device so soone,
Or new made fashion, of our choyce invention;
But if she like it, she will have the same,
Or study newer to exceed us both.[2]
Besides, she is so nice and so demure;
So sober, courteous, modest, and precise,
That all the Court hath worke ynough to do,
To talke how she exceedeth me and you.

---

[1] Shakespeare omits both Sc. 1 and this.
[2] Hence Kent calls Goneril 'Vanity the puppet', II.2.36. These are ancestors of Cinderella's envious sisters.

RAG.   What should I do? would it were in my power,
To find a cure for this contagious ill: 110
Some desperate medicine must be soone applyed,
To dimme the glory of her mounting fame;
Els ere't be long, sheele have both prick and praise,
And we must be set by for working dayes.
Doe you not see what severall choyce of Suters
She daily hath, and of the best degree?
Say, amongst all, she hap to fancy one,
And have a husband when as we have none:
Why then, by right, to her we must give place,
Though it be ne're so much to our disgrace.   120
    GON.   By my virginity, rather then she shall have
A husband before me,
Ile marry one or other in his shirt:
And yet I have made halfe a graunt already
Of my good will unto the King of Cornwall.[1]
    RAG.   Sweare not so deeply (sister) here commeth my L. *Skalliger*:
Something his hasty comming doth import.
                    [*Enter Skal.*
    SKAL.   Sweet Princesses, I am glad I met you heere so luckily,
Having good newes which doth concerne you both,
And craveth speedy expedition.   130
    RAG.   For Gods sake tell us what it is, my Lord,
I am with child untill you utter it.
    SKAL.   Madam, to save your longing, this it is:
Your father in great secrecy to day,
Told me, he meanes to marry you out of hand,
Unto the noble Prince of Cambria;
You, Madam, to the King of Cornwalls Grace:
Your yonger sister he would fayne bestow
Upon the rich King of Hibernia:
But that he doubts, she hardly will consent;   140
For hitherto she ne're could fancy him.
If she do yeeld, why then, betweene you three,
He will devide his kingdome for your dowries.
But yet there is a further mystery,[2]
Which, so you will conceale, I will disclose.
    GON.   What e're thou speakst to us, kind *Skalliger*,
Thinke that thou speakst it only to thy selfe.
    SKAL.   He earnestly desireth for to know,
Which of you three do beare most love to him,

---

[1] In *Lear* Regan marries Cornwall, Goneril Albany.
[2] Cf. I.1.36: 'our darker purpose'.

And on your loves he so extremely dotes,   150
As never any did, I thinke, before.
He presently doth meane to send for you,
To be resolv'd of this tormenting doubt:
And looke, whose answere pleaseth him the best,
They shall have most unto their marriages.[1]

    RAG.   O that I had some pleasing Mermayds voyce,
For to inchaunt his sencelesse sences with!

    SKAL.   For he supposeth that *Cordella* will
(Striving to go beyond you in her love)
Promise to do what ever he desires: 160
Then will he straight enjoyne her for his sake,
The Hibernian King in marriage for to take.
This is the summe of all I have to say;
Which being done, I humbly take my leave,
Not doubting but your wisdomes will foresee,
What course will best unto your good agree.

    GON.   Thanks, gentle *Skalliger*, thy kindnes undeserved,
Shall not be unrequited, if we live.

                         [Exit Skalliger.

    RAG.   Now have we fit occasion offred us,
To be reveng'd upon her unperceyv'd.   170

    GON.   Nay, our revenge we will inflict on her,
Shall be accounted piety in us:
I will so flatter with my doting father,
As he was ne're so flattred in his life.
Nay, I will say, that if it be his pleasure,
To match me to a begger, I will yeeld:
For why, I know what ever I do say,
He meanes to match me with the Cornwall King.

    RAG.   Ile say the like: for I am well assured,
What e're I say to please the old mans mind,   180
Who dotes, as if he were a child agayne,
I shall injoy the noble Cambrian Prince:
Only, to feed his humour, will suffice,
To say, I am content with any one
Whom heele appoynt me; this will please him more,
Then e're *Apolloes* musike pleased Jove.

    GON.   I smile to think, in what a wofull plight
Cordella will be, when we answere thus:
For she will rather dye, then give consent
To joyne in marriage with the Irish King: 190
So will our father think, she loveth him not,

---

[1] Not what Leir said (39), but what Skalliger suggested (37–8).

Because she will not graunt to his desire,
Which we will aggravate in such bitter termes,
That he will soone convert his love to hate:
For he, you know, is alwayes in extremes.[1]
    RAG.   Not all the world could lay a better plot,
I long till it be put in practice.

                                        [*Exeunt.*

       [Sc. 3]   *Enter Leir and Perillus.*

    LEIR.   *Perillus*, go seeke my daughters,
Will them immediately come and speak with me.   200
    PER.   I will, my gracious Lord.

                                          [*Exit.*

    LEIR.   Oh, what a combat feeles my panting heart,
'Twixt childrens love, and care of Common weale!
How deare my daughters are unto my soule,
None knowes, but he, that knowes my thoghts & secret deeds.
Ah, little do they know the deare regard,
Wherein I hold their future state to come:
When they securely sleepe on beds of downe,
These aged eyes do watch for their behalfe:
While they like wantons sport in youthfull toyes,   210
This throbbing heart is pearst with dire annoyes.
As doth the Sun exceed the smallest Starre,
So much the fathers love exceeds the childs.
Yet my complaynts are causlesse: for the world
Affords not children more conformable:
And yet, me thinks, my mind presageth still
I know not what; and yet I feare some ill.

     [*Enter Perillus, with the three daughters.*

Well, here my daughters come: I have found out
A present meanes to rid me of this doubt.   220
    GON.   Our royall Lord and father, in all duty,
We come to know the tenour of your will,
Why you so hastily have sent for us?
    LEIR.   Deare *Gonorill*, kind *Ragan*, sweet *Cordella*,
Ye florishing branches of a Kingly stocke,
Sprung from a tree that once did flourish greene,
Whose blossomes now are nipt with Winters frost,
And pale grym death doth wayt upon my steps,[2]

---

[1] Cf. I.1.289–300.
[2] Cf. I.1.41: 'crawl toward death'.

And summons me unto his next Assizes.
Therefore, deare daughters, as ye tender the safety   230
Of him that was the cause of your first being,
Resolve a doubt which much molests my mind,
Which of you three to me would prove most kind;
Which loves me most, and which at my request
Will soonest yeeld unto their fathers hest.
    GON.   I hope, my gracious father makes no doubt
Of any of his daughters love to him:
Yet for my part, to shew my zeale to you,
Which cannot be in windy words rehearst,
I prize my love to you at such a rate,   240
I thinke my life inferiour to my love.
Should you injoyne me for to tye a milstone
About my neck, and leape into the Sea,
At your commaund I willingly would doe it:
Yea, for to doe you good, I would ascend
The highest Turret in all Brittany,
And from the top leape headlong to the ground:
Nay, more, should you appoynt me for to marry
The meanest vassayle in the spacious world,
Without reply I would accomplish it: 250
In briefe, commaund what ever you desire,
And if I fayle, no favour I require.
    LEIR.   O, how thy words revive my dying soule!
    COR.   O, how I doe abhorre this flattery!
    LEIR.   But what sayth *Ragan* to her fathers will?
    RAG.   O, that my simple utterance could suffice,
To tell the true intention of my heart,
Which burnes in zeale of duty to your grace,
And never can be quench'd, but by desire
To shew the same in outward forwardnesse.   260
Oh, that there were some other mayd that durst
But make a challenge of her love with me;
Ide make her soone confesse she never loved
Her father halfe so well as I doe you.
I then, my deeds should prove in playner case,
How much my zeale aboundeth to your grace:
But for them all, let this one meane suffice,
To ratify my love before your eyes:
I have right noble Suters to my love,
No worse then Kings, and happely I love one: 270
Yet, would you have me make my choyce anew,
Ide bridle fancy, and be rulde by you.

LEIR.   Did never *Philomel* sing so sweet a note.

COR.   Did never flatterer tell so false a tale.

LEIR.   Speak now, *Cordella*, make my joyes at full,
And drop downe Nectar from thy hony lips.

COR.   I cannot paynt my duty forth in words,[1]
I hope my deeds shall make report for me:
But looke what love the child doth owe the father,
The same to you I beare, my gracious Lord.   280

GON.   Here is an answere answerlesse indeed:
Were you my daughter, I should scarcely brooke it.

RAG.   Dost thou not blush, proud Peacock as thou art,
To make our father such a slight reply?

LEIR.   Why how now, Minion, are you growne so proud?[2]
Doth our deare love make you thus peremptory?
What, is your love become so small to us,
As that you scorne to tell us what it is?
Do you love us, as every child doth love
Their father? True indeed, as some   290
Who by disobedience short their fathers dayes,
And so would you; some are so father-sick,
That they make meanes to rid them from the world;
And so would you: some are indifferent,
Whether their aged parents live or dye;
And so are you. But, didst thou know, proud gyrle,
What care I had to foster thee to this,
Ah, then thou wouldst say as thy sisters do:
Our life is lesse, then love we owe to you.

COR.   Deare father, do not so mistake my words,   300
Nor my playne meaning be misconstrued;
My toung was never usde to flattery.[3]

GON.   You were not best say I flatter: if you do,
My deeds shall shew, I flatter not with you.
I love my father better then thou canst.

COR.   The prayse were great, spoke from anothers mouth:
But it should seeme your neighbours dwell far off.

RAG.   Nay, here is one, that will confirme as much
As she hath sayd, both for my selfe and her.
I say, thou dost not wish my fathers good.   310

COR.   Deare father—

LEIR.   Peace, bastard Impe, no issue of King *Leir*,
I will not heare thee speake one tittle more.
Call not me father, if thou love thy life,[4]

---

[1] Cf. I.1.91–2: 'I cannot heave my heart into my mouth', and Text VII, St. 28.
[2] I.1.90.   [3] I.1.232–3.   [4] I.1.113–14.

Nor these thy sisters once presume to name:
Looke for no helpe henceforth from me nor mine;
Shift as thou wilt, and trust unto thy selfe:
My Kingdome will I equally devide
'Twixt thy two sisters to their royall dowre,
And will bestow them worthy their deserts: 320
This done, because thou shalt not have the hope,
To have a childs part in the time to come,
I presently will dispossesse my selfe,
And set up these upon my princely throne.
    GON.   I ever thought that pride would have a fall.
    RAG.   Plaine dealing, sister: your beauty is so sheene,
You need no dowry, to make you be a Queene.
                                [Exeunt Leir, Gonorill, Ragan.
    COR.   Now whither, poore forsaken, shall I goe,
When mine own sisters tryumph in my woe?   330
But unto him which doth protect the just,
In him will poore *Cordella* put her trust.
These hands shall labour, for to get my spending;
And so ile live untill my dayes have ending.
    PER.   Oh, how I grieve, to see my Lord thus fond,
To dote so much upon vayne flattering words.
Ah, if he but with good advice had weyghed,
The hidden tenure of her humble speech,[1]
Reason to rage should not have given place,
Nor poore *Cordella* suffer such disgrace.   340
                                  [Exit.

    [Sc. 4]   *Enter the Gallian King with Mumford, and three*
                        Nobles more.

    KING.   Disswade me not, my Lords, I am resolv'd,
This next fayre wynd to sayle for Brittany,
In some disguise, to see if flying fame
Be not too prodigall in the wonderous prayse
Of these three Nymphes, the daughters of King *Leir*.
If present view do answere absent prayse,
And eyes allow of what our eares have heard,
And *Venus* stand auspicious to my vowes,   350
And Fortune favour what I take in hand;
I will returne seyz'd of as rich a prize
As *Jason*, when he wanne the golden fleece.[2]
    MUM.   Heavens graunt you may; the match were ful of honor,

---

[1] Cf. Kent, I.1.149–54.
[2] This anticipates *MV*, I.1.169–72 (Bassanio on Portia).

And well beseeming the young Gallian King.
I would your Grace would favour me so much,
As make me partner of your Pilgrimage.
I long to see the gallant Brittish Dames,
And feed mine eyes upon their rare perfections:
For till I know the contrary, Ile say,   360
Our Dames in Fraunce are more fayre then they.
    KING.   Lord *Mumford*, you have saved me a labour,
In offring that which I did meane to aske:
And I most willingly accept your company.
Yet first I will injoyne you to observe
Some few conditions which I shall propose.
    MUM.   So that you do not tye mine eyes for looking
After the amorous glaunces of fayre Dames:
So that you do not tye my toung from speaking,
My lips from kissing when occasion serves,   370
My hands from congees, and my knees to bow
To gallant Gyrles; which were a taske more hard,
Then flesh and bloud is able to indure:
Commaund what else you please, I rest content.
    KING.   To bind thee from a thing thou canst not leave,
Were but a meane to make thee seeke it more:
And therefore speake, looke, kisse, salute for me;
In these my selfe am like to second thee.
Now heare thy taske. I charge thee from the time
That first we set sayle for the Brittish shore,   380
To use no words of dignity to me,
But in the friendliest maner that thou cast,
Make use of me as thy companion:
For we will go disguisde in Palmers weeds,
That no man shall mistrust us what we are.
    MUM.   If that be all, ile fit your turne, I warrant you. I am
some kin to the Blunts, and I think, the bluntest of all my
kindred; therfore if I bee too blunt with you, thank your selfe
for praying me to be so.
    KING.   Thy pleasant company will make the way seeme short. 390
It resteth now, that in my absence hence,
I do commit the government to you
My trusty Lords and faythfull Counsellers.
Time cutteth off the rest I have to say:
The wynd blowes fayre, and I must needs away.
    NOBLES.   Heavens send your voyage to as good effect,
As we your land do purpose to protect.
                             [*Exeunt.*

[Sc. 5]   *Enter the King of Cornwall and his man booted and*
spurd, a riding wand, and a letter in his hand.

CORN.   But how far distant are we from the Court?   400
SER.   Some twenty miles, my Lord, or thereabouts.
CORN.   It seemeth to me twenty thousand myles:
Yet hope I to be there within this houre.
SER.   Then are you like to ride alone for me.
                                        [*to himselfe.*
I thinke, my Lord is weary of his life.
CORN.   Sweet *Gonorill*, I long to see thy face,
Which hast so kindly gratified my love.

          Enter the King of Cambria booted and spurd, and his man
                      with a wand and a letter.
CAM.   Get a fresh horse: for by my soule I sweare,   410
                                        [*He lookes on the letter.*
I am past patience, longer to forbeare
The wished sight of my beloved mistris,
Deare *Ragan*, stay and comfort of my life.
SER.   Now what in Gods name doth my Lord intend?
                                        [*to himselfe.*
He thinks he ne're shall come at's journeyes end.
I would he had old *Dedalus* waxen wings,
That he might flye, so I might stay behind:
For e're we get to Troynouant, I see
He quite will tyre himselfe, his horse and me.

          [*Cornwall & Cambria looke one upon another, and start*
                    to see eche other there.   420

CORN.   Brother of Cambria, we greet you well,
As one whom here we little did expect.
CAM.   Brother of Cornwall, met in happy time:
I thought as much to have met with the Souldan of Persia,
As to have met you in this place, my Lord,
No doubt, it is about some great affayres,
That makes you here so slenderly accompanied.
CORN.   To say the truth, my Lord, it is no lesse,
And for your part some hasty wind of chance   430
Hath blowne you hither thus upon the sudden.
CAM.   My Lord, to break off further circumstances,
For at this time I cannot brooke delayes:
Tell you your reason, I will tell you mine.
CORN.   In fayth, content, and therefore to be briefe;

For I am sure my haste's as great as yours:
I am sent for, to come unto King *Leir*,
Who by these present letters promiseth
His eldest daughter, lovely *Gonorill*,
To me in mariage, and for present dowry,   440
The moity of halfe his Regiment.
The Ladies love I long ago possest:
But untill now I never had the fathers.
    CAM.   You tell me wonders, yet I will relate
Strange newes, and henceforth we must brothers call;
Witnesse these lynes: his honourable age,
Being weary of the troubles of his Crowne,
His princely daughter *Ragan* will bestow
On me in mariage, with halfe his Seigniories,
Whom I would gladly have accepted of,   450
With the third part, her complements are such.
    CORN.   If I have one halfe, and you have the other,
Then betweene us we must needs have the whole.
    CAM.   The hole! how meane you that? Zlood, I hope,
We shall have two holes between us.
    CORN.   Why, the whole Kingdome.
    CAM.   I, that's very true.
    CORN.   What then is left for his third daughters dowry,
Lovely *Cordella*, whom the world admires?
    CAM.   Tis very strange, I know not what to thinke,   460
Unlesse they meane to make a Nunne of her.
    CORN.   'Twere pity such rare beauty should be hid
Within the compasse of a Cloysters wall:
But howsoe're, if *Leirs* words prove true,
It will be good, my Lord, for me and you.
    CAM.   Then let us haste, all danger to prevent,
For feare delayes doe alter his intent.   [*Exeunt.*

[Sc. 6]   *Enter Gonorill and Ragan.*

    GON.   Sister, when did you see *Cordella* last,
That pretty piece, that thinks none good ynough
To speake to her, because (sir-reverence)   470
She hath a little beauty extraordinary?[1]
    RAG.   Since time my father warnd her from his presence,
I never saw her, that I can remember.
God give her joy of her surpassing beauty;
I thinke her dowry will be small ynough.

   [1] Shakespeare makes little of this rivalry in beauty.

GON.   I have incenst my father so against her,
As he will never be reclaymd agayne.

   RAG.   I was not much behind to do the like.

   GON.   Faith, sister, what moves you to beare her such good will? 480

   RAG.   In truth, I thinke, the same that moveth you;
Because she doth surpasse us both in beauty.

   GON.   Beshrew your fingers, how right you can gesse:
I tell you true, it cuts me to the heart.

   RAG.   But we will keepe her low enough, I warrant,
And clip her wings for mounting up too hye.

   GON.   Who ever hath her, shall have a rich mariage of her.

   RAG.   She were right fit to make a Parsons wife:
For they, men say, do love faire women well,
And many times doe marry them with nothing.   490

   GON.   With nothing! marry God forbid: why, are there any
     such?

   RAG.   I meane, no money.

   GON.   I cry you mercy, I mistooke you much:
And she is far too stately for the Church;
Sheele lay her husbands Benefice on her back,
Even in one gowne, if she may have her will.

   RAG.   In faith, poore soule, I pitty her a little.
Would she were lesse fayre, or more fortunate.
Well, I thinke long untill I see my *Morgan*,
The gallant Prince of Cambria, here arrive.   500

   GON.   And so do I, untill the Cornwall King
Present himselfe, to consummate my joyes.
Peace, here commeth my father.

          [Enter Leir, Perillus and others.

   LEIR.   Cease, good my Lords, and sue not to reverse
Our censure, which is now irrevocable.
We have dispatched letters of contract
Unto the Kings of Cambria and of Cornwall;
Our hand and seale will justify no lesse:
Then do not so dishonour me, my Lords,   510
As to make shipwrack of our kingly word.
I am as kind as is the Pellican,
That kils it selfe, to save her young ones lives:[1]
And yet as jelous as the princely Eagle,
That kils her young ones, if they do but dazell
Upon the radiant splendor of the Sunne.
Within this two dayes I expect their comming.

---

[1] Shakespeare reverses the idea in 'pelican daughters' (III.4.72-3).

[*Enter Kings of Cornwall and Cambria.*

But in good time, they are arriv'd already.
This haste of yours, my Lords, doth testify
The fervent love you beare unto my daughters: 520
And think your selves as welcome to King *Leir*,
As ever *Pryams* children were to him.
    CORN.   My gracious Lord, and father too, I hope,
Pardon, for that I made no greater haste:
But were my horse as swift as was my will,
I long ere this had seene your Maiesty.
    CAM.   No other scuse of absence can I frame,
Then what my brother hath inform'd your Grace:
For our undeserved welcome, we do vowe,
Perpetually to rest at your commaund.   530
    CORN.   But you, sweet Love, illustrious *Gonorill*,
The Regent, and the Soveraigne of my soule,
Is *Cornwall* welcome to your Excellency?
    GON.   As welcome, as *Leander* was to *Hero*,
Or brave *Aeneas* to the Carthage Queene:
So and more welcome is your Grace to me.
    CAM.   O, may my fortune prove no worse then his,
Since heavens do know, my fancy is as much.
Deare *Ragan*, say, if welcome unto thee,
All welcomes else will little comfort me.   540
    RAG.   As gold is welcome to the covetous eye,
As sleepe is welcome to the Traveller,
As is fresh water to sea-beaten men,
Or moystned showres unto the parched ground,
Or any thing more welcomer then this,
So and more welcome lovely *Morgan* is.
    LEIR.   What resteth then, but that we consummate
The celebration of these nuptiall Rites?
My Kingdome I do equally devide.
Princes, draw lots, and take your chaunce as falles.   550

[*Then they draw lots.*

These I resigne as freely unto you,
As earst by true succession they were mine.
And here I do freely dispossesse my selfe,
And make you two my true adopted heyres:
My selfe will sojorne with my sonne of Cornwall,[1]
And take me to my prayers and my beades.

   [1] Cf. I.1.127–39 where Lear is more demanding.

I know, my daughter *Ragan* will be sorry,
Because I do not spend my dayes with her:
Would I were able to be with both at once;   560
They are the kindest Gyrles in Christendome,
    PER.   I have bin silent all this while, my Lord,
To see if any worthyer then my selfe,
Would once have spoke in poore *Cordellaes* cause:
But love or feare tyes silence to their toungs.
Oh, heare me speake for her, my gracious Lord,
Whose deeds have not deserv'd this ruthlesse doome,
As thus to disinherit her of all.
    LEIR.   Urge this no more, and if thou love thy life:[1]
I say, she is no daughter, that doth scorne   570
To tell her father how she loveth him.
Who ever speaketh hereof to mee agayne,
I will esteeme him for my mortall foe.
Come, let us in, to celebrate with joy,
The happy Nuptialls of these lovely payres.
                        [Exeunt omnes, manet Perillus.
    PER.   Ah, who so blind, as they that will not see[2]
The neere approch of their owne misery?
Poore Lady, I extremely pitty her:
And whilst I live, eche drop of my heart blood,   580
Will I strayne forth, to do her any good.   *[Exit.*

    [Sc. 7]   *Enter the Gallian King, and Mumford, disguised
                        like Pilgrims.*

    MUM.   My Lord, how do you brook this Brittish ayre?
    KING.   My Lord? I told you of this foolish humour,
And bound you to the contrary, you know.
    MUM.   Pardon me for once, my Lord; I did forget.
    KING.   My Lord agayne? then let's have nothing else,
And so be tane for spyes, and then tis well.
    MUM.   Swounds, I could bite my toung in two for anger: 590
For Gods sake name your selfe some proper name.
    KING.   Call me *Tresillus*: Ile call thee *Denapoll*.
    MUM.   Might I be made the Monarch of the world,
I could not hit upon these names, I sweare.[3]
    KING.   Then call me *Will*, ile call thee *Jacke*.
    MUM.   Well, be it so, for I have wel deserv'd to be cal'd *Jack*.
    KING.   Stand close; for here a Brittish Lady commeth:

---

[1] I.1.154, 'Kent, on thy life, no more.'
[2] Cf. I.1.157–9: 'See better, Lear. . . .'
[3] Cf. *Supposes*, II.2. [Vol. I, p. 125]. Paquetto speaks similarly.

[Enter Cordella.

A fayrer creature ne're mine eyes beheld.

COR.   This is a day of joy unto my sisters,
Wherein they both are maried unto Kings;   600
And I, by byrth, as worthy as themselves,
Am turnd into the world, to seeke my fortune.
How may I blame the fickle Queene of Chaunce,
That maketh me a patterne of her power?
Ah, poore weake mayd, whose imbecility
Is far unable to indure these brunts.
Oh, father *Leir*, how dost thou wrong thy child,
Who alwayes was obedient to thy will!
But why accuse I fortune and my father?
No, no, it is the pleasure of my God: 610
And I do willingly imbrace the rod.

KING.   It is no Goddesse; for she doth complayne
On fortune, and th' unkindnesse of her father.

COR.   These costly robes ill fitting my estate,
I will exchange for other meaner habit.

MUM.   Now if I had a Kingdome in my hands,
I would exchange it for a milkmaids smock and petycoate,
That she and I might shift our clothes together.

COR.   I will betake me to my threed and Needle,
And earne my living with my fingers ends.   620

MUM.   O brave! God willing, thou shalt have my custome,
By sweet S. *Denis*, here I sadly sweare,
For all the shirts and night-geare that I weare.

COR.   I will professe and vow a maydens life.

MUM.   Then I protest thou shalt not have my custom.

KING.   I can forbeare no longer for to speak:
For if I do, I think my heart will breake.

MUM.   Sblood, *Wil*, I hope you are not in love with my
     Sempster.

KING.   I am in such a laborinth of love,
As that I know not which way to get out.   630

MUM.   You'l ne're get out, unlesse you first get in.

KING.   I prithy *Jacke*, crosse not my passions.

MUM.   Prithy *Wil*, to her, and try her patience.

KING.   Thou fairest creature, whatsoere thou art,
That ever any mortall eyes beheld,
Vouchsafe to me, who have o'reheard thy woes,
To shew the cause of these thy sad laments.

COR.   Ah Pilgrims, what availes to shew the cause.
When there's no meanes to find a remedy?

KING.   To utter griefe, doth ease a heart o'recharg'd.   640

COR.   To touch a sore, doth aggravate the payne.

KING.   The silly mouse, by vertue of her teeth,
Releas'd the princely Lyon from the net.

COR.   Kind Palmer, which so much desir'st to heare
The tragick tale of my unhappy youth:
Know this in briefe, I am the haplesse daughter
Of *Leir*, sometimes King of Brittany.

KING.   Why, who debarres his honourable age,
From being still the King of Brittany?

COR.   None, but himselfe hath dispossest himselfe,   650
And given all his Kingdome to the Kings
Of Cornwall and of Cambria, with my sisters.

KING.   Hath he given nothing to your lovely selfe?

COR.   He lov'd me not, & therfore gave me nothing,
Only because I could not flatter him:[1]
And in this day of tryumph to my sisters,
Doth Fortune tryumph in my overthrow.

KING.   Sweet Lady, say there should come a King,
As good as eyther of your sisters husbands,
To crave your love, would you accept of him?   660

COR.   Oh, doe not mocke with those in misery,
Nor do not think, though fortune have the power,
To spoyle mine honour, and debase my state,
That she hath any interest in my mind:
For if the greatest Monarch on the earth,
Should sue to me in this extremity,
Except my heart could love, and heart could like,
Better then any that I ever saw,
His great estate no more should move my mind,
Then mountaynes move by blast of every wind.   670

KING.   Think not, sweet Nymph, tis holy Palmers guise,
To grieved soules fresh torments to devise:
Therefore in witnesse of my true intent,
Let heaven and earth beare record of my words:
There is a young and lusty Gallian King,
So like to me, as I am to my selfe,
That earnestly doth crave to have thy love,
And joyne with thee in *Hymens* sacred bonds.

COR.   The like to thee did ne're these eyes behold;
Oh live to adde new torments to my griefe: 680

[1] I.1.231–4.

Why didst thou thus intrap me unawares?
Ah Palmer, my estate doth not befit
A kingly mariage, as the case now stands.
Whilome when as I liv'd in honours height,
A Prince perhaps might postulate my love:
Now misery, dishonour and disgrace,
Hath light on me, and quite reverst the case.
Thy King will hold thee wise, if thou surcease
The sute, whereas no dowry will insue.[1]
Then be advised, Palmer, what to do: 690
Cease for thy King, seeke for thy selfe to woo.

    KING.   Your birth's too high for any, but a King.

    COR.   My mind is low ynough to love a Palmer,
Rather then any King upon the earth.

    KING.   O, but you never can indure their life,
Which is so straight and full of penury.[2]

    COR.   O yes, I can, and happy if I might:
Ile hold thy Palmers staffe within my hand,
And thinke it is the Scepter of a Queene.
Sometime ile set thy Bonnet on my head,   700
And thinke I weare a rich imperiall Crowne,
Sometime Ile helpe thee in thy holy prayers,
And thinke I am with thee in Paradise.
Thus ile mock fortune, as she mocketh me,
And never will my lovely choyce repent:
For having thee, I shall have all content.

    KING.   'Twere sin to hold her longer in suspence,
Since that my soule hath vow'd she shall be mine.
Ah, deare *Cordella*, cordiall to my heart,
I am no Palmer, as I seeme to be,   710
But hither come in this unknowne disguise,
To view th' admired beauty of those eyes.
I am the King of Gallia, gentle mayd,
(Although thus slenderly accompanied)
And yet thy vassayle by imperious Love,
And sworne to serve thee everlastingly.

    COR.   What e're you be, of high or low discent,
All's one to me, I do request but this:
That as I am, you will accept of me,
And I will have you whatsoe're you be: 720
Yet well I know, you come of royall race,
I see such sparks of honour in your face.

[1] As does Burgundy in I.1.203–48.
[2] France pretends to be a poor Palmer; Edgar to be a mad beggar.

MUM. Have Palmers weeds such power to win fayre Ladies?
Fayth, then I hope the next that falles is myne:
Upon condition I no worse might speed,
I would for ever weare a Palmers weed.
I like an honest and playne dealing wench,
That sweares (without exceptions) I will have you.
These foppets, that know not whether to love a man or no,
except they first go aske their mothers leave, by this hand, I
hate them ten tymes worse then poyson.   730
    KING. What resteth then our happinesse to procure?
    MUM. Fayth, go to Church, to make the matter sure.
    KING. It shall be so, because the world shall say,
King *Leirs* three daughters were wedded in one day:
The celebration of this happy chaunce,
We will deferre, untill we come to Fraunce.
    MUM. I like the wooing, that's not long a doing.
Well, for her sake, I know what I know:
Ile never marry whilest I live,   740
Except I have one of these Brittish Ladyes.
My humour is alienated from the mayds of Fraunce.   [*Exeunt.*

[Sc. 8]   *Enter Perillus solus.*

    PER. The King hath dispossest himselfe of all,
Those to advaunce which scarce will give him thanks:
His youngest daughter he hath turnd away,
And no man knowes what is become of her.
He sojournes now in Cornwall with the eldest,[1]
Who flattred him, untill she did obtayne
That at his hands, which now she doth possesse: 750
And now she sees hee hath no more to give,
It grieves her heart to see her father live.
Oh, whom should man trust in this wicked age,
When children thus against their parents rage?
But he, the myrrour of mild patience,[2]
Puts up all wrongs, and never gives reply:
Yet shames she not in most opprobrious sort,
To call him foole and doterd to his face,
And sets her Parasites of purpose oft,
In scoffing wise to offer him disgrace.[3]   760
Oh yron age! O times! O monstrous, vilde,

---

[1] In Albany in *Lear*.
[2] Cf. II.4.271. Lear knows that he lacks patience.
[3] Hence Oswald, I.4.77–84.

When parents are contemned of the child!
His pension she hath halfe restrain'd from him,[1]
And will, e're long, the other halfe, I feare:
For she thinks nothing is bestowde in vayne,
But that which doth her fathers life maintayne.
Trust not alliance; but trust strangers rather,
Since daughters prove disloyall to the father.
Well, I will counsell him the best I can:
Would I were able to redresse his wrong.   770
Yet what I can, unto my utmost power,
He shall be sure of to the latest houre.   [*Exit.*

[Sc. 9]   *Enter Gonorill, and Skalliger.*

GON.   I prithy, *Skalliger*, tell me what thou thinkst:
Could any woman of our dignity
Endure such quips and peremptory taunts,
As I do daily from my doting father?[2]
Doth't not suffice that I him keepe of almes,
Who is not able for to keepe himselfe?
But as if he were our better, he should thinke   780
To check and snap me up at every word.
I cannot make me a new fashioned gowne,
And set it forth with more then common cost;
But his old doting doltish withered wit,
Is sure to give a sencelesse check for it.[3]
I cannot make a banquet extraordinary,
To grace my selfe, and spread my name abroad,
But he, old foole, is captious by and by,
And sayth, the cost would well suffice for twice.[4]
Judge then, I pray, what reason ist, that I   790
Should stand alone charg'd with his vaine expence,
And that my sister *Ragan* should go free,
To whom he gave as much, as unto me?
I prithy, *Skalliger*, tell me, if thou know,
By any meanes to rid me of this woe.
SKAL.   Your many favours still bestowde on me,
Binde me in duty to advise your Grace,
How you may soonest remedy this ill.
The large allowance which he hath from you,
Is that which makes him so forget himselfe: 800
Therefore abbridge it halfe, and you shall see,

---

[1] I.4.294.   [2] I.3.4–6.
[3] Did this suggest II.4.267–70?   [4] I.3.7–8.

That having lesse, he will more thankfull be:
For why, abundance maketh us forget
The fountaynes whence the benefits do spring.
  GON. Well, *Skalliger*, for thy kynd advice herein,
I will not be ungratefull, if I live:
I have restrayned halfe his portion already,[1]
And I will presently restrayne the other,
That having no meanes to releeve himselfe,[2]
He may go seeke elsewhere for better helpe.   [*Exit.*   810
  SKAL. Go, viperous woman, shame to all thy sexe:
The heavens, no doubt, will punish thee for this:
And me a villayne, that to curry favour,
Have given the daughter counsell 'gainst the father.
But us the world doth this experience give,
That he that cannot flatter, cannot live.   [*Exit.*

[Sc. 10]   *Enter King of Cornwall, Leir, Perillus & Nobles.*

  CORN. Father, what ayleth you to be so sad?[3]
Me thinks, you frollike not as you were wont.
  LEIR. The neerer we do grow unto our graves,   820
The lesse we do delight in worldly joyes.
  CORN. But if a man can frame himselfe to myrth,
It is a meane for to prolong his life.
  LEIR. Then welcome sorrow, *Leirs* only friend,
Who doth desire his troubled dayes had end.
  CORN. Comfort your selfe, father, here comes your daughter,
Who much will grieve, I know, to see you sad.   [*Enter Gonorill.*
  LEIR. But more doth grieve, I feare, to see me live.
  CORN. My *Gonorill*, you come in wished time,
To put your father from these pensive dumps.   830
In fayth, I feare that all things go not well.[4]
  GON. What do you feare, that I have angred him?
Hath he complaynd of me unto my Lord?
Ile provide him a piece of bread and cheese;
For in a time hee'l practise nothing else,
Then carry tales from one unto another.
Tis all his practise for to kindle strife,
'Twixt you, my Lord, and me your loving wife:
But I will take an order, if I can,

---

[1] Cf. I.4.246–51; 293–4.
[2] Cf. the two sisters, II.4.236–63.
[3] Albany, I.4.295.
[4] Cf. Gloucester, II.4.119.

To cease th' effect, where first the cause began.   840
    CORN.   Sweet, be not angry in a partiall cause,[1]
He ne're complaynd of thee in all his life.
Father, you must not weygh a womans words.
    LEIR.   Alas, not I: poore soule, she breeds yong bones,[2]
And that is it makes her so tutchy, sure.
    GON.   What, breeds young bones already! you will make
An honest woman of me then, belike.
O vild olde wretch! who ever heard the like,
That seeketh thus his owne child to defame?
    CORN.   I cannot stay to heare this discord sound.[3]   [*Exit.*   850
    GON.   For any one that loves your company,
You may go pack, and seeke some other place,[4]
To sowe the seed of discord and disgrace.   [*Exit.*
    LEIR.   Thus, say or do the best that e're I can,
Tis wrested straight into another sence.
This punishment my heavy sinnes deserve,
And more then this ten thousand thousand times:
Else aged *Leir* them could never find
Cruell to him, to whom he hath bin kind.
Why do I over-live my selfe, to see   860
The course of nature quite reverst in me?
Ah, gentle Death, if ever any wight
Did wish thy presence with a perfit zeale:
Then come, I pray thee, even with all my heart,
And end my sorrowes with thy fatall dart.[5]   [*He weepes.*
    PER.   Ah, do not so disconsolate your selfe,
Nor dew your aged cheeks with wasting teares.
    LEIR.   What man art thou that takest any pity
Upon the worthlesse state of old *Leir*?
    PER.   One, who doth beare as great a share of griefe,   870
As if it were my dearest fathers case.[6]
    LEIR.   Ah, good my friend, how ill art thou advisde,
For to consort with miserable men:[7]
Go learne to flatter, where thou mayst in time
Get favour 'mongst the mighty, and so clyme:
For now I am so poore and full of want,
As that I ne're can recompence thy love.

---

[1] Cf. I.4.312: 'I cannot be so partial, Goneril.'
[2] Cf. Lear, II.4.162: 'Strike her young bones'.
[3] Albany stays and asserts his innocence, I.4.273-4.
[4] This suggestion is Lear's at I.4.252-4.
[5] Lear is not cast down so easily.
[6] Cf. Kent, I.4.19-20.
[7] So the Fool, I.4.6-103.

PER.   What's got by flattery, doth not long indure;
And men in favour live not most secure.
My conscience tels me, if I should forsake you,   880
I were the hatefulst excrement on the earth:
Which well do know, in course of former time,
How good my Lord hath bin to me and mine.
    LEIR.   Did I ere rayse thee higher then the rest
Of all thy ancestors which were before?
    PER.   I ne're did seeke it; but by your good Grace,
I still injoyed my owne with quietnesse.
    LEIR.   Did I ere give thee living, to increase
The due revennues which thy father left?
    PER.   I had ynough, my Lord, and having that,   890
What should you need to give me any more?
    LEIR.   Oh, did I ever dispossesse my selfe,
And give thee halfe my Kingdome in good will?
    PER.   Alas, my Lord, there were no reason, why
You should have such a thought, to give it me.
    LEIR.   Nay, if thou talke of reason, then be mute;
For with good reason I can thee confute.
If they, which first by natures sacred law,
Do owe to me the tribute of their lives;
If they to whom I always have bin kinde,   900
And bountiful beyond comparison;
If they, for whom I have undone my selfe,
And brought my age unto this extreme want,
Do now reject, contemne, despise, abhor me,
What reason moveth thee to sorrow for me?[1]
    PER.   Where reason fayles, let teares confirme my love,
And speake how much your passions do me move.
Ah, good my Lord, condemne not all for one:
You have two daughters left[2] to whom I know
You shall be welcome, if you please to go.   910
    LEIR.   Oh, how thy words adde sorrow to my soule,
To thinke of my unkindnesse to *Cordella*!
Whom causelesse I did dispossesse of all,
Upon th' unkind suggestions of her sisters:
And for her sake, I thinke this heavy doome
Is falne on me, and not without desert:
Yet unto *Ragan* was I always kinde,
And gave to her the halfe of all I had:
It may be, if I should to her repayre,

[1] Cf. Lear, II.4.264–78: 'O! reason not the need . . .'
[2] Cf. I.4.254: 'Yet have I left a daughter'; 305.

She would be kinder, and intreat me fayre.   920
    PER.   No doubt she would, & practise ere't be long,
By force of Armes for to redresse your wrong.[1]
    LEIR.   Well, since thou doest advise me for to go,
I am resolv'd to try the worst of wo.   [*Exeunt.*

[Sc. 11]   *Enter Ragan solus.*

    RAG.   How may I blesse the howre of my nativity,
Which bodeth unto me such happy Starres!
How may I thank kind fortune, that vouchsafes
To all my actions, such desir'd event!
I rule the King of Cambria as I please: 930
The States are all obedient to my will;
And looke what ere I say, it shall be so;
Not any one, that dareth answere no.
My eldest sister lives in royall state,
And wanteth nothing fitting her degree:
Yet hath she such a cooling card withall,
As that her hony savoureth much of gall.
My father with her is quarter-master still,
And many times restraynes her of her will:
But if he were with me, and serv'd me so,   940
Ide send him packing some where else to go.
Ide entertayne him with such slender cost,
That he should quickly wish to change his host.   [*Exit.*

[Sc. 12]   *Enter Cornwall, Gonorill, and attendants.*

    CORN.   Ah, *Gonorill*, what dire unhappy chaunce
Hath sequestred thy father from our presence,
That no report can yet be heard of him?
Some great unkindnesse hath bin offred him,
Exceeding far the bounds of patience:
Else all the world shall never me perswade,   950
He would forsake us without notice made.
    GON.   Alas, my Lord, whom doth it touch so neere,
Or who hath interest in this griefe, but I,
Whom sorrow had brought to her longest home,
But that I know his qualities so well?[2]
I know, he is but stolne upon my sister
At unawares, to see her how she fares,
And spend a little time with her, to note

---

[1] Cf. Lear, I.4.305–8.
[2] Goneril is more masterful to Albany, I.4.341–6.

How all things goe, and how she likes her choyce:
And when occasion serves, heele steale from her,   960
And unawares returne to us agayne.
Therefore, my Lord, be frolick, and resolve
To see my father here agayne e're long.
    CORN.   I hope so too; but yet to be more sure,
Ile send a Poste immediately to know
Whether he be arrived there or no.   [*Exit.*
    GON.   But I will intercept the Messenger,
And temper him before he doth depart,
With sweet perswasions, and with sound rewards,
That his report shall ratify my speech,   970
And make my Lord cease further to inquire.
If he be not gone to my sisters Court,
As sure my mind presageth that he is,
He happely may, by travelling unknowne wayes,
Fall sicke, and as a common passenger,
Be dead and buried: would God it were so well;
For then there were no more to do, but this,
He went away, and none knowes where he is.
But say he be in Cambria with the King,
And there exclayme against me, as he will: 980
I know he is as welcome to my sister,
As water is into a broken ship.
Well, after him Ile send such thunderclaps
Of slaunder, scandall, and invented tales,
That all the blame shall be remov'd from me,
And unperceiv'd rebound upon himselfe.[1]
Thus with one nayle another Ile expell,
And make the world judge, that I usde him well.

       [*Enter the Messenger that should go to Cambria,[2] with a
                letter in his hand.*   990

    GON.   My honest friend, whither away so fast?
    MESS.   To Cambria, Madam, with letters from the king.
    GON.   To whom?
    MESS.   Unto your father, if he be there.
    GON.   Let me see them.   [*She opens them.*
    MESS.   Madam, I hope your Grace will stand
Betweene me and my neck-verse, if I be
Calld in question, for opening the Kings letters.[3]

---

[1] 1.4.332–40.
[2] Oswald is Goneril's messenger.
[3] Cf. Regan and Oswald, IV.5.21–3.

GON. 'Twas I that opened them, it was not thou.

MESS. I, but you need not care: and so must I, 1000
A hansome man, be quickly trust up,
And when a man's hang'd, all the world cannot save him.

GON. He that hangs thee, were better hang his father,
Or that but hurts thee in the least degree.
I tell thee, we make great account of thee.

MESS. I am o're-joy'd, I surfet of sweet words:
Kind Queene, had I a hundred lives, I would
Spend ninety nyne of them for you, for that word.

GON. I, but thou wouldst keepe one life still,
And that's as many as thou art like to have. 1010

MESS. That one life is not too deare for my good Queene;
this sword, this buckler, this head, this heart, these hands,
armes, legs, tripes, bowels, and all the members else whatsoever, are at your dispose; use me, trust me, commaund me:
if I fayle in any thing, tye me to a dung cart, and make a
Scavengers horse of me, and whip me, so long as I have any
skin on my back.

GON. In token of further imployment, take that.

[*Flings him a purse.*

MESS. A strong Bond, a firme Obligation, good in law,
good in law: if I keepe not the condition, let my necke be the
forfeyture of my negligence. 1020

GON. I like thee well, thou hast a good toung.

MESS. And as bad a toung if it be set on it, as any Oyster-
wife at Billinsgate hath: why, I have made many of my neighbours forsake their houses with rayling upon them, and go
dwell else where; and so by my meanes houses have bin good
cheape in our parish: My toung being well whetted with
choller, is more sharpe then a Razer of Palerno.

GON. O, thou art a fit man for my purpose.

MESS. Commend me not, sweet Queene, before you try me. 1030
As my deserts are, so do think of me.

GON. Well sayd, then this is thy tryall: Instead of carrying
the Kings letters to my father, carry thou these letters to my
sister, which contayne matter quite contrary to the other:
there shal she be given to understand, that my father hath
detracted her, given out slaundrous speaches against her; and
that hee hath most intollerably abused me, set my Lord and
me at variance, and made mutinyes amongst the commons.
These things (although it be not so)
Yet thou must affirme them to be true, 1040
With othes and protestations as will serve,

To drive my sister out of love with him,
And cause my will accomplished to be.[1]
This do, thou winst my favour for ever,
And makest a hye way of preferment to thee
And all thy friends.

    MESS.   It sufficeth, conceyt it is already done:
I will so toung-whip him, that I will[2]
Leave him as bare of credit, as a Poulter
Leaves a Cony, when she pulls off his skin.   1050

    GON.   Yet there is a further matter.

    MESS.   I thirst to heare it.

    GON.   If my sister thinketh convenient, as my letters im-
porteth, to make him away, hast thou the heart to effect it?[3]

    MESS.   Few words are best in so small a matter:
These are but trifles. By this booke I will.   [*kisses the paper.*

    GON.   About it presently, I long till it be done.

    MESS.   I fly, I fly.   [*Exeunt.*   1060

[Sc. 13]   *Enter Cordella solus.*

    I have bin over-negligent to-day,
In going to the Temple of my God,
To render thanks for all his benefits,
Which he miraculously hath bestowed on me,
In raysing me out of my meane estate,
When as I was devoyd of worldly friends,
And placing me in such a sweet content,
As far exceeds the reach of my deserts.
My kingly husband, myrrour of his time,   1070
For zeale, for justice, kindnesse, and for care
To God, his subjects, me, and Common weale,
By his appoyntment was ordayned for me.
I cannot wish the thing that I do want;
I cannot want the thing but I may have,
Save only this which I shall ne're obtayne,
My fathers love, oh this I ne're shall gayne.
I would abstayne from any nutryment,
And pyne my body to the very bones:
Bare foote I would on pilgrimage set forth   1080
Unto the furthest quarters of the earth,
And all my life time would I sackcloth weare,

---

[1] Cf. I.4.332–41.
[2] Cf. Lear, II.4.159, 'Struck me with her tongue.'
[3] Cf. Warner, ll.22–3 (Text VIII).

And mourning-wise powre dust upon my head:
So he but to forgive me once would please,
That his grey haires might go to heaven in peace.
And yet I know not how I him offended,
Or wherein justly I have deserved blame.
Oh sisters! you are much to blame in this,
It was not he, but you that did me wrong.
Yet God forgive both him, and you and me,   1090
Even as I doe in perfit charity.
I will to Church, and pray unto my Saviour,
That ere I dye, I may obtayne his favour.   [*Exit.*

[Sc. 14]   *Enter Leir and Perillus fayntly.*

PER.   Rest on me, my Lord, and stay your selfe,
The way seemes tedious to your aged lymmes.
    LEIR.   Nay, rest on me, kind friend, and stay thy selfe,
Thou art as old as I, but more kind.
    PER.   Ah, good my Lord, it ill befits, that I
Should leane upon the person of a King.   1100
    LEIR.   But it fits worse, that I should bring thee forth,
That had no cause to come along with me,
Through these uncouth paths, and tirefull wayes,
And never ease thy faynting limmes a whit.
Thou hast left all, I, all to come with me,
And I, for all, have nought to guerdon thee.
    PER.   Cease, good my Lord, to aggravate my woes,
With these kind words, which cuts my heart in two,
To think your will should want the power to do.
    LEIR.   Cease, good *Perillus*, for to call me Lord,   1110
And think me but the shaddow of my selfe.[1]
    PER.   That honourable title will I give,
Unto my Lord, so long as I do live.
Oh, be of comfort; for I see the place
Whereas your daughter keeps her residence.
And loe, in happy time the Cambrian Prince
Is here arriv'd, to gratify our comming.

[*Enter the Prince of Cambria, Ragan and Nobles: looke
upon them, and whisper together.*

    LEIR.   Were I best speak, or sit me downe and dye?   1120
I am asham'd to tell this heavy tale.
    PER.   Then let me tell it, if you please, my Lord:
Tis shame for them that were the cause thereof.

[1] Cf. Lear and Fool, I.4.229–31.

CAM.   What two old men are those that seeme so sad?[1]
Me thinks, I should remember well their lookes.
   RAG.   No, I mistake not, sure it is my father:
I must dissemble kindnesse now of force.[2]
            [She runneth to him, and kneels downe, saying:
Father, I bid you welcome, full of griefe,
To see your Grace usde thus unworthily,   1130
And ill befitting for your reverend age,
To come on foot a journey so indurable.
Oh, what disaster chaunce hath bin the cause,
To make your cheeks so hollow, spare and leane?
He cannot speake for weeping: for Gods love, come.
Let us refresh him with some needfull things,
And at more leysure we may better know,
Whence springs the ground of this unlookt for wo.
   CAM.   Come, father, e're we any further talke,
You shall refresh you after this weary walk.   1140
            [Exeunt, manet Ragan.
   RAG.   Comes he to me with finger in the eye,
To tell a tale against my sister here?
Whom I do know, he greatly hath abusde:
And now like a contentious crafty wretch,
He first begins for to complayne himselfe,
When as himselfe is in the greatest fault.
Ile not be partiall in my sisters cause,
Nor yet beleeve his doting vayne reports:
Who for a trifle (safely) I dare say,
Upon a spleene is stolen thence away: 1150
And here (forsooth) he hopeth to have harbour,
And to be moan'd and made on like a child:
But ere't be long, his comming he shall curse,
And truely say, he came from bad to worse:
Yet will I make fayre weather, to procure
Convenient meanes, and then ile strike it sure.[3]   *[Exit.*

[Sc. 15]   *Enter Messenger solus.*

   MESS.   Now happily I am arrived here,
Before the stately Palace of the Cambrian King:
If *Leir* be here safe-seated, and in rest,   1160

---

[1] In *Lear* the King sends Kent ahead with letters to Regan, I.5.1; II.1.123.
[2] Lear calls her 'tender-hefted' though she has refused to see him (II.4.87–90, 170–3).
[3] Cf. Goneril, I.3.25–6.

To rowse him from it I will do my best.[1]   *[Enter Ragan.*

Now bags of gold, your vertue is (no doubt)

To make me in my message bold and stout.

The King of heaven preserve your Majesty.

And send your Highnesse everlasting raigne.

    RAG.   Thanks, good my friend; but what imports thy
        message?

    MESS.   Kind greetings from the Cornwall Queene:

The residue these letters will declare.

              [She opens the letters.

    RAG.   How fares our royall sister?   1170

    MESS.   I did leave her at my parting, in good health.

        [She reads the letter, frownes and stamps.

See how her colour comes and goes agayne,

Now red as scarlet, now as pale as ash:

See how she knits her brow, and bytes her lips,

And stamps, and makes a dumbe shew of disdayne,

Mixt with revenge, and violent extreames.

Here will be more worke and more crownes for me.

    RAG.   Alas, poore soule, and hath he usde her thus?

And is he now come hither, with intent   1180

To set divorce betwixt my Lord and me?

Doth he give out, that he doth heare report,

That I do rule my husband as I list,

And therefore meanes to alter so the case,

That I shall know my Lord to be my head?

Well, it were best for him to take good heed,

Or I will make him hop without a head,

For this presumption, dottard that he is.

In Cornwall he hath made such mutinies,

First, setting of the King against the Queene;[2]   1190

Then stirring up the Commons 'gainst the King;

That had he there continued any longer,

He had bin call'd in question for his fact.

So upon that occasion thence he fled,

And comes thus slily stealing unto us:

And now already since his comming hither,

My Lord and he are growne in such a league,

That I can have no conference with his Grace:[3]

---

[1] In *Lear* Oswald arrives at the same time as Kent, and before the King.
(II.2.50.)

[2] Goneril's behaviour in I.4. turns Albany against her.

[3] Not so in *Lear*, where the fiery Duke puts Kent in the stocks, and supports his
wife.

I feare, he doth already intimate
Some forged cavillations 'gainst my state: 1200
Tis therefore best to cut him off in time,
Lest slaunderous rumours once abroad disperst,
It is too late for them to be reverst.
Friend, as the tennour of these letters shewes,
My sister puts great confidence in thee.[1]

    MESS.   She never yet committed trust to me.
But that (I hope) she found me alwayes faythfull:
So will I be to any friend of hers,
That hath occasion to imploy my helpe.

    RAG.   Hast thou the heart to act a stratagem,   1210
And give a stabbe or two, if need require?

    MESS.   I have a heart compact of Adamant,
Which never knew what melting pitty meant.
I weigh no more the murdring of a man,
Then I respect the cracking of a Flea,
When I doe catch her byting on my skin.
If you will have your husband or your father,
Or both of them sent to another world,
Do but commaund me doo't, it shall be done.

    RAG.   It is ynough, we make no doubt of thee: 1220
Meet us to morrow here, at nyne a clock:
Meane while, farewell, and drink that for my sake.   [*Exit.*

    MESS.   I, this is it will make me do the deed:
Oh, had I every day such customers,
This were the gainefulst trade in Christendome!
A purse of gold giv'n for a paltry stabbe!
Why, heres a wench that longs to have a stabbe.
Wel, I could give it her, and ne're hurt her neither.

    [Sc. 16]   *Enter the Gallian King, and Cordella.*

    KING.   When will these clouds of sorrow once disperse,   1230
And smiling joy tryumph upon thy brow?
When will this Scene of sadnesse have an end,
And pleasant acts insue, to move delight?
When will my lovely Queene cease to lament,
And take some comfort to her grieved thoughts?
If of thy selfe thou daignst to have no care
Yet pitty me, whom thy griefe makes despayre.

    COR.   O, grieve not you, my Lord, you have no cause:
Let not my passions move your mind a whit:

---

[1] Cf. IV.5.26–8.

For I am bound by nature, to lament   1240
For his ill will, that life to me first lent.
If so the stocke be dryed with disdayne,
Withered and sere the branch must needes remaine.
    KING.   But thou art now graft in another stock;
I am the stock, and thou the lovely branch:
And from my root continuall sap shall flow,
To make thee flourish with perpetuall spring.
Forget thy father and thy kindred now,
Since they forsake thee like inhumane beastes,
Thinke they are dead, since all their kindnesse dyes,   1250
And bury them, where black oblivion lyes.
Think not thou art the daughter of old *Leir*,
Who did unkindly disinherit thee:
But think thou art the noble Gallian Queene,
And wife to him that dearely loveth thee:
Embrace the joyes that present with thee dwell,
Let sorrow packe and hide her selfe in hell.
    COR.   Not that I misse my country or my kinne,
My old acquaintance or my ancient friends,
Doth any whit distemperate my mynd,   1260
Knowing you, which are more deare to me,
Then Country, kin, and all things els can be.
Yet pardon me, my gracious Lord, in this:
For what can stop the course of natures power?
As easy is it for foure-footed beasts,
To stay themselves upon the liquid ayre,
And mount aloft into the element,
And overstrip the feathered Fowles in flight:
As easy is it for the slimy Fish,
To live and thrive without the helpe of water: 1270
As easy is it for the Blackamoore,
To wash the tawny colour from his skin,
Which all oppose against the course of nature,
As I am able to forget my father.
    KING.   Myrrour of vertue, Phoenix of our age!
Too kind a daughter for an unkind father,
Be of good comfort; for I will dispatch
Ambassadors immediately for Brittayne,
Unto the King of Cornwalls Court, whereas
Your father keepeth now his residence,[1]   1280
And in the kindest maner him intreat,
That setting former grievances apart,

    [1] Kent in the stocks has a letter from Cordelia, II.2.163-70.

He will be pleasde to come and visit us.
If no intreaty will suffice the turne,
Ile offer him the halfe of all my Crowne:
If that moves not, weele furnish out a Fleet,
And sayle to Cornwall for to visit him;
And there you shall be firmely reconcilde
In perfit love, as earst you were before.

    COR.   Where toung cannot sufficient thanks afford,   1290
The King of heaven remunerate my Lord.

    KING.   Only be blithe, and frolick (sweet) with me:
This and much more ile do to comfort thee.

[Sc. 17]   *Enter Messenger solus.*

    MESS.   It is a world to see now I am flush,
How many friends I purchase every where!
How many seekes to creepe into my favour,
And kisse their hands, and bend their knees to me!
No more, here comes the Queene, now shall I know her mind,
And hope for to derive more crownes from her.   [*Enter Ragan.* 1300

    RAG.   My friend, I see thou mind'st thy promise well,
And art before me here, me thinks, to day.

    MESS.   I am poore man, and it like your Grace;
But yet I always love to keepe my word.

    RAG.   Wel, keepe thy word with me, & thou shalt see,
That of a poore man I will make thee rich.

    MESS.   I long to heare it, it might have bin dispatcht,
If you had told me of it yesternight.

    RAG.   It is a thing of right strange consequence,
And well I cannot utter it in words.   1310

    MESS.   It is more strange, that I am not by this
Beside my selfe, with longing for to heare it.
Were it to meet the Devill in his denne,
And try a bout with him for a scratcht face,
Ide undertake it, if you would but bid me.[1]

    RAG.   Ah, good my friend, that I should have thee do,
Is such a thing, as I do shame to speake;
Yet it must needs be done.

    MESS.   Ile speak it for thee, Queene: shall I kill thy father?
I know tis that, and if it be so, say.

    RAG.   I.   1320

    MESS.   Why, thats ynough.

    RAG.   And yet that is not all.

---

[1] This villain resembles Lightborn in Marlowe's *Edward II*, V.4.

N

MESS. What else?

RAG. Thou must kill that old man that came with him.

MESS. Here are two hands, for eche of them is one.

RAG. And for eche hand here is a recompence.

[*Give him two purses.*

MESS. Oh, that I had ten hands by myracle,
I could teare ten in pieces with my teeth,
So in my mouth yould put a purse of gold.   1330
But in what maner must it be effected?

RAG. To morrow morning ere the breake of day,
I by a wyle will send them to the thicket,
That is about some two myles from the Court,
And promise them to meet them there my selfe,
Because I must have private conference,
About some newes I have receyv'd from Cornwall.
This is ynough, I know, they will not fayle,
And then be ready for to play thy part:
Which done, thou mayst right easily escape,   1340
And no man once mistrust thee for the fact:
But yet, before thou prosecute the act,
Shew him the letter, which my sister sent
There let him read his owne inditement first,
And then proceed to execution:
But see thou faynt not; for they will speake fayre.

MESS. Could he speak words as pleasing as the pipe
Of *Mercury*, which charm'd the hundred eyes
Of watchfull *Argos*, and inforc'd him sleepe:
Yet here are words so pleasing to my thoughts, [*To the purse.* 1350
As quite shall take away the sound of his.   [*Exit.*

RAG. About it then, and when thou hast dispatcht,
Ile find a meanes to send thee after him.   [*Exit.*

[Sc. 18]   *Enter Cornwall and Gonorill.*

CORN. I wonder that the Messenger doth stay,
Whom we dispatcht for Cambria so long since:[1]
If that his answere do not please us well,
And he do shew good reason for delay,
Ile teach him how to dally with his King,
And to detayne us in such long suspence.   1360

GON. My Lord, I thinke the reason may be this:
My father meanes to come along with him;
And therefore tis his pleasure he shall stay,

---

[1] Cf. Lear, II.4.1-2.

For to attend upon him on the way.
   CORN.   It may be so, and therefore till I know
The truth thereof, I will suspend my judgement.

[*Enter Servant.*

   SER.   And't like your Grace, there is an Ambassador
Arrived from Gallia, and craves admittance to your Majesty.
   CORN.   From Gallia? what should his message   1370
Hither import? is not your father happely
Gone thither? well, whatsoere it be,
Bid him come in, he shall have audience.

[*Enter Ambassador.*

What newes from Gallia? speake Ambassador.
   AM.   The noble King and Queene of Gallia first salutes,
By me, their honourable father, my Lord *Leir*:
Next, they commend them kindly to your Graces,
As those whose wellfare they intirely wish.
Letters I have to deliver to my Lord *Leir*,   1380
And presents too, if I might speake with him.
   GON.   If you might speak with him? why, do you thinke,
We are afrayd that you should speake with him?
   AM.   Pardon me, Madam; for I thinke not so,
But say so only, 'cause he is not here.
   CORN.   Indeed, my friend, upon some urgent cause,
He is at this time absent from the Court:
But if a day or two you here repose,
Tis very likely you shall have him here,
Or else have certayne notice where he is.   1390
   GON.   Are not we worthy to receive your message?
   AM.   I had in charge to do it to himselfe.
   GON.   It may be then 'twill not be done in haste.
                              [*to herselfe.*
How doth my sister brooke the ayre of Fraunce?
   AM.   Exceeding well, and never sicke one houre,
Since first she set her foot upon the shore.
   GON.   I am the more sorry.
   AM.   I hope, not so, Madam.
   GON.   Didst thou not say, that she was ever sicke,
Since the first houre that she arrived there?   1400
   AM.   No, Madam, I sayd quite contrary.
   GON.   Then I mistooke thee.
   CORN.   Then she is merry, if she have her health.

AM.   Oh no, her griefe exceeds, untill the time,
That she be reconcil'd unto her father.

GON.   God continue it.

AM.   What, madam?

GON.   Why, her health.

AM.   Amen to that: but God release her griefe,
And send her father in a better mind,   1410
Then to continue alwayes so unkind.

CORN.   Ile be a mediator in her cause,
And seeke all meanes to expiat his wrath.

AM.   Madam, I hope your Grace will do the like.

GON.   Should I be a meane to exasperate his wrath
Against my sister, whom I love so deare? no, no.

AM.   To expiate or mittigate his wrath:
For he hath misconceyved without a cause.

GON.   O, I, what else?

AM.   Tis pity it should be so, would it were otherwise.   1420

GON.   It were great pity it should be otherwise.

AM.   Then how, Madam?

GON.   Then that they should be reconcilde againe.

AM.   It shewes you beare an honourable mind.

GON.   It shewes thy understanding to be blind,

                                        [*Speakes to herselfe.*
And that thou hadst need of an Interpreter:
Well, I will know thy message ere't be long,
And find a meane to crosse it, if I can.

CORN.   Come in, my friend, and frolick in our Court,
Till certayne notice of my father come.   [*Exeunt.*   1430

[Sc. 19]   *Enter Leir and Perillus.*

PER.   My Lord, you are up to day before your houre,
Tis newes to you to be abroad so rathe.

LEIR.   Tis newes indeed, I am so extreme heavy,
That I can scarcely keepe my eye-lids open.

PER.   And so am I, but I impute the cause
To rising sooner then we use to do.

LEIR.   Hither my daughter meanes to come disguis'd:
Ile sit me downe, and read untill she come.

                        [*Pull out a booke and sit downe.*   1440

PER.   Sheele not be long, I warrant you, my Lord:
But say, a couple of these they call good fellowes,
Should step out of a hedge, and set upon us,
We were in good case for to answere them.

LEIR.   'Twere not for us to stand upon our hands.

PER.   I feare, we scant should stand upon our legs.
But how should we do to defend our selves?
    LEIR.   Even pray to God, to blesse us from their hands:
For fervent prayer much ill hap withstands.
    PER.   Ile sit and pray with you for company;   1450
Yet was I ne're so heavy in my life.
                    [*They fall both asleepe.*

            Enter the Messenger or murtherer with two
                    daggers in his hands.[1]

    MESS.   Were it not a mad jest, if two or three of my profes-
sion should meet me, and lay me downe in a ditch, and play
robbe thiefe with me, & perforce take my gold away from
me, whilest I act this stratagem, and by this meanes the gray
beards should escape? Fayth, when I were at liberty againe,
I would make no more to do, but go to the next tree, and
there hang my selfe.   1460
            [*See them and start.*
But stay, me thinks, my youthes are here already,
And with pure zeale have prayed themselves asleepe.
I thinke, they know to what intent they came,
And are provided for another world.
            [*He takes their bookes away.*
Now could I stab them bravely, while they sleepe,[2]
And in a maner put them to no payne;
And doing so, I shewed them mighty friendship:
For feare of death is worse then death it selfe.   1470
But that my sweet Queene will'd me for to shew
This letter to them, ere I did the deed.
Masse, they begin to stirre: ile stand aside;
So shall I come upon them unawares.
            [*They wake and rise.*
    LEIR.   I marvell, that my daughter stayes so long.
    PER.   I feare, we did mistake the place, my Lord.
    LEIR.   God grant we do not miscarry in the place:
I had a short nap, but so full of dread,
As much amazeth me to think thereof.   1480
    PER.   Feare not, my Lord, dreames are but fantasies,
And slight imaginations of the brayne.
    MESS.   Perswade him so; but ile make him and you

---

[1] Perrett (*op. cit.*, p. 113) noted that in Lodge's *Euphues Shadow* (1592) the sorrow-ful Philamour 'entered a close thicket and in the mydst of his meditations fell a sleepe'. He was then attacked by robbers.
[2] Cf. 2nd Murderer in *R3*, I.4.110-11.

Confesse, that dreames do often prove too true.

    PER.   I pray, my Lord, what was the effect of it?
I may go neere to gesse what it pretends.

    MESS.   Leave that to me, I will expound the dreame.

    LEIR.   Me thought, my daughters, *Gonorill* & *Ragan*,
Stood both before me with such grim aspects,
Eche brandishing a Faulchion in their hand,   1490
Ready to lop a lymme off where it fell,
And in their other hands a naked poynyard,
Wherwith they stabd me in a hundred places,
And to their thinking left me there for dead:
But then my youngest daughter, fayre *Cordella*,
Came with a boxe of Balsome in her hand,
And powred it into my bleeding wounds,
By whose good meanes I was recovered well,
In perfit health, as earst I was before:
And with the feare of this I did awake,   1500
And yet for feare my feeble joynts do quake.[1]

    MESS.   Ile make you quake for something presently.
Stand, Stand.   [*They reele.*

    LEIR.   We do, my friend, although with much adoe.

    MESS.   Deliver, deliver.

    PER.   Deliver us, good Lord, from such as he.

    MESS.   You should have prayed before, while it was time,
And then perhaps, you might have scapt my hands:
But you, like faithfull watch-men, fell asleepe,
The whilst I came and tooke your Halberds from you.   1510
                  [*Shew their Bookes.*
And now you want your weapons of defence,
How have you any hope to be delivered?
This comes, because you have no better stay,
But fall asleepe, when you should watch and pray.

    LEIR.   My friend, thou seemst to be a proper man.

    MESS.   Sblood, how the old slave clawes me by the elbow!
He thinks, belike, to scape by scaping thus.

    PER.   And it may be, are in some need of money.

    MESS.   That to be false, behold my evidence.   1520
                  [*Shewes his purses.*

    LEIR.   If that I have will do thee any good,
I give it thee, even with a right good will.   [*Take it.*

    PER.   Here, take mine too, & wish with all my heart,
To do thee pleasure, it were twice as much.
         [*Take his, and weygh them both in his hands.*

[1] Cf. Clarence's dream in *R3*, I.4.9–63.

MESS.   Ile none of them, they are too light for me.
                    [*Puts them in his pocket.*
    LEIR.   Why then farewell: and if thou have occasion.
In any thing, to use me to the Queene,   1530
'Tis like ynough that I can pleasure thee.
                    [*They proffer to goe.*
    MESS.   Do you heare, do you heare, sir?
If I had occasion to use you to the Queene,
Would you do one thing for me I should aske?
    LEIR.   I, any thing that lyes within my power.
Here is my hand upon it, so farewell.   [*Proffer to goe.*
    MESS.   Heare you sir, heare you? pray, a word with you.
Me thinks, a comely honest ancient man
Should not dissemble with one for a vantage.   1540
I know, when I shall come to try this geare,
You will recant from all that you have sayd.
    PER.   Mistrust not him, but try him when thou wilt:
He is her father, therefore may do much.
    MESS.   I know he is, and therefore meane to try him:
You are his friend too, I must try you both.
    AMBO.   Prithy do, prithy do.   [*Proffer to go out.*
    MESS.   Stay gray-beards then, and prove men of your words:
The Queene hath tyed me by a solemne othe,
Here in this place to see you both dispatcht: 1550
Now for the safegard of my conscience,
Do me the pleasure for to kill your selves:
So shall you save me labour for to do it,
And prove your selves true old men of your words.
And here I vow in sight of all the world,
I ne're will trouble you whilst I live agayne.
    LEIR.   Affright us not with terrour, good my friend,
Nor strike such feare into our aged hearts.
Play not the Cat, which dallieth with the mouse;
And on a sudden maketh her a pray: 1560
But if thou art markt for the man of death
To me and to my *Damion*, tell me playne,
That we may be prepared for the stroke,
And make our selves fit for the world to come.
    MESS.   I am the last of any mortall race,
That ere your eyes are likely to behold,
And hither sent of purpose to this place,
To give a finall period to your dayes,
Which are so wicked, and have lived so long,
That your owne children seeke to short your life.   1570

LEIR.   Camst thou from France, of purpose to do this?

MESS.   From France? zoones, do I looke like a Frenchman?
Sure I have not mine owne face on; some body hath chang'd
faces with me, and I know not of it: But I am sure, my apparell
is all English. Sirra, what meanest thou to aske that question?
I could spoyle the fashion of this face for anger. A French face!

LEIR.   Because my daughter, whom I have offended,
And at whose hands I have deserv'd as ill,
As ever any father did of child,
Is Queene of Fraunce, no thanks at all to me,   1580
But unto God, who my injustice see.
If it be so, that shee doth seeke revenge,
As with good reason she may justly do,
I will most willingly resigne my life,
A sacrifice to mittigate her ire:[1]
I never will intreat thee to forgive,
Because I am unworthy for to live.
Therefore speake soone, & I will soone make speed:
Whether *Cordella* will'd thee do this deed?

MESS.   As I am a perfit gentleman, thou speakst French to me:
I never heard *Cordellaes* name before,
Nor never was in Fraunce in all my life:
I never knew thou hadst a daughter there,
To whom thou didst prove so unkind a churle:
But thy owne toung declares that thou hast bin
A vyle old wretch, and full of heynous sin.

LEIR.   Ah no, my friend, thou art deceyved much:
For her except, whom I confesse I wrongd,
Through doting frenzy, and o're-jelous love.
There lives not any under heavens bright eye,   1600
That can convict me of impiety.[2]
And therfore sure thou dost mistake the marke:
For I am in true peace with all the world.

MESS.   You are the fitter for the King of heaven:[3]
And therefore, for to rid thee of suspence,
Know thou, the Queenes of Cambria and Cornwall,
Thy owne two daughters, *Gonorill* and *Ragan*,
Appoynted me to massacre thee here.
Why wouldst thou then perswade me, that thou art
In charity with all the world? but now   1610
When thy owne issue hold thee in such hate,

[1] Cf. Lear to Cordelia, IV.7.72–5.
[2] Cf. Lear, III.2.59–60: 'I am a man / More sinn'd against than sinning.'
[3] Cf. *R3*, I.2.105–7.

That they have hyred me t'abbridge thy fate,
Oh, fy upon such vyle dissembling breath,
That would deceyve, even at the poynt of death.

    PER.   Am I awake, or is it but a dreame?

    MESS.   Feare nothing, man, thou art but in a dreame,
And thou shalt never wake untill doomes day,
By then, I hope, thou wilt have slept ynough.

    LEIR.   Yet, gentle friend, graunt one thing ere I die.

    MESS.   Ile graunt you any thing, except your lives.   1620

    LEIR.   Oh, but assure me by some certayne token,
That my two daughters hyred thee to this deed:
If I were once resolv'd of that, then I
Would wish no longer life, but crave to dye.

    MESS.   That to be true, in sight of heaven I sweare.[1]

    LEIR.   Sweare not by heaven, for feare of punishment:
The heavens are guiltlesse of such haynous acts.

    MESS.   I sweare by earth, the mother of us all.[2]

    LEIRE.   Sweare not by earth; for she abhors to beare
Such bastards, as are murtherers of her sonnes.   1630

    MESS.   Why then, by hell, and all the devils I sweare.

    LEIR.   Sweare not by hell; for that stands gaping wide,
To swallow thee, and if thou do this deed.

                [Thunder and lightning.

    MESS.   I would that word were in his belly agayne,
It hath frighted me even to the very heart:
This old man is some strong Magician:
His words have turned my mind from this exployt.
Then neyther heaven, earth, nor hell be witnesse;
But let this paper witnesse for them all.   1640

                [Shewes Gonorils letter.

Shall I relent, or shall I prosecute?
Shall I resolve, or were I best recant?
I will not crack my credit with two Queenes,
To whom I have already past my word.
Oh, but my conscience for this act doth tell,
I get heavens hate, earths scorne, and paynes of hell.

                [They blesse themselves.

    PER.   Oh just *Jehova*, whose almighty power
Doth governe all things in this spacious world,   1650
How canst thou suffer such outragious acts
To be committed without just revenge?[3]

---

[1] Clarence in *R3* is told that his two brothers hate him.
[2] Cf. *R3*, IV.4.369–89 for a series of oaths rejected.
[3] Cf. Albany's outcry, IV.2.46–50.

O viperous generation and accurst,
To seeke his blood, whose blood did make them first!

    LEIR.   Ah, my true friend in all extremity,
Let us submit us to the will of God:
Things past all sence, let us not seeke to know;
It is Gods will, and therefore must be so.
My friend, I am prepared for the stroke:
Strike when thou wilt, and I forgive thee here,[1]   1660
Even from the very bottome of my heart.

    MESS.   But I am not prepared for to strike.

    LEIR.   Farewell, *Perillus*, even the truest friend,
That ever lived in adversity:
The latest kindnesse ile request of thee,
Is that thou go unto my daughter Cordella,
And carry her her fathers latest blessing:
Withall desire her, that she will forgive me;
For I have wrongd her without any cause.
Now, Lord, receyve me, for I come to thee,   1670
And dye, I hope, in perfit charity.
Dispatch, I pray thee, I have lived too long.[2]

    MESS.   I, but you are unwise, to send an errand
By him that never meaneth to deliver it:
Why, he must go along with you to heaven:
It were not good you should go all alone.

    LEIR.   No doubt, he shal, when by the course of nature,
He must surrender up his due to death:
But that time shall not come, till God permit.

    MESS.   Nay, presently, to beare you company.   1680
I have a Passport for him in my pocket,
Already seald, and he must needs ride Poste.
               [*Shew a bagge of money.*

    LEIR.   The letter which I read, imports not so,
It only toucheth me, no word of him.

    MESS.   I, but the Queene commaunds it must be so,
And I am payd for him, as well as you.

    PER.   I, who have borne you company in life,
Most willingly will beare a share in death.
It skilleth not for me, my friend, a whit,   1690
Nor for a hundred such as thou and I.

    MESS.   Mary, but it doth, sir, by your leave; your good dayes
are past: though it bee no matter for you, tis a matter for me,
proper men are not so rife.

    PER.   Oh, but beware, how thou dost lay thy hand

[1] Cf. Gloucester to Oswald, IV.6.231–2.   [2] Cf. V.3.317.

Upon the high anoynted of the Lord:
O, be advised ere thou dost begin:
Dispatch me straight, but meddle not with him.
    LEIR.   Friend, thy commission is to deale with me,
And I am he that hath deserved all: 1700
The plot was layd to take away my life:
And here it is, I do intreat thee take it:
Yet for my sake, and as thou art a man,
Spare this my friend, that hither with me came:
I brought him forth, whereas he had not bin,
But for good will to beare me company.
He left his friends, his country and his goods,
And came with me in most extremity.
Oh, if he should miscarry here and dye,
Who is the cause of it, but only I?   1710
    MESS.   Why that am I, let that ne're trouble thee.
    LEIR.   O no, tis I. O, had I now to give thee
The monarchy of all the spacious world
To save his life, I would bestow it on thee:
But I have nothing but these teares and prayers,
And the submission of a bended knee.   [*kneele.*
O, if all this to mercy move thy mind,
Spare him, in heaven thou shalt like mercy find,
    MESS.   I am as hard to be moved as another, and yet me
thinks the strength of their perswasions stirres me a little.   1720
    PER.   My friend, if feare of the almighty power
Have power to move thee, we have sayd ynough:
But if thy mind be moveable with gold,
We have not presently to give it thee:
Yet to thy selfe thou mayst do greater good,
To keepe thy hands still undefilde from blood:
For do but well consider with thy selfe,
When thou hast finisht this outragious act,
What horrour still will haunt thee for the deed: 1730
Think this agayne, that they which would incense
Thee for to be the Butcher of their father,
When it is done, for feare it should be knowne,
Would make a meanes to rid thee from the world:
Oh, then art thou for ever tyed in chaynes
Of everlasting torments to indure,
Even in the hotest hole of grisly hell,
Such paynes, as never mortall toung can tell.
        [*It thunders. He quakes, and lets fall the Dagger next to*
                       Perillus.   1740

LEIR.　O, heavens be thanked, he wil spare my friend.
Now when thou wilt come make an end of me.

　　　　　　　　　　[*He lets fall the other dagger.*

　　PER.　Oh, happy sight! he meanes to save my Lord.
The King of heaven continue this good mind.

　　LEIR.　Why stayst thou to do execution?

　　MESS.　I am as wilfull as you for your life:
I will not do it, now you do intreat me.

　　PER.　Ah, now I see thou hast some sparke of grace.

　　MESS.　Beshrew you for it, you have put it in me:　　　1750
The parlosest old men, that ere I heard.
Well, to be flat, ile not meddle with you:
Here I found you, and here ile leave you:
If any aske you why the case so stands?
Say that your toungs were better then your hands.

　　　　　　　　　　　　　[*Exit Messenger.*

　　PER.　Farewell. If ever we together meet,
It shall go hard, but I will thee regreet.
Courage, my Lord, the worst is overpast;
Let us give thanks to God, and hye us hence.

　　LEIR.　Thou art deceyved; for I am past the best,　　　1760
And know not whither for to go from hence:
Death had bin better welcome unto me,
Then longer life to adde more misery.

　　PER.　It were not good to returne from whence we came,
Unto your daughter *Ragan* back againe.[1]
Now let us go to France, unto *Cordella*,
Your youngest daughter, doubtlesse she will succour you.

　　LEIR.　Oh, how can I perswade my selfe of that,
Since the other two are quite devoyd of love;
To whom I was so kind, as that my gifts,　　　1770
Might make them love me, if 'twere nothing else?

　　PER.　No worldly gifts, but grace from God on hye,
Doth nourish vertue and true charity.
Remember well what words *Cordella* spake,
What time you askt her, how she lov'd your Grace.
She sayd, her love unto you was as much,
As ought a child to beare unto her father.

　　LEIR.　But she did find, my love was not to her,
As should a father beare unto a child.

　　PER.　That makes not her love to be any lesse,　　　1780
If she do love you as a child should do:
You have tryed two, try one more for my sake,

　　　　[1] Cf. Gloucester's warning, III.6.93: 'I have o'erheard a plot of death upon him.'

Ile ne're intreat you further tryall make.
Remember well the dream you had of late,
And thinke what comfort it foretels to us.

    LEIR.   Come, truest friend, that ever man possest,
I know thou counsailst all things for the best:
If this third daughter play a kinder part,
It comes of God, and not of my desert.   [*Exeunt.*

[Sc. 20]   *Enter the Gallian Ambassador solus.*

    AM.   There is of late newes come unto the Court,   1791
That old Lord *Leir* remaynes in Cambria:
Ile hye me thither presently, to impart
My letters and my message unto him.
I never was lesse welcome to a place
In all my life time, then I have bin hither,
Especially unto the stately Queene,
Who would not cast one gracious looke on me,
But still with lowring and suspicious eyes,
Would take exceptions at each word I spake,   1800
And fayne she would have undermined me,
To know what my Ambassage did import:
But she is like to hop without her hope,
And in this matter for to want her will,
Though (by report) sheele hav't in all things else.
Well, I will poste away for Cambria:
Within these few dayes I hope to be there.   [*Exit.*

[Sc. 21]   *Enter the King and Queene of Gallia, & Mumford.*

    KING.   By this, our father understands our mind,
And our kind greetings sent to him of late: 1810
Therefore my mind presageth ere't be long,
We shall receyve from Brittayne happy newes.

    COR.   I feare, my sister will disswade his mind;
For she to me hath alwayes bin unkind.

    KING.   Feare not, my love, since that we know the worst,
The last meanes helpes, if that we misse the first:
If hee'le not come to Gallia unto us,
Then we will sayle to Brittayne unto him.

    MUM.   Well, if I once see Brittayne agayne,
I have sworne, ile ne're come home without my wench,   1820
And ile not be forsworne,
Ile rather never come home while I live.

COR. Are you sure, *Mumford*, she is a mayd still?

MUM. Nay, ile not sweare she is a mayd, but she goes for one:
Ile take her at all adventures, if I can get her.

COR. I, thats well put in.

MUM. Well put in? nay, it was ill put in; for had it
Bin as well put in, as ere I put in my dayes,
I would have made her follow me to Fraunce.

COR. Nay, you'd have bin so kind, as take her with you,   1830
Or else, were I as she,
I would have bin so loving, as Ide stay behind you:
Yet I must confesse, you are a very proper man,
And able to make a wench do more then she would do.

MUM. Well, I have a payre of slops for the nonce,
Will hold all your mocks.

KING. Nay, we see you have a hansome hose.

COR. I, and of the newest fashion.

MUM. More bobs, more: put them in still,
They'l serve instead of bumbast; yet put not in too many,   1840
lest the seames crack, and they fly out amongst you againe:
you must not think to outface me so easly in my mistris quarrel,
who if I see once agayne, ten teame of horses shall
not draw me away, till I have full and whole possession.

KING. I, but one teame and a cart will serve the turne.

COR. Not only for him, but also for his wench.

MUM. Well, you are two to one, ile give you over:
And since I see you so pleasantly disposed,
Which indeed is but seldome seene, ile clayme
A promise of you, which you shall not deny me: 1850
For promise is debt, & by this hand you promisd it me.
Therefore you owe it me, and you shall pay it me,
Or ile sue you upon an action of unkindnesse.

KING. Prithy, Lord *Mumford*, what promise did I make thee?

MUM. Fayth, nothing but this,
That the next fayre weather, which is very now,
You would go in progresse downe to the sea side,
Which is very neere.

KING. Fayth, in this motion I will joyne with thee,
And be a mediator to my Queene.   1860
Prithy, my Love, let this match go forward,
My mind foretels, 'twill be a lucky voyage.

COR. Entreaty needs not, where you may commaund,
So you be pleasde, I am right well content:
Yet, as the Sea I much desire to see,
So am I most unwilling to be seene.

KING.   Weele go disguised, all unknowne to any.
COR.   Howsoever you make one, ile make another.
MUM.   And I the third: oh, I am over-joyed!
See what love is, which getteth with a word,   1870
What all the world besides could ne're obtayne!
But what disguises shall we have, my Lord?
KING.   Fayth thus: my Queene & I wil be disguisde,
Like a playne country couple, and you shall be *Roger*
Our man, and wayt upon us: or if you will,
You shall go first, and we will wayt on you.
MUM.   'Twere more then time; this device is excellent.
Come let us about it.   [*Exeunt.*

[Sc. 22]   *Enter Cambria and Ragan with Nobles.*

CAM..   What strange mischance or unexpected hap   1880
Hath thus depriv'd us of our fathers presence?
Can no man tell us what's become of him,
With whom we did converse not two dayes since?
My Lords, let every where light-horse be sent,
To scoure about through all our Regiment.
Dispatch a Poste immediately to Cornwall,
To see if any newes be of him there;
My selfe will make a strickt inquiry here,
And all about our Cities neere at hand,
Till certayne newes of his abode be brought.   1890
RAG.   All sorrow is but counterfet to mine,
Whose lips are almost sealed up with griefe:
Mine is the substance, whilst they do but seeme
To weepe the losse, which teares cannot redeeme.
O, ne're was heard so strange a misadventure,
A thing so far beyond the reach of sence,
Since no mans reason in the cause can enter.
What hath remov'd my father thus from hence?
O, I do feare some charme or invocation
Of wicked spirits, or infernall fiends,   1900
Stird by *Cordella*, moves this innovation,
And brings my father timelesse to his end.
But might I know, that the detested Witch
Were certayne cause of this uncertayne ill,
My selfe to Fraunce would go in some disguise,
And with these nayles scratch out her hatefull eyes:[1]
For since I am deprived of my father,

[1] Cf. I.4.307–8; III.7.56–7.

I loath my life, and wish my death the rather.

 CAM. The heavens are just,[1] and hate impiety,
And will (no doubt) reveale such haynous crimes: 1910
Censure not any, till you know the right:
Let him be Judge, that bringeth truth to light.

 RAG. O, but my griefe, like to a swelling tyde,
Exceeds the bounds of common patience:
Nor can I moderate my toung so much,
To conceale them, whom I hold in suspect.

 CAM. This matter shall be sifted: if it be she,
A thousand Fraunces shall not harbour her.

     [Enter the Gallian Ambassador.

 AM. All happinesse unto the Cambrian King.   1920
 CAM. Welcom, my friend, from whence is thy Ambassage?
 AM. I came from Gallia, unto Cornwall sent,
With letters to your honourable father,
Whom there not finding, as I did expect,
I was directed hither to repayre.

 RAG. Frenchman, what is thy message to my father?
 AM. My letters, Madam, will import the same,
Which my Commission is for to deliver.

 RAG. In his absence you may trust us with your letters.
 AM. I must performe my charge in such a maner,   1930
As I have strict commaundement from the King.

 RAG. There is good packing twixt your King and you:
You need not hither come to aske for him,
You know where he is better then ourselves.

 AM. Madam, I hope, nor far off.
 RAG. Hath the young murdresse, your outragious Queene,
No meanes to colour her detested deeds,
In finishing my guiltlesse fathers dayes,
(Because he gave her nothing to her dowre)
But by the colour of a fayn'd Ambassage,   1940
To send him letters hither to our Court?
Go carry them to them that sent them hither,
And bid them keepe their scroules unto themselves:
They cannot blind us with such slight excuse,
To smother up so monstrous vild abuse.
And were it not, it is 'gainst law of Armes,
To offer violence to a Messenger,
We would inflict such torments on thy selfe,
As should inforce thee to reveale the truth.

[1] Cf. IV.2.78–9; V.3.171–2.

AM.   Madam, your threats no whit apall my mind,   1950
I know my conscience guiltlesse of this act;
My King and Queene, I dare be sworne, are free
From any thought of such impiety:
And therefore, Madam, you have done them wrong,
And ill beseeming with a sisters love,
Who in meere duty tender him as much,
As ever you respected him for dowre.
The King your husband will not say as much.
   CAM.   I will suspend my judgement for a time,
Till more apparance give us further light: 1960
Yet to be playne, your comming doth inforce
A great suspicion to our doubtful mind,
And that you do resemble, to be briefe,
Him that first robs, and then cries, Stop the theefe.
   AM.   Pray God some neere you have not done the like.
   RAG.   Hence, saucy mate, reply no more to us;
                                         [*She strikes him.*[1]
For law of Armes shall not protect thy toung.
   AM.   Ne're was I offred such discourtesy;
God and my King, I trust, ere it be long,
Will find a meane to remedy this wrong,   [*Exit Amb.* 1970
   RAG.   How shall I live, to suffer this disgrace,
At every base and vulgar peasants hands?
It ill befitteth my imperiall state,
To be thus usde, and no man take my part.   [*Shee weeps.*
   CAM.   What should I do? infringe the law of Armes,
Were to my everlasting obloquy:
But I will take revenge upon his master,
Which sent him hither, to delude us thus.
   RAG.   Nay, if you put up this, be sure, ere long,
Now that my father thus is made away,   1980
Sheele come & clayme a third part of your Crowne,
As due unto her by inheritance.
   CAM.   But I will prove her title to be nought
But shame, and the reward of Parricide,
And make her an example to the world,
For after-ages to admire her penance.
This will I do, as I am Cambriaes King,
Or lose my life, to prosecute revenge.
Come, first let's learne what newes is of our father,
And then proceed, as best occasion fits.   [*Exeunt.* 1990

---

[1] Cf. her violence in III.7.34, 80.

[Sc. 23]   *Enter Leir, Perillus, and two Marriners, in*
sea-gownes and sea-caps.

PER.   My honest friends, we are asham'd to shew
The great extremity of our present state,
In that at this time we are brought so low,
That we want money for to pay our passage.
The truth is so, we met with some good fellowes,
A little before we came aboord your ship,
Which stript us quite of all the coyne we had,
And left us not a penny in our purses: 2000
Yet wanting mony, we will use the meane,
To see you satisfied to the uttermost.   [*Looke on Leir.*
    1 MAR.   Heres a good gown, 'twould become me passing wel,
I should be fine in it.   [*Looke on Perillus.*
    2 MAR.   Heres a good cloke, I marvel how I should look in it.
    LEIR.   Fayth, had we others to supply their roome,
Though ne'er so meane, you willingly should have them.
    1 MAR.   Do you heare, sir? you looke like an honest man;
Ile not stand to do you a pleasure: here's a good strong motly
gaberdine, cost me xiiii. good shillings at Billingsgate; give me
your gowne for it, & your cap for mine, & ile forgive your   2010
passage.
    LEIR.   With al my heart, and xx. thanks. [*Leir & he changeth.*
    2 MAR.   Do you heare, sir? you shal have a better match
then he, because you are my friend: here is a good sheeps
russet sea-gowne, wil bide more stresse, I warrant you, then
two of his, yet for you seem to be an honest gentleman, I am
content to change it for your cloke, and aske you nothing for
your passage more.
                         [*Pull off Perillus cloke.*
    PER.   My owne I willingly would change with thee,
And think my selfe indebted to thy kindnesse: 2020
But would my friend might keepe his garment still.
My friend, ile give thee this new dublet, if thou wilt
Restore his gowne unto him back agayne.
    1 MAR.   Nay, if I do, would I might ne're eate powderd
beefe and mustard more, nor drink Can of good liquor whilst
I live. My friend, you have small reason to seeke to hinder me
of my bargaine: but the best is, a bargayne's a bargayne.
    LEIR.   Kind friend, it is much better as it is; [*Leir to Perillus.*[1]
For by this meanes we may escape unknowne,

---

[1] The exchange of garments may have suggested the several allusions to clothing
in III.4, III.6, IV.7.

Till time and opportunity do fit.   2030
   2 MAR. Hark, hark, they are laying their heads together,
Theile repent them of their bargayne anon,
'Twere best for us to go while we are well.
   1 MAR. God be with you, sir, for your passage back agayne,
Ile use you as unreasonable as another.
   LEIR. I know thou wilt; but we hope to bring ready money
With us, when we come back agayne.   [*Exeunt Mariners.*
Were ever men in this extremity,
In a strange country, and devoyd of friends,
And not a penny for to helpe our selves?   2040
Kind friend, what thinkst thou will become of us?
   PER. Be of good cheere, my Lord, I have a dublet,
Will yeeld us mony ynough to serve our turnes,
Untill we come unto your daughters Court:
And then, I hope, we shall find friends ynough.
   LEIR. Ah, kind *Perillus*, that is it I feare,
And makes me faynt, or ever I come there.
Can kindnesse spring out of ingratitude?
Or love be reapt, where hatred hath bin sowne?
Can Henbane joyne in league with Methridate?   2050
Or Sugar grow in Wormwoods bitter stalke?
It cannot be, they are too opposite:
And so am I to any kindnesse here.
I have throwne Wormwood on the sugred youth,
And like to Henbane poysoned the Fount,
Whence flowed the Methridate of a childs goodwil:
I, like an envious thorne, have prickt the heart,
And turnd sweet Grapes, to sowre unrelisht Sloes:
The causeless ire of my respectlesse brest,
Hath sowrd the sweet milk of dame Natures paps: 2060
My bitter words have gauld her hony thoughts,
And weeds of rancour chokt the flower of grace.
Then what remainder is of any hope,
But all our fortunes will go quite aslope?[1]
   PER. Feare not, my Lord, the perfit good indeed,
Can never be corrupted by the bad:
A new fresh vessell still retaynes the taste
Of that which first is powr'd into the same:
And therfore, though you name yourselfe the thorn,
The weed, the gall, the henbane & the wormewood;   2070
Yet sheele continue in her former state,
The hony milke, Grape, Sugar, Methridate.

   [1] Cf. IV.3.44–9.

LEIR. Thou pleasing Orator unto me in wo,
Cease to beguile me with thy hopefull speaches:
O joyne with me, and thinke of nought but crosses,
And then weele one lament anothers losses.

PER. Why, say the worst, the worst can be but death,[1]
And death is better then for to despaire:
Then hazzard death, which may convert to life;
Banish despaire, which brings a thousand deathes.   2080

LEIR. Orecome with thy strong arguments, I yeeld,
To be directed by thee, as thou wilt:
As thou yeeldst comfort to my crazed thoughts,[2]
Would I could yeeld the like unto thy body,
Which is full weake, I know, and ill apayd,
For want of fresh meat and due sustenance.

PER. Alack, my Lord, my heart doth bleed, to think
That you should be in such extremity.

LEIR. Come, let us go, and see what God will send;
When all meanes faile, he is the surest friend.   [*Exeunt.* 2090

[Sc. 24] *Enter the Gallian King and Queene, and Mumford,*
with a basket, disguised like Countrey folke.

KING. This tedious journey all on foot, sweet Love,
Cannot be pleasing to your tender joynts,
Which ne're were used to these toylesome walks.

COR. I never in my life tooke more delight
In any journey, then I do in this:
It did me good, when as we hapt to light
Amongst the merry crue of country folke,
To see what industry and paynes they tooke,   2100
To win them commendations 'mongst their friends.
Lord, how they labour to bestir themselves,
And in their quirks to go beyond the Moone,
And so take on them with such antike fits,
That one would think they were beside their wits!
Come away, *Roger*, with your basket.

MUM. Soft, Dame, here comes a couple of old youthes,
I must needs make my selfe fat with jesting at them.
                    [*Enter Leir & Perillus very faintly.*

COR. Nay, prithy do not, they do seeme to be   2110
Men much o'regone with griefe and misery.
Let's stand aside, and harken what they say.

---

[1] Cf. Edgar in IV.1.27–8, V.2.9–11, etc.
[2] 'impaired, sick thoughts', not 'insane'.

LEIR.   Ah, my *Perillus,* now I see we both
Shall end our dayes in this unfruitfull soyle.
Oh, I do faint for want of sustenance:
And thou, I know, in little better case.
No gentle tree affords one taste of fruit,
To comfort us, untill we meet with men:
No lucky path conducts our lucklesse steps
Unto a place where any comfort dwels.
Sweet rest betyde unto our happy soules;   2120
For here I see our bodies must have end.
   PER.   Ah, my deare Lord, how doth my heart lament,
To see you brought to this extremity!
O, if you love me, as you do professe,
Or ever thought well of me in my life,   [*He strips up his arme.*
Feed on this flesh, whose veynes are not so dry,
But there is vertue left to comfort you.
O, feed on this, if this will do you good,
Ile smile for joy, to see you suck my bloud.
   LEIR.   I am no Caniball, that I should delight   2130
To slake my hungry jawes with humane flesh:
I am no devill, or ten times worse then so,
To suck the bloud of such a peerelesse friend.
O, do not think that I respect my life
So dearely, as I do thy loyall love.
Ah, Brittayne, I shall never see thee more,
That hast unkindly banished thy King:
And yet not thou dost make me to complayne,
But they which were more neere to me then thou.
   COR.   What do I heare? this lamentable voyce,   2140
Me thinks, ere now I often times have heard.
   LEIR.   Ah, *Gonorill,* was halfe my Kingdomes gift
The cause that thou dist seeke to have my life?
Ah, cruell *Ragan,* did I give thee all,
And all could not suffice without my bloud?
Ah, poore *Cordella,* did I give thee nought,
Nor never shall be able for to give?
O, let me warne all ages that insueth,
How they trust flattery, and reject the trueth.
Well, unkind Girles, I here forgive you both,   2150
Yet the just heavens will hardly do the like;
And only crave forgivenesse at the end
Of good *Cordella,* and of thee, my friend;
Of God, whose Majesty I have offended,
By my transgression many thousand wayes:

Of her, deare heart, whom I for no occasion
Turn'd out of all, through flatterers perswasion:
Of thee, kind friend, who but for me, I know,
Hadst never come unto this place of wo.

    COR.   Alack, that ever I should live to see   2160
My noble father in this misery.[1]

    KING.   Sweet Love, reveale not what thou art as yet,
Untill we know the ground of all this ill.

    COR.   O, but some meat, some meat: do you not see,
How neere they are to death for want of food?

    PER.   Lord, which didst help thy servants at their need,
Or now or never send us helpe with speed.
Oh comfort, comfort! yonder is a banquet,
And men and women, my Lord: be of good cheare:
For I see comfort comming very neere.   2170
O my Lord, a banquet, and men and women![2]

    LEIR.   O, let kind pity mollify their hearts,
That they may helpe us in our great extreames.

    PER.   God save your, friends; & if this blessed banquet
Affordeth any food or sustenance,
Even for his sake that saved us all from death,
Vouchsafe to save us from the gripe of famine.

                        [She bringeth him to the table.

    COR.   Here father, sit and eat, here, sit & drink:
And would it were far better for your sakes.

               [Perillus takes Leir by the hand to the table.   2180

    PER.   Ile give you thanks anon: my friend doth faynt,
And needeth present comfort.   *[Leir drinks.*

    MUM.   I warrant, he ne're stayes to say grace:
O, theres no sauce to a good stomake.

    PER.   The blessed God of heaven hath thought upon us.

    LEIR.   The thanks be his, and these kind courteous folke,
By whose humanity we are preserved.

                     [They eat hungerly, Leir drinkes.

    COR.   And may that draught be unto him, as was
That which old *Eson* dranke, which did renue
His withered age, and made him young againe.[3]   2190
And may that meat be unto him, as was
That which *Elias* ate, in strength whereof

---

[1] Cf. Cordelia's stronger reaction in IV.7.26–42.
[2] Cf. Orlando and old Adam in *AYL*, II.6, 7.
[3] Aeson, Jason's father, old and infirm when his son returned with the Golden Fleece, had his youth renewed by Medea.

He walked fourty dayes, and never faynted.[1]
Shall I conceale me longer from my father?
Or shall I manifest my selfe to him?
   KING.   Forbeare a while, untill his strength returne,
Lest being over joyed with seeing thee,
His poore weake sences should forsake their office,[2]
And so our cause of joy be turnd to sorrow.
   PER.   What chere, my Lord? how do your feel yourselfe?   2200
   LEIR.   Me thinks, I never ate such savory meat:
It is as pleasant as the blessed Manna,
That raynd from heaven amongst the Israelites:
It hath recall'd my spirits home agayne,
And made me fresh, as earst I was before.
But how shall we congratulate their kindnesse?
   PER.   Infayth, I know not how sufficiently;
But the best meane that I can think on, is this:
Ile offer them my dublet in requitall;
For we have nothing else to spare.   2210
   LEIR.   Nay, stay, *Perillus*, for they shall have mine.
   PER.   Pardon, my Lord, I sweare they shall have mine.
         [Perillus proffers his dublet: they will not take it.
   LEIR.   Ah, who would think such kindnes should remayne
Among such strange and unacquainted men:
And that such hate should harbour in the brest
Of those, which have occasion to be best?
   COR.   Ah, good old father, tell to me thy griefe,
Ile sorrow with thee, if not adde reliefe.
   LEIR.   Ah, good young daughter, I may call thee so;   2220
For thou art like a daughter I did owe.
   COR.   Do you not owe her still? what, is she dead?
   LEIR.   No, God forbid: but all my interest's gone,
By shewing my selfe too much unnaturall:
So have I lost the title of a father,
And may be call'd a stranger to her rather.
   COR.   Your title's good still; for tis alwayes knowne,
A man may do as him list with his owne.
But have you but one daughter then in all?
   LEIR.   Yes, I have more by two, then would I had.   2230
   COR.   O, say not so, but rather see the end:
They that are bad, may have the grace to mend:
But how have they offended you so much?
   LEIR.   If from the first I should relate the cause,

---

[1] I *Kings* 19. 8.
[2] Cf. the Doctor, IV.7.78–82, and Gloucester's death, V.3.196–200.

'Twould make a heart of Adamant to weepe;
And thou, poore soule, kind-hearted as thou art,
Dost weepe already, ere I do begin.
    COR.   For Gods love tell it, and when you have done,
Ile tell the reason why I weepe so soone.
    LEIR.   Then know this first, I am a Brittayne borne,   2240
And had three daughters by one loving wife:
And though I say it, of beauty they were sped;
Especially the youngest of the three,
For her perfections hardly matcht could be:
On these I doted with a jelous love,
And thought to try which of them lov'd me best,
By asking them, which would do most for me?
The first and second flattred me with words,
And vowd they lov'd me better then their lives:
The youngest sayd, she loved me as a child   2250
Might do: her answere I esteeme'd most vild,
And presently in an outragious mood,
I turned her from me to go sinke or swym:
And all I had, even to the very clothes,
I gave in dowry with the other two:
And she that best deserv'd the greatest share,
I gave her nothing, but disgrace and care.
Now mark the sequell: When I had done thus,
I sojournd in my eldest daughters house,
Where for a time I was intreated well,   2260
And liv'd in state sufficing my content:
But every day her kindnesse did grow cold,
Which I with patience put up well ynough,
And seemed not to see the things I saw:[1]
But at the last she grew so far incenst
With moody fury, and with causlesse hate,
That in most vild and contumelious termes,
She bade me pack, and harbour somewhere else.
Then was I fayne for refuge to repayre
Unto my other daughter for reliefe,   2270
Who gave me pleasing and most courteous words;
But in her actions shewed her selfe so sore,
As never any daughter did before:
She prayd me in a morning out betime,
To go to a thicket two miles from the Court,
Poynting that there she would come talke with me:
There she had set a shaghayrd murdring wretch,

[1] Cf. I.4.66–70.

To massacre my honest friend and me.
Then judge your selfe, although my tale be briefe,
If ever man had greater cause of griefe.   2280
    KING.   Nor never like impiety was done,
Since the creation of the world begun.
    LEIR.   And now I am constraind to seeke reliefe
Of her, to whom I have bin so unkind;
Whose censure, if it do award me death,
I must confesse she payes me but my due:
But if she shew a loving daughters part,
It comes of God and her, not my desert.
    COR.   No doubt she will, I dare be sworne she will.
    LEIR.   How know you that, not knowing what she is?   2290
    COR.   My selfe a father have a great way hence,
Usde me as ill as ever you did her;
Yet, that his reverend age I once might see,
Ide creepe along, to meet him on my knee.
    LEIR.   O, no mens children are unkind but mine.
    COR.   Condemne not all, because of others crime:
But looke, deare father, looke behold and see
Thy loving daughter speaketh unto thee.   [*She kneeles.*
    LEIR.   O, stand thou up, it is my part to kneele,
And aske forgivenesse for my former faults.   [*he kneeles.*[1] 2300
    COR.   O, if you wish I should injoy my breath,
Deare father rise, or I receive my death.   [*he riseth.*
    LEIR.   Then I will rise to satisfy your mind,
But kneele againe, til pardon be resignd.   [*he kneeles.*
    COR.   I pardon you: the word beseemes not me:
But I do say so, for to ease your knee.
You gave me life, you were the cause that I
Am what I am, who else had never bin.
    LEIR.   But you gave life to me and to my friend,
Whose dayes had else had an untimely end.   2310
    COR.   You brought me up, when as I was but young,
And far unable for to helpe my selfe.
    LEIR.   I cast thee forth, when as thou wast but young,
And far unable for to helpe thy selfe.
    COR.   God, world and nature say I do you wrong,
That can indure to see you kneele so long.
    PER[2].   Let me breake off this loving controversy,
Which doth rejoyce my very soule to see.
Good father, rise, she is your loving daughter,   [*He riseth.*

---

[1] Cf. IV.7.57–9; 'No, sir, you must not kneel.'
[2] KING. *1605.*

And honours you with as respective duty,   2320
As if you were the Monarch of the world.
    COR.   But I will never rise from off my knee,   [*She kneeles.*
Untill I have your blessing, and your pardon[1]
Of all my faults committed any way,
From my first birth unto this present day.
    LEIR.   The blessing, which the God of *Abraham* gave
Unto the trybe of *Juda*, light on thee,
And multiply thy dayes, that thou mayst see
Thy childrens children prosper after thee.
Thy faults, which are just none that I do know,   2330
God pardon on high, and I forgive below.   [*She riseth.*
    COR.   Now is my heart at quiet, and doth leape
Within my brest, for joy of this good hap:
And now (deare father) welcome to our Court,
And welcome (kind *Perillus*) unto me,
Myrrour of vertue and true honesty.
    LEIR.   O, he hath bin the kindest friend to me,
That ever man had in adversity.
    PER.   My toung doth faile, to say what heart doth think,
I am so ravisht with exceeding joy.   2340
    KING.   All you have spoke: now let me speak my mind,
And in few words much matter here conclude: [*he kneeles.*
If ere my heart do harbour any joy,
Or true content repose within my brest,
Till I have rooted out this viperous sect,
And repossest my father of his Crowne,
Let me be counted for the perjurdst man,
That ever spake word since the world began.   [*rise.*
    MUM.   Let me pray to, that never pray'd before;
                             [*Mumford kneeles.*
If ere I resalute the Brittish earth,   2350
(As (ere't be long) I do presume I shall)
And do returne from thence without my wench,
Let me be gelded for my recompence.   [*rise.*
    KING.   Come, let's to armes for to redresse this wrong:
Till I am there, me thinks, the time seemes long.   [*Exeunt.*

                [Sc. 25]   *Enter Ragan sola.*

    RAG.   I feele a hell of conscience in my brest,
Tormenting me with horrour for my fact,
And makes me in an agony of doubt,

[1] Cf. IV.7.57–8; V.3.10–11.

For feare the world should find my dealing out.   2360
The slave whom I appoynted for the act,
I ne're set eye upon the peasant since:
O, could I get him for to make him sure,
My doubts would cease, and I should rest secure.
But if the old men, with perswasive words,
Have sav'd their lives, and made him to relent;
Then are they fled unto the Court of Fraunce,
And like a Trumpet manifest my shame.
A shame on these white-liverd slaves, say I,
That with fayre words so soone are overcome.   2370
O God, that I had bin but made a man;
Or that my strength were equall with my will!
These foolish men are nothing but meere pity,
And melt as butter doth against the Sun.
Why should they have preeminence over us,
Since we are creatures of more brave resolve?
I sweare, I am quite out of charity
With all the heartlesse men in Christendome.
A poxe upon them, when they are affrayd
To give a stab, or slit a paltry Wind-pipe,   2380
Which are so easy matters to be done.
Well, had I thought the slave would serve me so,
My selfe would have bin executioner:
Tis now undone, and if that it be knowne,
Ile make as good shift as I can for one.
He that repines at me, how ere it stands,
'Twere best for him to keepe him from my hands.   [*Exit.*

[Sc. 26]   *Sound Drums & Trumpets: Enter the Gallian King,*
Leir, Mumford and the army.

KING.   Thus have we brought our army to the sea,   2390
Whereas our ships are ready to receyve us:
The wind stands fayre, and we in foure houres sayle
May easily arrive on Brittish shore,
Where unexpected we may them surprise,
And gayne a glorious victory with ease.
Wherefore, my loving Countreymen, resolve,
Since truth and justice fighteth on our sides,
That we shall march with conquest where we go.
My selfe will be as forward as the first,
And step by step march with the hardiest wight: 2400
And not the meanest souldier in our Campe

Shall be in danger, but ile second him.
To you, my Lord, we give the whole commaund
Of all the army, next unto our selfe,
Not doubting of you, but you will extend
Your wonted valour in this needfull case,
Encouraging the rest to do the like,
By your approved magnanimity.

MUM.   My Lege, tis needlesse to spur a willing horse,
Thats apt enough to run himselfe to death: 2410
For here I sweare by that sweet Saints bright eye,
Which are the starres, which guide me to good hap,
Eyther to see my old Lord crown'd anew,
Or in his cause to bid the world adieu.

LEIR.   Thanks, good Lord *Mumford*, tis more of your good will,
Then any merit or desert in me.

MUM.   And now to you, my worthy Countrymen,
Ye valiant race of Genovestan Gawles,
Surnamed Red-shanks, for your chyvalry,
Because you fight up to the shanks in bloud;   2420
Shew your selves now to be right Gawles indeed,
And be so bitter on your enemies,
That they may say, you are as bitter as Gall.
Gall them, brave Shot, with your Artillery:
Gall them, brave Halberts, with your sharp point Billes,
Each in their poynted place, not one, but all,
Fight for the credit of your selves and Gawle.

KING.   Then what should more perswasion need to those,
That rather wish to deale, then heare of blowes?
Let's to our ships, and if that God permit,   2430
In foure houres sayle, I hope we shall be there.

MUM.   And in five houres more, I make no doubt,
But we shall bring our wish'd desires about.   [*Exeunt.*

[Sc. 27]   *Enter a Captayne of the watch, and two watchmen.*

CAP.   My honest friends, it is your turne to night,
To watch in this place, neere about the Beacon,
And vigilantly have regard,
If any fleet of ships passe hitherward:
Which if you do, your office is to fire
The Beacon presently, and raise the towne.   [*Exit.*   2440

1 WAT.   I, I, I, feare nothing; we know our charge, I
warrant: I have bin a watchman about this Beacon this xxx.
yere, and yet I ne're see it stir, but stood as quietly as might be.

2 WAT.   Fayth neighbour, and you'l follow my vice, in-

stead of watching the Beacon, wee'l go to goodman *Gennings*,
& watch a pot of Ale and a rasher of Bacon: and if we do not
drink our selves drunke, then so; I warrant, the Beacon will
see us when we come out agayne.

 1 WAT. I, but how if some body excuse us to the Captayne?

 2 WAT. Tis no matter, ile prove by good reason that we 2450
watch the Beacon: asse for example.

 1 WAT. I hope you do not call me asse by craft, neighbour.

 2 WAT. No, no, but for example: Say here stands the pot
of ale, thats the Beacon. 1 WAT. I, I, tis a very good Beacon.

 2 WAT. Well, say here stands your nose, thats the fire.

 1 WAT. Indeed I must confesse, tis somewhat red.

 2 WAT. I see come marching in a dish, halfe a score pieces
of salt Bacon. 1 WAT. I understand your meaning, thats
as much to say, half a score ships. 2 WAT. True, you con-
ster right; presently, like a faithfull watchman, I fire the
Beacon, and call up the towne. 2460

 1 WAT. I, thats as much as to say, you set your nose to the
pot, and drink up the drink. 2 WAT. You are in the right;
come, let's go fire the Beacon.[1]   *[Exeunt.*

   [Sc. 28] *Enter the King of Gallia with a stil march,*
      Mumford & soldiers.

 KING. Now march our ensignes on the Brittish earth,
And we are neere approaching to the towne:
Then looke about you, valiant Countrymen,
And we shall finish this exployt with ease.
Th'inhabitants of this mistrustfull place,
Are dead asleep, as men that are secure: 2470
Here shall we skirmish but with naked men,
Devoyd of sence, new waked from a dreame,
That know not what our comming doth pretend,
Till they do feele our meaning on their skinnes:
Therefore assaile: God and our right for us. *[Exeunt.*

   [Sc. 29] *Alarum, with men and women halfe naked:*
    Enter two Captaynes without dublets, with swords.

 1 CAP. Where are these villaines that were set to watch,
And fire the Beacon, if occasion serv'd,
That thus have suffred us to be surprisde, 2480
And never given notice to the towne?

[1] Contrast III.1.31–4.

We are betrayd, and quite devoyd of hope,
By any meanes to fortify our selves.

   2 CAP.   Tis ten to one the peasants are o'recome with
drinke and sleep, and so neglect their charge.

   I CAP.   A whirl-wind carry them quick to a whirl-poole,
That there the slaves may drinke their bellies full.

   2 CAP.   This tis, to have the Beacon so neere the Ale-house.

[Enter the watchmen drunke, with each a pot.

   I CAP.   Out on ye, villaynes, whither run you now?   2490

   I WAT.   To fire the towne, and call up the Beacon.

   2 WAT.   No, no, sir, to fire the Beacon.   *[He drinkes.*

   2 CAP.   What, with a pot of ale, you drunken Rogues?

   I CAP.   You'l fire the Beacon, when the towne is lost:
Ile teach you how to tend your office better.   *[draw to stab them.*

[Enter Mumford, Captaynes run away.

   MUM.   Yeeld, yeeld, yeeld.   *[He kicks downe their pots.*

   I WAT.   Reele? no, we do not reele:
You may lacke a pot of Ale ere you dye.

   MUM.   But in meane space, I answer, you want none.   2500
Wel, theres no dealing with you, y'are tall men, & wel weapond,
I would there were no worse then you in the towne.   *[Exit.*

   2 WAT.   A speaks like an honest man; my cholers past already.
Come, neighbour, let's go.

   I WAT.   Nay, first let's see and we can stand.   *[Exeunt.*
   Alarum, excursions, Mumford after them, and some halfe naked.

   [Sc. 30]   *Enter the Gallian King, Leir, Mumford, Cordella,
Perillus, and souldiers, with the chiefe of the towne bound.*

   KING.   Feare not, my friends, you shall receyve no hurt,
If you'l subscribe unto your lawfull King,   2510
And quite revoke your fealty from *Cambria*,
And from aspiring *Cornwall* too, whose wives
Have practisde treason 'gainst their fathers life.
Wee come in justice of your wronged King,
And do intend no harm at all to you,
So you submit unto your lawfull King.

   LEIR.   Kind Countrymen, it grieves me, that perforce,
I am constraind to use extremities.

   NOBLE.   Long have you here bin lookt for, good my Lord,

And wish'd for by a generall consent: 2520
And had we known your Highnesse had arrived,
We had not made resistance to your Grace:
And now, my gracious Lord, you need not doubt,
But all the Country will yeeld presently,
Which since your absence have bin greatly tax'd,
For to maintayne their overswelling pride.
Weele presently send word to all our friends;
When they have notice, they will come apace.

    LEIR.   Thanks, loving subjects; and thanks, worthy son,
Thanks, my kind daughter, thanks to you, my Lord,   2530
Who willingly adventured have your blood,
(Without desert) to do me so much good.

    MUM.   O, say no so:
I have bin much beholding to your Grace:
I must confesse, I have bin in some skirmishes,
But I was never in the like to this:
For where I was wont to meet with armed men,
I was now incountred with naked women.

    CORD.   We that are feeble, and want use of Armes,
Will pray to God, to sheeld you from all harmes.   2540

    LEIR.   The while your hands do manage ceaselesse toyle,
Our hearts shall pray, the foes may have the foyle.

    PER.   Weele fast and pray, whilst you for us do fight,
That victory may prosecute the right.

    KING.   Me thinks, your words do amplify (my friends)
And adde fresh vigor to my willing limmes: [*Drum.*
But harke, I heare the adverse Drum approch.
God and our right, Saint *Denis*, and Saint *George*.

    [*Enter Cornwall, Cambria, Gonorill, Ragan, and the army.*

    CORN.   Presumptuous King of Gawles, how darest thou   2550
Presume to enter on our Brittish shore?
And more then that, to take our townes perforce,
And draw our subjects hearts from their true King?
Be sure to buy it at as deare a price,
As ere you bought presumption in your lives.

    KING.   Ore-daring *Cornwall*, know, we came in right,
And just revengement of the wronged King,
Whose daughters there, fell vipers as they are,
Have sought to murder and deprive of life:
But God protected him from all their spight,   2560
And we are come in justice of his right.

CAM.   Nor he nor thou have any interest here,
But what you win and purchase with the sword.
Thy slaunders to our noble vertuous Queenes,
Wee'l in the battell thrust them down thy throte,
Except for feare of our revenging hands,
Thou flye to sea, as not secure on lands.

MUM.   Welshman, ile so ferrit you ere night for that word,
That you shall have no mind to crake so wel this twelvemonth.

GON.   They lye, that say, we sought our fathers death.   2570

RAG.   Tis meerely forged for a colours sake,
To set a glosse on your invasion.
Me thinks, an old man ready for to dye,
Should be asham'd to broache so foule a lye.

COR.   Fy, shamelesse sister, so devoyd of grace,
To call our father lyer to his face.

GON.   Peace (Puritan) dissembling hypocrite,
Which art so good, that thou wilt prove stark naught:
Anon, when as I have you in my fingers,
Ile make you wish your selfe in Purgatory.   2580

PER.   Nay, peace thou monster, shame unto thy sexe:
Thou fiend in likenesse of a humane creature.[1]

RAG.   I never heard a fouler spoken man.

LEIR.   Out on thee, viper, scum, filthy parricide,
More odious to my sight then is a Toade.
Knowest thou these letters?   [*She snatches them & teares them.*[2]

RAG.   Think you to outface me with your paltry scrowles?
You come to drive my husband from his right,
Under the colour of a forged letter.

LEIR.   Who ever heard the like impiety?   2590

PER.   You are our debtour of more patience:
We were more patient when we stayd for you,
Within the thicket two long houres and more.

RAG.   What houres? what thicket?

PER.   There, where you sent your servant with your letters,
Seald with your hand, to send us both to heaven,
Where, as I thinke, you never meane to come.

RAG.   Alas, you are growne a child agayne with age,
Or else your sences dote for want of sleepe.

PER.   Indeed you made us rise betimes, you know,   2600
Yet had a care we should sleepe where you bade us stay,
But never wake more till the latter day.

GON.   Peace, peace, old fellow, thou art sleepy still.

MUM.   Fayth, and if you reason till to morrow,

[1] Cf. Albany, IV.2.59–61.   [2] V.3.155–62.

You get no other answere at their hands.
Tis pitty two such good faces
Should have so little grace betweene them.
Well let us see if their husbands with their hands,
Can do as much, as they do with their toungs.

    CAM.   I, with their swords they'l make your toung unsay   2610
What they have sayd, or else they'l cut them out.

    KING.   Too't, gallants, too't, let's not stand brawling thus.
                                  [*Exeunt both armyes.*

    [Sc. 31]   *Sound alarum: excursions. Mumford must chase*
                  Cambria away: then cease. Enter Cornwall.

    CORN.   The day is lost,[1] our friends do all revolt,
And joyne against us with the adverse part:
There is no meanes of safety but by flight,
And therefore ile to Cornwall with my Queene.   [*Exit.*

                [*Enter Cambria.*   2620

    CAM.   I thinke, there is a devill in the Campe hath haunted
me to day: he hath so tyred me, that in a maner I can fight no
more.

                [*Enter Mumford.*

Zounds, here he comes, Ile take me to my horse.   [*Exit.*
        Mumford followes him to the dore, and returnes.

    MUM.   Farewell (Welshman) give thee but thy due,
Thou hast a light and nimble payre of legs:
Thou art more in debt to them then to thy hands:
But if I meet thee once agayne to day,
Ile cut them off, and set them to a better heart.   [*Exit.*   2630

    [Sc. 32]   *Alarums and excursions, then sound victory.*

    Enter Leir, Perillus, King, Cordella, and Mumford.

    KING.   Thanks be to God, your foes are overcome,
And you againe possessed of your right.

    LEIR.   First to the heavens, next, thanks to you, my sonne,
By whose good meanes I repossesse the same:
Which if it please you to accept your selfe,
With all my heart I will resigne to you:
For it is yours by right, and none of mine.
First, have you raisd, at your owne charge, a power   2640
Of valiant Souldiers; (this comes all from you)

   [1] Contrast V.2.6, 'King Lear hath lost!'
   O

Next have you ventured your owne persons scathe.
And lastly, (worthy *Gallia* never staynd)
My kingly title I by thee have gaynd.

    KING.   Thank heavens, not me, my zeale to you is such,
Commaund my utmost, I will never grutch.

    COR.   He that with all kind love intreats his Queene,
Will not be to her father unkind seene.

    LEIR.   Ah, my *Cordella*, now I call to mind,
The modest answere, which I tooke unkind: 2650
But now I see, I am no whit beguild,
Thou lovedst me dearely, and as ought a child.
And thou (*Perillus*) partner once in woe,
Thee to requite, the best I can, Ile doe:
Yet all I can, I, were it ne're so much,
Were not sufficient, thy true love is such.
Thanks (worthy, *Mumford*) to thee last of all,
Not greeted last, 'cause thy desert was small;
No, thou hast Lion-like layd on to day,
Chasing the Cornwall King and Cambria;
Who with my daughters, daughters did I say?   2660
To save their lives, the fugitives did play.
Come, sonne and daughter, who did me advaunce,
Repose with me awhile, and then for Fraunce.
      Sound Drummes and Trumpets.   [*Exeunt.*

X. Source

From
THE COUNTESSE OF PEMBROKES ARCADIA
by Sir Philip Sidney (1590)

A. [In Bk. II Ch. 10 Pyrocles and Musidorus have an adventure
'worthy to be remembered for the un-used examples therin, as well
of true natural goodnes, as of wretched ungratefulnesse'.]

It was in the kingdome of *Galacia*, the season being (as in the depth
of winter) very cold, and as then sodainely growne to so extreame
and foule a storme, that never any winter (I thinke) brought foorth
a fouler child: so that the Princes were even compelled by the haile,
that the pride of the winde blew into their faces, to seeke some
shrowding place within a certaine hollow rocke offering it unto them,

they made it their shield against the tempests furie.[1] And so staying there, till the violence thereof was passed, they heard the speach of a couple, who not perceiving them (being hidde within that rude canapy) helde a straunge and pitifull disputation which made them steppe out; yet in such sort, as they might see unseene. There they perceaved an aged man, and a young, scarcely come to the age of a man, both poorely arayed, extreamely weather-beaten;[2] the olde man blinde, the young man leading him: and yet through all those miseries, in both these seemed to appeare a kind of noblenesse, not sutable to that affliction. But the first words they heard, were these of the old man. Well *Leonatus* (said he) since I cannot perswade thee to lead me to that which should end my griefe, & thy trouble, let me now entreat thee to leave me: feare not, my miserie cannot be greater then it is, & nothing doth become me but miserie; feare not the danger of my blind steps, I cannot fall worse then I am. And doo not I pray thee, doo not obstinately continue to infect thee with my wretchednes. But flie, flie from this region, onely worthy of me. Deare father (answered he) doo not take away from me the onely remnant of my happinesse: while I have power to doo your service, I am not wholly miserable. Ah my sonne (said he, and with that he groned, as if sorrow strave to breake his harte,) how evill fits it me to have such a sonne, and how much doth thy kindnesse upbraide my wickednesse? These dolefull speeches, and some others to like purpose (well shewing they had not bene borne to the fortune they were in,) moved the Princes to goe out unto them, and aske the younger what they were? Sirs (answered he, with a good grace, and made the more agreable by a certaine noble kinde of pitiousnes) I see well you are straungers, that know not our miserie so well here knowne, that no man dare know, but that we must be miserable. In deede our state is such, as though nothing is so needfull unto us as pittie, yet nothing is more daungerous unto us, then to make our selves so knowne as may stirre pittie. But your presence promiseth, that cruelty shall not over-runne hate. And if it did, in truth our state is soncke below the degree of feare.

This old man (whom I leade) was lately rightfull Prince of this countrie of *Paphlagonia*, by the hard-harted ungratefulnes of a sonne of his, deprived, not onely of his kingdome (whereof no forraine forces were ever able to spoyle him) but of his sight, the riches which Nature graunts to the poorest creatures. Whereby, and by other his unnaturall dealings, he hath bin driven to such griefe, as even now he would have had me to have led him to the toppe of this rocke, thence to cast himselfe headlong to death: and so would have made

[1] This no doubt suggested the hovel in Lear's storm, III.2 and 4.
[2] Edgar has to disguise his nobleness, IV.1, etc.

me (who received my life of him) to be the worker of his destruction. But noble Gentlemen (said he) if either of you have a father, and feele what duetifull affection is engraffed in a sonnes hart, let me intreate you to convey this afflicted Prince to some place of rest and securitie. Amongst your worthie actes it shall be none of the least, that a King, of such might and fame, and so unjustly oppressed, is in any sort by you relieved.

But before they could make him answere, his father began to speake, Ah my sonne (said he) how evill an Historian are you, that leave out the chiefe knotte of all the discourse! my wickednes, my wickednes. And if thou doest it to spare my eares, (the onely sense nowe left me proper for knowledge) assure thy selfe thou dost mistake me. And I take witnesse of that Sunne which you see (with that he cast up his blinde eyes, as if he would hunt for light,) and wish my selfe in worse case then I do wish my selfe, which is as evill as may be, if I speake untruely; that nothing is so welcome to my thoughts, as the publishing of my shame. Therefore know you Gentlemen (to whom from my harte I wish that it may not prove ominous foretoken of misfortune to have mette with such a miser as I am) that whatsoever my sonne (O God, that trueth binds me to reproch him with the name of my sonne) hath said, is true. But besides those truthes, this also is true, that having had in lawful mariage, of a mother fitte to beare royall children, this sonne (such one as partly you see, and better shall knowe by my shorte declaration) and so enjoyed the expectations in the world of him, till he was growen to justifie their expectations (so as I needed envie no father for the chiefe comfort of mortalitie, to leave an other ones-selfe after me) I was caried by a bastarde sonne of mine (if at least I be bounde to beleeve the words of that base woman my concubine, his mother) first to mislike, then to hate, lastly to destroy, to doo my best to destroy, this sonne (I thinke you thinke) undeserving destruction. What waies he used to bring me to it, if I should tell you, I should tediously trouble you with as much poysonous hypocrisie, desperate fraude, smoothe malice, hidden ambition, and smiling envie, as in any living person could be harbored.[1] But I list it not, no remembrance, (no, of naughtines) delights me, but mine own; and me thinks, the accusing his traines might in some manner excuse my fault, which certainly I loth to doo. But the conclusion is, that I gave order to some servants of mine, whom I thought as apte for such charities as my selfe, to leade him out into a forrest, and there to kill him.

But those theeves (better natured to my sonne then my selfe) spared his life, letting him goe, to learne to live poorely: which he

[1] Shakespeare explains it by means of other material from Sidney (pp. 404–11).

did, giving himselfe to be a private souldier, in a countrie here by. But as he was redy to be greatly advaunced for some noble peeces of service which he did, he hearde newes of me: who (dronke in my affection to that unlawfull and unnaturall sonne of mine) suffered my self so to be governed by him, that all favors and punishments passed by him, all offices, and places of importance distributed to his favourites; so that ere I was aware, I had left my self nothing but the name of a King: which he shortly wearie of too, with many indignities (if any thing may be called an indignity, which was laid upon me) threw me out of my seat, and put out my eies; and then (proud in his tyrannie) let me goe, nether imprisoning, nor killing me: but rather delighting to make me feele my miserie;[1] miserie indeed, if ever there were any; full of wretchednes, fuller of disgrace, and fullest of guiltines. And as he came to the crowne by so unjust meanes, as unjustlie he kept it, by force of stranger souldiers in *Cittadels*, the nestes of tyranny, & murderers of libertie; disarming all his own countrimen, that no man durst shew himself a welwisher of mine: to say the trueth (I think) few of them being so (considering my cruell follie to my good sonne, and foolish kindnes to my unkinde bastard:) but if there were any who fell to pitie of so great a fall, and had yet any sparkes of unstained duety lefte in them towardes me, yet durst they not shewe it, scarcely with giving me almes at their doores;[2] which yet was the onelie sustenaunce of my distressed life, no bodie daring to shewe so much charitie, as to lende me a hande to guide my darke steppes:[3] Till this sonne of mine (God knowes, woorthie of a more vertuous, and more fortunate father) forgetting my abhominable wrongs, not recking danger, and neglecting the present good way he was in doing himselfe good, came hether to doo this kind office you see him performe towardes me, to my unspeakable griefe; not onely because his kindnes is a glasse even to my blind eyes, of my naughtines, but that above all griefes, it greeves me he should desperatly adventure the losse of his soul-deserving life for mine, that yet owe more to fortune for my deserts, as if he would cary mudde in a chest of christall. For well I know, he that now raigneth, how much soever (and with good reason) he despiseth me, of all men despised; yet he will not let slippe any advantage to make away him, whose just title (ennobled by courage and goodnes) may one day shake the seate of a never secure tyrannie. And for this cause I craved of him to leade me to the toppe of this rocke, indeede I must confesse, with meaning to free him from so Serpentine a companion

---

[1] Cf. Regan, III.7.93: 'Let him smell his way to Dover!' Edmund is not present but knows that his father is to be punished horribly.

[2] So Gloucester is ordered not to help Lear, III.3.1–6. But he does so.

[3] One of Gloucester's servants dies trying to save him; others 'get the Bedlam to lead him' (III.7.72ff.).

as I am. But he finding what I purposed, onely therein since he was
borne, shewed himselfe disobedient unto me.[1] And now Gentlemen,
you have the true storie, which I pray you publish to the world, that
my mischievous proceedinges may be the glorie of his filiall pietie,
the onely reward now left for so great a merite. And if it may be, let
me obtaine that of you, which my sonne denies me: for never was
there more pity in saving any, then in ending me; both because
therein my agonies shall ende, and so shall you preserve this excellent young man, who els wilfully folowes his owne ruine.

The matter in it self lamentable, lamentably expressed by the old
Prince (which needed not take to himselfe the gestures of pitie, since
his face could not put of the markes thereof) greatly moved the two
Princes to compassion, which could not stay in such harts as theirs
without seeking remedie. But by and by the occasion was presented:
for *Plexirtus* (so was the bastard called) came thether with fortie
horse, onely of purpose to murder this brother; of whose comming
he had soone advertisement, and thought no eyes of sufficient credite
in such a matter, but his owne; and therefore came him selfe to be
actor, and spectator. And as soone as he came, not regarding the
weake (as he thought) garde of but two men, commaunded some of
his followers to set their handes to his, in the killing of *Leonatus*. But
the young Prince (though not otherwise armed but with a sworde)
how falsely soever he was dealt with by others, would not betray
him selfe: but bravely drawing it out, made the death of the first
that assaulted him, warne his fellowes to come more warily after
him.[2] But then *Pyrocles* and *Musidorus* were quickly become parties
(so just a defence deserving as much as old friendship) and so did
behave them among that companie (more injurious then valiant)
that many of them lost their lives for their wicked maister.

Yet perhaps had the number of them at last prevailed, if the King
of Pontus (lately by them made so) had not come unlooked for to
their succour. Who (having had a dreame which had fixt his imagination vehemently upon some great daunger presently to follow
those two Princes whom he most deerely loved) was come in all hast,
following as well as he could their tracke with a hundreth horses in
that countrie, which he thought (considering who then raigned) a
fit place inough to make the stage of any Tragedie.

But then the match had ben so ill made for *Plexirtus*, that his ill-led
life, and worse gotten honour should have tumbled together to
destruction; had there not come in *Tydeus* and *Telenor*, with fortie
or fiftie in their suit, to the defence of *Plexirtus*. . . . And briefly so

[1] Edgar pretends to help his father to suicide, IV.6.

[2] Regan wants Gloucester 'cut off' (IV.5.37–8) and Oswald tries to kill him, but
is slain by Edgar (IV.6.227–54).

they did, that if they overcame not yet were they not overcome, but caried away that ungratefull maister of theirs to a place of securitie; howsoever the Princes laboured to the contrary.[1] But this matter being thus far begun, it became not the constancie of the Princes so to leave it; but in all hast making forces both in *Pontus* and *Phrygia*, they had in fewe dayes lefte him but only that one strong place where he was. For feare having bene the onely knot that had fastned his people unto him, that once untied by a greater force, they all scattered from him; like so many birdes, whose cage had bene broken.

In which season the blind King (having in the chief cittie of his Realme, set the crowne upon his sonne *Leonatus* head) with many teares (both of joy and sorrow) setting forth to the whole people, his owne fault and his sonnes vertue, after he had kist him, and forst his sonne to accept honour of him (as of his newe-become subject) even in a moment died, as it should seeme: his hart broken with unkindnes and affliction, stretched so farre beyond his limits with this excesse of comfort, as it was able no longer to keep safe his roial spirits.[2] But the new King (having no lesse lovingly performed all duties to him dead, then alive) pursued on the siege of his unnatural brother, asmuch for the revenge of his father, as for the establishing of his owne quiet. In which siege truly I cannot but acknowledge the prowesse of those two brothers, then whom the Princes never found in all their travell two men of greater habilitie to performe, nor of habler skill for conduct.

But *Plexirtus* finding, that if nothing els, famin would at last bring him to destruction, thought better by humblenes to creepe, where by pride he could not march. For certainely so had nature formed him, and the exercise of craft conformed him to all turnings of sleights, that though no man had lesse goodnes in his soule then he, no man could better find the places whence arguments might grow of goodnesse to another: though no man felt lesse pitie, no man could tel better how to stir pitie: no man more impudent to deny, where proofes were not manifest; no man more ready to confesse with a repenting manner of aggravating his owne evil, where denial would but make the fault fouler. Now he tooke this way, that having gotten a pasport for one (that pretended he would put *Plexirtus* alive into his hands) to speak with the King his brother, he him selfe (though much against the minds of the valiant brothers, who rather wished to die in brave defence) with a rope about his necke,[3] barefooted, came to offer himselfe to the discretion of *Leonatus*. Where what sub-

---

[1] Cf. Edmund's apparent victory (V.3) turned to defeat by Albany.

[2] Cf. Gloucester's death: 'Twixt two extremes of passion, joy and grief' (V.3.199).

[3] Cf. Edmund's orders to the captain to hang Cordelia and 'To lay the blame upon her own despair' (V.3.253-6).

mission he used, how cunningly in making greater the faulte he made
the faultines the lesse, how artificially he could set out the torments
of his owne conscience, with the burdensome comber he had found
of his ambitious desires, how finely seeming to desire nothing but
death, as ashamed to live, he begd life in the refusing it, I am not
cunning inough to be able to expresse; but so fell out of it, that
though at first sight *Leonatus* saw him with no other eie, then as the
murderer of his father; and anger already began to paint revenge in
many colours, ere long he had not only gotten pitie, but pardon, and
if not an excuse of the fault past, yet an opinion of a future amendment: while the poore villaines (chiefe ministers of his wickednes,
now betraied by the author thereof,) were delivered to many cruell
sorts of death; he so handling it, that it rather seemed, he had rather
come into the defence of an unremediable mischiefe already comit-
ted, then that they had done it at first by his consent.[1]

In such sort the Princes left these reconciled brothers (*Plexirtus* in
all his behaviour carying him in far lower degree of service, then the
ever-noble nature of *Leonatus* would suffer him) . . .

B. [Bk. II Ch. 15 tells the story of Plangus, a prince of Iberia who
at one time had been in love with the woman who became his
father's second wife. This stepmother tempted him to commit
adultery with her, and when he refused began to hate him.]

Therefore did she trie the uttermost of her wicked wit, how to overthrow him in the foundation of his strength, which was, in the favour
of his father: which because she saw strong both in nature and
desert, it required the more cunning how to undermine it. And therfore (shunning the ordinary trade of hireling sycophants) she made
her praises of him, to be accusations; and her advauncing him, to be
his ruine. For first with words (neerer admiration then liking) she
would extoll his excellencies, the goodlines of his shape, the power of
his witte, the valiantnes of his courage, the fortunatenes of his
successes: so as the father might finde in her a singular love towardes
him: nay, she shunned not to kindle some fewe sparkes of jelousie in
him. Thus having gotten an opinion in his father, that she was farre
from meaning mischiefe to the sonne, then fell she to praise him with
no lesse vehemencie of affection, but with much more cunning of
malice. For then she sets foorth the liberty of his mind, the high flying
of this thoughts, the fitnesse in him to beare rule, the singular love the
Subjects bare him; that it was doubtfull, whether his wit were
greater in winning their favors, or his courage in employing their
favours: that he was not borne to live a subject-life, each action of
his bearing in it Majestie, such a Kingly entertainement, such a

[1] Edmund accepts his end with some dignity (V.3.174–5).

Kingly magnificence, such a Kingly harte for enterprises: especially remembring those vertues, which in a successor are no more honoured by the subjects, then suspected of the Princes. Then would she by putting-of objections, bring in objections to her husbands head, already infected with suspition.[1] Nay (would she say) I dare take it upon my death, that he is no such sonne, as many of like might have bene, who loved greatnes so well, as to build their greatnes upon their fathers ruine. . . .

Then tooke she help to her of a servant neere about her husband, whom she knew to be of a hasty ambition, and such a one, who wanting true sufficiencie to raise him, would make a ladder of any mischiefe. Him she useth to deale more plainely in alleaging causes of jealousie, making him know the fittest times when her husband already was stirred that way. And so they two, with divers wayes, nourished one humour, like Musitians, that singing divers parts, make one musicke. He sometime with fearefull countenaunce would desire the King to looke to himselfe; for that all the court and Cittie were full of whisperings, and expectation of some suddaine change, upon what ground himselfe knew not. Another time he would counsell the King to make much of his sonne, and holde his favour, for that it was too late now to keepe him under. Now seeming to feare himselfe, because (he said) *Plangus* loved none of them that were great about his father. Lastly, breaking with him directly (making a sorrowful countenance, & an humble gesture beare false witnesse for his true meaning) that he found, not only souldiery, but people weary of his government, & al their affections bent upon *Plangus*. Both he and the Queene concurring in strange dreames, & each thing else, that in a mind (already perplexed) might breed astonishment: so that within a while, all *Plangus* actions began to be translated into the language of suspition. . . . But even while the doubtes most boiled, she thus nourished them.

She under-hand dealt with the principall men of that country, that at the great Parliament (which was then to be held) they should in the name of all the estates perswade the King (being now stept deeply into old age) to make *Plangus*, his associate in government with him:[2] assuring them, that not only she would joine with them, but that the father himself would take it kindly; chargeing them not to acquaint *Plangus* withal; for that perhaps it might be harmeful unto him, if the King should find, that he were a party. They (who thought they might do it, not only willingly, because they loved him, & truly, because such indeed was the minde of the people, but safely,

[1] This is Iago's technique with Othello; but there is a trace of it in Edmund's handling of Gloucester, I.2.
[2] Shakespeare substitutes Edmund's forged letter, I.2.29–62, and 72–7.

because she who ruled the King was agreed therto) accomplished her counsell: she indeed keeping promise of vehement perswading the same: which the more she & they did, the more she knew her husband would fear, & hate the cause of his feare. . . .

She caused that same minister of hers to go unto *Plangus*, & (enabling his words with great shew of faith, & endearing them with desire of secresie) to tell him, that he found his ruine conspired by his stepmother, with certain of the noble men of that country, the King himselfe giving his consent, and that few daies should passe, before the putting it in practize: with all discovering the very truth indeed, with what cunning his stepmother had proceeded. This agreing with *Plangus* his owne opinion, made him give him the better credit: yet not so far, as to flie out of his country (according to the naughty fellowes persuasion) but to attend, and to see further.[1] Whereupon the fellow (by the direction of his mistresse) told him one day, that the same night, about one of the clocke, the King had appointed to have his wife, & those noble men together, to deliberate of their manner of proceeding against *Plangus*: & therfore offered him, that if himselfe would agree, he would bring him into a place where he should heare all that passed;[2] & so have the more reason both to himselfe, and to the world, to seeke his safetie. The poore *Plangus* (being subject to that only disadvantage of honest harts, creditlie) was perswaded by him: & arming himself (because of his late going)[3] was closely conveied into the place appointed. In the meane time his stepmother, making all her gestures cunningly counterfait a miserable affliction, she lay almost groveling on the flower of her chamber, not suffering any body to comfort her; untill they calling for her husband, and he held of with long enquiry, at length, she told him (even almost crying out every word) that she was wery of her life, since she was brought to that plunge, either to conceale her husbands murther, or accuse her sonne, who had ever bene more deare, then a sonne unto her. Then with many interruptions and exclamations she told him, that her sonne *Plangus* (solliciting her in the old affection betweene them) had besought her to put her helping hand to the death of the King; assuring her, that though all the lawes in the world were against it, he would marrie her when he were King.

She had not fully said thus much, with many pitifull digressions, when in comes the same fellow, that brought *Plangus*: & runing himself out of breath, fell at the Kings feet, beseeching him to save himself, for that there was a man with sword drawen in the next

[1] Cf. II.1.21; II. 3.
[2] So Edmund at I.2.170–4.
[3] Cf. I.2.175–6, Edmund, 'If you do stir abroad, go armed.'

roome. The King affrighted, went out, & called his gard, who entring the place, found indeed *Plangus* with his sword in his hand, but not naked, but standing suspiciously inough, to one already suspicious.[1] The King (thinking he had put up his sworde because of the noise) never tooke leasure to heare his answer, but made him prisoner, meaning the next morning to put him to death in the market place.

But the day had no sooner opened the eies & eares of his friends & followers, but that there was a little army of them, who came, and by force delivered him; although numbers on the other side (abused with the fine framing of their report) tooke armes for the King. But *Plangus*, though he might have used the force of his friends to revenge his wrong, and get the crowne; yet the naturall love of his father, and hate to make their suspition seeme just, caused him rather to choose a voluntarie exile, then to make his fathers death the purchase of his life:[2] & therefore went he to *Tiridates*, whose mother was his fathers sister, living in his Court eleven or twelve yeares, ever hoping by his intercession, and his owne desert, to recover his fathers grace.

C. [Cecropia, wicked sister of King Basileus, has a son Amphialus, who was heir to the throne until his uncle married and had two daughters, Philoclea and Pamela. In Bk. III, Ch. 5, 6, 10 Cecropia tries in vain to persuade each of the two maidens to marry her son. Pamela's piety and patience are shown when her aunt overhears her meditating in her chamber (Ch. 6).]

And so she might perceave that *Pamela* did walke up and down, full of deep (though patient) thoughts. For her look and countenance was setled, her pace soft, and almost still of one measure, without any passionate gesture, or violent motion: till at length (as it were) awaking, & strengthning her selfe, Well (said she) yet this is the best, & of this I am sure, that how soever they wrong me, they cannot over-master God. No darkenes blinds his eyes, no Jayle barres him out. To whome then else should I flie, but to him for succoure? And therewith kneeling down, even in the same place where she stood, she thus said: 'O all-seeing Light, and eternal Life of all things . . . looke upon my miserie with thine eye of mercie,[3] and let thine infinite power vouchsafe to limite out some proportion of deliverance unto me, as to thee shall seem most convenient'.

[The long prayer is a complete surrender to God's will, and it moves even the obdurate Cecropia. But she attempts to break down

---

[1] Edmund arranges a struggle, II.1.29–37.

[2] Edgar is proclaimed an outlaw, II.1.81; II.3.1.

[3] Note the imagery of blindness and light, as well as the example of devout patience, not unlike Cordella in *Leir*.

Pamela's virtue by atheistical appeals to Nature and false reasoning, especially in Ch. 10.]

Therefore, employing the uttermost of her mischievous witte, and speaking the more earnestly, because she spake as she thought, she thus dealt with her. Deare neece, or rather, deare daughter (if my affection and wishe might prevaile therein) how much dooth it increase (trowe you) the earnest desire I have of this blessed match, to see these vertues of yours knit fast with such zeale of Devotion, indeede the best bonde, which the most politicke wittes have found, to holde mans witte in well doing? For, as children must first by feare be induced to know that, which after (when they doo know) they are most glad of: So are these bugbeares of opinions brought by great Clearkes into the world, to serve as shewelles to keepe them from those faults, whereto els the vanitie of the worlde, and weakenes of senses might pull them. But in you (Neece) whose excellencie is such, as it neede not to be helde up by the staffe of vulgar opinions, I would not you should love Vertue servillie for feare of I know not what, which you see not: but even for the good effects of vertue which you see. Feare, and indeede, foolish feare, and fearefull ignorance, was the first inventer of those conceates. For, when they heard it thunder, not knowing the naturall cause, they thought there was some angrie body above, that spake so lowde:[1] and ever the lesse they did perceive, the more they did conceive. Whereof they knew no cause, that grewe streight a miracle: foolish folks, not marking that the alterations be but upon particular accidents, the universalitie being alwaies one. Yesterday was but as to day, and to morrow will tread the same footsteps of his foregoers:[2] so as it is manifest inough, that all things follow but the course of their own nature, saving only Man, who while by the pregnancie of his imagination he strives to things supernaturall, meane-while he looseth his owne naturall felicitie. Be wise, and that wisedome shalbe a God unto thee; be contented, and that is thy heaven: for els to thinke that those powers (if there be any such) above, are moved either by the eloquence of our prayers, or in a chafe by the folly of our actions; caries asmuch reason as if flies should thinke, that men take great care which of them hums sweetest, and which of them flies nimblest.[3]

She would have spoken further to have enlarged & confirmed her discourse: but *Pamela* (whose cheeks were died in the beautifullest graine of vertuous anger, with eies which glistered forth beames of

---

[1] Cf. *Leir*, 1739–59; *King Lear*, III.2.49–51.

[2] Did Shakespeare remember this in *Macbeth*, 'Tomorrow and tomorrow...' (V. 5.18–21)?

[3] IV.1.36. 'As flies ...'

disdaine) thus interrupted her. Peace (wicked woman) peace, unworthy to breathe, that doest not acknowledge the breath-giver; most unworthy to have a tongue, which speakest against him, through whom thou speakest: keepe your affection to your self, which like a bemired dog, would defile with fauning. You say yesterday was as to day. O foolish woman, and most miserably foolish, since wit makes you foolish. What dooth that argue, but that there is a constancie in the everlasting governour? Would you have an inconstant God, since we count a man foolish that is inconstant? He is not seene, you say, and would you thinke him a God, who might be seene by so wicked eyes, as yours? which yet might see enough if they were not like such, who for sport-sake willingly hoodwincke themselves to receave blowes the easier. But though I speake to you without any hope of fruite in so rotten a harte, and there be no bodie else here to judge of my speeches, yet be thou my witnesse, O captivitie, that my eares shall not be willingly guiltie of my Creators blasphemie. You saie, because we know not the causes of things, therefore feare was the mother of superstition: nay, because we know that each effect hath a cause, that hath engendred a true & lively devotion. For this goodly worke of which we are, and in which we live, hath not his being by Chaunce; on which opinion it is beyond mervaile by what chaunce any braine could stumble. For if it be eternall (as you would seeme to conceive of it) Eternity, & Chaunce are things unsufferable together. . . .

Lastly, perfect order, perfect beautie, perfect constancie, if these be the children of Chaunce, or Fortune the efficient of these, let Wisedome be counted the roote of wickednesse, and eternitie the fruite of her inconstancie. But you will say it is so by nature, as much as if you said it is so, because it is so: if you meane of many natures conspiring together, as in a popular governement to establish this fayre estate; as if the Elementishe and ethereall partes should in their towne-house set downe the boundes of each ones office; then consider what followes: that there must needes have bene a wisedome which made them concurre: for their natures beyng absolute contrarie, in nature rather woulde have sought each others ruine, then have served as well consorted partes to such an unexpressable harmonie. For that contrary things should meete to make up a perfection without a force and Wisedome above their powers, is absolutely impossible; unles you will flie to that hissed-out opinion of Chaunce againe. . . .

This worlde therefore cannot otherwise consist but by a minde of Wisedome, whiche governes it, which whether you wil allow to be the Creator thereof, as undoubtedly he is, or the soule and governour thereof, most certaine it is that whether he governe all, or make all, his power is above either his creatures, or his government. And if his power be above all thinges, then consequently it must needes be infinite, since there is nothing above it to limit it. For beyond which there is nothing, must needes be boundlesse, and infinite: if his power be infinite, then likewise must his knowledge be infinite. . . .

Since then there is a God, and an all-knowing God, so as he sees into the darkest of all naturall secretes, which is the harte of Man; and sees therein the deepest dissembled thoughts, nay sees the thoughts before they be thought: since he is just to exercise his might, and mightie to performe his justice, assure thy selfe, most wicked woman (that hast so plaguily a corrupted minde, as thou canst not keepe thy sickenesse to thy selfe, but must most wickedly infect others) assure thy selfe, I say, (for what I say dependes of everlasting and unremooveable causes) that the time will come, when thou shalt knowe that power by feeling it, when thou shalt see his wisedome in the manifesting thy ougly shamelessnesse, and shalt onely perceive him to have bene a Creator in thy destruction.[1]

XI. Source

From A DECLARATION OF EGREGIOUS POPISH IMPOSTURES
by Samuel Harsnett (1603)[2]

CHAP. 10

The strange names of their devils

Now that I have acquainted you with the names of the Maister, and his twelve disciples, the names of the places wherein, and the names of the persons upon whom these wonders were shewed: it seemes not incongruent that I relate unto you the names of the devils, whom in this glorious pageant they did dispossesse. Wherein, we may call unto *Porphyrius, Proclus, Iamblicus*, and *Trismegistus*, the old Platonicall sect, that conversed familiarly, and kept company with devils, and

[1] So it is in *Leir*, but in Shakespeare the good suffer more than the bad. The wisdom and goodness of the gods are not made clear.

[2] Title page: 'A Declaration of egregious Popish Impostures, to with-draw the harts of her Majesties Subjects from their allegeance, and from the truth of Christian Religion professed in England, under the pretence of casting out devils. Practised by Edmunds, alias *Weston* a Jesuit, and divers Romish Priests his wicked associates. . . . At London Printed by James Roberts, dwelling in Barbican. 1603.'

desire their help to expound us these new devils names: and to tell us at what solemne feast, and meeting in hell, these devils were dubbed, and halowed with these new strange names. It cannot be but our holy devill-crue had surely met with *Menippus*, proclaiming himselfe new come out of hell: *ad sum profoundo Tartari emissus specu:* Else they could never have beene so deeply sighted, and acquainted with the Muster-booke of hell. Or else it may seeme that our vagrant devils heere did take theyr fashion of new names from our wandring Jesuits, who to dissemble themselves, have alwaies three, or foure odde conceited names in their budget: or els they did so plague the poore devils with theyr holy charmes, and enchaunted geare, and did so intoxicate them with their dreadful fumigations, as they made some so giddy-headed, that they gave themselves giddy names, they wist not what. Or else there is a confederation between our wandring Exorcists, and these walking devils, and they are agreed of certaine uncouth non-significant names, which goe currant amongst themselves, as the Gipsies are of gibridge,[1] which none but themselves can spell without a paire of spectacles. Howsoever it is, it is not amisse that you be acquainted with these extravagant names of devils, least meeting them otherwise by chance, you mistaken them for the names of Tapsters, or Juglers.

First then, to marshall them in as good order, as such disorderly cattell will be brought into, you are to understand, that there were in our possessed 5. Captaines, or Commaunders above the rest:[2] Captaine *Pippin, Marwoods* devill, Captaine *Philpot, Trayfords* devil, Captaine *Maho, Saras* devil, Captaine *Modu, Maynies* devill, and Captaine *Soforce, Anne Smiths* devil. These were not all of equal authoritie, & place, but some had more, some fewer under theyr commaund. *Pippin, Marwoods* devill was a Captaine, (marry either cassierd for some part of bad service hee had done, or else a male-content standing upon his worth) like some of our high Puntilios, scorned to sort himselfe with any of his ranke, and therefore like a melancholick *Privado,* he affects *Marwood* to lie in the fields, and to gape at the Moone, and so of a *Caesars* humor, he raignes in *Marwood* alone.

Captaine *Philpot, Trayfords* devill, was a Centurion, (as himselfe tels you) and had an hundred under his charge. Mary he was (as seemes) but a white-livered devill, for he was so hastie to be gone out of *Trayford,* for feare of the Exorcist, that hee would scarce give him leave, beeing a bed, to put on his breeches. The names of ther punie spirits cast out of *Trayford* were these,[3] *Hilco, Smolkin,*[4] *Hillio, Hiaclito,*

---

[1] gibberish, unintelligible language.
[2] *In margin:* 'See the booke of Miracles.'
[3] *In margin:* 'Booke of Miracles.'   [4] III.4.137.

and *Lustie huffe-cap*: this last seemes some swaggering punie devill, dropt out of a Tinkers budget. But *Hiaclito* may not be slipped over without your observation: for he scorning a great while (as the Author saith) to tell his name, at last he aunswered most proudly, *my name is* Hiaclito, *a Prince, & Monarch of the world.* And beeing asked by the Exorcist, what fellowes he had with him: hee said that *hee had no fellowes, but two men, and an urchin boy.*[1] It was little beseeming his state (I wis) beeing so mighty a Monarch, to come into our coasts so skurvily attended, except hee came to see fashions in England, and so made himselfe private till the Exorcist reveald him: or els that he was of the new Court cut, affecting no other traine then two crasie fellowes, and an urchin butter-flie boy.

Soforce, Anne Smiths possedent, was but a musty devill; there was neither mirth, nor good fellowship with him, affecting so much sullennesse, as he would hardlie speake. Yet as all melancholike creatures use to have, he had a restie tricke with him. For whether *Alexander* the Apothecarie had put too much *Assa Foetida* in the fumigation for the devill, or had done the devill some other shrewd turne with his drugges, sure it is that *Alexander* the Apothecarie, riding one day towards London, to fetch more Priests to *Denham*, his horse fell a plunging, and *Alexander* came downe: and returning to *Denham*, hee constantly affirmed, that it was *Anne Smiths* devill, that playd the Jade with him.

Modu, Ma: *Maynies* devill, was a graund Commaunder, Mustermaister over the Captaines of the seaven deadly sinnes:[2] *Cliton, Bernon, Hilo, Motubizanto,* & the rest, himselfe a Generall of a kind and curteous disposi[ti]on: so saith *Sara Williams,* touching this devils acquaintance with Mistres *Plater,* and her sister *Fid.*

Sara Williams had in her at a bare word, *all the devils in hell.*[3] The Exorcist askes *Maho, Saras* devil,[4] what company he had with him, and the devil makes no bones, but tels him in flat termes, *all the devils in hell.* Heere was a goodly fat *otium* this meane while in hell: the poore soules there had good leave to play: such a day was never seene since hell was hell: not a doore-keeper left, but all must goe a maying to poore *Saras* house. It was not kindly done of the devils, to leave the poore soules behind, especially going to make merry amongst theyr friends. But what if the soules had fallen a madding, or maying as fast, as the devils, and had gone a roming abroade amongst their good friends, had not this (trow we,) made a prettie peece of worke in hell?

[1] Somewhat like the mad Lear in III.4.
[2] III.4.141; IV.1.62.
[3] *In margin:* 'Booke of Miracles', p. 42.
[4] Cf. III.4.141; IV.1.62.

And if I misse not my markes, this *Dictator Modu* saith, hee had beene in *Sara* by the space of two yeeres, then so long hell was cleere, and had not a devill to cast at a mad dogge. And sooth, I cannot much blame the devils for staying so long abroade, they had taken up an Inne, much sweeter then hell: & an hostesse that wanted neither wit, nor mirth, to give them kinde welcome.

Heere, if you please, you may take a survey of the whole regiment of hell: at least the chiefe Leaders, and officers, as we finde them enrolled by theyr names.

First *Killico*, *Hob*, and a third *anonymos*, are booked downe for three graund Commaunders, every one having under him 300 attendants.[1]

Coronell *Portirichio* had with him two Captaines, & an hundred assistants, and this he affirmes to be true uppon his oath taken upon the blessed sacrament, & then you must believe him: an admirable new way to make the devil true, and cock-sure of his word, to offer him an oath upon the blessed sacrament, and then dog with a fiddle. But the devill is like some other good fellowes in the world, that will not sweare, except he allow theyr Commission[2] that tenders him his oath: and Commissioners for the devill, are onely holy Exorcists, and then it must be the sacrament of the Masse to, else I wis it is not all worth a beane.

Frateretto,[3] *Fliberdigibbet*,[4] *Hoberdidance*,[5] *Tocobatto* were foure devils of the round, or Morrice, whom *Sara* in her fits, tuned together, in measure and sweet cadence.[6] And least you should conceive, that the devils had no musicke in hell, especially that they would goe a maying without theyr musicke, the Fidler comes in with his Taber, & Pipe, and a whole Morice after him, with motly visards for theyr better grace. These foure had forty assistants under them, as themselves doe confesse.

Lustie Jollie Jenkin, (an other of *Saras* Captaine devils names) by his name should seeme to be foreman of the motly morrice: hee had under him, saith himselfe, forty assistants, or rather (if I misse not) he had beene by some old Exorcist allowed for the Master setter of Catches, or roundes, used to be sung by Tinkers, as they sit by the fire with a pot of good Ale betweene theyr legges: *Hey jolly Jenkin, I see a knave a drinking, et cæt.*

Delicat, an other Captaine, or vicenarie in *Sara*, having under him twenty assistants, seemes by his English name to be *yeoman* of the *Sprucery*, to see the devils motly visards, after they were soiled with

---

[1] *In margin:* 'Booke of Miracles', p. 34.
[2] Lear has a 'commission' of justice in III.6.39–58.
[3] III.6.6; IV.1.62–3.   [4] III.4.112; IV.1.61–3.   [5] III.6.31; IV.1.61.
[6] Cf. Edgar, IV.1.60: 'Five fiends have been in Poor Tom at once.'

Brimstone, and sweat, to be brusht up, and kept sweet, neate, &
cleane. These were the Officers, or Commaunders names, that had
taken up theyr lodging in *Sara Williams*, now the many, rascality, or
black-guard of hell, were God knows how many in her: for all were
there tag, and ragge, cut and long-tayle, yet divers of them it pleaseth
the holie Exorcist to commaund theyr names to doe them some grace,
others he lets goe out, leaving no names, but an ill savour behind
them. The names of such as the Exorcist thought good to favour,
were these, *Puffe*, and *Purre*,[1] the two fat devils, that had beene conjurd up for mony, anno 84, and would not home to hell againe, till
good company came for them. *Lustie Dickie, Cornerd-cappe, Nurre,
Molkin, Wilkin, Helcmodion, Kellicocam*. These were like the *Sporades
in via lactea*, having neither office, order, nor ranke; all these were
Saras devils.

     Maho was generall *Dictator* of hell: & yet for good manners sake,
hee was contented of his good nature to make shew, that himselfe
was under the check of *Modu*, the graund devil in Ma: *Maynie*. These
were all in poore *Sara* at a chop, with these the poore soule travailed
up and downe full two yeeres together; so as during those two yeeres,
it had beene all one to say, one is gone to hell, or hee is gone to *Sara
Williams*: for shee poore wench had all hell in her belly. And had had
it still to this day for any thing we know, if it had not pleased Fa:
Weston, and his twelve holy disciples, to have delivered her of that
devil-childe. But of this you shall heare heereafter: now I may
proceed (pp. 45–50).

CHAP. 14

[The exorcists made use of relics which included articles of clothing belonging to recent martyrs such as Fr. Edmund Campion,
hanged on 1 December 1581.][2]

. . . You are next to be informed, that this devil-killing vertue did
not lye in the priests head onely, as the poyson of an Adder doth;
nor yet in his taile alone, as the light of a Glow-worme; but was
universally diffused over all, and every part of his body, and so
transfused into all, and every part of the apparel, that came neere
his body. *Campians* girdle that he wore (as seemes) at *Tiburne*, (and I
wonder how they missed the roape, that embraced his holy necke)
being enritched with an outlandish grace, that it came from Jerusalem, (as Fa: *Edmunds* tells us,) and had there girded about the sepul-
cher of our Saviour Christ, shal tell you stranger newes, then
Dibdales stockins did.[3]

---

[1] 'Purr! the cat is grey.' (III.6.46.)
[2] Cf. Evelyn Waugh, *Edmund Campion*. Campion was canonized in 1970.
[3] Dibdale, a martyred priest whose hose were used as relics in exorcism.

Marwoods devil being a stiffe resty spirit, of kin (as seems) to a malt-horse of *Ware*, that will not out of his way: had beene conjured at *Hackney* by *Stemp*, and other priests, by the space of a moneth. *Mengus* his club, his whip, his scare-devil, had beene many, and sundry times assayed, the invocation of the blessed Trinity, many times used, *Missa de spiritu sancto* (*Edmunds* owne words) *celebrata*: *A choice Masse of the holy Ghost had beene celebrated*, deadfull infernall Exorcismes had been thundered abroad . . .[1] The sullen spirit, seemed not to care for it a rash. But when *Edmunds* came in . . . Taking in his hand, a certaine silken twist, which Fa: *Campion* did alwayes cary about with him, and used it at the celebration of the Masse; and which he often said, had beene at Jerusalem, and girded our Saviours tombe: applied the same gently to *Marwoods* side; at the touch whereof, he presently began to tremble, and turmoile, and the paine of his side shifted into a new place, whereby *Edmunds* discerned, that *Marwood* was a Demoniack indeede.

What a wonderfull Saint-maker is *Tyburne* by this, that in a quarter of an houre shall miscreate a Saint, whose girdle, or twist (provided it be worne by the old Saint at the gallowes) shal put downe, at scaring of a devil, *Mengus* his club-devil, whip-devil, scare-devil, the Masse, the invocation of God our Saviour Christ, the holy Ghost, and all . . .

[Harsnett gives 'a short, and sweet Dialogue, betweene the Jesuit, and the devil' in which the latter admits the power of the martyr's girdle.]

And now the devil was a Sainting, and that his hand was in, it was much overseene of *Edmunds* the Presenter, that he did not name him, Story, Felton, Sommervile, Arden, Parrie, and Lopez,[2] and the rest of that Saint-Traytorly crue, whom *Tiburne* and the devil were as familiar with-all, as with S. Campian I wis; and knew as wel the causes, motives, and end of their Saint-ships alike: the devil himselfe having beene the Author, and inspirer to them all . . . (pp. 82–5).

[Ch. 22 tells 'Of the admirable finall act of expelling the devils, and of their formes in theyr departing.']

The first devill that was disseised was *Smolkin*, *Trayfords* spirit, whom *Sara* espied (saith the Miraclist) to goe out at *Trayfords* right

---

[1] I omit the Latin but give Harsnett's translation.

[2] All these were Catholics condemned as traitors against the Queen's person. Dr Lopez was the Portuguese physician accused by Essex in 1594 and probably referred to in *The Merchant of Venice*. Arden was Edward Arden, a distant cousin of Shakespeare's mother, and High Sheriff of Warwickshire in 1575. In 1583 he was hanged for plotting with John Somerville to shoot the Queen. If Shakespeare was a Roman Catholic would he have drawn so much from Harsnett's book?

eare in the forme of a *Mouse*, and it made the poore wench at the sight of the Mouse almost out of her wits. The next devil dispossessed was *Hilcho* at *Uxbridge*, who appeared (saith our Authour) to the possessed parties at his going out, like *a flame of* fire, and lay glowing in the fire in *Trayfords* sight, till he had a new charge. The third was *Hoberdidance*, *Saras* dancing devil:[1] who appeared to the patient, like a *whirlwind*, turning round like a flame of fire,[2] & his voyce was heard by a Cooke, as he flew over the Larder. Captaine *Filpot* went his way in the likenes of a *smoke*, turning round, and so tooke his way up into the chimney. *Lusty Dicke* (as seemes) did slippe a button in one of his turnes above ground: for he went out in a foule unsavoury *stench*. *Delicate*, and *Lusty Jolly Jenkin* went out, one whirling like a *snake*, the other in a *vapor* not verie sweet. *Lusty Huffcappe* went out in the likenes of a *Cat*. Killico, Hob, and the third *Anonymos*, all Captaines, went out in a *wind*. Purre went out in a *little whirlewind*, Frateretto in a *smoke*.

Maister *Maynie* had in him (as you have heard) the Maister-devils of the seaven deadly sinnes,[3] and therefore his devils went out in the forme of those creatures, that have neerest resemblance unto those sinnes: as for example; the spirit of *Pride* went out in the forme of a *Peacocke* (forsooth), the spirit of *Sloth* in the likenesse of an *Asse*: the spirit of *Envy* in the similitude of a *Dog*: the spirit of *Gluttony* in the forme of a *Woolfe*.[4] But it is to be wondered at, that Generall *Maho*, at the last, and most dreadfull exorcisme of all, when hee was expelled with 22000 yeeres torment layd uppon his backe, hee slunke out without any similitude at all. And more, an ordinary Reader will wonder, that *Maho*, beeing Dictator of hell, is said in the Legend of Miracles, and so noted by Sara, to have chosen such a strange part in *Sara* for his passage out, as I dare not name: and yet devils, comedians, and their reporters, may have licence in all Courts to call all things by their name . . .[5] (pp. 140–1.)

---

[1] 'Hobbididance, prince of dumbness', IV.I.61.

[2] The Fool calls Gloucester 'a walking fire' at III.4.111.

[3] Cf. Edgar's vices and animal similitudes, III.4.83–92.

[4] III.4.91: 'wolf in greediness.'

[5] There is more about this 'fact', which together with the girdle of Fr. Campion mentioned above may have suggested, IV.6.127–8.

MACBETH

INTRODUCTION

MACBETH is not known to have been printed until the first Folio (1623) in which it follows *Julius Cæsar* and precedes *Hamlet*. Although it has twenty-seven scenes in F1 it is by far the shortest of the completed tragedies (2,108 lines), and this, with the presence of loose ends and unexplained references, has led some critics to regard it as a shortened play. Thus J. D. Wilson[1] considered that it was probably cut down by Shakespeare himself for a court performance when the King of Denmark, Christian IV, visited his brother-in-law in the summer of 1606. James I was certainly no lover of long plays, which bored him or sent him to sleep. We should, however, have to suppose that the shortened version was that used in the public theatre thenceforth, and that this was later subject to interpolations and other alterations.

The most obvious loose end is Lady Macbeth's surprising exclamation (I.7.47–52) 'What beast was't then, / That made you break this enterprise to me? / . . . Nor time nor place / Did then adhere . . .' which must mean that Macbeth had before our play opens suggested murdering Duncan. In our text Macbeth did not 'break the enterprise' to his wife in his letter, and there has been no intervening plan or opportunity since his arrival home. Shakespeare cannot have cut out a scene unless his play originally began before Donwald's revolt (and so before the chroniclers supplied any material), and this is most unlikely. Maybe Shakespeare put in the suggestion, regardless of previous scenes, to show that Macbeth was already guilty of more than 'fantastical' ambition. I.2 seems to have been cut somewhat; and why does Macbeth know nothing of Cawdor's treachery at I.3.72–3, although Ross knew of it (I.2.53) and suggests that he was with Norway when Macbeth defeated the latter? The stage directions are often confused. Loose ends and unevenness of style have been explained (without any external evidence) as

[1] *Camb.*, p. xxiiiff.

due to rapid composition for performance during the King of Denmark's visit. The Folio text is not always reliable, and the actors tinkered with the playbook.

At some stage after 1609 two songs from Thomas Middleton's *The Witch* (played by the King's Men at the Blackfriars Theatre and influenced by *Macbeth*) were interpolated into III.5. and IV.1, and it has been asserted that the Hecate passages (III.5; IV.1.39–43, 125–32) were written to introduce them. This is possible. Many critics have considered Hecate's speech 'too crude' for Shakespeare, and its rhythms differ from those of the Witches. But is III.5 any more 'unShakespearian' than many of his 'visionary' scenes? It links the play to the Senecan tradition which was in Shakespeare's mind while composing *Macbeth* (Cf. Medea's invoking of Hecate, p. 521); it makes a quasi-theological distinction between those who use the super-natural merely for their own profit and those who worship evil as a god (ll.12–13); it lets us know the nature of the 'illusions' to be seen by Macbeth; above all, the scene has an ironic function, showing, even before he moves against Macduff, the futility of Macbeth's search for 'security'. Moreover Hecate makes the Witches 'less solemn, less awe-inspiring',[1] and their malice more explicit when they appear in IV.1.

As they stand, the lines III.6.37–9 are inconsistent with IV.1.139–43, since they make Macbeth aware of Macduff's flight before he is told (to his surprise) after the Witches have vanished, that the thane has fled to England. The time-scale is wrong too, or else we are in 'double time' as in *Othello*. Again there is excellent irony if the audience knows that Macbeth's victim has escaped, before the tyrant is given pretended security in IV.1.[2]

Coleridge thought the Porter-scene an interpolation, but it is now generally recognized that this piece of grotesque comedy both relieves and intensified the tragedy. Moreover, it enunciates in a different key and with topical references (to Jesuits, the Gunpowder Plot, and corn-shortages) some of the

---

[1] R. L. Rogers, '*Double Profit*' in *Macbeth*, Melbourne, 1942, pp. 29–31. Cf. R. Flatter, 'Who wrote the Hecate Scene?', *ShJb*, xciii, 1957, pp. 196–210; J. R. Brown, 'Shakespeare: the Tragedy of Macbeth', *Studies in English*, No. 14, 1963, pp. 11–13. Contrast L. C. Knights, *Explorations*, 1946, pp. 30–1; J. M. Nosworthy, *RES*, April 1948, p. 138; K. Muir, *Arden*, p. xxxvi.

[2] Cf. R. L. Rogers, *op. cit.* pp. 25–9.

main themes of the tragedy, namely treachery, hypocrisy, and murder.[1]

Some other passages have been thought by various editors not to be by Shakespeare,[2] but they can all be explained as deliberate attempts at a different style by Shakespeare, or as contaminated by the actors.

The play was seen at the Globe by Dr Simon Forman in spring 1611, but there were echoes of it over three years earlier in *Lingua* (a sleepwalking scene), and references to a ghost like Banquo's in *The Puritaine* (IV.3.89) and *The Knight of the Burning Pestle* (V.1.26–32), the first two published and the last acted, in 1607. With its reference to 'twofold balls and treble sceptres' (IV.1.121) and touching for the King's Evil (IV.3.146) it must have been written after the accession of James I in 1603. The references to traitors and equivocation were obviously to the trials after the Gunpowder Plot, and especially to that of Father Garnet (March 1606), who after many of his denials had been countered, 'fell into a large Discourse of defending *Equivocations*, with many weak and frivolous Distinctions'.[3] So the allusions in the Porter-scene were written about that time, when the subject was topical. The late J. D. Wilson suggested that they were added for a court performance, but the idea of equivocation is so integral to the scene and to the play in general that I find this hard to believe. Resemblances between *Macbeth* and Marston's *Sophonisba* (played by the Children at Blackfriars and entered in the S.R. 17 March 1606), if due to Marston's imitating Shakespeare, would throw the date of *Macbeth* back into 1605 at least, but the debt was probably Shakespeare's. If imitating Shakespeare, Marston would probably have done more than take a few words here and there. Shakespeare on the other hand may well have remembered certain features of Marston's tragedy, of which the author declared 'I have not labored in this poeme, to tie myselfe to relate any thing as an historian, but to inlarge every thing as a Poet. To transcribe Authors, quote authorities, and translate Latin prose-orations into English blank-verse, hath . . . beene the least aime of my

---

[1] Muir, *Arden*, pp. xxvii–xxxiv writes well on this scene.
[2] Muir, *op. cit.* pp. xxvi–vii.
[3] Letter from John Chamberlaine to Winwood, 5 April 1606. R. Winwood, *Memorials*, 1725, II, pp. 205–6.

studies.'[1] This was no doubt aimed at Jonson's *Sejanus*, and Shakespeare would approve, for in *Macbeth* he followed Marston's example rather than Jonson's.

The main contacts with the *Macbeth* theme are by contrast.[2] Here is the story of a loving wife who shows her love by constancy in virtue; and of a husband who is noble and virtuous. Syphax the black-hearted Libyan goes in Act IV, Sc. 1, to a dark vault where a witch Erictho is described at length in terms taken from Lucan's *Pharsalia*. Erictho is powerfully conceived, a vampire who revels in corruption and disgusting filth both physical and moral ('Fair is foul and foul is fair' indeed). She promises Syphax that he shall possess Sophonisba, then deceives him with an illusion, herself taking Sophonisba's form to lie with the young prince. There is also the Ghost of Sophonisba's father Asdrubal who turned traitor and died by poison.

It may well be that Shakespeare's tragedy of treachery, witchcraft and a ghost, was a satisfying rival at the Globe in 1606 to Marston's *Sophonisba* at the Blackfriars. Shakespeare's witchcraft was modern, not classical, and his Ghost much more potent. Yet maybe memories of *Sophonisba* floated up as he penned the epic rhetoric of the 'bloody Captain' in I.2 (not unlike that of the wounded Carthalan in Marston's I.2), and Ross's image, 'Where the Norweyan banners flout the sky / And fan our people cold' (I.2.49–51) may echo Marston's description of the Roman ships coming against Carthage, 'Upon whose tops the *Roman* eagles streached / Their large spread winges, which fan'd the evening ayre / To us cold breath' (I.2).[3] Other verbal parallels are insignificant.[4]

Certainly Shakespeare did not write *Macbeth* only as a *riposte* to *Sophonisba*. Although there is no sure evidence to support Malone's conjecture that it was specially written for performance before James I and the King of Denmark during the

[1] 'To the Generall Reader', *Sophonisba*, in *The Plays of J. Marston* ed. H. Harvey Wood, 1938, II, p. 5 and p. xii.

[2] *Sophonisba* is a story found in Livy, Appian and many Renaissance historians and short-story tellers, about the noble Carthaginian bride of a young general who leaves her in order to fight the Romans, whereupon she is carried off by the Libyan King Syphax who twice tries to force her. There is much changing of sides in the war, and Sophonisba finally drinks poison with her husband's connivance.

[3] Cf. H. H. Wood, ed., *op. cit.* p. 13.

[4] Listed in K. Muir ed., *Arden*, pp. xxiin, xxiiin.

latter's visit (18 July–10 August), Shakespeare probably had an eye on Court performance. The theme was chosen to please the King by referring to his ancestry, his touching for the 'King's Evil', and his interest in witches and abnormal psychology. The most likely date of composition is in the spring and summer of 1606, between the execution of the Gunpowder Plotters (Henry Garnet 3 May) and August. The Plot made regicide topical; there was another alarm on 22 March when it was rumoured that an attempt had been made on the King's life;[1] and early in July Salisbury's agents uncovered a plot to persuade Captain William Neuce (who had led a company of Irish to enter Spanish service in the Low Countries) to hand over the keys of Sluys or Flushing and to kill the King when he was out hunting at Royston. According to the Venetian ambassador, Neuce insisted on asking a Catholic priest whether he could kill the King without endangering his soul: 'Accordingly it would seem, they arranged a colloquy between him and a Jesuit, who, in the garb of a Dominican Friar, lives as chaplain at the Spanish Embassy, where the interview took place. They say the Englishman was fully satisfied that he might undertake the deed without a single scruple'. Equivocation indeed! Neuce lost his enthusiasm (if indeed he was not an *agent provocateur* of Cecil's); at which his tempters gave him poisoned sweetmeats, which nearly killed him and his wife and two other women with whom he shared them. Depositions were still being taken during Christian IV's visit.[2]

If this does not prove anything about the date of *Macbeth* it demonstrates how suitable the atmosphere was for the composition and performance of the tragedy. One allusion in the play may help in dating: the First Witch's reference to the sailor's wife: 'Her husband's to Aleppo gone, master o' the Tiger' (I.3.7) and the threat, 'Though his bark can not be lost, yet it shall be tempest-toss'd.' A 'Tiger' had sailed for the east in 1604 and had a terrible voyage, arriving back in Milford Haven on 27 June 1606 and Portsmouth Road on 9 July.[3] This suggests that the witch-scene was written or augmented after the end of June.

---

[1] H. N. Paul, *The Royal Play of Macbeth*, 1950, p. 231.
[2] *C.S.P. Venetian*, 1603–7, pp. 375–6, 382; *C.S.P. Dom.*, 1603–10, pp. 323–5.
[3] Cf. M. A. Taylor, *ShQ*, xv, 1964, pp. 110–13; H. N. Paul, *op. cit.* pp. 302–3.

Macbeth was not the first Scottish play. In 1567 the Children of the Queen's Chapel played 'a tragedie of the King of Scottes, to which belonged the scenery of Scotland and a great castle on the other side', perhaps an edifying piece by their master William Hunnis. Robert Greene's *Scottish History of Jame IV* was an unhistorical romance; but Henslowe bought a *Malcolm King of Scotland* from the playwright Charles Massey in 1602. This was probably about Malcolm III and his Queen Margaret, an English princess; it may have included Macbeth and Edward the Confessor. In 1604 a play on the Gowrie conspiracy prepared for the anniversary of that affair on 5 August, was twice performed by the King's men, but it was thought unfit that Princes should be played on the stage in their lifetime . . . so 'tis thought it shall be forbidden'.[1]

The representation of contemporary history was frowned on, but the King suffered much from theatrical satire on his nation and even himself, and the French ambassador was shocked in June 1604 because the Queen attended 'these performances in order to enjoy the laugh against her husband'.[2] In 1605 Jonson and Chapman were imprisoned for satirizing the Scots in *Eastward Ho*, and in February 1606 John Day's *The Isle of Gulls*, played at the Blackfriars Theatre, got its sponsors into trouble for the same reason.

That some Englishmen not only disliked the Scots but regarded Scottish history as a chronicle of violence was shown in the 1606 Parliament when Sir Christopher Piggott, one of the Knights for the County of Bucks, rose in the House during a discussion on 23 February about the Union of the two countries and

'entered into a bye matter of invective against the Scots and Scottish nation; using words of scandal and obloquy, ill beseeming such an audience, and not pertinent to the matter in hand. As "let us not join murderers, thieves, and the roguish Scots, with the well deserving Scots. As much difference between them as between a judge and a thief. He would speak his conscience without flattery of any creature whatsoever. They have not suffered above two kings to die in their

[1] R. Winwood, *Memorials*, 1725, II, p. 41.
[2] E. K. Chambers, *ElSt*, I, p. 325.

beds, these 200 years. Our king hath hardly escaped them; they have attempted him.[1] Now he is come from amongst them, let us free him from such attempts hereafter, etc." The house, we are informed, were amazed at this speech, that they stood staring at one another, and took no notice of it at that time, but let it pass without tax or censure.'[2]

The King was furious, and protested against the House's inaction, so the egregious Sir Christopher was arrested and kept in the Tower for some time, and he was not allowed to sit in Parliament again.

It may well be that after these and other anti-Scottish outbursts the King's Men decided to set the balance right and to honour their royal patron without undue topicality by presenting a Scottish historical tragedy. But why choose the grim story of Macbeth?

There must have been a ballad about him by 1600 when William Kemp in *Nine Daies Wonder* mocked at 'a penny Poet whose first making was the miserable stolne story of Macdoel or Macdobeth or Macsomewhat: for I am sure a Mac it was, though I never had the maw to see it.'[3] Kemp advised him to 'leave writing these beastly ballets, make not good wenches Prophetesses, for litle or no profit'. Where the ballad-maker stole his material we do not know; but apparently the witches were there in some form.

On 27 August 1605, when the King visited Oxford, his cortège, approaching the city from Woodstock, halted near St John's College outside the north gate to hear a short Latin dialogue of welcome written by Dr Matthew Gwinn, Fellow of St John's.[4] In this, three Sibyls greeted King James as the descendant of Banquo (himself no king, but promised eternal rule for his descendants). Each hailed him on behalf of one of his kingdoms and welcomed the members of his family. He was also praised as the unifier of Britain, the restorer of 'the fourfold glory of Canute', and the bringer of peace. The Sibyls ended by praising the founder of St John's, Sir Thomas White, and wel-

---

[1] A reference to the Gowrie conspiracy.

[2] W. Cobbett, *Parliamentary History of England*, 1856, I., col. 1096–8.

[3] *Kemps nine daies wonder* . . . (1600), ed. G. B. Harrison, 1923, pp. 31–2.

[4] Printed in *Vertumnus sive Annus Recurrens Oxonii* . . . 1607. Since the Queen knew no Latin an English version was recited, but not published.

coming the King to the University (Text I). Macbeth was not mentioned. Doubtless the importance of his reign, for Dr Gwinn (and James himself) lay in the prophecy to Banquo and the escape of Fleance which resulted ultimately in the line of the Stuarts.

The several correspondences between this effusion and *Macbeth* have made scholars speculate that Shakespeare may have been there and have heard (and treasured) what the three Sibyls said.[1] But he could have heard details of the Oxford visit afterwards in London or Stratford, for it was much discussed as a splendid occasion. He *may* have been directed to the reign of Macbeth by hearing of Gwinn's dialogue—he may even have known Gwinn personally[2]—but he probably knew Holinshed better than the Doctor did, and he may have come upon the Macbeth story when tracing the King's ancestry in search of a theme which might please his royal patron.

K. Muir points to a parallel between Macbeth's dialogue with the Doctor in V.3.37 and a speech in Samuel Daniel's *Arcadia Reformed*, a pastoral tragicomedy produced by Gwinn before the Queen during the Oxford celebrations and published as *The Queenes Arcadia* in 1606 (S.R. 26 November 1605). It occurs in Act III after the unfaithful Daphne has consulted the quack doctor Alcon about her inability to sleep:

> what
> Can Phisicke doe to cure that hideous wound
> My lusts have given my Conscience? which I see
> Is that which onely is diseas'd within
> And not my body now, that's it doth so
> Disquiet all the lodging of my spirits
> As keeps me waking, that is it presents
> Those ougly formes of terror that affright
> My broken sleepes, that layes upon my heart
> This heavy loade that weighes it downe with griefe . . . (F2ᵛ)

[1] They have not forgotten the scandalous story that Sir William Davenant (son of an Oxford vintner) claimed to be Shakespeare's son, and that William D. was baptized on 3 March 1606.

[2] Gwinn (1588?–1627) began his Oxford career by teaching music, but gave it up because books were hard to get and 'the practice of that science was unusual if not useless'. Turning to medicine he became a celebrated physician. A friend of Florio and Bruno, he wrote and produced plays in the University but lived mainly in London.

This seems to be a remarkable instance of that give-and-take often noted in the relations between Daniel and Shakespeare. If the former's play was published early in 1606, Shakespeare may have read it while composing *Macbeth*.

Whether or not Shakespeare was influenced by Gwinn's work, the Oxford dialogue proves the topicality of the Banquo prophecies when Shakespeare wrote *Macbeth*.

Further evidence of the sudden English interest in Scottish history is afforded by the 1606 edition of *A Continuance of Albions England* by William Warner which added Books 14–16 to the work originally published in 1586. The new material, miscellaneous in nature and doggerel in style, included assertions of the essential unity of Great Britain through racial intermixture, flattery of the King, and in Book 15, Ch. 94 and 95, two companion pictures: the story of Macbeth and Fleance and that of the Gunpowder Plot. The former is intended mainly to set forth the origin of the Stuarts in the love of Fleance for the daughter of King Griffith of Wales, but mentions the murder of Banquo and the prophecy of the 'Fairies' or 'Weird-Elfes' (Text II). I print this as an analogue, but I suspect that it was influenced by Shakespeare's play, for it insists on Macbeth's 'guiltie Conscience' and 'selfe-tormenting mind', and that 'But to proceed in bloud he thought no safetie to find', which recalls III.4.135–8.

The story of Macbeth and his murder of Duncan goes back to the early eleventh century, when Scotland had largely been unified and the ideas of nationality and kingship were gradually developing. North of Inverness was mainly in Norwegian hands. In Moray the Macbeth family were the overlords (Mormaers) and our Macbeth's father Findlaech (Finlay)[1] was defeated by Sigurd of Orkney in Caithness when he tried to destroy the Viking's growing power. This was in the reign of Kenneth II, whose uneasy rule stretched from the Tweed to the Pentland Firth, with Strathclyde as a vassal state. Kenneth is said to have been slain by Fenella (the 'white shouldered') to avenge the execution of her rebel son, or it may have been because Kenneth had arbitrarily changed the law of royal succession. Previously there had been a complicated system of alternate succession by different branches of a family whereby a member of the family of the King's predecessor inherited when a monarch died. In

[1] Not Sinell, as in Hol. (p. 488), and Sinel (I.3.71).

addition there was an elective custom, for if an heir seemed too young or incapable to bear the rigours of leadership in that wild age, a more competent relative could be elected by the nobility. Kenneth II, anxious that his own son Malcolm should succeed him, introduced a law of primogeniture which was not universally agreeable. This is important for our knowledge of the historical Macbeth.

Malcolm II got the throne only after two others had reigned (Cullen and Kenneth III); then he proved an excellent ruler, beating an alliance of English and Danes in 1018 and taking all the Lowlands into his kingdom; but in 1031 he was forced to admit the supremacy of King Cnut, who invaded Alba.

Malcolm II had no son, but at least two daughters: one married Sigurd of Caithness and bore a redoubtable son, Thorfinn; another married Crinan, the Lord of Dunkeld, and bore Duncan. Some chroniclers tell that a third daughter Douda was the wife of Finlay and bore Macbeth, who was thus Duncan's cousin.

Duncan was only young and his reign (1034–40) was made unhappy by military defeats. His enemy the Earl of Northumberland devastated Strathclyde, and when Duncan in revenge besieged Durham, he lost all his foot-soldiers, whose heads were placed on stakes round the city marketplace. He was also unsuccessful against Thorfinn who invaded the north. Whether Duncan was rash or weak or saintly, or just unlucky, we cannot say, but there seems to have been little general regret when he was murdered by Macbeth and other nobles.

Macbeth himself had some claim to the throne by the obsolescent custom of alternate succession; so had his wife Gruoch, daughter of a son of Kenneth III who had been killed by Malcolm II in order to ensure Duncan's succession. After killing Duncan at Bothgouanan ('the smith's bothy') near Elgin, Macbeth reigned successfully for seventeen years (1040–57). Many good laws conducive to social order and royal power were ascribed to him; he was generous to the Church and especially to the holy hermits of Lochleven,[1] and in 1050 he went on a pilgrimage to Rome, where he scattered *largesse* 'like seed'.

[1] Cf. Lady Macbeth to Duncan, 'we rest your hermits' (I.6.20). Did Shakespeare transfer this generosity of Macbeth to Duncan?

After their father's murder Duncan's sons Malcolm Canmore ('Bighead') and Donald Bane ('the fair') were kept in Scotland for a time. (They must have been young children.) Malcolm then went to Siward of Northumbria, Duncan's brother-in-law, and in 1054 Siward invaded Scotland on his behalf, and Malcolm may have got a foothold in Strathclyde. After Siward's death Malcolm continued the struggle and in 1057 slew Macbeth at Lumphanan in Aberdeenshire.[1]

How many children had Lady Macbeth may seem unimportant to those students of Shakespeare who never 'look before and after, and sigh for what is not'; but by her first husband Gillecomgain she had at least one, Lulach, who was set up as King by Macbeth's party and was killed in 1058. Lulach had descendants in Moray, who opposed the line of Malcolm for many generations.

Malcolm III made good marriages—first with Ingibiorg (either widow or daughter of Thorfinn) so making peace with the Caithness Norsemen, second with the saintly Margaret (grand-daughter of Edward Ironsides and sister of Edward Atheling). Their daughter Edith (Matilda) married Henry I of England and so became the ancestress of a long line of English kings—as some of Shakespeare's audience would know. Malcolm had to do homage to William the Conqueror and William Rufus, but he frequently invaded England and was finally killed at Alnwick in 1093, after which there was a dynastic war between his brother Donald Bane[2] and other claimants.

Macbeth, if a murderer, was a good king;[3] but Malcolm's descendants and their court chroniclers would hardly think him so. Quite soon therefore he was treated as a villain, and since his good laws could not be ignored, he was said to have reigned well for ten years and then become a tyrant. When the Stewarts came to power and their obscure genealogy had to be extended,

---

[1] The *A–S Chronicle* (Land E) tells how Siward in 1054 invaded Scotland and 'put to flight their king Macbeth and slew the noblest in the land' (trans. Garmonsway, pp. 184–5). Material from Celtic sources is given by W. F. Skene, *Celtic Scotland*, Edinburgh, 1876, Vol. I, Ch. 7, 8.

[2] Donalbain is not with the English forces at V.2.7–8. He spent many years in Ireland.

[3] Highly praised by St. Berchan: 'The liberal king will possess Fortrenn / The red one was fair, yellow, tall; / Pleasant was the youth to me. / Plenteous was Alban east and west, / During the reign of the fierce red one.' (Skene, *op. cit.*, p. 406.)

P

it was done by inventing Banquo and his son Fleance.[1] Macduff was also probably the creation of later chroniclers.

The story of Macbeth as Shakespeare took it over, mainly from Holinshed, was the work of many chroniclers. Since claims have been made that he read several of them, something must be said about them, and a few excerpts will be supplied.

One of the earliest and most fascinating accounts of Macbeth was given by Andrew Wyntoun (*c.* 1350–1428), a Canon regular of St Andrews, in whose rhymed-chronicle of world and Scottish history (1406)[2] the 'historical' as distinct from the legendary part begins with the reign of Malcolm Canmore. His Duncan and Macbeth were a mixture of folklore and tradition (Text III).

Wyntoun tells how Duncan reigned for six years and begot two legitimate sons. But while out hunting he fell in love with the miller's daughter of Forteviot and by her he had a son, Malcolm. From this bastard child descended kings of England such as Henry II and a Pope, Clement VII.

According to Wyntoun Macbeth was incited to murder his cousin Duncan by a dream he had when out hunting with the King in which he saw three women ('weird sisteris') who made three prophecies; and 'the fantasy of this dreame / Muffit [moved] him for to slay his eme'. He made himself king and married Duncan's widow, disregarding the degrees of affinity. Macbeth reigned well and even went to Rome, but then he reverted to his origin, which was diabolic. Wyntoun explains that his mother had one day met a 'faire man' in the woods, who got a son on her and promised that 'na man suld be borne of wif / Of power to reif him his lyf'. The demon often visited her and told her many future things.

Wyntoun does not say how Duncan was murdered, but he describes the building of Macbeth's castle at Dunsinane and how when a yoke of Macduff's oxen failed to draw a load uphill the earl overheard the tyrant threaten to put his head in the yoke. So Macduff fled to England after bidding his wife tell

---

[1] Fleance was said to have fled to Wales where he seduced the daughter of King Griffyth. She bore a son Walter, whose valour took him to Scotland. There he behaved so doughtily that he was made Steward of Scotland. His line took that name. The link with the Welsh royal house also provided an Arthurian flavour.

[2] *The Original Chronicle of Andrew of Wyntoun*, ed. F. J. Amours, S.T.S., 1906, Vol. IV, pp. 254–301.

the King that he would return. Macbeth pursued Macduff, but the brave woman delayed him until her husband's boat was well away from land. In England Macduff tried in vain to persuade Duncan's legitimate sons to go back against Macbeth. He then approached the illegitimate Malcolm who tested him three times by pretending to be lecherous, covetous and false: 'I am so fals that na man may / Trow na word that ever I say'; whereat Macduff in despair and disgust cried, 'I compt his thrift all gane / In whom lawte [loyalty] restis nane.' Malcolm then promised to be true, and they united with Edward the Confessor and the Earl of Northumberland to invade Scotland.

Having heard that Macbeth 'in phantom fretis [ghostly superstitions] had good faith' and believed that he was safe till Birnam wood was brought to Dunsinane, they made every man carry a branch. When Macbeth saw this he fled, and a knight (not Macduff) slew him at the wood of Lumphanan, telling him 'I wes never of woman borne; / Of my moder for I wes schorne.' A Latin epigram rounds off the story.[1]

Noteworthy features of Wyntoun's poem include: the diabolical origin of Macbeth; his connection with prophecies, and his fatal reliance on them; the absence of a Lady Macbeth and Banquo. Macbeth is moved by his own ambition and the 'weird sisters'; the murder of King Duff by Donwald is not mentioned; that of Duncan is not described; Malcolm's test of Macduff is given at great length.

The earliest 'historical' account of Macbeth, however, came in the *Chronica Gentis Scotorum* of John of Fordun (died about 1384),[2] who tells briefly of the murder of Malcolm Duff, without giving Donwald's name. He tells how Kenneth III forced through a change in the system of royal succession to primogeniture, so that

'every king on his death, should be succeeded by his son or his daughter or his nephew or his niece, or by his brother or sister, in the collateral line; or in short by whoever was the nearest survivor in blood to the deceased king, even though

[1] *Rex Makabedus decim Scocie septem fit annis,/In cuis regno fertile tempus erat;/Hunc in Lumfanan truncatur morte crudeli/Duncani natus, nomine Malcolmus.*

[2] Johannis de Fordun, *Chronica*, in *The Historians of Scotland*, ed. W. F. Skene, Edinburgh, 1871, Vol. I, Bk. IV, Ch. 26. Translation in Vol. 4.

it were a babe a day old; for it is said, "A King's age consists in his subjects' faith"; and no law contrary to this has since prevailed.' (Bk. IV, Ch. 29)

Fordun also tells how Kenneth III was cunningly murdered by Fenella, daughter of the Earl of Angus. After Malcolm II's death there is a chapter (IV.42) 'Concerning vile treachery the basest of all vices, to be execrated and shunned by all'.

Duncan was a gentle soul: 'so good was he that no dissension ever broke out in his kingdom . . . among the princes but, hearing of it, he immediately brought peace.' He was killed through the wickedness of a family (the murderers of both his grandfather and great grandfather) the head of which was Machabeus, son of Finele. Duncan was 'so patient and remiss that he would not listen to rumours of conspiracy but would cover the suspects with his friendship'. The method of his murder is not told, nor is Lady Macbeth or Banquo mentioned. The building of Dunsinane Castle is ignored. Macduff hated Macbeth but hid his opinion of him. 'For what reason I do not know', Macbeth swore to put him under the yoke. So Macduff fled as soon as he could get a little boat. There is a pleasant account of the tyrant coming to a point of land where he saw the ship sailing away to safety. The exile of Macduff makes all men hate Macbeth. Malcolm tests Macduff lengthily. (Bk. V. Ch. 1–6.) They defeat Macbeth easily; he is driven north 'among the narrow passes of the country and the thickets of the woods'. His men abandon him in battle, knowing that Malcolm is their rightful lord. With Malcolm and Macduff in mind Fordun (Bk. V, Ch. 8) excuses those subjects of a tyrant who flee their country.

Neither Fordun nor Wyntoun was printed until long after Shakespeare's time, but the *Scotorum Historiae* of Hector Boethius (Boece) was published in about 1527, and several other editions, and a Scottish translation by John Bellenden in about 1536. Boece was Holinshed's main source and his account was incorporated in the narrative from which Text IV is taken. Certain features of his treatment deserve separate notice; and a few short passages not repeated in Holinshed must be given.

In describing the murder of King Duff, Boece develops the character of Donwald's wife, who pesters her husband until he admits his fury at the King's execution of his friends.

'This woman wes of unmercifull cruelte, havend na less hatrent þan hir housband had agains þe King, for sindry of hir freyndes were justifiit in þat samyn maner, throw quhilk hir venomous ire wes bolden ilk daye with mair indignacioun, noch knawing to quhom scho mycht oppen þe samyn. And quhen scho understude hir husband of þe samyn intencioun, scho exhortit him to be of gude chere, promitting to fynd þe waye how þir injuris mycht be best revengit, saying þe King was oft tymes familiarlie lugeitt with þame, and mycht þairfor be punesit at þair pleseir, quhilk suld be done but any tary . . .'[1]

Donwald's hypocrisy is also stressed, for he spent the night of the murder with the King's guards, telling them of the great kindness often shown him by the King. On the discovery of the murder he was assiduous 'above the measure of proper affecioun' in searching for the murderers, so that some nobles began to suspect him. Donwald's flight is explained as due to conscience: 'The mynde of every cursit tyran be naturall inclinacioun dredis all creature, schawing þame cryminabill ether in wlt[2] or contenance, and hes ay sik fere of þair lyfe þat þai geif to na man credit, eschewing all gude cumpany, and levand in obscure and schaymfull places.' Not all applicable to Macbeth.

When Macbeth and Banquo meet the three women, Boece calls them 'thre weird sisteris or wiches' and repeats 'wiches' several times. He also gives details of Lady Macbeth's pressure on her husband to kill Duncan speedily, 'þat scho mycht be ane qwene; calland him oft tymes debill cowart and nocht desyrus of honouris, sen he durst nocht assailʒe þe thing with manhede and curage quhilk is offerit to him be benevolence of fortoun, howbeit sindry utheris offeris þame to maist terribill jeopardeis, knawing na sikkirnes to succede þereftir.' Banquo is not mentioned as privy to the crime, and he is murdered only because Macbeth fears his posterity.

Macbeth ruled well for ten years, but 'þe samyn wes contrair his naturall inclinacioun' and he 'returnit to his innative cruelte, and became furious, as þe nature of all tyrannis is quhilkis conqueris realmes be wrangwis menis, traisting all pepill to doo

---

[1] *The Chronicle* . . . trans. J. Bellenden, ed. E. B. Batho and H. W. Husbands, STS. Vol. 2, 1941, P. 95.
[2] expression.

siclike cruelties to him as he did afoir to utheris.' Boece handed on to Holinshed the story of Fleance in Wales and his son Walter, with a long genealogy linking them with the Stewart kings; also the adventures of Macduff, the murder of his wife and children, his testing of Malcolm, and his slaying of Macbeth. The attitude of Lady Macbeth to her husband in Boece comes so close to Shakespeare that it seems likely that the dramatist knew the chronicle, either in Latin or in Bellenden's translation.

It is unlikely that Shakespeare read *The Buik of the Chronicles of Scotland* by William Stewart, not published until 1858,[1] although as J. D. Wilson points out, James VI possessed a Latin Boece and 'the Scottis Chronicle written with hand'. There is no evidence that Shakespeare had access to the King's private library at any time. There are parallels between Stewart's chronicle and the play, but they are indecisive and appear elsewhere.[2] Thus 'What! will the line stretch out to the crack of doom?' (IV.i.117) may well have been suggested by Holinshed's genealogy of the Stewarts before and after they came to the throne, and by loyal hopes for the new dynasty in England, hopes shared by James I himself, who prophesied that his line would 'rule over you to the world's end'. In his Oxford entertainment Gwinn wished '*imperium sine fine*' for the new King. Stewart insists on the persuasions of Macbeth's wife, who calls him a coward; but he got this from Hector Boece.

A more likely source is the *Rerum Scoticarum Historia* (1582) of George Buchanan, who had been tutor both to Mary, Queen of Scots, and to James VI, and whose work as reformer and historian was celebrated throughout Europe. There was no English translation of the *History*,[3] and it cannot be proved that Shakespeare used it, but it seems likely that he did, although he would find little in Buchanan which he could not have developed from Holinshed's narrative (Text V).

Shakespeare's Macbeth is very like Buchanan's in his 'sharp Wit', 'lofty spirit' and the stress laid on his cruelty. In Buchanan too he had previously 'conceived a secret Hope of the Kingdom

---

[1] Ed. W. B. D. D. Turnbull, Rolls Series, 3 vols. 1858.
[2] Cf. C. C. Stopes, *Shakespeare's Industry*, 1916, pp. 102–3, and J. D. Wilson, *Camb*, pp. xvii–xix; countered by K. Muir, *Shakespeare's Sources*, pp. 170–1.
[3] My excerpts are from the 1690 translation by T. Page.

in his mind' before he dreamed of the three august women. Like Buchanan's, Macbeth, in the play regarded the creation of Malcolm as Earl of Cumberland ('the first step to the Kingdom of Scotland') as a great obstacle: 'The Prince of Cumberland— that is a step / On which I must fall down, or else o'erleap, / For in my way it lies.'[1] Lady Macbeth's bitter words in I.8.35–60 recall the behaviour of Donwald's wife and the 'daily impor- tunities' of Macbeth's wife in Buchanan, but her calling him a coward is closer to Boece. In Buchanan Banquo was party to the killing of Duncan, and we learn little else of him than that he was a powerful and resourceful man and as successful a general as Macbeth. When Macbeth's brooding fears turned him to tyranny, Banquo was naturally their first target, not because 'in his royalty of nature / Reigns that which would be feared' (III.1.50–1), but because, being 'already stained with the blood of a king', he might imitate Macbeth's example.[2]

Shakespeare came especially close to Buchanan's description of Kenneth's haunting remorse (see p. 511), which was much fuller than in Boece or Holinshed. In III.2 before the feast Lady Macbeth says that they 'dwell in doubtful joy'[3] and has to urge her husband to be 'bright and jovial among your guests'. He lies 'on the torture of the mind / In restless ecstasy'.[4] He sleeps 'in the affliction of these terrible dreams / That shake us nightly'.[5] The voice Kenneth hears seems to be objective in Holinshed whereas Buchanan writes that it was 'either a true one, as some think; or else such a one as his disquieted Mind suggested . . . speaking to him, in his Sleep'. Compare Macbeth at II.2.36–44: 'Methought I heard a voice cry, "Sleep no more! Macbeth does murder sleep".' On which Lady Macbeth says scornfully, 'Who was it that thus cried?' and tells him not to think 'So brainsickly of things'.[6]

Buchanan was more critical than most previous chroniclers.

[1] Cf. K. Muir, *Shakespeare's Sources*, p. 172, and *N&Q*, 1955, pp. 511–12.

[2] H. N. Paul, *op. cit.* p. 218, like Page (1690), translated '*et regio iam sanguine imbutus*' as 'and with royal blood in his veins', which would suggest 'his royalty of nature'. Muir pointed out the error in translation and did not reject the possibility that Shakespeare made the same error.

[3,4] Buchanan wrote, '*Tamen animus, conscientia sceleris inquietus, nullum solidum et sincerum et gaudium esse, permittebat.*'

[5] '*per somnum obversantia, visa horroris plena quietam interpellabant.*'

[6] These parallels and others less close were drawn in Mark H. Liddell's edn. (1903). For his note see K. Muir, *op. cit.*, pp. 169–70n.

He rejected the story that the course of a stream was changed so that King Duffus' body could be buried without trace, and he reduced the coming of Birnam Wood to Dunsinane to a triumphant march of soldiers 'with green Boughs in their Helmets'. Sceptical about supernatural visitations, he turned the Witches into a dream of fair women prophesying. No prophecies were made about Macbeth's imperviousness or length of rule; the prophecy about Banquo's posterity was spread by the tyrant's ill-wishers. Buchanan knew the fabulous stories about Macbeth, but omitted them as 'like *Milesian* Tales, and fitter for the Stage, than an History'. Shakespeare certainly thought them fit for the stage, and the supernatural atmosphere of his tragedy owed nothing to Buchanan.

Nevertheless Shakespeare probably got one or two ideas from Buchanan. Another small but significant example occurs in Banquo's exclamation when doubting the objectivity of the Witches: 'have we eaten on the insane root / That takes the reason prisoner?' (I.3.84–5). Commentators have referred to hemlock roots, and Malone recalled Plutarch's *Life of Antony* in which his soldiers, starving in the Parthian war, ate a root 'that made them out of their wits'. More immediately Shakespeare, whose characters were returning home from defeating the Norsemen, had in his mind Duncan's cunning device at Perth, when he drugged the food and drink offered to the enemy (see p. 512). In Holinshed the Scots used 'the juice of mekilwoort berries', and insanity is not mentioned. Buchanan calls the plant 'Solanum', 'Nightshade', and describes its growth in detail. 'It hath a very small seed, as little as the Grains of a Fig. The Virtue of the Fruit, Root, and especially of the Seed, is *Soporiferous*: and will make men mad, if they be taken in too great Quantities.[1] Possibly the poet had Buchanan's sinister plant in mind when he made Banquo allude to 'the seeds of time' and 'which grain will grow and which will not' (I.3.58–9) as well as to 'the insane root'.

The familiarity with which Buchanan's Macbeth invited Banquo to the fatal feast has been thought to colour the tone of III.1.10–40, but this I doubt. Banquo is to be 'chief guest' at a 'solemn supper' (official banquet), and Macbeth's manner is formal.

---

[1] '*Semen habent perexiguum, velut fici grana, vis fructui, radici, ac maximè semini, somnifera, & quae in amentia, si largius sumantur, agat.*'

Another book which Shakespeare may have glanced through was *De Origine Scotorum* by John Leslie, Bishop of Ross (Rome, 1578). Shakespeare must have read it, if at all, in Latin.[1] Leslie makes no mention of Donwald's wife, but Macbeth's fosters his insane lust for power. The witches, devils in female form, are briefly mentioned in an account of Banquo and his line, and then only as prophesying the extinction of Macbeth's. The murder of Duncan is ascribed to Macbeth alone. Banquo has no part in it, and he is murdered because the tyrant fears him as he fears Macduff. Macduff is said to have 'cut off Macbeth's head and brought it as a gift to Malcolm' (Text VI).

As a staunch defender of his Queen both before and after her abdication, and of her rights to the succession of both the Scottish and English thrones, Leslie laid great stress on the 'unbroken succession of Kings in perpetual line' descended from Banquo, and gave a handsome family tree (Plate 2) headed 'Genealogy of the Royal Family of the Stuarts, who obtain the Scottish Sceptre in a direct line and Succession of eight Monarchs.'

H. N. Paul[2] argues that Shakespeare knew this tree and that it influenced the imagery of III.1. There Banquo 'sees himself "the root and father of many kings" (l. 5)' and 'Macbeth's fears stick deep (are deeply rooted) in Banquo (l. 49) because he is to be "father to a line of kings" (*series perpetuo filo contexta*).' Macbeth also refers to his 'fruitless crown' and 'barren sceptre', and 'the seed of Banquo'. 'And finally in the fourth Act it is a show of eight (not nine) kings, for the title of the cut speaks of a series "*octo posteriorum regum*"'. For Leslie, Mary was still Queen of Scots in 1578 and James 'still only "*Scotorum Princeps*"'. For Englishmen 'there were in 1578 nine Stuart kings in the direct line, not eight'; and certainly nine for Shakespeare in 1606.[3]

It is tempting to conclude that the dramatist based his show of kings upon Leslie's royal tree, and drew imagery from it; also that Leslie's account of Banquo supported Shakespeare's natural desire to present the ancestor of James VI as innocent of any crime.

[1] Leslie wrote the part dealing with 1436–1541 in Scots for Q. Mary (1568–70), then the whole in Latin. This was turned into Scots in 1596 by Fr James Dalrymple but not printed until 1884–95 (ed. E. G. Cody, S.T.S. 2 vols).

[2] *Op. cit.* pp. 174–5.

[3] But would Shakespeare dare to present an 'illusion' of James VI on the stage?

As Professor J. O. Wood has suggested,[1] a line in the Latin of Leslie's account of the discovery of the witches who troubled King Duff may help to solve the mystery of Hecate's 'drop profound' (III.5.24). The second witch was discovered murmuring spells and moistening a waxen image with a certain liquor, gradually, drop by drop: *'alteram carmina sub murmurantem, imaginem liquore quodam sensim instillato perfundere'* (Leslie, p. 193). *'Perfundere'*, to moisten, wet, sprinkle; Cf. 'profound' from *profundus*, 'from the bottom', 'from the depth', 'concealed'. The confusion of the two forms makes a pun characteristic of Shakespeare and it may well be that a reminiscence of Leslie's witches was at the bottom of it.

Although Leslie died near Brussels in 1596, King James had good reason always to be grateful to him, for he put forward his right to the English throne during James's youth. In his *Defence of the honour of the Princess Marie Queene of Scotlande* (1569)[2] he asserted her innocence of Darnley's murder and declared that by forcing her to abdicate her nobles had 'given to the subjects of other Princes such a wicked presidente, that yf theis other subjects treade fast upon your steppes, there will shortelie fewe Kings and Princes in Christendome have any sure and faste holde of their scepter and royall dignitie' (f. 53ᵛ). He tells the murder of Duffus by Donwald as analogous to that of Darnley by Moray, adding a few interesting details: 'when the kinge was a bedd in the Castle, wherof this Donwaldus had the keapinge, he banketed hys chamberlaines, and so sore oppressed them with immoderat surfeitynge and drinckinge,[3] that when they were ons gotten aboute midnight to sleep in theire bedds, ye might have ronge a greate bell over their heades, longe ere they woulde wake' (f. 41ʳ).

Shakespeare may have looked through these works, and it is possible that the insistence on bells—the small bell at II.1.31–2 and the alarm bell at II.3.75, 81–5, and even Macbeth's anguished comment on the knocking, 'Wake Duncan with thy knocking: I would thou couldst!' (II.2.74–5)—were suggested

---

[1] 'Hecate's "Vap'rous Drop profound"', *N&Q* n.s. II, 7, 1964, pp. 262–4.

[2] *A Defence of the Honour of the Right Highe, Mightye, and Noble Princesse Marie, Queene of Scotlande and Dowager of France; with a Declaration as well of her Right, Title, and Interest to the Succession of the Crowne of England, as that the Regimente of Women ys conformable to the Lawe of God and Nature*, 1569 (anon., reprinted 1571).

[3] Lady Macbeth does this: I.7.61–70.

by Leslie. But Shakespeare was quite as inventive as the Bishop.

From 1568 to 1572 Leslie was Mary's ambassador in England, hoping for help to get her restored to her throne. Later he re-wrote his argument about the succession, first in Latin (1580), then in English (1584),[1] adding the name of James VI as en-titled to be Elizabeth's heir. He had already in 1569 looked forward to 'a perfect and entire monarchie of this Ile of Britaine, united and incorporated after a most marvellous sorte, and in the worthie and excellente person of a Prince mete and capable of such a monarchie' (f. 147^v).

He now added 'An Exhortation to the English and Scottishe Nations' to unite 'under the regiment of one rightful Prince, and Catholique Religion of their Auncestors' (f. 71^r). He meant 'Roman Catholic' religion, of course. These words would not appeal to James VI, but Leslie anticipated, and may have influenced, James's sincere desire, not only to prove his heredi-tary right to both crowns, but to join the two countries in per-petual peace. Hence in addressing Parliament in 1603 he spoke of 'my Descent lineally out of the *Loynes* of Henry the Seventh', and of 'the Union of the two ancient and famous Kingdoms' in an 'inward Peace annexed to my Person'. Parliament, however, was strangely reluctant to treat the Scots as equal citizens, and when *Macbeth* was written the King was still hoping in vain for free trade between the two countries and the inter-naturaliza-tion of their subjects. Shakespeare shows the saintly King Edward of England aiding a legitimate Scottish heir, and Mac-beth sees among future kings some 'That two-fold balls and treble sceptres carry' (IV.i.121)—looking forward to King James I and his line.

Shakespeare seems to have been aware not only of the King's various interests but also of his immediate family history and royal connections. Suggestions have occasionally been made that the dramatist intended the audience to draw parallels between the murder of Duncan, that of Darnley by Bothwell; and even the Massacre of St Bartholomew in Paris in 1572.[2] Any

---

[1] *A Treatise touching the Right, Title and Interest of the most excellent Princesse Marie, Queene of Scotland, And of the most noble king James, her Graces Sonne, to the succession of the Crowne of England . . . by . . . John Lesley, Byshop of Rosse, An. 1584.*

[2] E.g. by Lilian Winstanley, *Macbeth, King Lear, and Contemporary History*, Cambridge, 1922.

obvious analogy between Lady Macbeth and Mary Queen of Scots would have displeased the King immensely. Nevertheless there are details of resemblance, and maybe Shakespeare], with that wonderful memory ever ready to float up, albeit unconsciously, associations from reading or hearsay, utilized in representing an ancient crime, with no desire to have them recognized, incidents connected with the King's father's death and his mother's French relatives.

The show of kings in IV.1 affords a significant instance of this possibility. In the chronicles the line of Banquo and Fleance is either described in words or shown as a genealogical tree. Looking for some more striking method of projection than a long prophetic catalogue of names, Shakespeare found it in an anecdote about Catherine de Medici (1519–89), who as Queen Mother of France had become as evil in English Protestant eyes as Lady Macbeth could be, for she was thought to have poisoned many rivals and to have instigated the Massacre of St Bartholomew.[1] She was the mother of Queen Mary's shortlived first husband, Francis II. Very superstitious, Catherine frequently consulted astrologers and magicians, including Nostradamus and Cosimo Ruggieri. According to one story, after the accidental death of her husband Henri II in 1559 she asked a magician to show her the future of the crown and of her family. Accounts varied as the legend grew. One relates that the conjuror took a concave steel mirror on the four corners of which were written in pigeon's blood four names, Jehovah, Mithras, Elohim and Adonai. At the first hour after sunset as the new moon rose over the Forest of Chaumont, he made Catherine look into the mirror, where she saw each of her sons circling round as many times as he would reign in years. François II went by rapidly (he reigned only one year, 1559–60); Charles IX (1560–74) made fourteen turns; Henri III (1574–89) fifteen. When her enemy Henry of Navarre appeared and made twenty turns (1589–1610), Catherine broke off the séance.[2]

Shakespeare must have seen a reference to this in Henry Howard's *A Defensative against the Poyson of supposed Prophecies*

---

[1] *Ane Merveillous discours Upon the lyfe, deides, and behaviours of Katherine de Medicis, Queene Mother . . .* Printed at Cracow [Edinburgh?], 1576, [By H. Estienne?].

[2] Cf. Jacques Castelnau, *Cathérine de Medici*, Paris, 1954; Eugène de France, *Cathérine de Medici, ses astrologues et ses médecins envoûteurs*, Paris, 1911.

(1583), a book attacking belief in witchcraft.[1] The dramatist may also have known a more detailed account, of the kind given (too late for use in *Macbeth*) by Simon Goulart in his *Trésors d'histoires admirables* (1607), and by Nicholas Pasquier in a letter written shortly after the assassination of Henri IV in 1610.[2] I cite two of the passages (Text VII). In Pasquier there is no mirror; the figures move round a magic circle.

Shakespeare combines a parade of kings from Robert II onwards and a mirror in which Macbeth can see more Stuarts, including rulers of the United Kingdom from James VI onwards. In the first Folio the mirror is carried by Banquo, in a stage direction, but this contradicts the text, where 'the eighth appears, who bears a glass / Which shows me many more'.

If Catherine was in Shakespeare's mind at this point of the play she may have entered it elsewhere. She was said to have urged on the vacillating Charles IX to order the massacre of Protestants in 1572. De Thou told how, after it had been decided that the signal for the massacre should be 'the tolling of the bell of the Palace-clock'

'The Queen, fearing lest the King, whom she thought she did observe, still wavering and staggering at the horridness of the enterprize, should change his mind, comes into his Bed chamber at midnight, whither presently Anjou, Nevers, Biragus, Tavannes, Radesianus, and after them Guise, came by agreement. There they immind the King, hesitating, and after a long discourse had to and fro, upbraided by his Mother, that by his delaying he would let slip a fair occasion offered him by God, of subduing his enemies. By which speech the King, finding himself accused of Cowardise, and being of himself of a fierce nature, and accustomed to bloud-shed, was inflamed, and gave command to put the thing in execution. Therefore the Queen, laying hold of his present heat, lest by delaying it should slack, commands that the sign which was to have been given at break of day should be hastened, and

---

[1] Cf. C. G. Harlow, 'The Authorship of *I Henry VI*', *S.E.L.*, V, 1965, 269–81. The particular parallel was noted by R. Farmer in Steevens's edn. *Works*, 1773, 1778, Vol. x, 490. I have not traced the passage. Howard was the Earl of Northampton, one of James's chief counsellors.

[2] Printed in *Oeuvres d'Estienne Pasquier*, 2 vols., Amsterdam 1723.

that the Bell of the nearer Church of St. German Auxerrois should be tolled.'[1]

The reverberations of that bell were heard by Protestants for generations. Moreover it was widely reported that Charles IX suffered great remorse, sleeplessness and hallucinations after the slaughter. There is no need to believe that Shakespeare consciously recalled St Bartholomew. His alarm bell is rung *after* the murder and would be found in most castles. Macbeth's remorse is based on Kenneth's and needs no other source. Yet the possibility remains.

Equally elusive are parallels with the Darnley–Bothwell murder (e.g. the Macbeths' behaviour after their crime, and Bothwell's). At the latter's trial on 25 March 1567/8, one of his servants deponed:

'My lord came into his lodgeing [i.e. Holyrood] and immediately callit for ane drink, and tuik off his cloathes incontinent, and geid to his bed, and tarriet in his bed about half an hour, quhen *Mr. George Hackett* come to the get [gate] and knocks, and desired to be in; and quhen he came in, he appeared to be in ane greit effray, and was black as any pik, and not ane word to speik. *My Lord* enquirit, "Quhat is the matter man?" And he answerit, "The Kingis house is blawn up, and I trow the King be slayn." And my lord cryit, "Fy, treasoun!" And than he raise and put on his claiths. And þareafter the Erle Huntley and mony came in to my lord, and þai geid into the Queen's house.'[2]

This comes nearer to Shakespeare than to Holinshed's account of the murder of King Duff, which was performed by hirelings. Donwald sat up the rest of the night with the guards; his wife apparently had no part in the deed itself. But neither Macbeth nor his wife goes to bed; they are interrupted by the

[1] *Illustris Viri Iac. August Thuani . . . Historiarum sui Temporis 1543–1607*, 4 vols., 1625. Vol. 1, p. 1075/1/B. Trans. in *Popish Policies and Practices*, Anon, 1674, pp. 28–31. Cf. L. Winstanley, *op. cit.*, Ch. 3, 7.

[2] *Criminal Trials in Scotland*, ed. Robert Pitcairn, 3 vols., 1833 edn., Vol. I, p. 494. 'Deposition of Wm. Powrie one of his servants.' G. Buchanan in *An Detection of the duinges of Marie Queene of Scottes*, (1571, 1572) insisted with heavy irony on her calm throughout. After the murder was reported 'scho hirself settilt hir to Rest with ane Countenance so quyet, and Mynde sa untroublit, that scho sweitly sleipit till the nixt Day at None.'

knocking and retire hastily to wash and don their night attire (II.2.58ff). All the resemblances in the play can be explained on dramatic and psychological grounds. Above all we must avoid any suggestion that Shakespeare intended the King to think of his mother, whom a Scottish Act of Parliament in December 1567 declared 'was previe, Airt and Pairt of the actuall Devise and Deid of the Murthair of the King hir lauchfull Husband, and Father to our Soverane Lord, committed be the said James, sumtyme Erle of Bothwell, his Complices and Pertakeris'.

It is clear that there was no lack of Scottish historical material available to Shakespeare, and that he may have consulted several modern works, but his main source was Hector Boece's narrative as modified by Holinshed in the second volume of his *Chronicles*, 'The Chronicle of Scotland'. I cite the 1587 edition, which the dramatist frequently used, but he may have seen the illustrations in the 1577 volume, examples of which I also give (Text IV, pp. 489 ff.). He did not confine his reading to the Macbeth episode, but ranged widely over early history, taking details and matter of importance from other places.

Thus, from the 'Description of Scotland', with its account of ancient Scottish life and customs and its suggestion that the native spartan ways degenerated through contact with the English, came Macbeth's scornful dismissal of the latter as 'the English epicures' (V.3.8). The description of Scottish women, (Text IVB), their insistence on suckling their own children, their participation in warfare and their readiness to drink the blood of their enemies, influenced the depiction of Lady Macbeth and her 'I have given suck,' etc. (I.7.54ff.). There were numerous stories in Holinshed about women fiercer than the Scottish princess in the Amleth-saga; e.g. the wife of Fergus III (A.D. 767) who strangled her husband because he neglected her for his concubines.

There were other prophetic witches besides Macbeth's. In A.D. 280 King Natholocus sent a trusted servant to consult a witch about the outcome of a rebellion. When the messenger was told that he would kill his master, this put him into a dilemma from which he escaped by first telling the King the witch's answer and then stabbing him to death. No doubt such episodes in the grim series of conspiracies, ambushes and treacherous attacks related by Holinshed helped to fill Shakespeare's mind with the horrific images with which he surrounded the Macbeth story. In that story he found much that was dramatic, but there were gaps and details that had to be altered. Banquo could not be the central figure, since he was removed long before the rightful king was restored. Moreover, in Holinshed he was an accessory in the murder of Duncan, and that would never do. He must remain guiltless; hence the nature of the murder must be changed from semi-public to private. There was also a lack of 'feminine interest' in the Macbeth story. The murderer's wife was dismissed in a parenthesis. Of course Shakespeare could have invented everything, but he never liked to do that, preferring always to remake suitable existing material. The story of the murder of King Duff by Donwald, after a very different encounter with witches, filled the gap, added to Macbeth's character, and also provided an ambitious, resentful wife whose part in the plot was defined more closely than in the original Macbeth story. Taking both from Macbeth and Donwald the idea of reluctant evil and the 'prick of conscience', Shakespeare developed the conflict between scruples and ambition, imagination and callousness into a major theme, picking out from the life of another ambitious murderer, Kenneth II, the account of his troubled sleep and hallucination. So the play could be truly said to present a composite picture of the darkest side of Scottish medieval history as viewed from the happy present in James's benign reign of unity and concord. But in addition, Shakespeare converted what might have been a catalogue of crime and bloodshed into a profound study of guilt and self-destruction in which poetry played as important a part as action and overt motivation.

Inevitably, in adapting his material he departed somewhat from the chronicle and invented much new detail. Thus, to make Macbeth's first crime more evil, Duncan is depicted not as a young and unsatisfactory monarch but as old and venerable. Lady Macbeth's character is almost entirely created by Shakespeare both in its internal convolutions and in its outward manifestations. The ambitious wives in Holinshed and other possible chronicle sources provided merely a sketchy outline which he filled in with such tempestuous chiaroscuro as to make Goneril and Regan seem cardboard figures by comparison.

Macbeth's claims to the throne by his own birth and through

his wife are not mentioned, so the reasons why the nomination of Malcolm as heir would so disturb him are not brought out—perhaps also because that would involve explaining the ancient tanist system of which Holinshed was aware. Macbeth's ambition therefore becomes wilder and less well-founded, and the Witches' prophecy more remarkable. His rise and fall and the speed of the play are intensified by telescoping the history of seventeen years into a few weeks. The good years of the reign are ignored and his beneficent laws. The cruelty mentioned by Holinshed is magnified: once on the throne he becomes a tyrant.

Other incidents are compressed. The three campaigns in Duncan's reign are run together (I.2), and the gradual building of Dunsinane Castle is omitted.

In Holinshed not only was Banquo involved in Duncan's murder, but there was the implication (more definitely made by other chroniclers) that he might serve Macbeth 'of the same cup as he had ministred to his predecessor'. This image produces the 'poison'd chalice' of I.7.11; but Shakespeare's Banquo is a noble soul who at the outset warns Macbeth against trusting the devil's 'honest trifles' (I.3.120–6) and later lets him know that he will not participate in any disloyal or dishonourable action (II.1.21–9). He soon suspects that Macbeth has played 'most foully' for the crown (III.1.3), and he is murdered shortly after the coronation. Macbeth fears not only the prophecy about his descendants but Banquo's very being: 'Under him my Genius is rebuk'd' (III.1.54–72). Bradley thought him tainted by ambition, an accessory after the fact, since he knew the Witches' prophecies, but the Witches did not say that Macbeth would murder Duncan, and Banquo knows no more about that deed than any other courtier. He represses all 'cursed thoughts' and will not try to make the prophecy about his line come true. The contrast between the two men isolates Macbeth in his wickedness.

Macduff's part in the action is increased, so we make his acquaintance early, when he comes on duty with Lennox to rouse the King, and discovers the crime (II.3). He severs relations at once with Macbeth when he goes home to Fife rather than to the coronation (II.4.35). Neither incident is in Holinshed, where he is first mentioned when he fails to accompany his workmen to the building of Dunsinane Castle, and so gains Macbeth's hatred. Shakespeare attributes this enmity to his failure to attend the Banquo-feast. In Holinshed Macbeth himself lays siege to Macduff's castle but is admitted at once by its inmates 'mistrusting none evill'. In Shakespeare he sends murderers (IV.2), and the pathos of Lady Macduff's death is increased by making her ignorant of her husband's flight or its cause. She blames him for unkindness to her and bitterly tells her son that his father is dead and a traitor. Shakespeare wishes us to see her complete innocence of any ill-will towards the tyrant, and how 'cruel are the times, when we are traitors, / And do not know ourselves' (IV.2.18). Her pathos is accentuated at the expense of making her husband's behaviour ambiguous.

In Holinshed Macduff apparently knows of his wife's death before he approaches Malcolm. By keeping him in ignorance until after he has persuaded Malcolm to attack Macbeth, Shakespeare makes his motive more purely patriotic and less personal, and the long scene of moral discussion rises to a fine dramatic climax when Ross comes and gradually discloses the grim tidings. Macduff's reception of the news also adds to the ethical force of the scene by showing how a good and brave man endures the shock of bereavement. This is not the self-conscious Stoicism of Brutus (*JC* IV.3: 'No man bears sorrow better'), but a man reeling under anguish, blaming himself, and preparing for a just revenge ('He has no children.') A worthy antagonist for the tyrant.

Unlike that of the 'history' plays (e.g. *Richard III*), the chronicle material behind *Macbeth* is deficient in detailed description of significant encounters, and especially in dialogue. Indeed we get a close and sustained transcript of the source only in one major scene, this long interview between Macduff and Malcolm, which some critics have called tedious. But it is important for its delineation of the two characters, Malcolm, full of wise caution and rightly mistrustful of anyone from Scotland, and Macduff in his growing desperation, which is finally transformed to hope and gratitude. In addition it lists the bad traits that every good king should avoid, and the appropriate antithesis is set forth in Malcolm's avowal of his innocence. The dramatist thus uses Holinshed adroitly to allude to one of James I's favourite topics, which he had discussed in his *Basilicon Doron*

(1599, reprinted 1603). The account of Edward the Confessor's gift of healing (IV.3.140–59) which is interpolated from the *Chronicles of England* (Text IVD) also makes a pleasant compliment to King James, who was persuaded to 'touch' victims of scrofula and heal them by his prayers—thus proving that he inherited 'the healing benediction' from King Edward and was truly of the English royal line.

Shakespeare's other major transformations of and additions to Holinshed (e.g. his use of the Witches, the Porter, Banquo's ghost) will be discussed in a brief survey of the action of the play as it develops, with special reference to the presentation of the two chief characters. Something must first be said, however, about Shakespeare's debt to the classical tragedies of Seneca.

Editors have pointed out that in *Macbeth* Shakespeare comes nearer to Seneca than elsewhere, using many Senecan devices and in a more concentrated way than previously. Faced with chronicle-material including deeds of bloodshed and darkness, magic, portents, murders, treachery, and a general atmosphere of evil stifling good, the dramatist recalled parallels in Latin plays which had been translated by Jasper Heywood and others.[1] There was no need to go to *Thyestes* for the portents and unnatural accompaniments of crime, since they were already in Holinshed and a commonplace of Elizabethan drama. But maybe the witches owed something to the horrid brew prepared by Medea with its serpents' venom, obscene birds, and baleful herbs (including one cut at midnight and another pinched off with a fingernail while muttering a charm). (*Medea*, 705–34.) Moreover, Medea invokes 'tri-form Hecate' (ll. 7, 577), offers her (as Phoebe) suitably sinister gifts (771–86) and says that Hecate has heard her prayers and 'raised her evil flames with baleful light' (Text VIIIA).

Lady Macbeth herself is like Medea (8–18, 740–51) when she summons up the powers of evil (I.5.40–54). In rejecting her own womanhood she also resembles Medea—'*pelle femineos metus*' (42)—and when she says that she would slay her child rather than not perform her oath (I.7.54–9), Shakespeare is probably remembering that Medea slew her two children despite some 'compunctious visitings of nature'.

[1] *Seneca his tenne tragedies*, ed. Thomas Newton (1581), 1927. Line numbers are those of the Latin text.

The nearest resemblances between *Macbeth* and Seneca's other plays are found in occasional ideas and phrases. In the *Agamemnon* Clytemnestra is a murderer, and one of her adages is transferred to Macbeth:

> CLYT. *per scelera semper sceleribus tutum iter*
> [The safest path to mischiefe is by mischiefe open still]
> MAC. Things bad begun make themselves strong by ill.
>
> (III.2.55)

But this is found in other plays too.[1]

When Cassandra foresees the murder of Agamemnon (V. 2615ff.) she asserts: 'No vision fond fantasticall my senses doth beguile', and 'The gobs of bloude downe dropping on the wynd shall powred bee', which K. Muir thinks may have suggested Macbeth's vision of the airy dagger:

> Art thou not, fatal Vision, sensible
> To feeling as to sight . . .
> . . . I see thee still,
> And on thy blade and dudgeon, gouts of blood
>
> (II.1.36–46)

as well as Banquo's query to the Witches, 'Are ye fantastical, or that indeed / Which outwardly ye show?' (1.3.53–4).

This tragedy of Seneca's seems especially to have seized on Shakespeare's imagination (Text VIII B). Thus the Chorus, Act I, presents a cluster of parallels in words as well as imagery (suggesting that the dramatist read the Studley translation) which are scattered through *Macbeth*.[2] They include 'hurlye burlye done', 'mynister releefe' and 'bloodye Bellon' (Text VIIIB). This last reminds us that Macbeth, who is called 'Bellona's bridegroom' (I.1.55) was accused by Leslie of conceiving Duncan's murder out of a vain desire of ruling.

Holinshed's account of Kenneth II's insomnia may have gained support from this Chorus:

> Sleep that doth overcome and breake the bonds of griefe,
> It cannot ease theyr hartes, nor mynister releefe.
>
> (Cf. II.2.38–41)

---

[1] J. Cunliffe, *The Influence of Seneca on Elizabethan Tragedy*, 1893, pp. 24–5.
[2] K. Muir, *op. cit.* pp. 180–3.

This was something of a Senecan commonplace; e.g. in *Hercules Furens* the Chorus prays that the insane hero may be restored to his senses by sleep.

This latter play, however, has one parallel which may well have come to Shakespeare's mind. When Hercules wakes to sanity and realizes that he has murdered his wife and children he cries (1321–30):

> What Tanais, or what Nilus els, or with his Persyan wave
> What Tigris violent of streame, or what fierce Rhenus flood,
> Or Tagus troublesome that flowes with Ibers treasures good
> May my right hande now wash from gylt? although Maeotis
>   colde
> The waves of all the Northern sea on me shed out now wolde,
> And al the water thereof sholde now passe by my two handes,
> Yet will the mischiefe deepe remayne. (2532–44)[1]

Cf. Macbeth, 'Will all great Neptune's ocean wash this blood / Clean from my hand'; and Lady Macbeth, 'All the perfumes of Arabia will not sweeten this little hand.' (V.1.53.) Macbeth seems also to be recalling a similar passage in *Phaedra*, 715–18:

> *Quis eluet me Tanais aut quae barbaris*
> *Maeotis undis Pontico incumbens mari?*
> *Non ipse toto magnus Oceano pater*
> *Tantum expiaris sceleris.*[2]

At times Shakespeare drew from Seneca suggestions not only for matter but also for rhetorical form. Thus, as Miss E. B. Lyle points out,[3] when Macbeth, expressing his horror at Banquo's ghost (III.4.99–105), lists the fierce animals he would rather meet:

> What man dare, I dare:
> Approach thou like the rugged Russian bear,
> The arm'd rhinoceros, or the Hyrcan tiger:
> Take any shape but that, and my firm nerves
> Shall never tremble . . .

[1] *The first Tragedie of Lucius Anneus Seneca, intituled Hercules newly . . . translated into English metre . . . by Jasper Heywood . . . 1561.*

[2] P. Simpson, *Studies in Elizabethan Drama*, 1955, pp. 51–4, gives other examples also.

[3] *English Studies*, 53, April, 1972.

he is indebted to *Hercules Oetaeus* where the frenzied victim of Nessus' shirt catalogues the agonies he could bear without crying out, and ends:

> Let meete a thousand savage beates and rent me al at once;
> Let Stymphal fowles with houing hoarse lay strokes upon my
> bones,
> Or scrowling bul on thother syde strike on with head and
> horne
> Or els of other serpentes wilde let all my partes be torne;
> With roring earthquakes, hugy lumpes be puffet upon me;
> With griping greefe let all my limmes to nothing pyned bee;
> Although I be to pouder crusht I wil with pacience peace
> In spite of beastes or brusing blowes my sighes and teares shal
> seace.[1]

Arguing, no doubt rightly, that Shakespeare referred to Seneca in the original Latin, Dr Lyle shows the close parallel in sentiment and construction between III.1.63–7, where Macbeth fears lest his aspiration to the crown should prove ultimately futile:

> If't be so,
> For Banquo's issue have I fil'd my mind,
> For them the gracious Duncan have I murder'd,
> Put rancours in the vessel of my peace,
> Only for them,

and the rage of Hercules' wife Deianira that his new bride Iole may have children, and will enjoy the reward of the prayers that Deianira has offered constantly for his safety:

> *Vota quae superis tuli*
> *cessere captae, paelici felix fui,*
> *illi meas audistis, o superi, preces,*
> *incolumis illi remeat* (292–5)[2]

These and other parallels make it seem likely that 'Shakespeare re-read Seneca's plays with the intention of writing a

---

[1] Transl by J. Studley, in Thomas Newton, *Seneca His Tenne Tragedies* (1581), ed. C. Whibley, 1927, II, p. 239.

[2] 'The prayers which to the heavenly ones I raised have been granted to a slave; for a harlot have I been fortunate; for her ye heard my prayers, O gods; for her is he safe returned.' (Loeb trans. by F. J. Miller, Vol. II, 1917, pp. 206–7.)

more classical play than his previous tragedies' (Muir, *op. cit.* p. 180). Yet it would be misleading to call *Macbeth* a Senecan drama. Some occasional tones, turns of style and moral comments go back to Seneca, but the presentation is not mainly through monologue, and the characters are not embodiments of passions or mythical figures, but suffering human beings with mixed motives and credible temptations. And the Roman's fatalism is not pervasive. Indeed, when Macbeth becomes fatalistic he is at the end of his tether.[1]

It is clear that Shakespeare set out to write a short, concentrated tragedy in which the two main characters would be portrayed in considerable detail and the others remain somewhat flat. There was to be a rapid rising movement until the middle of the play (III.4) followed by an equally rapid falling movement, for as Holinshed stated: 'After the contrived slaughter of Banquho, nothing prospered with the foresaid Makbeth.' 'His method seems to have been to work in short, swift scenes dominated by the great protagonist, interspersed with other scenes of slower movement.'[2] The aim was to give an impression of irresistible speed and inevitability; and as R. G. Moulton demonstrated,[3] the method is one of 'oracular action' as the Witches' prophecies are fulfilled through the voluntary acts of the characters, but always with an ironical inflection.

The prophecies are fulfilled, not because the Witches wish it, but through the duality of Macbeth's character. His high deserts and the King's gratitude make him Thane of Cawdor; his base ambition makes him wish to have the other prophecy come true; and the 'thought whose murder is yet but fantastical' is turned into action by the prompting of his wife. In Holinshed, both Donwald and Macbeth are cursed with ambitious wives, and the suggestion is made that neither would have fallen into crime without the woman's influence. Though Donwald had reason to hate Duff, he 'abhorred the act greatlie in his heart', but his wife 'showed him the meanes wherby he might accomplish' the murder of the King. Out of this circumstance Shakespeare created the relationship between Macbeth and Lady

---

[1] See the illuminating essay 'Macbeth et l'Influence de Sénèque' by P. Bacquet in *Bulletin de la Faculté des Lettres de Strasbourg*, May–June 1961, pp. 399–411.

[2] J. Munro, *The London Shakespeare*, Vol. VI, 1958, p. 1091.

[3] R. G. Moulton, *Shakespeare as a Dramatic Artist*, 1885, Ch. 6, pp. 125–43.

Macbeth, her indomitable courage, his vacillation, and her overriding of his qualms of conscience or fear. But Shakespeare develops both her character and his much further, and builds up a contrast between them by emphasizing the moral and psychological effects of their deeds. The man, ambitious yet afflicted with fears and scruples, is led to overcome them and, once in, wades ever deeper into blood despite the warnings of his imagination. The woman, less imaginative, eminently practical and devoted to his interests, rises magnificently to a crisis, but collapses into madness and suicide as her repressed fears and conscience get the upper hand.[1]

In Shakespeare indeed the tragedy becomes one of diseased imaginations and wills leading to self-damnation, and the method of presentation depends largely on irony. Irony is suggested by the source-material, since from the first things are bound to turn out differently from what the protagonist expects. As Banquo says:

> oftentimes, to woo us to our harm,
> The instruments of darkness tell us truths,
> Win us with honest trifles, to betray's
> In deepest consequence. (I.3.123–6)

Whether they already knew Macbeth's story or not, the Jacobean audience would expect topsy-turvy happenings from the moment when the Witches cried 'Fair is foul and foul is fair'.[2]

In the first half of the play everything goes in favour of the Macbeths' earthly rise and moral decline. The naming of Malcolm as Duncan's heir makes Macbeth decide on the murder which he has just rejected. The King comes to Macbeth's castle unexpectedly and gives Lady Macbeth the opportunity she wants. The flight of the two sons brings them under suspicion and lets Macbeth gain the throne at once with general consent. The riding of Banquo and Fleance gives an easy chance for their removal.

Yet the more secure Macbeth tries to make himself the more a reversal is assured. Malcolm returns to defeat him. Macduff

---

[1] Cf. A. C. Bradley, *Shakespearean Tragedy*, pp. 371–9.

[2] In his *Daemonologie* (1597) James VI had inveighed against witches and those who consulted them. His first Parliament passed an Act 'against Conjuration, Witchcraft, and dealing with evil and wicked Spirits' (based on 5 *Eliz.* ch. 16). Cf. H. N. Paul, *op. cit.* pp. 75—130, on the King's activities in this connection.

flees, and his innocent family is blotted out, but he will be the agent of Malcolm's return and himself Macbeth's executioner. Fleance, by escaping, ensures that Banquo's issue will succeed in time.

The second interview with the Witches seems to make Macbeth safe, since they lay down impossibilities as conditions of his downfall—a moving wood and a man not born of woman. But the impossibilities come to pass. All turns on the 'equivocation of the fiend', for the Witches 'are the agents of Nemesis working by means of ironical oracles'.[1]

The equivocation and irony shown in their utterances and the future facts they conceal appear in many details throughout the play, e.g. Duncan's wistful reference to Cawdor, also applicable to Macbeth: 'He was a gentleman on whom I built / An absolute trust' (I.4.13–14); his praise of Macbeth's 'great love' (I.5.23) and his castle with its 'temple-haunting martlet'; the hypocritical flattery extended to the King by his murderous hosts; Lady Macbeth's 'A little water clears us of this deed' (II.2.68); the lucubrations of the Porter (II.3); Macbeth's references to Banquo in the banquet-scene and the health he proposes—to which the Ghost so promptly responds (III.4); and the sarcastic speech of Lennox praising Macbeth (III.6), etc.

For Macbeth and Lady Macbeth as for the Witches, 'Fair is foul and foul is fair'. This reversal of nature, mirrored in the portents and abnormal occurrences surrounding Duncan's murder (taken over from the Donwald story in Holinshed), is basic to the characterization of the usurper and his Queen. In depicting them Shakespeare took further the inquiry into the 'mystery of iniquity' on which he had been engaged during the past few years. In *Othello* and *King Lear* the reasons for Iago's, Goneril's, Regan's and even Edmund's wickedness had not been deeply explored; they were postulated as evil and were little analysed in the course of the action. Now, however, the dramatist traces the development of evil and its effects in both deeds and minds, and educes from his source-material a tragedy in which the diseased imaginations of the evildoers respond to and reflect the evil in the supernatural world.

A passage in Robert Burton's *Anatomy of Melancholy* (1621) in

[1] R. G. Moulton, *op. cit.*

which he summed up contemporary ideas about the force of imagination is relevant here:

> ... And although this fantasy of ours be a subordinate faculty to reason, and should be ruled by it, yet in many men, through inward or outward distemperatures, defect of organs, which are unapt, or otherwise contaminated, it is likewise unapt, or hindred and hurt. This we see verified in sleepers, which by reason of humours and concourse of vapours troubling the fantasy, imagine many times absurd and prodigious things ... when there is nothing offends, but a concourse of bad humours, which trouble the fantasy. This is likewise evident in such as walk in the night in their sleep, and do strange feats: these vapours move the fantasy, the fantasy the appetite, which moving the animal spirits causeth the body to walk up and down as if they were awake. ... Those common apparitions in Bede and Gregory, Saint Bridget's revelations, Wier, *l.3 de lamiis, c.11.* Caesar Vanninus, in his Dialogues, &c reduceth (as I have formerly said) with all those tales of witches' progresses, dancing, riding, transformations, operations, &c. to the force of imagination and the devil's illusions. The like effects almost are to be seen in such as are awake: how many chimeras, antics, golden mountains and castles in the air do they build unto themselves? I appeal to painters, mechanicians, mathematicians. Some ascribe all vices to a false and corrupt imagination, anger, revenge, lust, ambition, covetousness, which prefer falsehood before that which is right and good, deluding the soul with false shows and suppositions. ... Lavater imputes the greatest cause of spectrums, and the like apparitions, to fear, which above all other passions begets the strongest imagination (saith Wierus), and so likewise, love, sorrow, joy, &c.
>
> (Pt. 1. Sec. 2. Mem. 3. Subs. 2)

The force of imagination could be swayed by diabolical agents such as witches, but the Devil himself could directly affect men's minds: 'He begins first with the fantasy, and moves that so strongly, that no reason is able to resist' (Pt. 1. Sec. 2. Mem. 1. Subs. 2).

How well this sums up much of what happens in *Macbeth*!

Having decided to combine the 'weird sisters', the 'witch' and 'wizzards' of Holinshed, with the fantastic hags of current folk-lore and witch-hunts, Shakespeare was led to ascribe to Macbeth the kind of corrupt imagination which was predisposed to encounter and take notice of their soothsaying.[1] The 'false shows and suppositions' native to his ambition, are strengthened by fear and the intermittent workings of a conscience which he admits but will not obey. So he is the victim of hallucinations in which, owing to the conflict in him, the inner and outward images are confused so that he can hardly distinguish the objective from the subjective—as in his vision of the 'air-drawn dagger', and the auditory hallucination of the voice that cried 'Sleep no more!'

On hearing the first prophecies Macbeth starts and admits to himself that his imagination has been set evilly at work:

> My thought whose murder yet is but fantastical
> Shakes so my single state of man, that function
> Is smother'd in surmise, and nothing is
> But what is not   (I.3.139–42)

Banquo asks the Witches, 'Are ye fantastical, or that indeed / What outwardly ye show' (*ibid.* 52–4). They are real women, not illusions, and they operate by working insidiously on Macbeth's predisposition. Lady Macbeth's imagination is less subtle, as her conscience is less active; but she wishes to be possessed by the powers of darkness, wishes herself no woman, and with images of 'knife', 'wound', 'blanket of the dark', indicates that she sees herself as stabbing the sleeping King through his bed-clothes (I.5.38–54). She fears not the sin nor the horror of its physical facts.

The great soliloquy in I.7 reveals the complexity of Macbeth's doubts. On the surface his scruples are not moral but expedient. He does not fear 'the life to come', only failure, 'judgement here'. In Holinshed the 'pricke of conscience' is due to fear lest 'he be served of the same cup as he had ministred to his predecessor'. Here the cup becomes a 'poisoned chalice', and the

---

[1] Cf. King James VI: 'it is most certaine, that God will not permit him [Satan] so to deceive his owne: but onely such, as first wilfully deceive them selves, by running unto him, whom God then suffers to fall in their owne snares, and justly permits them to be illuded with great efficacie of deceit . . .' *Daemonologie* (1597), Bk. I, Ch. 1 (*Workes*, 1616, p. 91).

suggestion of sacrilege betrays a deeper awareness of the wrong he proposes to commit. Macbeth's full consciousness of his villainy makes it worse: he is Duncan's kinsman and host; he knows the King's gentleness and ability which will ensure that his death will arouse universal grief and desire for justice. As he expatiates on this with images of heavenly justice ('angels trumpet-tongued') and pity ('naked new-born babe', etc.) the certainty of his 'deep damnation' combines with his realization that his only motive is ambition—which may not succeed. He tells his wife that he will not go on with the plan but rest content with his honours and present popularity.

His divided mind is ruled by her resolution, but before the murder his perverted will projects itself in the dagger which 'marshallest me the way that I was going', though he soon realizes that it is 'A dagger of the mind, a false creation / Proceeding from the heat-oppressed brain' (II.1.33–49). Such hallucinations were thought to be frequent in men made melancholy either by nature or events.[1] Dismissing the horrifying fantasy, Macbeth prepares himself for the crime in a ritualistic Senecan speech filled with sinister images of night (49–60). Yet he fears that the very stones might cry out, and realizes the 'present horror' of his misdeed, for he is deliberately denying the good in his nature, indeed, in Nature as a whole.

The murder is done off-stage, and so gains in imaginative suggestion as Lady Macbeth, waiting below, boasts of her (Dutch) courage (II.2.1–2) yet starts at the owl's shriek and her husband's call. She fears that he may fail, and she herself has had a moment of humanity: 'Had he not resembled my father as he slept, I had done't'. She is not as immune as she wishes from traces of 'human kindness'.

In II.2 the insistence is on Macbeth's state of mind as he comes down the stair in a daze of horror, and mazed by his narrow escape when, creeping through the anteroom where two courtiers were sleeping, he heard them stir and speak, 'As they

---

[1] 'It is a question moved by Scaliger; why men of a melancholick constitution be more subject to fears, fancies, and imaginations of devils and witches, than other tempers be. His answer is . . . because from their black and sooty blood, gloomie fuliginous spirits do fume into their brain, which bring black, gloomy, and frightful images, representations, and similitudes in them.' (S. Harsnett, *Declaration of Egregious Popish Impostures* (1603), Ch. 21, pp. 131–2; cited by H. N. Paul, *op. cit.* p. 54.)

had seen me with these hangman's hands'. The self-damned man could not join in their piety, though 'I had most need of blessing', he says with bitter naïvety. A voice cried 'Sleep no more . . .'. From this time on, sleeplessness afflicts him, and bad dreams; and in sleep Lady Macbeth's mind will wander perilously.

In this scene the practical wife rejects imagination and reflection. 'These deeds must not be thought / After these ways; so it will make us mad.' (34–5); and ''tis the eye of childhood / That fears a painted devil' (55–6). She has no fear of a corpse or blood, and goes to complete their purpose. When her husband, frenzied by the blood on his hands, thinks himself an Oedipus ('they pluck out mine eyes') and projects his ocean of guilt in the image of handwashing, she reduces everything to everyday normality: 'A little water clears us of this deed.'[1] The knocking does not scare her. There is nothing supernatural; people are at the south entry and must be prepared for. But Macbeth knows that this his crime is so horrible that he had better not think of its implications for his soul (74). '*Nosce teipsum*' would be too frightful a process.

The Porter-scene (II.3) plays on the idea of knocking (which appalled Macbeth) in a manner both comic and sinister when the tipsy porter drolly sees himself as the keeper of hell-gate besieged by all-too-many damned souls. The parallel between this scene and the Harrowing of Hell in the Mystery cycles has been rightly drawn.[2] In the medieval plays Christ after his Crucifixion beats down the gates of Hell to release the virtuous souls 'In bliss to dwell for ever more'.[3] Macbeth's castle is indeed

---

[1] See Text IXB for a remarkable fictional analogue, combining omens, premonitions, a hesitant murderer urged on by his wife, and (the victim's) hallucination of bloodstained hands, in Thomas Deloney's story *Thomas of Reading* (1600).

[2] E.g. by W. A. Armstrong in *Shakespeare's Typology: Miracle and Morality Motifs in 'Macbeth'*, Westfield College, 1970.

[3] I modernize from the Wakefield Pageant, where the minor devil Ribald is the gatekeeper:

JESUS. Lift your heads, O ye gates, and be ye lift up, ye everlasting doors, and the
    King of Glory shall come in.
RIBALD. What art thou that speakest so?
JESUS. A king of bliss that hight Jesus.
RIBALD.   Ye hence fast I rede thee go,
    And mell thee not with us.
BEELZEBUB.   Our gates I trow will last;
    They are so strong I ween;

an infernal place, but Macduff is no Christ when he enters jesting, only to discover that 'Most sacrilegious murder hath broke ope / The Lord's anointed temple.' The finding of the body and the tolling of the alarm bell introduce the associated imagery of Doomsday, with sleepers awakened in a fearful resurrection.[1] Lady Macbeth is as ready-witted as her husband, and if the 'gentle lady' faints at II.3.119, it is at the best moment to distract attention from Macbeth's over-elaborate excuses for killing the two grooms of the chamber.

That the minds of others are filled with images of horror appears in II.4, where the Old Man and Ross consider how unnatural events mirror the murder of Duncan, all the more unnatural since (apparently) done by his sons.

Act III, which historically would begin at least ten years after Macbeth's accession, starts soon after his coronation with Banquo suspicious but showing no sign of trying to make the Witches' prophecy to himself come true. Macbeth's treacherous duplicity is shown when, after calling Banquo 'our chief guest' and taking unusual interest in his riding expedition, he reveals in soliloquy his fear of Banquo's 'royalty of nature' and his superior 'Genius',[2] and especially resents the probability that 'For Banquo's issue have I fil'd my mind', and 'mine eternal jewel / Given to the common enemy of man' (III.1.48–71). There is no suggestion of repentance; his only remedy for his fears and 'the affliction of these terrible dreams / That shake us nightly' (III.2.16–19) is to do 'A deed of dreadful note' in removing Banquo and Fleance.

Macbeth no longer needs Lady Macbeth's urging to drive him to violence. Indeed she fears his obvious obsession with

---

But if our bars blast,
For thee they shall not twine.
JESUS. This stead shall stand no longer stoken [shut]
Open up and let my people pass.
RIBALD. Out, harro! our bailey's broken,
And burst are all our bands of brass.
BEELZEBUB. Harro! our gates begin to crack;
Asunder, I trow, they go.
And Hell, I trow, will all to-shake.
Alas, what I am wo!

[1] W. A. Armstrong, *op. cit.* pp. 12–14, with interesting suggestions for staging this scene.
[2] The Mark Antony-Octavius Caesar allusion anticipates *A&C*, II.3.18–23.

Banquo: 'You must leave this' (35). So he does not take her into his confidence, but in an invocation corresponding to hers, at III.2.46–54 he calls on the diabolical dark to destroy the bond of nature in him that keeps him 'pale' (does this mean 'weak' or 'less black than the Devil'?) One crime must be followed by another. Macbeth regards himself as already damned; henceforth he rushes on to his doom like a machine out of control; unlike a machine he knows what he is doing, and cannot will anything but death to others.

The banquet-scene (III.4), one of Shakespeare's finest inventions, scarcely needed a specific source, for there were many similar ghostly incidents. Thus the medieval *Alphabet of Tales*[1] told about an archdeacon who murdered his Bishop and succeeded him in his diocese, but was betrayed when his victim's head was seen at his inaugural feast (Text X). This tale was dramatized in France in one of the Miracles of Our Lady. Less close to *Macbeth* is a passage in *A Treatise of Specters* by P. de Loyer[2] in which the fears of tyrants are described: 'How often have they supposed and imagined, that they have seene sundry visions and apparitions of those whom they have murdered, or of some others whome they have feared?' De Loyer relates that Theodoric the Great (455–526), whose last years were tarnished by the judicial murders of Boethius and Symmachus, 'on an evening as he sat at supper [saw] the face of Simmachus in a most horrible shape and fashion, with great mustachioes, knitting his browes, frowning with his eyes, biting his lippes for very anger, and looking awry upon him.'[3] Macbeth's excitement grows from the moment when the First Murderer, with blood-stained face, reports their incomplete success. Recalled to his duties as host, he is about to take his seat, hypocritically regretting Banquo's absence, when he sees the Ghost in his place. His efforts to exculpate himself show that he knows a murder has

---

[1] E.E.T.S. 126, 1904, p. 60. Cf. B. D. Brown, *PMLA*, l, 1935, pp. 700–14; and Société des anciens textes français, 1876, i, p. 101.

[2] *A Treatise of Specters or strange Sights, Visions and Apparitions appearing sensibly unto men*, trans. Z. Jones, 1605, Ch. 11, pp. 112–13. Cited by H. N. Paul, *op. cit.* pp. 57–9.

[3] The story in Procopius *De bello italico* is more bizarre, for there Theodoric sees the head of a fish served up at table turn into that of the murdered orator. Plutarch in *De sera numinis vindicta* tells how the parricide Bessus betrayed his guilt when at a feast he suddenly struck at a nest of swallows with his sword because (he cried) they were reproaching him.

occurred—though only he of those present sees the Ghost.[1] His horrified defiance becomes frenzy.

Lady Macbeth, who in III.2.4–7 has admitted to herself that her desire has been 'got without content', rises to the occasion as usual, acting the good hostess, soothing the alarmed guests, and trying to calm her husband while covering up for him. He has long had these fits of disordered fancy, she says. Him she upbraids with her favourite taunt: 'Are you a man?', and treats the Ghost as a hallucination like the air-drawn dagger. But Macbeth knows better, and when, recovering himself, the King drinks to his victim and the Ghost reappears, he is unmanned, as he admits, and his wild looks and speech are too much even for his wife's courage. She dismisses the guests swiftly, just in time, for Macbeth is saying: 'Blood will have blood', and referring to the strange ways in which murders have been disclosed.

Yet at this turning-point of the play Macbeth's diseased imagination makes him resolve to wade still deeper into blood, and he seizes on Macduff as the next object of his suspicious fear. He will send for the reluctant Earl, and 'betimes' consult the Witches to learn 'By the worst means the worst'. The ever-practical Lady Macbeth ascribes his overwrought behaviour to lack of sleep, but he now blames his visions on lack of practice in bloodshed: 'We are yet young in deed'. The mind must learn to take such crimes as a matter of course.

Macbeth's second encounter with the Witches shows his imagination in league with the suggestions of the supernatural agents, when (after a scene, III.5, perhaps not wholly by Shakespeare) he is shown

> such artificial sprites
> As by the strength of their illusion
> Shall draw him on to his confusion. (III.5.27–9)

In Act I Macbeth was sought out by the Witches; now he seeks them, for he has fallen into their power.

The Apparitions are forms taken by the Witches' masters. The first, 'an armed Head', reminds one of the brazen head

---

[1] W. C. Curry (*Shakespeare's Philosophical Patterns*, pp. 73–5) thinks it is an illusion of the devils to help destroy Macbeth. Disbelievers in ghosts such as James I would believe this; many spectators would regard it as Banquo's accusing spirit.

made by Friar Bacon in Greene's comedy,[1] and the head of
Mahomet in his *Alphonsus, King of Aragon* (Act IV), which by its
prophecies helps make Amuracke march against Alphonsus and
be defeated. It may symbolize Macbeth's beheading by Macduff; that is what he must avoid ('beware Macduff'). The
second Apparition, 'a bloody Child', takes shape from Macduff's strange birth, 'from his mother's womb, untimely ripp'd'
and may also foretell the murder of Macduff's children. The
third, 'a child crowned, with a tree in his hand', signifies, not
only young Malcolm and Birnam Wood, but Banquo's seed and
the tree of Stewart descent (found in Leslie's history).

When Macbeth wants more he is given 'a show of Eight
Kings; the last with a glass in his hand; Banquo's Ghost following'. In the glass are shown those who from James VI will rule
the United Kingdom. Banquo's Ghost is here certainly a devilish illusion. The effect is to dismay Macbeth by the final glimpse
of Banquo's royal line, and to confirm him in his personal
security, while making him decide to destroy Macduff. He is
now completely isolated and at the mercy of his passions, all
caution and self-control cast aside. When we next see him in
V.3 he is raging at friend and foe, veering from self-pity to
defiance as all dissolves around him until he is left with nothing
but the prophecies to support him.

The sleep-walking scene was invented to bring Lady Macbeth back into the play and to supply a parallel to her husband's
degeneration. Hers appears more abrupt, for the transitions are
omitted, and we glimpse her collapse in mind and body as her
suppressed fears and remorse break through the savage guard
of her will. For the Elizabethans, as we have noted, bad dreams
and sleep-walking were symptoms of a grave perturbation of
spirit, an ill-directed imagination outside the control of reason.[2]

---

[1] *Friar Bacon and Friar Bungay:*

> Poring upon dark Hecat's principles,
> I have fram'd out a monstrous head of brass,
> That by the enchanting forces of the Devil,
> Shall tell out strange and uncouth aphorisms,
> And girt fair England with a wall of brass. (Sc. xi, 16–20).

Did Shakespeare know of Sir John Harington's interview with James I in 1604 in
which the King spoke 'of those who by second sight had seen the bloody head of
Mary Stuart dancing in the air before her execution; he admitted that he had himself sometimes sought to find, 'out of certain books, a way to know the future'.
(Harington's *Letters* (to Amyas Paulet) cited in C. Williams, *James I*, 1934, p. 202.)

[2] Cf. p. 458 (R. Burton).

Q

No doubt King James would enjoy the scene, for he was interested in abnormal mental phenomena, and investigated numerous cases. Recently (1605) he had looked into the pretensions of Richard Haydock, a medical doctor of New College, Oxford, who preached excellent sermons while apparently asleep. The King had him to Court and sat up two nights to hear him. After making him confess his fraud he forgave Haydock.[1]

There were medieval as well as classical parallels to Lady Macbeth's attempts to wash the blood-guilt from herself; e.g. the Queen who cut the throat of the baby born of her incest. Some blood fell on to her left palm, and she could not get rid of it until she confessed her crime (Text IXA).[2] Shakespeare had used the idea at the end of *Richard II* where Bolingbroke declares: 'I'll make a voyage to the Holy Land / To wash this blood off from my guilty hand' (V.6.49–50).

In *Macbeth* the doctor's professional coolness gives place to horror and pity as the Queen lets out that she shares her husband's guilt in the murders of Duncan, Banquo, and Lady Macduff. As he says, her 'sorely charg'd heart' 'more needs the divine than the physician'. So she fades from view, and in the last lines of the tragedy it is believed that she 'by self and violent hands / Took off her life' (V.7.99–100).

By V.3 Macbeth too is on the verge of breakdown as, awaiting the enemy in his strongly fortified castle, he realizes his total loss of honour and friends, and asks the doctor to cure his wife and himself by ministering to their diseased minds and 'Cleanse the stuff'd bosom of that perilous stuff / Which weighs upon the heart' (V.3.37–45). The doctor's reply is by implication the same as that he made about Lady Macbeth: 'Therein the patient / Must minister to himself'. At this Macbeth bursts out in rage, and suggests that his land is sick, not he. But he has nothing left but his courage.

When Seton brings word of his wife's death, Macbeth's reaction accords well with his assertion that he is so sated with horrors that he has lost the power to feel. 'She should have died hereafter'—not just before the siege. She has let him down; he cannot mourn; but with her passing he experiences the empti-

---

[1] See my article in *London Review* 3, Spring, 1968.
[2] See B. D. Brown, *PMLA*, I, 1935, pp. 700–14.

ness of existence (V.5.16–28). News that Birnam Wood is moving shakes him from his apathy; yet his resolution wanes and he begins (too late) 'to doubt the equivocation of the fiend, / That lies like truth' (43–4). His doom is upon him and, with despair in his heart, 'At least we'll die with harness on our back.'

In Holinshed Macbeth flees north and is overtaken and slain by Macduff at Lumphanan in Aberdeenshire. In the play he is unable to flee and perishes outside his castle after brief battle-passages in which young Siward is killed by Macbeth himself, Macduff pursues the tyrant, 'the castle's gently render'd', and Macbeth refuses to 'play the Roman fool, and die / On mine own sword' (like Brutus and Antony). Face to face with Macduff, he wishes not to fight with him, (V.7.34–5), and he boasts of his immunity. When he learns of Macduff's unnatural birth[1] his faith in the Witches is finally shattered: 'And be these puzzling fiends no more believ'd, / That palter with us in a double sense'. Irony comes full circle as Banquo's early warning proves true. It only remains to show the high cost of virtue's triumph, in the proud grief of Siward for his son, and for Malcolm as the chosen King of Scotland to distribute honours and punishments as they are deserved.

As W. C. Curry has argued, the tragedy is organized to show 'a human soul on its way to the devil and progressively surrendering its free will under the effects of guilt'.[2] At first Macbeth seems able to make his own decisions, but he is influenced 'by inordinate passion, by reason impaired through disordered imagination, by his wife, and by such evil influences as are symbolized in the Weird Sisters'.

The play is conceived in terms of unnatural forces at work on Macbeth, his wife and others. Shakespeare found numerous ingredients ready to hand in Holinshed: the Weird Sisters and

[1] The manner of Julius Caesar's birth gave its name to the 'Caesarian section'. Sigurd's ancestor Volsung was born thus. There were many other stories of strange births; e.g. Antonio de Torquemada in *The Spanish Mandevile of Miracles*, trs. F. Walker (1600), tells of 'the birth of *Don Sanches Garcia*, King of Navarre, whose mother Donna Ursaca, being at a place called Baraban, to take her pleasure in the fields, was by certaine Moores which of a sudden came thither to spoile and make booty, thrust into the body with a speare ... Which her servants perceiving, opened the wound a little more, and tooke the Infant out, causing him to be nourished, the which prospered so well, that he afterwards came to attaine the royall Diademe, and raigned many yeeres.' (fol. 8.)

[2] W. C. Curry, *Shakespeare's Philosophical Patterns*, Baton Rouge, 1937, p. 105.

their prophecies, the ominous darkness and portents and dis-
locations of the natural order, the mysterious voice accusing
Macbeth, his belief in the prophecies of his immunity, etc. He
added other material of the same kind, insisting more, however,
on mental than physical abnormalities; and all these additions
were devised to shape the historical material into a tragedy
permeated by a sense of moral horror which extends through
incidents and characters into the imagery of the entire piece.[1]
The imagery of *Macbeth*, indeed, does more than in some of the
other tragedies to bind the whole play together. This may well
be because so many images were suggested by the source-
material. For Holinshed contains allusions to the wax images
and other enchantments taught to witches 'by evill spirits', to
hypocrisy (Donwald's), blood (King Duff's chamber), terrifying
darkness, sleep and the 'unquiet mind', 'the pricke of conscience',
fear, 'illusion of the devil', etc. All of these fructified in Shakespeare's imagination and were combined with images from his
knowledge of the supernatural, medical psychology, and Senecan drama to suffuse plot, character and thought with a singular
unity of poetic feeling.

There may also be slighter reflections of Holinshed, as in
Lady Macbeth's 'But screw your courage to the sticking place /
And we'll not fail' (I.7.60–1), in the 'bending' images after in
the same scene and II.2.44–6; also in the reference to 'Fate hid
in an augur-hole' at II.3.123. As Professor J. O. Wood has
ingeniously argued, these may have been suggested by the
murder of Kenneth III by Fenella by means of concealed cross-
bows (see p. 487).[2]

Another minor instance occurs when Ross, telling Lady Macduff of her husband's flight, speaks of the fears which make men
'float upon a wild and violent sea' (IV.2.21). This may possibly
be a reminiscence of Buchanan's account of Macduff's escape
'in a small boat' (*navicula*).

I referred (p. 447) to Miss M. C. Bradbrook's suggestion

[1] Cf. G. Wilson Knight, *The Wheel of Fire*, 1930.
[2] J. O. Wood, 'Lady Macbeth's Secret Weapon', *N&Q*, n.s. 12, March 1965,
pp. 98–100. He believes that Shakespeare may have used Leslie's account. The
augur-hole, however, may refer to the sinking of ships by boring holes in their hulls,
as in the folk-song 'The Golden Vanity', where the cabin-boy sank 'the Spanish
Galleon / As she lay in the Low-lands low'. 'He bored with the augur, he bored
once and twice', etc.

that Lady Macbeth's 'I have given suck' in her cruel speech at
I.7.54–9 is a memory of the passage in Boece's *Description of
Scotland* (Text IVB) where the loving care of Scottish mothers
for their children is closely followed by an account of their
bloodthirstiness in war.[1] Shakespeare makes her pervert even
maternal tenderness into murderous intent.

Neither Macbeth nor Lady Macbeth shows any sign of
repentance, and one of the dramatist's major problems was to
prevent their being the monstrous figures of evil they seem to
their enemies. His method was to insist, as so often before, on
the 'mixed nature' of human beings and, by entering into their
minds and letting them express their doubts and revulsions, to
suggest that their evil behaviour was a wasteful misdirection of
energy which might easily have been turned to good; so he
preserves a modicum of sympathy for them even at their worst
moments. He presents the paradox that however much Macbeth
and Lady Macbeth try to dehumanize themselves, they cannot
entirely do so. The soul of man, however low it falls, still retains
(like Milton's Lucifer) some sparks of its divine origin; indeed
damnation is made more grievous by the consciousness of loss.
So Lady Macbeth wishes to unsex herself and become an
embodiment of direst cruelty, yet she cannot murder Duncan;
she suffers constant unease and perturbations of mind; she walks
in her sleep, and kills herself. In Macbeth too, abused nature
retaliates as his reason and freewill are sapped. He drops almost
to the animal level; almost, but not quite, for his imagination
never ceases to trouble him, and even when he likens himself to
a bear tied to a stake (V.7) he is not ignoble in his desperation;
and when he meets Macduff he is surely sincere when he wishes
not to fight him because 'my soul is too much charg'd / With
blood of thine already' (V.7.34–5). Butcher though he is, he can
no more than his wife destroy the bonds that tie him to humanity, and he lives to the last with an energy whose violence sur-
passes anything in *Richard III*, *Julius Caesar*, or *Othello*.

[1] Shakespeare may also have recalled the savage story from Bandello in Fenton's
Certaine Tragicall Discourses (1567) in which (Disc. III) Pandora, left pregnant by
her lover Parthenope, brings on a premature birth, then dashes out the child's
brains and tears it to pieces in a mad fury.

I. Analogue

From
VERTUMNUS SIVE ANNUS RECURRENS
[by Matthew Gwinn] 1607; translated by the editor

Vertumnus sive Annus recurrens, Oxonii, xxix Augusti, Anno. 1605. Coram Jacobo Rege, Henrici Principe, Proceribus. A Joannensibus in Scena. . . . Nicholas Dokes, 1607.

[After this very academic play in Latin comes a short address]

'*Ad Regis introitum, è Ioannensi Collegio extra portam Urbis Borealem sito, tres quasi Sibyllae, sic (Ut é sylva) salutarunt.*'

1   Fatidicas olim fama est cecinisse Sorores
    Imperium sine fine tuae, REX Inclyte, stirpis.[1]
    Banquonem agnovit generosa *Loquabria Thanum:*
    Nec tibi *Banquo,* tuis sceptra nepotibus illae
    Immortalibus immortalia vaticinatae:
    In saltum, ut latens, dum *Banquo* recedis ab Aula.
    Tres eadem pariter canimus tibi fata, tuisque,
    Dum spectande tuis, e saltu accedis ad Urbem:
    Teq; salutamus: Salve, cui *Scotia* servit.
2   *Anglia* cui, salve.   3   Cui servit *Hibernia,* salve.
1   *Gallia* cui titulos, terras dant caetera, salve.
2   Quem, divisa prìus, colit una *Britannia,* salve.
3   Summe Monarcha *Britannice, Hibernice, Gallice,* salve.
1   ANNA parens Regum, soror, uxor, filia, salve.
2   Salve HENRICE Hæres, Princeps pulcherrime, salve.
3   Dux CAROLE, & perbella Polonice Regule,[2] salve.
1   Nec metas fatis, nec tempora ponimus istis;
    Quin Orbis regno, famae sint terminus astra:
    CANUTUM referas regno quadruplice clarum:
    Maior Avus; sequanda tuis diademate solis.
    Nec ferimus caedes, nec bella, nec anxia corda:
    Nec furor in nobis; sed agente calescimus illo

[1] *In margin: Reg. Sct. Duncan (on a cancel) Ang. Canub. Wall. Llhewelyn ap Sitsylht.*
[2] The future Charles I, not yet five, was a sickly child still unable to walk upright or speak properly. Who was the 'Polish Princess'?

Numine, quo THOMAS WHITUS per somnia motus,
Londinensis Eques, Musis haec tecta dicavit:[1]
Musis? imò Deo, tutelarique Ioanni
Ille Deo charum, & curam, prope praetereuntem
Ire salutatum, Christi Precursor, ad Ædem
Christi pergentem, jussit. Dicta ergo salute,
Perge, tuo aspectu sit leta Academia, perge.

M.G.

Translation.
   At the King's entry. From John's College, sited outside the North Gate of the city, three (as it were) Sibyls thus saluted him as if from a wood.

1   Fame says the fatal Sisters once foretold
    Power without end, great Monarch, to thy stock.
    One greeted Banquo, proud Lochaber's Thane:
    Not to thee Banquo, but to thy descendants
    Eternal rule was promised by immortals,
    Hid in a glade as Banquo left the Court.
    We three same Fates so chant to thee and thine
    As, watched by all, from fields thou near'st the City;
    And thus we greet thee: Hail, whom Scotland serves!
2   Whom England, hail!   3   Whom Ireland serves, all hail!
1   Whom France gives titles, lands besides, all hail!
2   Hail, whom divided Britain join'st in one!
3   Hail, mighty Lord of Britain, Ireland, France!
1   Hail Anne, of Kings the mother, sister, wife
    And daughter too!
2   Hail Henry, Prince and Heir!
3   Duke Charles, and lovely Polish princess, hail!
1   We set no times nor limits to the fates;
    In worldly rule fame's goal may be the stars.
    Thou dost restore the fourfold glory of Canute,
    Great ancestor, his crowns and royal thrones.
    Nor shall we bear wars, slaughter, anxious hearts,
    Or fury 'gainst ourselves; but we'll grow warm
    With love and peace through prompting of that spirit
    By which the Knight of London, Thomas White,
    Moved in his sleep, these roofs named to the Muses—
    The Muses? Nay, to God and our patron John.

---

[1] Thomas White (1492–1567), a clothier and founder of St. John's College, Oxford, in 1555. He was said to have been told in a dream to build it on the site of a Cistercian monastery outside the city walls. Before he died White sent a letter to the members of the College begging them to set brotherly love before religious differences.

He, when for his great love and care for God
One passing hailed him, 'Harbinger of Christ',
Bade his well-wisher seek the Temple of Christ.
So now, our greetings done, proceed, and may
Our Colleges be happy in thy sight.[1]

M.G.

II. Analogue

From A CONTINUANCE OF ALBIONS ENGLAND
by William Warner (1606)

Bk. XV. Ch. 94

ONE *Makebeth*, who had traitrously his sometimes Sovereigne
    slaine,
And like a Monster not a Man usurpt in *Scotland* raigne,
Whose guiltie Conscience did itselfe so feelingly accuse,[2]
As nothing not applide by him against himselfe he vewes,
No whispring but of him, gainst him all weapons feares he
    borne,
All beings jointly to revenge his Murthers thinks he sworne,
Wherefore (for such are ever such in selfe-tormenting mind)
But to proceed in bloud he thought no safetie to find.[3]
All Greatnesse therefore, save his owne, his driftings did infest:
Wit so is wisedomes Excrement, and dangerously transgrest.   10
But Pomp, nor Policie, the poore in spirit shall be blest,
When at the generall Doome our Soules and Sathan shall
    contest.
One *Banquho*, powrefulst of the Peers, in popular affection
And prowesse great, was murthred by his tyrannous direction.
Fleance therefore this *Banquhos* sonne fled thence to *Wales* for
    feare,
Whome *Gruffyth* kindly did receive, and cherisht nobly there.
This grew so rare in Court, as him did every Eie and Eare

---

[1] Anthony Nixon, in *Oxford's Triumph: in the royall entertainment of his Majestie*
(1605), described the occasion thus: 'his Majestie passed along till hee came before
Saint John's college, when three little boyes, coming foorth of a castle made all of
ivie, drest like three nymphes (the concept whereof the king did very much
applaude) delivered three orations, first in Latine to the king, then in English to
the queene and young prince; which being ended, his Majestie proceeded towards
the east gate of the citie.'

[2] Cf. III.1.64–9; III.2.19–22.

[3] Cf. III.4.135–8.

Desier to see for person, for discourse delight to heare.
King *Gruffyths* Daughter, Paragon for bewtie and for wit,
He followed with such Offices to complet Courtship fit,   20
That each to other sympathiz'd such setled liking, as
Her heart to his, his heart to hers transplantively did passe.
In other Courts for either Sexe not amorous to appeare
Was not to be a Courtior, but such boldnesse faulted theare:
Her lov'd of him, him lov'd of her, was patent to them both,
Yet dombly so, and either that should th'other noote it loth.
Not he, by Sonnets passonate, did give the world to wit
That he was turnd *Hermaphrodit*, and she the cause of it:
Nor borrowed she of *Phaos* box thereby to seeme more faire,
As those that fondly rob themselves by Arte of that they are.   30
Through this occasion lastly thus he nakt to her his heart:
   I pree thee, *Fleance*, tell quoth she, which I have heard in part,
The Storie of *Fairies* that foretold thy Fathers fate,
For why? I know not why, but sure it throbs my heart of late.
Throb may it so it thrive, quoth he, in you to that event
Divind by them, nor hope I you can Destinie prevent:
But howsoever thus it was. King *Duncane* when alive,
To *Makbeth* and my father did great Dignities derive,
As chiefest for their births, their wit, and valour, also they
Held friendship long, and luckily in *Scotch* affaires did sway.   40
Three *Fairies* in a private walke to them appeared, who
Saluted *Makbeth* King, and gave him other Titles too:
To whom my father, laughing, said they dealt unequall dole,[1]
Behighting nought thereof to him, bot to his Friend the whole.
When of the *Weird-Elfes*[2] one of them, replying, said that he
Should not be King, but of his Streene a many Kings should be.
So vanish they: and what they said of *Makbeth* now we see.
But murdred is my father, and of him remaines but me,
Nor shall what they divin'd effect, unlesse, sweet Sweet, by thee.
What, blush you, Lady, pree thee let me busse that blush away,   50
He said, and did it, She to seeke even of a womans Nay.
   When Lovers opportunely meet to chaffer fire and flaxe,
Will sometimes falles too soone a worke, and Wit thereof doth
   taxe:
This amourous Couples close Contract perform'd such earnest
   sport,
As worser newes than would their tongues her belly did report.
The fault apparant, *Fleance* was by furious *Gruffyth* kild,

---

[1] In the play Banquo does not jest, but in Hol. both he and Macbeth would jest about the prophecies until Macbeth began to consider the last one seriously.
[2] Cf. Hol., 'the weird sisters . . . or else some nymphs or feiries.'

And she, delivered of a Sonne, was in affliction hild.

The rather for an Aliant had prevailed in that case,

Than which amongst the *Welsh-men* then was nothing more disgrace.

And, soothly, unto these our times in *Europe* scarce is knowne　　60

As North-*Wales* is, a Nation more intirely People-one,

But that so long in one same Land have hild them thinke I none,

If be not naturall *Irish* for abode and Breede out-worne.

From these so haplesse Parents yet an happie Sonne procceded,

Well educated of the King, and proving nobly deeded,

At age admir'd for active, and for high imployments apt:

But for the vertuous to have bin envied ever hapt.

One taxing him of Bastardie, words more than he could brooke,

Was slaine by him: who fearing Law his flight to *Scotland* tooke.

Where *Walter* (for it was his name) exact of noble blood,　　70

And Grand-sonne to the King of *Wales*, in publique favour stood.

Amongst great honors, which his great Achivements well did merit,

He was Lord *Steward* of the Land: which Sur-name all inherit

Of him descended to this day: which Surname, and which Streene

Hath blest the *Scots* with Princes eight, Ours also numbers neene:[1]

Great Monarke of great *Britaine* now, so amply never any:

Long may he live an happie King, of him may Kings be many.

Boast of his triple royall blood from you yee *Cambrian Brutes*,

Which to his high descents else-where not lowest ranked sutes.

For *Tudor* from *Cadwallader*, and *James* from *Tudor* claimes,

From *Gruffyths* royall Daughter too himselfe a *Brute* he names,　　80

From *Gladys*, *Mortimer* his wife Prince *Davids* sister and

Undoubted heire, he also hath in blood and ownes your Land.

Great *Britaine*, sith a *Briton* doth remonarchize thy Throne,

Remaund thy name: *Brute* had, *James* hath the whole, as els had none.

　　What then remaines, sith all is One's, but all be one in all,

And Schismes be reconcilde or scourg'd, for God quaints not[2] with *Baal*.

The great Surname of *Steward*, how it royaliz'd shall rest

For amplier Storie, and of *Wales* shall be awhile digrest.

[1] 'Streene': strain; 'neene' nine.

[2] 'quaints not': is not familiar with.

III. Analogue

From THE CHRONICLE OF ANDREW WYNTOUN[1]

Book VI. Ch. 16.

[In A.D. 1034 Malcolm II died and his grandson Duncan reigned for six years and begot two legitimate sons. While out hunting the King sought the hospitality of the Miller of Teviot and fell in love with the miller's daughter.]

And that ilk nycht, þat þe king
Tuke with þe myllar his gestnyng,
In to the bed with hir he lay,
And gat a sone on hir or day,
That callit wes Malcome Canmore,
Thare eftir crounit King þar for.   1670
   This woman he wald haif put till hycht,
To gret stait and to meikle mycht,
But Fynlaw Makbeth, his sister sone
Lettit þat purpos to be done.
And uthere gretare purposs als:
For till his eme he wes full fals,
That fosterit him full tendrely,
And gaif him rentes and senȝeory.
He murtherit his eme in Elgyne,
And usurpit his kinrik syne . . .   1680

[From the bastard Malcolm III descended kings of England such as Henry II, and a Pope, Clement VII. After turning aside to describe the death of Edmund Ironside (Bk. VI, Ch. 17), Wyntoun returned to Macbeth and the dream which led him to murder his cousin.]

Book VI. Ch. 18

A nycht him thocht in his dremyng   1895
That he wes sittand neire the king,
At a seit in hunting swa,

[1] *The Original Chronicle of Andrew of Wyntoun*, ed. F. J. Amours, S.T.S., 6 vols, 1903–14. Vol. IV, 1906, pp. 254–301. I cite the Wemyss text. Both Wyntoun and Fordun used a chronicle in a Register at the Priory of St. Serf in St. Andrews— written in the fourteenth century, and not seen since about 1660.

And in a lesche had grewhundis twa.
Him thocht, till he wes sittand,
He saw thre women by gangand,   1900
And þai thre women þan thocht he
Thre werd sisteris like to be.
    The first he herd say gangand by:
Lo, ȝonder the thayne of Crumbaghty!
    The tother sister said agane:
Of Murray ȝonder I see the thayne.
    The thrid said: ȝonder I se the King.
All þis herd he in his dremyng.
Sone efter þat, in his youth-heid,
Of thai þayndomes þe thayne wes maid;   1910
Then thocht he nixt for to be King,
Fra Duncanis dais had tane ending.
And þus the fantasy of þis dreme
Muffit him for to sla his eme,
As he did falsly in deid,
As ȝe have herd, befor þis reid.
    Syne with his awne emys wif
He lay, and with hir led his lif,
And held hir baith his wif and quene,
Rycht as scho forouth þat had bene   1920
Till his eme the King liffand,
Quhen he wes King with croune regnand;
For litill taill þat tyme gaif he
Of the greis of affinite.
And þusgatis quhen his eme wes dede,
He succedit in his steid,
And XVII winter wes regnand
As King with crowne in till Scotland.

[Macbeth ruled well and even went on pilgrimage to Rome. But
his origin was strange.]

    His moder to woddis wald oft repair   1941
For þe delite of hailsum aire.
Sa, as scho went apon a day
To wod all be hir ane to play,
Scho met of caiss with a faire man,
Never nane sa faire, as scho thocht an,
Sa mekle, sa strang, sa faire by sycht,
Scho never nane befor, I hecht,

Proportiound weill in all mesour,
Off lyme and lyth a faire figour.   1950
In sic aquaytans þare þai fell
That, schortly þarof to tell,
Thare in þare gamyn and thare play
That persone by þat woman lay,
And on hir þat tyme a sone gat,
This Makbeth, þat efter that
Grew to gret stait and to hicht,
And to gret powere and to mycht.
As befor ȝe haif herd said.
And fro his persone had wiþ hir plaid,   1960
And had þe jurnay with hir done,
And gottin had on hir a sone,
He said he a devill was at him gat,
And bad hir nocht be fleit of þat,
For he said þat his sone suld be
A man of hie stait and pouste,
And na man suld be borne of wif
Off power to reif him his lif;
And þare apon in takynnyng
He gaif his lemman þare a ring,   1970
And bad þat scho suld keip it weill,
And for his luf had þat joweill.
And efter þat oft usit he
To deill with hir in prevate,
And tald hir mony things suld fall
That scho trowit suld haif bene all.
      At hir tyme scho wes lichtare,
And þat sone at he gat scho bare,
And callit him Fynlaw Makbeth to name,
That grew, as ȝe herd, to gret fame.   1980
      Thusgate wes Makbethis ofspring,
That maid himefter of Scotland king,
As of him sum story sais;
Bot quheþer it sa were or oþer wais,
As to be gottin naturaly,
As oþer men ar generaly,
I wait nocht, bot his dedis were fell,
As ȝe may heire, and hes herd tell.

[For a summary of the rest of the story see pp. 434–5.]

IV. Source

From
THE CHRONICLES OF ENGLAND,
SCOTLANDE, AND IRELAND
by R. Holinshed (1587 edn.)

A. From Vol. II. THE CHRONICLE OF SCOTLAND

[69/1/41] [Natholocus, King of Scotland (A.D. 242–80), learned that a revolt was being fomented against him.]

. . . for that he was desirous to understand somewhat of the issue of this trouble, he sent one of his trustie servaunts, being a gentleman of that countrie, unto a woman that dwelt in the Ile of Colmekil (otherwise called Iona), esteemed very skilfull in foreshewing of things to come, to learne of hir what fortune should hap of this warre, which was alreadie begunne.

The Witch consulting with hir spirits, declared in the end how it should come shortlie to passe,[1] that the king shoulde bee murthered, not by his own enimies, but by the hands of one of his most familiar friendes, in whome he had reposed an especiall trust.[2] The messenger demanding by whose hands that should be? Even by thine, saith she, as it shall be well knowen within these fewe daies. The gentleman hearing these wordes, railed against hir verie bitterly, bidding hir go lyke an old witch; for he trusted to see hir burnt before he should commit so villanous a deed. And departing from hir, he went by and by to signifie what answere he had received; but before he came where the king lay, his mind was altered,[3] so that what for doubt on the one side that if he should declare the trueth as it was told him, the king might happelie conceyve some greate suspicion, that it should follow by his means as she had declared, and thereupon put him to death first; and for feare on the other side that if he keepe it secret, it might happen to be revealed by some other, and then he to run in as much danger of life as before; he determined with himselfe to worke the surest way,[4] and so comming to the king, he was led aside by him into his privie chamber, where al other being commaunded to avoid, he declared how he had sped; and

---

[1] *In margin:* 'The witches answer.'
[2] Cf. Duncan, of the traitor Cawdor, I.4.13–14.
[3] *In margin:* 'What happened by giving credit to the woords of a witch.'
[4] Cf. *Macbeth*, I.5.18: 'To catch the nearest way.'

then falling foorthwith upon Natholocus, with his dagger he slue him outright, and threw his bodie into a privie, and afterwards getting out by a backe doore, and taking his horsse which he had there readie, he fled with all speed unto the campe of the conspirators, and was the firste that brought news unto them of this act thus by him atchieved.[1]

[King Duff (952–67), son of Malcolm I, put down pirates, rogues and vagabonds, and set all men to work. After a while he fell sick.]

[149/1/61] In the meane time the king [Duff] fell into a languishing disease, not so greevous as strange, for that none of his physicians could perceive what to make of it. For there was seene in him no token, that either choler, melancholie, flegme, or any other vicious humor did any thing abound, whereby his bodie should be brought into such decaie and consumption (so as there remained unneth anie thing upon him save skin and bone.) . . .

[149/2/27] But about that present time there was a murmuring amongst the people, how the king was vexed with no naturall sicknesse, but by sorcerie and magicall art, practised by a sort of witches dwelling in a towne of Murreyland, called Fores.[2]

Whereupon, albeit the author of this secret talke was not knowne: yet being brought to the kings eare, it caused him to send foorthwith certeine wittie persons thither, to inquire of the truth. They that were thus sent, dissembling the cause of their jornie, were received in the darke of the night into the castell of Fores by the lieutenant of the same, called Donwald, who continuing faithfull to the king, had kept that castell against the rebels to the kings use. Unto him therefore these messengers declared the cause of their comming, requiring his aid for the accomplishment of the kings pleasure.

The souldiers, which laie there in garrison had an inkling that there was some such matter in hand as was talked of amongst the people; by reason that one of them kept as concubine a yoong woman, which was daughter to one of the witches as his paramour, who told him the whole maner used by hir mother & other hir companions, with their intent also, which was to make awaie the king. The souldier having learned this of his lemman, told the same to his fellowes, who made report to Donwald, and hee shewed it to the kings messengers, and therwith sent for the yoong damosell

---

[1] *Hol.* 1577 has a picture of the messenger murdering Natholocus, with the Witch pointing to them and standing in a circle set with cabalistic signs, and a spotted toad squatting behind her.

[2] *In margin:* 'Wiches in Fores.' Hence I.3.39.

which the souldier kept, as then being within the castell, and caused hir upon streict examination to confesse the whole matter as she had seene and knew.[1] Whereupon learning by hir confession in what house in the towne it was where they wrought there mischiefous mysterie,[2] he sent foorth souldiers, about the middest of the night, who breaking into the house, found one of the witches rosting upon a woodden broch[3] an image of wax at the fier, resembling in each feature the kings person, made and devised (as is to be thought) by craft and art of the divell: an other of them sat reciting certaine words of inchantment, and still basted the image with a certeine liquor verie busilie.

The souldiers finding them occupied in this wise, tooke them togither with the image, and led them into the castell, where being streictlie examined for what purpose they went about such manner of inchantment, they answered, to the end to make away the king: for as the image did waste afore the fire, so did the bodie of the king breake foorth in sweat. And as for the words of inchantment, they served to keepe him still waking from sleepe, so that as the wax ever melted, so did the kings flesh: by the which meanes it should have come to passe, that when the wax was once cleane consumed, the death of the king should immediatlie follow. So were they taught by evill spirits, and hired to worke the feat by the nobles of Murrey land.[4] The standers by, that heard such an abhominable tale told by these witches, streightwaies brake the image, and caused the witches (according as they had well deserved) to bee burnt to death.[5]

It was said, that the king, at the verie same time that these things were a dooing within the castell of Fores, was delivered of his languor, and slept that night without anie sweat breaking foorth upon him at all, & the next daie being restored to his strength, was able to doo anie maner of thing that lay in man to doo, as though he had not beene sicke before anie thing at all.[6] But howsoever it came to passe, truth it is, that when he was restored to his perfect health, he gathered a power of men, & with the same went into Murrey land against the rebels there, and chasing them from thence, he pursued them into Rosse, and from Rosse into Cathnesse, where apprehending them, he brought them backe unto Fores, and there caused them to be hanged up, on gallows and gibets.[7]

[1] *In margin:* 'A witches daughter is examined.'
[2] *In margin:* 'The witches are found out.'
[3] broach, spit. *In margin:* 'An image of wax rosting at the fire.'
[4] *In margin:* 'The nobles of the countie set the witches on work.'
[5] *In margin:* 'The witches were burnt.'
[6] Cf. I.7.46. *In margin:* 'The king is restored to health.'
[7] *In margin:* 'The rebels are executed.'

Amongest them there were also certeine yoong gentlemen, right beautifull and goodlie personages, being neere of kin unto Donwald capteine of the castell, and had beene persuaded to be partakers with the other rebels, more through the fraudulent counsell of diverse wicked persons, than of their owne accord: whereupon the foresaid Donwald lamenting their case, made earnest labor and sute to the king to have begged their pardon; but having a plaine deniall, he conceived such an inward malice towards the king,[1] (though he shewed it not outwardlie at the first) that the same continued still boiling in his stomach, and ceased not, till through setting on of his wife, and in revenge of such unthankefulnesse, hee found meanes to murther the king within the foresaid castell of Fores where he used to sojourne. For the king being in that countrie, was accustomed to lie most commonlie within the same castell, having a speciall trust in Donwald,[2] as a man whom he never suspected.

But Donwald, not forgetting the reproch which his linage had susteined by the execution of those his kinsmen, whome the king for a spectacle to the people had caused to be hanged, could not but shew manifest tokens of great griefe at home amongst his familie: which his wife perceiving, ceassed not to travell with him, till she understood what the cause was of his displeasure. Which at length when she had learned by his owne relation, she as one that bare no lesse malice in hir heart towards the king, for the like cause on hir behalfe, than hir husband did for his friends, counselled him (sith the king oftentimes[3] used to lodge in his house without anie gard about him, other than the garrison of the castell, which was wholie at his commandement) to make him awaie, and shewed him the meanes wherby he might soonest accomplish it.[4]

Donwald thus being the more kindled in wrath by the words of his wife, determined to follow hir advise in the execution of so heinous an act. Wherupon devising with himselfe for a while, which way hee might best accomplish his cursed intent, at length he gat opportunitie, and sped his purpose as followeth. It chanced that the king upon the daie before he purposed to depart foorth of the castell,[5] was long in his oratorie at his praiers, and there continued till it was late in the night.[6] At the last, comming foorth, he called such afore him as had faithfullie served him in pursute and apprehension

---

[1] *In margin:* 'Captein Donwald craved pardon for them but not granted.' 'Donwald conceived hatred against the king.'

[2] Cf. Duncan, I.4.13–14.

[3] In the play a special occasion: I.4.42–7.

[4] *In margin:* 'Donwald's wife counselled him to murther the king.' 'The womans evill counsell is followed.' (I.5.60–73; I.7.61–72.)

[5] A one-night stay in *Mac*, I.5.59–60.

[6] Not in the play; he is tired with 'his day's hard journey' (I.7.62).

of the rebels, and giving them heartie thanks,[1] he bestowed sundrie honorable gifts amongst them, of the which number Donwald was one, as he that had beene ever accounted a most faithfull servant to the king.

At length, having talked with them a long time, he got him into his privie chamber, onelie with two of his chamberlains, who having brought him to bed,[2] came foorth againe, and then fell to banketting with Donwald and his wife,[3] who had prepared diverse delicate dishes, and sundrie sorts of drinks for their reare[4] supper or collation, wherat they sate up so long, till they had charged their stomachs with such full gorges, that their heads were no sooner got to the pillow, but asleepe they were so fast, that a man might have remooved the chamber over them, sooner than to have awaked them out of their droonken sleepe.[5]

Then Donwald, though he abhorred the act greatlie in his heart,[6] yet through instigation of his wife, hee called foure of his servants unto him (whome he had made privie to his wicked intent before, and framed to his purpose with large gifts)[7] and now declaring unto them, after what sort they should worke the feat, they gladlie obeied the instructions, & speedilie going about the murther, they enter the chamber (in which the king laie) a little before cocks crow,[8] where they secretlie cut his throte as he lay sleeping, without anie buskling at all:[9] and immediatlie by a posterne gate they caried foorth the dead bodie into the fields, and throwing it upon an horsse there provided readie for that purpose, they convey it unto a place, about two miles distant from the castell, where they staied, and gat certeine labourers to helpe them to turne the course of a little river running through the fields there, and digging a deepe hole in the chanell, they burie the bodie in the same, ramming it up with stones and gravell so closelie, that setting the water in the right course againe, no man could perceive that anie thing had beene newlie digged there.[10] This they did by order appointed them by Donwald as is reported, for that the bodie should not be found, & by bleeding (when Donwald should be present) declare him to be guiltie of the

---

[1] *In margin:* 'The king rewarded his friends.' (II.1.12–17.)

[2] *In margin:* 'The king went to bed.' (II.1.12; I.7.63 'two chamberlains').

[3] *In margin:* 'The chamberleins went to banketting.' With Lady Macbeth, apparently: I.7.64; II.2.1–2.

[4] late.

[5] So at I.7.63–70; II.2.6–9.

[6] Hence Macbeth's complicated emotions.

[7] The Macbeths are more secret.

[8] Cf. II.1.5; II.2.4.

[9] *In margin:* 'The suborned servants cut the kings throte.'

[10] *In margin:* 'The king his buriall.'

murther. For such an opinion men have, that the dead corps of anie man being slaine, will bleed abundantlie if the murtherer be present. But for what consideration soever they buried him there, they had no sooner finished the worke, but that they slue them whose helpe they used herein, and streightwaies thereupon fled into Orknie.

Donwald, about the time that the murther was in dooing, got him amongst them that kept the watch, and so continued in companie with them all the residue of the night.[1] But in the morning when the noise was raised in the kings chamber how the king was slaine, his bodie conveied awaie, and the bed all beraied with bloud; he with the watch ran thither, as though he had knowne nothing of the matter,[2] and breaking into the chamber, and finding cakes of bloud in the bed, and on the floore about the sides of it,[3] he foorthwith slue the chamberleins, as guiltie of that heinous murther, and then like a mad man running to and fro,[4] he ransacked everie corner within the castell, as though it had beene to have seene if he might have found either the bodie, or anie of the murtherers hid in anie privie place: but at length comming to the posterne gate, and finding it open, he burdened the chamberleins, whome he had slaine, with all the fault, they having the keies of the gates committed to their keeping all the night, and therefore it could not be otherwise (said he) but that they were of counsell in the committing of that most detestable murther.

Finallie, such was his over earnest diligence in the severe inquisition and triall of the offendors heerein, that some of the lords began to mislike the matter, and to smell foorth shrewd tokens, that he should not be altogither cleare himselfe.[5] But for so much as they were in that countrie, where hee had the whole rule, what by reason of his friends and authoritie togither, they doubted to utter what they thought, till time and place should better serve thereunto, and heereupon got them awaie everie man to his home. For the space of six moneths togither, after this heinous murther thus committed, there appeered no sunne by day, nor moone by night in anie part of the realme, but still was the skie covered with continuall clouds, and sometimes suche outragious windes arose, with

---

[1] *In margin:* 'Donwald kept himselfe amongst the watchmen.' Boece adds: 'schawing þame of þe grete humanite done to him sindry tymes be þe Kingis grace.'

[2] *In margin:* 'Donwald a verie dissembler.'

[3] Hence the 'blood' imagery in II.2., II.3. and elsewhere.

[4] II.3.107–19; Macbeth pretends temporary madness.

[5] *In margin:* 'Some wiser than other. The matter suspected.' Boece adds: 'because he maid sic deligence in serching of þe auctours of þis tresoun, above þe mesoure of just affeccioun.'

lightenings and tempests, that the people were in great feare of present destruction.[1]

Monstrous sights also that were seene within the Scotish kingdome that yeere were these, horsses in Louthian, being of singular beautie and swiftnesse, did eate their owne flesh, and would in no wise taste anie other meate. In Angus there was a gentlewoman brought foorth a child without eies, nose, hand or foot. There was a sparhawke also strangled by an owle.

[Culen succeeded Duff but his coronation was marred by these portents and bad weather, which the bishops declared would not cease until the murderers of King Duff were punished. Culen therefore set off for Moray, and Donwald, fearing exposure, fled 'without making his wyfe privie to his departure.'[2]]

[151/1/71] Culene . . . passed over Spey water, and taking the castell of Fores, slewe all that he found therein, and put the house to sacke and fire. Donwalds wife with his three daughters were taken; for Culene commanded, that whosoever could light upon them, should in anie wise save their lives, and bring them unto him. Which being done, he had them to the racke, where the mother upon hir examination confessed the whole matter.[3] how by hir procurement chieflie hir husband was mooved to cause the deed to be doone, who they were that by his commandement did it, and in what place they had buried the bodye. Heere would the multitude have torne hir in peeces, but that they were restreined by Commandement of an officer at armes . . .

[Donwald was shipwrecked within four miles of the castle, and was captured and tried along with his wife and the four murderers, who were also taken.]

They were first scourged by the hangman, and then bowelled.[4] Their entrails being throwen into a fire, the other parts of their bodies were cut into quarters, and sent unto the chiefest cities of the realme, and there set up aloft upon the gates and highest towers, for example sake to all such as should come after, how heinous a thing it is to pollute their hands in the sacred blood of their prince.

This dreadfull end had Donwald and his wife, before he saw anie sunne after the murder was committed, and that by the appointment of the most righteous God, the creator of that heavenlie

---

[1] *In margin:* 'Prodigious weather.' Shakespeare transfers the prodigies to Duncan's murder, II.4.1–20.

[2] Like Macduff in the play, IV.2.1–8.

[3] *In margin:* 'The murther is wholie confessed.'

[4] *In margin:* 'Donwald with his confederats are executed.'

planet and all other things, who suffereth no crime to be unrevenged . . .

[The body of King Duff was taken up and reburied at Colmekill (Iona).]

[151/2/65] As soone as it was brought above the ground the aire began to cleere up, and the sunne brake foorth, shining more brighter than it had beene seene aforetime, to anie of the beholders remembrance. And that which put men in most deepe considera-tion of all, was the sight of manifold flowers, which sprang foorth over all the fields immediatlie thereupon, cleane contrarie to the time and season of the yeere.

[Unfortunately Culen proved a bad king, falling into gross sensuality, till he was murdered by a thane whose daughter he had ravished. After him reigned Kenneth, a good monarch who however was determined that his own son should succeed him and not his nephew Malcolm (son of King Duff) Prince of Cumberland and heir apparent. He poisoned Malcolm secretly, and got the nobles to agree that succession should henceforth be by primogeniture. During Kenneth's reign came the Danish invasion during which the husbandman Hay and his two sons turned the tide of battle[1]. The King's conscience troubled him about his murder of Malcolm.]

[158/1/19] Thus might he seeme happie to all men, . . . but yet to himselfe he seemed most unhappie[2] as he that could not but still live in continuall feare, least his wicked practise concerning the death of Malcome Duffe should come to light and knowledge of the world. For so commeth it to passe, that such as are pricked in conscience for anie secret offense committed, have ever an unquiet mind.[3] And (as the fame goeth) it chanced that a voice was heard as he was in bed in the night time to take his rest, uttering unto him these or the like woords in effect:[4] 'Thinke not Kenneth that the wicked slaughter of Malcome Duffe by thee contrived, is kept secret from the knowledge of the eternall God. Thou art he that didst conspire the innocents death, enterprising by traitorous meanes to

---

[1] The incident was used for *Cymbeline*, V.3.14–52.

[2] *In margin:* 'The king had a giltie conscience.'

[3] Macbeth fears only 'judgment here' at I.7.8. Boece says that Kenneth 'had every royndyng and qwyete commonyng, quhen he saw þe samyn amang þe pepill, in suspicion.'

[4] *In margin:* 'A voice heard by the king.' Boece adds: 'O þou unhappy tiran, quhilk for þe desyre of þe croune hes slayne ane innocent, invading þi nychtboure with þi tresonable murder . . . þrou quhilk þou hes incurrit sik hatred aganis God þat baith þou and þi sonnes salbe haistly slayne!' Cf. II.2.36–44.

doo that to thy neighbour, which thou wouldest have revenged by cruell punishment on anie of thy subjects, if it had beene offered to thy selfe. It shall therefore come to passe, that both thou thy selfe, and thy issue, through the just vengeance of almightie God, shall suffer woorthie punishment, to the infamie of thy house and familie for evermore. For even at this present are there in hand secret practises to dispatch both thee and thy issue out of the waie, that other maie injoy this kingdome which thou doost indevour to assure unto thine issue.' The king with this voice being striken into great dread and terror, passed that night without anie sleepe comming in his eies.

[He confessed his crime to a holy Bishop and did great penance, but he was murdered in the following way by Fenella in revenge for the execution of her son.]

[158/1/57] It chanced heereupon, that within a short time after he had beene at Fordune, a towne in Mernes, to visit the reliks of Paladius which remaine there,[1] he turned a little out of the waie to lodge at the castell of Fethircarne, where as then there was a forrest full of all manner of wild beasts that were to be had in anie part of Albion.[2] Here was he received by Fenella ladie of the house, whose son (as ye have heard) he caused to be put to death, for the commotion made betwixt them of Mernes and Angus. She was also of kin unto Malcolme Duffe,[3] whome the king had made awaie, and in like manner unto Constantine and Grime, defrauded of their right to the crowne, by the craftie devise of the king (as before is partlie mentioned.) This woman therefore being of a stout stomach, long time before having conceived an immortall grudge towards the king, upon the occasions before rehearsed (namelie aswell for the death of hir sonne Cruthlint, as having some inkling also of the impoisoning of Malcolme Duffe, though no full certeintie therof was knowne) imagined night and day how to be revenged.[4]

She understood that the king delighted above measure in goodlie buildings, and therefore to the end to compasse hir malicious intent,[5] she had caused a tower to be made, joining unto hir owne lodging within the foresaid castell of Fethircarne. The which tower was covered over with copper finelie ingraven with diverse flowers and images. Heereto was it hoong within with rich cloths of arras wrought with gold and silke, verie faire and costlie. Behind the same

[1] *In margin:* 'The king went to Fordune in pilgrimage.' Palladius was sent by Pope Celestine (A.D. 430) as 'first bishop' to Irish Christians.
[2] *In margin:* 'A parke with wild beasts at the castell of Fethircarne.'
[3] *In margin:* 'Fenella was of kin unto Malcolme.'
[4] *In margin:* 'She was desirous for to revenge.'
[5] *In margin:* 'Fenella hir malicious intent.'

were there crossebowes set readie bent with sharpe quarrels in them.[1] In the middest of the house there was a goodlie brasen image also, resembling the figure of king Kenneth, holding in the one hand a faire golden apple set full of pretious stones, devised with such art and cunning, that so soone as anie man should draw the same unto him, or remoove it never so little anie waie foorth, the crossebowes would immediatlie discharge their quarrels upon him with great force and violence.

Fenella therefore being thus provided aforehand, after meate desired the king to go with hir into that inner chamber,[2] into the which being entered, he could not be satisfied of long with the behold-ing of the goodlie furniture, aswell of the hangings as of diverse other things. As the last having viewed the image which stood (as is said) in the midst of the chamber, he demanded what the same did signifie? Fenella answered, how that image did represent his person, and the golden apple set so richlie with smaragds, jacincts, saphires, topases, rubies, turkasses, and such like pretious stones, she had pro-vided as a gift for him, and therefore required him to take the same, beseeching him to accept it in good part, though it were not in value woorthie to be offered unto his princelie honor and high dignitie. And heerewith she hirselfe withdrew aside, as though she would have taken some thing foorth of a chest or coffer, thereby to avoid the danger.

But the king delighted in beholding the gems and orient stones, at length remooving the apple, the better to advise it, incontinentlie the crossebowes discharged their quarrels so directlie upon him, that striking him through in sundrie places, he fell downe starke dead, and lay flat on the ground.[3] Fenella as soone as she beheld him fall to the ground readie to die, she got foorth by a backe doore into the next woods, where she had appointed horsses to tarie for hir, by meanes wherof she escaped[4] out of all danger of them that pursued hir, yer the death of the king were openlie knowne unto them. His servants still waiting for his comming foorth in the utter chamber, at length when they saw he came not at all, first they knocked at the doore softlie, then they rapped hard therat:[5] lastlie, doubting that which had happened, they brake open doore after doore, till at length they came into the chamber where the king lay cold dead upon the floor.[6]

The clamor and crie heereupon was raised by his servants, and

[1] *In margin:* 'Crossebowes readie bent, hidden.' Cf. I.7.60, 79–80.
[2] *In margin:* 'Fenella had the king into the inner chamber.'
[3] *In margin:* 'The king was slaine with the crosse bowes.'
[4] *In margin:* 'Fenella escaped from them all.'
[5] *In margin:* 'His servants looked for their king.' Cf. the knocking at the gate in *Macbeth*, II.3.
[6] *In margin:* 'The doores broken open, they find him dead.'

Fenella curssed and sought for in everie place, that had committed so heinous and wicked a deed: but the ungratious woman was conveied so secretlie out of the waie, that no where could she be heard of.[1] Some supposed that she fled first unto Constantine, by whose helpe she got over into Ireland.[2]

[Kenneth II's son Malcolm II reigned from 1005 to 1034, after killing Kenneth III, son of King Duff.]

[168/2/12] After Malcolme succeeded his nephue Duncane, the sonne of his daughter Beatrice: for Malcolme had two daughters, the one which was this Beatrice, being given in mariage unto one Abbanath Crinen, a man of great nobilitie, and thane of the Isles and west parts of Scotland, bare of that mariage the foresaid Duncane; The other called Doada, was maried unto Sinell[3] the thane of Glammis, by whom she had issue one Makbeth a valiant gentleman, and one that if he had not beene somewhat cruell of nature,[4] might have beene thought most woorthie the government of a realme. On the other part, Duncane was so soft and gentle of nature,[5] that the people wished the inclinations and maners of these two cousins to have beene so tempered and enterchangeablie bestowed betwixt them, that where the one had too much of clemencie, and the other of crueltie, the meane vertue betwixt these two extremities might have reigned by indifferent partition in them both, so should Duncane have proved a woorthie king, and Makbeth an excellent capteine. The beginning of Duncans reigne was verie quiet and peaceable, without anie notable trouble; but after it was perceived how negligent he was in punishing offendors, manie misruled persons tooke occasion thereof to trouble the peace and quiet state of the common-wealth, by seditious commotions which first had their beginnings in this wise.

Banquho the thane of Lochquhaber, of whom the house of the Stewards is descended,[6] the which by order of linage hath now for a long time injoied the crowne of Scotland, even till these our daies, as he gathered the finances due to the king, and further punished

[1] *In margin:* 'Fenella could not be found.'

[2] *In margin:* 'Fenella got hirselfe into Ireland by the helpe of Constantine.'

[3] Should be 'Finele' or 'Finley'. 'Macbeth's father was Findlaech, Mormaer of Moray' (H. N. Paul, *op. cit.* p. 209n). 'Sinele' was a copyist's error in the thirteenth century, which Boece, Bellenden and Holinshed follow, 'Both Fordun and Wyntoun retain the initial "F"'. This suggests to Paul that Shakespeare did not read either of them.

[4] Hinted in I.2.

[5] *In margin:* 'Duncan of too soft a nature.' But our Macbeth does not blame him; I.7.16–20.

[6] *In margin:* 'The house of the Stewards.'

somewhat sharpelie such as were notorious offendors, being assailed by a number of rebels inhabiting in that countrie, and spoiled of the monie and all other things, had much a doo to get awaie with life, after he had received sundrie grievous wounds amongst them. Yet escaping their hands, after hee was somewhat recovered of his hurts and was able to ride, he repaired to the court, where making his

complaint to the king in most earnest wise, he purchased at length that the offendors were sent for by a sergeant at armes,[1] to appeare to make answer unto such matters as should be laid to their charge: but they augmenting their mischiefous act with a more wicked deed, after they had misused the messenger with sundrie kinds of reproches, they finallie slue him also.

Then doubting not but for such contemptuous demeanor against the kings regall authoritie, they should be invaded with all the power the king could make, Makdowald one of great estimation among them, making first a confederacie with his neerest friends and kinsmen, tooke upon him to be chiefe capteine of all such rebels, as would stand against the king, in maintenance of their grievous offenses latelie committed against him.[2] Manie slanderous words also, and railing tants this Makdowald uttered against his prince, calling him a faint-hearted milkesop, more meet to governe a sort of idle moonks in some cloister, than to have the rule of such valiant and hardie men of warre as the Scots were. He used also such subtill

[1] *In margin:* 'A sergeant at armes slaine by the rebels.' Perhaps the origin of the 'bleeding sergeant's' rank in I.2. Shakespeare recalled that Banquo had enemies at III.1.115.

[2] *In margin:* 'Makdowald offereth himself to be capteine of the rebels.'

persuasions and forged allurements, that in a small time he had gotten togither a mightie power of men: for out of the westerne Isles there came unto him a great multitude of people, offering themselves to assist him in that rebellious quarell, and out of Ireland in hope of the spoile came no small number of Kernes and Gallo-glasses,[1] offering gladlie to serve under him, whither it should please him to lead them.

Makdowald thus having a mightie puissance about him, incountered with such of the kings people as were sent against him into Lochquhaber, and discomfiting them,[2] by mere force tooke their capteine Malcolme, and after the end of the battell smote off his head. This overthrow being notified to the king, did put him in woonderfull feare, by reason of his small skill in warlike affaires.[3] Calling therefore his nobles to a councell, he asked of them their best advise for the subduing of Makdowald & other the rebels. Here, in sundrie heads (as ever it happeneth) were sundrie opinions, which they uttered according to everie man his skill. At length Makbeth speaking much against the kings softnes, and overmuch slacknesse in punishing offendors, whereby they had such time to assemble togither, he promised notwithstanding, if the charge were committed unto him and unto Banquho, so to order the matter, that the rebels should be shortly vanquished & quite put downe, and that not so much as one of them should be found to make resistance within the countrie.

And even so it came to passe: for being sent foorth with a new power,[4] at his entring into Lochquhaber, the fame of his comming put the enimies in such feare, that a great number of them stale secretlie awaie from their capteine Makdowald, who neverthelesse inforced thereto, gave battell unto Makbeth, with the residue which remained with him: but being overcome, and fleeing for refuge into a castell (within the which his wife & children were inclosed) at length when he saw how he could neither defend the hold anie longer against his enimies, nor yet upon surrender be suffered to depart with life saved, hee first slue his wife and children, and lastlie himselfe, least if he had yeelded simplie, he should have beene executed in most cruell wise for an example to other.[5] Makbeth entring into the castell by the gates, as then set open, found the carcasse of Makdowald lieng dead there amongst the residue of the slaine bodies, which when he beheld, remitting no peece of his cruell

---

[1] I.2.12–13.

[2] *In margin:* 'Makdowald discomfiteth the kings power.' (I.2.14–15.)

[3] *In margin:* 'The smal skill of the king in warlike affaires.'

[4] *In margin:* 'Makbeth and Banquho are sent against the rebels.'

[5] Contrast I.2.16–22: Macbeth slays him in single combat.

nature with that pitifull sight, he caused the head to be cut off, and set upon a poles end, and so sent it as a present to the king who as then laie at Bertha.[1] The headlesse trunke he commanded to bee hoong up upon an high paire of gallowes.

Them of the westerne Isles suing for pardon, in that they had aided Makdowald in his tratorous enterprise, he fined at great sums of moneie: and those whome he tooke in Lochquhaber, being come thither to beare armor against the king, he put to execution. Herupon the Ilandmen conceived a deadlie grudge towards him, calling him a covenant-breaker, a bloudie tyrant, & a cruell murtherer of them whome the kings mercie had pardoned.[2] With which reprochfull words Makbeth being kindled in wrathfull ire against them, had passed over with an armie into the Isles, to have taken revenge upon them for their liberall talke, had he not beene otherwise persuaded by some of his friends, and partlie pacified by gifts presented unto him on the behalfe of the Ilandmen, seeking to avoid his displeasure. Thus was justice and law restored againe to the old accustomed course, by the diligent means of Makbeth.[3] Immediatlie whereupon woord came that Sueno king of Norway was arrived in Fife with a puissant armie, to subdue the whole realme of Scotland[4]. . . . the pretense of his comming was to avenge the slaughter of his uncle

[1] *In margin:* 'Makdowalds head sent to the king. Makbeths crueltie.' Cf. I.2.23: 'upon our battlements'.

[2] *In margin:* 'Makbeth defamed by the Ilandmen.'

[3] *In margin:* 'Justice and law restored.' (I.2.29–30.)

[4] *In margin:* 'Sueno king of Norway landed in Fife.' I.2.31–33: 'a fresh assault'. Holinshed has described previous invasions.

Camus, and other of the Danish nations slaine at Barre, Crierdane and Cernmer.

The crueltie of this Sueno was such, that he neither spared man, woman, nor child, of what age, condition or degree soever they were.[1] Whereof when K. Duncane was certified, he set all slouthfull and lingering delaies apart, and began to assemble an armie in most speedie wise, like a verie valiant capteine: for oftentimes it happeneth, that a dull coward and slouthfull person, constreined by necessitie, becommeth verie hardie and active. Therefore when his whole power was come togither, he divided the same into three battels. The first was led by Makbeth, the second by Banquho, & the king himselfe governed in the maine battell or middle ward, wherein were appointed to attend and wait upon his person the most part of all the residue of the Scottish nobilitie.

The armie of Scotishmen being thus ordered, came unto Culros, where incountering with the enimies, after a sore and cruell foughten battell, Sueno remained victorious, and Duncane with his Scots discomfited.[2] Howbeit the Danes were so broken by this battell, that they were not able to make long chase on their enimies, but kept themselves all night in order of battell, for doubt least the Scots assembling togither againe, might have set upon them at some advantage. On the morrow, when the fields were discovered, and that it was perceived how no enimies were to be found abrode, they gathered the spoile, which they divided amongst them, according to the law of armes. Then was it ordeined by commandement of Sueno, that such no souldier should hurt either man, woman, or child, except as were found with weapon in hand readie to make resistance, for he hoped now to conquer the realme without further bloudshed.

But when knowledge was given how Duncane was fled to the castell of Bertha,[3] and that Makbeth was gathering a new power to withstand the incursions of the Danes, Sueno raised his tents & comming to the said castell, laid a strong siege round about it. Duncane seeing himselfe thus environed by his enimies, sent a secret message by counsell of Banquho to Makbeth, commanding him to abide at Inchcuthill, till he heard from him some other newes. In the meane time Duncane fell in fained communication with Sueno, as though he would have yeelded up the castell into his hands,[4] under certeine conditions, and this did he to drive time, and to put his enimies out of all suspicion of anie enterprise ment against

[1] *In margin:* 'The crueltie of Sueno king of Norwaie.' Hence I.2.49–52.
[2] *In margin:* 'Sueno vanquisheth the Scots.' Hence the 'dismal conflict', I.2.54.
[3] *In margin:* 'Duncane fled to the castell of Bertha [Perth].'
[4] *In margin:* 'Fained treatie.'

them, till all things were brought to passe that might serve for the purpose. At length, when they were fallen at a point for rendring up the hold, Duncane offered to send foorth of the castell into the campe greate provision of vittels to refresh the armie, which offer was gladlie accepted of the Danes, for that they had beene in great penurie of sustenance manie daies before.

[170/2/21] The Scots heereupon tooke the juice of mekilwoort berries, and mixed the same in their ale and bread, sending it thus spiced & confectioned, in great abundance unto their enimies.[1] They rejoising that they had got meate and drinke sufficient to satisfie their bellies, fell to eating and drinking after such greedie wise, that it seemed they strove who might devoure and swallow up most, till the operation of the berries spread in such sort through all the parts of their bodies, that they were in the end brought into a fast dead sleepe, that in manner it was unpossible to awake them. Then foorthwith Duncane sent unto Makbeth, commanding him with all diligence to come and set upon the enimies, being in easie point to be overcome. Makbeth making no delaie, came with his people to the place, where his enimies were lodged, and first killing the watch, afterwards entered the campe, and made such slaughter on all sides without anie resistance, that it was a woonderfull matter to behold, for the Danes were so heavie of sleepe, that the most part of them were slaine and never stirred:[2] other that were awakened either by the noise or other waies foorth, were so amazed and dizzie headed upon their wakening, that they were not able to make anie defense: so that of the whole number there escaped no more but onelie Sueno himselfe and ten other persons, by whose helpe he got to his ships lieng at rode in the mouth of Taie[3]. . . .

The Scots having woone so notable a victorie, after they had gathered & divided the spoile of the field, caused solemne processions to be made in all places of the realme, and thanks to be given to almightie God, that had sent them so faire a day over their enimies. But whilst the people were thus at their processions, woord was brought that a new fleet of Danes was arrived at Kingcorne, sent thither by Canute king of England, in revenge of his brother Suenos overthrow.[4] To resist these enimies, which were alreadie

[1] *In margin:* 'Spiced cups prepared for the Danes.' Buchanan wrote that not only the berries but also the roots were a drug bringing 'sleep, and if consumed largely, madness'. Hence maybe the 'insane root', I.3.84–5.

[2] *In margin:* 'Makbeth assaileth the campe of the Danes, being overcome with drink and sleepe.'

[3] *In margin:* 'The slaughter of Danes. Sueno with ten others escaped.'

[4] *In margin:* 'A power of Danes arrive at King corne out of England.' Cf. I.2.49–61. The two campaigns are compressed into one.

landed, and busie in spoiling the countrie; Makbeth and Banquho were sent with the kings authoritie, who having with them a convenient power, incountred the enimies, slue part of them, and chased the other to their ships.[1] They that escaped and got once to their ships, obteined of Makbeth for a great summe of gold, that such of their friends as were slaine at this last bickering, might be buried in saint Colmes Inch.[2] In memorie wherof, manie old sepultures are yet in the said Inch, there to be seene graven with the armes of the Danes, as the maner of burieng noble men still is, and heeretofore hath been used.

A peace was also concluded at the same time betwixt the Danes and Scotishmen,[3] ratified (as some have written) in this wise: That from thencefoorth the Danes should never come into Scotland to make anie warres against the Scots by anie maner of meanes. And these were the warres that Duncane had with forren

enimies, in the seventh yeere of his reigne. Shortlie after happened a strange and uncouth woonder, which afterward was the cause of much trouble in the realme of Scotland, as ye shall after heare. It fortuned as Makbeth and Banquho journied towards Fores, where the king then laie, they went sporting by the waie togither without other companie, save onelie themselves, passing thorough the woods and fields, when suddenlie in the middest of a laund, there met them three women in strange and wild apparell, resembling creatures of

[1] *In margin:* 'The Danes vanquished by Makbeth and Banquho.' (I.2.33ff.)
[2] *In margin:* 'Danes buried in S. Colmes Inche' (I.2.62–4.)
[3] *In margin:* 'A peace concluded betwixt Scots and Danes.'

elder world,[1] whome when they attentivelie beheld, woondering much at the sight, the first of them spake and said; All haile Makbeth, thane of Glammis (for he had latelie entered into that dignitie and office by the death of his father Sinell.[2]) The second of them said; Haile Makbeth thane of Cawder. But the third said; All haile Makbeth that heereafter shalt be king of Scotland.

Then Banquho; What manner of women (saith he) are you, that seeme so little favourable unto me, whereas to my fellow heere, besides high offices, ye assigne also the kingdome, appointing foorth nothing for me at all? Yes (saith the first of them) we promise greater benefits unto thee, than unto him, for he shall reigne in deed, but with an unluckie end: neither shall he leave anie issue behind him to succeed in his place, where contrarilie thou in deed shalt not reigne at all, but of thee those shall be borne which shall govern the Scottish kingdome by long order of continuall descent.[3] Herewith the foresaid women vanished immediatlie out of their sight.[4] This was reputed at the first but some vaine fantasticall illusion by Mackbeth and Banquho, insomuch that Banquho would call Mackbeth in jest, king of Scotland; and Mackbeth againe would call him in sport likewise, the father of manie kings.[5] But afterwards the common opinion was, that these women were either the weird sisters,[6] that is (as ye would say) the goddesses of destinie, or else some nymphs or feiries, indued with knowledge of prophesie by their necromanticall science, bicause everie thing came to passe as they had spoken. For shortlie after, the thane of Cawder being condemned at Fores of treason against the king committed;[7] his lands, livings, and offices were given of the kings liberalitie to Mackbeth.

The same night after, at supper, Banquho jested with him and said; Now Mackbeth thou hast obteined those things which the two former sisters prophesied, there remaineth onelie for thee to purchase that which the third said should come to passe. Whereupon Mackbeth revolving the thing in his mind, began even then to devise how he might atteine to the kingdome:[8] but yet he thought with himselfe that

[1] I.3.39–42. *In margin:* 'The prophesie of three women supposing to be the weird sisters or feiries.' Cf. Boece: 'thai mett be þe gaitt thre weird sisteris or wiches, quhilk come to þame with elrege clething.'

[2] I.3.71.

[3] I.3.57–69.

[4] *In margin:* 'A thing to wonder at.'

[5] *In margin:* 'Banquho the father of manie kings.'

[6] Cf. I.3.32. Bellenden: 'Nocht þeless, becaus all thinges come as þir wiches divinit, the pepill traistit þeme to be werd sisteris.'

[7] *In margin:* 'The thane of Cawdor condemned of treason.' (I.3.103–16.) 'Makbeth made thane of Cawdor.'

[8] *In margin:* 'Mackbeth deviseth howhe might atteine the kingdome.' (I.3.127–64.)

he must tarie a time, which should advance him thereto (by the divine providence) as it had come to passe in his former preferment. But shortlie after it chanced that king Duncane, having two sonnes by his wife which was the daughter of Siward earle of Northumberland,[1] he made the elder of them called Malcolme prince of Cumberland, as it were thereby to appoint him his successor in the kingdome, immediatlie after his deceasse.[2] Mackbeth sore troubled herewith, for that he saw by this means his hope sore hindered (where, by the old lawes of the realme, the ordinance was, that if he that should succeed were not of able age to take the charge upon himselfe, he that was next of bloud unto him should be admitted) he began to take counsell how he might usurpe the kingdome by force,[3] having a just quarell so to doo (as he tooke the matter) for that Duncane did what in him lay to defraud him of all maner of title and claime, which he might in time to come, pretend unto the crowne.

The woords of the three weird sisters also (of whom before ye have heard) greatlie incouraged him hereunto,[4] but speciallie his wife lay sore upon him to attempt the thing, as she that was verie ambitious, burning in unquenchable desire to beare the name of a queene.[5] At length therefore, communicating his purposed intent with his trustie friends, amongst whome Banquho was the chiefest,[6] upon confidence of their promised aid, he slue the king at Enverns, or (as some say) at Botgosuane, in the sixt yeare of his reigne. Then having a companie about him of such as he had made privie to his enterprise, he caused himselfe to be proclaimed king, and foorthwith went unto Scone,[7] where (by common consent) he received the investure of the kingdome according to the accustomed maner. The bodie of Duncane was first conveied unto Elgine, & there buried in kinglie wise; but afterwards it was removed and conveied unto Colmekill,[8]

[1] *In margin:* 'The daughter of Siward earle of Northumberland wife to king Duncane.'

[2] I.4.35–42.

[3] *In margin:* 'Mackbeth studieth which way he may take the kingdom by force.' (I.4.48–53.)

[4] *In margin:* 'Prophesies moove men to unlawfull attempts.'

[5] *In margin:* 'Women desirous of high estate.' Not emphasized in I.5, though implied. Cf. Boece: 'his wyfe, impacient of lang tarie, as wemen ar to all thing quhair þai sett þame, gaif him gret artacioun [instigation] to persew þe samyn, þat scho mycht be ane quene, calland him oft tymes febill cowart and nocht desyrous of honouris, sen he durst nocht assailȝe þe thing with manhede and corage quhilk is offert to him be benevolence of fortoun.' (I.5.15–30; I.7.35–59.)

[6] *In margin:* 'Mackbeth sleaeth king Duncane.' Boece does not mention Banquo here, and Shakespeare makes him loyal, II.1.26–9.

[7] *In margin:* 'Mackbeth usurpeth the crowne.' Cf. II.4.29–31.

[8] Iona.

and there laid in a sepulture amongst his predecessors, in the yeare
after the birth of our Saviour, 1046.

Malcolme Cammore and Donald Bane the sons of king Duncane,
for feare of their lives (which they might well know that Mackbeth
would seeke to bring to end for his more sure confirmation in the
estate) fled into Cumberland,[1] where Malcolme remained, till time
that saint Edward the sonne of Etheldred recovered the dominion
of England from the Danish power, the which Edward received
Malcolme by way of most friendlie enterteinment:[2] but Donald
passed over into Ireland, where he was tenderlie cherished by the
king of that land. Mackbeth, after the departure thus of Duncanes
sonnes, used great liberalitie towards the nobles of the realme,[3]
thereby to win their favour, and when he saw that no man went
about to trouble him, he set his whole intention to mainteine
justice,[4] and to punish all enormities and abuses, which had chanced
through the feeble and slouthfull administration of Duncane.
[Macbeth punished murderers sternly] in such sort, that manie
yeares after all theft and reiffings were little heard of, the people
injoieng the blissefull benefit of good peace and tranquillitie.
Mackbeth ... was accounted the sure defense and buckler of innocent people; and hereto he also applied his whole indevor,[5] to cause
young men to exercise themselves in vertuous maners, and men of the

---

[1] *In margin:* 'Malcolme Cammore and Donald Bane flee into Cumberland.'
[2] *In margin:* 'Malcolm Cammore received by Edward king of England.' (III.1.31.)
[3] *In margin:* 'Mackbeths liberalitie.'
[4] *In margin:* 'Mackbeth studieth to advance justice.'
[5] *In margin:* 'A kinglie endevor.'

R

church to attend their divine service according to their vocations . . .
He made manie holesome laws and statutes for the publike weale of
his subjects.

[These laws included many to strengthen the king's power, but also
authorized tithes for the church, gave a daughter the right to inherit,
failing a male heir, and a lord's widow a third part of her husband's
lands. Knights were to swear an oath 'to defend ladies, virgins,
widows, orphans, and the communaltie. And he that is made King
shall be sworne in semblable maner.']

[173/2/21] These and the like commendable lawes Makbeth caused
to be put as then in use, governing the realme for the space of ten
yeares in equall justice. But this was but a counterfet zeale of equitie
shewed by him, partlie against his naturall inclination to purchase
thereby the favour of the people.[1] Shortlie after, he began to shew
what he was, in stead of equitie practising crueltie. For the pricke
of conscience (as it chanceth ever in tyrants, and such as atteine to
anie estate by unrighteous means) caused him ever to feare,[2] least he
should be served of the same cup as he had ministred to his predecessor. The woords also of the three weird sisters, would not out of his
mind, which as they promised him the kingdome, so likewise did
they promise it at the same time unto the posteritie of Banquho.[3]
He willed therefore the same Banquho with his sonne named
Fleance, to come to a supper that he had prepared for them, which
was in deed, as he had devised, present death at the hands of certeine
murderers, whom he hired to execute that deed,[4] appointing them
to meete with the same Banquho and his sonne without the palace,
as they returned to their lodgings, and there to slea them, so that
he would not have his house slandered, but that in time to come he
might cleare himselfe, if anie thing were laid to his charge upon anie
suspicion that might arise.

It chanced yet by the benefit of the darke night, that though the
father were slaine, the sonne yet by the helpe of almightie God
reserving him to better fortune, escaped that danger:[5] and afterwards having some inkeling (by the admonition of some friends which
he had in the court) how his life was sought no lesse than his fathers,
who was slaine not by chancemedlie (as by the handling of the matter

---

[1] *In margin:* 'Makbeths counterfeit zeale and equitie.' Shakespeare ignores the
ten years of good rule between Acts II and III.

[2] *In margin:* 'Makbeth's guiltie conscience.' Shakespeare changes the cup image
to 'chalice'. I.7.10–12.

[3] Cf. III.148–72.

[4] *In margin:* 'Makbeths devise to slea Banquho and his sonne.' (III.1.11–44;
74ff.)

[5] *In margin:* 'Banquho is slaine, but his sonne escapeth.' (III.3.)

Makbeth woould have had it to appeare) but even upon a prepensed devise: whereupon to avoid further perill he fled into Wales.[1]

[Holinshed now traces the line of descent from Banquo through Fleance's bastard son by a Welsh princess, Walter, made Steward of Scotland, down to James V and his daughter, 'Marie queene of Scotland[2] that tooke to husband Henrie Steward lord Darnlie, by whome she had issue Charles James now king of Scotland'.]

[1741/1/26] But to returne unto Makbeth, in continuing the historie, and to begin where I left, ye shall understand that after the contrived slaughter of Banquho, nothing prospered with the foresaid Makbeth: for in maner everie man began to doubt his owne life, and durst unneth appeare in the kings presence; and even as there were manie that stood in feare of him, so likewise stood he in feare of manie,[3] in such sort that he began to make those awaie by one surmised cavillation or other, whome he thought most able to worke him anie displeasure.[4]

At length he found such sweetnesse by putting his nobles thus to death, that his earnest thirst after bloud in this behalfe might in no wise be satisfied: for ye must consider he wan double profite (as hee thought) hereby: for first they were rid out of the way whome he feared, and then againe his coffers were inriched by their goods which were forfeited to his use, whereby he might the better mainteine a gard of armed men about him to defend his person from injurie of them whom he had in anie suspicion. Further, to the end he might the more cruellie oppresse his subjects with all tyrant like wrongs, he builded a strong castell on the top of an hie hill called Dunsinane,[5] situate in Gowrie, ten miles from Perth, on such a proud height, that standing there aloft, a man might behold well neere all the countries of Angus, Fife, Stermond, and Ernedale, as it were lieng underneath him. This castell then being founded on the top of that high hill, put the realme to great charges before it was finished, for all the stuffe necessarie to the building, could not be brought up without much toile and businesse. But Makbeth being once determined to have the worke go forward, caused the thanes of each shire within the realme, to come and helpe towards that building, each man his course about.

At the last, when the turne fell unto Makduffe thane of Fife to

---

[1] *In margin:* 'Fleance Banquho's sonne fleeth into Wales.'

[2] According to Scottish authorities Duncan was the 84th king, Mary Stuart the 106th. The line was indeed a long one.

[3] *In margin:* 'Makbeths dread.' (III.4.122ff.) III.6 shows other men's fears of him.

[4] *In margin:* 'His crueltie caused through feare.'

[5] *In margin:* 'The castell of Dunsinane builded.' Its erection is not in the play.

build his part,[1] he sent workemen with all needfull provision, and commanded them to shew such diligence in everie behalfe, that no occasion might bee given for the king to find fault with him, in that he came not himselfe as other had doone, which he refused to doo, for doubt least the king bearing him (as he partlie understood) no great good will, would laie violent handes upon him, as he had doone upon diverse other. Shortly after, Makbeth comming to behold how the worke went forward, and bicause he found not Makduffe there, he was sore offended,[2] and said; I perceive this man will never obeie my commandements, till he be ridden with a snaffle: but I shall provide well inough for him. Neither could he afterwards abide to looke upon the said Makduffe, either for that he thought his puissance over great; either else for that he had learned of certeine wizzards,[3] in whose words he put great confidence (for that the prophesie had happened so right, which the three fairies or weird sisters had declared unto him) how that he ought to take heed of Makduffe,[4] who in time to come should seeke to destroie him.

And suerlie hereupon had he put Makduffe to death, but that a certeine witch, whome hee had in great trust, had told that he should never be slaine with man borne of anie woman, nor vanquished till the wood or Bernane came to the castell of Dunsinane.[5] By this prophesie Makbeth put all feare out of his heart, supposing he might doo what he would, without anie feare to be punished for the same, for by the one prophesie he beleeved it was unpossible for anie man to vanquish him, and by the other unpossible to slea him. This vaine hope[6] caused him to doo manie outragious things, to the greevous oppression of his subjects. At length Makduffe, to avoid perill of life, purposed with himselfe to passe into England, to procure Malcolme Cammore to claime the crowne of Scotland. But this was not so secretlie devised by Makduffe, but that Makbeth had knowledge given him thereof: for kings (as is said) have sharpe sight like unto Lynx, and long ears like unto Midas.[7] For Makbeth had in everie noble mans house one slie fellow or other in fee with him,[8] to reveale all that was said or doone within the same, by

---

[1] *In margin:* 'Makduffe thane of Fife.'

[2] *In margin:* 'Makbeth is offended with Makduffe.' In the play, because he did not attend the feast, and refused to help in war: III.6.21–3, 39–43.

[3] *In margin:* 'Makbeths confidence in wizzards.' (III.4.132–5.) Boece has no wizards, but 'or elles schawin to him be prophesy of þe forsaid wyches þat Makduff suld wound him with displeserr.'

[4] IV.1.69–74.

[5] IV.1.77–94.

[6] Cf. Hecate, III.5.27–33. Boece has 'þir fals illusions of devill.'

[7] *In margin:* 'Lynxs eies and Midas eares.' *Hol.* adds these images to Boece's 'scharp sycht and lang eares.'

[8] III.4.131–2.

which slight he oppressed the most part of the nobles of his realme.

Immediatlie then, being advertised whereabout Makduffe went, he came hastily with a great power into Fife, and foorthwith besieged the castell where Makduffe dwelled, trusting to have found him therein. They that kept the house, without anie resistance opened the gates, and suffered him to enter, mistrusting none evill. But neverthelesse Makbeth most cruellie caused the wife and children of Makduffe, with all other whom he found in that castell, to be slaine.[1] Also he confiscated the goods of Makduffe, proclaimed him traitor, and confined him out of all the parts of his realme; but Makduffe was alreadie escaped out of danger, and gotten into England unto Malcolme Cammore,[2] to trie what purchase hee might make by means of his support to revenge the slaughter so cruellie executed on his wife, his children, and other friends. At his comming unto Malcolme, he declared into what great miserie the estate of Scotland was brought, by the detestable cruelties exercised by the tyrant Makbeth,[3] having committed manie horrible slaughters and murders, both as well of the nobles as commons, for the which he was hated right mortallie of all his liege people, desiring nothing more than to be delivered of that intollerable and most heavie yoke of thraldome, which they susteined at such a caitifes hands.[4]

Malcolme hearing Makduffes woords, which he uttered in verie lamentable sort, for meere compassion and verie ruth that pearsed his sorowfull hart, bewailing the miserable state of his countrie, he fetched a deepe sigh;[5] which Makduffe perceiving, began to fall most earnestlie in hand with him, to enterprise the delivering of the Scotish people out of the hands of so cruell and bloudie a tyrant, as Makbeth by too manie plaine experiments did shew himselfe to be: which was an easie matter for him to bring to passe, considering not onelie the good title he had, but also the earnest desire of the people to have some occasion ministred, whereby they might be revenged of those notable injuries, which they dailie susteined by the outragious crueltie of Makbeths misgovernance. Though Malcolme was verie sorrowfull for the oppression of his countriemen the Scots, in maner as Makduffe had declared; yet doubting whether he were come as one that ment unfeinedlie as he spake, or else as sent from Makbeth to betraie him, he thought to have some further

---

[1] *In margin:* 'Makbeth's crueltie used against Makduffs familie.' (IV.1.150ff; IV.2.) Lady Macduff is warned, but too late.

[2] *In margin:* 'Makduffe escapeth into England unto Malcolme Cammore.' (III.6.29ff.)

[3] *In margin:* 'Makduffs words unto Malcolme.' (IV.3.)

[4] III.6.32-7; 45-9.

[5] *In margin:* 'Malcome sigheth.' Cf. IV.3.1-2.

triall, and thereupon dissembling his mind at the first, he answered as followeth.[1]

I am truelie verie sorie for the miserie chanced to my countrie of Scotland, but though I have never so great affection to relieve the same, yet by reason of certeine incurable vices, which reigne in me, I am nothing meet thereto. First, such immoderate lust and voluptuous sensualitie (the abhominable founteine of all vices) followeth me, that if I were made king of Scots, I should seeke to defloure your maids and matrones, in such wise that mine intemperancie should be more importable unto you than the bloudie tyrannie of Makbeth now is. Heereunto Makduffe answered: this suerly is a verie evill fault, for manie noble princes and kings have lost both lives and kingdomes for the same;[2] neverthelesse there are women enow in Scotland, and therefore follow my counsell, Make thy selfe king, and I shall conveie the matter so wiselie, that thou shalt be so satisfied at thy pleasure in such secret wise, that no man shall be aware thereof.

Then said Malcolme, I am also the most avaritious creature on the earth, so that if I were king, I should seeke so manie waies to get lands and goods, that I would slea the most part of all the nobles of Scotland by surmised accusations, to the end I might injoy their lands, goods, and possessions; and therefore to shew you what mischiefe may insue on you through mine unsatiable covetousnes, I will rehearse unto you a fable.[3] There was a fox having a sore place on him overset with a swarme of flies, that continuallie sucked out hir bloud: and when one that came by and saw this manner, demanded whether she would have the flies driven beside hir, she answered no: for if these flies that are alreadie full, and by reason thereof sucke not verie eagerlie, should be chased awaie, other that are emptie and fellie an hungred, should light in their places, and sucke out the residue of my bloud farre more to my greevance than these, which now being satisfied doo not much annoie me. Therefore saith Malcolme, suffer me to remaine where I am, least if I atteine to the regiment of your realme, mine inequenchable avarice may proove such; that ye would thinke the displeasures which now grieve you, should seeme easie in respect of the unmeasurable outrage, which might insue through my comming amongst you.[4]

Makduffe to this made answer, how it was a far woorse fault than the other: for avarice is the root of all mischiefe,[5] and for that crime

[1] *In margin:* 'Malcolme Cammore his answer.' Shakespeare's Malcolm lets his doubts appear, IV.3.8–31.

[2] *In margin:* 'Makduffes answer.' In the play he does not offer to be Malcolm's pandar, IV.3.66–76.

[3] *In margin:* 'A fable of a fox.' Not in *Mac.*   [4] IV.3.76–84.

[5] *In margin:* 'Covetousnesse the root of all mischieve.' (IV.3.84–90.)

the most part of our kings have been slaine and brought to their finall end. Yet notwithstanding follow my counsell, and take upon thee the crowne, There is gold and riches inough in Scotland to satisfie thy greedie desire. Then said Malcolme againe, I am furthermore inclined to dissimulation, telling of leasings, and all other kinds of deceit, so that I naturallie rejoise in nothing so much, as to betraie & deceive such as put anie trust or confidence in my woords.[1] Then sith there is nothing that more becommeth a prince than constancie, veritie, truth, and justice, with the other laudable fellowship of those faire and noble vertues which are comprehended onelie in soothfastnesse, and that lieng utterlie overthroweth the same; you see how unable I am to governe anie province or region: and therefore sith you have remedies to cloke and hide all the rest of my other vices, I praie you find shift to cloke this vice amongst the residue.

Then said Makduffe: This yet is the woorst of all, and there I leave thee, and therefore saie; Oh ye unhappie and miserable Scotishmen, which are thus scourged with so manie and sundrie calamities, ech one above other![2] Ye have one curssed and wicked tyrant that now reigneth over you, without anie right or title, oppressing you with his most bloudie crueltie. This other that hath the right to the crowne, is so replet with the inconstant behaviour and manifest vices of Englishmen, that he is nothing woorthie to injoy it: for by his owne confession he is not onelie avaritious, and given to unsatiable lust, but so false a traitor withall, that no trust is to be had unto anie woord he speaketh. Adieu Scotland, for now I account my selfe a banished man for ever, without comfort or consolation: and with those woords the brackish teares trickled downe his cheekes verie abundantlie.[3]

At the last, when he was readie to depart, Malcolme tooke him by the sleeve, and said: Be of good comfort Makduffe,[4] for I have none of these vices before remembred, but have jested with thee in this manner, onelie to proove thy mind: for diverse times heeretofore hath Makbeth sought by this manner of meanes to bring me into his hands, but the more slow I have shewed my selfe to condescend to thy motion and request, the more diligence shall I use in accomplishing the same. Incontinentlie heereupon they imbraced ech other,[5] and promising to be faithfull the one to the other, they fell in

---

[1] *In margin:* 'Dissimulation and delighting in lies.' Malcolm at IV.3.91–100 substitutes for these a long list of other vices.

[2] *In margin:* 'Makduffes exclamation.' IV. 3.100–8, where he does not insult the English.

[3] *In margin:* 'Makduffe weepeth.' Cf. IV.3.108–14.

[4] *In margin:* 'Malcolme comforteth Makduffe.' At IV.3.114–37 he makes more of his own virtues.

[5] *In margin:* 'Makduffe and Malcolme imbrace ech other.'

consultation how they might best provide for all their businesse, to bring the same to good effect. Soone after, Makduffe repairing to the borders of Scotland, addressed his letters with secret dispatch unto the nobles of the realme,[1] declaring how Malcolme was confederat with him, to come hastilie into Scotland to claime the crowne, and therefore he required them, sith he was right inheritor thereto, to assist him with their powers to recover the same out of the hands of the wrongfull usurper.

In the meane time, Malcolme purchased such favor at king Edwards hands, that old Siward earle of Northumberland, was appointed with ten thousand men to go with him into Scotland, to support him in this enterprise, for recoverie of his right.[2] After these newes were spread abroad in Scotland, the nobles drew into two severall factions, the one taking part with Makbeth, and the other with Malcolme.[3] Heereupon insued oftentimes sundrie bickerings, & diverse light skirmishes: for those that were of Malcolmes side, would not jeopard to joine with their enimies in a pight field, till his comming out of England to their support. But after that Makbeth perceived his enimies power to increase, by such aid as came to them foorth of England with his adversarie Malcolme,[4] he recoiled backe into Fife, there purposing to abide in campe fortified, at the castell of Dunsinane,[5] and to fight with his enimies, if they ment to pursue him;[6] howbeit some of his friends advised him, that it should be best for him, either to make some agreement with Malcolme, or else to flee with all speed into the Iles,[7] and to take his treasure with him, to the end he might wage sundrie great princes of the realme to take his part, & reteine strangers, in whome he might better trust than in his owne subjects, which stale dailie from him: but he had such confidence in his prophesies, that he beleeved he should never be vanquished, till Birnane wood were brought to Dunsinane; nor yet to be slaine with anie man, that should be or was borne of anie woman.[8]

Malcolme following hastilie after Makbeth, came the night before the battell unto Birnane wood, and when his armie had rested for a while there to refresh them, he commanded everie man to get a bough of some tree or other of that wood in his hand,[9]

---

[1] *In margin:* 'Makduffe writeth letters to his friends in Scotland.'

[2] *In margin:* 'Siward earle of Northumberland.' (IV.3.133–5; 189–92.)

[3] *In margin:* 'The nobles of Scotland divided.' Shakespeare omits this.

[4] Boece adds, 'and his freyndis grow less.'

[5] *In margin:* 'Makbeth recoileth.' (V.2.12; V.3.)

[6] Boece has: 'with purpose to fecht with his enemyss erar þan to fle out of þe realme schamefullie but ony straik.'

[7] *In margin:* 'Makbeth is counselled to fle into the Iles.' Not in Shakespeare.

[8] *In margin:* 'Makbeths trust in prophesies.' (V.3.1–10.)

[9] *In margin:* 'Branches of trees.' (V.4.3–8.)

as big as he might beare, and to march foorth therewith in such wise, that on the next morrow they might come closelie and without sight in this manner within viewe of his enimies. On the morrow when Makbeth beheld them comming in this sort, he first marvelled what the matter ment, but in the end remembred himselfe that the prophesie which he had heard long before that time, of the comming of Birnane wood to Dunsinane castell, was likelie to be now fulfilled. Neverthelesse, he brought his men in order of battell,[1] and exhorted them to doo valiantlie, howbeit his enimies had scarsely cast from them their boughs, when Makbeth perceiving their numbers, betooke him streict to flight,[2] whom Makduffe pursued with great hatred even till he came unto Lunfannaine, where Makbeth perceiving that Makduffe was hard at his backe, leapt beside his horsse, saieng; Thou traitor, what meaneth it that thou shouldest thus in vaine follow me that am not appointed to be slaine by anie creature that is borne of a woman, come on therefore, and receive thy reward which thou hast deserved for thy paines, and therwithall he lifted up his swoord thinking to have slaine him.[3]

But Makduffe quicklie avoiding from his horsse, yer he came at him, answered (with his naked swoord in his hand) saieng: It is true Makbeth, and now shall thine insatiable crueltie have an end, for I am even he that thy wizzards have told thee of, who was never borne of my mother, but ripped out of her wombe: therwithall he stept unto him, and slue him in the place.[4] Then cutting his head from his shoulders, he set it upon a pole, and brought it unto Malcolme. This was the end of Makbeth, after he had reigned 17 yeeres over the Scotishmen. In the beginning of his reigne he accomplished manie woorthie acts, verie profitable to the commonwealth, (as ye have heard) but afterward by illusion of the divell, he defamed the same with most terrible crueltie. He was slaine in the yeere of the incarnation 1057, and in the 16 yeere of king Edwards reigne over the Englishmen.

Malcolme Cammore thus recovering the relme (as ye have heard) by support of king Edward, in the 16 yeere of the same Edwards reigne, he was crowned at Scone the 25 day of Aprill, in the yeere of

---

[1] *In margin:* 'Makbeth setteth his men in order of battell.' (V.5.29ff).

[2] *In margin:* 'Makbeth fleeth, and is pursued of Makduffe.' In the play he does not flee, but note V.7.32, 46–51. Macbeth was probably slain at Lumphanan three years after Dunsinane, i.e. 1057.

[3] Cf. Boece: 'on quhome followit Makduff with gret haitrent, saying: "Traitour, now þi insaciabill crewelte sall have ane end." þan sayis Makbeth, "þou followis me in vaine, for nane þat is borne of ane wife may slay me." þan said Makduff: "I am þe samyn man for I was schorne out of my moderis wayme" & incontinent schure of his heid, and brocht þe samyn on a staik to Malcolme.'

[4] *In margin:* 'Makbeth is slaine.'

our Lord 1057.[1] Immediatlie after his coronation he called a parlement at Forfair,[2] in the which he rewarded them with lands and
livings that had assisted him against Makbeth, advancing them to
fees and offices as he saw cause, & commanded that speciallie those
that bare the surname of anie offices or lands, should have and injoy
the same. He created manie earles, lords, barons, and knights.
Manie of them that before were thanes, were at this time made
earles,[3] as Fife, Menteth, Atholl, Levenox, Murrey, Cathnes, Rosse,
and Angus. These were the first earles that have beene heard of
amongst the Scotishmen, (as their histories doo make mention.)

B. From Vol. II. The Description of Scotland, written at the first by Hector Boece, and afterwarde translated into the Scotish speech by John Bellenden . . . and now finallie into English by R.H.

[20/1/63] Our elders, although they were right vertuous both in
warre abroad and at home in peace, were yet neverthelesse in
conversation and behaviour very temperat, which is the fountaine
and originall of all vertues. In sleepe they were competent, in meate
and drinke sober, and contented with such food as was readie at
hand and prepared with little cost. [They had shaven heads, went
barefooted and were simply clad.] They slept moreover either upon
the bare floore or pallets of straw, teaching their children even from
their infancie to eschew ease, and practise the like hardnesse; and
sith it was a cause of suspicion of the mothers fideltie toward hir
husband, to seeke a strange nurse for hir children (although hir
milke failed) each woman would take intollerable paines to bring
up and nourish hir owne children. They thought them furthermore
not to be kindlie fostered, except they were so well nourished after
their births with the milke of their brests, as they were before they
were borne with the bloud of their owne bellies, nay they feared
least they should degenerat and grow out of kind, except they gave
them sucke themselves,[4] and eschewed strange milke, therefore in
labour and in painfulnesse they were equall, and neither sex regarded
the heat in summer or cold in winter, but travelled barefooted . . .
[21/1/71] In these daies also the women of our countrie were of no
lesse courage than the men, for all stout maidens and wives (if they
were not with child) marched well in the field as did the men, and

---

[1] V.7.103-4.
[2] *In margin:* 'A parlement at Forfair.'
[3] *In margin:* 'Thanes changed into earles.' (V.7.89-93.)
[4] This adds force to Lady Macbeth's strong words at I.7.54-9.

so soone as the armie did set forward, they slue the first living creature that they found, in whose bloud they not onelie bathed their swords, but also tasted thereof with their mouthes, with no less religion and assurance conceived, than if they had alreadie beene sure of some notable and fortunat victorie. When they saw their owne bloud run from them in the fight, they waxed never a whit astonished with the matter, but rather doubling their courages, with more egernesse they assailed their enimies[1]. . . .

[22/1/33] In processe of time . . . and cheeflie about the daies of Malcolme Canmore, our manner began greatlie to change and alter. [Through contact with the English the Scots began] through our dailie trades and conversation with them, to learne also their maners, and therewithall their language . . . Thereby shortlie after it came also to passe, that the temperance and vertue of our ancestors grew to be judged worthie of small estimation amongst us,[2] notwithstanding that a certein idle desire of our former renowme did still remaine with us.

C. From Vol. I THE CHRONICLES OF ENGLAND. Bk. VIII, Ch. 5.

[The death of young Siward]

[192/1/27] About the thirteenth yeare of king Edward his reigne (as some write) or rather about the nineteenth or twentieth yeare, as should appeare by the Scotish writers, Siward the noble earle of Northumberland with a great power of horssemen went into Scotland, and in battell put to flight Mackbeth that had usurped the crowne of Scotland, and that doone, placed Malcolme surnamed Camoir, the sonne of Duncane, sometime king of Scotland, in the governement of that realme, who afterward slue the said Macbeth, and then reigned in quiet. Some of our English writers say, that this Malcolme was king of Cumberland, but other report him to be sonne to the king of Cumberland. . . . It is recorded also, that in the foresaid battell, in which earle Siward vanquished the Scots, one of Siwards sonnes chanced to be slaine, wherof although the father had good cause to be sorrowfull, yet when he heard that he died of a wound which he had received in fighting stoutlie in the forepart of his bodie, and that with his face towards the enimie, he greatlie rejoised thereat, to heare that he died so manfullie. But here is to be noted,

---

[1] Lady Macbeth, unlike her husband, is not a whit afraid of Duncan's blood. (II.22–3, 47–66.)

[2] Cf. Macbeth, 'Then fly, false thanes, / And mingle with the English epicures' (V.3.8).

that not now, but a little before (as Henrie Hunt.[1] saith) that earle Siward, went into Scotland himselfe in person, he sent his sonne with an armie to conquere the land, whose hap was there to be slaine: and when his father heard the newes, he demanded whether he received the wound whereof he died, in the forepart of the bodie, or in the hinder part: and when it was told him that he received it in the forepart; I rejoise (saith he) even with all my heart, for I would not wish either to my sonne nor to my selfe any other kind of death.[2]

D. From Vol. I THE CHRONICLES OF ENGLAND

[The character of Edward the Confessor.]

[195/1/33] In diet and apparell he was spare and nothing sumptuous: and although on high feasts he ware rich apparell, as became the majestie of his royall personage: yet he shewed no proud nor loftie countenance, rather praising God for his bountiful goodnesse towards him extended, than esteeming heerein the vaine pompe of the world.[3] The pleasure that he tooke chieflie in this world for refreshing of his wits, consisted onelie in hawking and hunting, which exercises he dailie used, after he had first beene in the church at divine service. In other things he seemed wholie given to a devout trade of life, charitable to the poore, and verie liberall, namelie to hospitals and houses of religion in the parties of beyond the sea, wishing ever that the moonks and religious persons of his realme would have followed the vertue and holinesse of life used amongst them of forren parties. As hath beene thought he was inspired with the gift of prophesie, and also to have had the gift of healing infirmities and diseases. He used to helpe those that were vexed with the disease, commonlie called the kings evill, and left that vertue as it were a portion of inheritance unto his successors the kings of this realme.[4]

[1] Henry of Huntingdon, a chronicler (*c.* 1084–1155).

[2] V.7.68–82.

[3] Cf. Boece: 'This Edward wes ane man but any rancour, and sa reuthfull to þe pepill þat he was repute ane mirrour of vertew.'

[4] Cf. IV.3.139–59.

V. Probable Source

From
RERUM SCOTICARUM HISTORIA
by George Buchanan[1]
translated by T. Page

The History of Scotland. Written in Latin by George
Buchanan. Faithfully Rendered into English by T. Page
... London ... 1690.

[From Book VI. The Murder of King Duffus. Buchanan concludes his account of the bewitching of Duffus:]

These things I deliver, as I receiv'd them from our Ancestors: What
to think of this sort of Witchcraft, I leave to the Judgment of the
Reader, only minding him, That this story is found amongst our
Ancient *Archives* and Records. Amidst these things, the fear of the
King being laid aside, because they hoped he would shortly die,
many Robberies and Murders were committed, every where.
Duffus, having recovered his strength, followed the Robbers thro'
Murray, Ross, and Caithnes, and slew many of them, at occasional
Onsets; but he brought the Chief of them to Forres, That so, their
Punishment might be the more conspicuous, in that Town. There
Donaldus, Governor of the Town and Castle petitioned the King to
pardon some of his Relations, who were of the Plot; but, being
denied, he conceived great Indignation against the King, as if he had
been highly wronged; whereupon, he was wholly intent on Thoughts
of Revenge; for he judged, That his deserts from the King were so
great, that, whatever he asked of him, he ought not to be denied:
And besides, the Wife of *Donald*, seeing some of her Kindred too
were like to suffer, did further inflame the already disaffected
Heart of her Husband, by bitter words; Moreover exciting him to
attempt the Kings Death, affirming, That, seeing he was Governor
of the Castle, The Kings Life was in his Power; and, having that
Power, he might not only perpetrate the Fact, but conceal it, after
it was committed: Hereupon, when the King, tired with business,
was sounder asleep than ordinary, and his Attendants, being made
Drunk by *Donald*, were in a Dead-sleep also; he sent in *Assassins*,

[1] Edinburgi, ap A. Arbuthnetum 1582.

no man being aware, and, after they had Murdered the King, they carried him out so cunningly, a back way, that not so much as a drop of Blood appeared; and so he was buried two Miles from the Abby of *Kinloss,* under a little Bridge, in a blind place, having Grassy-Turfs of Earth cast over him, that there might be no sign of any Ground, that was digg'd up. This seems a more likely story to me, than what others write, that the course of the River was turned, and so his Body was cast into a hole at Bottom; but when the Waters were returned again to their own Chanel, then his Grave, such as it was, was covered. Also the Actors of that bloody Fact were sent away, because there is an Opinion, received from our Ancestors, which as yet obtains amongst the Vulgar, *That blood will Issue from a dead Body, many days after the party was murdered, if the murderer be present, as if the fact had been but newly committed.* The day after, when the Report was spread abroad, that the King was missing, and that his Bed was besprinkled with blood, *Donald,* as if he had been surpriz'd at the atrocity of the Fact, flys into the Kings Bed-Chamber; and, as if he had been mad with Anger and Revenge, he slew the Officers appointed to attend him; after that, he presently made diligent inquiry every where, if any discovery of the dead Body might be made. The rest, being amazed at the Fact, and afraid too of their own selves, returned every one to his own house. Thus this Good King was wickedly slain, in the Flower of his Age, after he had Reigned 4 Years and 6 Months; and as soon as they conveniently could, the Estates Assembled to create a New King.

[This King, Culene, was soon succeeded by Kenneth III, who poisoned Duffus' son Malcolm, in order to ensure that his own son, and line, would succeed him.]

Other Laws were also made, *viz. That as the Kings Eldest Son should succeed his Father; so, if the Son died before the Father, the Nephew should succeed the Grandfather: That when the King was under Age, a Tutor or Protector should be Chosen, some Eminent Man for Interest and Power, to Govern in the Kings Name and stead, till he came to Fourteen Years of Age, and then he had Liberty to choose Guardians for Himself.* And besides, many other Things were Enacted concerning the Legitimate Succession of Heirs, which ran in common to the whole Nobility, as well as to the King. The King having thus, by indirect and evil Practises, setled the Kingdom on his Posterity, as he thought; yet, his Mind was not at rest. For, though he were very Courteous to all, and highly Beneficial and Obliging to a great many; and withal, did so manage the Kingdom, that no one Part of a good King was wanting in him; yet, his Mind being disquieted with the guilt of his Offence, suffered him to enjoy no sincere or solid Mirth; but in the

Day, he was vexed with the Thoughts of that foul Wickedness, which did inject themselves; and in the Night, terrible Apparitions disturbed his Rest. At last, a Voice was heard from Heaven, either a true one, as some think; or else, such an one, as his disquieted Mind suggested, (as it commonly happens to Guilty Consciences) speaking to him, in his Sleep, to this Sense: *Dost thou think, That the Murder of* Malcolm, *an Innocent Man, secretly and most impiously Committed by thee, is either unknown to me, or, That thou shalt go unpunished for the same: Nay, there are already Plots laid against thy Life, which thou canst not avoid; neither shalt thou leave a Firm and Stable Kingdom to thy Posterity, as thou thinkest to do, but a Tumultuous and Stormy one.* The King being terrified by this dreadful Apparition, betimes in the Morning hastned to the *Bishops* and *Monks*, to whom he declared the Confusion of his Mind, and his Repentance for his Wickedness. They, instead of prescribing him a *true* Remedy, according to the Doctrine of *Christ*, (being then degenerated, themselves, from the Piety and Simplicity of their Ancestors) enjoyned him those absurd and fallacious ones, which Evil and Self-minded Men had devised for their own Gain.

[Kenneth's penitent practices ended when he was murdered by Fenella, though Buchanan did not believe the story of her booby-trap.]

[From Book VII. Duncan and Macbeth. Duncan, grandson of Malcolm II, proved a gentle and passive ruler, unable to repress rebels such as Macduald of the Isles. He was glad when his cousin Mackbeth came to his aid] promising, that, if the Command or Generalship were bestowed on him and *Bancho*, who was well acquainted with that Country, he would quickly subdue all, and quiet things. This *Mackbeth* was of a sharp Wit, and of a very lofty Spirit; and, if Moderation had accompanied it, he had been worthy of a Command, tho an eminent one. But, in punishing Offenders, he was so severe, that having no respect to the Laws, he seemed soon likely to degenerate into Cruelty. When the chief Command of the Army was conferred upon him, many were so terrified, that, casting aside their Hopes, which they had conceived by reason of the Kings Slothful Temper, they hid themselves in Holes and Corners. The *Islanders* and the *Irish*, their Flight being stopp'd, were driven into great Despair, and in a fierce Fight were every one of them slain; *Macduald* himself, with a few others flying into a Neighbour Castle, being past all hopes of Pardon, redeemed Himself and His from the Opprobriousness of his Enemies, by a voluntary death. *Mackbeth*, not content with that punishment, cut off his Head, and sent it to the King at *Perth*, and hung up the rest of his Body, for all to behold, in a conspicuous place. Those of the *Redshanks*, which he took, he caused to be hanged.

This Domestick Sedition being appeased, a far greater Terror succeeded, and seized on him, occasioned by the *Danes*. For *Sueno*, the powerful King of the *Danes*, dying, left Three Kingdoms to his Three Sons; *England* to *Harold*; *Norway* to *Sueno*; and *Denmark* to *Canutus*. *Harold* dying soon after, *Canutus* succeeded him in the Realm of *England*. *Sueno*, (or *Swain*) King of *Norway*, being Emulous of his Brothers Glory, crossed the Seas with a great Navy, and Landed in *Fife*; upon the Bruit of his coming, *Machbeth* was sent to Levy an Army; *Bancho*, the other General, staying in the Interim, with the King. *Duncanus*, or *Donald*, as if he had been rouzed from a fit of Sluggishness, was forced to go meet the Enemy. They fought near Culross, with such obstinate Courage, that as One Party was scarce able to fly; so the Other had no heart to pursue. The *Scots*, who look'd upon themselves as overcome, rather by the Incommodiousness of the Place, than by the Valour of their Enemies, retreated to *Perth*; and there staid with the Relicts of their conquered Forces, waiting for the Motions of the Enemy.

[During negotiations with the Norsemen, Duncan offered to send them food, which they accepted.]

Whereupon, a great deal of Bread and Wine was sent, both Wine pressed out of the Grape, and also strong Drink made of Barly-Malt, mixed with the juice of a Poysonous Herb, whereof abundance grows in *Scotland*, called, *Somniferous Night-shade*. The Stalk of it is above two Foot Long, and in its upper part spreads into Branches, the Leaves are broadish, acuminated on the outside, and faintly Green. The Berrys are great and of a Black Colour when they are ripe, which proceed out of the Stalk under the bottom of the Leaves. Their Taste is sweetish, and almost insipid. It hath a very small seed, as little as the Grains of a Fig. The Virtue of the Fruit, Root, and especially of the Seed, is *Soporiferous*; and will make men mad,[1] if they be taken in too great Quantities. With this Herb all the Provision was infected, and they that carried it, to prevent all suspition of Fraud, tasted of it before, and invited the *Danes* to drink huge Draughts thereof. *Swain* himself, in token of Good will, did the same, according to the custom of his Nation. But *Duncan*, knowing that the force of the Potion would reach to their very Vitals, whilst they were asleep, had in great silence admitted *Mackbeth*, with his Forces into the City, by a Gate which was furthest off from the Enemies Camp; and, understanding by his Spies, that the Enemy was fast asleep and full of Wine, he sent *Bancho* before, who well knew all the Avenues

[1] Cf. Banquo, I.3.84-5, 58-9.

both of that Place, and of the Enemies Camp too, with the greatest part of the Army; placing the rest in Ambush. He, entring their Camp, and making a great Shout, found all things in a greater Posture of Negligence than he imagined, before. There were a few raised up at the Noise, who running up and down, like Mad-men, were slain as they were met; the others were killed, sleeping.

[Almost at once Banquo had to go out against a fleet of Danes, whom he defeated heavily.]

'Tis Reported, that the *Danes*, having made so many unlucky Expeditions into *Scotland*, bound themselves by a Solemn Oath, never to return, as Enemies, thither, any more. When Matters thus prosperously succeeded with the *Scots*, both at home and abroad, and all things flourished in Peace, *Mackbeth*, who had always a Disgust at the un-active Slothfulness of his Cousin; and thereupon had conceived a secret Hope of the Kingdom in his Mind, was further encouraged in his Ambitious Thoughts, by a Dream which he had: For one Night, when he was far distant from the King, he seemed to see Three Women, whose Beauty was more August and Surprizing than bare Womans useth to be, of which, one Saluted him, *Thane* of *Angus*; another, *Thane of Murray*; and a Third, King of *Scotland*. His Mind, which was before Sick betwixt Hope and Desire, was mightily encouraged by this Dream, so that he contrived all possible ways, by which he might obtain the Kingdom; in order to which, a just occasion was offered him, as he thought. *Duncan* begat two Sons on the Daughter of *Sibert*, a petty King of *Northumberland*; *Malcolm*, Sirnamed *Cammorus*, (which is as much as *Jolt-head*,) and *Donaldus*, Sirnamed *Banus*, i.e. *White*: Of these, he made *Malcolm*, scarce yet out of his Childhood, Governor of *Cumberland*. *Mackbeth* took this matter mighty Hainously; in regard, he look'd upon it as Obstacle of Delay to him, in his obtaining the Kingdom; for, having arrived at the Enjoyment of his other Honours, promised him by his Dream; by this means, he thought, that either he should be secluded altogether from the Kingdom; or else, should be much retarded in the Enjoyment thereof; in regard the Government of *Cumberland* was always look'd upon, as the first step to the Kingdom of *Scotland*.[1] Besides, his Mind, which was feirce enough of it self, was spurred on, by the daily Importunities of his Wife, (who was Privy to all his Counsels.) Whereupon, communicating the matter to his most intimate Friends, amongst whom *Bancho* was one, he got a fit opportunity, at *Innerness*, to way-lay the King, and so slew him in the Seventh year of his Reign; and gathering a Company together, went to *Scone*, and under the shelter of popular Favour, made himself

[1] Cf. I.4.48–50.

King. *Duncan*'s Children were astonished at this sudden Disaster. They saw their Father was slain, the Author of the Murder in the Throne, and Snares laid for them, to take away their Lives; that so, by their Deaths, the Kingdom might be confirmed to *Mackbeth*: Whereupon, they shifted up and down, and hid themselves, and thus, for a time, escaped his Fury. But perceiving that no place could long secure them from his Rage; and that, being of a feirce Nature, there was no hope of Clemency to be expected from him, they fled several ways; *Malcolm*, into *Cumberland*, and Donald, to the Kindred of his Father, in the Aebudae Islands.[1]

Mackbeth, *The Eighty Fifth King*.

Mackbeth, to confirm the ill-gotten Kingdom to himself, procured the favour of the Nobles by great Gifts, being secure of the Kings Children because of their Age, and of his Neighbouring Princes, in regard of their mutual Animosities, and Discords. Thus having engaged the great Men, he determined to procure the favour of the Vulgar by Justice and Equity, and to retain it by Severity, if nothing else would do. Whereupon, he determined with himself to punish the Free-booters or Thieves, who had taken courage from the Lenity of *Duncan*. [By cunning and main force he got rid of these and other enemies.] The publick Peace being thus restored, he applied his mind to make Laws, (a thing almost wholly neglected by former Kings) and indeed, he Enacted many good and useful ones, which now are either wholly unknown, or else lie unobserved, to the great damage of the Publick. In a word, he so managed the Government for ten years, that, if he had not obtained it by Violence, he might have been accounted inferior to none of the former Kings. But when he had so strengthned himself with the Aid and Favour of the Multitude, that he feared no Force to disturb him; the Murder of the King (as 'tis very probable) hurried his Mind into dangerous Precipices, so that he converted his Government, got by Treachery, into a Cruel Tyranny. He vented the first Shock of his Inhumanity upon *Bancho*, who was his Companion in the Kings Parricide. Some ill Men had spread a kind of Prophecie abroad among the Vulgar, *That hereafter his Posterity should enjoy the Kingdom*; whereupon, fearing lest he, being a powerful and active Man, and also of the Blood Royal,[2] should imitate the Example proposed by himself, he courteously[3] invited him and his Son to Supper, but, in his return, he caused him to be slain, as if a sudden Fray and Tumult had

---

[1] The Hebrides. To Ireland in *Hol.* and II.3.139.

[2] Properly 'already stained with blood of a king' (*'regio iam sanguine imbutus'*).

[3] Lat. *'familiariter'*.

arisen. His Son *Fleanchus*, being not known in the dark, escaped the Ambush, and, being informed by his Friends how his Father was treacherously slain by the King, and that his Life was also sought after, he fled secretly into *Wales*. Upon that Murder, so cruelly and perfidiously committed, the Nobles were afraid of themselves, insomuch, that they all departed to their own homes, and came but few of them, and those very seldom, to Court. So that the Kings Cruelty being partly discovered by some, and partly vehemently suspected by all, mutual Fear and Hatred sprung up betwixt him and the Nobility. Whereupon, seeing the matter could no longer be concealed, he broke forth into open Tyranny, and the Rich and Powerful for light, frivolous, and, many times, but pretended, Causes, were put to Death. Their Confiscated Goods helped to maintain a Band of *Debauchees*, which he had about him under the name of a Guard. And yet, he thought, that his Life was not sufficiently secured by them neither, so that he resolved to build a Castle on the top of the Hill *Dunsinnan*, where there was a large Prospect all over the Country; which Work proceeding but slowly on, by reason of the difficulty of Carriage of Materials thither, he commanded in all the *Thanes* of the whole Kingdom, and so dividing the Task amongst them, They themselves were to oversee, that the Labourers did their Duty. At that time *Mackduff* was the *Thane* of *Fife*, a very powerful Man in his Country; He, being loth to commit his Life unto the Kings hands, went not himself, but sent thither many Workmen, and some of them his intimate Friends, to press on the Work. The King, either out of a desire (as was pretended) to see how the Building proceeded, or else to apprehend *Mackduff*, (as he himself feared) came to view the Structure, and by chance spying a Teem of *Mackduff*'s Oxen, not able to draw up their Load against a steep Hill, he took thence a willing occasion to vent his Passion against the *Thane*, saying, *That he knew well enough, before, his disobedient Temper, and therefore was resolved to punish it; and, to make him an Example, he threatened to lay the Yoke upon his own Neck, instead of his Oxen.* *Mackduff*, hearing of it, commended the Care of his Family to his Wife, and, without any delay, fitted up a small Vessel, as well as the streights of Time permitted, and so passed over into *Lothian*, and from thence into *England*. The King hearing that he intended to fly, made haste into *Fife*, with a strong Band of Men to prevent him; but, he being departed before, the King was presently admitted into his Castle, where he poured out all his Fury upon the *Thane's* Wife and Children, who were there present. His Goods were confiscated, He himself was proclaimed Traitor, and a grievous Punishment was threatened to any, who dared to converse with, or entertain, him. He exercised also great Cruelty against others, if they were either Noble or Rich, without distinction. For now the Nobility was despised by him, and he managed the Government by Domestick Counsels. In the mean time, *Macduff*, arriving in *England*, found *Malcolm* there, Royally treated by King *Edward*. For *Edward*, when the *Danes* Power was broken in *England*, being recalled from Banishment, did favour *Malcolm*, who was brought to him by *Sibert*, (his Grandfather by the Mother side)[1] for many Reasons. . . .

[In a long discourse Macduff tried to persuade Malcolm to raise an army against Macbeth.]

Besides, he told him, That King *Edward* was so Gracious a Prince, That he would not be wanting to him, his Friend, and Suppliant; That the People did also favour Him and hated the Tyrant; In fine, *That Gods Favour would attend the Good, against the Impious, if he were not wanting to himself.* But *Malcolm*, who had often before been persuaded, and solicited to return, by Messengers secretly sent to him from *Mackbeth*; That he might not be ensnared, before he committed so great a Concern to Fortune, resolved to try the Faithfulness of *Mackduff*;

[Malcolm thereupon accused himself of such horrible vices that Macduff in despair and anger 'was about to fling away'.]

Then Malcolm took him by the hand, and declared the Cause of this his Dissimulation . . .

Thus they, plighting their Faith one to another, consulted concerning the destruction of the Tyrant, and advised their Friends of it, by secret Messages. King *Edward* assisted him with Ten Thousand Men, over whom *Malcolm*'s Grandfather, by the Mothers side,[2] was made General. At the Report of this Armies March, there was a great combustion in *Scotland*, and many flock'd in daily to the new King; *Mackbeth* being deserted by almost all his Men, in so suddain a Revolt, not knowing what better course to take, shut up himself in the Castle of *Dunsinnan*, and sent his Friends into the *Æbudæ*, and into *Ireland*, with Money to hire Soldiers. *Malcolm* understanding his Design, makes up directly towards him, the People praying for him all along as he went, and, with joyful Acclamations, wishing him good Success. His Soldiers took this as an *Omen* of Victory, and thereupon stuck up green Boughs in their Helmets, representing an Army Triumphing, rather than going to Fight. *Mackbeth* being terrified at the Confidence of his Enemy, immediately fled; and his Soldiers, forsaken by their Leader, surrendred themselves up to

---

[1] Siwald, a great Danish warrior, actually Malcolm's uncle, as in V.2.2, V.6.2. (H. N. Paul, *op. cit.* pp. 156, 224).

[2] Siwald is meant.

2 The line of Banquo. From J. Leslie, *De Origine, Moribus, et Rebus Gestis Scotorum*, Rome, 1578.

Malcolm; Some of our Writers do here Record many Fables, which are like *Milesian* Tales, and fitter for the Stage, than an History; and therefore I omit them. *Mackbeth* reigned Seventeen Years. In the first Ten, he performed the Duty of a very good King; in the last Seven, he equalled the Cruelty of the worst of Tyrants.

Malcolm, III. *The Eighty Sixth King.*

Malcolm, having thus recovered his Fathers Kingdom, was Declared King at *Scone*, the *25th* day of *April*, in the Year of our Redemption, 1057. At the entrance of his Reign, he convened an Assembly of the Estates at *Forfar*; where the First thing he did, was, to restore to the Children their Father's Estates, who had been put to death by *Mackbeth*; He is thought by some to have been the *First*, that introduced New and Foreign Names, as distinguishments of Degrees in Honour, which he borrowed from his Neighbor-Nations, and are no less Barbarous than the former were: Such as are *Dukes, Marquesses, Earls, Barons, Riders* or *Knights. Mackduff*, the *Thane* of *Fife*, was the First who had the Title of *Earl*, conferred upon him, and many others afterwards, according to their respective Merits, were honoured with New Titles[1]. . . .

VI. Possible Source

From DE ORIGINE, MORIBUS, ET REBUS GESTIS SCOTORUM
by John Leslie (1578)[2]
translated by the editor

Book V.   LXXXIIII DUNCAN

Duncan, Malcolm's nephew, was made King with the consent of all: a man in whom clearly nature had placed nothing of cruelty, no moroseness, no bitterness, so that he would not avenge the deepest injury done to him. Having such marvellous lenity of mind, when the populace, like wild beasts loosed from all restraint, had impiously abused it with sinful licence, because he could in no way lay aside his clemency,[3] he handed over the cares of administering the kingdom to Macbeth, a man rather more inclined to severity than himself.

---

[1] V.7.91–3.
[2] *De Origine Moribus, et Rebus Gestis Scotorum Libri Decem . . . Authore Ioanne Leslaeo, Scoto, Episcopo Rossensi.* Romae. MDLXXVIII.
[3] *In margin*: 'His too great lenity brought on civil wars.'

Who first of all, to discourage the criminal licence of the rest, punished the inhabitants of Lochaber with extreme cruelty because they had grievously wounded Banquo, the King's thane, and robbed him of the King's taxes and a large sum of money.

In addition Macbeth pursued Macdonald of the Isles, who had upheld with arms the hostile behaviour of those robbers, into the Castle of Lochaber, and besieged him so strictly that all way of escape was shut off. Whereby Macdonald was so struck with fear of the punishment which he thought he would have to undergo if he fell into his enemy's power that, blinded by obstinacy, he laid violent hands on his wife, children, and himself.

At that time the King of Norway[1] crossed to Scotland with an army on the pretext (for waging unjust war) that he must avenge the deaths of those of his subjects who had previously been slain in Scotland. . . . [The Siege of Perth and Macbeth's defeat of Sueno, the Norwegian King, are briefly described.][2]

But not long afterwards vainglory of spirit puffed up Macbeth, filling his mind with an insane lust for rule, insomuch that (his wife urging him on, when he was fearful, with hope of a happy outcome) he impiously murdered the saintly (*sanctissimum*) King Duncan, who had adorned him with so much honour, in the sixth year of his reign[3]. . . .

Book V.   LXXXV MACBETH.

Macbeth, son of Doada, daughter of Malcolm the second of that name, seized the kingdom by force. This man, abounding in warlike glory, was urged on by his innate ferocity to needless cruelty. But he calmed with wisdom the kingdom which he had won evilly, striving to win over the nobility with gifts and the people with kindness, punishing all lawless persons, making salutary laws and binding all men to him with the strictest benevolence. Yet—since the heaviest punishment is imposed by God on the most sinful souls—in the end, troubled in conscience by the crime he had committed, he began to fear those around him so greatly that, departing from the agreeable nature he had hitherto shown, he either savagely slew his nobles with open violence or by secret counsels incited them to slaughter one another.

Thus when he thought himself in danger from Banquo and Macduff, he first of all slew the former, then laid snares craftily for the latter. What more needs be said? Like a true tyrant he fears

[1] *In margin:* 'The Danes again invade Scotland.' [They are Norwegians in *Macbeth*, I.2.31].

[2] *In margin:* 'The Danes are defeated at the town of Perth.'

[3] *In margin:* 'Duncan is cut off by Macbeth in the 6th year of his reign.' (A.D. 1046.)

everybody and is feared by all. So it was that the people, anxious for the state of the realm and their own imminent peril, prudently sent Macduff to England, to invite Malcolm Canmore, who was in exile there, to come and regain his paternal inheritance, binding themselves faithfully and solemnly to aid him against Macbeth.

Understanding this, Malcolm, liberally provided with ten thousand Englishmen by King Edward, returns to Scotland and meets Macbeth, first at Dunsinane, then at Lunfanan, in fiercest battle. At Lunfanan Macduff, Thane of Fife (whose wife and sons he had had killed some time before) cut off Macbeth's head and brought it as a gift to Malcolm, who loaded him with rich rewards.[1]

Book VII.   XCVIII DAVID.

[David II, only son of Robert the Bruce, succeeded his father in 1329 and ruled until 1371, when, having no issue, he was succeeded by his sister's son, Robert II.]

After the death of David there was no male of the Bruce family, of legitimate birth, to succeed in the normal way, so by agreement of the nobles, government of the realm was given to the Stuarts, who from then until now have ruled successfully. This occasion seems to require that I say something more about the origin of the Stuarts, to make it manifest to all how justly our Kings have descended from their ancestor-Kings, and how gloriously both in peace and in war the Stuart family has ever flourished. This stock (to follow the matter from its fountain-head) took their origin from Banquo, the King's lieutenant (*praeside*, the Romans say) in Lochaber, a man adorned with many titles. How his descendants came to reach regal dignity will appear from what follows. Macbeth, whose life we discussed above, understood, by the prophecy of some women—or rather Demons who assumed the likeness of women and were the sure causes of treason, hatred and strife—that after his line was extinct that of Banquo would flourish and reign for a long time. So he resolved to invite Banquo and his son Fleance to a feast and to eliminate them in such a way that no guilt should be attached to him. Wherefore he set men in ambush who were secretly to kill Banquo and Fleance when returning from the feast. For if he had committed so foul a deed himself, openly violating the laws of hospitality and friendship, he would have alienated all minds from him. Those cut-throats to whom this business had been entrusted, accosted Banquo and Fleance, and murdered Banquo the father, but Fleance, seizing the opportunity afforded by the dark night which

[1] *In margin:* 'Macbeth is slain in the 16th year of his reign, A.D. 1061.'

concealed everything, escaped by running away, and having reached Wales, gave himself into the protection, and the family, of the man who ruled that country.

By that man's daughter, a very beautiful woman, he begat a son, Walter, who, increasing to their utmost the qualities inherited from his forbears, was led by a natural inclination to Scotland, to serve the King in his wars. There he conquered the Hebrideans, and destroyed others who were treacherously plotting against the King; and on his return as inspirer and general of that great victory, he was declared Governor of the King's Palace (In the vulgar tongue we call it Steward).

[Walter had other triumphs, after which he assumed the family name Steward (Stuart). Leslie traces his descendants down to Robert II, and provides the family tree (plate 2).]

VII. Analogues

[THE SHOW OF KINGS]

A. From A DEFENSATIVE AGAINST THE POYSON OF SUPPOSED PROPHECIES
by Henry Howard (1583)

I coulde alledge one notable example of a Conjurer, if that be true, which is reported in the memories of Fraunce, who representing to a Lady of greate calling, all those personnes, as it were in a dumbe showe, which should possesse the crowne in this our age, caused the king of Navarre, or rather a wicked spirite in his stedde to appeare in the fifth place, to none other ende (as I beleeve) then that she might attempt, the rydding him out of the way, by greater store of indirect devises, whom the destinies reserved to so great and honour.

B. From a Letter of Nicolas Pasquier[1]

[The assassination of Henri IV of France reminds Pasquier that his reign and sudden death were frequently prophesied, e.g. in some Latin lines by Helvaeus Rosselin, Doctor in Alsace.]

Verses which are confirmed by the curiosity of the late Queen Mother [Catherine de Medici], who, desiring to know if her children would come to the throne, a Magician (in the Château de Chaumont, which is situated on the bank of the River Loire between Blois and

---

[1] From *Les Oeuvres d'Estienne Pasquier*, 2 vols., Amsterdam, 1723. Vol. II, Livre I, Lettre I, 'To M. d'Ambeville; on the death of Great Henry, with some prognostications bearing on his death.' (Col. 1057). Henri III reigned 1574–89, Henry IV, 1589–1610. Louis XIII was 9 when he succeeded, and reigned 1610–43.

Amboise), showed her in a room, round a circle which he had drawn, all the Kings of France who had been and would be; and they made as many turns round the circle as the number of years they had reigned or would reign; and after Henri III had made fifteen turns, behold the late King enters the course, gay and hearty, and made twenty complete turns, but in trying to finish the twenty-first, he disappeared. After him came a little Prince of eight or nine years old, who made thirty-seven or thirty-eight turns, and after that everything became invisible, because the Queen Mother did not want to see any more.

I can tell you that six months before his death there fell into my hands an Almanach, which marked the 14th of this month of May with these words: 'Dies illa, dies irae, calamitatis et miseriae;' at which I began to laugh. And this same Almanach promised that a young Prince would come, who would re-establish the State, and would set it in sweet repose; at which I was amazed, seeing that our King was healthy and strong, and had no premonition of death.

VIII. Possible Sources

A. From the MEDEA of Seneca
translated by John Studley (1566)[1]

(i) Act I.

Medea invokes the gods.

O Gods whose grace doth guide their ghostes that joy in wedlocke
    pure,
O *Juno* thou *Lucina* hyght, on whom the chary cure
Alotted is of those, that grone in paynfull chyldbed bandes,

      ......

O threfolde shapen *Hecate* that sendest furthe thy lyght,
Unto thy sylent Sacryfyse that offered is by nyght,
By whom my *Jason* sware to me, O heavenly powers all,
And ye on whom *Medea* maye with safer conscience call,
O Dungeon darke, moste dredfull den of everlastyng nyghte,
O dampned ghostes: o kyngdome set agaynste the gods aryghte:
O Lord of sad and lowrynge lakes, O Ladye dire of Hell,
(Whom though that *Pluto* stale by force yet did his troth excell
The ficle fayth of *Jasons* love, that he to me dothe beare,)

[1] *The seventh Tragedie of Seneca, Entituled Medea: Translated out of Latin into English, by John Studley* . . . 1566, ed. E. M. Spearing, *Materialien*, xxxviii, 1913.

With cursed throte I conjure you, O gryslye ghostes appeare.
Come out, come out, ye hellish hagges, revenge this deede so dire,
Bryng in your scratting pawes a burnyng brande of deadly fyre.
Rise up ye hiddious divelish feendes,[1] as dreadfull as ye weare,
When unto me in wedlocke state ye did sometyme appeare.

(ii) Act IV.

Medea's brew

She mumbling conjures up by names of illes the rable rowte,
In hugger mugger cowched longe, kept close, unserched oute:
All pestlent plagues she calles uppon, what ever Libie lande
In frothy boylyng stream doth worke, or muddye belchynge sande:
What teryng torments *Taurus* bredes, wyth snowes unthawed styll
Where winter flawes, and hory froste knyt harde the craggy hyll,
She layes her crossynge handes upon eache monstrus conjurd
    thynge,
And over it her magicke verse wyth charmyng dothe she synge:

     ......

This herbe abode the edge of knyfe in dawnnynge of the daye.
Ere *Phebus* face gan pepe, bedecte wyth glyttryng goulden spraye
His slender stalke was snepped of in depe of sylent nyght,
Hys corne was cropt, whyle she wyth charm her poisned nailes did
    dight.
She chops the dedlie herbes, & wrings the squesed clottered blood
Of serpentes out: & fylthye byrds of irksom mirye mud
She tempers wyth the same: and eake she brayes the harte of owle,
Foreshewing death with glaring eyes and moapyng visage foule.
Of shryke owle hoarce alyve she takes the durtye stynkyng guttes,
Al these the framer of this feate in dyvers percels puttes.[2]
This hath in it devouryng force of gredye spoylynge flame,
The frosen eysye dullyng colde engenders by the same.
She chantes on those the magicke verse that workes no lesser
    harme,
With bustling frantickelie she stampes, and ceaseth not to charme.

B. From the AGAMEMNON of Seneca translated by John Studley (1566)[3]

From Chorus. Act I.

[1] Cf. Lady Macbeth, I.5.40ff.
[2] Cf. IV.1.4–38.
[3] *The Eyght Tragedie of Seneca, Entituled Agamemnon. Translated out of Latin in to English, by John Studley* ... 1566. ed. E. M. Spearing, *Materialien*, xxxviii, 1913.

O Fortune, that dost fayle the great estate of kynges,
on slyppery slydyng seat thou placest loftie thynges
    And sytst on tottring sort, where peryls do abounde
yet never kyngdome calme, not quyet could be founde:
    No day to scepters sure, doth shyne, that they myght saye,
To morow shall we rule, as we have don to daye.
    One clod of croked care another bryngeth in,
One hurlye burlye done,[1] another doth begin:

      ......

O how doth fortune tosse And tomble in her whele
The staggring states of kynges, that reddye be to rele?
    Fayne wold they dreded be, and yet not setled so
When as they feared are, they feare and lyve in woe.
    The sylent Ladye nyght so sweete to man and beast,
Can not bestow on them her safe and quyet rest:
    Slepe that doth overcom and breake the bondes of greefe,[2]
It cannot ease theyr hartes, nor mynister releefe:[3]
    What castell stronglye buylt, what Bulwark, tower, or towne,
Is not by mischyfes meanes, brought topsye turvey downe?
    What ramperd walls are not made weake by wicked war?
From statelye courtes of kynges doth justice flye afar:
    In pryncelye pallacies, of honestie the lore,
And wedlock now devoute, is set by lytle store.
    The bloodye Bellon[4] those doth haunt with gorye hand,
Whose lyght and vayne conceit in paynted pomp doth stand.
    And those *Erinnys* wood turmoyles with frensyes fitts,
That ever more in proud and hautie howses sitts,
    Which fycle fortunes hand in twynklyng of an eye,
From hygh and proud degre dryves down in dust to lye.

IX. Analogues

[BLOODSTAINED HANDS]

A. From GESTA ROMANORUM,

Anon. (Fourteenth century)[5]; translated by the editor

Ch. 13. *Of Guilty Love.*

There was once an emperor who had a beautiful wife whom he
loved beyond measure. She conceived in the first year and bore a

---

[1] Cf. I.1.3.   [2] II.2.38–41.   [3] V.4.40.   [4] Cf. I.1.55.
[5] *Gesta Romanorum*, von Hermann Oesterly, Berlin, 1872, pp. 291–2.

son whom the mother adored so much that some nights she lay in the same bed with him. When he was only three years old, however, the king died, and great mourning was made for his death. The Queen mourned many days; but when he had been placed in his grave, she dwelt by herself in a castle with her son, and delighted in him so much that she could not bear to be away from him. They both continued to lie together until the boy was eighteen years old.

The Devil, seeing such great love between mother and son, tempted them to abominable behaviour, to such an extent that the son had intercourse with his mother. The queen, in fact, at once conceived. But when she became pregnant the son in deep grief abandoned his kingdom completely and went off to distant parts. When the time of her labour arrived, the mother bore a most beautiful male child, but seeing the little one born, she at once cut its throat, slitting its windpipe in the middle. Some blood from the baby's throat fell on to the palm of the queen's left hand, and made there four circles like this: O O O O. The queen could by no means remove the circles from her hand, and because of this she was so ashamed that she always had a glove on that hand, so that nobody could see the spots of blood.

Now the queen was very devoted to the Blessed Virgin, yet she was so ashamed because she had conceived by her own son and had killed her own child, that she could not bring herself to confess it, although every fifteen days she went and confessed her other sins, She also distributed generous alms for love of the Blessed Virgin Mary, and was beloved by all for her graciousness to everybody. It happened one night that her confessor was saying five Ave Maries on his knees by his bedside, when the Blessed Virgin appeared to him and said: 'I am the Virgin Mary. I have something secret to tell you.' The confessor was very glad and said: 'Dearest Lady, tell your servant whatever you please.' She said: 'The queen of this realm confesses to you; but she has committed one sin which she does not dare to lay before you for very shame. Tomorrow she will come to you to make her confession. Tell her from me that her alms and prayers have been brought to the notice of my son, and accepted. I order her to confess that sin which she committed privately in her chamber, because of which she killed her son. I have prayed for her and her sin is remitted if she will confess it. If however she will not agree to what you say, ask her to take the glove from her left hand, and in her palm you will find evidence of the sin which she has committed and not confessed. If she will not, take off the glove by force.'

With these words the Blessed Virgin vanished. Next morning the queen made humble confession of all her sins except that one. And when she had told everything that she wanted to tell her confessor said: 'Dear Lady, many people are wondering greatly why you always have a glove on your left hand. Be so bold as to show me your hand so that I may see if it hides anything unpleasing to God.' But she: 'Master, my hand is not healthy and for that reason I do not want to show it to you.'

On hearing this he seized her by the arm and, much against her will, drew off the glove, saying: 'Do not be afraid, my Lady, the Blessed Virgin, who loves you dearly, has commanded me to do this.' And when he saw her open hand he perceived four round bloody spots. In the first circle were four C C C C, the second four D D D D, in the third four M M M M, in the fourth four R R R R. Around each circle, as on a seal, was a red superscription, running as follows: 'Casu Cecidisti Carne Cecata': 'Demoni Dedisti Dona Donata'; 'Monstrat Manifeste Manus Maculata'; 'Recedit Rubigo Regina Rogata' (i.e. By occasion thou hast fallen blinded in flesh; Thou hast given to the Devil the gifts bestowed on thee; A stained hand shows itself clearly; The scarlet (of sin) disappears through the prayers of the Queen of Heaven).[1]

When the queen saw this she fell at her confessor's feet and with tears humbly confessed the sin she had committed. She received absolution and did her penance, and after a few days she slept in the Lord. And at her death there was great mourning in the city.

B. From THOMAS OF READING
by Thomas Deloney (1600)

[Thomas Cole of Reading comes to the inn at Colnbrook, and is welcomed by the host and hostess, who intend to kill him. He feels unaccountably sad, even when musicians play for him.]

This musicke comes very well (said Cole) and when he had listned a while thereunto, he said, Methinks these instruments sound like the ring of S. Mary Overies belles, but the base drownes all the rest: and in my eare it goes like a bell that rings a forenoones knell. For Gods sake let them leave off, and beare them this simple reward.

The musitians being gone, his hoste asked if now it would please him to go to bed; for (quoth he) it is welneare eleven of the clocke.

---

[1] There were many parables showing the importance of Confession. This story is found in Vincent of Beauvais, *Speculum Historiae*, Lib. 7, 93. Cf. a similar, shorter tale, about a sinful woman who was told in a vision by Jesus to confess her sin, and next morning she 'looked on her hand, and it was all bloody, that no hot water could, nor any other liquid, wash it away' until she had confessed and done penance; 'Anon the blood was away from her hand, revealing her sin.' *Gesta Romanorum, Early English Versions*, ed. S. J. H. Herrtage, E.E.T.S, Ex. Ser. xxxiii, 1879, p. 393. Our story is followed by a long religious application, from which I construct the interpretations of the cryptic words.

S

With that Cole behoulding his host and hostesse earnestly, began to start backe, saying, What aile you to looke so like pale death? Good Lord, what have you done, that your hands are thus bloody?

What, my hands (said his host)? Why, you may see they are neither bloudy nor foule: either your eies doe greatly dazell, or else fancies of a troubled minde do delude you . . .

Good Lord (said he) I am not sicke, I praise God, but such an alteration I find in my selfe as I never did before. With that the scritch owle cried piteously, and anone after the night raven sate croking hard by his window.

Jesu have mercy upon me (quoth hee) what an ill favoured cry doe yonder carrion birds make, and therewithall he laid him downe in his bed, from whence he never rose againe.[1]

His host and hostesse, that all this while noted his troubled mind, began to commune betwixt themselves thereof. And the man said, he knew not what were best to be done. By my consent (quoth he) the matter should passe, for I thinke it is not best to meddle on him.

What, man (quoth she) faint you now? have you done so many and doe you shrinke at this? . . . Her wicked counsell was followed . . .

X. Analogue

From
AN ALPHABET OF TALES
(Fifteenth century)[2]

LXXVIII. *An Archdeacon aspiring to the Bishopric committed murder*

We read in the 'Book of the Gift of Fear' how once there was in Germany an Archdeacon who desired greatly to be a Bishop, and plotted therefore his Bishop's death; and he laid a great stone above the gate by which the Bishop used to go into the church; and over the gate there was an image of Our Lady. On a time, as he went before his company and set himself down on his knees to worship the image, this stone was made to fall, and it smote out his brains. And soon after, this Archdeacon was made Bishop, and held a great feast at his installation. At this feast there was a great Prince who served him, and suddenly this man was ravished into a vision, in

---

[1] How differently Shakespeare used the popular superstitions brought together in this passage! Text is from 1623 edn.

[2] *An Alphabet of Tales: An English 15th-Century translation of the Alphabetum Narrationum of Estienne de Besançon*, ed. Mary Macleod Banks, Pt. I, E.E.T.S., Orig. Ser. 126, 1904, p. 60.

which he saw Our Lady with a great multitude of angels and saints, bearing the Bishop's head that the brains were struck out of; and she presented it to Almighty God saying after this manner: 'Dear Son! This my servant's head is still bleeding, and yet his slayer the murderer who made him die, enjoys the dignity that he has after him.' And then Our Lord asked her whom he should send unto him. And she said, 'Lo! yonder is his server.' And then Our Lord commanded him on pain of death that he should without delay tell that Bishop all that he had both heard and seen. Then he came to himself and wept, and went in and publicly told the Bishop, before all who were there, what he had both heard and seen. And when the Bishop had heard him openly before all men, he grew mad and died.

BIBLIOGRAPHY

I. General Critical Works
(Only a small selection is given here. For others see the Bibliographies in previous volumes and Vol. VIII)

BATTENHOUSE, R. W. 'Shakespearean Tragedy: A Christian Interpretation', in *The Tragic Vision and the Christian Faith*, ed. N. A. Scott, N.Y., 1957.

BOWERS, F. T. *Elizabethan Revenge Tragedy*, Princeton, 1940, 1966.

BRADLEY, A. C. *Shakespearian Tragedy*, 1904, etc.

BRIGGS, K. M. *The Anatomy of Puck*, 1959.

BRIGGS, K. M. *Pale Hecate's Team*, 1962.

CAMPBELL, L. B. *Shakespeare's Tragic Heroes, Slaves of Passion*, Cambridge, 1930, 1961.

CHARLTON, H. B. *Shakespearian Tragedy*, Cambridge, 1948.

CURRY, W. C. *Shakespeare's Philosophical Patterns*, Baton Rouge, 1937.

DANIEL, P. A. *Time-Analysis of Shakespeare's Plays*, 1877-9.

FRYE, N. *Fools of Time*, Toronto, 1967.

GRANVILLE-BARKER, H. *Prefaces to Shakespeare*, 4 vols, 1930, 1963.

GREG, W. W. *The Shakespeare First Folio*, Oxford, 1955.

HAWKES, T. *Shakespeare and the Reason*, 1964.

Henslowe's Diary, ed. R. A. Foakes and R. T. Rickert, Cambridge, 1961.

HUNTER, G. K. 'The Last Tragic Heroes', in *Later Shakespeare. Stratford-upon-Avon Studies 8*, 1966, 11-28.

HUNTER, G. K. 'Seneca and the Elizabethans', *Sh Survey*, *20*, Cambridge, 1967, 17-26.

KNIGHT, G. W. *The Wheel of Fire*, 1930.

KNIGHT, G. W. *The Imperial Theme*, 1930.

LAWLOR, J. *The Tragic Sense in Shakespeare*, 1960.

LEECH, C. 'The "Capability" of Shakespeare', *ShQ*, xi, 1960, 123-36.

LERNER, L. *Shakespeare's Tragedies: An Anthology of Modern Critics*, 1963.

MOULTON, R. G. *Shakespeare as a Dramatic Artist*, 1885.

MUIR, K. *Shakespeare's Sources*, Vol. I, 1957.

NOSWORTHY, J. M. *Shakespeare's Occasional Plays*, 1965.

OPPEL, H. 'Shakespeare und das Leid', *ShJb*, xciii, 1957, 38-81.

RIGHTER, A. *Shakespeare and the Idea of the Play*, 1962, 1967.

ROSSITER, A. P. *Angel with Horns*, 1961.

SIEGEL, P. N. *Shakespearean Tragedy and the Elizabethan Compromise*, N.Y., 1957.

SIMROCK, M. K. *Remarks on the Plots of Shakespeare's Plays*, ed. H. O. Halliwell, Sh.Soc. 1850.

SISSON, C. J. *Shakespeare's Tragic Justice*, 1962.

SPENCER, T. J. B. 'The Sophistry of Shakespeare', *English Studies Today*, iv, 1966, 169–85.

SPRAGUE, A. C. *Shakespeare and the Actors*, 1944.

STEWART, J. I. M. *Character and Motive in Shakespeare*, 1949.

TRAVERSI, D. A. *An Approach to Shakespeare*, 3rd. edn., Vol. 2, 1969.

VICKERS, B. *The Artistry of Shakespeare's Prose*, 1968.

WALKER, A. *Textual Problems of the First Folio*, 1953.

WATSON, C. B. *Shakespeare and the Renaissance Concept of Honor*, Princeton 1960.

WEST, R. H. *The Invisible World*, Athens, Georgia, 1939.

WEST, R. H. *Shakespeare and the Outer Mystery*, Lexington, 1968.

WILSON, H. S. *On the Design of Shakespearian Tragedy*, Toronto, 1957.

II. Editions and Criticism of Individual Plays

Hamlet

1. Editions of the play

Q1 1603. *The Tragicall Historie of Hamlet Prince of Denmarke By William Shake-speare. As it hath beene diverse times acted by his Highnesse servants in the Cittie of London: as also in the two Universities of Cambridge and Oxford, and else-where.* At London printed for N. L. and John Trundell. 1603.

    Modern edns.: W. Griggs (facs.) 1880; W. A. Wright, 1893; F. G. Hubbard, 1920; G. B. Harrison, 1923; Scolar Press, 1969.

Q2 1604. *The Tragicall Historie of Hamlet, Prince of Denmarke. By William Shakespeare. Newly imprinted and enlarged to almost as much againe as it was, according to the true and perfect Coppie.* At London, Printed by I.R. for N.L. and are to be sold at his shoppe under Saint Dunstons Church in Fleetstreet,1604.

    Modern edns.: W. Griggs (facs.) 1880; Van Damm, 1924; J. D. Wilson, 1930; T. M. Parrott and H. Craig, 1938; O. J. Campbell (facs.) 1938; Scolar Press, 1969.

Q3 1611. Q4 n.d. Q5 1637.

F1 1623. Modern edns.: Facs. in F1 ed. J. O. Halliwell-Phillips, 1876, F1 ed. H. Kökeritz and C. T. Prouty, 1955; F1 ed. C. Hinman, 1968; Scolar Press facs. 1969. Parallel texts: S. Timmins, Q1, Q2, 1860; E. P. Vining, Q1, F1, 1890;

W. Viëtor, Q1, Q2, F1, 1891. Most modern edns. give conflated texts. H. H. Furness, *Var*, 1877; E. K. Chambers, 1894; E. Dowden, *Arden*, 1899, 1928; J. Q. Adams, 1929; J. D. Wilson, *Camb*, 1934, 1936; G. L. Kittredge, 1939; C. F. T. Brooke, *Yale*, 1947; W. Farnham, *Pelican*, 1957; K. Muir, *New Penguin*, 1968.

2. Major Sources and Analogues
(*a*) *Editions*
Saxo Grammaticus

Saxo Grammaticus. *Danorum Regum Heroumque Historie* . . ., Paris, 1514, Basle, 1534, Frankfurt, 1576.
Modern edn.: F. W. Horn, 2 vols, Copenhagen, 1898. Trans.: O. Elton, *The First Nine Books of the Danish History*, 1894; 1930 (part). Bk. III trans. in *Var*, 1877; Gollancz, *The Sources of Hamlet*, 1926. See also collections below.

Belleforest

Belleforest, F. de. *Le Cinquiesme livre des histoires tragiques.* 1570, 1576, 1582, 1601, etc.
Modern edns.: see collections below. Eng. trans.: Anon, *The Hystorie of Hamblet, 1608.* Modern edns.: *Var*, 1877, *ShLib*, 1875.
Collections of above sources, etc.: *ShLib*, 1875, Vol. ii; R. Gericke, *Shakespeares Hamlet-Quellen*, Leipzig, 1881; M. Moltke, *Hamlet-Quellen*, Leipzig, 1881; J. Schick, *Corpus Hamleticum*, 4 vols, Berlin, 1912–38; I. Gollancz, *The Sources of Hamlet*, 1926; J. D. Wilson, ed., *Hamlet* (Cranach Press), Weimar, 1930.

Fratricide Punished

Anon. *Tragoedia der bestrafte Brudermord oder Prinz Hamlet aus Dännemark* (MS in Library of Gotha), ed. H. A. O. Reichard, *Olla Potrida*, ii. 18, Berlin, 1781; A. Cohn, *Shakespeare in Germany*, 1865 (with Eng. trans.); trans. in Furness, *Var.* ii, 1877; W. Creizenach, *Die Schauspiele der englischen Komödianten*, 1889; trans. in E. Brennecke, *Shakespeare in Germany, 1590–1710*, Chicago, 1964.

Seneca

Seneca, L.A. *Tragoediae*, 1589; ed. T. Farnaby, 1613. *Troas: The sixt tragedie of L. A. Seneca, entituled Troas*, trans. Jasper Heywood, 1559, 1560?; *Thyestes: The second tragedie of Seneca: Thyestes*, trans. J. Heywood, 1560. *Agamemnon: The eyght tragedie of Seneca: Agamemnon*, trans. J. Studley, 1566. *Seneca his tenne tragedies translated into Englysh*, ed. T. Newton, 1581. Modern edns.: J. Leigh (Spenser Society), 1887; C. Whibley, 2 vols, 1927. *Troas* and *Thyestes* ed H. de Vocht in *Materialien*, xli, 1913; *Agamemnon* by E. M. Spearing, *Materialien*, xxxviii. 1913.

Spanish Tragedy

[Kyd, T.] *The Spanish Tragedie, Containing the lamentable end of Don Horatio, and Bel-Imperia: with the pittiful death of olde Hieronimo*, n.d.; 1594, 1599, 1602, 1610. etc.
Modern edns.: R. Dodsley, 1744, 1875 etc.: J. M. Manly, 1897; J. Shick, 1898; F. S. Boas, *Works of T. Kyd*, Oxford, 1901; P. Edwards, 1959.

(b) Critical studies of major sources

CARRÈRE, F. *Le Théâtre du Thomas Kyd*, Toulouse, 1951.

CORBIN, J. *The Elizabethan Hamlet*, 1895.

CORBIN, J. 'The German *Hamlet* and the earlier English versions', *Harvard Studies*, v, 1896.

CREIZENACH, W. '*Der bestrafte Brudermord* and its relation to Shakespeare's *Hamlet*', *MPhil*, ii, 1905, 249–60.

CREIZENACH, W. 'Hamletfragen.' *ShJb*, xlii, 1906, 76–85.

EVANS, G. LL. 'Shakespeare, Seneca, and the Kingdom of Violence', in *Roman Drama*, ed. T. A. Dorey and D. R. Dudley, 1965.

EVANS, M. B. '*Der bestrafte Brudermord* and Shakespeare's *Hamlet*', *MPhil*, ii, 1905, 433–9.

FITZGERALD, J. D. *The Sources of the Hamlet Tragedy*, 1909.

FREUDENSTEIN, R. *Der bestrafte Brudermord. Shakespeares Hamlet auf der Wanderbühne des 17 Jahrhunderts*, Hamburg, 1958.

GOLLANCZ, I. *Hamlet in Iceland*, 1898.

GOLLANCZ, I. *The Sources of Hamlet, with an essay on the Legend*, Oxford, 1926.

HANSEN, G. P. *The Legend of Hamlet as found in Saxo Grammaticus and other writers of the Twelfth Century*, Chicago, 1951.

HATCHER, O. L. 'The Ur-Hamlet Problem', *MLN*, xxi, 1906, 177–80.

HOOK, F. S. *The French Bandello, U. of Missouri Studies*, xxii, Columbus, 1948.

JACK, A. E., 'Thomas Kyd and the *Ur-Hamlet*', *PMLA*, xx, n.s. 13, 1905, 729–48.

KNIGHT, A. H. J. '*Der bestrafte Brudermord* and *Hamlet*, Act V', MLR, xxxi, 1936, 385–91.

LATHAM, R. G. *Two Dissertations on the Hamlet of Saxo Grammaticus*, 1872.

LEWIS, C. M. *The Genesis of Hamlet*, N.Y., 1907.

MACCALLUM, M. W. 'The authorship of the early *Hamlet*', in *An English Miscellany*, Oxford, 1901, 282–95.

MALONE, K. *The Literary History of Hamlet*, Heidelberg, 1923.

MUIR, K. 'Seneca and Shakespeare', *N&Q*, June 1956, 243–4.

ØSTERBERG, V. *Studier over Hamlet-teksterne*, Copenhagen, 1920.

SARRAZIN, G. 'Die Entstehung der Hamlet-Tragödie', *Anglia*, Bd. 12, 1889, 143–57; Bd. 13, 1891, 117–39.

SCHICK, J. 'Die Entstehung des *Hamlet*', *ShJb*, xxxix, 1902, 13–48.

SCHULTZE, F. W. *Hamlet: Geschichtsubstanzen zwischen Rohstoff und Endform des Gedichts*, Halle, 1956.

STABLER, A. P. 'The Histoires Tragiques of F. de Belleforest', Ph.D. Dissertation, U. of Virginia, 1959.

STABLER, A. P. 'The Sources of *Hamlet*: Some Corrections of the Record', *Renaissance Studies*, xxxii, 1964, 207–16.

STABLER, A. P. 'Melancholy, Ambition, and Revenge in Belleforest's Hamlet', *PMLA*, lxxxi, 1966, 207–13.

STAMM, R. '*The Spanish Tragedy* and *Hamlet*', in *The Shaping Powers at Work*, Heidelberg, 1967.

TANGER, G. '*Der bestrafte Brudermord* und sein Verhältnis zu Shakespeares *Hamlet*', *ShJb*, xxiii, 1888, 224–45.

3. Minor Sources, etc.: editions and critical studies

Alphonsus, Emperor of Germany (Anon.) (?1594–9) 1654.
    Modern edns.: K. Elze, 1867; H. F. Schwartz, 1912; collections of G. Chapman. Bowers, F. T. '*Alphonsus, Emperor of Germany* and the *Ur-Hamlet*', *MLN*, xlviii, 1933, 101–8.

BURTON, ROBERT, *The Anatomy of Melancholy*, Oxford, 1621, 1624, 1628. Modern edns.: A. R. Shilleto, 1893; H. Jackson, 1932.

G. J. (John Gordon) *Henrici Scotorum Regis Manes / Ad Jacobum VI^um Filium*, in G. Lambin, 'Une Première Ebauche d'*Hamlet* (mars 1587)', *Les Langues Modernes*, xlix, Paris, 1955, 37–45.

GOSLICIUS, L. GRIMALDUS. *De Optimo Senatore*, Venice, 1568, Basle, 1593. English trans.: Anon. *The Counsellor. Exactly pourtraited in two Bookes*, prd. Richard Bradocke, 1598.
    Modern edn. in W. Chwalewik, *Anglo-Polish Renaissance Texts*, Warsaw, 1968 (facs.). Cf. I. Gollancz, 'Bits of Timber', in *A Book of Homage*, 1916.

GRAY, H. D. 'Did Shakespeare write a Tragedy of Dido?', *MLR*, xv, 1920, 217–20.

KRANTZ, ALBERT, *Chronica Regnorum Aquilonarium*, Strasbourg, 1545 (German), 1548 (Latin) etc.

LIVIUS T. *The Romane Historie*, trans. Philemon Holland, 1600.

MARLOWE, C. *The Tragedie of Dido Queene of Carthage*, 1594. Modern edn.: C. F. T. Brooke, 1930.

Reine Chatiée, La, in J. F. Bladé, *Contes populaires de la Gascoigne*, 3 vols, Paris, 1886, i. 57–66.

Krappe, A. H. 'Sh. in Romance Folk-lore', *Neuphilologische Mitteilungen*, xxvii, Helsinki, 1926, 65–70.

M. Lüthi, 'Hamlet in der Gascoigne', *ShJb*, 1951/2, 48–57.

St. Albans Chronicle (1406–20), ed. V. H. Galbraith, Oxford, 1937 (Appendix).

SIDNEY, SIR PHILIP, *The Countesse of Pembrokes Arcadia*, 1590. Modern edn.: A Feuillerat, 1922.

Sir Bevis of Hampton. 1550 (Copland). Modern edn. in G. Ellis, *Specimens of Early English Metrical Romances*, 1848, ed. H. O. Halliwell. Study by R. Zecker, *Boece-Amlethus*, Berlin, 1905.

TACITUS, P. C. *The Annales* [trans. R. Greneway], 1598, 1604, 1605. W. Montgomerie, 'More an antique Roman than a Dane', *Hibbert Journal*, lix, 1960, 67–96.

Tarltons newes out of Purgatorie, 1590, 1630. Modern edn.: J. O. Halliwell, 1844.

VALERIUS MAXIMUS. *Romae Antiquae Descriptio*, trans. S. Speed, 1617, 1678.

VIRGIL. *The whole xii bookes of the Aeneidos*, trans. T. Phaer and T. Twyne, 1573, 1584. Modern trans. J. Conington, 1884. C. Leech, 'The Hesitation of Pyrrhus', in *The Morality of Art*, ed. D. W. Jefferson, 1969.

Warning for Faire Women, A. Anon., 1599. Modern edns.: R. Simpson, 1878; J. S. Farmer, *TFT*, 1912.

WOODES, N. *The Conflict of Conscience*, 1581. Modern edn.: *MalSoc*, 1952.

ZACHARASIEWICZ, W. 'Der perfekte Rachemord', in *Festschrift für R. Palgen*, 1971.

4. Political and Historical Background
(a) *Scotland, Scandinavia, Poland*

BLACK, J. B. *The Reign of Elizabeth*, Oxford, 1936, 1959.

BROWN, KEITH. 'Hamlet's Place on the Map', *Sh Studies*, iv, 1968 ed. J. L. Barroll, Vanderbilt U., Dubuque, Iowa, 160–82.

CHAMBERLAIN, JOHN. *Letters*, ed. N. E. McClure, Philadelphia, 1939.

CRANSTOUN, J. *Satirical Poems of the Time of the Reformation*, *STS*, 2 vols, 1891.

HENDERSON, T. F. *Mary. Queen of Scots*, 1905.

HORSEY, SIR JEROME. *A Relacion or Memorial* ed. E. A. Bond, Hakluyt Soc, 1856.

LARSEN, K. *A History of Norway*, N.Y., 1948.

OLSSON, Y. 'In Search of Yorick's Skull', *Sh Studies*, iv, 1968, 183–220.

POLLARD, A. F. *Political History of England, 1547–1603*, 1913.

ROWSE, A. L. *The Expansion of Elizabethan England*, 1955.

SJÖGREN, G. 'The Danish Background in *Hamlet*', *Sh Studies*, iv, 221–30.

STEVENSON, J. *Selections from Unpublished MSS . . . illustrating the Reign of Mary, Q. of Scotland*, Maitland Club, 1837.

WINSTANLEY, L. *Hamlet and the Scottish Succession*, 1921.

WRIGHT, T. *Queen Elizabeth and her Times: a series of Original Letters*, 2 vols, 1838.

(*b*) *Italy and* 'The Murder of Gonzago'

AFFÒ, P. IRENEO. *Vita di Luigi Gonzaga, detto Rodomonte*, Parma, 1780.

ARETINO. *Lettere*, 1542. Modern edn.: *Il Secondo Libro delle Lettere*, ed. F. Nicolini, Bari, 1916.

BEMBO P. *Opere*, Venice, 1729.

BROWNE, C. ELLIOT. 'Notes on Shakespeare's Names', *Athenaeum*, 29 July 1876.

BULLOUGH, G. 'The Murder of Gonzago', *MLR*, xxx, 1935, 433–44.

CHILDS, R. DE S. 'Influence of Court Tragedy on the Play Scene'. *JEGP*, xxxii. 1933, 44–50.

DENNISTOUN, J. *Memoirs of the Dukes of Urbino*, 3 vols, 1851, 1909.

FERGUSON, E. L. 'The Play-scene in *Hamlet*', *MLR*, xiv, 1919, 370–9.

GIOVIO, P. *Pauli Jovii. Elogia Virorum bellica virtute illustrium et nunc ex cuiusdem Musae ad vivum expressus exornata*, Basel, 1575. Italian trans., *Gli Elogi, Vite brevemente scritte d'huomini illustri . . .*, 1554.

GIROLAMO MARIA DA VENETIA, *Fra Cronica della Città d'Ugubbio;* in *Rerum Italicarum Scriptores*, ed. L. A. Muratori, T. XXI, Pt. 4, Città di Castello, 1902.

GREG, W. W. 'A critical mouse-trap', in *A Book of Homage*, ed. I. Gollancz, 1916, 179–80.

LEONI, G. *Vita di Francesco Maria I di Urbino*, Venice, 1605.

MARCOLINI, C. *Notizie Storiche della Provincia de Pesaro e Urbino*, Pesaro, 1868.

REBORA, P. *Echi della Cultura di Urbino nelle Letteratura inglese, Studi Urbinati*, Urbino, 1938; reprd. in *Momenti di Cultura Italiana e Inglese*, Mazara, 1952.

SANSOVINO FR. *Dell'Origine delle Case Illustri d'Italia*, Venice, 1582, 1609.

SARRAZIN, G. 'Neu Italienische Skizzen zu Shakespeare', *ShJb*, xxxi, 1895, 169–76.

SISMONDI, J. C. L. *Histoire des Républiques italiennes du moyen-âge*, 1826 edn.

VIANI, ELISA. *L'Avvelenatura di Francesco Maria, Duca di Urbino*, Mantua 1902.

5. Other Relevant Criticism

ALEXANDER, N. 'Critical Disagreement about Oedipus and Hamlet', *Sh Survey 20*, Cambridge, 1967, 33–40.

ALEXANDER, P. *Hamlet, Father and Son*, Oxford, 1955.

BATTENHOUSE, R. W. *Hamlet without Tears*, Dubuque, Iowa, 1946.

BATTENHOUSE, R. W. 'The Ghost in *Hamlet*: a Catholic "Linchpin"?', *S Phil*, xlviii, 1951, 161–92.

BEVINGTON, T. M. ed. *Twentieth Century Interpretations of Hamlet*, N.J., 1968.

BONJOUR, A. 'The Question of Hamlet's grief', *Eng. Studies*, xliii, 1962, 336–43.

BRADBY, G. F. *The Problems of Hamlet*, 1928.

CHAKRAVORTY, J. 'Shakespearian Transmutation of Revenge', in *Shakespeare: A Book of Homage*, Jadavpur U., Calcutta, 1964.

CHATTERJEE, V. 'T. S. Eliot and the Problems of *Hamlet*', *Shakespeare: A Book of Homage*, Jadavpur V., Calcutta, 1964.

DUTHIE, G. I. *The 'Bad Quarto' of Hamlet*, Cambridge, 1941.

ELIOT, T. S. 'Hamlet and his Problems' in *The Sacred Wood*, 1920.

ELLIOTT, G. R. *Scourge and Minister*, Durham, N. C., 1951.

GARDNER, HELEN. 'Lawful Espials', *MLR*, xxxiii, 1938, 344–55.

GOLLANCZ, I. 'Bits of Timber' in *A Book of Homage*, 1916.

GREG, W. W. 'Hamlet's Hallucination', *MLR*, xii, 1917.

HERFORD C. H. and WIDGERY W. H. *The Fist Quarto edition of Hamlet (1603)*, 1880.

HONIGMANN, E. A. J. '*The Date of Hamlet*.' *Sh Survey 9*, 1958, 24–34.

HONIGMANN, E. A. J. 'The Politics in *Hamlet* and the World of the Play', *Stratford-upon-Avon Studies*, 5, 1963, 129–47.

JENKINS, H. 'The Tragedy of Revenge in Shakespeare and Webster', *Sh Survey 14*, 1961, 45–55.

JENKINS, H. 'Hamlet and Ophelia', *Proc. Brit. Acad.*, 1963, 135–51.

JORGENSEN, P. A. 'Hamlet and the Restless Renaissance', in *Shakespearean Essays*, ed. A. Thaler and N. Sanders, U. of Tennessee, Knoxville, 1964, 131–43.

JOSEPH, B. L. *Conscience and the King*, 1953.

JOSEPH, MIRIAM. 'Discerning the Ghost in *Hamlet*', *PMLA*, lxxvi, 1961, 493–502.

JUMP, J. D. ed. *Hamlet: A Casebook*, 1968.

KITTO, H. D. F. *Form and Meaning in Drama*, 1956.

KNIGHTS, L. C. *An Approach to Hamlet*, 1960.

LAWLOR, J. J. 'The Tragic Conflict in *Hamlet*', *RES*, n.s. 1, 1950, 97–113.

LAWRENCE, W. W. *Shakespeare's Workshop*, Oxford, 1928.

LEWIS, C. S. 'Hamlet, the Prince or the Poem?', *Proc. Brit. Acad.*, 1943.

MCKERROW, R. B. *The Works of Thomas Nashe*, 5 vols, 1904–10.

MUIR, K. *Shakespeare: Hamlet*, 1963.

NOWOTTNY, W. 'Shakespeares Tragedies', in *Shakespeare's World*, ed. J. R. Sutherland and J. Hurstfield, 1964.

PALMER, D. J. 'Stage Spectators in *Hamlet*', *Eng. Studies*, xlvii, 1966, 423–30.

PROSSER, E. *Hamlet and Revenge*, Stanford, Cal., 1967.

RABKIN, N. *Shakespeare and the Common Understanding*, N.Y., 1967.

ROBERTSON, J. M. *The Hamlet Problem*, 1919; *Hamlet once More*, 1923.

SEMPER, I. J. 'The Ghost in *Hamlet*, Pagan or Christian?' *The Month*, 1953, 230–1.

SHEPARD, W. V. 'Hoisting the Engineer with his own Petard', *ShQ*, vii, 1956, 281–5.

STOLL, E. E. *Hamlet, a Comparative Study*, 1919.

STOLL, E. E. *Art and Artifice in Shakespeare*, 1935.

THORNDIKE, A. H. 'The Relation of *Hamlet* to Contemporary Revenge Plays', *PMLA*, xvii, 1902, 125–220.

VAN LAAN, T. F. 'Ironic Reversal in *Hamlet*', *SEL*, vi, 1966, 247–52.

WALDOCK, A. J. A. *Hamlet: A Study in Critical Method*, Cambridge, 1931.

WALCUTT, C. C. '*Hamlet*—The Plot's the Thing', *Michigan Q. Rev.*, v, 1966.

WEST, R. H. 'King Hamlet's Ambiguous Ghost', *PMLA*, lxx, 1955, 1107–17. Reprd. in *Shakespeare and the Outer Mystery*, U. of Kentucky, Lexington, 1968.

WILSON, J. DOVER. *What Happens in Hamlet*, Cambridge, 1935.

Othello

1. Editions of the play

Q1 1622. Facs. J. O. Halliwell, 1864; H. A. Evans, 1885.

Q2 1630. Facs. ed. H. A. Evans, 1885.

Q3 1655.

F1 1623. Facs. in F1, J. O. Halliwell-Phillips, 1876; F1, H. Kökeritz and C. T. Prouty, 1959; C. Hinman, 1968.

Parallel texts: Q1 and F1, T. R. Price, N.Y. 1890: M. M. A. Schröer, Heidelberg, 1909.

Modern edns.: H. H. Furness, *Var*, 1886; H. C. Hart, *Arden*, 1903; 1928; L. Mason, *Yale*, 1918; C. H. Herford, *Warwick*, 1920; G. L. Kittredge, 1941; M. Sales, N.Y. 1946; A. Walker and J. D. Wilson, *Camb.* 1957; M. R. Ridley, *New Arden*, 1958; K. Muir, *New Penguin*, 1968.

2. Sources and analogues

BANDELLO, M. *Novelle: La prima (secunda, terza) parte de le Novelle del Bandello*, Lucca, 1554; augmented later, 1560, 1566, 1573, etc.

Modern edn.: F. Flora, 2 vols, Milan, 1934–5.

English trans.: John Payne, 6 vols, 1890. French trans.

Histoires tragiques extraites de l'Italien de Bandel, 1559, etc.
Pt. i by P. Boaistuau, Pt. ii (containing the Albanian captain,
no. 4) by F. de Belleforest, *Continuation des Histoires Tragiques...*
Paris, 1559, 1560 etc. Eng. trans.: G. Fenton, *Certaine Tragi-
call Discourses written oute of French and Latin* . . . 1567, 1579.
Modern edn.: R. L. Douglas, 2 vols (Tudor Trans.) 1898;
(Broadway Trans.) 1924.

BIZARI, P. *Cyprium bellum, inter Venetos, et Selymum Turcarum, imperatorem
gestum* . . . Basle, 1573. French trans.: F. de Belleforest, *Histoire
de la Guerre qui c'est passée entre les Venétiens* . . . *contre les Turcs pour
l'Ile de Cypre*, Paris, 1573.

BOTERO, G. *Relationi Universali*, Ferrara, 1592, 1595, 1599, 1602.
Trans.: I.R. (Robt. Johnson) *The Travellers Breviat*, 1601; *An
Historicall Description of the most famous Kingdomes and Common-
weales in the Worlde*, trans. R.I. 1603, 1608, etc.

BRANCACCIO, LELIO. *Il Brancatio, della vera disciplina, et arte militare*,
Venetia, 1582, 1585; *I Carichi Militari*, Antwerp, 1610, etc.

CINTHIO, G. B. GIRALDI. *Selene*, 1583, and in *Le Tragedie*, Venice, 1583.

CINTHIO, G. B. GIRALDI. *De Gli Hecatommithi*, Mondori, 1565, 2 vols,
Venice, 1566, 1574, 1580, 1593, etc. French trans.: G. Chappuys,
Premier Volume des Cent Excellentes Novelles, 1584, 2 vols. English
trans. of Moor story: *The Story of the Moor of Venice*, 1795, by W.
Parr; used in *Collier*, 1843 and *ShLib*. 1875; J. E. Taylor, *The
Moor of Venice*, 1855; Furness, *Var.* 1886; Ridley, *New Arden*,
1958, etc. T. J. B. Spencer, *Elizabethan Love Stories*, 1968, gives a
new trans.

CONTARINI, G. *De Magistratibus Republica Vinetorum, libri quinque*,
Paris, 1543, etc. Ital. trans.: E. Auditimi, Venice, 1544, 1548,
etc. Eng. trans.: Lewis Lewkenor, *The Commonwealth and Government of Venice*, 1599.

CONTARINI, G. P. *Historia della Guerra*, 1572; *De Bello Turcico contra
Venetos*, Basle, 1573.

JAMES VI. *His Majesties Poeticall Exercises at Vacant Houres*, Edinburgh,
1591, 1603. Modern edn.: J. Craigie, *The Poems of James VI of
Scotland*, S.T.S. 1955– .

KNOLLES, SIR RICHARD. *History of the Turkes*, 1603, 1611.

LEO AFRICANUS. *The History and Description of Africa*, trans. J. Pory,
1600. Modern edn.: R. Brown, 3 vols, Hakluyt Soc., 1896.

Lust's Dominion: or The Lascivious Queen, Anon. (*c.* 1600), 1657.
Modern edns.: C. W. Dilke, 1814; Hazlitt-Dodsley, xiv,
1876; J. G. Brereton, *Materialien*, n.s. 5, 1931.

MASUCCIO SALERNITANO. *Il Novellino*, 1483, 1484, many later edns.
Modern edn.: A. Mauro, 1940; trans. W. G. Waters, 2 vols,
1895.

MOLMENTI, P. G. *Venetia nella Vita privata* . . . Bergamo, 1905–8; trans. H. F. Brown, 1906–8.

MOLMENTI, P. G. *Vecchie Storie*, Venice, 1882.

PETTIE, G. *A Petite Pallace of Pettie His Pleasure*, 1576, 1578? 1580? Modern edn.: I. Gollancz, 2 vols, 1908.

PLINY. *The Historie of the World*, trans. Philemon Holland, 2 vols, 1601, 1634. Modern selection: Paul Turner, 1962.

RICH, B. *A Pathwaie to Military Practise*, 1587.

SANUTO, MARINO. *I Diarii*, 58 vols. Venice 1879–1903; Bologna, 1969–70.

SAVORGNANO, M. *Arte Militare Terrestre e Maritimo*, Venice, 1599, 1614.

THOMAS, W. *The Historye of Italy*, 1549, 1561. Modern edn.: G. P. Parks, Ithaca, N.Y., 1963.

VALLE, B. DELLA. *Vallo. Libro Continente apperteniente ai Capitani.* . . . Venice, 1524, 1529, 1535, etc. French trans. Lyon, 1554.

3. Critical Studies

ALEXANDER, N. 'Thomas Rymer and Othello', *Sh Survey 21*, 1968.

ALEXANDER, P. 'Under which king, Bezonian?', in *Eliz. and Jacob. Studies presented to F. P. Wilson*, Oxford, 1959, 67–77.

ALLEN, N. B. 'The Two Parts of *Othello*', *Sh Survey 21*, 1968, 13–29.

ARNOLD, A. 'The Function of Brabantio in *Othello*', *ShQ*, viii, 1957, 51–6.

BROWN, RAWDON, *Ragguagli sulla Vita e sulle Opere di Marin Sanuto*, Venice, 1837.

BULLOCK, W. A. 'The Sources of *Othello*', *MLN*, xl, 1925, 226.

DA MOSTO, A. 'Il Moro di Venezia', *Bolletino degli Studi inglesi in Italia*, ii, Florence, 1933, 3–10.

DE FONBLANQUE, E. M. 'The Italian Sources of *Othello*', *Fort. Rev.*, xcvi, 1911, 907–18.

DORAN, M. 'Good Name in *Othello*', *SEL*, vii, 1967, 195–217.

DRAPER, J. W. 'Honest Iago', *PMLA*, xlvi, 1931.

DRAPER, J. W. 'This Poor Trash of Venice', *JEGP*, xxx, 1931.

DRAPER, J. W. 'Captain General Othello', *Anglia*, lv, 1931.

DRAPER, J. W. 'Othello and Elizabethan Army Life', *Rev. Anglo-Américaine*, ix, 1932.

DRAPER, J. W. 'Desdemona: a Compound of Two Cultures', *Rev. de Litt. Comparée*, xiii, 1933.

DRAPER, J. W. 'Patterns of Tempo and Humour in Othello', *Eng. Studies*, xxviii, 1947.

DRAPER, J. W. 'Shakespeare and the Turk', *JEGP*, lv, 1956, 523–32.

DRAPER, J. W. 'Shakespeare and Barbary', *Etudes Anglaises*, xiv, 1961, 306–13.

ELLIOTT, G. R. *Flaming Minister*, Durham, N. C., 1953.

EMPSON, W. *The Structure of Complex Words*, 1951.

ENGEL, E. 'Zur Urgeschichte des *Othello*', *ShJb*, xxxv, 1899, 271.

GARDNER, H. 'The Noble Moor', *Proc. Brit. Acad.*, xli, 1956, 189–205.

GARDNER, H. 'Othello: A Retrospect, 1900–67', *Sh Survey 21*, 1968.

GERARD, A. 'Egregiously an Ass', *Sh Survey 10*, 1957, 98–104.

GILBERT, A. H. 'Scenes of Discovery in *Othello*', *PhilQ*, v, 1926.

HALLSTEAD, R. N. 'Idolatrous Love: a New Approach to Othello', *ShQ*, xix, 1968, 107–24.

HARRIS, B. 'A Portrait of a Moor', *Sh Survey 11*, 1958, 89–97.

HEILMAN, R. B. *Magic in the Web*, Lexington, 1956.

HIBBARD, G. '*Othello* and the Pattern of Shakespeare's Tragedy', *Sh Survey 21*, 1968.

HONIGMANN, E. A. J. '*Othello*, Chappuys and Cinthio'. *N&Q*, n.s. xiii, 1966, 136–7.

HUBLER, E. 'The Damnation of Othello', *ShQ*, ix, 1958, 295–300.

HUNTER, G. K. 'Othello and Colour Prejudice', *Proc. Brit. Acad.*, lvii, 1968, 139–63.

JONES, ELDRED. *Othello's Countrymen: The African in English Renaissance Drama*, 1965.

JONES, EMRYS. '*Othello*, *Lepanto*, and the Cyprus Wars', *Sh Survey 21*, 1968, 47–52.

JORGENSEN, P. A. 'Honesty in *Othello*', *St Phil*, xlvii, 1950.

JORGENSEN, P. A. *Shakespeare's Military World*, Berkeley and Los Angeles, 1956.

KAULE, D. 'Othello Possessed', *Sh Studies*, II, 1966, 112–32.

KRAPPE, A. H. 'A Byzantine Source of Sh's Othello', *MLN*, xxxix, 1924, 156–61.

LEAVIS, F. R. 'Diabolic Intellect and the Noble Hero', *Scrutiny*, vi, 1938; repd. in *The Common Pursuit*, 1952, 1963.

LEES, F. N. 'George Meredith and Othello', *N&Q*, n.s. 12, 1965, 96.

LERNER, L. 'The Machiavel and the Moor', *Essays in Crit.*, ix, 1959, 339–60.

MAUGERI, A. *Otello e la storia del capitano moro*, Messina, 1947.

MCCARRON, W. E. '*Othello* and Fenton—An Addendum', *N&Q*, n.s. 13, 1966, 137–8.

MCGEE, A. 'Othello's Motive for Murder', *ShQ*, xv, 1964, 45–55.

MENDONÇA, B. H. DE. 'Othello: A Tragedy built on a Comic Structure', *Sh Survey 21*, 1968.

MEYERSTEIN, E. H. W. 'Othello and C. Furius Cresinus', *TLS*, Feb. 7, 1942, 72.

MONEY, J. 'Othello's "It is the Cause . . ." An Analysis', *Sh Survey 6*, 1953.

MOORE, J. K. 'The Character of Iago', in *Studies in Honor of A. H. R. Fairchild*, Columbia, Miss. 1946.

MOULTON, R. G. '*Othello* as a type of Plot', *Trans. New Sh. Soc.*, 1887–92.

MUIR, K. 'The Jealousy of Iago', *English Misc.* 2, Rome, 1951.

MURPHY, G. N. 'A Note on Iago's Name', in *Literature and Society*, ed. B. Slote, Lincoln, Neb. 1964.

O'CONNELL, R. 'Desdemona in the Flesh', *N&Q*, 6 Ser. xi, 1885, 147.

POIRIER, M. 'Le Double Temps dans *Othello*', *Etudes Anglaises*, v. 1952.

POISSON, R. '*Othello*, V. 2. 347', *MLR*, lxii, 1967, 209–11.

PRAGER, L. 'The Clown in *Othello*', *ShQ*, xl, 1960, 3–11.

RANALD, M. L. 'The Indiscretions of Desdemona', *ShQ*, xiv, 1963, 127–39.

REBORA, P. 'Nuove Fonti Italiane di Shakespeare', in *Momenti di Cultura Italiana e Inglese*, Mazara, 1952.

ROSENBERG, M. *The Masks of Othello*, Berkeley and Los Angeles, 1961.

RYMER, T. *A Short View of Tragedy*, 1693. See J. E. Spingarn, *Critical Essays of the 17th Century*, Oxford, 1908, Vol. ii.

SEGRE, C. *Relazioni Litterarie fra Italia e Inghilterra*, Florence, 1911.

SHAFFER, E. S. 'Iago's Malignity Motivated', *ShQ*, xix, 1968, 195–203.

SIEGEL, P. N. 'The Damnation of Othello', *PMLA*, lxviii, 1953.

SIEGEL, P. N. 'A New Source for *Othello*?', *PMLA*, lxxv, 1960.

SPIVACK, B. *Shakespeare and the Allegory of Evil*, Columbia U.P., 1958.

STIRLING, B. 'Psychology in *Othello*', *Sh. Assoc. Bull.*, xix, 1944.

STOLL, E. E. *Othello, an Historical and Comparative Study*, Minneapolis, 1915.

STOLL, E. E. *Art and Artifice in Shakespeare*, 1933.

STOLL, E. E. 'Source and Motive in *Macbeth* and *Othello*', *RES*, xix, 1943.

WALTON, J. K. '"Strength's Abundance". A view of Othello', *RES*, n.s. xi, 1960, 8–17.

WEBB, H. J. 'The Military Background in *Othello*', *PhilQ*, xxx, 1951.

WHITNEY, L. 'Did Shakespeare know Leo Africanus?', *PMLA*, xxxvii, 1922.

WILSON, E. M. '*Othello*, a Tragedy of Honour', *Listener*, June 5, 1952.

WILSON, E. M. 'Family Honour in the Plays of Shakespeare's Predecessors and Contemporaries', *Essays and Studies*, 1953, 19–40.

WOKATSCH, W. 'Zur Quelle des Othello', *Archiv*, Bd. 162, 1932, 118–19.

King Lear

1. Editions of the play

Q1. 1608. *M. William Shakespeare: His True Chronicle Historie of the life and death of King Lear and his Three Daughters.* . . . Facs. J. O. Halliwell, 1868; C. Praetorius, 1885; *Sh.Q. Facs.* 1939.

Q2. 1619 (dated 1608) Facs. J. O. Halliwell, 1867: C. Praetorius 1885.

Q3. 1655.
F1. 1623. Facs. J. D. Wilson, 1928, and in facs. of F1.
   Parallel Texts: Q1 and F1, A. A. Adee, 1890; W. Vietor,
   1892.
   Modern edns.: H. H. Furness, *Var*, 1880, 1964; A. W. Verity,
   1897; W. J. Craig, *Arden*, 1901, 1927; D. Nichol Smith,
   Warwick, 1902; W. L. Phelps, *Yale*, 1917; G. I. Duthie, 1949;
   K. Muir, *New Arden*, 1952; A. Harbage, *Pelican*, 1958; G. I.
   Duthie and J. D. Wilson, *Camb*, 1960.

2. Sources and analogues
[Anon] *The True Chronicle History of King Leir, and his three daughters,
   Gonorill, Ragan, and Cordella . . .*, 1605.
   Modern edns.: J. Nichols, 1779; W. C. Hazlitt, *ShLib.*,
   1875; W. W. Greg, *MalSoc*, 1907; S. Lee, 1909; J. S. Farmer,
   TFT, 1910; R. Fischer, 1914.
CAMDEN, W. *Remaines Concerning Britaine*, 1605, 1614, etc.
GEOFFREY OF MONMOUTH. *Historia Regium Britanniae (c. 1139)*, Paris,
   1508, 1517, 1585.
   Modern ed.: San Marte (A Schulz) Halle, 1854, Trans.: A.
   Thompson, 1718; J. A. Giles in *Six Old English Chronicles*,
   1878, 1896; S. Evans, 1903, 1912.
HARRISON, W. *An Historical Description of the Iland of Britaine*, Printed in
   Holinshed, q.v.
HARSNETT, S. *A Declaration of Egregious Popish Impostures*, 1603.
HIGGINS, JOHN. *The First parte of the Mirour for Magistrates . . .*, 1574.
   Modern edn.: L. B. Campbell, *Parts Added to the Mirror for
   Magistrates*, Cambridge, 1946.
HOLINSHED, R. *Chronicles*, 1577, 1587, *The History of England*.
   Modern edn.: 1808. Relevant parts in *Var*, 1880; G. Boswell-
   Stone, *Shakspere's Holinshed*, 1896, 1907, A. and J. Nicoll,
   Holinshed's Chronicle as used in Shakespeare's Plays, and some
   modern edns., e.g. *New Arden*.
SIDNEY, SIR P. *The Countesse of Pembrokes Arcadia*, 1590.
   Modern edns.: Facs. H. O. Sommer, A. Feuillerat, 1922.
SPENSER, E. *The Faerie Queene*, 1596, (Bk. II).
   Modern edns.: R. Morris, *Globe*, 1893: J. C. Smith, 2 vols,
   Oxford, 1909, 1961.
WARNER, W. *Albions England*, 1589, 1592, 1596, 1601, 1606.

3. Critical Studies relating to Sources, etc.
ATKINSON, D. F. '*King Lear*: Another Contemporary Account', *ELH*,
   iii, 1936. (G. Legh's *Accedens of Armoury*, 1562).
BODE, E. *Die Lear Sage vor Shakespeare*, Göttingen, 1904.

BONHEIM, H. ed. *The King Lear Perplex*, Belmont, Cal., 1960. (excerpts from many critics since J. Warton).

BULLOUGH, G. '*King Lear* and the Annesley Case', *Festschrift Rudolf Stamm*, Berne, 1969, 43–50.

DORAN, M. 'Elements in the Composition of *King Lear*', *SPhil*, xxx, 1933, 34–58.

FISCHER, R. ed. *Quellen zu König Lear*, Bonn, 1914.

GREG, W. W. 'The Date of *King Lear* and Shakespeare's Use of Earlier Versions of the Story', *Library*, 4, Ser. xx, 1940.

LAW, R. A. 'Holinshed as a Source for *Henry V* and *King Lear*', *Texas U. Studies*, xiv, 1934.

LAW, R. A. 'Holinshed's *Leir* Story and Shakespeare's', *SPhil*, xlvii, 1950.

MENDONÇA, B. H. C. DE. 'The Influence of *Gorboduc* on *King Lear*', *Sh Survey 13*, 1960, 41–8.

MUIR K. and DANBY J. F. '*Arcadia* and *King Lear*', *N&Q*, Feb. 4, 1950.

MUIR, K. 'Samuel Harsnett and *King Lear*', *RES*, n.s. ii, 1951, 11–21.

PERKINSON, R. H. 'Shakespeare's Revision of the Lear Story and the Structure of *King Lear*', *PhilQ*, xxii, 1943, 315–29.

PERRETT, W. *The Story of King Lear from Geoffrey of Monmouth to Shakespeare*, Berlin, 1904.

PYLE, F. '*Twelfth Night*, *King Lear*, and *Arcadia*', *MLR*, xliii, 1948, 449–55.

RIBNER, I. 'Sidney's *Arcadia* and the Structure of *King Lear*', *Studia Neophilologica*, xxiv, 1952.

4. Other Relevant Critical Studies

BALD, R. C. '"Thou Nature art my Goddess": Edmund and Renaissance Free Thought', in *J. Q. Adams Memorial Studies*, Washington, 1948.

BENNETT, J. W. 'The Storm Within: The Madness of Lear', *ShQ*, xiii, 1962, 137–55.

BICKERSTETH, G. 'The Golden World of *King Lear*', *Proc. Brit. Acad.*, xxxiv, 1947.

BLOK, A. 'Shakespeare's *King Lear*', in *Shakespeare in the Soviet Union*. ed. R. Samarin and A. Nikolyukin, Moscow, 1966.

CAMPBELL, O. J. 'The Salvation of King Lear', *ELH*, xv, 1948, 93–109.

CHAMBERS, R. W. *King Lear* (W. P. Ker Memorial Lec.), Glasgow. 1940.

CRAIG, H. 'The Composition of *King Lear*', *Renaissance Papers 1961*, ed. G. W. Williams, Durham N. C., 1962, 57–61.

DANBY, J. F. *Shakespeare's Doctrine of Nature: A Study of King Lear*, 1949.

DRAPER, J. W. 'The Occasion of *King Lear*', *SPhil*, xxxiv, 1937, 176–85.

ELTON, W. R. '*King Lear*' and the Gods, San Marino, 1966.

FRICKER, R. A. 'Shakespeare und das Drama des Absurden', *ShJb(W)*, 1966, 7–29.

GARDNER, HELEN, *King Lear* (John Coffin Mem. Lec.), Athlone Press, 1967.

HEILMAN, R. B. *This Great Stage: Image and Structure in King Lear*, Baton Rouge, 1948.

KEAST, W. R. 'Imagery and Meaning in the Interpretation of *King Lear*', *MPhil*, xlvii, 1949, 45–64.

KERNODLE, G. F. 'The Symphonic Form of *King Lear*', in *Elizabethan Studies*, Boulder, Col., 1945.

KIRSCHBAUM, L. 'Albany', *Sh Survey 13*, 1960, 20–29.

MACLEAN, H. 'Disguise in *King Lear*', *ShQ*, xi, 1960, 49–54.

MUIR, K. 'Madness in *King Lear*', *Sh Survey 13*, 1960, 30–40.

NOSWORTHY, J. M. '*King Lear*. The Moral Aspect', *Eng. Studies*, xxi, 1939, 260–68.

ORWELL, GEORGE. 'Lear, Tolstoy, and the Fool', in *Shooting an Elephant*, 1950.

PRICE, T. R. '*King Lear*: A Study of Shakespeare's Dramatic Method', *PMLA*, ix, 1894, 165–81.

ROSENBERG, J. D. 'King Lear and his Comforters', *Essays in Crit.*, xvi, 1966, 135–46.

SCHOFF, F. G. 'King Lear: Moral Example or Tragic Protagonist?', *ShQ*, xiii, 1962, 157–72.

SHAW, J. '*King Lear*: The Final Lines', *ShQ*, xiii, 1962, 261–7.

SMITH, R. M. '*King Lear* and the Merlin Tradition', *Mod. Lang. Q.*, vii, 1946.

STEWART, J. I. M. 'The Blinding of Gloster', *RES*, xxi, 1945, 264–70.

STUART, B. K. 'Truth and Tragedy in *King Lear*', *ShQ*, xviii, 1967, 167–80.

TOLSTOY, LEO. 'Shakespeare and the Drama' (Introduction to E. Crosby, *Shakespeare and the Working Classes*, 1903).

WALTON, J. K. 'Lear's Last Speech', *Sh Survey 13*, 1960, 11–19.

ZANDVOORT, R. W. '*King Lear*: The Scholars and the Critics', *Mededelingen der Nederlandse Akademie van Wetenschappen . . .*, xix, 1956, 229–44.

Macbeth

1. Editions of the Play

F1. 1623. Facs. in edns. of F1 by J. O. Halliwell-Phillips, 1876; Kökeritz and C. T. Prouty, 1955; C. Hinman, 1968. Facs. J. D. Wilson, 1928.

Modern edns.: W. G. Clark and W. A. Wright, *Oxford*, 1869; *Var.* 1873, 1903; E. K. Chambers, *Warwick*, 1893; J. M. Manly, 1896; M. H. Liddell, 1903; H. Conrad, 1907;

H. Cunningham, *Arden*, 1912, 1928; C. M. Lewis, *Yale*, 1918; G. C. Taylor and R. Smith, 1936; W. D. Sargeaunt, 1937; G. L. Kittredge, 1939; J. D. Wilson, *Camb.* 1947; K. Muir, *New Arden*, 1951; E. M. Waith, *Yale*, 1954; A. Harbage, *Pelican* 1956; G. K. Hunter, *New Penguin*, 1967.

2. Sources and analogues

BESANÇON, ESTIENNE DE. *Alphabeticum Narrationum.*
  Trans.: *An Alphabet of Tales: An English Fifteenth-Century Translation*, ed. M. M. Banks, EETS, orig. ser., 126, 1904.

BOECE, HECTOR, *Scotorum Historiae*, Paris, 1526, 1574, 1575. Scots.: John Bellenden, 1536? Modern edns.: T. Maitland, 1821; STS, 1941.

BUCHANAN, G. *Rerum Scoticarum historia*, Edinburgh, 1582, London, 1583. Eng. trans.: T. Page, 1690; J. Aikman, 6 vols, Glasgow, 1827. *Ane Detectioun of the Duinges of Marie Quene of Scottes*, 1571; St Andrews, 1572, 1583, 1592, etc.

DANIEL, S. *The Queenes Arcadia*, 1606. Also in *Certain Small Workes* ... 1607, 1611. Modern edn.: *Complete Works* ed. A. B. Grosart, 5 vols. (Vol. iii, 1885).

DELONEY, T. *Thomas of Reading*, 1600, 1602. Modern edns. *Works*, ed. F. Q. Mann, Oxford, 1912. G. Saintsbury, 1929.

[ESTIENNE. H.?] *Ane Merveillous discours Upon the lyfe deedes and behaviours of Katherine de Medicis* ... Cracow [Edinburgh], 1576.

FORDUN, J. DE, *Chronica*, ed. W. F. Skene, *Historians of Scotland*, 1871, Vols I, 4.

GREENE, R. *Friar Bacon and Friar Bungay* (c. 1589), 1594. Modern edns. J. S. Farmer, *TFT*, 1914; W. A. Neilson, 1911. *The Comicall Historie of Alphonsus, King of Aragon*, (c. 1587), 1599. Both plays in J. C. Collins, *Plays and Poems of R. G.*, 2 vols, 1905.

[GWINN, M.] *Vertumnus sive Annus Recurrens Oxonii xxix Augusti. Anno 1605*, 1607. Modern edn.: *Var.* 1873.

HOLINSHED, R. *The Chronicles of England, Scotland, and Ireland*, 2 vols, 1577, 1587. Modern edn.: H. Ellis, 1807–8. Selection in W. G. Boswell-Stone, *Shakspere's Holinshed* 1896, 1907; A. and J. Nicoll, *Holinshed's Chronicle as used in Shakespeare's Plays*, 1927.

HOWARD, H. *A Defensative against the Poyson of Supposed Prophecies*, 1583.

JAMES, I. *Daemonologie, in form of a Dialogue*, 1597, 1603. *The Workes of the Most High and Mightie Prince James*, 1616.

LESLIE, JOHN. *A Defence of the Honour of the* ... *Princesse Marie Quene of Scotlande*, 1569, 1571. Modern edn.: in J. Anderson, *Collections relating to Queen Mary*, 1727, Vol. 1. *A Treatise touching the Right, Title and Interest of the Princesse Marie* ... *and of the most Noble King*

James... 1584. *De Origine, Moribus et Rebus Gestis Scotorum,* Rome 1578. Modern edn.: T. Thomson, Bannatyne Club, Edinburgh, 1830. Scots trans.: J. Dalrymple (1596) ed. E. G. Cody, *STS,* 2 vols, Edinburgh, 1888–95.

LIVY, T. *Titi Livii Patavini Romanae Historiae Principis, Libri Omnes,* 1589. Trans.: Ph. Holland, *The Romane Historie,* 1600.

[NIXON, A.] *Oxford's Triumph.* ... 1605.

SKENE, W. F. *Celtic Scotland,* Edinburgh, 1876, Vol. I.

STEWART, W. *The Buik of the Cronicles of Scotland,* Rolls Series, 1858.

THOU, J. A. DE. *Illustris Viri Iac. Augusti Thuani* ... *Historiarum sui Temporis 1543–1607,* 4 vols, 1625. Relevant part trans. in *Popish Policies and Practices* ... Anon. 1674.

VITRY, J. DE. *The Exempla, or illustrative Sermons from the Sermones Vulgares,* ed. T. F. Crane, Folk-Lore Soc. xxvi, 1890.

WARNER, W. *A Continuance of Albions England,* 1606.

WYNTOUN, A. *The Original Chronicle of Andrew Wyntoun,* ed. F. J. Amours, S.T.S., 6 vols, 1903–14, Vol. IV.

3. Critical Studies of Sources, etc.

ANDERSON, R. L. 'The Pattern of Behaviour culminating in *Macbeth*' *SEL,* iii, 1963, 151–74.

ARMSTRONG, W. A. *Shakespeare's Typology: Miracle and Morality Motifs in Macbeth,* Westfield College, London, 1970.

BACQUET, P. 'Macbeth et l'influence de Sénéque', *Bull. de la Fac. des Lettres de Strasbourg,* 1961, 399–411.

BRADBROOK, M. C. 'The Sources of *Macbeth*', *Sh Survey 4,* 1951.

BRANDL, A. 'Zur Quelle des *Macbeth*', *Eng. Studien,* lxx, 1935.

BROWN, B. D. 'Exemplum Materials underlying *Macbeth*', *PMLA,* l, 1935, 700–14.

BULLOUGH, G. '*Macbeth,* James I and Abnormal Psychology', *London Review,* iii, Spring 1968.

CALHOUN, H. V. 'James I and the Witch Scenes', *Sh. Assoc. Bull.,* xvii, 1942.

DEFRANCE, E. *Catherine de Medicis, ses Astrologues et ses Magiciens envoûteurs,* Paris, 1911.

DRAPER, J. W. 'Macbeth as a Compliment to James I', *Eng. Studien,* lxxii, 1938, 207–20.

DRAPER, J. W. 'The Gracious Duncan.' *MLR,* xxxvi, 1941, 495–9.

EWBANK, I.-S. 'The Fiend-like Queen: A Note on *Macbeth* and Seneca's *Medea*', *Sh Survey 19,* 1961, 82–94.

FLATTER, R. 'Who wrote the Hecate-scene?', *ShJb,* xciii, 1957, 196–210.

GODSHALL, W. L. 'Livy's Tullia: A Classical Prototype of Lady Macbeth', *ShQ,* xvi, 1965, 240–1.

HARCOURT, J. B. 'I pray you remember the Porter', *ShQ*, xii, 1961, 393–402.

HARLOW, G. 'The Authorship of *Henry VI*', *SEL*, v, 1965, 31–47; 269–81.

HUNTLEY, F. L. '*Macbeth* and the Background of Jesuitical Equivocation', *PMLA*, lxxix, 1964, 390–400.

KITTREDGE, G. L. *Witchcraft in Old and New England*, Cambridge, Mass., 1929.

KRÖGER, E. *Die Sage von Macbeth bis zu Shakespeare*, Palaestra, 292, Berlin, 1904.

LAW, R. A. 'The Composition of *Macbeth* with Reference to Holinshed', *SEL*, xxxi, 1952.

LOOMIS, E. A. 'Master of the Tyger', *ShQ*, vii, 1956, 457.

LYLE, E. 'Two Parallels in *Macbeth* to Seneca's *Hercules Oetaus*', *Eng. Studies*, 53, April 1972.

PARISH, E. *Hallucinations and Illusions*, 1897.

PAUL, H. N. *The Royal Play of Macbeth*, 1950.

SARRAZIN, G. 'Shakespeares *Macbeth* und Kyds *Spanish Tragedy*', *Eng. Studien*, xxi, 1895, 328–40.

SCHANZER, E. 'Four Notes on *Macbeth*', *MLR*, lii, 1957, 223–7.

SMITH, F. M. 'The Relation of *Macbeth* to *Richard III*', *PMLA*, lx, 1945.

SPARGO, J. W. 'The Knocking at the Gate in *Macbeth*', in *J. Q. Adams Memorial Studies*, Washington, 1948.

STOPES, C. C. 'The Scottish and English Macbeth', in *Shakespeare's Industry*, 1897.

THALER, A. 'The Lost Scenes of *Macbeth*', *PMLA*, xlix, 1934, 835–47.

URE, P. '*Macbeth* and Warner's *Albion's England*', *N&Q*, 1949, 232–3.

WICKHAM, G. 'Hell-Gate and its Door-Keeper', *Sh Survey 19*, 1966, 68–74.

WINSTANLEY, L. *Macbeth, King Lear, and Contemporary History*, 1922.

WOOD, J. O. 'Hecate's "Drop profound"', *N&Q*, n.s. xi, 1964, 262–4.

WOOD, J. O. 'Lady Macbeth's Secret Weapon', *N&Q*, n.s. xii, 1965, 98–100.

4. Other Relevant Studies

BROOKS, C. 'The Naked Babe and the Cloak of Manliness', in *The Well Wrought Urn*, 1947.

CUNNINGHAM, D. G. '*Macbeth*: The Tragedy of the Hardened Heart', *ShQ*, xiv, 1963, 39–47.

CURRY, W. C. 'The Demonic Metaphysics of *Macbeth*', *SPhil*, xxx, 1933, 395–426.

CURRY, W. C. '*Macbeth's* Changing Character', *JEGP*, xxxiv, 1935, 311–38.

DORAN, M. 'That Undiscovered Country', *PhilQ*, xx, 1941, 413–27.

DUTHIE, G. I. 'Antithesis in *Macbeth*', *Sh Survey 19*, 1966, 25–33.

DYSON, P. 'The Structural Function of the Banquet Scene', *ShQ*, xiv, 1963, 369–78.

ELLIOTT, G. R. *Dramatic Providence in Macbeth*, Princeton, 1958.

EMPSON, W. 'Dover Wilson on *Macbeth*', *Kenyon Rev.*, xiv, 1952, 84–102.

HALES, J. W. 'On the Porter in *Macbeth*', *Trans. New Sh Soc.*, 1874.

HEILMAN, R. B. 'The Criminal as Tragic Hero', *Sh Survey 19*, 1966, 12–24.

HUNTER, E. R. '*Macbeth* as a Morality', *Sh Assoc. Bull.*, 1937.

HUNTER, G. K. '*Macbeth* in the Twentieth Century', *Sh Survey 19*, 1966, 1–11.

KIRSCHBAUM, L. 'Banquo and Edgar—Character or Function?', *Essays in Crit.*, 1957, 1–21. Cf. C. Gillie, 322–4, F. W. Bateson, 324–5, on the same theme.

KNIGHTS. L. C. 'How many Children had Lady Macbeth?', *Scrutiny*, 1933; reprd. in *Explorations*, 1946, 1964.

MERCHANT, W. M. 'His Fiend-like Queen', *Sh Survey 19*, 1966, 75–81.

MUIR, K. 'Image and Symbol in *Macbeth*', *Sh Survey 19*, 1966, 45–54.

NOTESTEIN, W. *History of Witchcraft in England, 1553–1718*, Washington, 1911.

ROGERS, R. L. '*Double Profit*' in *Macbeth*, Melbourne U.P., 1942.

SANDERS, W. *The Dramatist and the Received Idea*, Cambridge, 1968, Ch. 13, 14.

SCHOLDERER, V. 'Illustrations of the First Edition of Holinshed' in *Edinburgh Bib. Soc. trans. Vol. II*, Edinburgh, 1946, 398–403.

WALKER, R. '*The Time is Free*': *A Study of Macbeth*, 1949.

ZANDVOORT, R. W. 'Dramatic Motivation in *Macbeth*', *Langues Modernes*, xlv, 1951; repd. in *Collected Papers*, Gröningen, 1954.

INDEX TO THE INTRODUCTIONS